FUNDAMENTALS OF

ELECTRICITY

AND

MAGNETISM

FUNDAMENTALS OF ELECTRICITY AND MAGNETISM

R B SINGH
Former Head
Deptartment of Phyics UNPG College
Padrauna, DDU Gorakhpur University
Gorakhpur (UP)

A K Shukla
Associate Professor
Department of Pure and Applied Physics
Guru Ghasidas Vishwavidyalaya
Bilaspur, (CG)

NEW AGE INTERNATIONAL (P) LIMITED, PUBLISHERS
LONDON • NEW DELHI • NAIROBI
Bangalore • Chennai • Cochin • Guwahati • Hyderabad • Kolkata • Lucknow • Mumbai
Visit us at www.newagepublishers.com

Published by New Age International (P) Ltd., Publishers
First Edition: 2012
Reprint: 2018

GLOBAL OFFICES

- **New Delhi** — **NEW AGE INTERNATIONAL (P) LIMITED, PUBLISHERS**
  7/30 A, Daryaganj, New Delhi-110002, (INDIA)
  Tel.: (011) 23253771, 23253472, **Telefax:** 23267437, 43551305
  E-mail: contactus@newagepublishers.com • Visit us at www.newagepublishers.com
- **London** — **NEW AGE INTERNATIONAL (UK) LTD.**
  27 Old Gloucester Street, London, WC1N 3AX, UK
  E-mail: info@newacademicscience.co.uk • Visit us at www.newacademicscience.co.uk
- **Nairobi** — **NEW AGE GOLDEN (EAST AFRICA) LTD.**
  Ground Floor, Westlands Arcade, Chiromo Road (Next to Naivas Supermarket)
  Westlands, Nairobi, KENYA, **Tel.:** 00-254-713848772, 00-254-725700286
  E-mail: kenya@newagepublishers.com

BRANCHES

- **Bangalore** — 37/10, 8th Cross (Near Hanuman Temple), Azad Nagar, Chamarajpet, Bangalore- 560 018
  Tel.: (080) 26756823, **Telefax:** 26756820, **E-mail: bangalore@newagepublishers.com**
- **Chennai** — 26, Damodaran Street, T. Nagar, Chennai-600 017, **Tel.:** (044) 24353401, **Telefax:** 24351463
  E-mail: chennai@newagepublishers.com
- **Cochin** — CC-39/1016, Carrier Station Road, Ernakulam South, Cochin-682 016, **Tel.:** (0484) 2377303, **Telefax:** 4051304
  E-mail: cochin@newagepublishers.com
- **Guwahati** — Hemsen Complex, Mohd. Shah Road, Paltan Bazar, Near Starline Hotel, Guwahati-781 008,
  Tel.: (0361) 2513881, **Telefax:** 2543669, **E-mail: guwahati@newagepublishers.com**
- **Hyderabad** — 105, 1st Floor, Madhiray Kaveri Tower, 3-2-19, Azam Jahi Road, Near Kumar Theater, Nimboliadda Kachiguda, Hyderabad-500 027, **Tel.:** (040) 24652456, **Telefax:** 24652457
  E-mail: hyderabad@newagepublishers.com
- **Kolkata** — RDB Chambers (Formerly Lotus Cinema) 106A, 1st Floor, S N Banerjee Road, Kolkata-700 014
  Tel.: (033) 22273773, **Telefax:** 22275247, **E-mail: kolkata@newagepublishers.com**
- **Lucknow** — 16-A, Jopling Road, Lucknow-226 001, **Tel.:** (0522) 2209578, 4045297, **Telefax:** 2204098
  E-mail: lucknow@newagepublishers.com
- **Mumbai** — 142C, Victor House, Ground Floor, N.M. Joshi Marg, Lower Parel, Mumbai-400 013
  Tel.: (022) 24927869, **Telefax:** 24915415, **E-mail: mumbai@newagepublishers.com**
- **New Delhi** — 22, Golden House, Daryaganj, New Delhi-110 002, **Tel.:** (011) 23262368, 23262370, **Telefax:** 43551305
  E-mail: sales@newagepublishers.com

ISBN: 978-81-224-3272-5
C-17-07-10572

Printed in India at Krishna Printers & Binders, Delhi.
Typeset at In-house, New Delhi.

NEW AGE INTERNATIONAL (P) LIMITED, PUBLISHERS
7/30 A, Daryaganj, New Delhi-110002
Visit us at **www.newagepublishers.com**
(CIN: U74899DL1966PTC004618)

Preface

Electricity and Magnetism often called electromagnetism is one of the core course of Physics at undergraduate level. With the advancement of extensive science teaching most of the courses taught at undergraduate level in the past have now been shifted to lower classes. The concept of magnetic pole in magnetism has been almost abandoned and teaching of magnetism is done in terms of circulating current or spinning charge. For this reason the subjects of electricity and magnetism are not taught separately but as a single unit called *electromagnetism.*

Electromagnetic phenomena are most elegantly and compactly described in vector notation. A sound knowledge vector calculus is a prerequisite for the study of electromagnetism. To meet this end, adequate material on vector calculus has been given in appendix.

In our opinion, SI units are most suitable for the description of electromagnetic quantities. So we have used this system of units throughout the book. A sufficiently large number of solved examples have been added at appropriate places to make the readers feel confident in applying the basic principles discussed in the text.

We are of the opinion that it is a difficult task to write a book without being in contact with those for whom the book is written. Also interaction with colleagues and students helps in veiwing the same thing at different angles. We have received some valuable inputs in this way. Of course, the importance of extensive reading of different standard books on the subject cannot be underestimated because it broadens the mental horizon of the reader. All these things and our long teaching experience has been the prime source of matter of this book.

This is the first edition of the book and in spite of all our precautions chances of errors, omissions and misinterpretation of phenomena are always there. Hence our request to readers is to help us by pointing them out so that they may be removed in next edition.

The writing of book needs a lot of patience not only of authors but also to their family members. We are thankful to them for their patience and help in their own way.

We hope that this book will be helpful not only to undergraduate students of science and engineering but also to all those who are preparing for competitive examinations.

We wish to express my thanks to Mr. Saumya Gupta, Managing Director, New Age International (P) Limited, Publishers, as well as editorial department for their untiring effort to complete this project within a short period.

—R.B. Singh

—A.K. Shukla

Contents

PHYSICAL CONSTANTS

Speed of light in vacuum	$c = 2.998 \times 10^{8}\ ms^{-1}$
Gravitational constant	$G = 6.67 \times 10^{-11}\ Nm^{2}\ kg^{-2}$
Avogadro constant	$N = 6.022 \times 10^{23}\ mol^{-1}$
Loschmidt number	$N_L = 2.687 \times 10^{25}\ m^{-3}$
Molar gas constant	$R = 8.31\ J\,mol^{-1}\ K^{-1}$
Boltzmann constant	$k = 1.38 \times 10^{-23}\ J\ K^{-1}$
Faraday constant	$F = 9.648 \times 10^{4}\ C\ mol^{-1}$
Permittvity of vaccum	$\varepsilon_0 = 8.85 \times 10^{-12}\ F\ m^{-1}$
Vaccum permeability	$\mu_0 = 4\pi \times 10^{-7}\ H\ m^{-1} = 1.257 \times 10^{6}\ H\ m^{-1}$
Electron rest mass	$m_e = 9.109 \times 10^{-31}\ kg$
Proton rest mass	$m_p = 1.673 \times 10^{-27}\ kg$
Neutron rest mass	$m_n = 1.675 \times 10^{-27}\ kg$
Charge of proton	$e = 1.602 \times 10^{-19}\ C$
Electron charge-to-mass ratio	$e/m_e = 1.759 \times 10^{11}\ C\ kg^{-1}$
Ratio of proton and electron masses	$m_p/m_e = 1836.15$
Atomic mass unit	$1\ amu = 1.660 \times 10^{-27}\ kg$
Planck's constant	$h = 6.626 \times 10^{-34}\ J.s$
	$\hbar = 1.054 \times 10^{-34}\ J.s$
Stefan-Boltzmann constant	$\sigma = 5.67 \times 10^{-8}\ W\ m^{-2}\ K^{-4}$
Wien constant	$b = 2.897 \times 10^{-3}\ m.K$
Rydberg constant (for hydrogen)	$R_H = 1.097 \times 10^{7}\ m^{-1}$
Triple point of water	$T = 273.16\ K\ (= 0.01\ ^{\circ}C)$

MISCELLANEOUS CONSTANTS

Coulomb constant $1/4\pi\varepsilon_0 = 9 \times 10^9$ m F^{-1}

$GM_e = 4 \times 10^{14}$ J. m

$\pi = 3.14$, $\pi^2 = 9.86$, $\sqrt{\pi} = 1.772$, $\sqrt{2} = 1.41$, $\sqrt{3} = 1.73$, $e = 2.72$, $1/e = 0.368$

$\log_{10} e = 0.434$, $\ell_n 10 = 2.302$, $\ell_n x = 2.3026 \log_{10} x$

$180° = \pi$ radian, 1 radian = 57.3°

1 nautical mile = 1852 meter, 1 light year = 9.46×10^{12} km, 1 Par sec = 3.084×10^{13} km

1 year = 3.11×10^7 sec

1 atmospheric pressure = 1.01×10^5 N m^{-2}

1 bar = 100 kPa

1 calorie = 4.18 J

1 A° = 10^{-10} m

1 fermi = 10^{-15} m

1 barn = 10^{-28} m^2

1 eV = 1.6×10^{-19} J

1 amu = 931.4 MeV

1 CHAPTER

Electrostatics: Electric Field and Potential

1.1. INTRODUCTION

The science of electricity and magnetism was developed in bits and pieces. Prior to Oersted (1820) and Ampere (1820) discovery of magnetic effect of current, electricity and magnetism were considered as two separate subjects. In 1831, Faraday showed that a changing magnetic field produces an electric field. The works of these physicists established that electricity and magnetism could no longer be treated as separate subjects but they were the two aspects of the same subject – *electromagnetism*. This synthesis is regarded as one of the most important events in the history of physics. In 1865 again a British physicist J.C. Maxwell made another synthesis – the synthesis of electromagnetism and optics. About this synthesis Nobel Laureate R.P. Feynman, the founder of Quantum Electrodynamics (QED), said: 'From a long view of the history of mankind - seen from today, say, ten thousand years now – there can be little doubt that the most significant event of the 19th century will be judged as Maxwell's discovery of the laws of electrodynamics. The American Civil War will pale into provincial significance in comparison with this important event of the same decade.

The concept of electric charge plays a central role in electromagnetic phenomena. We now know that matter is composed of three kinds of particles, electrons, protons and neutrons. Experiments show that two electrons repel each other. This is also true for two protons. A proton attracts an electron. In order to understand these two types of interaction, it is assumed that there exist two kinds of electric charges. Conventionally an electron is assigned a negative charge and a proton positive charge. Neutron is assumed to carry no charge. The magnitude of charge on electron and proton has the same value, $| e | = 1.6 \times 10^{-19}$ Coulomb. An object containing equal number of electrons and protons is electrically neutral. Deficiency of electrons in an object gives it positive charge and excess of electrons a negative charge. The charge on an object is always integral multiple of electronic charge. In other words, electric charge is quantized. The charge on an object has the same magnitude in all inertial frames *i.e.* the magnitude of charge is relativistically invariant. The total charge on an isolated system always remains the same. Appearance of charge at one place is accompanied by disappearance at the other. The charge on an isolated object is conserved.

The interaction of electric charges is described in terms of *field*. According to this view, *an electric charge distorts the space or creates a condition in the space around it. When another charge is placed nearby it, the distorted condition of space exerts a force on the second charge and vice-versa. We call the distorted condition of space as an electric field. Thus two charged particles interact via an electric field.*

Electric charge 1 $\leftrightarrow$ *electric field* $\leftrightarrow$ *electric charge* 2

The concept of *field* is a very useful formulation for describing electromagnetic phenomena.

We shall begin our study of electromagnetism with electrostatics in which the electric charges—the sources of electric fields are assumed to be static relative to the observer and the charge density is independent of time.

1.2. COULOMB'S LAW

Coulomb's law is a statement describing the magnitude and direction of the force acting between two static point charges. The law states that the force between two static point charges q_1 and q_2 separated by a distance r_{12} is proportional to the product of charges and is inversely proportional to the square of the distance between them. The force acts along the line joining the charges. Thus the electric force is central force. Between the like charges, the force is repulsive; and between unlike charges, the force is attractive. If $\mathbf{F}_{12}$ is the force on charge q_1 due to q_2 and $\mathbf{F}_{21}$ is the force on q_2 due to q_1 and r_{12} is the separation between them then the Coulomb's law can be expressed as

$$\mathbf{F}_{12} = const.\ \frac{q_1 q_2}{r_{12}^2}(-\hat{\mathbf{r}}_{12}), \quad \mathbf{F}_{21} = const.\ \frac{q_1 q_2}{r_{12}^2}\hat{\mathbf{r}}_{12} \qquad \text{...(1.1)}$$

$$\mathbf{F}_{21} = -\mathbf{F}_{12}$$

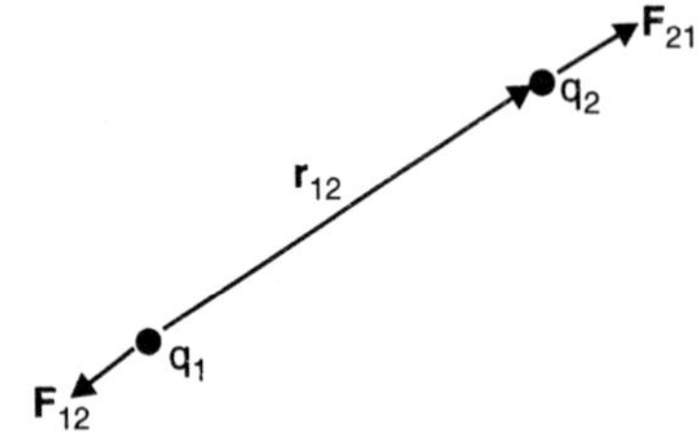

Fig. 1.1. Electrostatic between two point charges.

Where $\hat{\mathbf{r}}_{12}$ is unit vector along the position vector $\mathbf{r}_{12}$. In SI system of units, the constant of proportionality is written as $\frac{1}{4\pi\varepsilon_0} = 9 \times 10^9 \,\text{Nm}^2\text{C}^{-2}$. The constant ε_0 is called permittivity of vaccum.

It looks odd to introduce the factor 4π in the proportionality constant, but once we have introduced it in Coulomb's law, the fundamental laws of electrodynamics-the Maxwell's Equations are free from them.

1.3. PRINCIPLE OF SUPERPOSITION

This is another fact of nature which states that the force between two charges is unaffected by the presence of other charges. If there are several point charges q_1, q_2, q_3, ... then the force on a charge q is the vector sum of Coulomb forces exerted by all other charges.

$$\mathbf{F_q} = \mathbf{F_1} + \mathbf{F_2} + \mathbf{F_3} \ldots$$

$$= \frac{1}{4\pi\varepsilon_0}\left(\frac{q_1 q}{r_1^2}\hat{\mathbf{r}}_1 + \frac{q_2 q}{r_2^2}\hat{\mathbf{r}}_2 + \frac{q_3 q}{r_3^2}\hat{\mathbf{r}}_3 + \ldots\right) \quad \ldots(1.2)$$

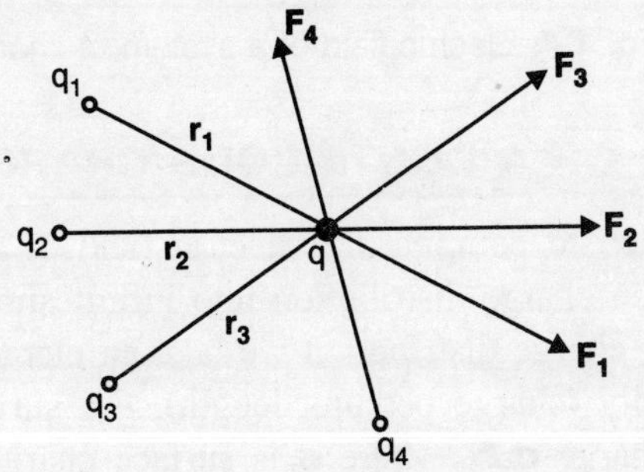

Fig. 1.2. Principle of superposition.

Equation (1.2) is the mathematical statement of the principle of superposition. Coulomb's law and the principle of superposition are the only basic laws of electrostatics. The rest of the electrostatics is nothing but the mathematical elaboration of these laws.

1.4. ELECTRIC FIELD VECTOR E

Experiment shows that a test charge q_0 placed nearby a point charge q, experiences a force **F**. The ratio $\mathbf{F}/q_0$ is defined as the electric field **E**.

$$\mathbf{E} = \frac{\mathbf{F}}{q_0} \quad \ldots(1.3)$$

q ——r——> o q_0 ——> E

Fig. 1.3.

The electric field **E** at a point **r** due to a point charge q is

$$\mathbf{E} = \frac{1}{4\pi\varepsilon_0}\frac{q}{r^2}\ \hat{\mathbf{r}} \quad \ldots(1.4)$$

If we have a system of discrete point charges q_1, q_2, q_3, ... then the electric field at point P due to these charges is given by the principle of superposition

$$\mathbf{E} = \mathbf{E}_1 + \mathbf{E}_2 + \mathbf{E}_3 + \cdots = \frac{1}{4\pi\varepsilon_0}\left(\frac{q_1}{r_1^2}\hat{\mathbf{r}}_1 + \frac{q_2}{r_2^2}\hat{\mathbf{r}}_2 + \frac{q_3}{r_3^2}\hat{\mathbf{r}}_3 + \cdots\right) = \frac{1}{4\pi\varepsilon_0}\sum_i \frac{q_i}{r_i^2}\hat{\mathbf{r}}_i \qquad ...(1.5)$$

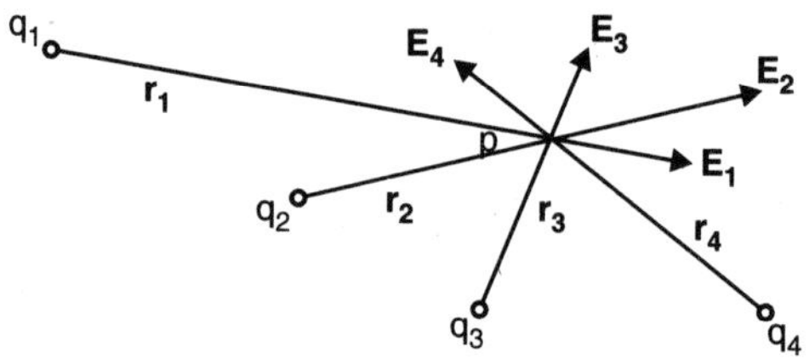

Fig. 1.4. Electric field of a system of charges.

1.5. ELECTRIC FIELD OF A CONTINUOUS CHARGE DISTRIBUTION

Equation (1.5) may be extended to compute the electric field of a continuous charge distribution. To this end we divide the given charge distribution into infinitesimal pieces and treat each of them as a point charge. For a linear charge distribution we take an element of length dl with charge λdl, where λ is linear charge density (charge per unit length). For surface charge distribution, we take an element of area dS with charge σdS, where σ is surface charge density (charge per unit area). For volume distribution of charge, we take an element of $d\tau$ with charge $\rho d\tau$, where ρ is volume density of charge (charge per unit volume). In order to calculate the electric field due to entire charge distribution, following transformations are made in equation (1.5).

$$\sum_i \frac{q_i}{r_i^2}\hat{\mathbf{r}}_i \rightarrow \int \frac{\lambda dl}{r^2}\hat{\mathbf{r}} \quad \text{(Linear distribution)}$$

$$\rightarrow \int \frac{\sigma dS}{r^2}\hat{\mathbf{r}} \quad \text{(Surface distribution)}$$

$$\rightarrow \int \frac{\rho d\tau}{r^2}\hat{\mathbf{r}} \quad \text{(Volume distribution)}$$

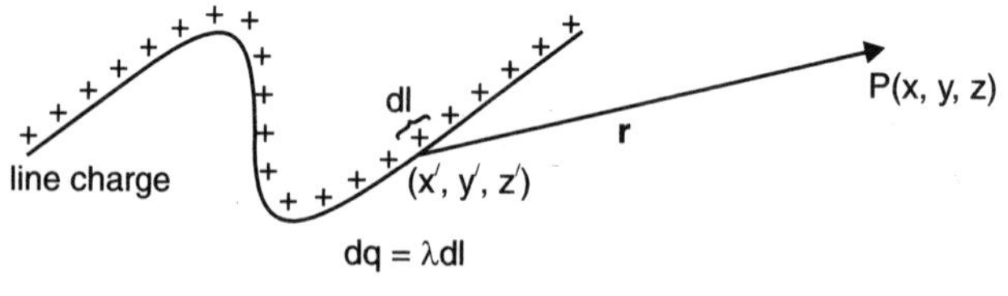

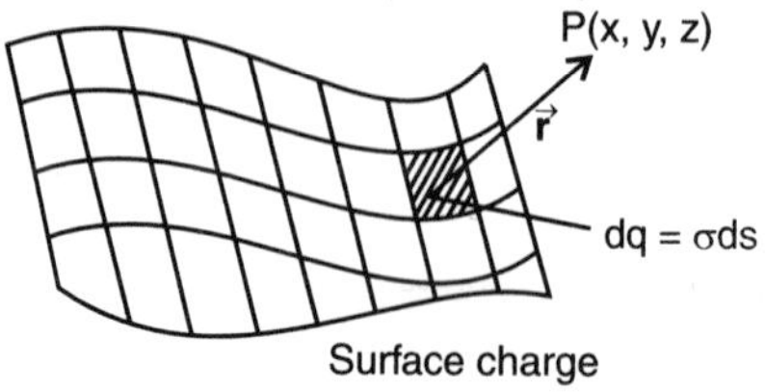

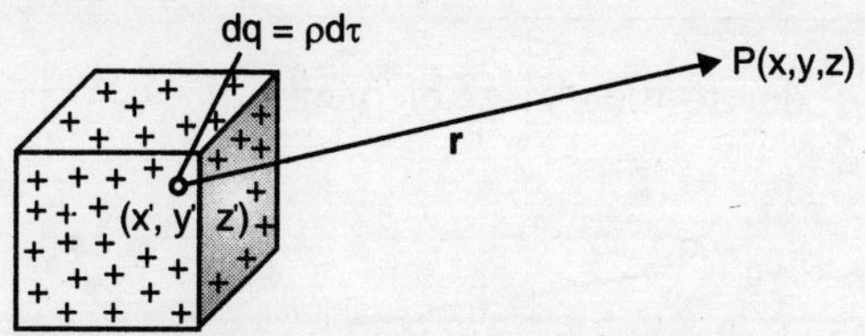

Fig. 1.5. Continuous charge distribution.

Thus the expressions for the electric field for the continuous charge distributions become

$$\mathbf{E}(x,y,z) = \frac{1}{4\pi\varepsilon_0}\int \frac{\lambda dl}{r^2}\hat{\mathbf{r}} \qquad \text{(linear)} \qquad ...(1.6)$$

$$\mathbf{E}(x,y,z) = \frac{1}{4\pi\varepsilon_0}\int \frac{\sigma dS}{r^2}\hat{\mathbf{r}} \qquad \text{(surface)} \qquad ...(1.7)$$

$$\mathbf{E}(x,y,z) = \frac{1}{4\pi\varepsilon_0}\int \frac{\rho d\tau}{r^2}\hat{\mathbf{r}} \qquad \text{(volume)} \qquad ...(1.8)$$

In above expressions r is the distance from the location element of charge (x', y', z') to the field point (x, y, z).

$$\mathbf{r} = (x - x')\mathbf{i} + (y - y')\mathbf{j} + (z - z')\mathbf{k} \qquad ...(1.9)$$

In eqns. (1.6), (1.7), (1.8) the integration is to be carried over the region occupied by the charge distribution i.e. the variables in the integrand are the source coordinates x', y', z'. Since the integrands involve vector quantities, the problem reduces to the evaluation of three scalar integrals corresponding to the three components E_{x}, E_{y}, E_{z}.

1.6. ELECTRIC FIELD OF A LINEAR CHARGE DISTRIBUTION

Consider a thin wire of length L with charge q uniformly distributed over its entire length. The linear charge density on the wire is $\lambda = q/L$. We shall calculate the electric field produced by the wire at a point P lying on the perpendicular bisector of the wire at a distance z from it. Consider a line element dl at a distance l from the point O, the foot of perpendicular drawn from P to the wire.

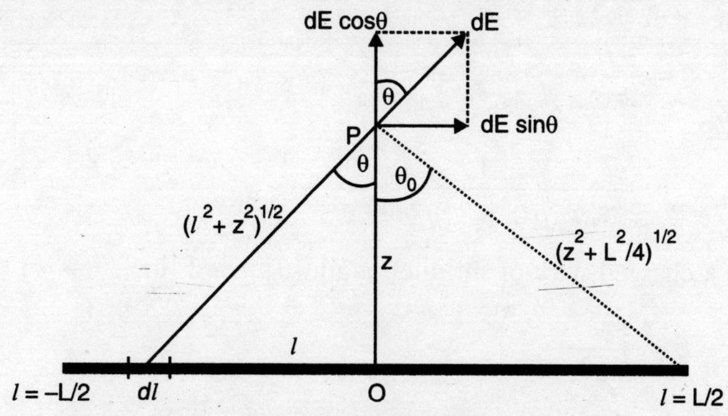

Fig. 1.6. Line charge.

The electric field at point P due to the charge element λdl is

$$dE = \frac{1}{4\pi\varepsilon_0}\frac{\lambda dl}{l^2 + z^2} \quad ...(1.10)$$

The components of dE parallel and perpendicular to wire are $dE \sin\theta$ and $dE \cos\theta$ respectively. A charge element symmetrically situated on the other side of point O produces electric field whose component parallel to the wire is opposite to that considered in the figure and the component perpendicular to the rod adds up. This happens for every charge element. Hence

$$\int dE \sin\theta = 0$$

Thus the electric field of the wire is perpendicular to the wire and is given by

$$E = \int dE\cos\theta = \frac{\lambda}{4\pi\varepsilon_0}\int \frac{dl}{l^2 + z^2}\cos\theta$$

$$= \frac{\lambda}{4\pi\varepsilon_0}\int \frac{z}{(l^2 + z^2)^{1/2}}\frac{dl}{(l^2 + z^2)}$$

$$= \frac{\lambda}{4\pi\varepsilon_0}\int \frac{zdl}{(l^2 + z^2)^{3/2}}$$

The electric field due to charged wire is

$$E = \frac{\lambda z}{4\pi\varepsilon_0}\int_{-L/2}^{L/2}\frac{dl}{(l^2 + z^2)^{3/2}} = \frac{2\lambda z}{4\pi\varepsilon_0}\int_{0}^{L/2}\frac{dl}{(l^2 + z^2)^{3/2}}$$

$$= \frac{2\lambda}{4\pi\varepsilon_0 z}\int_0^{\theta_0}\cos\theta\, d\theta, \quad l = z\tan\theta,\ dl = z\sec^2\theta\, d\theta, \quad \sin\theta_0 = \frac{L/2}{\sqrt{z^2 + L^2/4}}$$

$$= \frac{\lambda}{2\pi\varepsilon_0 z}\sin\theta_0$$

$$= \frac{\lambda}{2\pi\varepsilon_0 z}\frac{L/2}{\sqrt{z^2 + L^2/4}}$$

$$= \frac{\lambda}{2\pi\varepsilon_0 z}\frac{1}{\sqrt{1 + 4z^2/L^2}} \quad ...(1.11a)$$

The electric field of a charged wire of infinite length ($\theta_0 = \pi/2$ or $L \to \infty$) is

$$E = \frac{\lambda}{2\pi\varepsilon_0 z} \quad ...(1.11b)$$

The electric field of a charged wire points normal to it and varies inversely as the distance of field point from the wire.

1.7. ELECTRIC FIELD OF A CIRCULAR RING

Consider a circular ring of radius a carrying a charge q uniformly distributed over its circumference. Our aim is to calculate the electric field at an axial point. We take z-axis along the axis of the ring. The linear charge density on the ring is $\lambda/2\pi a$. The charge dq on a line dl is λdl. The electric field due to this charge element at an axial point lying at a distance z from the center of the ring is

$$dE = \frac{1}{4\pi\varepsilon_0}\frac{dq}{a^2+z^2} = \frac{\lambda}{4\pi\varepsilon_0}\frac{dl}{a^2+z^2} \qquad ...(1.12)$$

The projection of dE parallel and perpendicular to the axis of the ring are $dE\cos\theta$ and $dE\sin\theta$ respectively. The perpendicular component cancels out with its counterpart produced by charge element situated diametrically opposite to it. Thus

$$\int dE\sin\theta = 0$$

The components of dE parallel to the axis add up. Hence the total electric field of the ring is along the axis and is given by

$$E = \int dE\cos\theta = \frac{\lambda}{4\pi\varepsilon_0}\int\frac{dl}{(a^2+z^2)}\cdot\frac{z}{(a^2+z^2)^{1/2}} = \frac{\lambda z}{4\pi\varepsilon_0(a^2+z^2)^{3/2}}\int dl$$

$$= \frac{\lambda z}{4\pi\varepsilon_0(a^2+z^2)^{3/2}}2\pi a$$

$$= \frac{qz}{4\pi\varepsilon_0(a^2+z^2)^{3/2}} \qquad ...(1.13)$$

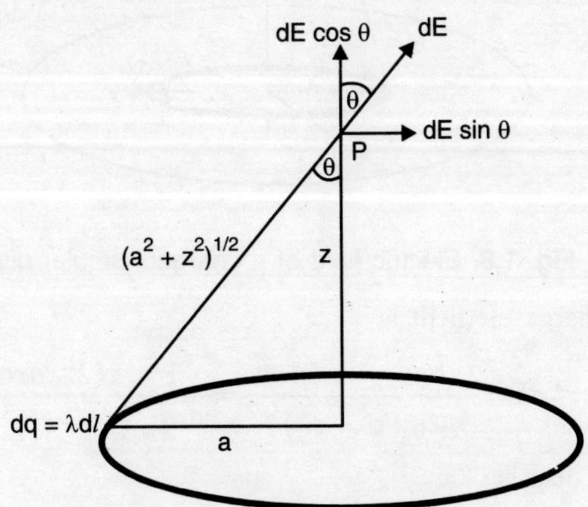

Fig. 1.7. Electric field of a charged ring.

The electric field is maximum at a point given by

$$\left(\frac{\partial E}{\partial z}\right)_{z=z_m} = 0$$

This gives $$z_m = \frac{a}{\sqrt{2}} \quad ...(1.14)$$

The maximum value of electric field is

$$E_{\max} = \frac{2q}{4\pi\varepsilon_0 3\sqrt{3}a^2} \quad ...(1.15)$$

From Eqn. (1.13) it can be easily seen that when the dimensions of the ring is very small in comparison to the distance z ($a/z \to 0$) the expression for the electric field of a charged ring reduces to that of point charge. Thus from a point far away from the ring it looks like a point charge.

1.8. ELECTRIC FIELD OF A CHARGED CIRCULAR DISC

Consider a uniformly charged circular disc of radius a with surface charge density $\sigma = q/\pi a^2$. We shall calculate the electric field of such a charged disc at a point lying on the axis of symmetry. We divide the disc into a large number of concentric rings with increasing radii. Consider one of the rings having radius x and width dx. Area of this ring is $2\pi x dx$ and charge on it is $dq = 2\pi x dx \sigma$.

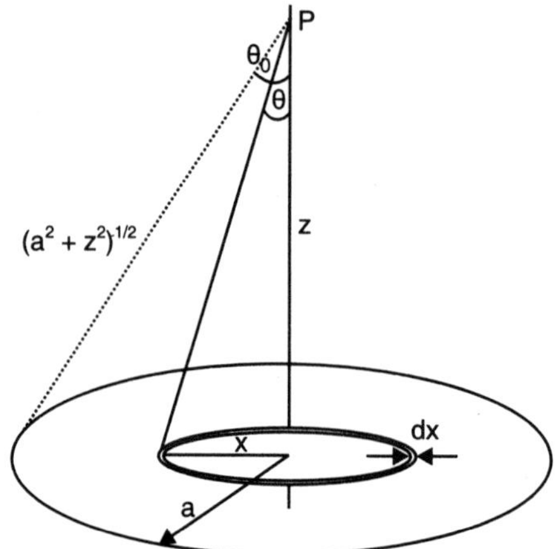

Fig. 1.8. Electric field of a charged circular disc.

The electric field of this charge element is

$$dE = \frac{1}{4\pi\varepsilon_0}\frac{zdq}{(x^2+z^2)^{3/2}} = \frac{1}{4\pi\varepsilon_0}\frac{z(2\pi x dx\sigma)}{(x^2+z^2)^{3/2}}$$

The electric field of entire disc is

$$E = \frac{1}{4\pi\varepsilon_0}.2\pi\sigma \; z\int_0^a \frac{xdx}{(x^2+z^2)^{3/2}} = \frac{\sigma z}{2\varepsilon_0}\left[\frac{-1}{(x^2+z^2)^{1/2}}\right]_0^a$$

$$= \frac{\sigma}{2\varepsilon_0}\left[1 - \frac{z}{(a^2+z^2)^{1/2}}\right] \qquad ...(1.16)$$

$$= \frac{\sigma}{2\varepsilon_0}[1 - \cos\theta_0] \qquad ...(1.17)$$

Where θ_0 is the angle subtended by the radius of the disc at the field point.

Infinite Charged Plane: In the limit $a \to \infty$, $\cos\theta_0 \to 0$, the disc becomes an infinite plane. The electric field in this limit is given by

$$E = \frac{\sigma}{2\varepsilon_0} \qquad ...(1.18)$$

At a very large distance ($z >> a$) the electric field is given by

$$E = \frac{\sigma}{2\varepsilon_0}\left[1 - \left(1 + \frac{a^2}{z^2}\right)^{-1/2}\right]$$

$$= \frac{\sigma}{2\varepsilon_0}\left[1 - \left(1 - \frac{a^2}{2z^2}\right)\right]$$

$$= \frac{1}{4\pi\varepsilon_0} \cdot \frac{q}{z^2} \qquad ...(1.19)$$

Thus the field of a circular disc at a point far away from the disc is that of a point charge.

1.9. ELECTRIC FLUX

Given the charge distribution, we can in principle calculate the resulting electric field by the methods described earlier. Sometimes the integral involved in such calculations turn out to be very tedious even for symmetric charge distribution. It was *F.* Gauss, a German mathematician, who discovered an ingenious method for calculating electric field produced by symmetric charge distribution. Gauss's method involves the concept of flux which we shall illustrate first.

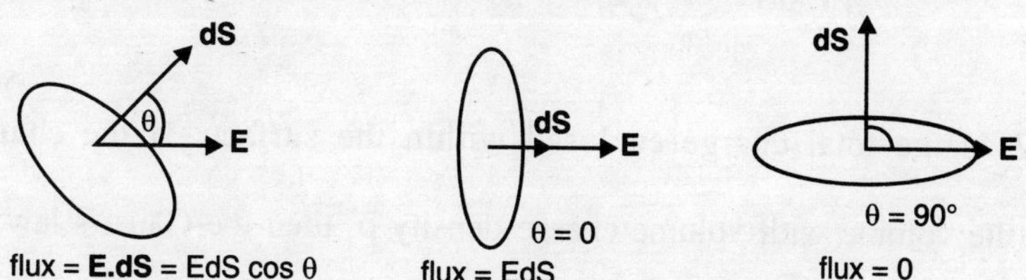

Fig. 1.9. Electric flux through an element of surface.

Now imagine an element of surface dS at point **r** (x, y, z). The electric field at point **r** is **E.** The scalar product **E·dS** = EdS cosθ is defined as the flux of electric field **E** over the surface **dS,** where θ is the angle between vector **E** and the normal to the surface dS. In other words the flux is defined as the product of normal component of electric field and the magnitude of surface area.

If we have a large surface S and the electric field varies from point to point over the surface then the electric flux over the surface S is given by surface integral

$$\text{flux} \quad \Phi = \int_S \mathbf{E}\cdot d\mathbf{S} = \int_S E\cos\theta \ dS \qquad ...(1.20)$$

If the surface S is closed one, the electric flux is written as

$$\text{flux} \quad \Phi = \oint_S \mathbf{E}\cdot d\mathbf{S} = \oint_S E\cos\theta \ dS \qquad ...(1.21)$$

Example 1. *A point charge q is located at the center of a sphere. Calculate the electric flux through the surface of sphere.*

Solution: The electric field E at the surface of the sphere is

$$E = \frac{q}{4\pi\varepsilon_0 R^2}, \qquad R \text{ is radius of sphere.}$$

The electric field has the same magnitude at every point on the sphere and is normal to it. Therefore,

$$\mathbf{E}\cdot\mathbf{dS} = EdS$$

Hence

$$\text{flux} \quad \Phi = \oint_S EdS = \oint_S \frac{q}{4\pi\varepsilon_0 R^2} dS = \frac{q}{4\pi\varepsilon_0 R^2}\oint_S dS = \frac{q}{4\pi\varepsilon_0 R^2} 4\pi R^2 = \frac{q}{\varepsilon_0}$$

1.10. GAUSS'S LAW

Gauss's law states that the total electric flux through a closed surface equals $\frac{1}{\varepsilon_0}$ *times the net charge enclosed within the surface.*

$$\oint_S \mathbf{E}\cdot\mathbf{dS} = \frac{1}{\varepsilon_0}\sum_i q_i \qquad ...(1.22)$$

Where $\sum_i q_i$ is the total charge enclosed within the surface. If the charges are uniformly distributed over the volume with volume charge density ρ, then the Gauss's law is expressed as

$$\oint_S \mathbf{E}\cdot\mathbf{dS} = \frac{1}{\varepsilon_0}\int_V \rho d\tau \qquad ...(1.23)$$

Proof. Suppose that we have a closed surface S that encloses a system of discrete charges q_1, q_2, q_3,... etc. Consider an element of surface **dS**. Let $\mathbf{E_1}$ be the electric field at **dS** due to charge q_1. Let $\mathbf{r_1}$ be the position vector from q_1 to **dS**. Then

$$\mathbf{E}_1 = \frac{q_1}{4\pi\varepsilon_0 r_1^3}\mathbf{r}_1$$

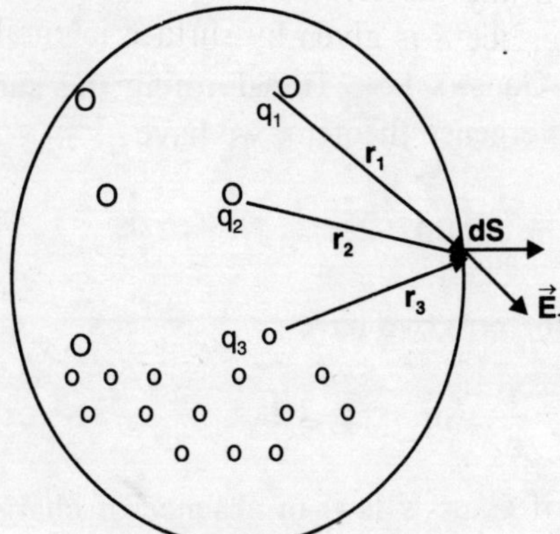

Fig. 1.10. Gauss's law.

The electric flux of vector $\mathbf{E_1}$ through the surface S is

$$\Phi_1 = \oint_S \mathbf{E}_1\cdot\mathbf{dS} = \oint_S \frac{q_1}{4\pi\varepsilon_0 r_1^3}\mathbf{r}_1\cdot\mathbf{dS} = \frac{q_1}{4\pi\varepsilon_0}\oint_S \frac{\mathbf{r}_1\cdot\mathbf{dS}}{r_1^3} = \frac{q_1}{4\pi\varepsilon_0}\oint_S d\Omega = \frac{q_1}{4\pi\varepsilon_0}(4\pi) = \frac{q_1}{\varepsilon_0}$$

Similarly, the flux of electric field $\mathbf{E_2}$, $\mathbf{E_3}$,... produced by charges q_2, q_3... respectively can be calculated and the results can expressed as

$$\Phi_2 = \oint_S \mathbf{E}_2\cdot\mathbf{dS} = \frac{q_2}{\varepsilon_0}$$

$$\Phi_3 = \oint_S \mathbf{E}_3\cdot\mathbf{dS} = \frac{q_3}{\varepsilon_0}$$

The total electric flux due to all charges enclosed within the surface is

$$\oint_S \mathbf{E}_1\cdot\mathbf{dS} + \oint_S \mathbf{E}_2\cdot\mathbf{dS} + \oint_S \mathbf{E}_3\cdot\mathbf{dS} + ... = \frac{q_1}{\varepsilon_0} + \frac{q_2}{\varepsilon_0} + \frac{q_3}{\varepsilon_0} + ...$$

$$\oint_S (\mathbf{E}_1 + \mathbf{E}_2 + \mathbf{E}_3 ...)\cdot\mathbf{dS} = \frac{1}{\varepsilon_0}(q_1 + q_2 + q_3 + ...)$$

$$\oint_S \mathbf{E}\cdot\mathbf{dS} = \frac{1}{\varepsilon_0}\sum_i q_i$$

Where $\mathbf{E} = \mathbf{E_1} + \mathbf{E_2} + \mathbf{E_3} + ...$ represents the resultant electric field at the center of surface element **dS** produced by all charges.

If the charge distribution is continuous with volume density ρ, then

$$\sum_i q_i = \int_V \rho\, d\tau$$

The Gauss's law then assumes the form

$$\oint_S \mathbf{E}\cdot d\mathbf{S} = \frac{1}{\varepsilon_0}\int_V \rho d\tau$$

This is the integral form of Gauss's law. Transforming the surface integral on the left hand side into volume integral using divergence theorem, we have

$$\int_V div\mathbf{E}\, d\tau = \frac{1}{\varepsilon_0}\int_V \rho d\tau$$

Since volume element $d\tau$ is not zero, we have

$$div\mathbf{E} = \frac{\rho}{\varepsilon_0} \quad \text{or} \quad \nabla\cdot\mathbf{E} = \frac{\rho}{\varepsilon_0} \qquad ...(1.24)$$

This is the differential form of Gauss's law. In absence of charges, Gauss's law reads

$$div\mathbf{E} = 0 \quad \text{or} \quad \nabla\cdot\mathbf{E} = 0 \qquad ...(1.25)$$

Equation (1.25) reads that in the region devoid of charges, the electric field is *solenoidal.*

It is worth to note that the Gauss's law is a powerful tool for computing electric field of symmetric charge distribution which we shall witness in the following sections. It should also be understood that the Gauss's law is not an independent law but it is a modification of Coulomb's law. Either of them may be regarded as the fundamental law of electrostatics. Gauss's law is the consequence of the inverse square and radial nature of the electric field. A field varying as $1/r^n$, $n \neq 2$, would not give Gauss's law.

1.11. APPLICATIONS OF GAUSS'S LAW

1.11.1. Electric Field of a Line Charge

Let us calculate the electric field of a line charge of infinite length at a distance z from it. Construct a coaxial cylindrical Gaussian surface of radius z and length l. By symmetry, we can guess that the electric field points normal to the charge distribution. The electric flux through the flat surface of the Gaussian is zero. At the curved surface, the electric field is everywhere normal to it. The charge enclosed within the Gaussian surface is λl, where λ is linear charge density. According to Gauss's law.

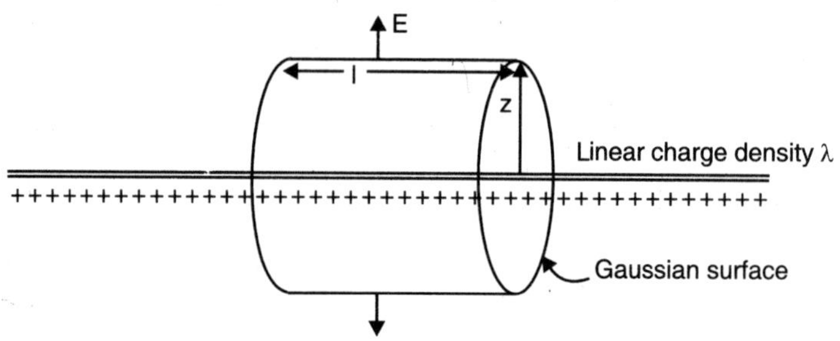

Fig. 1.11. Electric field of a line charge.

$$\oint_S \mathbf{E}\cdot d\mathbf{S} = \frac{q}{\varepsilon_0}$$

$$E(2\pi z l) = \frac{\lambda l}{\varepsilon_0}$$

$$E = \frac{\lambda}{2\pi\varepsilon_0 z} \qquad ...(1.26)$$

The electric field near a line charge varies inversely as the distance of the field point from it.

1.11.2. Electric Field of Charged Plane

Consider an infinite plane with uniform surface charge density σ. We have to calculate the electric field of this charged plane near it. Construct a cylindrical Gaussian surface (pill-box), half of which lies on one side of the plane and the remaining half on the other side with flat faces parallel to the plane as shown in the figure. By symmetry, the electric field E is everywhere normal to the plane. The electric flux through the curved surface of the Gaussian surface is zero. Let A be the area of the flat surface. The charge enclosed within the Gaussian surface is $q = \sigma A$.

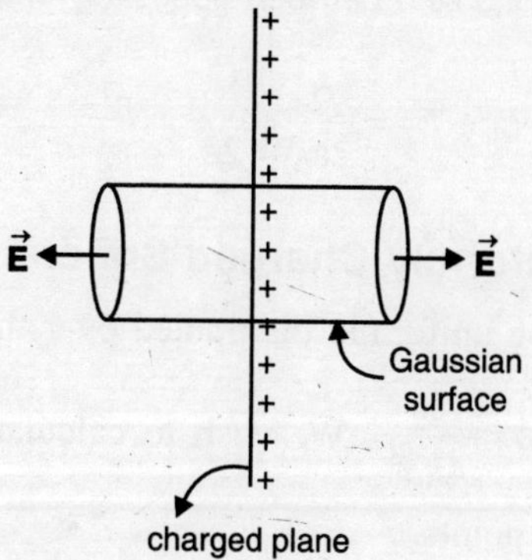

Fig. 1.12. Electric field of a charged plane.

Applying Gauss's theorem we have

$$EA + EA = \frac{\sigma A}{\varepsilon_0}$$

$$E = \frac{\sigma}{2\varepsilon_0} \qquad ...(1.27)$$

The electric field points away from the plane if the plane carries positive charge and towards the plane if the plane carries negative charge. We see that the electric field near a charged plane is independent of the distance of the field point from the plane.

1.11.3. Electric Field Between Two Planes Carrying Opposite Charge

Consider two oppositely charged parallel planes separated by a small distance. We shall calculate the electric field between the planes. Outside the planes, the electric field $\mathbf{E}_1$ due to the left plane cancels the electric field $\mathbf{E}_2$ of the right plane. In between the planes the electric fields of the two planes add up. Hence the total electric field between the planes is

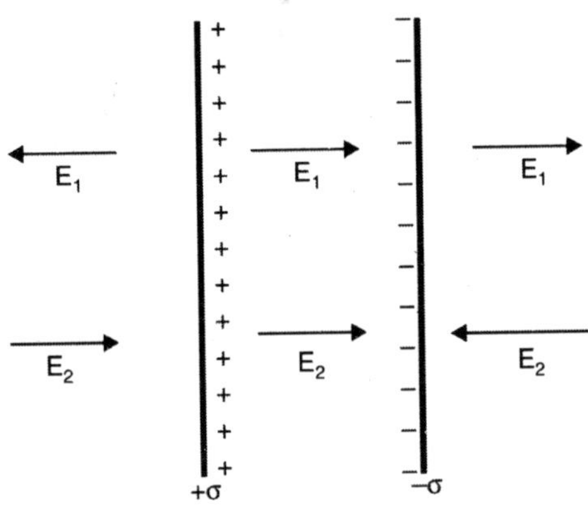

Fig. 1.13. Electric field between oppositely charged planes.

$$E = E_1 + E_2 = \frac{\sigma}{2\varepsilon_0} + \frac{\sigma}{2\varepsilon_0} = \frac{\sigma}{\varepsilon_0} \qquad ...(1.28)$$

1.11.4. Electric Field of Uniformly Charged Sphere

Let a certain amount of charge q be uniformly distributed over the volume of a sphere of radius a. The volume density of charge is $\rho = \frac{3q}{4\pi a^3}$. We wish to calculate the electric field of this charge distribution at internal and external points.

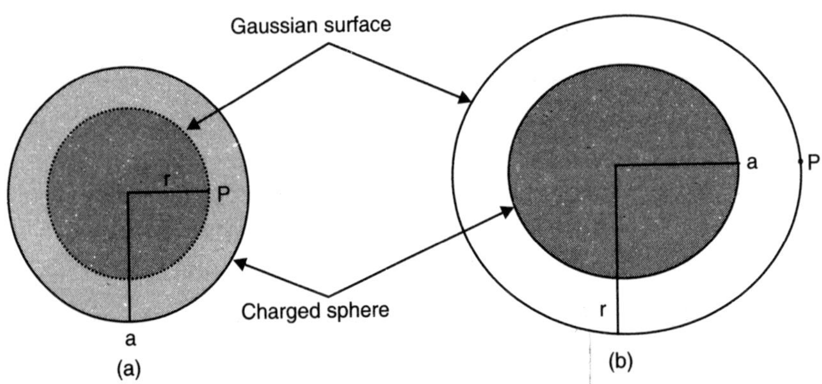

Fig. 1.14. (a) Field point lies inside the sphere (b) Field point lies outside the sphere.

Internal Point

Let the field point be at a distance r from the center of the sphere. Construct a spherical Gaussian surface of radius r with its center coinciding with that of the charged sphere. The total charge enclosed by the Gaussian surface is $\frac{4}{3}\pi r^3\rho$.

Applying Gauss's law we have

$$\oint_S \mathbf{E}\cdot d\mathbf{S} = \frac{1}{\varepsilon_0}\left(\frac{4}{3}\pi r^3\rho\right)$$

$$E(4\pi r^2) = \frac{4\pi r^3\rho}{3\varepsilon_0}$$

$$E = \frac{\rho r}{3\varepsilon_0} \qquad ...(1.29)$$

Thus the electric field inside a uniformly charged sphere varies directly as distance of the field point from the center.

External Point

When the field point lies outside the sphere, we construct the Gaussian surface through that point. In this case the Gaussian surface encloses the entire charge of the sphere. According to Gauss's theorem

$$\oint_S \mathbf{E}\cdot d\mathbf{S} = \frac{q}{\varepsilon_0}$$

$$E(4\pi r^2) = \frac{q}{\varepsilon_0}$$

$$E = \frac{q}{4\pi\varepsilon_0 r^2} \qquad ...(1.30)$$

Thus the electric field at an external point is the same as it would have been if the total charge of the sphere were concentrated at its center. The electric field at the surface is

$$E = \frac{q}{4\pi\varepsilon_0 a^2} \qquad ...(1.31)$$

1.11.5. Electric Field of a Charged Spherical Shell

Internal Point

Suppose we have a spherical shell of radius a with charge q uniformly distributed over its surface. The surface charge density is $\sigma = \frac{q}{4\pi a^2}$. Construct a Gaussian surface with center coinciding with that of the shell and radius equal to the distance of the field point from the center of the shell.

The Gaussian surface encloses no charge within it. Let **E** be the electric field at the internal point. Applying Gauss's theorem we have

$$\oint_S \mathbf{E}\cdot d\mathbf{S} = 0$$

$$E = 0$$

Thus the electric field at all internal points of a shell is zero.

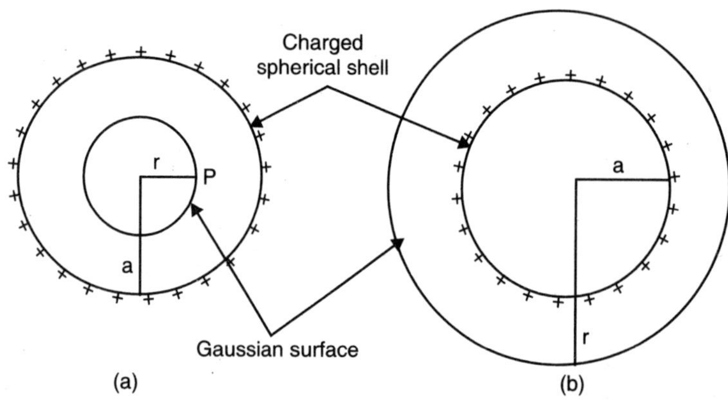

Fig. 1.15. (a) Electric field at internal point (b) Electric field at external point.

External Point

In order to calculate electric field at an external point, construct a Gaussian surface passing through the field point. This Gaussian surface encloses the entire charge lying on the spherical shell. Let **E** be the electric field at the point of observation. Applying Gauss's law we have

$$\oint_S \mathbf{E}\cdot d\mathbf{S} = \frac{q}{\varepsilon_0}$$

$$E(4\pi r^2) = \frac{q}{\varepsilon_0}$$

$$E = \frac{q}{4\pi\varepsilon_0 r^2} \qquad ...(1.32)$$

The electric field at an external point is the same as if the total charge of the shell were concentrated at the centre of the shell.

At the surface of the shell, the electric field is given by

$$E = \frac{q}{4\pi\varepsilon_0 a^2} \qquad ...(1.33)$$

1.12. ELECTRIC FIELD OF A CHARGED CONDUCTOR

There exists a class of materials whose constituent atoms or molecules contribute at least one charge carrier each of which is free to move throughout the body of the material. Such materials are called *conductors*. In metals the free charge carriers are electrons. In electrolytes free charge carriers are positive and negative ions. In semiconductors electrons and holes act like free charge carriers. These free charge carriers are capable of moving under the influence electric field however small.

When a neutral conductor is placed in an external field, the charge carriers are set into motion. The positive charge move in the direction of the electric field and the negative ones in opposite direction. These positive and negative charges pile up at the opposite ends of the outer surface of the conductor. These charges are called *induced charges*. These induced charges lying at the opposite ends of the conductor produce their own electric field which acts in a direction opposite to the external electric field. Thus the electric field of induced charges tends to cancel the external electric field. The movement of charge carriers under the action external electric field takes place until the electric field of induced charges completely cancels the external electric field within the conductor. The entire process is almost instantaneous.

From the above discussion we see that the introduction of conductor in electric field modifies the electric field in its vicinity. The lines of force of electric field terminate on the negative induced charge and begin again on the positive induced charge. *The electric field inside the conductor is zero and outside it electric field is normal to the surface of the conductor.*

$$\mathbf{E}_{\text{inside}} = 0, \quad \text{E}_{\text{outside}} = E_n$$

Since $\mathbf{E}_{\text{inside}} = 0$, equation $\nabla.E = \rho/\varepsilon_0$ indicates that $\rho_{\text{inside}} = 0$.

This means that any net charge given to the conductor spreads entirely over its surface. The fact $\mathbf{E}_{\text{inside}} = 0$ implies that the surface of the conductor is an equipotential surface.

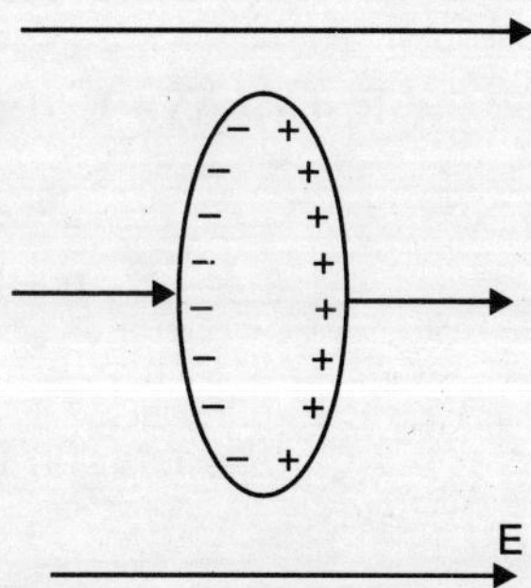

Fig. 1.16. A conductor in electric field.

Consider a conductor with surface charge density σ over its surface. We are interested in electric field outside the conductor in direct proximity to it. Now consider a disc like volume element whose surface constitutes the Gaussian surface. The disc is imagined to be so arranged that its one flat face is just outside the conductor and the other inside the conductor. The thickness of the disc is vanishingly small and is arranged normal to the conducting surface. Outside the conductor the electric field is normal to the conducting surface. Let E be the magnitude of the electric field at the centre of the flat face of the disc. The flux of electric field through the flat face of the disc lying inside the conductor is zero because $E = 0$. Because of the infinitesimal thickness of the disc, its curved surface is negligible and hence the flux through it may be taken to be zero. The flux of electric field through the outer flat face is $E\Delta S$, where ΔS is the area of the flat face. According to Gauss's theorem

$$E\Delta S = \frac{\sigma \Delta S}{\varepsilon_0}$$

$$E = \frac{\sigma}{\varepsilon_0} \qquad \text{... (1.34)}$$

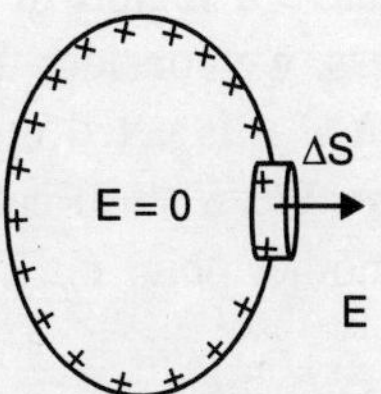

Fig. 1.17. Electric field outside a charged conductor.

This equation gives the magnitude of the electric field in the proximity of a charged conductor. The direction of E is along the normal to the surface of the conductor.

The above deduction of electric field due to a charged conductor is a special case of the result which we are going to derive now.

Consider a charged interface which separates two media 1 and 2. The surface charge density on the interface is σ. Let $\mathbf{E}_1$ and $\mathbf{E}_2$ be the electric fields on the two sides of the interface as shown in the figure. We construct a thin disc like volume element of infinitesimally small thickness such that one of the flat faces lies in the medium 1 and the other in medium 2. The flux of electric field through the curved surface of the disc is zero because of the infinitesimal thickness of the disc. The electric flux through the flat faces of the disc are $\mathbf{E}_1\cdot(-\mathbf{n}\Delta S)$ and $\mathbf{E}_2\cdot(\mathbf{n}\Delta S)$, where $\mathbf{n}$ is unit vector normal to the interface and ΔS is the area of the interface lying within the disc. Applying Gauss's law to the surface of the disc we have

$$\mathbf{E}_1\cdot(-)\mathbf{n}\Delta S + \mathbf{E}_2\cdot(\mathbf{n}\Delta S) = \frac{\sigma\Delta S}{\varepsilon_0}$$

$$\mathbf{E}_2\cdot\mathbf{n} - \mathbf{E}_1\cdot\mathbf{n} = \frac{\sigma}{\varepsilon_0} \quad \text{...(1.35)}$$

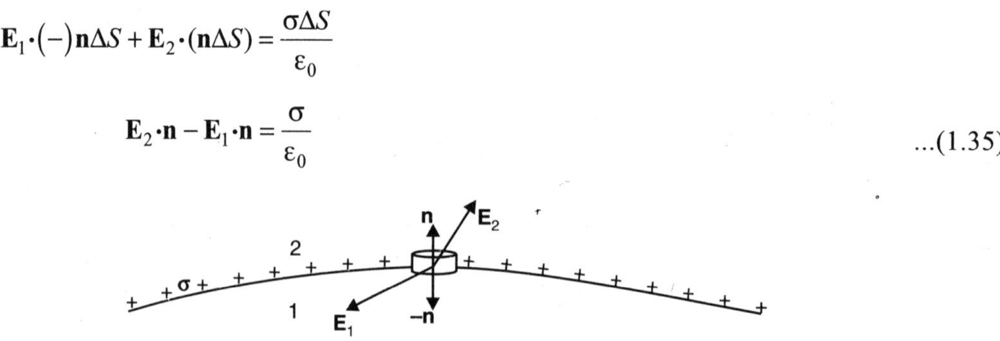

Fig. 1.18. Relationship between the normal components of electric field on the two sides of a charged interface.

Thus the difference of normal components of electric field at the charged interface equals the surface charged density divided by ε_0.

If one of the media, say 1, is conductor then $\mathbf{E}_1 = \mathbf{0}$ then

$$\mathbf{E}_2.\mathbf{n} = \frac{\sigma}{\varepsilon_0} \quad \text{...(1.36)}$$

This gives the electric field outside a conductor carrying charge with surface charge density σ.

1.13. ELECTRIC FIELD IS A CO–SERVATIVE FIELD

Suppose we have a region in which there exists an electric field which varies from point to point. For definiteness, we consider the electric field produced by a point charge q. If we place a test charge q_0 in this region, it is acted upon by a force $\mathbf{F} = q_0\mathbf{E}$, where $\mathbf{E}$ is the electric field at the location of the test charge. We wish to calculate the work done by the field in carrying the test charge from one point $\mathbf{r}_A$, to another point $\mathbf{r}_B$. The work done by the electric field in this process is

$$W_{AB} = \int_A^B q_0\mathbf{E}\cdot d\mathbf{l} \quad \text{...(1.37)}$$

Now we shall show that this work is independent of path connecting the points A and B and depends only on the positions of the end point A and B. Out of many conceivable paths we choose a path which consists of an arc of circle AA_1 and a radial path A_1A_2, then an arc of circle A_2A_3 and a radial path A_3A_4 and so on. See Fig. 1.19. Since the electric field is perpendicular to the arcs, no work is done by the electric field in carrying the test charge along these arcs. The contributions to total work come from the radial paths A_1A_2, A_3A_4 and A_5A_6. Thus

$$W_{AB} = q_0\int_A^B \mathbf{E\cdot dl} = q_0\left[\int_{A_1=A}^{A_2} \mathbf{E\cdot dl} + \int_{A_3}^{A_4} \mathbf{E\cdot dl} + \int_{A_5}^{A_6=B} \mathbf{E\cdot dl}\right]$$

$$= \frac{qq_0}{4\pi\varepsilon_0}\left[\int_{r_A}^{r_2}\frac{dr}{r^2} + \int_{r_3=r_2}^{r_4}\frac{dr}{r^2} + \int_{r_4=r_5}^{r_6=r_B}\frac{dr}{r^2}\right]$$

$$= \frac{qq_0}{4\pi\varepsilon_0}\left[\frac{1}{r_A} - \frac{1}{r_B}\right] \qquad ...(1.38)$$

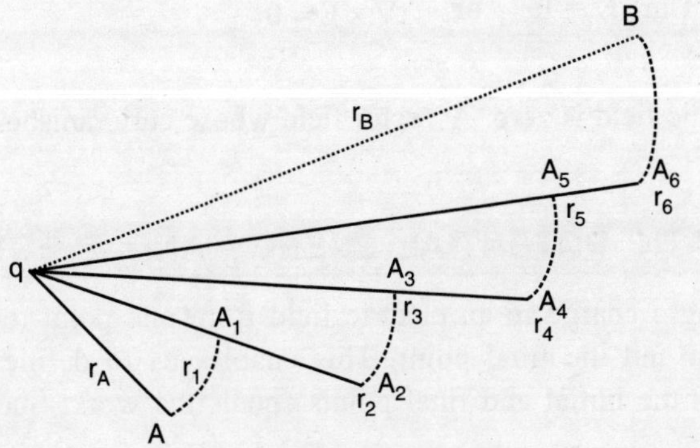

Fig. 1.19.

The right hand side of eqn. (1.38) depends only on the position of the end points A and B and not on the path joining these points. Thus we have proved a very important result:

$$\int_A^B \mathbf{E\cdot dl} \text{ is independent of path} \qquad ...(1.39)$$

A vector field whose line integral is independent of path is called a *conservative field.* So the electric field of a stationary charge is a *conservative field.* Now we shall prove that the line integral of electric field around a closed path is zero.

Now connect the points A and B by two paths 1 and 2. Since $\mathbf{E}$ is conservative,

$$\underset{\text{path 1}}{\int_A^B \mathbf{E\cdot dl}} = \underset{\text{path 2}}{\int_A^B \mathbf{E\cdot dl}}$$

$$\int_{A}^{B} \mathbf{E}\cdot\mathbf{dl} - \int_{A}^{B} \mathbf{E}\cdot\mathbf{dl} = 0$$

path 1 path 2

$$\int_{A}^{B} \mathbf{E}\cdot\mathbf{dl} + \int_{B}^{A} \mathbf{E}\cdot\mathbf{dl} = 0$$

path 1 path 2

Fig. 1.20.

$$\oint_{\text{closed path ABA}} \mathbf{E}\cdot\mathbf{dl} = \mathbf{0} \quad \text{...(1.40)}$$

Using Stokes theorem, eqn. (1.40) can be written as

$$\int \text{curl } \mathbf{E}\cdot\mathbf{dS} = 0$$

$$\text{Curl } \mathbf{E} = \mathbf{0} \quad \textbf{or} \quad \nabla \times \mathbf{E} = 0 \quad \text{...(1.41)}$$

The curl of electrostatic field is zero. A vector field whose curl vanishes is also called *irrotational field.*

1.14. ELECTROSTATIC POTENTIAL ENERGY AND ELECTRIC POTENTIAL

The work done in moving a charge in an electric field from one point to another depends only on the position of the initial and the final point. This enables us to define a function such that the difference of its values at the initial and final points equals the work. Such a function is called the potential energy function

If the source of electric field is a point charge q then the electric field **E** at point **r** is

$$\mathbf{E} = \frac{q}{4\pi\varepsilon_0 r^2}\hat{\mathbf{r}}$$

The force of electric field on the test charge + q_0 is

$$\mathbf{F} = q_0\mathbf{E} = \frac{qq_0}{4\pi\varepsilon_0 r^2}\hat{\mathbf{r}}$$

When the test charge + q_0 is moved from point A to point B, the work done by the force of electric field on the test charge is

$$W_{A\to B} = \int_{r_A}^{r_B} F(r)\hat{\mathbf{r}}.\mathbf{dl} = \int_{r_A}^{r_B} F(r)dr$$

Here **dl** is elementary displacement of the test charge and $\hat{\mathbf{r}}.\mathbf{dl} = dr$ is the magnitude of increment in position vector **r**.

Now,

$$W_{A\to B} = \frac{qq_0}{4\pi\varepsilon_0}\int_{r_A}^{r_B}\frac{dr}{r^2} = \frac{qq_0}{4\pi\varepsilon_0}\left(\frac{1}{r_A}-\frac{1}{r_B}\right) \qquad ...(1.42)$$

The work done by electric field (which is a conservative field) is defined as the decrement of potential energy of the test charge. Thus,

$$W_{A\to B} = U_A - U_B \qquad ...(1.43)$$

Comparison of eq. (1.42) and (1.43) gives

$$U_A = \frac{qq_0}{4\pi\varepsilon_0 r_A}, \qquad U_B = \frac{qq_0}{4\pi\varepsilon_0 r_B}$$

In general, we can write

$$U = \frac{1}{4\pi\varepsilon_0}\frac{qq_0}{r} + const.$$

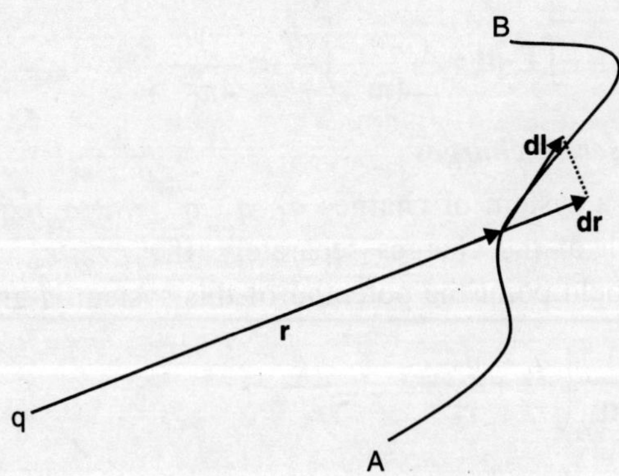

Fig. 1.20. Potential energy of a point charge q in the field of point charge q.

The value of constant is so chosen that U is zero at r = ". With this convention, the constant comes out to be zero. Hence

$$U = \frac{1}{4\pi\varepsilon_0}\frac{qq_0}{r}$$

This is the expression for the potential energy of a pair of charges q and q_0 separated by a distance r. For a pair of charges q_1 and q_2 separated by a distance r_{12} is given by

$$U = \frac{1}{4\pi\varepsilon_0}\frac{q_1 q_2}{r_{12}} \qquad ...(1.44)$$

The potential energy of a system in a given configuration is defined with respect to some arbitrarily chosen standard configuration. Notice that the difference of potential energies and not its absolute value is defined. The above analysis leads us to the following definition of potential energy.

In an electric field, the potential energy of a point charge at a point **r** *is defined with respect to its value at infinity, which is taken to be zero.* Thus the potential energy of a point charge q_2 lying at point **r** in an electric field **E** produced by a point charge q_1 located at the origin is, by definition,

$$U(\mathbf{r}) = -q_2\int_{\infty}^{r} \mathbf{E}\cdot d\mathbf{l} = -q_2\int_{\infty}^{r} \frac{q_1}{4\pi\varepsilon_0 r^2}dr = \frac{1}{4\pi\varepsilon_0}\frac{q_1 q_2}{r} \qquad ...(1.45)$$

Electrostatic Potential φ

The electrostatic potential at a point **r** *in the electric field of a point charge q located at the origin of position vector* **r** *is defined as the negative work done by the electric field in bringing a unit positive charge from infinity to that point.* In other words the electrostatic potential equals the potential energy per unit charge. Thus

$$\varphi(r) = -\int_{\infty}^{r} \mathbf{E}\cdot d\mathbf{l} = -\frac{q}{4\pi\varepsilon_0}\int_{\infty}^{r}\frac{dr}{r^2} = \frac{1}{4\pi\varepsilon_0}\frac{q}{r} \qquad ...(1.46a)$$

Potential of a system of discrete charges

The potential produced by a system of charges $q_1, q_2, q_3, \ldots\ldots q_N$ equals the algebraic sum of the potentials produced by each of the charges separately. If $r_1, r_2, r_3, \ldots\ldots r_N$ are the distances from each of the charges to the field point the potential of this system is given by

$$\varphi = \frac{1}{4\pi\varepsilon_0}\left(\frac{q_1}{r_1} + \frac{q_2}{r_2} + \ldots\ldots\ldots \frac{q_N}{r_N}\right)$$

$$= \frac{1}{4\pi\varepsilon_0}\sum_{i=1}^{N}\frac{q_i}{r_i} \qquad ...(1.46b)$$

1.15. ELECTRIC FIELD AS GRADIENT OF POTENTIAL (E = –grad φ = –∇φ)

Consider two points A (x, y, z) and B $(x + dx, y + dy, z + dz)$ at infinitesimally small separation. Let φ and $\varphi + d\varphi$ be the potentials at A and B respectively. By definition,

$$\varphi_B - \varphi_A = -W_{A\to B} \text{ (By electric field)}$$

$$= -E.dl$$

$$d\varphi = -E.dl$$

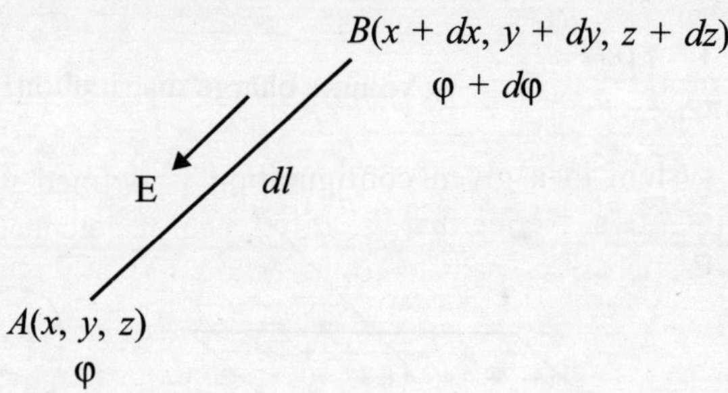

or, $$\left(\frac{\partial\varphi}{\partial x}dx + \frac{\partial\varphi}{\partial y}dy + \frac{\partial\varphi}{\partial z}dz\right) = -\left(E_x dx + E_y dy + E_z dz\right)$$

This gives

$$E_x = -\frac{\partial\varphi}{\partial x}, \quad E_y = -\frac{\partial\varphi}{\partial y}, \quad E_z = -\frac{\partial\varphi}{\partial z} \qquad ...(1.47)$$

The electric field **E** in terms of components is expressed as

$$\mathbf{E} = -\left(\mathbf{i}\frac{\partial\varphi}{\partial x} + \mathbf{j}\frac{\partial\varphi}{\partial y} + \mathbf{k}\frac{\partial\varphi}{\partial z}\right) = -\nabla\varphi \qquad ...(1.48)$$

1.16. POTENTIAL OF CONTINUOUS CHARGE DISTRIBUTION

The potential of a system of discrete charges is equal to the sum of potentials of individual charges and is given by

$$\varphi = \frac{1}{4\pi\varepsilon_0}\sum_i \frac{q_i}{r_i} \qquad ...(1.49)$$

Let us write expressions for the potential produced by continuous charge distributions. If the charges are distributed on a line with linear charge density λ (charge per unit length) the potential is given by

$$\varphi = \frac{1}{4\pi\varepsilon_0}\int \frac{\lambda dl}{r} \qquad \text{(Linear charge distribution)} \qquad ...(1.50)$$

If the charges are distributed over the surface with surface charge density σ, the potential is given by

$$\varphi = \frac{1}{4\pi\varepsilon_0}\int \frac{\sigma dS}{r} \qquad \text{(Surface charge distribution)} \qquad ...(1.51)$$

For a volume distribution of charges with volume density of charge ρ

$$\varphi = \frac{1}{4\pi\varepsilon_0}\int\frac{\rho d\tau}{r} \qquad \text{(Volume charge distribution)} \qquad ...(1.52)$$

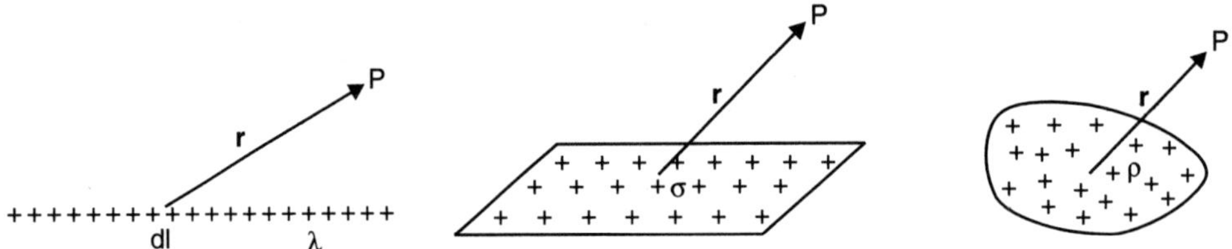

Fig. 1.22. Line, surface and volume distribution of charges.

1.17. ELECTROSTATIC ENERGY OF A CHARGED DISTRIBUTION

The potential energy of a charged distribution is defined as the work done in assembling its constituent particles from infinity to the given configuration. For a pair of charged particles q_1 and q_2 separated by a distance r_{12}, the potential energy is

$$U = W = \frac{1}{4\pi\varepsilon_0}\frac{q_1 q_2}{r_{12}}$$

For a system of three charges

$$U = W = \frac{1}{4\pi\varepsilon_0}\left(\frac{q_1 q_2}{r_{12}} + \frac{q_2 q_3}{r_{23}} + \frac{q_3 q_1}{r_{31}}\right) \qquad ...(1.53)$$

The above expression can be written as

$$U = \frac{1}{4\pi\varepsilon_0}\cdot\frac{1}{2}\cdot\sum_{i=1}^{3}\sum_{j=1, i\neq j}^{3}\frac{q_i q_j}{r_{ij}} \qquad ...(1.54)$$

In above equation, the summation over i and j contains each pair of charges twice like $\frac{q_1 q_2}{r_{12}}$ and $\frac{q_2 q_1}{r_{21}}$. The factor ½ corrects the over-counting of pairs. For a system of N discrete charges the expression for potential energy becomes

$$U = \frac{1}{2}\cdot\frac{1}{4\pi\varepsilon_0}\sum_{i=1}^{N} q_i \sum_{j=1}^{N}\frac{q_j}{r_{ij}} \qquad ...(1.55)$$

or $$U = \frac{1}{2}\sum_{i}^{N} q_i \varphi_i \qquad ...(1.56)$$

Where $$\varphi_i = \frac{1}{4\pi\varepsilon_0}\sum_{j=1}^{N}\frac{q_j}{r_{ij}} \qquad ...(1.57)$$

Φ_i represents the potential at the location of charge q_i due to all other charges. For continuous charge distribution the above expression for potential energy becomes

$$U = \frac{1}{2}\int \varphi\rho d\tau \qquad \text{(Volume distribution of charge)} \qquad ...(1.58)$$

$$U = \frac{1}{2}\int \varphi\sigma ds \qquad \text{(Surface distribution of charge)} \qquad ...(1.59)$$

$$U = \frac{1}{2}\int \varphi\lambda dl \qquad \text{(Line distribution of charge)} \qquad ...(1.60)$$

1.18. ELECTROSTATIC ENERGY DENSITY

According to one interpretation the energy of a charge distribution is stored in the system itself. Change in energy occurs when the configuration of the system undergoes change. Now we shall give another interpretation according to which the energy of the system resides in space in the form of electric field.

The energy of a volume distribution of charge characterized by volume density of charge ρ is given by

$$U = \frac{1}{2}\int \varphi\rho d\tau \qquad ....(1.61)$$

Making use of Gauss's law $\nabla\cdot\mathbf{E} = \rho/\varepsilon_0$, we write

$$U = \frac{1}{2}\varepsilon_0\int(\nabla\cdot\mathbf{E})\varphi\, d\tau \qquad ...(1.62)$$

We now use the following vector identity to replace $\nabla\cdot\mathbf{E}$ in eqn. (1.62)

$$\nabla\cdot\varphi\mathbf{E} = \nabla\varphi\cdot\mathbf{E} + \varphi\nabla\cdot\mathbf{E} = -\mathbf{E}\cdot\mathbf{E} = -E^2 + \varphi\nabla\cdot\mathbf{E}$$

Doing so we obtain

$$U = \frac{1}{2}\varepsilon_0\left[\int(\nabla\cdot\varphi\mathbf{E})d\tau + \int E^2 d\tau\right] \qquad ...(1.63)$$

The first volume integral on the right hand side of eqn. (1.63) in now transformed into surface integral using divergence theorem of vector analysis. This gives

$$U = \frac{1}{2}\varepsilon_0\left[\int \varphi\mathbf{E}\cdot dS + \int E^2 d\tau\right] \qquad ...(1.64)$$

In eqn. (1.61) the integration extends over the volume occupied by the charged distribution. Any volume larger than this is not going to affect the value of integral because outside the charge distribution $\rho = 0$ and hence the integral contributes nothing to the potential energy. By increasing the volume, we increase the area of the bounding surface and its distance from the charge distribution. In the integrand of the surface integral, the first factor viz φ varies as $1/r$, the second factor E varies as $1/r^2$ and the third factor dS varies as r^2. So the integrand goes over as $1/r$. So if we integrate eqn. (1.64) over infinite volume, the first integral contributes nothing to energy and then the energy of the system comes out to be

$$U = \frac{1}{2}\varepsilon_0 \int_{\text{all space}} E^2 d\tau \qquad \text{...(1.65)}$$

Equation (1.65) allows us to interpret that the electrostatic energy of charge distribution resides in all space, the energy density being

$$u = \frac{U}{\text{volume}} = \frac{1}{2}\varepsilon_0 E^2 \qquad \text{...(1.66)}$$

1.19. ELECTROSTATIC ENERGY OF A CHARGED SPHERE

Consider a sphere of radius R with charge q distributed uniformly over its volume. The volume charge density of the sphere is $\rho = \frac{3q}{4\pi R^3}$. A sphere may be imagined to be built up by successive addition of spherical layers of increasing radii. In the intermediate process, suppose we have built up a sphere of radius r. The electric potential on the surface of this sphere is

$$\varphi = \frac{1}{4\pi\varepsilon_0}\frac{\frac{4}{3}\pi r^3 \rho}{r} \qquad \text{...(1.67)}$$

Let an element of charge dq be added over the surface of this sphere in form of spherical layer of thickness dr. The charge $dq = 4\pi r^2\, dr\, \rho$. The work done in process is

$$dW = \varphi dq = \left(\frac{1}{4\pi\varepsilon_0}\frac{\frac{4}{3}\pi r^3 \rho}{r}\right)\left(4\pi r^2 dr \rho\right)$$

$$= \frac{4\pi\rho^2}{3\varepsilon_0} r^4 dr$$

The work done in assembling the total charge in the form of a sphere of radius R is

$$W = \frac{4\pi\rho^2}{3\varepsilon_0}\int_0^R r^4 dr = \frac{1}{4\pi\varepsilon_0}\cdot\frac{3}{5}\cdot\frac{q^2}{R} \qquad \text{...(1.68)}$$

This work is stored as the potential energy of sphere. This amount of energy is emanated when the sphere is dismantled so that its fragments are infinitely far apart.

$$U = \frac{1}{4\pi\varepsilon_0} \cdot \frac{3}{5} \frac{q^2}{R} \qquad ...(1.69)$$

1.20. CLASSICAL RADIUS OF ELECTRON

In the expression for the potential energy of charged solid sphere the factor 3/5 is the characteristics of spherical charge distribution. We know nothing about the charge distribution in electron hence the factor 3/5 may be omitted. The electrostatic energy of electron may be written as

$$U = \frac{1}{4\pi\varepsilon_0} \frac{e^2}{r_0}$$

Assuming that the electrostatic energy of electron equals the rest energy m_0c^2, we have

$$\frac{1}{4\pi\varepsilon_0} \frac{e^2}{r_0} = m_0 c^2$$

Therefore,
$$r_0 = \frac{1}{4\pi\varepsilon_0} \frac{e^2}{m_0 c^2} = 2.82 \times 10^{-15} \text{ m} \qquad ...(1.70)$$

This distance r_0 is called the classical radius of electron.

1.21. ELECTROSTATIC ENERGY OF A CHARGED SPHERICAL SHELL

Let a charge q be uniformly distributed over the surface of a spherical shell of radius R. The surface charge density is $\sigma = q/4\pi R^2$. The electrostatic energy of the shell is

$$U = \frac{1}{2}\int \varphi\sigma dS = \frac{1}{2}\int \left(\frac{q}{4\pi\varepsilon_0 R}\right)\left(\frac{q}{4\pi R^2}\right) dS = \frac{q^2}{8\pi\varepsilon_0 R(4\pi R^2)}\int dS = \frac{q^2}{8\pi\varepsilon_0 R} \qquad ...(1.71)$$

The same result may also be obtained using the field concept. The electrostatic energy around the spherical shell is

$$U = \frac{1}{2}\varepsilon_0 \int E^2 d\tau$$

The integration is to be carried overall the space occupied by the electric field. Consider the volume element $d\tau$ in the form of a spherical shell of radius r and thickness dr then $d\tau = 4\pi r^2 dr$. Thus

$$U = \frac{1}{2}\varepsilon_0 \int_R^\infty \left(\frac{q}{4\pi\varepsilon_0 r^2}\right)^2 (4\pi r^2 dr) = \frac{q^2}{8\pi\varepsilon_0 R} \qquad ...(1.72)$$

1.22. FORCE OF ATTRACTION BETWEEN PLATES OF A CHARGED CAPACITOR

The plates of oppositely charged capacitor attract each other. Let F be the force of attraction between the plates. If the plate separation is increased by dx, the work needed is

$$dW = Fdx \quad ...(1.73)$$

This work appears as increase in potential energy of the capacitor. The potential energy of the capacitor with charge q, area A and plate separation x is

$$U = \frac{q^2}{2C} = \frac{q^2}{2\varepsilon_0 A}x$$

When the plate separation is increased by dx, the potential energy is increased by amount

$$dU = \frac{q^2}{2\varepsilon_0 A}dx$$

Since $dW = dU$, we have

$$F = \frac{q^2}{2\varepsilon_0 A} = \frac{1}{2}\varepsilon_0 AE^2 \quad ...(1.74)$$

The force acting per unit area of the plate is

$$\frac{F}{A} = \frac{1}{2}\varepsilon_0 E^2 \quad ...(1.75)$$

The same result can also be obtained as follows. The electrostatic energy between the plates of the capacitor is

$$U = (energy\ density)(volume) = \left(\frac{1}{2}\varepsilon_0 E^2\right)(Ax)$$

The force is negative gradient of potential energy, hence

$$F = \left(-\frac{dU}{dx}\right) = \frac{1}{2}\varepsilon_0 AE^2$$

1.23. PRESSURE ON A CHARGED SURFACE

A charged surface because of its own charge experiences an outward pressure regardless of the sign of charge. Consider a body of conductor. When a charge is given to a conducting body, the entire charge resides on its surface. The electric field inside the body of conductor is zero and just outside is σ/ε_0. The electric field at a point outside the conductor may be assumed to be the vector sum of the field $\mathbf{E}_1$ due to elementary part dA near the point and the field $\mathbf{E}_2$ due to the remaining part of the conductor.

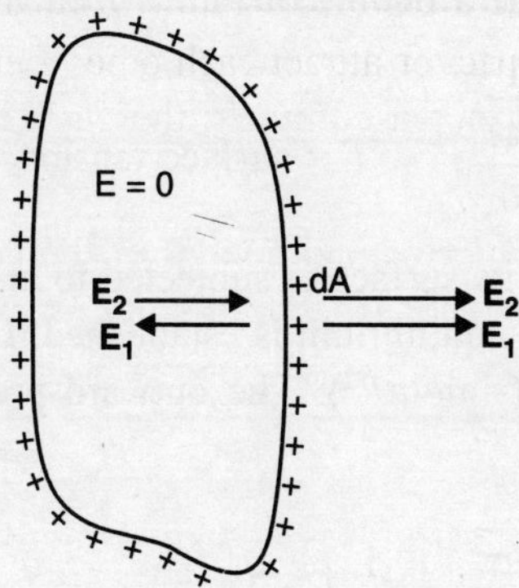

Fig. 1.23. The electric field inside and outside a charged conducting body.

Outside the conductor, the field $\mathbf{E_1}$ and $\mathbf{E_2}$ have the same direction and hence add up. Inside the conductor, the fields $\mathbf{E_1}$ and $\mathbf{E_2}$ are oppositely directed and hence cancel each other.

$$E_{\text{outside}} = E_1 + E_2 = \frac{\sigma}{\varepsilon_0} \quad ...(1.76)$$

$$E_{\text{inside}} = E_1 - E_2 = 0 \quad ...(1.77)$$

From (1.77) we have $E_1 = E_2$.

Therefore, $$E_{\text{outside}} = 2E_2 = \frac{\sigma}{\varepsilon_0}$$

or $$E_2 = \frac{\sigma}{2\varepsilon_0} \quad ...(1.78)$$

Due to the electric field E_2, an elementary area dA experiences a force

$$F = \sigma dA E_2 = \frac{\sigma^2}{2\varepsilon_0} dA \quad \text{(in outward direction)}$$

The force per unit area or pressure on the surface is

$$P = \frac{F}{dA} = \frac{\sigma^2}{2\varepsilon_0} = \frac{1}{2}\varepsilon_0 E_{\text{outside}}^2 \quad ...(1.79)$$

1.24. CHARGED BUBBLE

The outward excess pressure p inside a bubble of radius r balances the pressure of surface tension. Thus

$$p = \frac{4T}{r}, \qquad T = \text{surface tension of liquid}$$

If the bubble is gently charged, its surface is subjected to an additional outward pressure, which makes the bubble expand and a new equilibrium is established. Let R be the new radius. The surface charge density on the bubble is σ ($= q/4\pi R^2$). The outward pressure on the surface of the bubble due to the charge is

$$p_E = \frac{\sigma^2}{2\varepsilon_0} = \frac{1}{2\varepsilon_0}\left(\frac{q}{4\pi R^2}\right)^2 = \frac{q^2}{32\varepsilon_0 \pi^2 R^4}$$

Let p' be the new value of excess pressure. Hence

$$p' + p_E = \frac{4T}{R}$$

If the mechanical pressure p' is to vanish, the charge q_0 needed to obtain this condition is given by

$$\frac{q_0^{\,2}}{32\varepsilon_0 \pi^2 R^4} = \frac{4T}{R}$$

$$q_0 = 8\pi R\sqrt{2\varepsilon_0 RT} \qquad \text{...(1.80)}$$

The potential of the bubble in this case is

$$\varphi = \frac{q_0}{4\pi\varepsilon_0 R} = \sqrt{\frac{8RT}{\varepsilon_0}} \qquad \text{...(1.81)}$$

1.25. POTENTIAL OF A CHARGED RING

Consider circular ring of radius a with charge q uniformly distributed over its circumference. The linear charge density is $\lambda = q/2\pi a$. The charge on a line element of length dl is λdl. The potential due to the charge element at an axial point lying at distance z from the centre of the ring is

$$d\varphi = \frac{1}{4\pi\varepsilon_0}\frac{\lambda dl}{(a^2 + z^2)^{1/2}}$$

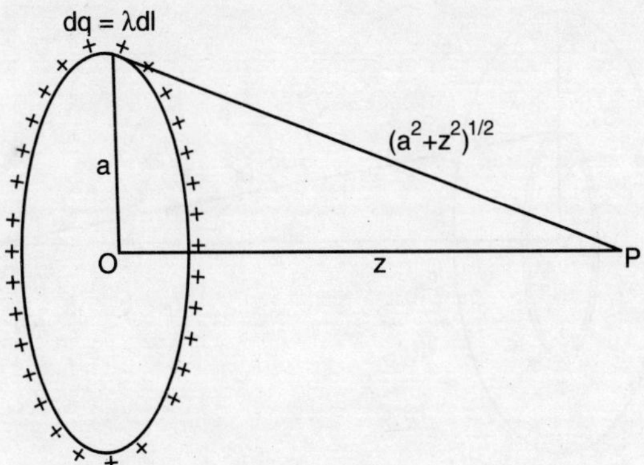

Fig. 1.24. Potential of charged circular ring.

Potential of entire ring is

$$\varphi = \frac{\lambda}{4\pi\varepsilon_0 (a^2 + z^2)^{1/2}} \int dl = \frac{\lambda(2\pi a)}{4\pi\varepsilon_0 (a^2 + z^2)^{1/2}}$$

or
$$\varphi(z) = \frac{q}{4\pi\varepsilon_0 (a^2 + z^2)^{1/2}} \qquad ...(1.82)$$

The electric field at point P is given by

$$E_z = -\frac{\partial\varphi}{\partial z} = \frac{qz}{4\pi\varepsilon_0 (a^2 + z^2)^{3/2}} \qquad ...(1.83)$$

1.26. POTENTIAL OF A CHARGED CIRCULAR DISC

Consider a circular disc of radius a carrying a charge q uniformly distributed over its surface. The surface density of charge is $\sigma = q/\pi a^2$. We want to calculate the potential of this disc at an axial point at a distance z from its center. We divide the circular disc into a large number of concentric rings and consider one of them having radius x and width dx. The charge on this element is $dq = 2\pi x dx \sigma$. Every point of this element is at a distance $(x^2 + z^2)^{1/2}$ from the point of observation P. The potential of the elementary ring at point P is

$$d\varphi = \frac{1}{4\pi\varepsilon_0} \frac{2\pi x dx \sigma}{(x^2 + z^2)^{1/2}}$$

The potential of entire disc is

$$\varphi = \frac{\sigma}{2\varepsilon_0} \int_0^a \frac{x dx}{(x^2 + z^2)^{1/2}} = \frac{\sigma}{2\varepsilon_0} \left[(x^2 + z^2)^{1/2} \right]_0^a$$

$$= \frac{\sigma}{2\varepsilon_0} \left[\sqrt{a^2 + z^2} - z \right] \qquad ...(1.84)$$

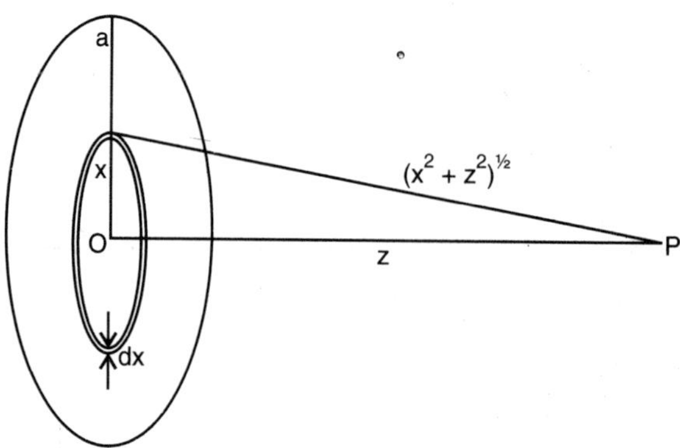

Fig. 1.25. Potential of a charged circular disc.

If the point of observation is far away ($z >> a$) from the disc, we can use the following approximation.

$$(a^2 + z^2)^{1/2} = z\left(1 + \frac{a^2}{z^2}\right)^{1/2} \approx z\left(1 + \frac{1}{2}\frac{a^2}{z^2}\right)$$

Then the potential at a very large distance is given by

$$\varphi = \frac{\sigma}{2\varepsilon_0}\left(\frac{a^2}{2z}\right) = \frac{1}{4\pi\varepsilon_0}\frac{q}{z}$$

Thus, at points far away from the disc, it behaves like a point charge.

The electric field at an axial point is

$$E_z = -\frac{\partial\varphi}{\partial z} = \frac{\sigma}{2\varepsilon_0}\left(1 - \frac{z}{\sqrt{a^2 + z^2}}\right) \qquad \text{...(1.85)}$$

1.27. POTENTIAL OF A CHARGED SPHERICAL SHELL

Consider a spherical shell of radius R carrying a charge q uniformly distributed over its surface. The surface charge density is $\sigma = q/4\pi R^2$. We wish to calculate the electric potential of this shell at external and internal points.

External Point

Let the point of observation lie at a distance r from the center O of the shell. Join OP. Consider a portion of the shell between two closely spaced parallel planes perpendicular to OP at angular positions θ and $\theta + d\theta$ as shown in the figure. This portion of the shell is in the form of a ring of radius $R \sin\theta$ and width $R\, d\theta$. It has surface area $dS = (2\pi R\sin\theta)\, Rd\,\theta$ and charge $dq = \sigma\,(2\pi R\sin\theta)\, Rd\theta$. Let x denote the distance from the ring to the point of observation P. From the figure

$$x^2 = r^2 + R^2 - 2rR\cos\theta \qquad \text{...(1.86)}$$

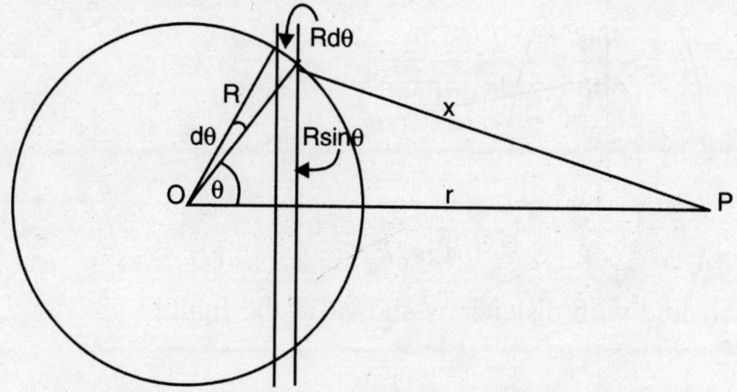

Fig. 1.26. Potential of charged spherical shell.

The potential of the ring at point P is

$$d\varphi = \frac{1}{4\pi\varepsilon_0}\frac{dq}{x} = \frac{1}{4\pi\varepsilon_0}\frac{2\pi R\sin\theta\, Rd\theta\,\sigma}{x} \quad ...(1.87)$$

Differentiation of Eqs. (1.86) gives

$$xdx = rR\sin\theta d\theta \quad ...(1.88)$$

Making use of (1.88) we eliminate θ from (1.87) to get

$$d\varphi = \frac{1}{4\pi\varepsilon_0}\frac{2\pi R\sigma}{r}dx$$

Potential of the entire shell

$$\varphi = \frac{1}{4\pi\varepsilon_0}\frac{2\pi R\sigma}{r}\int_{r-R}^{r+R} dx = \frac{1}{4\pi\varepsilon_0}\frac{4\pi R^2\sigma}{r} \quad ...(1.89)$$

$$\varphi = \frac{1}{4\pi\varepsilon_0}\frac{q}{r} \quad ...(1.90)$$

Thus the potential of a charged spherical shell at an external point is the same as if its total charge were concentrated at its centre.

Internal Point

If the point of observation P lies inside the shell, the new limits of integration in eqn. (1.88) are $x = (R - r)$ to $x = (R + r)$. Thus

$$\varphi = \frac{1}{4\pi\varepsilon_0}\frac{2\pi R\sigma}{r}\int_{R-r}^{R+r} dx$$

or,

$$\varphi = \frac{1}{4\pi\varepsilon_0}\frac{q}{R} \quad ...(1.91)$$

The potential inside the spherical shell is constant everywhere.

The electric field at *external point* is

$$E = -\frac{\partial \varphi}{\partial r} = -\frac{\partial}{\partial r}\left(\frac{q}{4\pi\varepsilon_0 r}\right) = \frac{1}{4\pi\varepsilon_0}\frac{q}{r^2} \qquad ...(1.92)$$

And at *internal point* is

$$E = -\frac{\partial \varphi}{\partial r} = -\frac{\partial}{\partial r}\left(\frac{q}{4\pi\varepsilon_0 R}\right) = 0$$

The variation of potential with distance is shown in the figure.

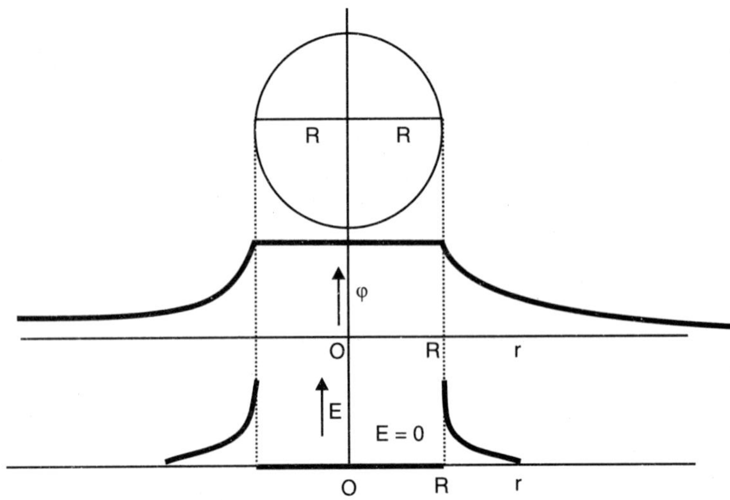

Fig. 1.27. Variation of electric potential and field with distance.

Aliter: From the definition of potential, the potential of a charged shell at an external point is

$$\varphi(r) = -\int_{\infty}^{r} \mathbf{E}\cdot d\mathbf{l} = -\frac{q}{4\pi\varepsilon_0}\int_{\infty}^{r}\frac{dr}{r^2} = \frac{q}{4\pi\varepsilon_0 r}$$

The potential at an internal point is

$$\varphi(r) = -\int_{\infty}^{r} \mathbf{E}\cdot d\mathbf{l} = -\int_{\infty}^{R}\frac{q\,dr}{4\pi\varepsilon_0 r^2} - \int_{R}^{r}(0)dr = \frac{q}{4\pi\varepsilon_0 R}$$

1.28 POTENTIAL OF A CHARGED SOLID SPHERE

Let a (dielectric) solid sphere of radius R carry a charge q uniformly distributed over its volume. The volume charge density is $\rho = 3q/4\pi R^3$. The sphere may be imagined to be made up of thin concentric spherical shells with varying radii from zero to R. A typical shell of radius x and thickness dx is shown in the Fig. 1.28. The charge contained in this shell is

$$dq = 4\pi x^2 dx\rho \qquad ...(1.93)$$

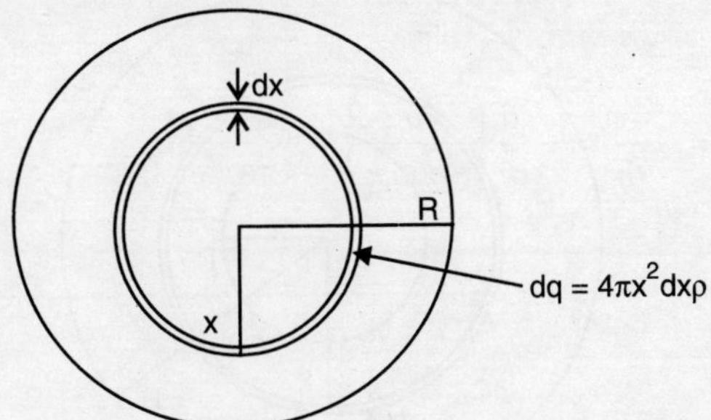

Fig. 1.28. Solid sphere may be imagined to made up of concentric spherical shells.

The potential of this spherical shell at an external point at a distance r from its center is

$$d\varphi = \frac{1}{4\pi\varepsilon_0}\frac{dq}{r} = \frac{1}{4\pi\varepsilon_0}\frac{4\pi x^2\,dx\rho}{r} \qquad \text{...(1.94)}$$

The potential of the entire sphere is

$$\varphi = \frac{1}{4\pi\varepsilon_0}\frac{4\pi\rho}{r}\int_0^R x^2\,dx$$

or,

$$\varphi = \frac{1}{4\pi\varepsilon_0}\frac{q}{r} \qquad \text{...(1.95)}$$

The electric field at an external point is

$$E = -\frac{\partial\varphi}{\partial r} = \frac{1}{4\pi\varepsilon_0}\frac{q}{r^2} \qquad \text{...(1.96)}$$

Thus the electric field produced by a charged sphere is equivalent to field produced by a point charge of the same amount placed at the center of the sphere.

Internal Point

Let us find an expression for the potential of a sphere at an internal point at a distance $r (r < R)$. Imagine a concentric solid sphere of radius r such that the point of observation lies at the surface of this sphere, which we shall call inner sphere. The potential at an internal point due to the entire sphere consists of two terms: φ_1 due to inner sphere and φ_2 due to the remaining part, which we shall call outer part. The charge contained within the inner sphere is $q_1 = \frac{4}{3}\pi r^3\rho$. The potential of inner sphere at the internal point is

$$\varphi_1 = \frac{1}{4\pi\varepsilon_0}\frac{q_1}{r} = \frac{\rho r^2}{3\varepsilon_0} = \frac{q}{4\pi\varepsilon_0 R^3}r^2 \qquad \text{...(1.97)}$$

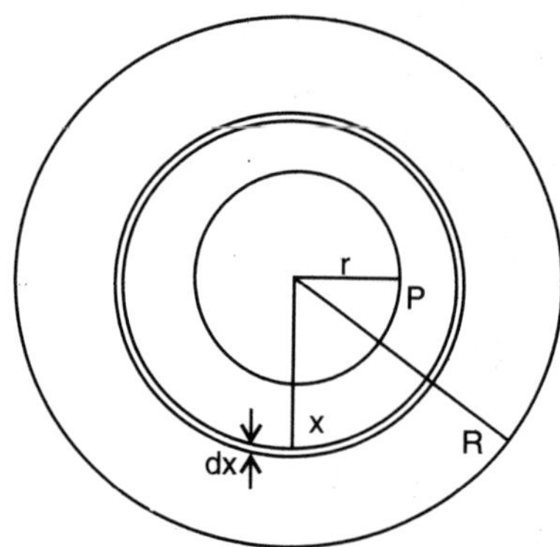

Fig. 1.29. Electric field of a charged sphere at an internal point.

In order to calculate φ_2, we consider a spherical shell of radius x and thickness dx such that $r < x < R$. The charge on this shell is $dq = 4\pi x^2 dx\rho$. The point of observation lies inside this shell and hence potential of this shell at an internal point is

$$d\varphi_2 = \frac{1}{4\pi\varepsilon_0}\frac{dq}{x} = \frac{1}{4\pi\varepsilon_0}4\pi\rho x dx$$

The potential of the outer part of the sphere is

$$\varphi_2 = \frac{1}{4\pi\varepsilon_0}4\pi\rho\int_r^R x dx = \frac{\rho}{2\varepsilon_0}(R^2 - r^2) = \frac{q}{4\pi\varepsilon_0 R^3}\frac{3}{2}(R^2 - r^2) \qquad ...(1.98)$$

Total potential of the solid sphere at an internal point is

$$\varphi = \varphi_1 + \varphi_2 = \frac{\rho r^2}{3\varepsilon_0} + \frac{\rho(R^2 - r^2)}{2\varepsilon_0} = \frac{\rho}{2\varepsilon_0}\left(R^2 - \frac{r^2}{3}\right)$$

or

$$\varphi = \frac{q}{4\pi\varepsilon_0 R^3}\left(\frac{3}{2}R^2 - \frac{1}{2}r^2\right) \qquad ...(1.99)$$

The electric field at an internal point of a charge sphere is

$$E = -\frac{\partial\varphi}{\partial r} = \left(\frac{q}{4\pi\varepsilon_0 R^3}\right) r = \frac{\rho r}{3\varepsilon_0} \qquad ...(1.100)$$

This is a very important result: *the electric field of charged sphere is proportional to the distance from the centre to field point.*

1.29. MONOPOLE, DIPOLE, QUADRUPOLE AND OCTUPOLE

A point charge q at origin is called a *monopole*. Electric potential of monopole at a point **r** is

$$\Phi^{(0)} = \frac{1}{4\pi\varepsilon_0}\frac{q}{r}$$

A system of two equal and opposite charges separated by a finite distance is called an *electric dipole*. The product of magnitude of one of the charges and the distance between them is defined as the dipole moment. The direction from the negative charge to the positive charge is taken as the direction of dipole moment. If two charges $-q$ and $+q$ are separated by a distance d, the dipole moment $\mathbf{p} = q\mathbf{d}$.

Fig. 1.30. An electric dipole.

For a system of N discrete charges $q_1, q_2, q_3,\ldots$ positioned at points $\mathbf{r}_1, \mathbf{r}_2, \mathbf{r}_3\ldots$ the dipole moment is given by

$$\mathbf{p} = q_1\mathbf{r}_1 + q_2\mathbf{r}_2 + q_3\mathbf{r}_3 + \ldots = \sum_i q_i\mathbf{r}_i \qquad \ldots(1.101)$$

For a system of two charges $-q$ and $+q$ with position vectors $\mathbf{r}_-$ and $\mathbf{r}_+$, the dipole moment is

$$\mathbf{p} = (-q)\mathbf{r}_- + (+q)\,\mathbf{r}_+ = q\,(\mathbf{r}_+ - \mathbf{r}_-) = q\mathbf{d}$$

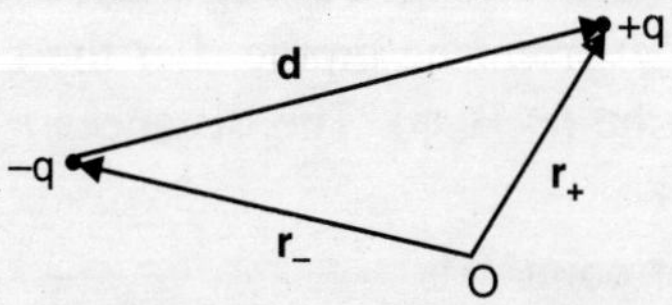

Fig. 1.31. An electric dipole.

For a continuous charge distribution characterized by volume charge density ρ, the dipole moment is given by

$$\mathbf{p} = \int \mathbf{r}'\rho(\mathbf{r}')d\tau' \qquad \ldots(1.102)$$

The prime indicates that the integration is to be carried over the volume occupied by the charge distribution i.e. variables of integration are the source coordinates.

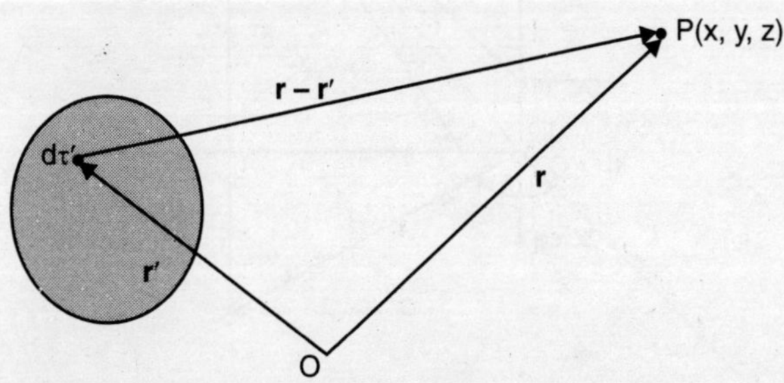

Fig. 1.32. Dipole moment of a continuous charge distribution.

A system of four dipoles, arranged as shown in the Fig. 1.33b, constitutes a *quadrupole.* This system consists of a pair of equal and opposite dipoles. Notice that the total dipole moment of a quadrupole is zero.

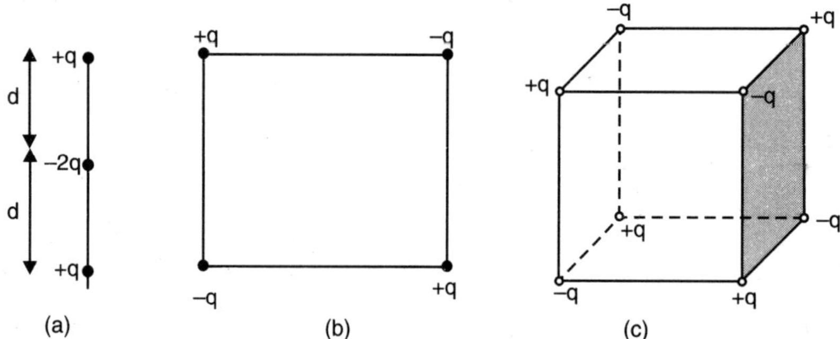

Fig. 1.33. (a) Linear quadrupole (b) Two-dimensional quadrupole (c) An octupole.

A octupole consists of eight dipoles arranged along the sides of a cube as shown in the Fig. 1.33(c).

1.30. ELECTRIC POTENTIAL AND FIELD OF A DIPOLE

Consider an electric dipole with its axis arranged along *z*-axis. We have to find an expression for potential at a point far away ($r >> d$) from the dipole. Let the coordinates of point of observation in spherical polar coordinate system be (r, θ, φ). The distances r_+ , r_-, r and angle θ are defined in the Fig. 1.34.

The potential of the dipole at the point P is

$$\Phi(r, \theta, \varphi) = \frac{1}{4\pi\varepsilon_0}\left(\frac{q}{r_+} - \frac{q}{r_-}\right) \qquad ...(1.103)$$

Fig. 1.34. Potential of an electric dipole.

Now $\quad r_\pm^2 = r^2 + (d/2)^2 \mp rd\cos\theta = r^2\left(1 \mp \frac{d}{r}\cos\theta + \frac{d^2}{4r^2}\right)$

Since we are interested in potential at a point far away from the dipole, $r \gg d$ so the term $d^2/4r^2$ may be neglected. Under this approximation,

$$\frac{1}{r_\pm} = \frac{1}{r}\left(1 \mp \frac{d}{r}\cos\theta\right)^{-1/2} = \frac{1}{r}\left(1 \pm \frac{d}{2r}\cos\theta\right)$$

From this result we have

$$\frac{1}{r_+} - \frac{1}{r_-} = \frac{d}{r^2}\cos\theta$$

Hence
$$\Phi = \frac{1}{4\pi\varepsilon_0}\frac{qd\cos\theta}{r^2} = \frac{1}{4\pi\varepsilon_0}\frac{p\cos\theta}{r^2} \quad ...(1.104)$$

or,
$$\Phi = \frac{1}{4\pi\varepsilon_0}\frac{\mathbf{p}.\hat{\mathbf{r}}}{r^2} \quad ...(1.105)$$

The electric field of a dipole is given by

$$E_r = -\frac{\partial\Phi}{\partial r} = \frac{2p\cos\theta}{4\pi\varepsilon_0 r^3} \quad ...(1.106)$$

$$E_\theta = -\frac{1}{r}\frac{\partial\Phi}{\partial\theta} = \frac{p\sin\theta}{4\pi\varepsilon_0 r^3} \quad ...(1.107)$$

$$E_\varphi = -\frac{1}{r\sin\theta}\frac{\partial\Phi}{\partial\varphi} = 0 \quad ...(1.108)$$

or,
$$\mathbf{E} = \frac{p}{4\pi\varepsilon_0 r^3}\left(2\cos\theta\,\hat{\mathbf{r}} + \sin\theta\,\hat{\boldsymbol{\theta}}\right) \quad ...(1.109)$$

or,
$$E = \left(E_r^2 + E_\theta^2\right)^{1/2} = \frac{p}{4\pi\varepsilon_0 r^3}\sqrt{3\cos^2\theta + 1} \quad ...(1.110)$$

Cartesian Components of E

$$\Phi = \frac{p\cos\theta}{4\pi\varepsilon_0 r^2} = \frac{p}{4\pi\varepsilon_0}\frac{z}{r^3}, \qquad (\because z = r\cos\theta) \quad ...(1.111)$$

Making use of the results, $r^2 = x^2 + y^2 + z^2$, $\frac{\partial r}{\partial x} = \frac{x}{r}$, $\frac{\partial r}{\partial y} = \frac{y}{r}$, $\frac{\partial r}{\partial z} = \frac{z}{r}$, we have

$$E_x = -\frac{\partial\Phi}{\partial x} = -\frac{\partial\Phi}{\partial r}\frac{\partial r}{\partial x} = \frac{p}{4\pi\varepsilon_0}\left(\frac{3xz}{r^5}\right) \quad ...(1.112)$$

$$E_y = -\frac{\partial\Phi}{\partial y} = -\frac{\partial\Phi}{\partial r}\frac{\partial r}{\partial y} = \frac{p}{4\pi\varepsilon_0}\left(\frac{3yz}{r^5}\right) \quad ...(1.113)$$

$$E_z = -\frac{\partial\Phi}{\partial z} = -\frac{\partial\Phi}{\partial r}\frac{\partial r}{\partial z} = \frac{p}{4\pi\varepsilon_0}\left(\frac{3z^2 - r^2}{r^5}\right) \quad ...(1.114)$$

Dipole Potential as Gradient

The dipole potential is

$$\Phi = \frac{\mathbf{p}\cdot\mathbf{r}}{4\pi\varepsilon_0 r^3} \qquad ...(1.115)$$

Making use of the result: $\nabla\left(\frac{1}{r}\right) = -\frac{\mathbf{r}}{r^3}$ we can write dipole potential as

$$\Phi = -\frac{1}{4\pi\varepsilon_0}\mathbf{p}\cdot\nabla\left(\frac{1}{r}\right) \qquad ...(1.116)$$

Electric Field in Coordinate-free Form

$$\mathbf{E} = -\nabla\Phi = -\frac{1}{4\pi\varepsilon_0}\nabla\left(\frac{\mathbf{p}\cdot\mathbf{r}}{r^3}\right) = -\frac{1}{4\pi\varepsilon_0}\left[\frac{1}{r^3}\nabla(\mathbf{p}\cdot\mathbf{r}) + (\mathbf{p}\cdot\mathbf{r})\nabla\left(\frac{1}{r^3}\right)\right]$$

$$= -\frac{1}{4\pi\varepsilon_0}\left[\frac{1}{r^3}\mathbf{p} + (\mathbf{p}\cdot\mathbf{r})\left(-\frac{3\mathbf{r}}{r^5}\right)\right] \qquad \because \nabla(\mathbf{a}\cdot\mathbf{r}) = \mathbf{a}, \quad \mathbf{a} \text{ is const.}$$

$$= \frac{1}{4\pi\varepsilon_0 r^3}\left[\frac{3(\mathbf{p}\cdot\mathbf{r})\mathbf{r}}{r^2} - \mathbf{p}\right] \qquad ...(1.117)$$

1.31. DIPOLE IN AN ELECTRIC FIELD

When an electric dipole is placed in a uniform electric field, it is acted upon by a torque $\mathbf{N} = \mathbf{p} \times \mathbf{E}$. This torque tends to align the dipole parallel to the field. The work done by the electric field in rotating the dipole through the angle $d\theta$ is

$$dW = Nd\theta = pE\sin\theta\, d\theta$$

If the dipole is rotated from initial position θ_1 to the final position θ_2, the workdone is

$$W = \int_{\theta_1}^{\theta_2} pE\sin\theta \; d\theta = pE(\cos\theta_1 - \cos\theta_2) \qquad ...(1.118)$$

This work is regarded as increase in electrostatic potential energy of the dipole.

$$U_2 - U_1 = pE(\cos\theta_1 - \cos\theta_2)$$

Usually, when the dipole is at right angles to the electric field ($\theta_1 = 90°$), the potential energy is taken to be zero ($U_1 = 0$). With this convention, the potential energy of the dipole in position θ is

$$U(\theta) = -pE\cos\theta = \mathbf{p}.\mathbf{E} \qquad ...(1.119)$$

If the dipole is placed in a non-uniform field, in addition to torque there will be also a net force on it. The net force on the dipole is

$$\mathbf{F} = q\mathbf{E}_+ - q\mathbf{E}_- = q\mathbf{dE}$$

Where **dE** is the difference of the electric fields at the positive end and the negative end. We know that

$$\mathbf{dE} = (d)_x \frac{\partial \mathbf{E}}{\partial x} + (d)_y \frac{\partial \mathbf{E}}{\partial y} + (d)_z \frac{\partial \mathbf{E}}{\partial z}$$

$$= \left((d)_x \frac{\partial}{\partial x} + (d)_y \frac{\partial}{\partial y} + (d)_z \frac{\partial}{\partial z} \right) \mathbf{E}$$

$$= (\mathbf{d} \cdot \nabla)\mathbf{E}$$

Making use of this result, we can write the force on an electric dipole in a non-uniform field as

$$\mathbf{F} = (\mathbf{p} \cdot \mathbf{E})\mathbf{E} \qquad \text{...(1.120)}$$

1.32. MULTI-POLE EXPANSION–POTENTIAL DUE TO A CHARGE DISTRIBUTION OF ARBITRARY SHAPE AT A LARGE DISTANCE

Suppose that we have a charge distribution of an arbitrary shape characterized by volume charge density $\rho(r)$. Our aim is to find the potential of this charge distribution at a very large distance. Relative to origin O, let the point of observation be at a distance r. By large distance we mean that the distance r of point of observation is very large in comparison to the dimensions of the region occupied by the charge distribution. The potential at point r due to entire charge distribution is

$$\Phi(r) = \frac{1}{4\pi\varepsilon_0} \int \frac{\rho(r')d\tau'}{|\mathbf{r} - \mathbf{r}'|} \qquad \text{...(1.121)}$$

In eqn. (1.121) the integration is performed over the region occupied by the charge distribution.

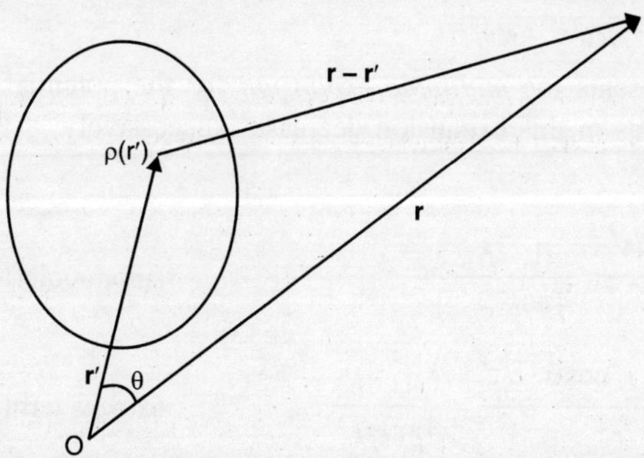

Fig. 1.35. Potential of a charge distribution at very large distance.

Now
$$|\mathbf{r} - \mathbf{r}'|^2 = r^2 + r'^2 - 2r\,r'\cos\theta$$

$$= r^2 \left[1 + \left(\frac{r'}{r}\right)^2 - 2\left(\frac{r'}{r}\right)\cos\theta \right]$$

$$= r^2\left[1+\frac{r'}{r}\left(\frac{r'}{r}-2\cos\theta\right)\right]$$

$$= r^2[1+\alpha], \qquad \alpha = \frac{r'}{r}\left(\frac{r'}{r}-2\cos\theta\right) \qquad ...(1.122)$$

Since $r >> r'$, α is a very small quantity. From eqn. (1.122) we have

$$\frac{1}{|\mathbf{r}-\mathbf{r}'|} = \frac{1}{r(1+\alpha)^{1/2}} = \frac{1}{r}(1+\alpha)^{-1/2} = \frac{1}{r}\left[1-\frac{1}{2}\alpha+\frac{3}{8}\alpha^2-\frac{5}{16}\alpha^3+......\right]$$

$$= \frac{1}{r}\left[1-\frac{1}{2}\frac{r'}{r}\left(\frac{r'}{r}-2\cos\theta\right)+\frac{3}{8}\left(\frac{r'}{r}\right)^2\left(\frac{r'}{r}-2\cos\theta\right)^2-\frac{5}{16}\left(\frac{r'}{r}\right)^3\left(\frac{r'}{r}-2\cos\theta\right)^3+.......\right]$$

$$= \frac{1}{r}\left[1+\frac{r'}{r}\cos\theta+\left(\frac{r'}{r}\right)^2\left(\frac{3}{2}\cos^2\theta-\frac{1}{2}\right)+\left(\frac{r'}{r}\right)^3\left(\frac{5}{2}\cos^3\theta-\frac{3}{2}\cos\theta\right)+......\right] \qquad ...(1.123)$$

In view of eqn. (1.123) we can write eqn. (1.121) as follows.

$$\Phi(r) = \frac{1}{4\pi\varepsilon_0}\left[\frac{\int\rho(r')d\tau'}{r}+\frac{\int\rho(r')\ r'\cos\theta d\tau'}{r^2}+\frac{\int\rho(r')\ r'^2\left(\frac{3}{2}\cos^2\theta-\frac{1}{2}\right)d\tau'}{r^3}+.........\right] \qquad ...(1.124)$$

$$= \Phi^{(0)}+\Phi^{(1)}+\Phi^{(2)}+\Phi^{(3)}+\Phi^{(4)}+........ \qquad ...(1.125)$$

Equation (1.124) represents the *multipole expansion* for the potential of a charge distribution. The magnitudes of the terms in this expansion decreases successively.

The terms

$$\Phi^{(0)} = \frac{1}{4\pi\varepsilon_0}\frac{\int\rho(r')d\tau'}{r} = \frac{1}{4\pi\varepsilon_0}\frac{K_0}{r} \qquad \text{(monopole term)} \qquad ...(1.126)$$

$$\Phi^{(1)} = \frac{1}{4\pi\varepsilon_0}\frac{\int\rho(r')\ r'\cos\theta\ d\tau'}{r^2} = \frac{1}{4\pi\varepsilon_0}\frac{K_1}{r^2} \qquad \text{(dipole term)} \qquad ...(1.127)$$

$$\Phi^{(2)} = \frac{1}{4\pi\varepsilon_0}\frac{\int\rho(r')\ r'^2\left(\frac{3}{2}\cos^2\theta-\frac{1}{2}\right)d\tau'}{r^3} = \frac{1}{4\pi\varepsilon_0}\frac{K_2}{r^3} \qquad \text{(quadrupole term)} \qquad ...(1.128)$$

are called the *monopole, dipole, quadrupole* terms respectively. The quantities defined by

$$K_0 = \int\rho(r')d\tau' \qquad \text{(monopole)} \qquad ...(1.129)$$

$$K_1 = \int (r' \cos\theta) \rho(r') d\tau' \text{ (dipole moment)} \quad ...(1.130)$$

$$K_2 = \int r'^2 \left(\frac{3}{2}\cos^2\theta - \frac{1}{2} \right) \rho(r') d\tau' \quad \text{(quadrupole moment)} \quad ...(1.131)$$

depend only on the configuration of the charge distribution and are called *monopole, dipole moment, quadrupole moment* respectively.

The quantity $K_0 = \int \rho(r') d\tau'$ represents the total charge of the distribution. If $K_0 \neq 0$, then the potential at large distances is dominated by the monopole term and is given by

$$\Phi^{(0)} = \frac{1}{4\pi\varepsilon_0} \frac{\int \rho(r') d\tau'}{r} = \frac{1}{4\pi\varepsilon_0} \frac{K_0}{r} = \frac{1}{4\pi\varepsilon_0} \frac{q}{r}$$

If the charge distribution contains equal amount of positive and negative charge, the monopole term vanishes. In that case, to find the potential we have to look for the other terms of the expansion.

If $K_0 = 0$, then the dominant term in the multipole expansion is the dipole term and the potential is given by eqn. (1.128). If $K_1 = 0$, then the potential is given by quadrupole term and the potential is given by eqn. (1.129).

This analysis shows that an arbitrary charge distribution may be thought of as made up of monopole, dipole, quadrupole, octupole etc. This view point is displayed in the Fig. 1.36.

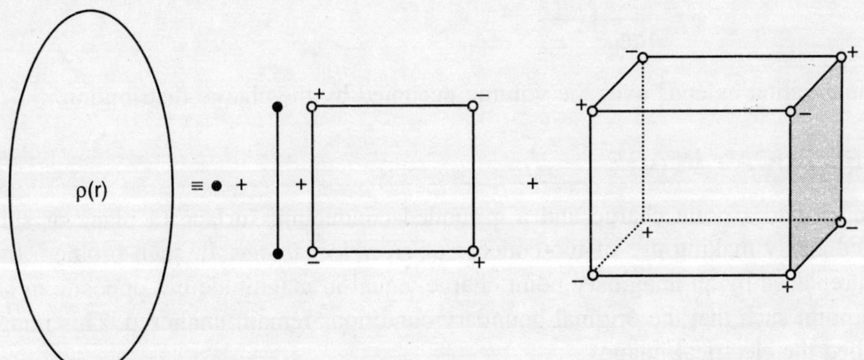

Fig. 1.36. Equivalence of an arbitrary charge distribution to a combination of point monopole, point dipole, quadrupole, octupole etc.

1.33. LAPLACE'S AND POISSON'S EQUATIONS

The electrostatic field of a charge distribution satisfies the equations

$$\nabla \cdot \mathbf{E} = \rho / \varepsilon_0 \quad ...(1.132)$$

And $$\nabla \times \mathbf{E} = 0 \quad ...(1.133)$$

A vector field whose curl vanishes may be expressed as the gradient of some scalar function and we already found a relation between electric field **E** and scalar potential φ which reads as

$$\mathbf{E} = -\nabla\varphi \qquad ...(1.134)$$

Equation (1.134) is not a new equation. It is equivalent to $\nabla \times E = 0$. Equations (1.132) and (1.133) are Maxwell's equations for electrostatics. These two equations may be combined into a single equation as follows. Substituting $\mathbf{E} = -\nabla\varphi$ in eqn. (1.132) we have

$$\nabla\cdot(-\nabla\varphi) = \rho/\varepsilon_0$$

or $$\nabla^2\varphi = -\rho/\varepsilon_0 \quad \text{(Poisson's Equation)} \qquad ...(1.135)$$

Equation (1.135) is known as Poisson's equation. Solution of this equation gives the electrostatic potential at the location of source charge density. In space outside the charge distribution where ρ is zero, Poisson equation becomes

$$\nabla^2\varphi = 0 \qquad \text{(Laplace's equation)} \qquad ...(1.136)$$

Equation (1.136) is known as Laplace's equation. It gives the potential of charge distribution at points outside the charge distribution. Mathematically, whole of the electrostatics is the study of Laplace's and Poisson's equations with appropriate boundary conditions. Once the potential function is obtained, the electric field is computed from the relation $\mathbf{E} = -\nabla\varphi$. The solution of Poisson's equation is

$$\varphi = \frac{1}{4\pi\varepsilon_0}\int\frac{\rho d\tau}{r} \qquad ...(1.137)$$

Where integration extends over the volume occupied by the charge distribution.

1.34. ELECTRICAL IMAGE

The potential due to a point charge and a grounded conducting surface (a plane or spherical) can be determined easily making use of the concept of *electrical image.* In such problem the grounded conductor is replaced by an imaginary point charge, equal in magnitude but opposite in sign, located at a suitable point such that the original boundary conditions remain unaltered. This imaginary point charge is called the electrical image.

1.35. POINT CHARGE NEAR A CONDUCTING PLANE

Let a point charge $+q$ be placed at a distance d from an infinite conducting plane. We assume that the conducting plane is earthed. We wish to calculate the potential and field at a point P on the same side of the plane as the point charge q. The electric field at the point P is produced by the charge q and the induced charges on the plane.

Boundary conditions:

(*i*) As the conducting plane is grounded, the electric potential at every point on the conductor is zero.

(*ii*) The electric potential at infinitely far point is zero.

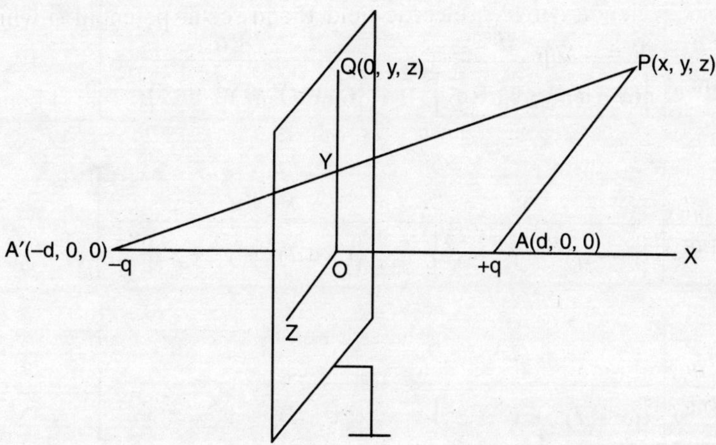

Fig. 1.37. A point charge and grounded conductor.

These conditions can be satisfied if we replace the grounded conductor by a point charge (image charge) $-q$ at a distance d to the left of the conductor such that the line joining the image charge and the actual charge intersects the plane conductor at right angles.

The potential at any point $Q(0, y, z)$ on the conductor due to real charge q and image charge $-q$ is

$$\varphi(0, y, z) = \frac{1}{4\pi\varepsilon_0}\left(\frac{q}{QA} + \frac{-q}{QA'}\right) = 0$$

Thus the first boundary condition is satisfied. The image charge $-q$ placed at point A' does not alter the potential at infinitely far points. The second boundary condition is also satisfied.

The real charge q at A and the image charge $-q$ at A' will produce the same electric field on the right hand side of the plane as that produced by real charge $+q$ and the charges induced on the grounded conductor.

Force between point charge +q and the grounded conductor

The force between the point charge $+q$ and the earthed conductor is the same as that between the charge $+q$ and the image charge $-q$.

$$F = \frac{1}{4\pi\varepsilon_0}\frac{q^2}{(2d)^2} \qquad \text{(Attractive force)} \qquad ...(1.138)$$

Electric field and potential at point (x, y, z)

The potential φ at a point $P(x, y, z)$ due to point charge $+q$ and the earthed conductor is the same as that due to point charge $+q$ and its image charge $-q$.

$$\varphi(x, y, z) = \frac{1}{4\pi\varepsilon_0}\left[\frac{q}{\sqrt{(x-d)^2 + y^2 + z^2}} - \frac{q}{\sqrt{(x+d)^2 + y^2 + z^2}}\right] \qquad ...(1.139)$$

Electric field $E(E_x, E_y, E_z)$ is given by

$$E_x = -\frac{\partial \varphi}{\partial x} = \frac{q}{4\pi\varepsilon_0}\left[\frac{x-d}{\left\{(x-d)^2+y^2+z^2\right\}^{3/2}} - \frac{x+d}{\left\{(x+d)^2+y^2+z^2\right\}^{3/2}}\right] \quad ...(1.140)$$

$$E_y = -\frac{\partial \varphi}{\partial y} = \frac{q}{4\pi\varepsilon_0}\left[\frac{y}{\left\{(x-d)^2+y^2+z^2\right\}^{3/2}} - \frac{y}{\left\{(x+d)^2+y^2+z^2\right\}^{3/2}}\right] \quad ...(1.141)$$

$$E_z = -\frac{\partial \varphi}{\partial z} = \frac{q}{4\pi\varepsilon_0}\left[\frac{z}{\left\{(x-d)^2+y^2+z^2\right\}^{3/2}} - \frac{z}{\left\{(x+d)^2+y^2+z^2\right\}^{3/2}}\right] \quad ...(1.142)$$

Thus $\mathbf{E} = \mathbf{i}E_x + \mathbf{j}E_y + \mathbf{k}E_z, \qquad E = \sqrt{E_x^2 + E_y^2 + E_z^2}$ ...(1.143)

Electric field at conductor (x = 0)

$$E_{x=0} = -\frac{qd}{2\pi\varepsilon_0}\frac{1}{(d^2+y^2+z^2)^{3/2}} \quad ...(1.144)$$

$$E_{y0} = 0, \qquad E_{z0} = 0$$

Surface charge on conductor

Let σ be the induced surface charge density on the conducting plane. The electric field at point $Q(0, y, z)$ is

$$E = (E_x)_{x=0} = \frac{\sigma}{\varepsilon_0}$$

$$\therefore \qquad \sigma = \varepsilon_0 (E_x)_{x=0} = -\frac{qd}{2\pi\left(d^2+y^2+z^2\right)^{3/2}} = -\frac{qd}{2\pi a^3} \quad ...(1.145)$$

Where a is the distance of point Q from the real charge q.

Total charge induced on the conducting plane

Consider a ring of radius r and width dr on the conducting plane around the origin. Let σ be the surface charge density on the plane.

The charge on the ring is $dq = 2\pi r dr\sigma$. The total charge on the plane is

$$q = \int 2\pi r dr\sigma = -\int 2\pi r dr\left(\frac{qd}{2\pi a^3}\right) = -qd\int_0^\infty \frac{rdr}{(r^2+d^2)^{3/2}} = -q\int_0^{\pi/2} \sin\theta\, d\theta = -q$$

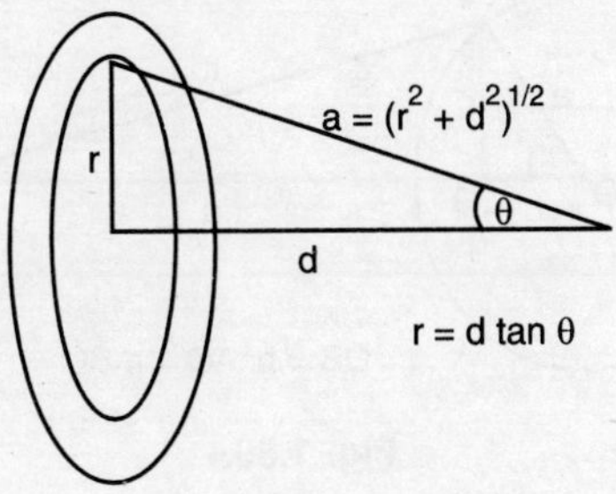

Fig. 1.38.

1.36. A POINT CHARGE AND A CONDUCTING SPHERE

Consider a point charge $+q$ placed at a distance d from the centre O of a grounded conducting sphere of radius a such that $a < d$. We wish to find the electric field outside the sphere and the distribution of the induced charges on the surface of sphere. As the conducting sphere is grounded, the boundary conditions are:

(*i*) The electric field and potential at every point on the surface of sphere is zero *i.e.* $\varphi = 0$ at $r = a$.

(*ii*) The electric potential at infinitely far points is zero *i.e.* $\varphi = 0$ at $r = \infty$.

Let us suppose that the image charge q' placed at point B such that $OB = b$. The real charge q and image charge q' with conducting sphere removed, produce zero potential at any point Q on the surface of the sphere. Thus

$$\varphi(Q) = \frac{1}{4\pi\varepsilon_0}\left[\frac{q}{r} + \frac{q'}{r'}\right] = 0$$

$$qr' = -q'r$$

or $$q^2 r'^2 = q'^2 r^2$$

or $$q^2(a^2 + b^2 - 2ab\cos\theta) = q'^2(a^2 + d^2 - 2ad\cos\theta) \quad \text{...(1.146)}$$

This equation is valid for all values of θ. Equating the coefficient of cos θ we get

$$q^2 ab = q'^2 ad$$

or, $$b = \frac{q'^2}{q^2} d = \alpha d, \qquad \alpha = \frac{q'^2}{q^2} \quad \text{... (1.147)}$$

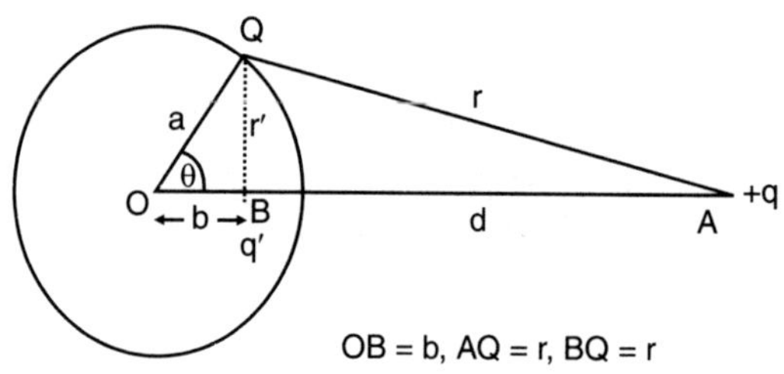

Fig. 1.39.

Equation (1.146) becomes

$$q^2(a^2 + b^2) = q'^2(a^2 + d^2)$$

$$q^2(a^2 + \alpha^2 d^2) = \alpha^2 q^2(a^2 + d^2)$$

$$d^2\alpha^2 - (a^2 + d^2)\alpha + a^2 = 0$$

This gives $\alpha = 1 \quad \text{or} \quad \alpha = \dfrac{a^2}{d^2}$ ...(1.148)

Now $\alpha = \dfrac{q'^2}{q^2} = 1 \Rightarrow q' = \pm q \quad \text{and} \quad b = d$ ...(1.149)

This shows that $b > a$.

For $\alpha = \dfrac{a^2}{d^2}$, we have $\dfrac{a^2}{d^2} = \dfrac{q'^2}{q^2}$

which implies $q' = \pm \dfrac{a}{d} q$

To make $\varphi = 0$ at the surface of sphere, we must choose the negative sign. Hence

$$q' = -\frac{a}{d}q \quad \text{and} \quad b = \frac{a^2}{d} \qquad ...(1.150)$$

This gives the magnitude, sign and the location of the image charge.

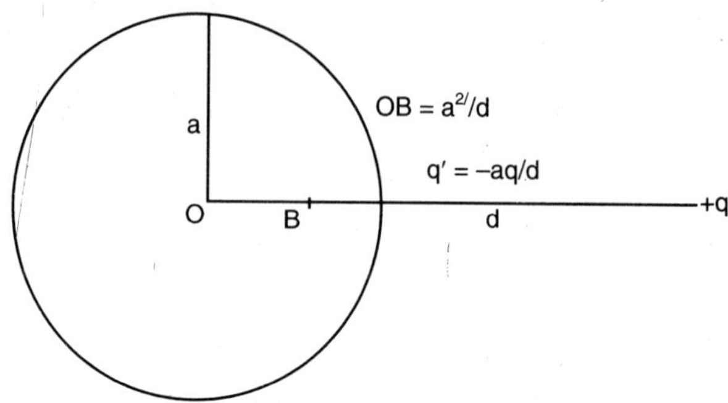

Fig. 1.40.

Electrical potential and field at external point

Potential at an external point is

$$\varphi(r) = \frac{1}{4\pi\varepsilon_0}\left[\frac{q}{AP} + \frac{q'}{BP}\right] = \frac{1}{4\pi\varepsilon_0}\left[\frac{q}{AP} - \frac{qa/d}{BP}\right]$$

$$= \frac{q}{4\pi\varepsilon_0}\left[\frac{1}{(r^2 + d^2 - 2rd\cos\theta)^{1/2}} - \frac{a/d}{(r^2 + b^2 - 2rb\cos\theta)^{1/2}}\right]$$

$$= \frac{q}{4\pi\varepsilon_0}\left[\frac{1}{(r^2 + d^2 - 2rd\cos\theta)^{1/2}} - \frac{a/d}{\{r^2(a/d)^2 - 2r(a^2/d)\cos\theta\}^{1/2}}\right]$$

$$= \frac{q}{4\pi\varepsilon_0}\left[\frac{1}{(r^2 + d^2 - 2rd\cos\theta)^{1/2}} - \frac{1}{\{(d^2/a^2)r^2 + a^2 - 2rd\cos\theta\}^{1/2}}\right] \quad ...(1.151)$$

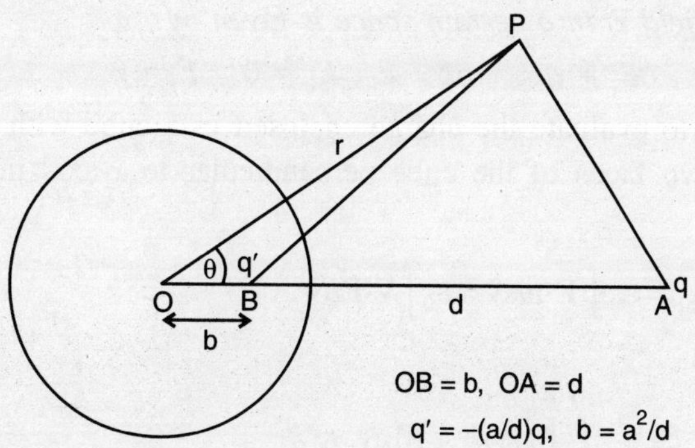

Fig. 1.41.

Radial component of E

$$E_r = -\frac{\partial r}{\partial r} = \frac{q}{4\pi\varepsilon_0}\left[\frac{r - d\cos\theta}{(r^2 + d^2 - 2rd\cos\theta)^{3/2}} - \frac{(d^2/a^2)r - d\cos\theta}{\{(d^2/a^2)r^2 + a^2 - 2rd\cos\theta\}^{3/2}}\right]$$

Transverse component of E

$$E_\theta = -\frac{1}{r}\frac{\partial\varphi}{\partial\theta} = \frac{q}{4\pi\varepsilon_0}\left[\frac{d\sin\theta}{(r^2 + d^2 - 2rd\cos\theta)^{3/2}} - \frac{d\sin\theta}{\{(d^2/a^2)r^2 + a^2 - 2rd\cos\theta\}^{3/2}}\right]$$

$$E = \sqrt{E_r^2 + E_\theta^2} \quad ...(1.152)$$

Electrical potential and field on the surface of sphere

At the surface of the sphere $r = a$,

$$(E_r)_{r=a} = \frac{q}{4\pi\varepsilon_0}\left[\frac{a - d\cos\theta}{(a^2 + d^2 - 2ad\cos\theta)^{3/2}} - \frac{(d^2/a) - d\cos\theta}{(a^2 + d^2 - 2ad\cos\theta)^{3/2}}\right]$$

$$= \frac{q}{4\pi\varepsilon_0 a}\left[\frac{a^2 - d^2}{(a^2 + d^2 - 2ad\cos\theta)^{3/2}}\right] \qquad ...(1.153)$$

E_θ at $r = a$ is zero.

Therefore, $$E = \frac{q}{4\pi\varepsilon_0 a}\left[\frac{a^2 - d^2}{(a^2 + d^2 - 2ad\cos\theta)^{3/2}}\right] \qquad ...(1.154)$$

Potential at the surface is zero.

Surface charge density

The normal component of E at the surface of sphere is $E = -\sigma/\varepsilon_0$. Therefore,

$$\sigma = -\varepsilon_0 E$$

Solved Examples

***Example* 1:** *The electric field* **E** *in a certain space is given by*

$$E_x = ax^2 + bx + c, \quad E_y = 0, \quad E_z = 0$$

Use Gauss's theorem to evaluate the charge enclosed in a cube with one of its sides of length L along the x-axis, the two faces of the cube perpendicular to x-axis lie in the planes $x = l$ and $x = l + L$.

***Solution*:** $$q_{\text{total}} = \varepsilon_0 \oint_S \mathbf{E}\cdot\mathbf{n}dS = \varepsilon_0 \int_V \nabla\cdot\mathbf{E}dV$$

$$= \varepsilon_0 \int_l^{l+L}\int_0^L\int_0^L (2ax + b)\,dx\,dy\,dz$$

$$= \varepsilon_0 L^3\left\{a(L + 2l) + b\right\}$$

***Example* 2:** *The electric field at any point in a space is directed radially outward along the line joining the point to a fixed point* (r = 0) *and is given by* ($ar + br^2$). *Evaluate the amount of charge enclosed in a sphere of radius R with the fixed point* (r = 0) *as centre.*

***Solution*:** From Gauss's law

$$q_{\text{total}} = \varepsilon_0 \oint_S \mathbf{E}\cdot\mathbf{n}dS = \varepsilon_0 \oint_S EdS$$

$$= \varepsilon\oint\left(aR + bR^2\right)dS$$

$$= \varepsilon_0 \left(aR + bR^2\right)\oint dS$$

$$= 4\pi\varepsilon_0 R^3\left(a + bR\right)$$

Aliter: The charge density ρ is given by

$$\rho = \varepsilon_0 \nabla \cdot \vec{E} = \varepsilon_0 \nabla \cdot \left\{ \left(a + br^2\right) \frac{\vec{r}}{r} \right\}$$

$$= \varepsilon_0 \left[\nabla \cdot a\vec{r} + \nabla \cdot (br\vec{r}) \right]$$

$$= \varepsilon_0 \left[3a + b(r + 3r) \right]$$

$$= \varepsilon_0 (3a + 4br)$$

The charge within a spherical shell of radius r and thickness dr is

$$dq = (4\pi r^2 dr)\rho = (4\pi r^2 dr)\varepsilon_0 (3a + 4br)$$

The total charge within the sphere of radius R is

$$Q = 4\pi\varepsilon_0 \int_0^R (3a + 4br) r^2 dr = 4\pi\varepsilon_0 (a + bR) R^3$$

***Example* 3:** *The charge density in a given space is given by ρ = (a/r) + b. Calculate the electric field at distance r′ from origin.*

***Solution*:**

According to Gauss's law

$$\oint \mathbf{E} \cdot \mathbf{n} dS = \frac{1}{\varepsilon_0} \int \rho dV$$

Consider a Gaussian surface of radius r' with centre at origin. The electric field is everywhere normal to the Gaussian surface. Hence the left hand side of above equation becomes

$$\oint_S \mathbf{E} \cdot \mathbf{n} dS = \oint_S E dS = E \oint_S dS = E\left(4\pi r'^2\right)$$

In order to evaluate the right hand side of Gauss's law, consider a spherical shell of radius r and thickness dr with centre at the origin. The quantity of charge within this spherical shell is $dq = 4\pi r^2 dr \rho$. Hence the total charge inside the sphere of radius r' is

$$q = \int \rho dV = \int_0^{r'} \left(4\pi r^2\right)\left(\frac{a}{r} + b\right) dr$$

$$= 4\pi \left(\frac{ar'^2}{2} + \frac{br'^3}{3} \right)$$

Therefore $$E = \frac{1}{\varepsilon_0}\left(\frac{a}{2} + \frac{br'}{3} \right)$$

***Example* 4:** *The electrostatic field at a distance r from a point charge q is given by*

$$\mathbf{E} = \frac{q}{4\pi\varepsilon_0} \frac{\mathbf{r}}{r^3}$$

Show that (*i*) **E** *is solenoidal in the region devoid of charges* (*ii*) **E** *is irrotational or conservative.*

Solution: (*i*) A vector field is solenoidal if its divergence vanishes. Now,

$$\nabla\cdot\mathbf{E} = \frac{q}{4\pi\varepsilon_0}\nabla\cdot\frac{\mathbf{r}}{r^3} = \frac{q}{4\pi\varepsilon_0}\left[\nabla r^{-3}\cdot\mathbf{r} + r^{-3}\nabla\cdot\mathbf{r}\right] = \frac{q}{4\pi\varepsilon_0}\left[-3r^{-5}\mathbf{r}\cdot\mathbf{r} + 3r^{-3}\right]$$

$$= \frac{q}{4\pi\varepsilon_0}\left[-3r^{-3} + 3r^{-3}\right] = 0$$

Hence **E** is solenoidal.

The function $\mathbf{r}/r^3$ becomes indeterminate at $r = 0$. The nature of divergence at $r = 0$ can be examined using divergence theorem, according to which

$$\int \nabla\cdot\frac{\mathbf{r}}{r^3} = \oint_S \frac{\mathbf{r}}{r^3}\cdot\mathbf{n}dS$$

Now imagine a small sphere of radius R with centre at $r = 0$. We shall evaluate the above surface integral over this surface. Thus

$$\oint_S \frac{\mathbf{r}}{r^3}\cdot\mathbf{n}dS = \oint_S \frac{dS}{R^2} = \frac{1}{R^2}\oint_S dS = \frac{1}{R^2}4\pi R^2 = 4\pi$$

Hence,

$$\oint_S \nabla\cdot\frac{\mathbf{r}}{r^3} = 4\pi$$

The divergence of function $\mathbf{r}/r^3$ is most elegantly expressed in terms of Dirac delta function which defined as follows.

$$\delta(r) = 0 \quad \text{at} \quad r \neq 0$$

$$\delta(r) = 4\pi \quad \text{at} \quad r = 0$$

$$\int \delta(r)\ d\tau = 1$$

In terms of δ-function we have

$$\oint \nabla\cdot\frac{\mathbf{r}}{r^3}d\tau = 4\pi\int\delta(r)d\tau$$

or

$$\nabla\cdot\frac{\mathbf{r}}{r^3} = 4\pi\delta(r)$$

(*ii*) A vector field is *irrotational* if its curl vanishes. Now

$$\nabla\times\mathbf{E} = \frac{q}{4\pi\varepsilon_0}\nabla\times\frac{\mathbf{r}}{r^3} = \frac{q}{4\pi\varepsilon_0}\left[\nabla r^{-3}\times\mathbf{r} + r^{-3}\nabla\times\mathbf{r}\right]$$

$$= \frac{q}{4\pi\varepsilon_0}\left[-3r^{-5}\mathbf{r}\times\mathbf{r} + 0\right] = 0$$

Hence **E** is irrotational.

***Example* 5:** *In a certain region the charge density varies according to the law* $\rho = \frac{\rho_0}{r}$*, where* ρ_0 *is constant and r is distance from the origin of coordinates. Find the electric field* **E** *as a function of position vector* **r**.

***Solution*:** Consider a spherical Gaussian surface of radius r with centre at the origin. Gauss's theorem gives

$$\oint \mathbf{E}\cdot d\mathbf{S} = \frac{1}{\varepsilon_0}\int \rho\, d\tau$$

$$E(4\pi r^2) = \frac{1}{\varepsilon_0}\int \frac{\rho_0}{r}(4\pi r^2 dr)$$

$$E = \frac{\rho_0}{2\varepsilon_0}$$

or
$$\mathbf{E} = \frac{\rho_0 \mathbf{r}}{2\varepsilon_0 r}$$

***Example* 6:** *The charge density in a spherical shell of inner radius a and outer radius b varies as* $\rho = \rho_0/r^2$ *in the region* $a \le r \le b$*. Find the electric field in the region (i)* $0 < r \le a$*, (ii)* $a \le r \le b$*, (iii)* $r \ge b$.

***Solution*:** (*i*) A Gaussian surface constructed entirely in the region $0 \le r \le a$ encloses no charge, hence the electric field in this region is zero.

(*ii*) Construct a spherical Gaussian surface of radius r such that $a \le r \le b$ with centre at the origin. Gauss's theorem gives

$$\oint \mathbf{E}\cdot d\mathbf{S} = \frac{1}{\varepsilon_0}\int \rho\, d\tau$$

$$E(4\pi r^2) = \frac{1}{\varepsilon_0}\int_a^r \frac{\rho_0}{r^2}(4\pi r^2 dr)$$

$$E = \frac{\rho_0}{\varepsilon_0}\left(\frac{r-a}{r^2}\right)$$

(*iii*) Construct a spherical Gaussian surface of radius $r \ge b$. Gauss's theorem when applied to this surface gives

$$\oint \mathbf{E}\cdot d\mathbf{S} = \frac{1}{\varepsilon_0}\int \rho\, d\tau$$

$$E(4\pi r^2) = \frac{1}{\varepsilon_0}\int_a^b \frac{\rho_0}{r^2}(4\pi r^2 dr)$$

$$E = \frac{\rho_0}{\varepsilon_0}\left(\frac{b-a}{r^2}\right)$$

***Example* 7:** *Two uniformly charged spheres, one with positive charge +q and the other with negative charge –q, are placed with their centres at a distance d apart. Calculate the electric field in the region of overlap.*

***Solution*:** The charged spheres are shown in Fig. 1.42. Let P be a point in the region of overlap and r be the distance from the centre C_1 of the left sphere. Construct a spherical Gaussian surface S_1 passing through the point P with centre at C_1. Let E_1 be the electric field at the point P due to the charges enclosed within the surface S_1. Applying Gauss's law to this surface we have

$$\oint_{S_1} \mathbf{E}_1 \cdot d\mathbf{S} = \frac{1}{\varepsilon_0} \int_{V_1} \rho d\tau$$

$$E_1 = \frac{\rho r}{3\varepsilon_0} \qquad \text{(towards left)}$$

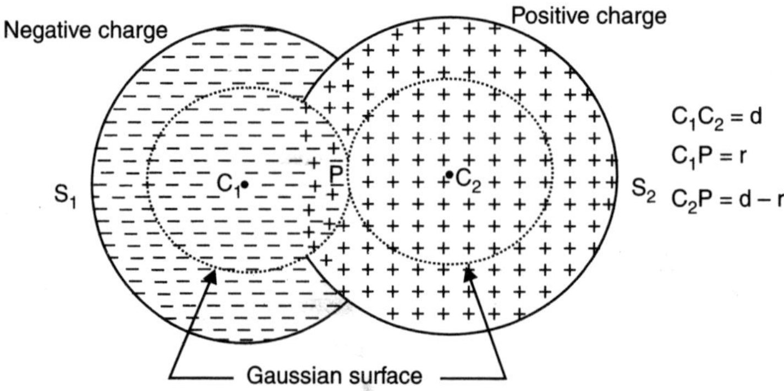

Fig. 1.42.

Construct another spherical Gaussian surface S_2 of radius $(d - r)$ with centre at the centre of other charge sphere. Let $\mathbf{E}_2$ be electric field at point P due to charges enclosed within the surface S_2. Using Gauss's theorem we have

$$\oint_{S_2} \mathbf{E}_2 \cdot d\mathbf{S} = \frac{1}{\varepsilon_0} \int_{V_2} \rho d\tau$$

$$E_2 = \frac{\rho(d-r)}{3\varepsilon_0} \qquad \text{(towards left)}$$

Total electric field at point P

$$E = E_1 + E_2 = \frac{\rho d}{3\varepsilon_0} = \frac{1}{4\pi\varepsilon_0} \frac{qd}{R^3}$$

where R is the radius of either charged sphere.

***Example* 8:** *The electrostatic potential due to a certain charge distribution is given by* $\varphi = ar^2 + b$ *where a and b are constant. Find the density of space charge distribution.*

***Solution*:** From Poisson's equation

$\rho = -\varepsilon_0 \nabla^2 \varphi = -\varepsilon_0 \nabla^2 (ar^2 + b) = -\varepsilon_0 a \nabla^2 r^2 = -6\varepsilon_0 a$

***Example* 9:** *Show that the field*

$$\mathbf{E} = 2xyz\,\mathbf{i} + x^2z\,\mathbf{j} + x^2y\,\mathbf{k}$$

is a potential field. Obtain its potential function.

***Solution*:** A vector field is a potential field if it can be expressed as gradient of some scalar field. This implies that the curl of the vector field must vanish.

Now,

$$\nabla \times \mathbf{E} = \begin{vmatrix} \vec{i} & \vec{j} & \vec{k} \\ \dfrac{\partial}{\partial x} & \dfrac{\partial}{\partial y} & \dfrac{\partial}{\partial z} \\ 2xyz & x^2z & x^2y \end{vmatrix} = 0$$

The potential function is given by

$$\varphi(x, y, z) = \int_0^x E_1 dx + \int_0^y E_2 dy + \int_0^z E_3 dz$$

$$= \int_0^x (2xyz)_{\substack{y=0\\z=0}} dx + \int_0^y \left(x^2 z\right)_{z=0} dy + \int_0^z x^2 y dz = x^2 yz$$

Hence the potential function is $\varphi(x, y, z) = x^2 yz + c$

***Example* 10:** *The electric field at any point (x, y, z) is given by*

$$\mathbf{E} = 2x\,\mathbf{i} + 2y\,\mathbf{j} + 2z\,\mathbf{k}$$

Derive an equation for the equipotential surface.

***Solution*:** The potential function is given by

$$\varphi(x, y, z) = \int_0^x 2x dx + \int_0^y 2y dy + \int_0^z 2z dz$$

$$\therefore \qquad \varphi = x^2 + y^2 + z^2$$

Equation of equipotential surface is

$$x^2 + y^2 + z^2 = c \qquad \text{(sphere)}$$

***Example* 11:** *A certain charge distribution has the potential function of the form*

$$\varphi = a(x^2 + y^2) + bz^2$$

Where a and b are constants. Find the magnitude and direction of the electric field. What is the shape of equipotential surface?

***Solution*:**

$$\mathbf{E} = -\nabla\varphi = -\left(2ax\mathbf{i} + 2ay\mathbf{j} + 2bz\mathbf{k}\right)$$

$$|\mathbf{E}| = 2\sqrt{a^2(x^2 + y^2) + b^2 z^2}$$

Equation of equipotential surface

$$ax^2 + ay^2 + bz^2 = \text{cons.} = \varphi_0 \qquad \text{(say)}$$

or
$$\frac{x^2}{\varphi_0 / a} + \frac{y^2}{\varphi_0 / a} + \frac{z^2}{\varphi_0 / b} = 1$$

This equation represents an ellipsoid.

Example 12: *A conducting sphere of radius R_0 carries a charge q in vacuum. (i) Calculate the total electrostatic energy stored in the surrounding space (ii) What is the radius of a sphere within which half of energy is confined?*

Solution: (*i*) The electric field within the conducting sphere is zero. At points $r > R_0$ the electric field is given by

$$E = \frac{q}{4\pi\varepsilon_0 r^2}$$

Energy density at point r is

$$u = \frac{1}{2}\varepsilon_0 E^2 = \frac{q^2}{32\pi^2\varepsilon_0 r^4}$$

Now consider a spherical shell of radius r and thickness dr. The energy within this shell is

$$du = u d\tau = u(4\pi r^2 dr) = \frac{q^2}{8\pi\varepsilon_0}\frac{dr}{r^2}$$

Total energy in the surrounding space is

$$U = \int du = \frac{q^2}{8\pi\varepsilon_0}\int_{R_0}^{\infty}\frac{dr}{r^2} = \frac{q^2}{8\pi\varepsilon_0 R_0}$$

(*ii*) Let R be the radius of the sphere such that half of the total energy lies within this sphere. Thus

$$\int_{R_0}^{R} du = \frac{U}{2}$$

$$\frac{q^2}{8\pi\varepsilon_0}\int_{R_0}^{R}\frac{dr}{r^2} = \frac{1}{2}\cdot\frac{q^2}{8\pi\varepsilon_0 R_0}$$

$$\frac{1}{2R_0} = -\frac{1}{R} + \frac{1}{R_0}$$

$$R = 2R_0$$

Example 13: *A charge q* = 100μμ *C is distributed over the volume of a sphere of radius* R_0 = 1.00 *cm. Calculate*

(*i*) *the energy of the sphere*

(ii) the energy confined within the sphere (iii) the energy confined in the space surrounding the sphere.

Solution: (*i*) Energy of the sphere

$$U = \frac{3}{5} \cdot \frac{1}{4\pi\varepsilon_0} \cdot \frac{q^2}{R_0}$$

Substituting the data we find $U = 5.4 \times 10^{-9}$ J

(*ii*) Electric field inside the sphere

$$E = \frac{\rho r}{3\varepsilon_0}$$

Energy inside the sphere

$$U_1 = \int u d\tau = \frac{1}{2}\varepsilon_0 \int_0^{R_0} \left(\frac{\rho r}{3\varepsilon_0}\right)^2 (4\pi r^2 dr) = \frac{1}{10} \cdot \frac{q^2}{4\pi\varepsilon_0 R_0} = \frac{U}{6} = 0.9 \times 10^{-9} \text{ J}$$

(*iii*) Energy in the surrounding space

$$U_2 = U - \frac{U}{6} = \frac{5U}{6} = 4.5 \times 10^{-9} \text{ J}$$

QUESTIONS AND PROBLEMS

Electric Field

1. An infinitely long line charge has uniform charge density λ per unit length. Obtain an expression for the electric field at a distance r from the line.

2. Obtain an expression for the magnitude of electric field at an axial point due to a ring of radius a and carrying a charge q. At what distance from the centre, electric field is maximum? Find the magnitude of maximum electric field.

3. A thin circular disc of radius a carries charge q. Find an expression for the electric field of this disc at an axial point at a distance z from its centre. Investigate the case in the limit $a \to 0$ and $z \to \infty$.

4. Prove that $\nabla \cdot \mathbf{E} = 0$ and $\nabla \times \mathbf{E} = 0$, $r \neq 0$, where $\mathbf{E} = \dfrac{q}{4\pi\varepsilon_0} \dfrac{\mathbf{r}}{r^3}$ is the electric field of a point charge q at a distance r.

5. What do you mean by electric flux? In a certain region, electric field is given by

$$\mathbf{E} = 8\mathbf{i} + 4\mathbf{j} + 3\mathbf{k}$$

Calculate the electric flux through a surface of area 100 units in the *xy*-plane.

Hint: Since the area lies in *xy*-plane, only *z*-component of electric field contribute to the total flux.

$$\text{flux} \quad \Phi = \oint_S \mathbf{E} \cdot d\mathbf{S} = \int E_x dydz + \int E_y dxdz + \int E_z dxdy = \int E_z dxdy$$

$$= 3\Delta x \Delta y = 3 \times 100 = 300 \text{ units}$$

6. State and prove Gauss's theorem in electrostatics. Show that $div\,\mathbf{E} = \frac{\rho}{\varepsilon_0}$.
7. Show that at every point of space, the divergence of electric field strength is proportional to the density of charge at that point.
8. State and prove Gauss's theorem in electrostatics. Find an expression for the electric field intensity at any point near a charged plane sheet.
9. A point charge q is located on the axis of a charged ring of radius a. Show that the electric flux through the ring is given by

$$\Phi = \frac{q}{2\varepsilon_0}[1 - \cos\theta_0]$$

Where θ_0 is the angle which the radius of the ring subtends at the field point.
10. Use Gauss's theorem to obtain electric field of a charged spherical shell at a point (*i*) inside, (*ii*) outside the shell.
11. Use Gauss's theorem to obtain electric field of a uniformly charged solid sphere at a point (*i*) inside, (*ii*) outside the shell.
12. Obtain the integral and differential forms of Gauss's law. What is the flux of **E** through a hemisphere of radius R if the electric field is uniform and parallel to axis of the hemisphere.
13. Calculate the electric field intensity due to a spherical charge distribution given by

$$\rho = \rho_0\left(1 - \frac{r}{a}\right) \text{ for } r < a \text{ and } \rho = 0 \text{ for } r > a.$$

Find the value of r for which E is maximum.
14. In a certain region, the electric field is given by $\mathbf{E} = [a\exp(-\mu r)]\hat{\mathbf{r}}$ where a and μ are constants. Find the total charge in a spherical volume of radius R with centre at origin.

Electric Potential

1. Explain what do you mean by gradient of a scalar function. Show that the electric field is the negative gradient of potential. Hence prove that curl $\mathbf{E} = \mathbf{0}$.
2. Obtain an expression for the potential at an axial point due to a charged ring. Hence find the electric field.
3. Obtain an expression for the potential at an axial point due to a charged circular disc. Hence find the electric field.
4. Calculate the potential due to a uniformly charged spherical shell at an external and internal point. Sketch the variation of potential and electric field with distance from the centre of the shell.
5. Obtain expression for potential and hence the electric field due to a uniformly charged solid sphere at an internal and external point. Sketch the variation of potential and electric field with distance from the centre of the sphere.
6. Obtain an expression for the electrostatic potential due to an electric dipole placed in free space. Find the components of electric field both in polar and cartesian coordinate system.
7. What do you mean by multipole expansion for potential due to an arbitrary charge distribution? Obtain an expression for potential of an arbitrary charge distribution as a multipole expansion. Interpret the various terms. Sketch the charge distribution in a quadrupole and octupole.

8. Show that the electrostatic energy of a charged configuration is given by $U = \frac{1}{2}\int \rho\varphi \, d\tau$, where the symbols have their usual meanings.

9. Show that the energy density in an electric field in vacuum is given by $u = \frac{1}{2}\varepsilon_0 E^2$.

10. Show that the electrostatic energy of a charged sphere of radius R in which charge q is uniformly distributed over its volume is $U = \frac{3}{5}\frac{1}{4\pi\varepsilon_0}.\frac{q^2}{R}$.

11. Is the field represented by $\mathbf{E} = (y + z)\mathbf{i} + (x + z)\mathbf{j} + (x + y)\mathbf{k}$ is a potential field. Find the potential describing this field.

Ans. $\varphi = xy + yz + zx + c$

12. Calculate the curl of the following fields

(*i*) $\mathbf{E} = yz\,\mathbf{i} + zx\,\mathbf{j} + xy\,\mathbf{k}$

(*ii*) $\mathbf{E} = xy^2 z\,\mathbf{i} + x^2 yz\,\mathbf{j} + \frac{1}{2}x^2 y^2\mathbf{k}$

(*iii*) $\mathbf{E} = a(y\,\mathbf{i} - x\,\mathbf{j})$

13. A sphere of radius R carries positive charge whose volume density varies according to the law $\rho = \rho_0\left(1 - \frac{r}{R}\right)$ where ρ_0 is a constant, r is the distance measured from the centre of the sphere. Find (*i*) magnitude of the electric field as a function of r both inside and outside the sphere (*ii*) maximum value of E and the corresponding distance.

Ans. (*i*) $E = \frac{\rho_0}{3\varepsilon_0}\frac{r}{}\left(1 - \frac{3r}{4R}\right)$ for $r < R$

$E = \frac{\rho_0 R^3}{12\varepsilon_0 r^2}$ for $r > R$

(*ii*) $E_{max} = \frac{\rho_0 R}{9\varepsilon_0}$, $r_{max} = \frac{2}{3}R$

14. Find the electric field at points inside and outside a spherically symmetric charge distribution $\rho = \rho_0 r^2$ for $r < r_0$ and $\rho = 0$ for $r > r_0$.

15. In a certain region charge density varies with r according to the law $\rho = \rho_0 \exp(-\alpha r^3)$ where ρ_0 and α are constants. Find E as a function of r.

Investigate the nature of electric field for $\alpha r^3 << 1$ and $\alpha r^3 >> 1$.

$$\mathbf{E} = \frac{\rho_0 \mathbf{r}}{3\varepsilon_0 \alpha r}\left[1 - \exp(-\alpha r^3)\right],$$

Ans. $E \propto r$ for $\alpha r^3 << 1$, and $E \propto \frac{1}{r^2}$ for $\alpha r^3 >> 1$.

16. The electric field in a region is given by $\mathbf{E} = Cr^n\,\hat{\mathbf{r}}$, where C is a constant. Find (*i*) the charge density as a function of r

(*ii*) the total charge enclosed within a sphere of radius r_0 centred at origin.

Ans. (*i*) $\rho = C\varepsilon_0 (n+2)\, r^{n-1}$ (*ii*) $q = 4\pi\varepsilon_0 C r_0^{n+2}$

17. The potential field in a certain region of space depends only on the x-coordinate as $\varphi = -ax + b$, where a and b are constants. Find the space charge distribution $\rho(x)$.

Ans. $\rho(x) = 6\varepsilon_0 ax$

18. The potential field inside a charged sphere varies with distance from the centre as $\varphi = ar^2 + b$, where a and b are constants. Find the space charge distribution $\rho(r)$ inside the sphere.

Hint: $\nabla\cdot\nabla\varphi = -\dfrac{\rho}{\varepsilon_0} \quad \Rightarrow \quad \rho = -6\varepsilon_0 a$

19. Calculate the potentials inside a spherically symmetric charge distribution given by

(*i*) $\rho = \rho_0 r$, for $r \le r_0$ and $\rho = 0$, for $r \ge r_0$

(*ii*) $\rho = \dfrac{\rho_0}{r}$, for $r \le r_0$ and $\rho = 0$, for $r \ge r_0$

(*iii*) $\rho = \rho_0 r \exp(-\alpha r)$ for $r \le r_0$ and $\rho = 0$ for $r \ge r_0$.

20. The electric potential at any point in the xy-plane is given by

$$\varphi = 5x(x^2 + y^2)^{1/2} + y(x^2 + y^2)^{-1/2}$$

Find the Cartesian components of the electric field.

21. The potential field of a certain charge distribution is $\varphi = 3x + 2y + z$. Find the electric field.

22. A charge q is distributed uniformly throughout a non-conducting spherical volume of radius R. Show that the potential at a distance $r (r < R)$ is given by

$$\varphi = \frac{q}{4\pi\varepsilon_0}\cdot\frac{3R^2 - r^2}{2R^2}$$

Hint:

$$\varphi = -\int_{\infty}^{r} \mathbf{E}\cdot d\mathbf{r} = -\left[\int_{\infty}^{R} \mathbf{E}_{\text{out}}\cdot d\mathbf{r} + \int_{R}^{r} \mathbf{E}_{\text{inside}}\cdot d\mathbf{r}\right]$$

$$\varphi = -\left[\int_{\infty}^{R} \frac{q}{4\pi\varepsilon_0}\frac{\mathbf{r}}{r^3}\cdot d\mathbf{r} + \int_{R}^{r} \frac{\rho r}{3\varepsilon_0}\hat{\mathbf{r}}\cdot d\mathbf{r}\right] = -\left[\frac{q}{4\pi\varepsilon_0}\int_{\infty}^{R}\frac{dr}{r^2} + \frac{\rho}{3\varepsilon_0}\int_{R}^{r} r\,dr\right]$$

$$\varphi = \frac{q}{4\pi\varepsilon_0}\left(\frac{3R^2 - r^2}{2R^3}\right)$$

23. An electric field is represented by potential $\phi = ax^2 - by^2$, where a and b are constants. (i) find the components of electric field (ii) find the coordinates of the point where potential is minimum (iii) where is the electric field minimum?

Ans. (*i*) $\mathbf{E} = (-2ax,\ 3by,\ 0)$, (*ii*) (0, 0), (*iii*) (0, 0)

Properties of Dielectric Materials

Dielectrics are those materials which have no free (mobile) charge carriers, they are bound to their parent atoms or molecules. How do dielectric materials respond to electric field will be the subject matter of our study in this chapter.

2.1. ELECTRIC POLARIZATION

Consider a parallel plate capacitor with free charges $+q$ and $-q$ on its plates and plate separation d. The potential difference between the plates is φ_0. The electric field between the plates is $E_0 = \varphi_0 / d$. The capacitance of the capacitor is $C_0 = q / \varphi_0$. Now the space between the plates is filled with a dielectric. It is observed that the potential difference and electric field are reduced by a certain factor, say K, and the capacitance is increased by the same factor. If φ, E and C denote the new values of potential difference, electric field and capacitance then we can express these observations as

$$E = \frac{E_0}{K}, \qquad \varphi = \frac{\varphi_0}{K}, \qquad C = KC_0 \qquad \text{...(2.1)}$$

The constant K (also denoted by ε_r) is called the dielectric constant (or relative permittivity) of the dielectric. The product $\varepsilon_0 K = \varepsilon$ is called permittivity of the medium.

The reduction of electric field inside the dielectric can be understood as follows. When a dielectric is subjected to an electric field, positive and negative charges appear on its faces normal to the electric field. *The phenomenon of appearance of charges on the faces of the dielectric under the action of electric field is called electric polarization and the charges so induced are called bound or polarization charges.*

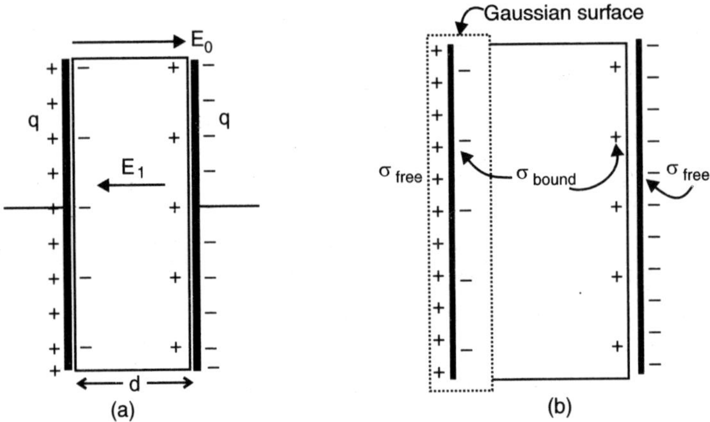

Fig. 2.1. Polarization of dielectric.

The bound charges produce their own electric field $\mathbf{E}_1$ which acts opposite to the applied field $\mathbf{E}_0$. The vector sum of $\mathbf{E}_0$ and $\mathbf{E}_1$ represents the net electric field **E**, which is, obviously, less than applied field.

Table 2.1: Dielectric constant of some materials

Material	Dielectric constant K	Material	Dielectric constant K
Vacuum	1.0	Bakelite	4.8
Air	1.0	Puby mica	5.4
Teflon	2.1	NaCl	5.6
Polyethylene	2.3	Porcelain	6.5
Polystyrene	2.6	Pure silicon	12.0
Amber	2.7	Pure Ge	16.0
Paper	3.5	Pure water	78
Fused quartz	3.8	Titanium oxide	100
		Metals	∞

2.2. MAGNITUDE OF POLARIZATION CHARGES

Let us obtain a relation between the magnitude of free and bound charges. Let A be the area of the capacitor plate and σ_f and σ_b be the surface densities of free and bound charges. Construct mentally a Gaussian surface shown dotted in the Fig. 2.1(b). The flux of electric field **E** over the Gaussian surface is

$$EA = \frac{1}{\varepsilon_0}\left(\sigma_f - \sigma_b\right)A$$

$$E = \frac{\sigma_f}{\varepsilon_0} - \frac{\sigma_b}{\varepsilon_0} \qquad \text{...(2.2)}$$

Since $E = \frac{E_0}{K} = \frac{\sigma_f}{\varepsilon_0 K}$, we have from eqn. (2.2)

$$\frac{\sigma_f}{\varepsilon_0 K} = \frac{\sigma_f}{\varepsilon_0} - \frac{\sigma_b}{\varepsilon_0}$$

or $$\sigma_b = \left(1 - \frac{1}{K}\right) \sigma_f \qquad \text{...(2.3)}$$

Since $K > 1$, the magnitude of bound charge is always less than the free charge.

2.3. POLARIZATION VECTOR P

The state of polarization of a dielectric is described by polarization vector **P**. *It is defined as the dipole moment per unit volume.* The polarization P is related to its source bound charge density.

Consider a cylindrical block of dielectric placed in an electric field with its flat faces normal to the electric field as shown in the Fig. 2.2(a). Let A and l denote the area of cross section and the length of the cylinder. The electric field induces positive and negative charges on the flat faces of the cylinder. Let the surface density of bound charge be σ_b. The dipole moment of the block is $(lA\sigma_b)$.

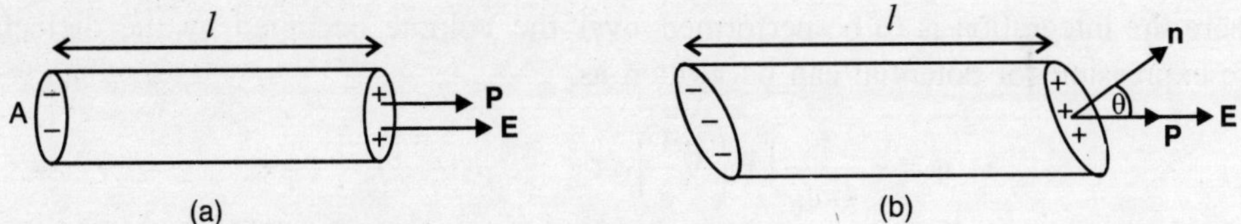

Fig. 2.2.

The dipole moment per unit volume is

$$P = \frac{lA\sigma_b}{lA} = \sigma_b \qquad \text{...(2.4)}$$

Thus *the magnitude of polarization vector is equal to the surface density of bound charge.*

Now consider a cylindrical block of dielectric with its flat faces inclined to its axis. It is placed in an electric field which acts along the axis of the cylinder. The dipole moment of this block is $(lA\sigma_b)$ and its volume is $(lA \cos\theta)$. The polarization is given by

$$P = \frac{lA\sigma_b}{lA\cos\theta} = \frac{\sigma_b}{\cos\theta}$$

$$\sigma_b = P\cos\theta = \mathbf{P}\cdot\mathbf{n} \qquad \text{...(2.5)}$$

Where **n** is unit vector normal to the flat face of the cylinder. From eqn. (2.5) we see that *the surface density of bound charge equals the normal component of polarization vector.*

If the polarization is uniform, the induced charges appear only on the surface of the dielectric. In case of non-uniform polarization, bound charges also induced within the body of the dielectric. In the following section we shall show that the volume density of bound charge equals the negative divergence of polarization vector **P**.

2.4. FIELD OF A POLARIZED PIECE OF DIELECTRIC

This section is devoted to the determination of electric field due to a piece of polarized dielectric at an external point. To determine the field, it is sufficient to know the potential. Consider a volume element $d\tau$ at point $\mathbf{r}'(x', y', z')$ inside the dielectric. The point of observation P lies at point $\mathbf{r}''(x'', y'', z'')$. The position vector of field point P relative to volume element (source point) $d\tau$ is $\mathbf{r}(= \mathbf{r}'' - \mathbf{r}')$. The dipole moment associated with the volume element is $\mathbf{P}d\tau$, where **P** is polarization vector. The potential at point P due to charge in volume element is

$$d\varphi = \frac{1}{4\pi\varepsilon_0}\frac{\mathbf{P}\cdot\mathbf{r}}{r^3}d\tau$$

Hence the potential of entire piece of polarized material is

$$\varphi = \frac{1}{4\pi\varepsilon_0}\int\frac{\mathbf{P}\cdot\mathbf{r}}{r^3}d\tau$$

where the integration is to be performed over the volume occupied by the dielectric piece. The above expression for potential can be written as

$$\varphi = -\frac{1}{4\pi\varepsilon_0}\int\mathbf{P}.\left(\nabla\frac{1}{r}\right)d\tau \qquad ...(2.6)$$

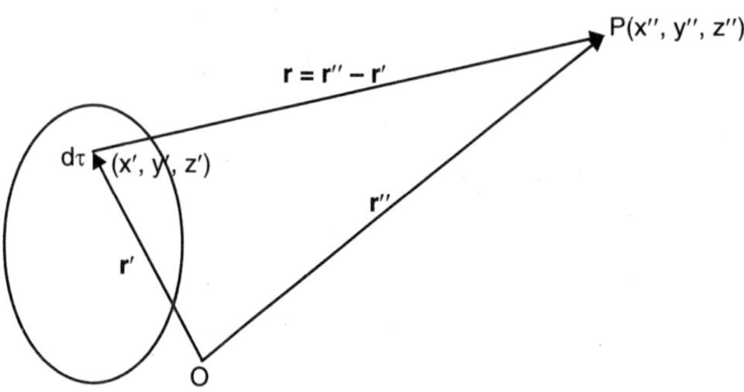

Fig. 2.3. Potential of a piece of polarized dielectric.

Here the operator ∇ involves differentiation with respect to observer's coordinates (x'', y'', z'')

$$\nabla = \mathbf{i}\frac{\partial}{\partial x''} + \mathbf{j}\frac{\partial}{\partial y''} + \mathbf{k}\frac{\partial}{\partial z''}$$

We define $$\nabla' = \mathbf{i}\frac{\partial}{\partial x'} + \mathbf{j}\frac{\partial}{\partial y'} + \mathbf{k}\frac{\partial}{\partial z'}$$

Which involves differentiation with respect to source coordinates (x', y', z'). It can be shown that

$$\nabla = -\nabla'$$

Making use of this result we can write eqn. (2.6) as

$$\varphi = \frac{1}{4\pi\varepsilon_0}\int \mathbf{P}\cdot\nabla'\left(\frac{1}{r}\right)d\tau \qquad ...(2.7)$$

To transform eqn. (2.6) into more convenient form we make use of the following identity

$$\nabla'(\varphi\mathbf{A}) = \nabla'\varphi\cdot\mathbf{A} + \varphi\nabla'\cdot\mathbf{A}$$

To use this result we make the following replacement. $\mathbf{A} \to \mathbf{P}$, $\varphi \to \frac{1}{r}$. Doing so we obtain

$$\mathbf{P}\cdot\nabla'\frac{1}{r} = \nabla'\left(\frac{\mathbf{P}}{r}\right) - \frac{1}{r}\nabla'\cdot\mathbf{P} \qquad ...(2.8)$$

In view of eqn. (2.8) we can write eqn. (2.7) as

$$\varphi = \frac{1}{4\pi\varepsilon_0}\int\left[\nabla'\left(\frac{\mathbf{P}}{r}\right) - \frac{1}{r}\nabla'\cdot\mathbf{P}\right]d\tau$$

$$= \frac{1}{4\pi\varepsilon_0}\int \nabla'\cdot\frac{\mathbf{P}}{r}d\tau - \frac{1}{4\pi\varepsilon_0}\int\frac{\nabla'\cdot\mathbf{P}}{r}d\tau \qquad ...(2.9)$$

Transforming the first integral on the right hand side into surface integral by *divergence theorem* we have

$$\varphi = \frac{1}{4\pi\varepsilon_0}\int\frac{\mathbf{P}\cdot\mathbf{n}}{r}d\mathbf{S} + \frac{1}{4\pi\varepsilon_0}\int\frac{-\nabla\cdot\mathbf{P}}{r}d\tau \qquad ...(2.10)$$

The first term on the right hand side of eqn. (2.10) looks like the potential due to a surface charge distribution with surface charge density

$$\sigma_b = \mathbf{P}\cdot\mathbf{n} \qquad ...(2.11)$$

And the second term looks like the potential due to a volume charge distribution with volume charge density

$$\rho_b = -\nabla\cdot\mathbf{P} \qquad ...(2.12)$$

In terms of newly defined charge densities σ_b and ρ_b the potential of the polarized dielectric is

$$\varphi = \frac{1}{4\pi\varepsilon_0}\int\frac{\sigma_b dS}{r} + \frac{1}{4\pi\varepsilon_0}\int\frac{\rho_b d\tau}{r} \qquad ...(2.13)$$

Proof of result $\nabla = -\nabla'$

$$\mathbf{r} = \mathbf{r}'' - \mathbf{r}' = (x'' - x')\mathbf{i} + (y'' - y')\mathbf{j} + (z'' - z')\mathbf{k}$$

$$r^2 = (x'' - x')^2 + (y'' - y')^2 + (z'' - z')^2$$

$$2r\frac{\partial r}{\partial x'} = -2(x'' - x') \quad \Rightarrow \quad \frac{\partial r}{\partial x'} = -\frac{x'' - x'}{r}$$

Similarly, $$\frac{\partial r}{\partial y'} = -\frac{y'' - y'}{r} \quad \text{and} \quad \frac{\partial r}{\partial z'} = -\frac{z'' - z'}{r}$$

Now $$\nabla'\left(\frac{1}{r}\right) = \mathbf{i}\frac{\partial}{\partial x'}\left(\frac{1}{r}\right) + \mathbf{j}\frac{\partial}{\partial y'}\left(\frac{1}{r}\right) + \mathbf{k}\frac{\partial}{\partial z'}\left(\frac{1}{r}\right)$$

$$= -\frac{1}{r^2}\frac{\partial r}{\partial x'}\mathbf{i} - \frac{1}{r^2}\frac{\partial r}{\partial y'}\mathbf{j} - \frac{1}{r^2}\frac{\partial r}{\partial z'}\mathbf{k}$$

$$= \frac{1}{r^2}\frac{x'' - x'}{r}\mathbf{i} + \frac{1}{r^2}\frac{y'' - y'}{r}\mathbf{j} + \frac{1}{r^2}\frac{z'' - z'}{r}\mathbf{k}$$

$$= \frac{\mathbf{r}}{r^3}$$

$$= -\nabla\left(\frac{1}{r}\right)$$

Hence $$\nabla' = -\nabla$$

2.5. GAUSS'S LAW IN DIELECTRICS: DISPLACEMENT VECTOR

Gauss's law which relates electric field **E** to its source charge density ρ reads

$$\nabla\cdot\mathbf{E} = \frac{\rho}{\varepsilon_0}$$

We want to write this law in dielectric. Let there be a piece of non-uniformly polarized dielectric with volume charge density $\rho_b = -\nabla\cdot\mathbf{P}$. Apart from these bound charges, we also introduce some extraneous charges, call it free charges, having charge density ρ_f. We call it free charges because they can be removed at will and they do not have any role in the structure of the dielectric. Both kinds of charges produce electric field. If **E** is the electric field inside the dielectric, we have

$$\nabla\cdot\mathbf{E} = \frac{\rho_{total}}{\varepsilon_0} = \frac{\rho_f + \rho_b}{\varepsilon_0} = \frac{\rho_f - \nabla\cdot\mathbf{P}}{\varepsilon_0}$$

$$\nabla\cdot(\varepsilon_0\mathbf{E} + \mathbf{P}) = \rho_f$$

or $$\nabla \cdot \mathbf{D} = \rho_f, \quad \text{...(2.14)}$$

where

$$\mathbf{D} = \varepsilon_0 \mathbf{E} + \mathbf{P} \quad \text{...(2.15)}$$

The vector **D** defined by eqn. (2.15) is called *displacement vector* and is measured in coulomb/metre^2. It is not a fundamental vector but is a mathematical construct introduced to simplify the electrostatic equations of dielectric theory. It plays a very important role when the concept of displacement current is introduced. The integral form of eqn. (2.14) is

$$\oint_S \mathbf{D} \cdot \mathbf{n} dS = \int_V \rho_f d\tau \quad \text{...(2.16)}$$

Equations (2.14) and (2.15) are the Gauss's law in dielectric in differential and integral form respectively. It is worth to note that

(*i*) Vector **D** is related to its source ρ_f. The field lines of **D** originate from and end on free charges only.

(*ii*) Vector **E** has its origin in both free and bound charges.

(*iii*) Vector **P** has its origin in bound charges only and hence the field lines of **P** originate from and end on polarization charges.

In the region outside dielectric, the polarization **P** = 0 and **D** = ε_0**E**. Thus in free space **D** and **E** are identical except for a constant factor ε_0.

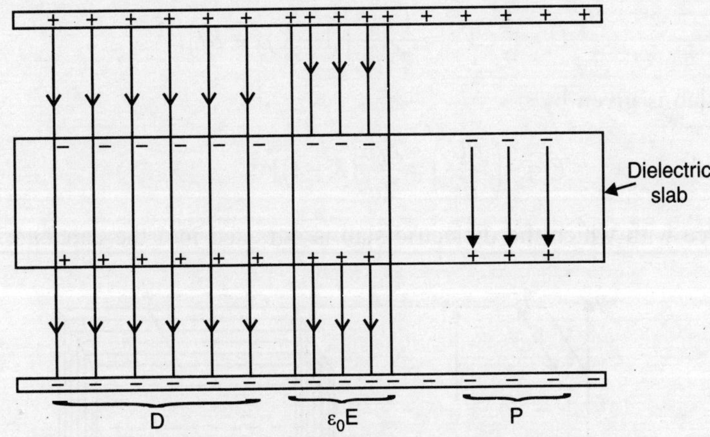

Fig. 2.4. Field lines of vector **E, P, D.**

2.6. MACROSCOPIC DIELECTRIC PARAMETERS

The electric field in dielectric **E**, the displacement vector **D**, polarization vector **P**, dielectric constant K (= ε_r), permittivity ε(= $\varepsilon_0 K = \varepsilon_0\ \varepsilon_r$) and electric susceptibility are called macroscopic dielectric parameters. In a homogeneous isotropic linear medium the polarization vector **P** is proportional to electric field **E**. The relation between **P** and **E** is written as

$$\mathbf{P} = \varepsilon_0 \chi_e \mathbf{E} \qquad ...(2.17)$$

The proportionality constant χ_e is called *electric susceptibility*. In above equation ε_0 is introduced to make the susceptibility dimensionless. Thus

$$\mathbf{D} = \varepsilon_0 \mathbf{E} + \mathbf{P} = \varepsilon_0 \mathbf{E} + \varepsilon_0 \chi_e \mathbf{E} = \varepsilon_0 (1 + \chi_e) \mathbf{E} = \varepsilon_0 K \mathbf{E} = \varepsilon \mathbf{E} \qquad ...(2.18)$$

Where $\quad K = 1 + \chi_e \quad$ or $\quad \chi_e = K - 1 \qquad ...(2.19)$

In terms of K, the polarization vector is expressed as

$$\mathbf{P} = \varepsilon_0 (K - 1) \mathbf{E} \qquad ...(2.20)$$

2.7. FORCE EXERTED BY A CAPACITOR ON A DIELECTRIC SLAB

Consider a parallel plate capacitor with plate separation d and dimensions l and b. A dielectric slab of thickness d is partially inserted between the plates so that it fills the space between the plates up to a distance $(l - x)$ as shown in the Fig. 2.5. The plates are maintained at constant potential V. The system shown in the figure can be viewed as two capacitors connected in parallel and its total capacitance is given by

$$C = \frac{\varepsilon_0 lbx}{d} + \frac{\varepsilon_0 K(l - b)x}{d} = \frac{\varepsilon_0 b}{d}[(1 - K)x + Kl]$$

Energy of the capacitor is

$$U = \frac{1}{2} CV^2 = \frac{1}{2} \frac{\varepsilon_0 b}{d} [(1 - K)x + Kl] V^2$$

Force on the slab is given by

$$F = -\left(\frac{dU}{dx}\right) = \frac{\varepsilon_0 b}{2d}(K - 1)V^2 \qquad ...(2.21)$$

This is the force with which the dielectric slab is attracted into the capacitor.

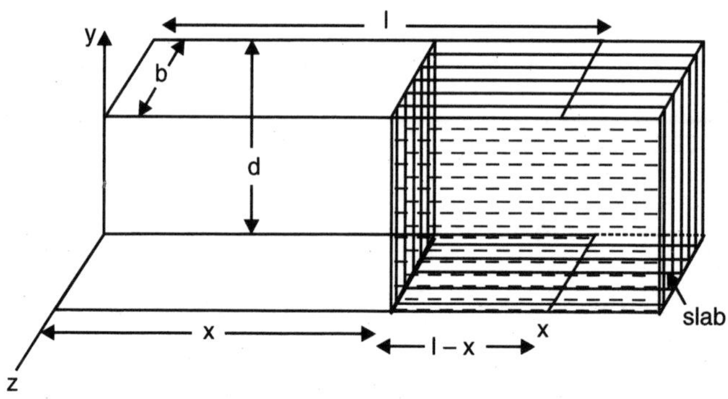

Fig. 2.5. A dielectric slab partially filling the space between the plates of a capacitor.

MICROSCOPIC THEORY OF DIELECTRICS

In order to understand the behaviour of dielectric material, it is essential to relate its macroscopic parameter with parameters of its basic constituents. Only through these connections, we shall be able to explain the variation of dielectric constant and other parameters with frequency and strength of applied electric field, temperature, pressure etc.

2.8. THE CONCEPT OF MICROSCOPIC UNIT

Dielectric material, like other matter, may occur in any of the three forms, gas, liquid and solid. All these materials are made of certain pattern unit. The smallest unit which can be thought of as the building block of the material may be termed, in general, a *microscopic unit*. Thus, in inert gases the microscopic unit is the atom of the gas. In gases like hydrogen, oxygen, carbon dioxide etc. the microscopic units are the molecules of the gas. In crystalline solid the microscopic unit is the unit cell. The basic requirement which a microscopic unit must have is that the total charge in the volume covered by it must be zero. The electric dipole moment of a microscopic unit is defined by the relation

$$\mathbf{p} = \int \rho(r)\,\mathbf{r}\,d\tau$$

For discrete charges

$$\mathbf{p} = \sum_i q_i \mathbf{r}_i$$

Where $\mathbf{r}_i$ is the vector indicating the position of charge q_i from a chosen origin.

2.9. POLAR AND NON-POLAR DIELECTRICS

If the microscopic unit (atom, molecule, unit cell) of a dielectric material has no permanent electric dipole moment, the dielectric material is referred to as non-polar dielectric. Inert gases (He, Ar, Ne, Kr), homo-nuclear diatomic molecules (H_2, N_2, O_2), symmetrical molecules like C_6H_6, elemental solids like carbon, silicon etc. are the examples of non-polar dielectrics. In inert gases, the centres of positive and negative charges in each atom coincide and thus possess no dipole moment. In homo-nuclear diatomic molecules the distribution of electron cloud is such that the centre of positive charge coincides with the centre of the negative charge and hence the molecule has no dipole moment.

If the microscopic unit of dielectric material possesses a permanent electric dipole moment, then the dielectric material is called polar dielectric (para-electric). HCl gas, water (H_2O), acetone, crystalline solids in which centre of symmetry lacks in unit cell are examples of polar dielectric materials. In hetero-nuclear molecule (such as HCl) the electron cloud is shifted towards the more electronegative atom Cl and thus the molecule acquires an electric dipole moment. Water is a good example of polar liquid. In this material, the microscopic unit of water is H_2O molecule. In this molecule, the OH bonds are inclined at an angle of 104°. Because of higher electronegativity of oxygen, the OH bonds acquire polarity with negative end at oxygen and positive end at hydrogen. If p_0 is the dipole moment of OH bond, the electric dipole moment p of water molecule is

$$p = \sqrt{p_0^2 + p_0^2 + 2p_0^2 \cos\theta}, \qquad \theta = 104°$$

2.10. INTERNAL ELECTRIC FIELD OR LOCAL ELECTRIC FIELD

The basic constituents of matter, in general, are atoms, molecules and unit cell, which are collectively called microscopic units. When a dielectric material is subjected to an electric field, the microscopic unit get polarized. These polarized units will create their own electric field. Thus the electric field at any point in the dielectric will be the sum of the electric field applied externally and the resultant electric field created by all other polarized units at that point. This field is often called *internal or local field* $\mathbf{E}_i$. Obviously this field will be quite different from the external field.

2.11. LORENTZ FORMULA FOR INTERNAL OR LOCAL ELECTRIC FIELD

It was Lorentz who for the first time derived a formula for the internal electric field. Consider a point within the dielectric at which the internal field is to be evaluated. A polarized dielectric may be imagined to be made up of a large number of point dipoles separated from each other by a distance of the order of nanometer. The electric field due to these dipoles will be inversely proportional to the square of its distance from the point under consideration. Thus, as we go away from the point under consideration, the contribution of dipoles towards electric field at the point decreases. Beyond a certain distance, their contribution becomes negligibly small and hence their presence may be ignored. Keeping this in mind, Lorentz took a small spherical region around the point at which the electric field is to be obtained. The radius of this cavity is chosen large enough to ignore the effect of dipoles lying outside it. Therefore, in evaluating the internal field we have to consider the contribution of dipoles lying within the cavity only. The resultant electric field $\mathbf{E}_i$ at a point within the polarized dielectric is the vector sum of following field:

(*i*) Applied Electric Field $\mathbf{E}_0$ (*ii*) Depolarization Field $\mathbf{E}_1$ (*iii*) Lorentz Field $\mathbf{E}_2$ (*iv*) Field of Dipoles within the Cavity $\mathbf{E}_3$

$$\mathbf{E}_i = \mathbf{E}_0 + \mathbf{E}_1 + \mathbf{E}_2 + \mathbf{E}_3 \qquad \text{...(2.22)}$$

(*i*) **Applied External Field $\mathbf{E}_0$:** This is the electric field created by the free charges external to the dielectric. For example, if the dielectric is polarized by electric field produced between the plates of a charged capacitor, the sources of this field are the charges lying on the capacitor plates. If the $\mathbf{E}$ is the macroscopic electric field within the dielectric and K is dielectric constant, then $\mathbf{E}_0$ is related to $\mathbf{E}$ through the relation

$$\mathbf{E} = \frac{\mathbf{E}_0}{K} \quad \text{or} \quad \mathbf{E}_0 = K\mathbf{E} \qquad \text{...(2.23)}$$

(*ii*) **Depolarization Field $\mathbf{E}_1$:** This field is produced by polarization charges induced on the outer surface of the dielectric. This field always opposes the external field $\mathbf{E}_0$. Its value depends on the geometrical shape of the dielectric. For a thin slab of dielectric it is given by

$$\mathbf{E}_1 = -\frac{\mathbf{P}}{\varepsilon_0} = -(K-1)\mathbf{E} \qquad ...(2.24)$$

(iii) **Lorentz Field $\mathbf{E}_2$:** This field is created by induced polarization charges at the inner surface of the spherical cavity. Let a be the radius of the cavity. The surface density of polarization charges at a point on the inner surface of cavity having angular position θ with respect to the direction of vector **P** is $\sigma = \mathbf{P}\cdot\mathbf{n} = -P\cos\theta$ where **n** is unit vector normal to the surface of cavity and pointing towards the centre of cavity. Now consider a ring between the radius vectors at angles θ and θ + dθ. The radius of the ring is $a\sin\theta$ and width is $ad\theta$. The surface area of the ring is $ds = 2\pi a \sin\theta \cdot a d\theta$. Charge on this ring is

$$|dq| = \sigma ds = 2\pi a \sin\theta \cdot a d\theta \cdot \sigma = 2\pi a^2 P \sin\theta \cos\theta \, d\theta$$

The magnitude of electric field at the centre of cavity due to this ring is

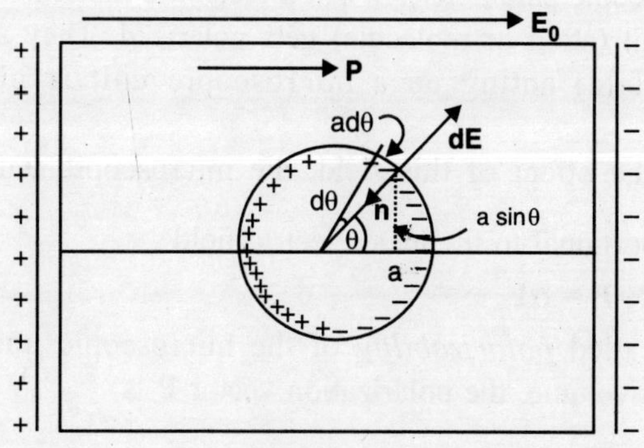

Fig. 2.6

$$dE = \frac{1}{4\pi\varepsilon_0} \cdot \frac{dq}{a^2} = \frac{2\pi a^2 P \sin\theta\cos\theta\, d\theta}{4\pi\varepsilon_0 a^2} = \frac{P}{2\varepsilon_0}\sin\theta\cos\theta\, d\theta$$

The resolved part of dE parallel to **P** is dE cos θ and perpendicular to **P** is dE sin θ. The cavity may be divided into a large number of such rings. The total field due to all rings will be $\sum dE\cos\theta$ parallel to **P** and $\sum dE \sin\theta$ perpendicular to **P**. Due to symmetry of the cavity, the perpendicular component $\sum dE\sin\theta$ will be equal to zero. Hence the total field due to charges on the surface of the cavity is parallel to polarization **P** and its magnitude is given by the expression

$$E_2 = \int dE\cos\theta = \frac{P}{2\varepsilon_0}\int_0^{\pi} \cos^2\theta \, \sin\theta\, d\theta$$

Substituting cos θ = x in above integral we have

$$E_2 = \frac{P}{2\varepsilon_0}\int_1^{-1} (-x^2)dx = \frac{P}{3\varepsilon_0}$$

In vector form

$$\mathbf{E}_2 = \frac{\mathbf{P}}{3\varepsilon_0} = \frac{K-1}{3}\mathbf{E} \qquad \text{...(2.25)}$$

(*iv*) The electric field $\mathbf{E}_3$ due to point dipoles inside the cavity vanishes for crystalline solids having cubic symmetry and also for neutral molecules having random arrangements.

Thus the internal field $\mathbf{E_i}$ at a point inside the polarized dielectric is given by the expression

$$\mathbf{E}_i = K\mathbf{E} - (K-1)\mathbf{E} + \frac{(K-1)}{3}\mathbf{E} = \left(\frac{K+2}{3}\right)\mathbf{E} \qquad \text{...(2.26)}$$

2.12. CLAUSIUS-MOSOTTI EQUATION

Clausius and Mosotti were the first to relate dielectric constant K (a macroscopic parameter) with polarizability α (a microscopic parameter). When a dielectric material is subjected to external electric field, the microscopic unit (atom or molecule) gets polarized. They assumed that the internal field $\mathbf{E_i}$ (also called local field) acting on a microscopic unit is given by Lorentz expression $\mathbf{E}_i = \frac{(K+2)}{3}\mathbf{E}$. Under the effect of this field, the microscopic unit acquires an induced dipole moment **p**, which is proportional to the local electric field

$$\mathbf{P} = \alpha\mathbf{E}_i \qquad \text{...(2.27a)}$$

The quantity α is called *polarizability* of the microscopic unit. For medium containing N microscopic unit per unit volume, the polarization vector **P** is

$$\mathbf{P} = N\mathbf{p} = N\alpha\mathbf{E}_i \qquad \text{...(2.27b)}$$

The polarization vector **P** is related to macroscopic electric field **E** through the relation

$$\mathbf{P} = \varepsilon_0(K-1)\mathbf{E} \qquad \text{...(2.27c)}$$

For dilute medium, the mutual interaction between dipoles is negligibly small the internal field $\mathbf{E_i}$ has the same value as the macroscopic field **E.**

Combining eqns. (2.27b) and (2.27c) we get

$$K = 1 + \frac{N\alpha}{\varepsilon_0} \qquad \text{...(2.27d)}$$

This equation can be used to determine the microscopic parameter α by measuring the macroscopic parameter K.

If the dielectric medium contains several kinds of microscopic units viz. N_j microscopic units per unit volume of *j*th kind, then the polarization vector **P** is given by

$$\mathbf{P} = \alpha_j\mathbf{E}_i^j \qquad \text{...(2.27e)}$$

The quantity α_j is called the *polarizability* of microscopic unit of *j*th kind and $\mathbf{E}_i^j$ is the local field on this unit. In general it is a tensor. For a symmetrical unit it is a scalar quantity.

$$\mathbf{P} = \sum_j N_j \alpha_j \mathbf{E}_i^j \qquad ...(2.28)$$

For an isotropic dielectric medium, the local field has the same value throughout the medium. So we can write eqn. (2.28) as

$$\mathbf{P} = \mathbf{E}_i \sum_j N_j \alpha_j = \left(\frac{K+2}{3}\right) \mathbf{E} \sum_j N_j \alpha_j \qquad ...(2.29)$$

Substituting the expression $\mathbf{P} = \varepsilon_0 (K-1)\mathbf{E}$ in eq. (2.29) we get

$$\frac{K-1}{K+2} = \frac{\sum_j N_j \alpha_j}{3\varepsilon_0} \qquad ...(2.30a)$$

This is the Clausius-Mosotti equation.

A medium with molar mass M and density ρ, has molar volume $\frac{M}{\rho}$. Molar volume contains N_A (Avogadro's number) molecules. Then the number of molecules per unit volume is $N = \frac{N_A}{(M/\rho)}$.

The Clausius-Mosotti equation for substance made up of single type of molecules is

$$\frac{K-1}{K+2} \cdot \frac{M}{\rho} = \frac{1}{3\varepsilon_0} N_A \alpha \qquad ...(2.30b)$$

2.13. KINDS OF POLARIZABILITY

There are three kinds of polarizabilities viz. (*i*) electronic or atomic polarizability (*ii*) ionic polarizability (*iii*) dipolar or orientational polarizability.

Electronic Polarizability (α_e)

The electronic polarization takes place due to shift of centres of negative charge and positive charge in an atom under the action of external electric field. In absence of external field the centre of negatively charged electron cloud in an atom coincides with that of positively charged nucleus. The dipole moment of the atom is zero. When an electric field is applied, the atom experiences an electric field $\mathbf{E_i}$. This electric field pulls the electron cloud of the atom in one direction and the nucleus in opposite direction and as a result of which they are displaced from their original position. The nucleus being much heavier in comparison to the electron cloud, it remains practically at rest, only electron cloud shifts through a small distance. The separation of electron cloud and the nucleus is opposed by the attractive Coulomb force between them. As a result of which, an equilibrium is established. Let x be the separation of the centre of electron cloud and the nucleus, Z the atomic number of atom, a the radius of the atom. The electric field produced by the electron cloud at the location of nucleus is

$$E = \frac{\rho x}{3\varepsilon_0} = \frac{Zex}{4\pi\varepsilon_0 a^3} = \frac{p_i}{4\pi\varepsilon_0 a^3} \qquad ...(2.31)$$

Where $p_i = Zex$ is induced dipole moment in the atom and $\rho = \dfrac{Ze}{(4/3)\pi a^3}$ = volume density of charge in electron cloud. In equilibrium $|E| = |E_i|$. Therefore,

$$E_i = \frac{Zex}{4\pi\varepsilon_0 a^3} = \frac{p_i}{4\pi\varepsilon_0 a^3} \qquad \text{...(2.32)}$$

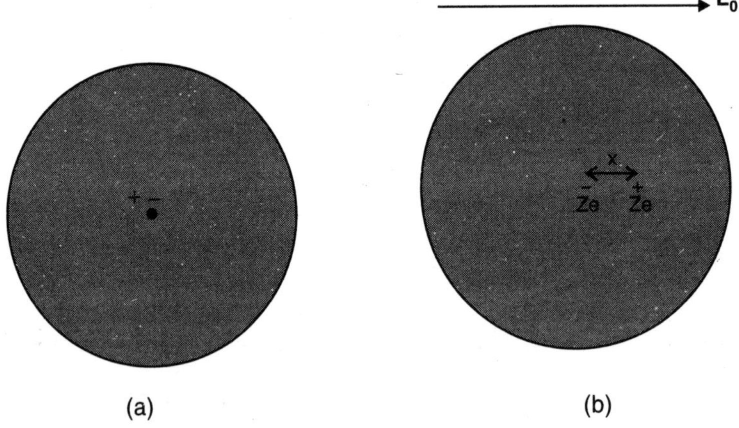

Fig. 2.7. (a) In absence of centre of positive charge coincides with that of negative charge. (b) Under the influence of external electric field centres of positive and negative charge get separated.

The electronic polarizability α_e of the atom is given by

$$p_i = \alpha_e E_i$$

Hence

$$\alpha_e = \frac{p_i}{E_i} = 4\pi\varepsilon_0 a^3 \qquad \text{...(2.33)}$$

Thus the *electronic polarizability* is proportional to the volume of the atom.

Table 2.2: Experimental values of electronic polarizabilities of some atoms ($\times 10^{-30}$ m^3)

Atoms	H	He	Li	Be	C	Ne	Na	Ar	K
$\alpha/4\pi\varepsilon_0$	0.667	0.205	24.3	5.60	1.76	0.396	24.7	1.64	43.4

Frequency Dependence of Electronic Polarizability

The electronic polarizability of a dielectric medium when subjected to an alternating electric field becomes frequency dependent. Let an electromagnetic radiation of frequency ω be propagating in a gaseous medium. The radiation consists of oscillating electric field $E = E_0 \cos \omega t$. Each electron in the molecule is bound with a restoring force $-sx$ characterized by force constant s, where x is displacement of oscillator. Thus, in this model each electron is treated as a classical oscillator with frequency $\omega_0 = \sqrt{\dfrac{s}{m}}$, m being the mass of electron. Under the action of oscillating electric field, the electron performs forced oscillation with frequency ω and in doing so it radiates energy. The energy of electron thus decays with time. The oscillating electron also loses energy while making collision with neighbouring particles of the medium. This loss of energy may be taken into account by introducing a damping term in the equation of motion for electron. We assume that the damping term is proportional to the velocity of the oscillator. The equation of motion of electron is

$$m\frac{d^2x}{dt^2} = -sx - m\gamma\frac{dx}{dt} + qE_0\cos\omega t, \quad ...(2.34)$$

q is charge of electron

For convenience we write this equation in complex form. The displacement x now becomes a complex quantity. In fact the above equation is the real part of the following complex equation

$$\ddot{\tilde{x}} + \gamma\dot{\tilde{x}} + \omega_0^2\tilde{x} = \frac{qE_0}{m}e^{-i\omega t} \quad ...(2.35)$$

The solution of eq. (2.35) may be obtained in the form

$$\tilde{x} = \tilde{x}_0 e^{-i\omega t} \quad ...(2.36)$$

The amplitude of vibration $\tilde{x}_0$ may be obtained by substituting (2.36) in (2.35). Doing so we obtain

$$\tilde{x}_0 = \frac{q/m}{\omega_0^2 - \omega^2 - i\gamma\omega}E_0 \quad ...(2.37)$$

Therefore,

$$\tilde{x} = \frac{q/m}{\omega_0^2 - \omega^2 - i\gamma\omega}E_0 e^{-i\omega t} \quad ...(2.38)$$

A deviation of electron from the equilibrium position results in a dipole moment. We consider a rarefied medium (gas) in which the electric field acting on the electron may be taken equal to that of the electromagnetic wave. The dipole moment induced in the electron oscillator is

$$\tilde{p} = q\tilde{x} = \frac{q^2/m}{\omega_0^2 - \omega^2 - i\gamma\omega}\tilde{E} \quad ...(2.39)$$

The coefficient of $\tilde{E}$ in above equation is complex electronic polarizability $\tilde{\alpha}_e$. Thus

$$\tilde{\alpha}_e = \frac{q^2/m}{\omega_0^2 - \omega^2 - i\gamma\omega} \quad ...(2.40)$$

Writing $\tilde{\alpha}_e = \alpha'_e + i\alpha''_e$, we have

$$\alpha'_e = \frac{q^2}{m}\frac{\omega_0^2 - \omega^2}{(\omega_0^2 - \omega^2)^2 + \gamma^2\omega^2} \quad ...(2.41)$$

$$\alpha''_e = \frac{q^2}{m}.\frac{\gamma\omega}{(\omega_0^2 - \omega^2)^2 + \gamma^2\omega^2} \quad ...(2.42)$$

If there are N electrons per unit volume then the dipole moment per unit volume $\tilde{P}$ (polarization) is

$$\tilde{P} = N\tilde{\alpha}_e\tilde{E} = N\frac{q^2/m}{\omega_0^2 - \omega^2 - i\gamma\omega}\tilde{E} \quad ...(2.43)$$

In a molecule all the electrons do not experience the same force constant and the same damping. Let us suppose that a fraction of f_k electrons have resonant frequency ω_k and damping constant γ_k. Of course $\sum_k f_k = 1$. Incorporating this modification, the expressions for electronic polarizability and dielectric constant become

$$\tilde{\alpha}_e = \frac{q^2}{m}\sum_k \frac{f_k}{\omega_k^2 - \omega^2 - i\gamma_k\omega}$$

Therefore,

$$\tilde{P} = \sum_k N f_k p_k = \frac{Nq^2}{m}\sum_k \frac{f_k}{\omega_k^2 - \omega^2 - i\gamma_k\omega} \quad ...(2.44)$$

In dilute medium (such as gases)

$$\tilde{P} = \varepsilon_0(\tilde{\varepsilon}_r - 1)\tilde{E} = N\tilde{\alpha}_e\tilde{E}$$

Where $\tilde{\varepsilon}_r$ is complex dielectric constant. From this equation we have

$$\tilde{\varepsilon}_r = 1 + \frac{N\tilde{\alpha}_e}{\varepsilon_0} = 1 + \frac{Nq^2}{\varepsilon_0 m}\sum_k \frac{f_k}{\omega_k^2 - \omega^2 - i\gamma_k\omega} \quad ...(2.45)$$

Separating the real and imaginary part of complex dielectric constant we have

$$\tilde{\varepsilon}_r = \varepsilon_r' + \varepsilon_r'' \quad ...(2.46)$$

$$\varepsilon_r' = 1 + \frac{Nq^2}{\varepsilon_0 m}.\sum_k \frac{f_k\left(\omega_k^2 - \omega^2\right)}{(\omega_k^2 - \omega^2)^2 + \gamma_k^2\omega^2} \quad ...(2.47)$$

$$\varepsilon_r'' = \frac{Nq^2}{\varepsilon_0 m}.\sum_k \frac{f_k\gamma_k\omega}{(\omega_k^2 - \omega^2)^2 + \gamma_k^2\omega^2} \quad ...(2.48)$$

The electromagnetic wave equation in a dielectric medium admits plane wave solution of the form

$$\tilde{E} = E_0 e^{i(\tilde{k}z - \omega t)} \quad ...(2.49)$$

Equation (2.49) represents a wave of frequency ω and wave vector $\tilde{k}$ propagating in z-direction. The complex propagation vector $\tilde{k}(= k' + ik'')$ is related to complex index of refraction $\tilde{n}(= n' + in'')$ through the relation

$$\tilde{k} = \frac{\omega}{c}\tilde{n}, \text{ with } k' = \frac{\omega}{c}n' \text{ and } k'' = \frac{\omega}{c}n'' \quad ...(2.50)$$

In terms of k' (or n') and k'' (or n'') the equation of electromagnetic wave becomes

$$\tilde{E} = E_0 e^{-k''z} e^{i(k'z-\omega t)} = E_0 e^{-\omega n'' z/c} e^{i[\omega n' z/c - \omega t]} \qquad \text{...(2.51)}$$

The exponential term $e^{i[\omega n' z/c - \omega t]}$ represents a wave travelling with phase velocity c/n'. The number n' represents what we normally call the index of refraction. The amplitude of the wave viz. $E_0 e^{-\omega n'' z/c}$, which contains n'', the imaginary part of $\tilde{n}$, decreases exponentially with z. Thus the imaginary part of complex index of refraction is responsible for the attenuation of the wave. The intensity I of the wave is proportional to the square of the amplitude, so

$$I \propto e^{-2\omega n'' z/c}$$

or

$$I \propto e^{-\beta z}, \quad \beta = \frac{2\omega n''}{c} \qquad \text{...(2.52)}$$

The quantity $\beta = \frac{2\omega n''}{c}$ is called the *absorption coefficient.*

Let us find a relation between the index of refraction $\tilde{n}$ and dielectric constant $\tilde{\varepsilon}_r$ and the electronic polarizability $\tilde{\alpha}_e$. We know that $n = \frac{c}{v} = c\sqrt{\mu\varepsilon} = c\sqrt{\mu_0\varepsilon_0\mu_r\varepsilon_r} = \sqrt{\mu_r\varepsilon_r} = \sqrt{\varepsilon_r}$. Where we have used the fact that for non-magnetic materials $\mu_r \approx 1$. In complex notation

$$\tilde{n} = \sqrt{\tilde{\varepsilon}_r} = \left(1 + \frac{N\tilde{\alpha}_e}{\varepsilon_0}\right)^{1/2} \approx 1 + \frac{N\tilde{\alpha}_e}{2\varepsilon_0}$$

In above equation we have assumed that the quantity $N\tilde{\alpha}_e/\varepsilon_0 << 1$. This is nearly true for gases. Then

$$\tilde{n} = 1 + \frac{Nq^2}{2\varepsilon_0 m}\sum_k \frac{f_k}{\omega_k^2 - \omega^2 - i\gamma_k\omega} \qquad \text{...(2.53)}$$

Obviously,

$$n' = 1 + \frac{Nq^2}{2\varepsilon_0 m}\sum_k \frac{f_k(\omega_k^2 - \omega^2)}{\left(\omega_k^2 - \omega^2\right)^2 + \gamma_k^2\omega^2} \qquad \text{...(2.54)}$$

and

$$n'' = \frac{Nq^2}{2\varepsilon_0 m}\sum_k \frac{f_k\gamma_k\omega}{\left(\omega_k^2 - \omega^2\right)^2 + \gamma_k^2\omega^2} \qquad \text{...(2.55)}$$

$$\beta = \frac{2\omega n''}{c} = \frac{Nq^2\omega^2}{\varepsilon_0 mc}\sum_k \frac{f_k\gamma_k}{\left(\omega_k^2 - \omega^2\right)^2 + \gamma_k^2\omega^2} \qquad \text{...(2.56)}$$

The complex index of refraction $\tilde{n}(=n'+in'')$, complex dielectric constant $\tilde{\varepsilon}_r(=\varepsilon'+i\varepsilon'')$ and polarizability $\tilde{\alpha}_e(=\alpha_e'+i\alpha_e'')$ are mutually related in the following way.

$$\tilde{n}=\sqrt{\tilde{\varepsilon}_r}, \qquad \tilde{\varepsilon}_r=1+\frac{N\tilde{\alpha}_e}{\varepsilon_0}, \qquad \tilde{\alpha}_e=\frac{q^2}{m}\sum_k \frac{f_k}{\omega_k^2-\omega^2-i\gamma_k\omega}$$

So the curves showing frequency dependence of these parameters have identical shapes. In Fig. 2.8, we have shown the variation of real and imaginary parts of $\tilde{n}$ viz. n' and n'' with driving frequency ω in the vicinity of one of the resonant frequency ω_k. It can easily be seen that the index of refraction n' rises gradually with increasing frequency ω. Near the resonant frequency ω_k, the index of refraction drops sharply. Notice that in this region, imaginary part n'', which describes power absorption, becomes maximum. This is not surprising. When the driving frequency ω coincides with the resonant frequency ω_k, the oscillator is driven at its most favourite frequency and consequently it dissipates maximum power due to damping. The sudden fall of index of refraction (n') near the resonant frequency (ω_k) is called *anomalous dispersion*.

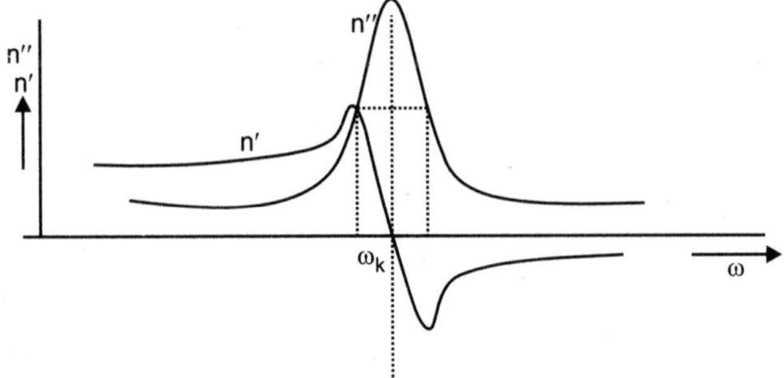

Fig. 2.8. Frequency dependence of n′ and n″.

When the driving frequency is far away from the resonant frequency, the damping term can be ignored and the formula for index of refraction becomes

$$n'=1+\frac{Nq^2}{2\varepsilon_0 m}\sum_k \frac{f_k}{\omega_k^2-\omega^2} \qquad ...(2.57)$$

For transparent materials, the resonant frequency lies in ultraviolet region and $\omega \ll \omega_k$, we make following approximation.

$$\frac{1}{\omega_k^2-\omega^2}=\frac{1}{\omega_k^2\left(1-\dfrac{\omega^2}{\omega_k^2}\right)}=\frac{1}{\omega_k^2}\left(1-\frac{\omega^2}{\omega_k^2}\right)^{-1}\cong\frac{1}{\omega_k^2}\left(1+\frac{\omega^2}{\omega_k^2}\right)$$

Then

$$n'=1+\frac{Nq^2}{2\varepsilon_0 m}\sum_k \frac{f_k}{\omega_k^2}\left(1+\frac{\omega^2}{\omega_k^2}\right)$$

$$= 1 + \left(\frac{Nq^2}{2\varepsilon_0 m}\sum_k \frac{f_k}{\omega_k^2}\right) + \left(\frac{Nq^2}{2\varepsilon_0 m}\sum_k \frac{f_k}{\omega_k^4}\right)\omega^2, \ \omega = \frac{2\pi c}{\lambda}$$

$$= A + \frac{B}{\lambda^2} \quad \text{...(2.58)}$$

Where the constant A is called coefficient of refraction and B is called the coefficient of absorption. Formula (2.58) is known as Cauchy's formula.

Ionic Polarizability (α_i)

This kind of polarizability is common to all ionic solids. Such materials consist of chain of positive and negative ions separated from each other by some fixed distance a_0 as shown in the Fig. 2.8(a).

(a) ⊖∿∿⊕∿∿⊖∿∿⊕∿∿⊖∿∿⊕ ⟵ a_0 ⟶

(b) E = o ∿∿⊖∿∿⊕∿∿ ⟵ a_0 ⟶

(c) E = E_i ⊖∿∿∿∿⊕ ⟵ $a_0 + \delta x$ ⟶

Fig. 2.8. (a) Linear chain of ions (b) One particular bond with E = 0 (c) Increase in length of bond under the action of electric field.

When an electric field is applied to such materials, the positive ions are pulled in one direction and negative ions in other direction. In equilibrium condition, the separation between the ions becomes $(a_0 + \delta x)$. Usually $\delta x << a_0$. This leads to an induced dipole moment p_i, which can be written as

$$p_i = q_i \delta x$$

Where q_i is the magnitude of charge on each ion. The increase in separation δx and hence p_i depends on the internal electric field E_i. Thus

$$p_i = \alpha_i E_i$$

or $$\alpha_i = \frac{q_i\,\delta x}{E_i}$$

α_i is called the *ionic polarizability*. When ions are displaced, a restoring force produced due to this deformation starts acting on them, which tries to bring the ions back to their original positions. This force is proportional to the displacement and can be written as $f_c\,\delta x$, where f_c is the force constant. Equilibrium is achieved when the restoring force becomes equal to $q_i E_i$, the force due to E_i. Thus

$$f_c \delta x = q_i E_i$$

or $$\delta x = \frac{q_i}{f_c} E_i$$

Hence $$\alpha_i = \frac{q_i^2}{f_c} = \frac{n_i^2 e^2}{f_c} \quad \text{...(2.59)}$$

Where n_i is an integer whose value depends on the ion. For Na^+, $n_i = 1$, for Cl^{-1}, $n_i = -1$ and so on.

Dipolar or Orientational Polarizability (α_d)

The microscopic units (atoms or molecules) of polar dielectrics possess permanent electric dipole moment. In absence of external field, these dipoles have random orientation and hence the material in bulk has no net dipole moment. When a static electric field is applied to such a substance, these dipoles experience a field $\boldsymbol{E}_i$. This field applies a torque on each dipole. Under the action of this torque, they will tend to rotate and align in the direction of $\boldsymbol{E}_i$. But this is opposed by thermal energy which tries to maintain random orientation. When the equilibrium is reached, in this condition every dipole is rotated a bit in the direction of the field. In an assembly of dipoles (whose number is about 10^{28}), it is not possible to obtain the induced dipole moment due to rotation of each dipole. However, we can say on average, each dipole acquires an induced electric dipole moment p_i in the direction of the effective internal field $\boldsymbol{E}_i$. We define dipolar polarizability α_d by the relation

$$\alpha_d = \frac{p_i}{E_i} \qquad \text{...(2.60)}$$

Debye Theory of Dipolar Polarization

Debye in 1912 obtained an expression for α_d making use of the following assumptions:

(*i*) All elementary dipoles of the material are identical and possess permanent dipole moment **p**.

(*ii*) Elementary dipoles are free to rotate inside the material.

(*iii*) Elementary dipoles do not interact with each other.

Let E_i be the static electric field acting on each dipole. Under the action of this field, each dipole undergoes a rotation until the equilibrium is reached. The dipoles which are inclined at angle θ with the internal field will have potential energy

$$U = -\mathbf{p}\cdot\mathbf{E}_i = -pE_i\cos\theta \qquad \text{...(2.61)}$$

All the dipoles whose inclination lies between θ and $\theta + d\theta$ have the same energy U. The number of such dipoles dn, according to Maxwell-Boltzmann statistics, is proportional to $\exp(-U/kT)$ and the solid angle $d\Omega = 2\pi \sin\theta\, d\theta$. Thus we can write

$$dn = C\exp\left(-\frac{U}{kT}\right)(2\pi\sin\theta\, d\theta)$$

$$= C\exp\left(\frac{pE_i\cos\theta}{kT}\right)\sin\theta\, d\theta \qquad \text{...(2.62)}$$

The factor 2π has been absorbed in constant C. All the dipoles falling in this group have component $p\cos\theta$ of dipole moment in the field direction. Thus the total dipole moment of these dn dipoles in the field direction is ($p\cos\theta\, dn$). The average contribution of each dipole towards the dipole moment in the field direction is

$$\bar{p} = \frac{\text{total dipole moment in the field direction}}{\text{total number of dipoles}} = \frac{\int (p\cos\theta)\, dn}{\int dn}$$

Where the integral extends overall possible orientations. Substituting the expression for dn in above expression we have

$$\bar{p} = \frac{p\int_0^\pi \exp\left(\frac{pE_i \cos\theta}{kT}\right).\cos\theta.\sin\theta\, d\theta}{\int_0^\pi \exp\left(\frac{pE_i \cos\theta}{kT}\right).\sin\theta\, d\theta} \qquad ...(2.63)$$

Put $\frac{pE_i}{kT} = a$ and $\cos\theta = x$ we have

$$\bar{p} = \frac{p\int_{-1}^{1} x \;\; e^{ax} dx}{\int_{-1}^{1} e^{ax} dx}$$

$$= p\left[\frac{e^a + e^{-a}}{e^a - e^{-a}} - \frac{1}{a}\right]$$

$$= p\left[\cot h\, a - \frac{1}{a}\right]$$

$$= p\; L(a) \qquad ...(2.64)$$

$L(a)$ is called *Langevin's function*. This function is such that it tends to become unity for large value of $a \left(= \frac{pE_i}{kT}\right)$ and becomes $\frac{a}{3}$ for values of a approaching zero or $a << 1$. At the electric field which we can apply to dielectric without its breakdown in laboratory at room temperature, the parameter $a = \frac{pE_i}{kT}$ is very small in comparison to unity and we can write

$$\bar{p} = p.\frac{a}{3} = \frac{p^2 E_i}{3kT}$$

Hence $$\alpha_d = \frac{p_i}{E_i} = \frac{p^2}{3kT} \qquad ...(2.65)$$

However, for large value of E_i and at low temperature $a >> 1$, $\bar{p} = p$ and it does not increase.

2.14. COMPLEX DIELECTRIC CONSTANT

When an alternating field is applied to a dielectric, the polarization vector **P,** and displacement vector **D** become oscillatory. Polarization takes finite time to grow and at any instant, it does not attain the value it should have corresponding to field. Thus it lags behind the electric field. Similarly, **D** also lags behind the applied field. In general, the expressions for **E, P** and **D** can be written as

$$E = E_0 e^{i\omega t} \quad ...(2.66)$$

$$P = P_0 e^{i(\omega t - \delta)} \quad ...(2.67)$$

$$D = D_0 e^{i(\omega t - \delta)}$$

E_0, P_0 and D_0 are the time independent amplitudes of electric field, polarization and displacement vectors respectively and δ is the phase difference. The complex dielectric constant of the material is defined by

$$\tilde{\varepsilon}_r = \frac{D}{\varepsilon_0 E} = \frac{D_0 e^{i(\omega t - \delta)}}{\varepsilon_0 E_0 e^{i\omega t}} = \frac{D_0}{\varepsilon_0 E_0} e^{-i\delta} \quad ...(2.68)$$

Writing complex dielectric constant as

$$\tilde{\varepsilon}_r = \varepsilon' - i\varepsilon''$$

We have

$$\varepsilon' = \frac{D_0}{\varepsilon_0 E_0} \cos\delta \quad \text{and} \quad \varepsilon'' = \frac{D_0}{\varepsilon_0 E_0} \sin\delta \quad \text{and} \quad \tan\delta = \frac{\varepsilon''}{\varepsilon'} \quad ...(2.69)$$

The real and imaginary parts of dielectric constants ε' and ε'' both depend on the frequency of the applied electric field. At low frequency $\varepsilon' = \varepsilon_s$, where ε_s is called static dielectric constant and at high frequency $\varepsilon'' = \varepsilon_\infty$, where ε_∞ is called optical dielectric constant.

Now we shall show that ε'' is related to the average power absorbed by the dielectric from the applied field. This justifies the name of ε'' as dielectric loss. Suppose that the space between the plates of a parallel plate capacitor is filled with the dielectric material. The plates carry free charges $+q$ and $-q$, the surface charge density being σ. The power absorbed is a real quantity, so we take the real part of electric field and electric displacement.

$$E = E_0 \cos\omega t \quad ...(2.70)$$

$$D = D_0 \cos(\omega t - \delta) \quad ...(2.71)$$

The electric displacement is related to free surface charge density σ. The time rate of change of D gives the current density J in the dielectric. Thus

$$J = \frac{dD}{dt} = -D_0\omega \sin(\omega t - \delta) = -D_0\omega\left[\sin\omega t\cos\delta - \cos\omega t\sin\delta\right]$$

$$= \varepsilon_0 \omega E_0 \left[-\varepsilon' \sin\omega t + \varepsilon'' \cos\omega t\right] \quad ...(2.72)$$

The average power absorbed per unit volume of the dielectric is

$$P = \frac{1}{T}\int_0^T E\,J\,dt$$

Where $T = 2\pi/\omega$ is the time period of the applied field. Substituting the expressions for E and J we have

$$P = \frac{1}{T}\int_0^T E_0 \cos\omega t\left[-\omega\varepsilon_0 E_0 \varepsilon'' \sin\omega t + \omega\varepsilon_0 E_0 \varepsilon'' \cos\omega t\right] dt$$

$$= \frac{1}{2}\varepsilon_0 E_0^2 \omega\varepsilon'' \qquad \text{...(2.73)}$$

Thus the imaginary part of dielectric constant is the measure of energy absorbed by the dielectric from the applied electric field.

SOLVED EXAMPLES

***Example* 1:** *A parallel plate capacitor has area $A = 1\ m^2$ of each plate, plate separation $d = 5$ mm. The plates carry equal and opposite charge of magnitude 20 microcoulomb. A dielectric slab with dielectric constant 2 fills the space between the plates. Calculate*

(*i*) *The electric field strength with and without dielectric between the plates.*

(*ii*) *Surface density of bound charges.*

(*iii*) *Polarization P*

(*iv*) *Electric displacement D*

(*v*) *Capacitance of the capacitor*

Solution:

(*i*) Electric field between the plates without dielectric

$$E_0 = \frac{q}{\varepsilon_0 A} = \frac{20\times10^{-6}\,C}{8.85\times10^{-12}\,\text{F m}^{-1}\times 1\,\text{m}^2} = 2.26\times10^6\,\text{V m}^{-1}$$

Electric field in presence of dielectric

$$E = \frac{E_0}{K} = \frac{2.26\times10^6\,\text{V m}^{-1}}{2} = 1.13\times10^6\,\text{V m}^{-1}$$

(*ii*) Surface density of bound charge

$$\sigma_b = \left(1-\frac{1}{K}\right)\sigma_f = \left(1-\frac{1}{2}\right)\times 20\times10^{-6} = 10\times10^{-6}\,\text{C m}^{-2}$$

(*iii*) Polarization P

$$P = \varepsilon_0(K-1)E = 8.85\times10^{-12}(2-1)\times1.13\times10^6 = 10\times10^{-6}\,\text{C m}^{-2}$$

or $$P = |\sigma_b|$$

(*iv*) Electric displacement

$$D = \varepsilon_0 KE = 8.85\times10^{-12}\times 2\times1.13\times10^6 = 20\times10^{-6}\,\text{C m}^{-2}$$

or $$D = |\sigma_f|$$

(*v*) Capacitance in absence of dielectric

$$C_0 = \frac{\varepsilon_0 A}{d} = \frac{8.85\times10^{-12}\times1}{5\times10^{-3}} = 1.77\times10^{-9}\,\text{F}$$

Capacitance with dielectric

$$C = KC_0 = 3.54\times10^{-9}\,\text{F}$$

***Example* 2:** *The plates of a parallel plate capacitor are 5 mm apart and 4 × 10² cm². The space between the plates is filled with two sheets, one 2 mm thick of dielectric constant 5 and other 3 mm thick of dielectric constant 2. Calculate*

(*i*) *Electric displacement D inside the two sheets*

(*ii*) *Electric field E inside the dielectric sheets*

(*iii*) *Polarization in both sheets*

(*iv*) *Potential difference between the plates*

(*v*) *Capacitance of the capacitor.*

The plates are oppositely charged with 20 microcoulomb charge.

Solution: Surface density of free charges on the plates

$$\sigma = \frac{q}{A} = \frac{20\times10^{-6}C}{4\times10^{-4}\text{m}^2} = 5\times10^{-4}\ \text{C m}^{-2}$$

(*i*) Displacement D depends on free charges, hence its value has the same value in both the dielectrics

$$D_1 = D_2 = \sigma = 5\times10^{-4}\ \text{C m}^{-2}$$

(*ii*) Electric field inside the first dielectric

$$E_1 = \frac{D_1}{\varepsilon_0 K_1} = \frac{5\times10^{-4}}{8.85\times10^{-12}\times5} = 1.13\times10^{7}\ \text{V m}^{-1}$$

Electric field inside the second dielectric

$$E_2 = \frac{D_2}{\varepsilon_0 K_2} = \frac{5\times10^{-4}}{8.85\times10^{-12}\times2} = 2.825\times10^{7}\ \text{V m}^{-1}$$

(*iii*) Polarization in the first dielectric

$$P_1 = \varepsilon_0(K_1-1)E_1 = 8.85\times10^{-12}(5-1)\times1.13\times10^{7} = 4\times10^{-4}\ \text{C m}^{-2}$$

Polarization in the second dielectric

$$P_2 = \varepsilon_0(K_2-1)E_2 = 8.85\times10^{-12}(2-1)\times2.825\times10^{7} = 2.5\times10^{-4}\ \text{C m}^{2}$$

Alternatively,

$$P_1 = \sigma_{b1} = \left(1-\frac{1}{K_1}\right)\sigma = 4\times10^{-4}\ \text{C m}^{2}$$

$$P_2 = \sigma_{b2} = \left(1 - \frac{1}{K_2}\right)\sigma = 2.5\times10^{-4}\ \text{C m}^{-2}$$

(*iv*) Potential difference between the plates

$$V = E_1 d_1 + E_2 d_2 = 1.13\times10^{7}\times2\times10^{-3} + 2.825\times10^{7}\times3\times10^{-3}$$

$$= 10.735 \times 10^4\ \text{V}$$

(*v*) Capacitance $C = \frac{q}{V} = \frac{20\times10^{6}}{10.735\times10^{4}} = 1.86\times10^{-10}\ \text{F} = 186\,\text{pF}$

***Example* 3:** *A homogeneous and isotropic infinite dielectric sheet of uniform thickness has dielectric constant 5 and is placed in a homogeneous electric field $E_0 = 1 \times 10^3\ V\ m^{-1}$. The sheet is oriented perpendicular to the electric field. Calculate*

(*i*) *The electric field E and displacement D inside the plate*

(*ii*) *The polarization P in the dielectric*

(*iii*) *Surface density of bound charges*

Solution: (*i*) Electric field inside the dielectric

$$E = \frac{E_0}{K} = \frac{1\times10^3}{5} = 200\ \text{V m}^{-1}$$

Electric displacement

$$D = \varepsilon_0 K E = 8.85\times10^{-12}\times5\times200 = 8.85\times10^{-9}\ \text{C m}^{-2}$$

(*ii*) Polarization $P = \varepsilon_0(K-1)E = 8.85\times10^{-12}(5-1)\times200 = 7.08\times10^{-9}\ \text{C m}^{-2}$

(*iii*) Surface charge density $\sigma = \pm P = \pm 7.08\times10^{-9}\ \text{V m}^{-2}$

***Example* 4:** *A point charge q is placed within an isotropic and homogeneous dielectric of infinite extent. Calculate the polarization at a distance r from the point charge.*

Solution: Construct a spherical Gaussian surface of radius r concentric with the point charge q. Let **D** be the electric displacement vector on the surface of the Gaussian surface. By symmetry, **D** radial. Hence

$$\oint_S \mathbf{D}\cdot d\mathbf{S} = q$$

$$D(4\pi r^2) = q$$

$$D = \frac{q}{4\pi r^2}$$

and

$$E = \frac{D}{\varepsilon_0 K} = \frac{q}{4\pi\varepsilon_0 K r^2}$$

Hence $$P = \varepsilon_0(K-1)E = \left(\frac{K-1}{K}\right)\frac{q}{4\pi r^2}$$

***Example* 5:** *A point charge q is located at the centre of a homogeneous and isotropic dielectric sphere with dielectric constant K. Find the polarization P as a function of **r**, the radius vector relative to the centre of sphere. Calculate the bound charges enclosed inside a sphere of radius less than the radius of the dielectric sphere.*

Solution: The electric field at a distance r from the point charge

$$\mathbf{E} = \frac{q}{4\pi\varepsilon_0 K}\frac{\mathbf{r}}{r^3} \quad ...(2.74)$$

Polarization $$\mathbf{P} = \varepsilon_0(K-1)\mathbf{E} = \left(\frac{K-1}{K}\right)\frac{q}{4\pi}\frac{\mathbf{r}}{r^3} \quad ...(2.75)$$

Imagine a sphere of radius R, less than the radius of the dielectric sphere. We have to calculate the magnitude of bound charges inside this sphere.

Volume density of bound charges $\rho_b = -div\ \mathbf{P} = \left(\frac{K-1}{4\pi K}\right)q\left(div\frac{\mathbf{r}}{r^3}\right) = 0$

Surface density of bound charges $\sigma_b = (|\mathbf{P}\cdot\mathbf{n}|)_{r=R} = |P|_{r=R} = \left(\frac{K-1}{4\pi K}\right)\frac{q}{R^2}$

Surface charge on the sphere of radius R $q' = \sigma_b(4\pi R^2) = \left(\frac{K-1}{K}\right)q$

***Example* 6:** *An infinite slab of thickness d is placed in uniform electric field* $\mathbf{E_0}$ *as shown in the fig. The dielectric constant of the slab varies linearly along the thickness from the value* K_1 *at the left boundary to* K_2 *at the right one. Calculate*

(*i*) ***E*** *and div* ***E***

(*ii*) *The volume density of bound charge.*

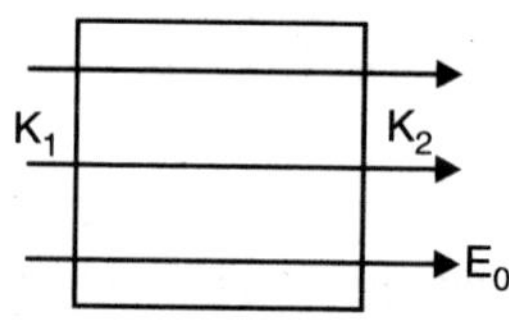

Fig. 2.9

Solution:

(*i*) Let us choose the origin at the left face of the slab and x-axis along the thickness of the slab. The dielectric constant at a distance x is given by

$$K = K_1 + \left(\frac{K_2 - K_1}{d}\right)x$$

Electric field at a distance x is

$$E = \frac{E_0}{K} = \frac{E_0}{K_1 + (K_2 - K_1)\ x/d}$$

Electric field is directed along x-axis.

$$div\mathbf{E} = \frac{\partial E_x}{\partial x} = \frac{\partial}{\partial x}\left[\frac{E_0}{K_1 + (K_2 - K_1)\ x/d}\right]$$

$$= -\frac{E_0}{[K_1 + (K_2 - K_1)\ \ x/d]^2}\left[\frac{K_2 - K_1}{d}\right]$$

(*ii*) Volume density of bound charge $\rho = -div\mathbf{P} = -\varepsilon_0 div(K-1)\mathbf{E}$

$$\rho = -\varepsilon_0 div\left(\frac{K-1}{K}\right)\mathbf{E}_0$$

or
$$\rho = -\varepsilon_0 E_0 \frac{\partial}{\partial x}\left[1 - \frac{1}{K}\right] = -\varepsilon_0 E_0 \frac{1}{K^2}\frac{dK}{dx}$$

or
$$\rho = -\frac{\varepsilon_0 E_0}{[K_1 + (K_2 - K_1)\ \ x/d]^2}\left(\frac{K_2 - K_1}{d}\right)$$

Example 7: *A sphere of radius R carries a polarization* $\mathbf{P} = \frac{C}{r}\hat{\mathbf{r}}$ *where C is a constant and r is the distance from the centre of the sphere. Calculate*

(*i*) *Surface and volume charge densities of bound charges*
(*ii*) *Electric field inside and outside the sphere.*

Solution: (*i*) Surface density of bound charge

$$\sigma_b = \mathbf{P}\cdot\mathbf{n} = \frac{C}{r}\hat{\mathbf{r}}\cdot\mathbf{n} = \frac{C}{r}$$

Volume density of bound charge

$$\rho_b = -\nabla\cdot\mathbf{P} = -\nabla\cdot\frac{C\hat{\mathbf{r}}}{r} = -C\nabla\cdot\frac{\mathbf{r}}{r^2} = -\frac{C}{r^2}$$

(*ii*) Electric field inside the polarized sphere

$$\mathbf{E} = -\frac{\mathbf{P}}{3\varepsilon_0} = -\frac{C}{3\varepsilon_0 r}\hat{\mathbf{r}}$$

For external points, the polarized sphere acts like a dipole of dipole moment $\mathbf{p} = \frac{4}{3}\pi R^3\mathbf{P}$. The electrostatic potential outside ($r > R$) the polarized sphere is given by

$$\varphi = \frac{1}{4\pi\varepsilon_0}\frac{\mathbf{P}\cdot\mathbf{r}}{r^3} = \frac{1}{4\pi\varepsilon_0}\left(\frac{4}{3.}\pi R^3\right)\frac{\mathbf{P}\cdot\mathbf{r}}{r^3} = \frac{C}{3\varepsilon_0}\frac{R^3}{r^3}$$

Electric field outside the sphere ($r > R$)

$$E = -\frac{\partial\varphi}{\partial r} = \frac{CR^3}{\varepsilon_0 r^4}$$

Example 8: *A uniform isotropic sphere of radius R = 5 cm is made of a material with dielectric constant K = 5. Electric field E = 500 V m*$^{-1}$ *exists inside the sphere. Find the maximum surface density of bound charges and the total bound charges of one sign.*

Solution: Polarization $P = \varepsilon_0(K-1)E$

$$P = 8.85\times10^{-12}\times(5-1)\times500 = 1.77\times10^{-8}\ \text{C m}^{-2}$$

Surface density of bound charge $\sigma_b = |\mathbf{P}\cdot\mathbf{n}| = P\cos\theta$

Maximum value of σ is $\sigma_{max} = P = 1.77\times10^{-8}\ \text{C m}^{-2}$

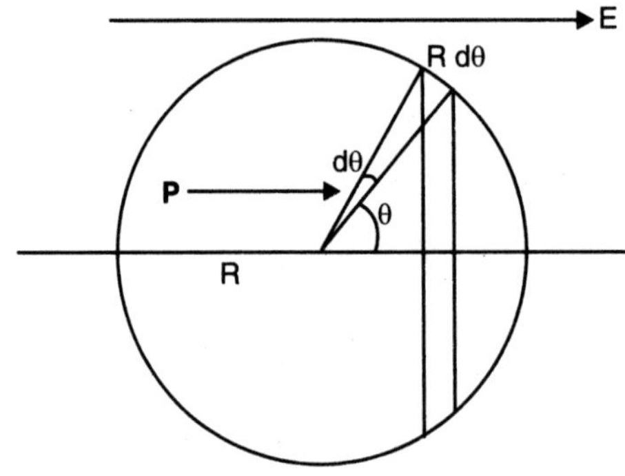

Fig. 2.10.

Total surface charge of one sign

$$q = \int \sigma dS = \int_0^{\pi/2} P\cos\theta\cdot 2\pi R\sin\theta\cdot R d\theta = \pi R^2 P$$

$$= 3.14\times5^2\times1.77\times10^{-8} = 1.39\times10^{-6}\ \text{C}$$

***Example* 9:** *A long dielectric cylinder is polarized so that* $\mathbf{P} = a\mathbf{r}$ *where a is constant and r is distance from the axis. Find the volume density of polarization charges as a function of r.*

Solution:

Consider a cylindrical Gaussian surface of radius r and length l with axis same as the axis of given cylinder. Let ρ_b be the volume density of bound charges. Using Gauss's theorem we have

$$\oint_S \mathbf{P}\cdot d\mathbf{S} = -\int \rho_b d\tau$$

$$\oint_S a\mathbf{r}\cdot d\mathbf{S} = -\rho_b(\pi r^2 l)$$

$$ar\oint_S dS = -\pi r^2 l\rho_b$$

$$ar(2\pi rl) = -\pi r^2 l\rho_b$$

$$\rho_b = -2a \quad (\textit{independent of } r)$$

Aliter: Taking x-axis along the axis of polarized cylinder, we can write vector **r** as

$$\mathbf{r} = y\mathbf{j} + z\mathbf{k}$$

Volume density of bound charges

$$\rho_b = -\nabla\cdot\mathbf{P} = -a\nabla\cdot\mathbf{r} = -a\left(\frac{\partial y}{\partial y}+\frac{\partial z}{\partial z}\right) = -2a$$

***Example* 10:** *An isolated metal sphere of radius a has free charge q on its surface. The sphere is covered with a dielectric layer of inner radius a and outer radius b. Calculate*

(*i*) *The electric displacement D and electric field E in the dielectric layer*

(*ii*) *The potential at the centre of the metallic sphere*

(*iii*) *The polarization surface charge density on the inner and outer surfaces of the dielectric layer*

(*iv*) *Volume density of polarization charges inside the dielectric.*

Solution: (*i*) The electric field E inside the metal sphere is zero and so are the electric displacement D and polarization P. By symmetry, the electric displacement is radial.

We construct a Gaussian surface of radius r such that $a < r < b$, and concentric with the metal sphere. Applying Gauss's theorem we have

$$\oint_S \mathbf{D}\cdot d\mathbf{S} = q_{free}$$

$$D(4\pi r^2) = q$$

$$\mathbf{D} = \frac{q}{4\pi r^2}\hat{\mathbf{r}} \qquad a<r<b \qquad \text{...(2.76)}$$

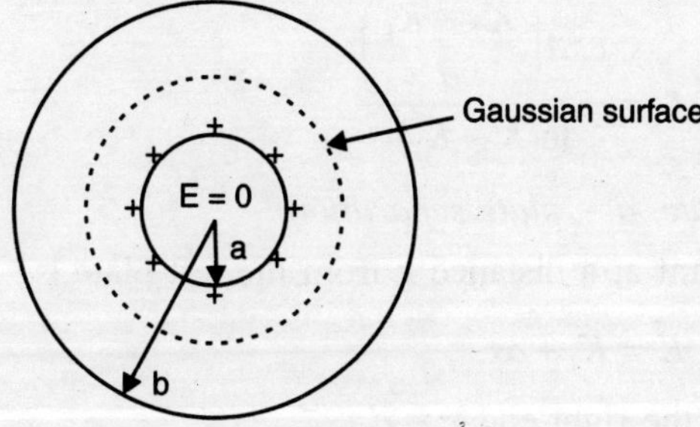

Fig. 2.11

Electric field in the dielectric layer

$$\mathbf{E} = \frac{\mathbf{D}}{\varepsilon_0 K} = \frac{q}{4\pi\varepsilon_0 K r^2}\hat{\mathbf{r}} \qquad a<r<b \qquad \text{...(2.77)}$$

Outside the dielectric layer

$$\mathbf{E}_0 = \frac{q}{4\pi\varepsilon_0 r^2}\hat{\mathbf{r}} \qquad r>b \qquad \text{...(2.78)}$$

(*ii*) Potential at the centre ($r = 0$)

$$V = -\int_\infty^r \mathbf{E}\cdot d\mathbf{r} = -\left[\int_\infty^b \frac{q\,dr}{4\pi\varepsilon_0 r^2} + \int_b^a \frac{q\,dr}{4\pi\varepsilon_0 K r^2} + \int_a^0 0\,dr\right]$$

$$= \frac{q}{4\pi\varepsilon_0}\left[\frac{1}{b} + \frac{1}{K}\left(\frac{1}{a} - \frac{1}{b}\right)\right] \qquad ...(2.79)$$

(*iii*) Polarization inside the dielectric

$$\mathbf{P} = \varepsilon_0(K-1)\mathbf{E} = \frac{q(K-1)}{4\pi K}\frac{\mathbf{r}}{r^3} \qquad ...(2.80)$$

Surface density of bound charges at the inner surface of the dielectric

$$\sigma_b = -\mathbf{P}\cdot\mathbf{n} = -P_{r=a} = -\frac{q(K-1)}{4\pi K a^2} \qquad ...(2.81)$$

At the outer surface

$$\sigma_b = P_{r=b} = \frac{q(K-1)}{4\pi K b^2} \qquad ...(2.82)$$

(*iv*) Volume density of bound charges

$$\rho_b = -\nabla\cdot\mathbf{P} = -\frac{q(K-1)}{4\pi K}\nabla\cdot\frac{\mathbf{r}}{r^3} = 0 \qquad ...(2.83)$$

***Example* 11:** *The space between the plates of a parallel plate capacitor is occupied by a dielectric whose dielectric constant varies linearly from K_1 at the left plate to K_2 at the right plate. Show that the capacitance is given by*

$$C = \frac{\varepsilon_0 A\left(\dfrac{K_2 - K_1}{d}\right)}{\ln(K_2/K_1)}$$

Where A = area of the plate, d = plate separation.

Solution: The dielectric constant at a distance x from the left plate is

$$K = K_1 + ax,$$

Where a is a constant. At the right end $x = d$

$$K_2 = K_1 + ad$$

Therefore, $$a = \frac{K_2 - K_1}{d}$$

And $$K = K_1 + \frac{K_2 - K_1}{d}x \qquad ...(1)$$

Electric field at a distance x

$$E = \frac{E_0}{K} = \frac{\sigma}{\varepsilon_0 K} = \frac{q}{\varepsilon_0 K A} \qquad ...(2)$$

Where q is the charge on the capacitor plate.

Potential difference between the plates is

$$V = -\int_d^0 E dx = -\int_d^0 \frac{q}{\varepsilon_0 K A} dx = -\frac{q}{\varepsilon_0 A}\int_d^0 \frac{dx}{K_1 + ax}$$

$$= -\frac{q}{\varepsilon_0 A a}\left[\ln(K_1 + ax)\right]_d^0 = \frac{q}{\varepsilon_0 K a}\ln\frac{K_1 + ad}{K_1}$$

$$= \frac{q}{\varepsilon_0 A}\left(\frac{d}{K_2 - K_1}\right)\ln\frac{K_2}{K_1}$$

Capacitance of the capacitor

$$C = \frac{q}{V} = \frac{\varepsilon_0 A\left(\dfrac{K_2 - K_1}{d}\right)}{\ln(K_2/K_1)}$$

***Example* 12:** *The radii of a spherical capacitor are* $r_1 = 5$ *cm and* $r_2 = 6$ *cm. The space between the plates is filled with a dielectric whose dielectric constant varies with distance r from the centre of the capacitor according to the law* $K = K_0\left(\frac{r_1}{r}\right)$ *where* $K_0 = 2$. *Calculate the capacitance of the capacitor.*

Solution: The electric field at a distance r from the centre of the capacitor

$$E = \frac{E_0}{K} = \frac{q}{4\pi\varepsilon_0 K r^2}, \qquad r_1 < r < r_2$$

Potential difference between the plates

$$V = -\int_{r_1}^{r_2} E dr = -\frac{q}{4\pi\varepsilon_0 K_0 r_1}\int_{r_1}^{r_2}\frac{dr}{r} = \frac{q}{4\pi\varepsilon_0 K_0 r_1}\ln\frac{r_2}{r_1}$$

Capacitance of the capacitor

$$C = \frac{q}{V} = \frac{4\pi\varepsilon_0 K_0 r_1}{\ln(r_2/r_1)} = \frac{2\times 5}{9\times 10^9 \ln(6/5)} = 6.1\times 10^{-9}\,\text{F}$$

***Example* 13:** *Initially, the space between the plates of a parallel plate capacitor is filled with air and the electric field and electric displacement in the gap are* **E** *and* **D**. *The half of the gap is filled with a uniform dielectric with dielectric constant K. Find the magnitudes of* **E** *and* **D** *in both parts of the capacitor if (i) the charge on the plates remains constant (ii) the voltage across the plates remains constant.*

***Solution:* (*i*) Constant *q* case:**

Electric displacement D is related to its source free charges. Since magnitude of free charges is constant, D has the same value in both the regions. Let E_1 and E_2 be the electric fields in the two regions. Then

$$D_1 = D_2 = D = \varepsilon_0 E,$$

where $D_1 = \varepsilon_0 E_1 = \varepsilon_0 E, \quad D_2 = \varepsilon_0 K E_2 = \varepsilon_0 E$

From above equations

$$E_1 = E$$

$$E_2 = \frac{E}{K}$$

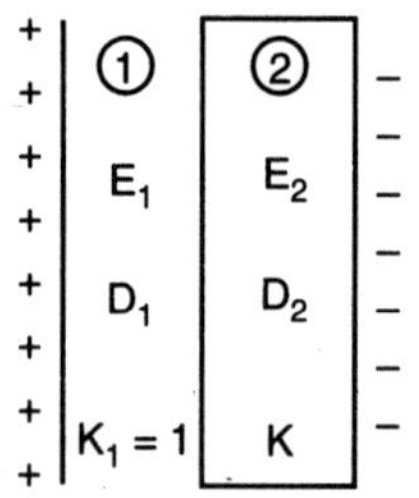

Fig. 2.12

(*ii*) Constant V case:

Initial value of electric field

$$E = \frac{V}{d}$$

In constant V case the charge on the capacitor increases when the dielectric sheet is inserted into the capacitor. The magnitude of charge on the plates with half gap filled with dielectric is

$$q = CV = \left(\frac{\varepsilon_0 A}{d - \frac{d}{2} + \frac{d}{2K}} \right) V = \frac{2\varepsilon_0 A}{\left(1 + \frac{1}{K}\right)} \left(\frac{V}{d} \right) = \left(\frac{2\varepsilon_0 K A}{K+1} \right) E$$

Charge density on plates

$$\sigma = \frac{q}{A} = \left(\frac{2\varepsilon_0 K}{K+1} \right) E$$

Electric displacement is related to free charges only, hence D has the same value in both the regions. Therefore,

$$D_1 = D_2 = \sigma = \left(\frac{2\varepsilon_0 K}{K+1} \right) E$$

and

$$E_1 = \frac{D_1}{\varepsilon_0} = \left(\frac{2K}{K+1} \right) E,$$

$$E_2 = \frac{D_2}{\varepsilon_0 K} = \left(\frac{2}{K+1} \right) E$$

***Example* 14:** *A parallel plate capacitor without any medium between its plates is fed to a source of* 100 *V. The plate separation between the plates is 1 mm. If capacitor is filled with a thin sheet of mica with dielectric constant 5, evaluate the macroscopic parameters of the dielectric.*

***Solution*:** Electric field between the plates without dielectric

$$E_0 = \frac{V}{d} = \frac{100}{1\times10^{-3}} = 1\times10^5 \text{ V m}^{-1}$$

Magnitude of electric displacement vector

$$D = \varepsilon_0 E = 8.85\times10^{-12}\times10^5 = 8.85\times10^{-7} \text{ C m}^{-2}$$

Electric field between the plates with dielectric

$$E = \frac{E_0}{K} = \frac{1\times10^5}{5} = 2\times10^4 \text{ V m}^{-1}$$

Magnitude of polarization vector

$$P = \varepsilon_0(K-1)E = 8.85\times10^{-12}(5-1)\times2\times10^4 = 7.08\times10^{-7}\text{C m}^{-2}$$

Electric permittivity of dielectric

$$\varepsilon = \varepsilon_0 K = 8.85\times10^{-12}\times5 = 4.43\times10^{-11}\text{F m}^{-1}$$

Electric susceptibility of dielectric material

$$\chi = \frac{P}{\varepsilon_0 E} = K-1 = 5-1 = 4$$

***Example* 15:** *A slab of dielectric material of dielectric constant* 10 *and thickness* 5 *mm is placed between the plates of a parallel plate capacitor. If a potential difference of* 1000 *V is applied to the capacitor, evaluate the internal field (Lorentz field).*

***Solution*:** Electric field between the plates of capacitor without dielectric

$$E_0 = \frac{V}{d} = \frac{1000}{5\times10^{-3}} = 2\times10^5 \text{ V m}^{-1}$$

Electric field in dielectric

$$E = \frac{E_0}{K} = \frac{2\times10^5}{10} = 2\times10^4 \text{ V m}^{-1}$$

Internal electric field (local or Lorentz field)

$$E_i = \frac{K+2}{3}E = \left(\frac{10+2}{3}\right)\times2\times10^4 = 8\times10^4 \text{ V m}^{-1}$$

***Example* 16:** *A hydrogen atom with diameter* 1 Å *is subjected to an electric field of* 5 × 10^5 *V m*^-1. *Evaluate (i) change in the relative positions of the centres of the nucleus and electron cloud (ii) electronic polarizability (iii) induced dipole moment in the atom.*

Solution: (*i*) The separation of positive and negative charge

$$x = \frac{4\pi\varepsilon_0 a^3}{Ze} E_i, \quad Z = 1$$

$$= \frac{(5\times 10^{-11})^3}{9\times 10^9 \times 1.6\times 10^{-19}} \times 5\times 10^5 = 4.3\times 10^{-17} \text{ m}$$

(*ii*) Electronic polarizability

$$\alpha_e = 4\pi\varepsilon_0 a^3 = \frac{(5\times 10^{-11})^3}{9\times 10^9} = 1.4\times 10^{-41} \text{ F·m}^2$$

(*iii*) Induced dipole moment

$$p = \alpha_e E_i = 1.4\times 10^{-41} \times 5\times 10^5 = 7.0\times 10^{-36} \text{C·m}$$

***Example* 17:** *The solid argon contains* 5 × 10^27 *atoms/m*^3. *If the polarizability of argon atom is* 1.7 × 10^-40 *F·m*^2, *evaluate the dielectric constant of argon.*

Solution: According to Clausius-Mosotti equation

$$\frac{K-1}{K+2} = \frac{n\alpha_e}{3\varepsilon_0}$$

$$\frac{K-1}{K+2} = \frac{5\times 10^{27} \times 1.7\times 10^{-40}}{3\times 8.85\times 10^{-12}} = 3.2\times 10^{-2}$$

$$\therefore \quad K = 1.1$$

QUESTIONS AND PROBLEMS

1. Explain the terms polarization vector, displacement vector, dielectric constant, dielectric permittivity, electrical susceptibility. Obtain relation between these parameters for an isotropic dielectric.
2. What do you mean by polarization of a dielectric material? Explain how the electric field inside the dielectric is reduced when it is polarized under the action of external electric field.
3. Show that the electric effect due to polarized dielectric material are the same as those produced by surface charge density **P·n** together with a volume charge density –∇·**P**. Symbols have their usual meaning.

4. Explain the meaning of polar and non polar units. Which of the following are polar units: H_2, HCl, N_2, Cl_2, H_2O, CO_2, NH_3 molecules?

5. Explain the terms electric susceptibility, dielectric constant and permittivity of a dielectric medium.

(*i*) Show that the surface density of polarization charges in a uniformly polarized dielectric is $\sigma_b = \mathbf{P \cdot n}$.

(*ii*) Show that the volume density of polarization charges in case of non-uniform polarization is $\rho_b = -\nabla \cdot \mathbf{P}$.

6. Obtain Gauss's theorem in a dielectric material. Show that $\nabla . \mathbf{D} = \rho_{free.}$

7. The plates of a parallel plate capacitor carry free charges + *q* and – *q*. The space between the plates is filled with a dielectric slab with *d. e. c. K*. Show that the magnitude of bound charges is given by

$$q_b = \left(1 - \frac{1}{k}\right) q$$

8. Show that the energy density in a dielectric medium is $u = \frac{1}{2}\varepsilon_0 K E^2$.

9. What do you mean by electronic, ionic and orientational polarizability. Obtain Debye expression for orientational polarizability.

10. What is Lorentz internal electric field (local electric field)? Using this concept establish Clausius-Mosotti equation for dielectrics.

11. A piece of dielectric material carries polarization as shown in the figure. Calculate the surface charge densities at its surfaces S_1, S_2 and S_3.

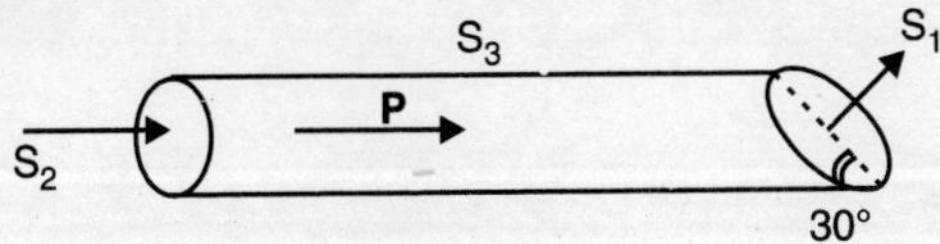

Fig. 2.13.

12. A dielectric sphere has uniform polarization **P** in z-direction. Find the total polarization charges of one kind.

Hint: $\sigma_b = P\cos\theta, \quad q = \int \sigma dS = \int_0^{\pi/2} P\cos\theta(2\pi a \sin\theta \cdot a d\theta)$

13. At a point inside an isotropic dielectric with *d. e. c. K*, the displacement vector is **D.** Show that at this point $\mathbf{P} = \left(\frac{K-1}{K}\right)\mathbf{D}$.

14. In a dielectric medium with polarization $\mathbf{P} = C\frac{\hat{\mathbf{r}}}{r^3}$. Show that the volume density of bound charges is zero.

15. Extraneous (free) charges are uniformly distributed with space density $\rho(>0)$ over a sphere of radius R made of uniform isotropic dielectric with *d. e. c.* K. Show that

$$E = \frac{\rho r}{3\varepsilon_0 K}, \quad r < R$$

$$= \frac{\rho R^3}{3\varepsilon_0 r^2}, \quad r > R$$

$$\rho_b = -\left(\frac{K-1}{K}\right)\rho \quad r < R$$

$$\rho_b = \rho R\left(\frac{K-1}{3K}\right) \quad r > R$$

OOO

3 CHAPTER

Steady Current and Magnetostatics

3.1. INTRODUCTION

Experiments show that the electric current or ordered motion of charge carriers in a conducting medium produces magnetic field. A magnetized material such as a magnet also produces magnetic field. The magnetic field produced by an electric current or that produced by magnetized material are identical in all respect. In fact the source of magnetism in magnetized material has its origin in microscopic currents which arise from the orbital and spin motion of electrons. Thus the ultimate source of magnetic field is the electric current. The microscopic current differs from the conventional current in one respect: the former cannot be measured by current measuring devices such as ammeter. In this chapter we shall study the static properties of magnetic field. Before doing so we shall give a brief description of steady current, a current that does not depend on time.

3.2. CURRENT AND CURRENT DENSITY

The current in a conduction medium is defined as the quantity of electric charge passing per unit time through a point inside the conducting medium.

$$I = \frac{dq}{dt} \qquad \text{...(3.1)}$$

It is measured in ampere. The direction of current is taken as the direction of motion of positive charge or opposite to direction of motion of negative charge (electron).

The current density **J** at a point in the conducting medium is defined as a vector whose magnitude equals the current per unit area held normal to the direction of flow of charge and direction is the same as the flow of positive charge. If dI denotes the current flowing through an infinitesimal area $dS_\perp$ then the magnitude of current density is

$$J = \frac{dI}{dS_\perp} \quad \text{or} \quad dI = J\,dS_\perp = \mathbf{J}\cdot\mathbf{n}\,dS_\perp \qquad \text{...(3.2)}$$

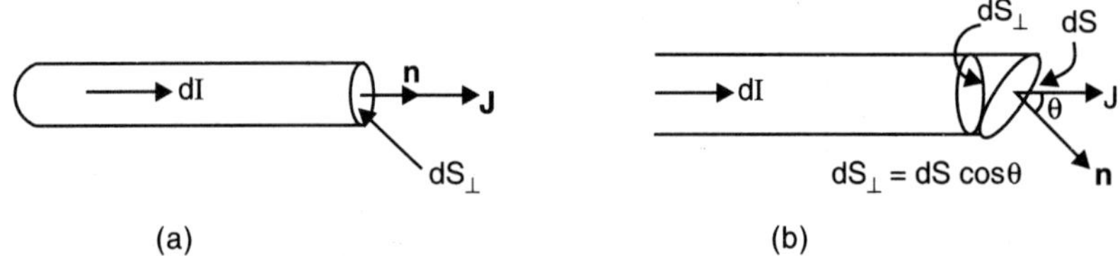

Fig. 3.1. Relation between current and current density.

Here **n** is unit vector normal to the surface area $dS_{\perp}$

3.3. ELECTRICAL CONDUCTIVITY

An electrical conductor is a material in which large current can be set up by applying even a small potential difference. *In steady state and at a constant temperature, the current I through a conductor is proportional to the voltage V applied across its end.* This statement is known as Ohm's law and is written as

$$I \propto V \quad \text{or} \quad I = GV \qquad ...(3.3)$$

Where G is a constant and is called conductance of the conductor. The reciprocal of conductance G is called resistance R of the conductor. Resistance is measured in ohm denoted by Ω.Thus $R = G^{-1}$. If a conductor is in the shape of a wire of length l and cross-section A then the current density in it is given by

$$J = \frac{I}{A} = \frac{G}{A}V = \frac{Gl}{A}.\frac{V}{l} = \sigma E \qquad ...(3.4)$$

Where σ is conductivity of the material and E is strength of electric field. σ is an important parameter in electric charge conduction and is measured in $(\Omega{\cdot}\text{m})^{-1}$. The reciprocal of conductivity σ is called resistivity $\rho(=1/\sigma)$. The electrical conductivity of some of the materials is given in the Table 3.1.

Table 3.1: Conductivities of some materials at room temperature

Material	Conductivity $(\Omega.\text{m})^{-1}$	Material	Conductivity $(\Omega{\cdot}\text{m})^{-1}$
Silver	6.2×10^7	Water	2×10^{-4}
Copper	5.8×10^7	Wood	10^{-9}
Pure Iron	1.0×10^7	Glass	10^{-11}
Mercury	10^6	Polyethylene	10^{-15}
Silicon	10^{-2}	Fused quartz	10^{-17}

Let the cross-sectional area dS of the conductor is inclined to the current density vector **J** as shown in the Fig. 3.1(b). In this case $dS_{\perp} = dS\cos\theta$ where θ is angle which the unit vector **n** normal to dS makes with the current density vector **J**. By definition

$$J = \frac{dI}{dS} = \frac{dI}{dS\cos\theta} \quad ...(3.5)$$

$\therefore$ $$dI = JdS\cos\theta$$

or $$dI = \mathbf{J}\cdot\mathbf{n}\,dS \quad ...(3.6)$$

The current through an extended surface S is given by

$$I = \int \mathbf{J}\cdot\mathbf{n}\,dS \quad ...(3.7)$$

The current density defined above is referred to as the *volume current density.*

If the current I is confined only to the surface of a conductor, we define another current density referred to as *surface current density*. Imagine a ribbon like surface running parallel to the current I as shown in Fig. 3.2. Let dI be the current flowing through length $dl_{\perp}$ of ribbon perpendicular to I. The surface current density **K** is defined as

$$\mathbf{K} = \frac{dI}{dl_{\perp}}\mathbf{n} \quad ...(3.8)$$

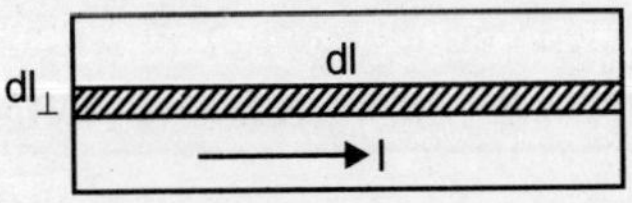

dI

$dl_{\perp}$

I

Fig. 3.2. Definition of surface current density K.

Where **n** is unit vector in the direction of current (or perpendicular to $dl_{\perp}$). Obviously.

$$dI = Kdl_{\perp} = \mathbf{K}\cdot\mathbf{n}\,dl$$

The current over an extended surface is

$$I = \int \mathbf{K}\cdot\mathbf{n}\,dl \quad ...(3.9)$$

The volume and surface current densities can be expressed in terms of drift velocity **v** as

$$\mathbf{K} = \sigma\mathbf{v} \quad ...(3.10a)$$

$$\mathbf{J} = nq\mathbf{v} = \rho\mathbf{v} \quad ...(3.10b)$$

Where n is number of charge carriers per unit volume. σ the surface density of charge. ρ the volume density of charge and q the charge on a charge carrier.

3.4. EQUATION OF CONTINUITY

The equation of continuity is the statement of the law of conservation of charge in mathematical form. Suppose we have a closed surface S which encloses a body of charge specified by volume density ρ. Let charges be made mobile. The moving charges through the surface constitute a current which will be given by the expression,

$$I = \oint \mathbf{J}\cdot d\mathbf{S}$$

The law of conservation of charge demands that the charges must decrease at the same rate inside the volume V bounded by the surface. Thus

$$\oint \mathbf{J}\cdot d\mathbf{S} = -\frac{dQ_{in}}{dt} = -\frac{d}{dt}\int_V \rho d\tau \qquad ...(3.11)$$

where ρ is the volume charge density and $d\tau$ is elementary volume. Equation 3.11 is referred to as the integral form of equation of continuity. Changing the surface integral of eqn. 3.11 into volume integral we get

$$\int_V \nabla\cdot\mathbf{J}d\tau = -\int_V \frac{d\rho}{dt}d\tau \qquad ...(3.12)$$

From eqn. 3.12, we get

$$\nabla\cdot\mathbf{J} + \frac{d\rho}{dt} = 0 \qquad ...(3.13)$$

This is the differential form of the equation of continuity. When the charge density is time dependent the current density J is a non steady current. If the charge density is independent of time, then we get the steady current. In this case we have

$$\nabla\cdot\mathbf{J} = 0 \qquad ...(3.14)$$

3.5. MAGNETIC INDUCTION OF MAGNETIC INDUCTION FIELD

The source of magnetic field **B** are some kinds of currents. Without going into the details of the source currents, we assume that **B** is present in a certain region. In this region, we fire a test charge q with velocity $\boldsymbol{v}$. Keeping the magnitude of the velocity constant, the direction of $\boldsymbol{v}$ is varied. It is observed that, in general, the test charge is deflected from its original direction of motion. There is one direction of $\boldsymbol{v}$ (and also the opposite one) for which the test charge *'feels'* no force when moving in this direction. By convention, this direction is taken as the direction of the magnetic field **B**. It is also observed that the force acting on the test charge is proportional to the component of $\boldsymbol{v}$ perpendicular to **B**. The force is maximum when the test charge is moving perpendicular to the direction of **B**. (This can be verified by measuring the magnitude of the deviation of the test charge). Let F be the force on the test charge when it is moving with velocity $\boldsymbol{v}$ at an angle θ with **B**. The magnitude of magnetic field B is defined by the ratio,

$$B = \frac{F}{qv\sin\theta} \qquad ...(3.15)$$

or by equation

$$F = qvB\sin\theta \qquad ...(3.16)$$

The sense of **B** is so chosen that if a right-handed screw is rotated from $\boldsymbol{v}$ to **B**, its head advances in the direction of the force **F**. With this convention, eqn. (3.16) can be written as

$$\mathbf{F} = q(\mathbf{v}\times\mathbf{B}) \qquad ...(3.17)$$

Equation 3.17 gives the force on a moving charge in magnetic field. The force is velocity dependent.

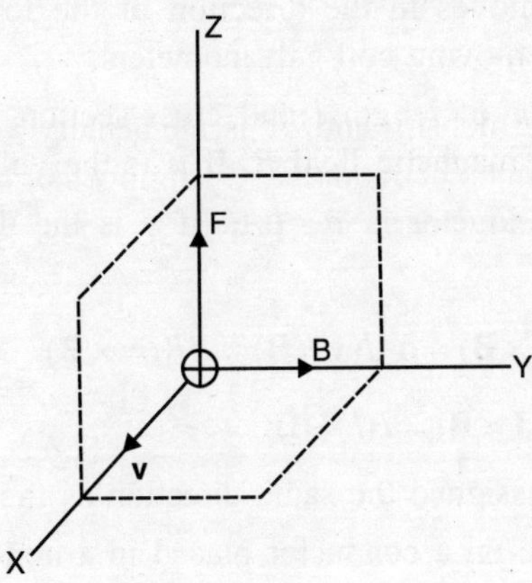

Fig. 3.3

If an electric field **E** is also present, the total force acting on the test charge is,

$$\mathbf{F} = q\mathbf{E} + q(\mathbf{v} \times \mathbf{B}) \qquad ...(3.18)$$

The force **F** given by eqn. 3.18 is called the **Lorentz force**. Equation 3.18 is an axiom of the theory of electrodynamics. Its validity can be tested by experiments alone. Indeed, it has been verified in a large number of experiments. In S.I. units, **B** is expressed in Newton/Ampere-metre or Weber/meter^2 or Tesla.

3.6. WORK DONE BY MAGNETIC FIELD B

The magnetic force acting on a moving charge in magnetic field **B** is always perpendicular to the direction of motion and hence it does no work on the charged particle. The magnetic field merely changes the direction of motion and not its magnitude. Mathematically, the work done by the magnetic force is given by

$$W = \mathbf{F} \cdot d\mathbf{l} = q(\mathbf{v} \times \mathbf{B}) \cdot \mathbf{v}dt = 0 \qquad ...(3.19)$$

[*by property of scalar triple product*]

3.7. FORCE ON A CURRENT CARRYING CONDUCTOR

When a current carrying conductor is placed in a magnetic field, the moving charges within the conductor *'feel'* magnetic forces. Since the moving charges can not leave the conductor, the magnetic forces are transmitted to the conductor as a whole.

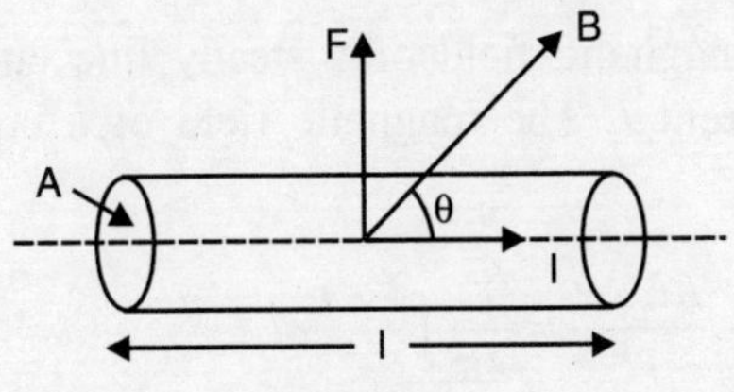

Fig. 3.4

If the conductor is free, it moves in the direction of the force. This phenomenon has been used in the design of motors and moving coil galvanometers.

Consider a straight conductor of length l and cross-section A. Let it carry a current **I**. The conductor is placed in a uniform magnetic field B. If ρ is the volume density of free charges, the total amount of charge in the conductor is $q = \rho Al$. If **v** is the drift-velocity of the free charges, the force on the conductor is

$$\mathbf{F} = q(\mathbf{v} \times \mathbf{B}) = \rho Al(\mathbf{v} \times \mathbf{B}) = Al(\rho\mathbf{v} \times \mathbf{B}) \qquad ...(3.20)$$

or
$$\mathrm{F} = Al(\mathbf{J} \times \mathbf{B}) = I(l \times \mathbf{B}) \qquad ...(3.21)$$

where the length vector **l** is assigned the same direction as the current.

In order to calculate the force on a conductor placed in a non-uniform magnetic field, we first calculate the force $d\mathbf{F}$ on a current element $Id\mathbf{l}$ and then integrate it over the entire length of the conductor.

$$d\mathbf{F} = I(d\mathbf{l} \times \mathbf{B})$$

$$\mathbf{F} = \int I(d\mathbf{l} \times \mathbf{B}) = \int (\mathbf{I} \times \mathbf{B})dl \qquad ...(3.22)$$

The force on surface current distribution is,

$$\mathbf{F} = \int \sigma ds(\mathbf{v} \times \mathbf{B}) = \int (\mathbf{K} \times \mathbf{B})ds \qquad ...(3.23)$$

And the force on volume current distribution is

$$\mathbf{F} = \int \sigma d\tau(\mathbf{v} \times \mathbf{B}) = \int (\mathbf{J} \times \mathbf{B})d\tau \qquad ...(3.24)$$

Equations (3.22), (3.23) and (3.24) give a transition rule.

$$\mathbf{I}dl \longleftrightarrow \mathbf{K}ds \longleftrightarrow \mathbf{J}d\tau \qquad ...(3.25)$$

3.8. AMPERE'S LAW

Ampere's law is a relationship between magnetic field and its source strength, namely the current. Analogous to Gauss's law, Ampere's law is one of the most important laws of electromagnetism. There are many equivalent laws which connect the magnetic field to its source strength. We shall call them all Ampere's law, since it was Ampere who gave the law the most thorough treatment at the time of its discovery. Ampere's law has been experimentally verified by innumerable measurements of the fields produced by many types of current distributions.

Biot-savart Law (First Form of Ampere Law)

Biot and Savart law gives the magnetic field of a steady line current element. Consider a linear conductor carrying a steady current I. The magnetic field of a current element dl at a distance r from it is,

$$d\mathbf{B} = \frac{\mu_0}{4\pi} \cdot \frac{Id\mathbf{l} \times \mathbf{r}}{r^3} = \frac{\mu_0}{4\pi} \cdot \int \frac{\mathbf{I} \times \mathbf{r}}{r^3} dl \qquad ...(3.26)$$

where the proportionality constant has been taken in the form $\frac{\mu_0}{4\pi}$ for the sake of convenience and has value 10^{-7} N/A^2. Other symbols are defined in the Fig. 3.5.

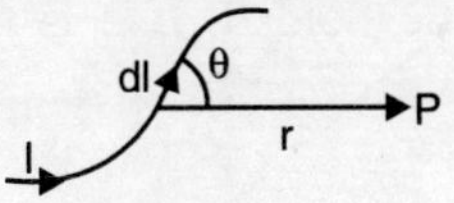

Fig. 3.5

Using the transition rule,

$$\mathbf{I}dl \longleftrightarrow \mathbf{K}ds \longleftrightarrow \mathbf{J}d\tau$$

we can write the magnetic field of surface and volume current elements as follows :

$$d\mathbf{B} = \frac{\mu_0}{4\pi} \cdot \frac{\mathbf{K} \times \mathbf{r}}{r^3} ds \qquad \text{...(3.27)}$$

$$d\mathbf{B} = \frac{\mu_0}{4\pi} \cdot \frac{\mathbf{J} \times \mathbf{r}}{r^3} d\tau \qquad \text{...(3.28)}$$

The magnetic fields of extended current distributions are given by

$$\mathbf{B} = \frac{\mu_0}{4\pi} \int \frac{\mathbf{I} \times \mathbf{r}}{r^3} dl \qquad \text{(Linear)} \qquad \text{...(3.29)}$$

$$\mathbf{B} = \frac{\mu_0}{4\pi} \int \frac{\mathbf{K} \times \mathbf{r}}{r^3} ds \qquad \text{(Surface)} \qquad \text{...(3.30)}$$

$$\mathbf{B} = \frac{\mu_0}{4\pi} \int \frac{\mathbf{J} \times \mathbf{r}}{r^3} d\tau \qquad \text{(Volume)} \qquad \text{...(3.31)}$$

The integrations in eqns. (3.29), (3.30) and (3.31) are to be performed over the regions occupied by the current.

3.9. CALCULATION OF MAGNETIC FIELDS USING BIOT AND SAVART LAW

3.9.1 Magnetic Field of a Straight Infinite Linear Conductor

Let us calculate the magnetic field at a distance a from a long straight conductor carrying a current I. Let O be the foot of perpendicular drawn from the point of observation P to the conductor. Consider a current element dl at a distance l from point O. Let $\mathbf{r}$ be the position vector of the point of observation relative to the current element. The angle between $\mathbf{r}$ and $\mathbf{dl}$ is θ. The magnetic field at the field point due to this current element is

$$d\mathbf{B} = \frac{\mu_0 I}{4\pi} \frac{d\mathbf{l} \times \mathbf{r}}{r^3}$$

Let the angular position of current element relative line PO be φ and those of the initial and end points of the conductor be φ_1 and φ_2 respectively. Refer to Fig. 3.6(a) in which $l = a \tan \varphi$, $r = a \sec \varphi$, $\theta = \frac{\pi}{2} + \varphi$.

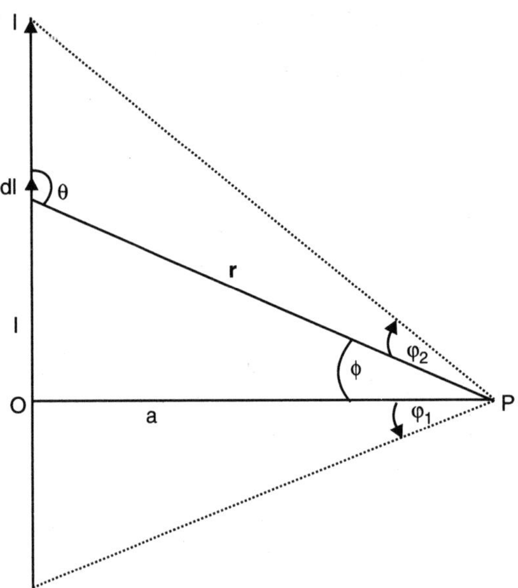

Fig. 3.6(a) Magnetic field of a straight conductor.

The magnitude of this field is

$$dB = \frac{\mu_0 I}{4\pi} \cdot \frac{r \sin\theta \, dl}{r^3}$$

The direction of this field is normal to the plane of drawing and points into the page. The magnetic field of the whole conductor is

$$B = \int dB = \frac{\mu_0 I}{4\pi} \int \frac{\sin\theta}{r^2} dl = \frac{\mu_0 I}{4\pi} \int_{\varphi_1}^{\varphi_2} \frac{\sin\left(\frac{\pi}{2} + \varphi\right)}{(a \sec\varphi)^2} a \sec^2 \varphi \, d\varphi$$

$$= \frac{\mu_0 I}{4\pi a} \int_{\varphi_1}^{\varphi_2} \cos\varphi \, d\varphi$$

$$B = \frac{\mu_0 I}{4\pi a} (\sin\varphi_2 - \sin\varphi_1)$$

We use the following convention for angles φ_1 and φ_2. These angles are measured from the reference line *PO*. The angle φ measured from *PO* in clockwise direction is taken positive and that measured in counter-clockwise is taken negative.

The magnetic field of an infinite conductor $(\varphi_1 \to -\pi/2, \ \varphi_2 \to +\pi/2)$ is

$$B = \frac{\mu_0 I}{2\pi a}$$

The magnetic field of a very long current carrying thin conductor is inversely proportional to its distance of field point. The lines of B encircle the wire, the sense being given by right hand rule: *grab the wire with your right hand with thumb pointing in the direction of the current, the fingers give the direction of the magnetic field.*

SPECIAL CASES

(*i*) *Magnetic field in front one end of infinite straight wire*

In this case $\varphi_1 = 0,\ \varphi_2 = \pi/2$.

$$B = \frac{\mu_0 I}{4\pi a}$$

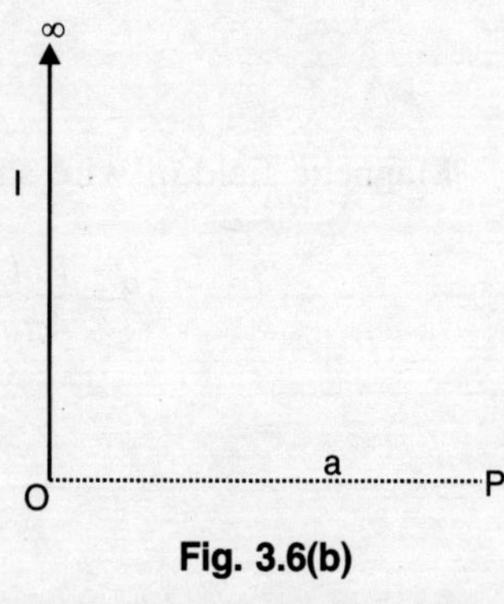

Fig. 3.6(b)

(*ii*) *Magnetic field in front of one end of finite straight wire*

In this case $\varphi_1 = 0,\ \varphi_2 = \varphi$.

$$B = \frac{\mu_0 I}{4\pi a}(\sin\phi) = \frac{\mu_0 I}{4\pi a}.\frac{L}{\sqrt{L^2 + a^2}}$$

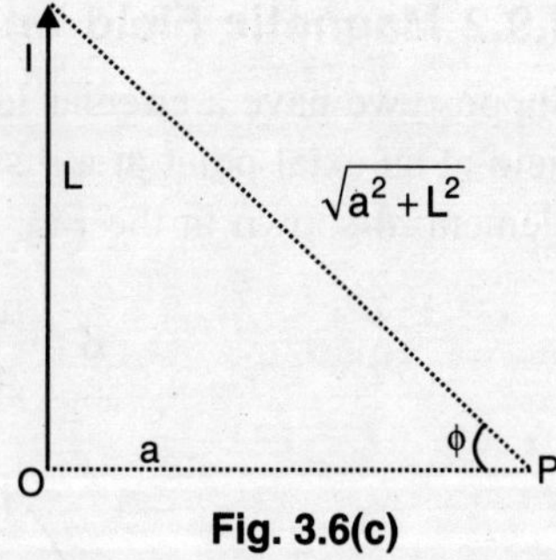

Fig. 3.6(c)

(*iii*) *Magnetic field in front of mid point of finite wire*

$$B = \frac{\mu_0 I}{4\pi a}\left[\sin\varphi + \sin(\varphi)\right]$$

$$B = \frac{\mu_0 I}{4\pi a}(2\sin\varphi) = \frac{\mu_0 I}{2\pi a}\frac{L}{\sqrt{L^2 + 4a^2}}$$

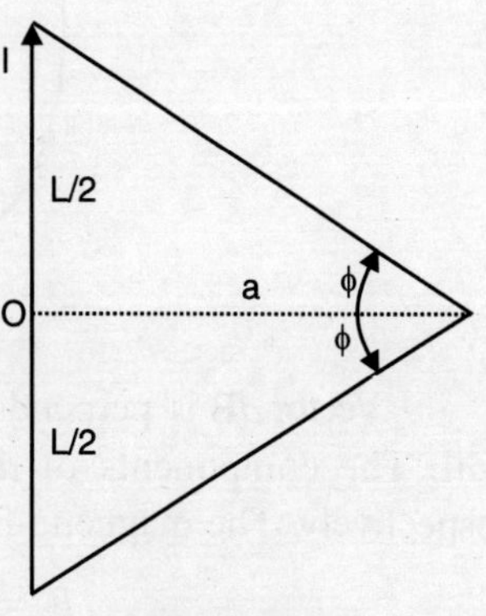

Fig. 3.6(d)

(*iv*) *Magnetic field of a finite segment of wire shown in Fig 3.6(e).*

Magnetic field of wire shown in Fig. 3.6(d)

$$B = \frac{\mu_0 I}{4\pi a}\left[\sin 60° - \sin 30°\right] = \frac{\mu_0 I}{4\pi a}\left(\frac{\sqrt{3}-1}{2}\right)$$

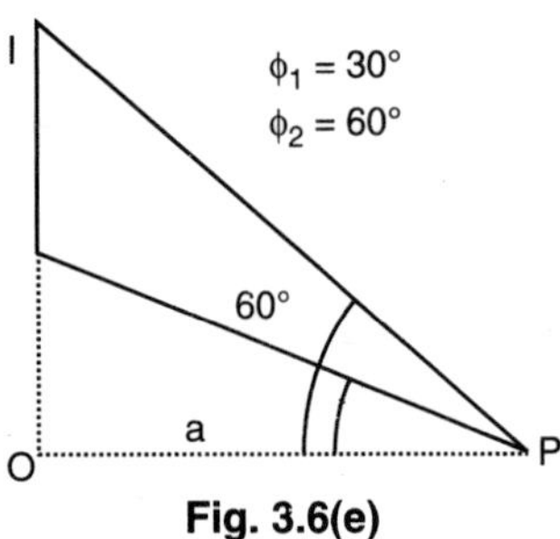

Fig. 3.6(e)

Magnetic field of wire shown in Fig. 3.6(e)

$$B = \frac{\mu_0 I}{4\pi a}\left[\sin(-30) - \sin(-60)\right] = \frac{\mu_0 I}{4\pi a}\left(\frac{\sqrt{3}-1}{2}\right)$$

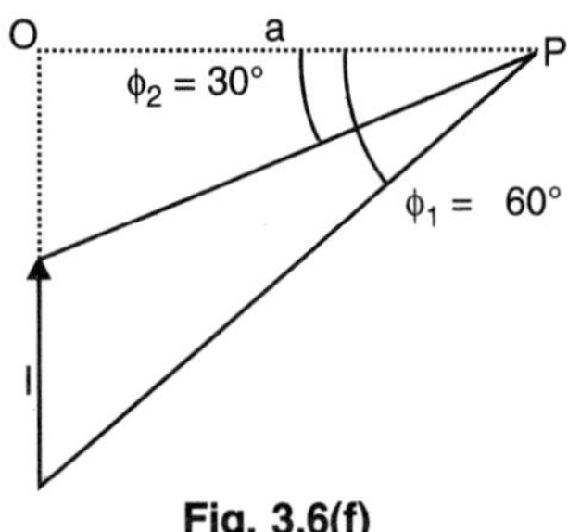

Fig. 3.6(f)

3.9.2 Magnetic Field on the Axis of a Circular Loop

Suppose we have a circular loop of radius R carrying a current I. We want to calculate the magnetic field at an axial point at a distance x from the centre of the coil. The magnetic field due to a current element $d\mathbf{l}$ shown in the Fig. 3.7 is

$$\mathbf{B} = \frac{\mu_0 I}{4\pi} \cdot \frac{d\mathbf{l} \times \mathbf{r}}{r^3} \qquad ...(3.32)$$

Fig. 3.7

Vector $d\mathbf{B}$ is perpendicular to vectors $\mathbf{r}$ and $d\mathbf{I}$. Let it make an angle α with the axis of the coil. The components of $d\mathbf{B}$ parallel and perpendicular to the axis are $dB\cos\alpha$ and $dB\sin\alpha$ respectively. The magnetic field of the entire loop is given by,

$$B_{\|} = \Sigma\, dB \cos\alpha$$

$$B_{\perp} = \Sigma\, dB \sin\alpha$$

The contributions to $\sum dB \sin\alpha$ from the various current elements which are symmetrically distributed about the axis sum up to zero.

$$B_{\perp} = \sum dB \sin\alpha = 0$$

Thus the total field of the loop is parallel to the axis and is given by,

$$B = B_{\parallel} = \sum dB \cos\alpha$$

$$= \sum \frac{\mu_0 I}{4\pi}\left(\frac{r dl \sin\theta}{r^3}\right)\cos\alpha \qquad \left[\theta = \pi/2\right]$$

$$= \frac{\mu_0 I}{4\pi}\cdot\frac{\cos\alpha}{r^2}\cdot\sum dl = \frac{\mu_0 I}{4\pi}\frac{\sin(90-\alpha)}{r^2}\cdot 2\pi R = \frac{\mu_0 I}{4\pi}\cdot\frac{R}{r^3}\cdot 2\pi R$$

$$= \frac{\mu_0 I}{2}\frac{R^2}{\left(R^2 + x^2\right)^{3/2}} \qquad ...(3.33)$$

If the loop contains N turns, the field is increased by a factor N. The magnetic field at the centre ($x = 0$) of the coils is,

$$B\,(\text{centre}) = \frac{\mu_0 I}{2R} \qquad ...(3.34)$$

At distances very large compared to the dimension of the loop (i.e. $x >> R$), the magnetic field is given by

$$B = \frac{1}{2}\mu_0 I \frac{R^2}{x^3} = \frac{\mu_0}{2\pi}\cdot\frac{IA}{x^3} \qquad ...(3.35)$$

Where $A = \pi R^2$ is the area of the loop.

3.9.3 Magnetic Field on the Axis of Helmholtz Coil and Helmholtz Galvanometer

A pair of identical coaxial circular coils separated by a distance equal to the coil radius are called Helmholtz coils. The importance of such an arrangement is that if both the coils carry equal currents in the same direction, are resultant magnetic field at a point on their common axis mid-way between their centres is almost uniform.

The magnetic field of one coil decreases with distance from its centre. The curve representing the variation of B with distance x is shown in the Fig. 3.8. The part of the curve AP is concave towards the point O_1, the centre of the coil, and beyond P it is convex. The point where the curvature changes sign is called the point of inflexion and at this point $\frac{d^2B}{dx^2} = 0$. In other words, at the *point of inflexion*, the space rate of variation of magnetic field is constant.

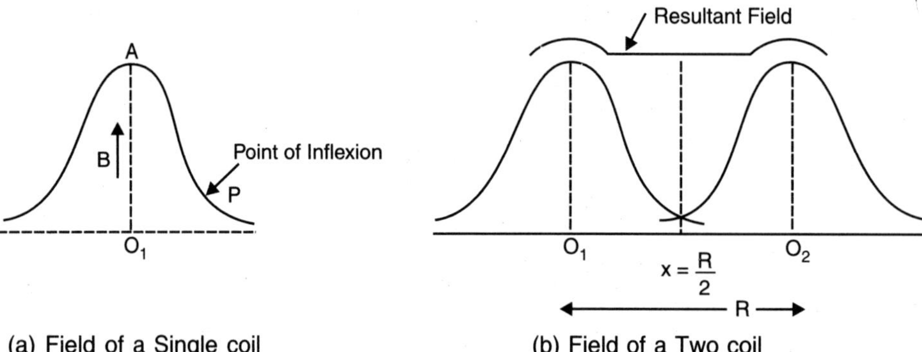

(a) Field of a Single coil (b) Field of a Two coil

Fig. 3.8

For one coil,

$$B = \frac{\mu_0 NI}{2} \cdot \frac{R^2}{\left(R^2 + x^2\right)^{3/2}}$$

$$\frac{dB}{dx} = \frac{\mu_0 NIR^2}{2} \cdot \left(-\frac{3}{2}\right)(R^2 + x^2)^{-5/2} \cdot 2x$$

At the point of inflexion,

$$\frac{d^2B}{dx^2} = 0 = -\frac{3}{2}\mu_0 NIR^2 \left[\left(-\frac{5}{2}\right)\left(R^2 + x^2\right)^{-7/2} \cdot 2x \cdot x + \left(R^2 + x^2\right)^{-5/2}\right]$$

$$\left(R^2 + x^2\right)^{-5/2}\left[-5x^2\left(R^2 + x^2\right)^{-2} + 1\right] = 0$$

$$1 - \frac{5x^2}{R^2 + x^2} = 0$$

$$x = \frac{R}{2} \qquad ...(3.36)$$

Thus the rate of change of magnetic field is constant midway between the coils. At this point, the decrease in the field of one coil is compensated by an equal increase in field of the other coil. Thus the magnetic field midway between the coils is uniform. This property of Helmholtz coils has been used in the construction of Helmholtz Galvanometer.

At the middle point between the centre of the coils, the resultant magnetic field is given by,

$$B = 2\left[\frac{\mu_0 NI}{2} \cdot \frac{R^2}{\left[R^2 + (R/2)^2\right]^{3/2}}\right]$$

$$= \frac{8\mu_0 NI}{5\sqrt{5}R} \qquad ...(3.37)$$

If the coils are set in magnetic meridian and a small magnetic needle placed mid-way between the coils shows a deflection θ with horizontal component of earth's magnetic field *H,* then

$$B = H \tan\theta \qquad \text{[Tangent law]}$$

$$\frac{8\mu_0 NI}{5\sqrt{5}R} = H \tan\theta$$

$$I = \left(\frac{5\sqrt{5}RH}{8\mu_0 N}\right)\tan\theta = K\tan\theta \qquad ...(3.38)$$

where $$K = \frac{5\sqrt{5}RH}{8\mu_0 N}$$

The constant *K* is called the reduction factor of the galvanometer.

3.9.4 Magnetic Field on the Axis of a Solenoid

A solenoid is a helical coil with closely spaced windings. When a current is made to flow in its windings, a magnetic field is produced in the space around it. We are interested in the magnetic field produced at an axial point of the solenoid. Let N = total number of turns, L = length of the solenoid, R = radius of the solenoid, I = current in its windings. The number of turns per unit length on the solenoid is $n = N/L$.

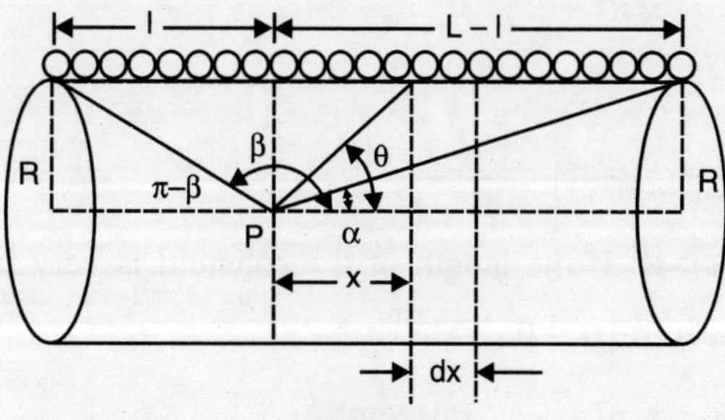

Fig. 3.9

Let the point of observation *P* be at a distance *l* from the left end of the solenoid. Consider an element of length *dx* of the solenoid at a distance *x* from the point *P*. This element contains *ndx* turns. The magnetic field at point *P* due to this element is,

$$dB = \frac{\mu_0 IR^2 (n\,dx)}{2\left(R^2 + x^2\right)^{3/2}} \qquad ...(3.39)$$

Let us change the variable *x* to θ where θ is the angular position of the current element.

$$x = R\cot\theta$$

$$dx = -R\,\text{cosec}^2\theta\, d\theta$$

In view of these relations, eqn. 3.39 becomes

$$dB = -\frac{1}{2}\mu_0 nI \sin\theta \, d\theta \qquad ...(3.40)$$

The magetic field due to the whole solenoid is

$$B = \frac{1}{2}\mu_0 nI \int_{\beta}^{\alpha} (-\sin\theta \, d\theta)$$

$$B = \frac{1}{2}\mu_0 nI (\cos\alpha - \cos\beta) \qquad ...(3.41)$$

or

$$B = \frac{1}{2}\mu_0 nI \left[+ \frac{L-l}{\sqrt{R^2 + (L-l)^2}} + \frac{l}{\sqrt{R^2 + l^2}} \right] \qquad ...(3.42)$$

The magnetic field at the centre $(l = L/2)$ of the solenoid is

$$B = \frac{1}{2}\mu_0 nI \left[\frac{L}{\sqrt{R^2 + L^4/4}} \right] \quad \text{(centre)} \qquad ...(3.43)$$

If the point P is at the left end of the solenoid, we have $\beta = \pi/2$ and

$$\cos\alpha = \frac{L}{\sqrt{R^2 + L^2}}$$

then the field is given by

$$B(\text{end}) = \frac{1}{2}\mu_0 nI \left[\frac{L}{\sqrt{R^2 + L^2}} \right] \qquad ...(3.44)$$

Very Long Solenoid, L>>R. If the length of the solenoid is very large in comparison with the radius, then the field at the centre $[\alpha = 0, \beta = \pi]$ is

$$B = \mu_0 nI \quad \text{(at centre)} \qquad ...(3.45)$$

At the end $[\alpha = 0, \beta = \pi/2]$ of a very long solenoid, the magnetic field is given by

$$B = \frac{1}{2}\mu_0 nI \quad \text{(at end)} \qquad ...(3.46)$$

Thus the magnetic field at the end of a long solenoid is just one half that at the centre. The direction of the magnetic field is the same at that in which a right handed screw advances when rotated in the sense of circulation of current.

In eqn. (3.45), nI is the current per unit length and is called the solenoid current density J. Thus

$$B(\text{centre}) = \mu_0 nI = \mu_0 J$$

3.10. CIRCUITAL FORM OF AMPERE'S LAW

Circuital form of Ampere's law states that *the circulation of magnetic field* **B** *around* a closed curve equals μ_0 times the current through the curve.

$$\oint_c \mathbf{B} \cdot d\mathbf{l} = \mu_0 I \qquad \text{Ampere's Law} \qquad ...(3.47)$$

If the closed curve C is threaded by more than one current carrying conductors, then the current I in eqn. (3.47) represents the algebraic sum of currents.

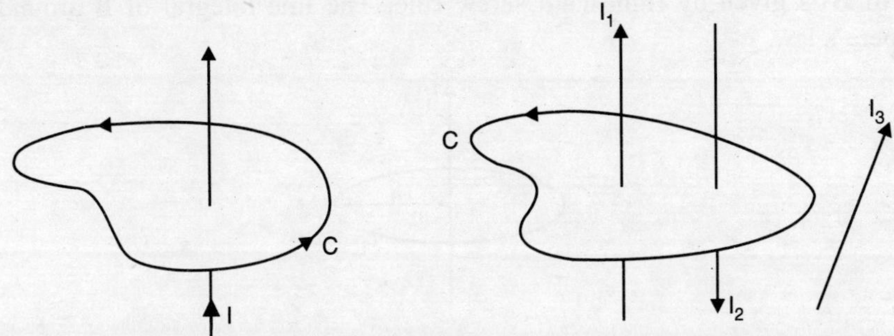

Fig. 3.10

The circuital form of Ampere's law is a highly significant deduction for *steady currents.* Like Gauss's law, Ampere's law in magnetostatics offers an extraordinary efficient method for calculating the magnetic field of highly symmetric current distributions.

Equation 3.47 can be written as

$$\oint_C \mathbf{B} \cdot d\mathbf{l} = \mu_0 \int_S \mathbf{J} \cdot d\mathbf{S} \qquad ...(3.48)$$

Where S is the surface bounded by the curve C. Equation (3.48) is known as the *integral* form of *Ampere's law.* Changing the line integral of eqn. (3.48) into surface integral using *Stoke's Theorem* we have

$$\int_S \nabla \times \mathbf{B} \cdot d\mathbf{S} = \mu_0 \int_S \mathbf{J} \cdot d\mathbf{S}$$

or

$$\nabla \times \mathbf{B} = \mu_0 \mathbf{J} \qquad ...(3.49)$$

This equation is known as the *differential form of Ampere's Law.*

Taking divergence of equation 3.49 we have

$$\nabla \cdot \nabla \times \mathbf{B} = \mu_0 \nabla \cdot \mathbf{J} \qquad ...(3.50)$$

Left hand side of equation 3.50 is identically zero.Thus

$$\nabla \cdot \mathbf{J} = 0 \qquad \text{Steady currents} \qquad ...(3.51)$$

Equation (3.51) which follows from Ampere's law and holds for steady currents and hence Ampere's law in the form 3.49 applies to steady currents only.

3.11. APPLICATION OF CIRCUITAL FORM OF AMPERE'S LAW

1. Magnetic Field of Infinite Straight Conductor

Consider a long straight conductor carrying a current I. The magnetic field of this wire has cylindrical symmetry; it has the same magnitude at all points which are at equal distance from the wire. The field lines are circles centred on the wire. We have to calculate magnetic field at a distance a from the wire. We now imagine a circle of radius a lying in a plane perpendicular to the wire. This circle is often called Amperian loop. The field lines are tangential to the Amperian loop and the direction of **B** is given by right-hand screw rule. The line integral of **B** around the circle is given by Ampere's law.

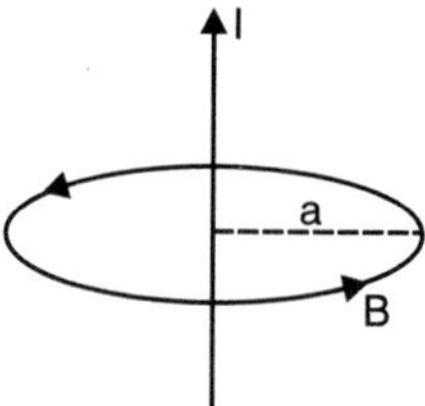

Fig. 3.11

$$\oint \mathbf{B} \cdot d\mathbf{l} = \mu_0 I$$

$$B(2\pi a) = \mu_0 I$$

$$B = \frac{\mu_0 I}{2\pi a} \qquad \text{...(3.52)}$$

2. Magnetic Field of a Solenoid

Now we shall calculate the magnetic field of a long solenoid. A long solenoid means one whose length is very large compared to its diameter. The entire magnetic field of such a solenoid is confined to inside and is constant over to the axis of the solenoid. The direction of B is given by right-hand screw rule: *If we rotate the screw in the direction of current in the solenoid windings, the direction of motion of the screw gives the direction of B.*

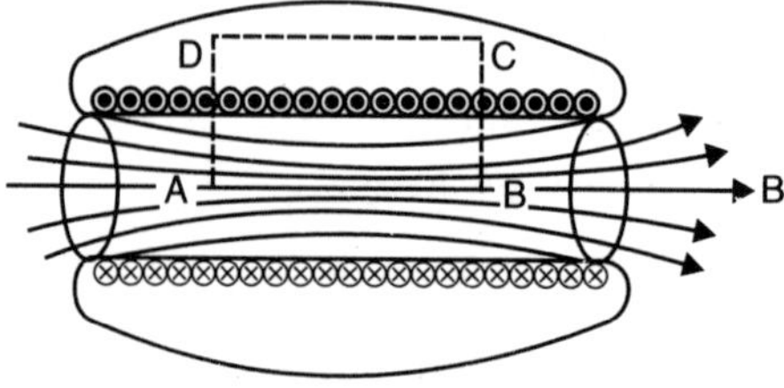

Fig. 3.12

We now imagine a rectangular Amperian loop $ABCD$. If n is the number of turns per unit length and L is the length of side AB of the rectangle, then the Amperian loop is threaded by nL turns. The line integral of B around the rectangle $ABCD$ is given by Ampere's law.

$$\oint \mathbf{B}.d\mathbf{l} = \mu_0 nLI$$

$$\int_{AB} \mathbf{B}.d\mathbf{l} + \int_{BC} \mathbf{B}.d\mathbf{l} + \int_{CD} \mathbf{B}.d\mathbf{l} + \int_{AD} \mathbf{B}.d\mathbf{l} = \mu_0 nLI$$

The magnetic field B is perpendicular to sides BC and AD and hence the second and the fourth integral vanish. The field outside the solenoid is nearly zero and hence the third integral also vanish. Now we are left with

$$\int_{AB} \mathbf{B}.d\mathbf{l} = \mu_0 nLI$$

$$BL = \mu_0 nLI \qquad ...(3.53)$$

$$B = \mu_0 nI$$

3. Magnetic Field of a Toroid

A toroid is a solenoid (of circular or rectangular cross-section) bent into the form of a circle with its ends joined together. The windings are so closely spaced that there is no axial component of current. The magnetic field of toroid is circumferential at all points. Almost all the magnetic field is confined to the interior of the toroid. To calculate **B** inside it we construct an Amperian loop in the form of a circle of radius r whose centre coincides with that of the toroid. If the loop lies inside the toroid, it encloses the current $2\pi RnI$ (R is the mean radius of the toroid, n = number of turns per unit length and I current in the windings).

According to Ampere's law,

$$\oint \mathbf{B}\cdot d\mathbf{l} = \mu_0(2\pi RnI)$$

$$B(2\pi r) = \mu_0(2\pi RnI)$$

$$B = \mu_0 nI\left(\frac{R}{r}\right) \qquad ...(3.54)$$

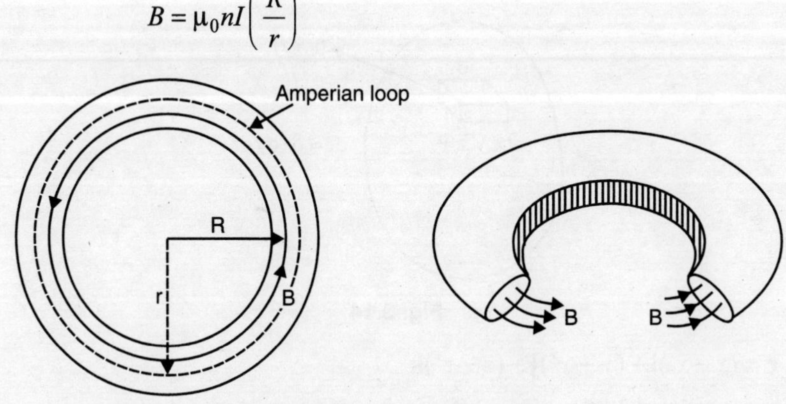

Amperian loop R r B B B

Fig. 3.13. A toroid top view.

The magnetic field is not constant over the cross-section of the toroid. If the Amperian loop lines outside the toroid, it encloses no current. Hence

$$\oint \mathbf{B}\cdot d\mathbf{l} = 0$$

$$B = 0$$

Thus the magnetic field outside a toroid is zero.

For a toroid of very small cross-section, the ratio R/r is almost equal to unity and the field of such a toroid is

$$B = \mu_0 nI \qquad (R/r \to 1)$$

Which is the field of a long solenoid.

3.12. DIVERGENCE OF MAGNETIC FIELD

The field lines of magnetic field are always closed, they have no beginning and no end. In other words, like electric charges, *isolated magnetic charges (poles) do not exist.* If we imagine closed surface in a magnetic field, the number of lines entering the surface equals the number of lines going out. The net magnetic flux through the closed surface is zero.

$$\oint \mathbf{B}\cdot d\mathbf{S} = 0 \qquad \text{...(3.55)}$$

Using divergence theorem, we can transform the surface integral into volume integral.

$$\int \nabla\cdot\mathbf{B}\, d\tau = 0$$

$$\nabla\cdot\mathbf{B} = 0 \qquad \text{...(3.56)}$$

The same result is obtained from Biot-Savart law. The magnetic field due to a volume distribution of current is

$$\mathbf{B}(x, y, z) = \frac{\mu_0}{4\pi}\int \frac{\mathbf{J}\times\mathbf{r}}{r^3}\, d\tau \qquad \text{...(3.57)}$$

Where $\mathbf{r}$ is the radius vector from the volume element $d\tau$ to the observer's point (x, y, z)

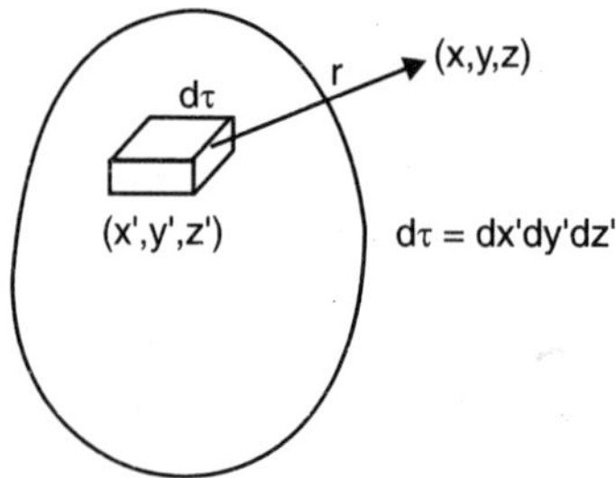

Fig. 3.14

$$\mathbf{r} = (x - x')\mathbf{i} + (y - y')\mathbf{j} + (z - z')\mathbf{k} \qquad \text{...(3.58)}$$

The current density $\mathbf{J}$ is function of source coordinates $\mathbf{J}(x', y', z')$

Taking divergence of eqn. (3.57) with respect to observer's coordinates (x, y, z) we have

$$\nabla\cdot\mathbf{B} = \frac{\mu_0}{4\pi}\int \nabla\cdot\left(\mathbf{J}\times\frac{\mathbf{r}}{r^3}\right) d\tau \qquad \text{...(3.59)}$$

Making use of the identity

$$\nabla\cdot(\mathbf{a}\times\mathbf{b}) = \mathbf{b}\cdot\nabla\times\mathbf{a} - \mathbf{a}\cdot\nabla\times\mathbf{b}$$

We can write eqn. (3.59) as

$$\nabla\cdot\mathbf{B} = \frac{\mu_0}{4\pi}\int\left(\frac{\mathbf{r}}{r^3}\cdot\nabla\times\mathbf{J} - \mathbf{J}\cdot\nabla\times\frac{\mathbf{r}}{r^3}\right)d\tau \qquad ...(3.60)$$

Since $\mathbf{J}$ is independent of $(x, y, z), \nabla\times\mathbf{J} = 0$ and $\nabla\times\frac{\mathbf{r}}{r^3} = 0$

Therefore $$\nabla\cdot\mathbf{B} = 0 \qquad ...(3.61)$$

3.13. CURRENT LOOP IN A MAGNETIC FIELD

When a loop carrying a current I is placed in a magnetic field $\mathbf{B}$, it experiences a force $\mathbf{F}$ which is given by,

$$\mathbf{F} = I\oint d\mathbf{l}\times\mathbf{B} \qquad ...(3.62)$$

In a uniform magnetic field, $\mathbf{B}$ = constant; the force on the loop is zero.

$$\mathbf{F} = I\left(\oint d\mathbf{l}\times\mathbf{B}\right) = 0 \qquad ...(3.63)$$

because the net displacement $\oint d\mathbf{l}$ around the closed loop vanishes.

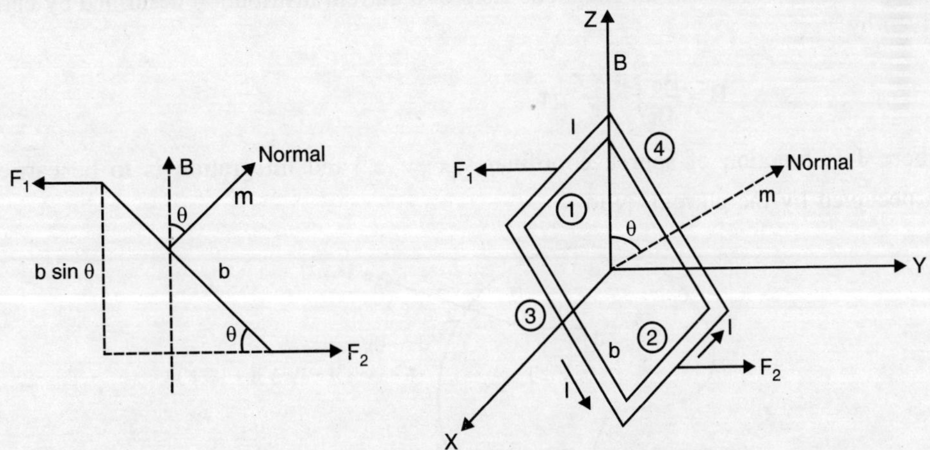

Fig. 3.15. A current loop in a magnetic field behaves like a magnetic dipole. The dipole moment of the current loop is **m** = I**An** where A is area of the loop and $\hat{n}$ is unit vector normal to the loop.

Now let us calculate the torque on a current loop in a uniform magnetic field. For the sake of convenience, we shall take the loop in the form of a rectangle. We take the origin at the centre of the loop and the z-direction along the field **B**. The loop is so tilted that the normal to its plane makes an angle θ with **B**. Since **B** is uniform, there is no net force on the loop. The forces F_3 and F_4 acting on the sides marked 3 and 4 respectively are equal in magnitude and are oppositely directed along the same line of action. Thus they do not have any tendency to rotate the loop. However the forces F_1 and F_2 marked on the sides 1 and 2 are equal in magnitude and are oppositely directed but their line of action are at a distance $b\sin\theta$, b being the length of side 3 or 4. Thus the forces F_1 and F_2 constitute a couple.

Thus $\quad F_1 = F_2 = IlB$

The moment arm of couple is $b\sin\theta$.

The torque of the couple is

$$\tau = (IlB)(b\sin\theta) = (IA)B\sin\theta = mB\sin\theta \quad ...(3.64)$$

where $\quad A = lb =$ Area of the loop

and $\quad m = IA \quad$ dipole moment ...(3.65)

Keeping in view the vector nature of the magnetic dipole moment, we can write the torque on the current loop as

$$\boldsymbol{\tau} = \mathbf{m} \times \mathbf{B} \quad ...(3.66)$$

This result is similar to the equation $\boldsymbol{\tau} = \mathbf{p} \times \mathbf{E}$ describing the torque on an electric dipole in a uniform electric field. *Thus a current behaves like a magnetic dipole.*

3.14. CURL OF MAGNETIC FIELD B

According to Biot-Savart law, the magnetic field of a current distribution described by current density **J** is given by

$$\mathbf{B} = \frac{\mu_0}{4\pi}\int \frac{\mathbf{J} \times \mathbf{r}}{r^3} d\tau.$$

where **J** is function of source coordinates (x', y', z') and integration is to be carried over the region occupied by the current. Now

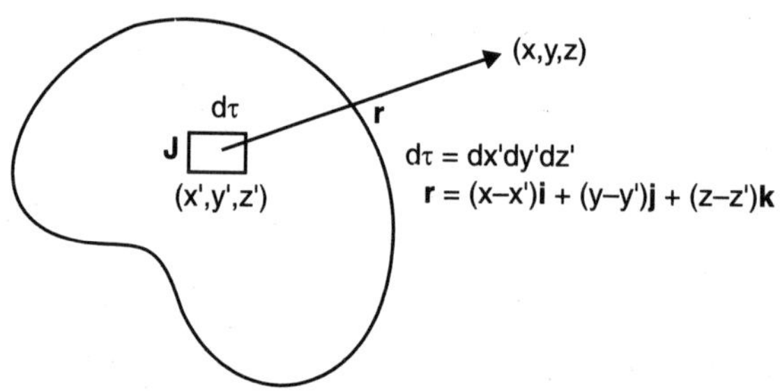

Fig. 3.16

$$\nabla \times \mathbf{B} = \frac{\mu_0}{4\pi}\int \nabla \times \left(\mathbf{J} \times \frac{\mathbf{r}}{r^3}\right) d\tau \quad ...(3.67)$$

Using the vector identity,

$$\nabla \times (\mathbf{A} \times \mathbf{B}) = (\nabla \cdot \mathbf{B})\mathbf{A} - (\nabla \cdot \mathbf{A})\mathbf{B} + (\mathbf{B} \cdot \nabla)\mathbf{A} - (\mathbf{A} \cdot \nabla)\mathbf{B}$$

We have $\nabla\times\left(\mathbf{J}\times\frac{\mathbf{r}}{r^3}\right)=\left(\nabla\cdot\frac{\mathbf{r}}{r^3}\right)\mathbf{J}-(\nabla\cdot\mathbf{J})\frac{\mathbf{r}}{r^3}+\left(\frac{\mathbf{r}}{r^3}\cdot\nabla\right)\mathbf{J}-(\mathbf{J}\cdot\nabla)\frac{\mathbf{r}}{r^3}$

Since ∇ involves differentiation with respect to observer's coordinates (x,y,z) and $\mathbf{J}$ is function of source coordinates (x',y',z') only, the second and third term on the right hand side of above equation vanish. We are then left with,

$$\nabla\times\left(\mathbf{J}\times\frac{\mathbf{r}}{r^3}\right)=\left(\nabla\cdot\frac{\mathbf{r}}{r^3}\right)\mathbf{J}-(\mathbf{J}\cdot\nabla)\frac{\mathbf{r}}{r^3} \qquad ...(3.68)$$

Now using the result $\nabla=-\nabla'$ where ∇' involves differentiation with respect to x',y',z' we can write

$$(\mathbf{J}\cdot\nabla)\frac{\mathbf{r}}{r^3}=-(\mathbf{J}\cdot\nabla')\frac{\mathbf{r}}{r^3} \qquad ...(3.69)$$

Let us simplify the x-component of the quantity on the right hand side of eqn. (3.69), viz.

$$\left[(\mathbf{J}\cdot\nabla')\frac{\mathbf{r}}{r^3}\right]_x=-(\mathbf{J}\cdot\nabla')\left(\frac{x-x'}{r^3}\right) \qquad ...(3.70)$$

Using the identity $\qquad \nabla\cdot\phi\mathbf{A}=\nabla\phi\cdot\mathbf{A}+\phi\nabla\cdot\mathbf{A}$

We have $\qquad \nabla'\cdot\left(\frac{x-x'}{r^3}\right)\mathbf{J}=\nabla'\left(\frac{x-x'}{r^3}\right)\cdot\mathbf{J}+\left(\frac{x-x'}{r^3}\right)\nabla'\cdot\mathbf{J}$

For steady current $\nabla'\cdot\mathbf{J}=0$ therefore,

$$\nabla'\cdot\left(\frac{x-x'}{r^3}\right)\mathbf{J}=\mathbf{J}\cdot\nabla'\left(\frac{x-x'}{r^3}\right) \qquad ...(3.71)$$

Integrating this equation over the volume occupied by current we have

$$\int_{volume}\nabla'\cdot\left(\frac{x-x'}{r^3}\right)\mathbf{J}d\tau'=\int_{volume}\mathbf{J}\cdot\nabla'\left(\frac{x-x'}{r^3}\right)d\tau$$

or $\qquad \displaystyle\int_{surface}\left(\frac{x-x'}{r^3}\right)\mathbf{J}\cdot d\mathbf{S}=\int_{volume}\mathbf{J}\cdot\nabla'\left(\frac{x-x'}{r^3}\right)d\tau$

If the surface over which the integration is to be evaluated, is taken so large that $\mathbf{J}$ is zero everywhere on it, the left hand side vanishes. So

$$\int\mathbf{J}\cdot\nabla'\left(\frac{x-x'}{r^3}\right)d\tau=0$$

Similar results holds for other components. Hence

$$\int(\mathbf{J}\cdot\nabla')\frac{\mathbf{r}}{r^3}d\tau=0 \qquad ...(3.72)$$

and then $\nabla\times\left(\mathbf{J}\times\frac{\mathbf{r}}{r^3}\right)=\left(\nabla\cdot\frac{\mathbf{r}}{r^3}\right)\mathbf{J}$ ...(3.73)

From eqn. (3.67) we have

$$\nabla\times\mathbf{B}=\frac{\mu_0}{4\pi}\int\nabla\cdot\left(\frac{\mathbf{r}}{r^3}\right)\mathbf{J}d\tau=\frac{\mu_0}{4\pi}\int\nabla\cdot\frac{\mathbf{r}}{r^3}d\tau$$

$$=\frac{\mu_0\mathbf{J}}{4\pi}(4\pi)\ \text{for } r=0$$

$$\nabla\times\mathbf{B}=\mu_0\mathbf{J} \quad ...(3.74)$$

3.15. MAGNETIC MOMENT OF A CURRENT LOOP

The magnetic moment of a small current loop carrying a current I is defined by

$$d\mathbf{m}=I\,d\mathbf{S} \quad ...(3.75)$$

where $d\mathbf{S}=\mathbf{n}dS$ is the area of the loop. A large current loop may be imagined to be made up of a large number of elementary loops each carrying the same current and in the same direction as the original one. The combined effect of all the elementary loops is the same as that of the original loop because of the cancellation of currents in the common branch of adjacent loops. The magnetic moment of a large loop is then given by

$$m=\int d\mathbf{m}=I\int\mathbf{n}dS \quad ...(3.76)$$

Now consider a plane loop with a current I. Referring to an origin O in the plane of the loop, let $\mathbf{r}$ and $\mathbf{r}+d\mathbf{l}$ be the radius vectors of the initial and tesrminal points of a current element. The area of the shaded part is

$$d\mathbf{S}=\frac{1}{2}\mathbf{r}\times(\mathbf{r}+d\mathbf{l})=\frac{1}{2}\mathbf{r}\times d\mathbf{l}$$

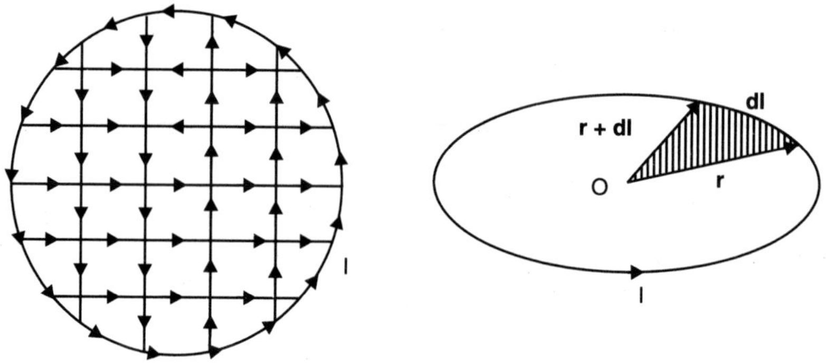

I

dl
r + dl
O
r
I

Fig. 3.17

The magnetic moment of the current loop is given by

$$\mathbf{m}=\frac{1}{2}I\oint\mathbf{r}\times d\mathbf{l} \quad ...(3.77)$$

For volume current density distribution, above expression becomes

$$\mathbf{m} = \frac{1}{2}\oint \mathbf{r} \times \mathbf{J} d\tau \qquad \text{... (3.78)}$$

Where **r** is the radius vector of the volume element . The magnetic moment is a vector quantity, pointing along the positive normal to the plane of the loop and its sense is given by right hand screw rule: *if a screw is rotated in the direction of current, the direction in which the screw advances coincides with the direction of* **m**.

3.16. POTENTIAL ENERGY OF A CURRENT LOOP IN A MAGNETIC FIELD

We have seen that a current loop experiences a torque in a uniform magnetic field given by

$$\tau = mB\sin\theta$$

This torque tends to align the magnetic moment **m** parallel to the magnetic field **B**. In order to increase the angle θ, an external torque must be applied. The work done by the external torque in increasing the angle by $d\theta$ is

$$dW = \tau d\theta = mB\sin\theta \, d\theta$$

This work is stored as potential energy of the current loop.

Gain in potential energy $dU = mB\sin\theta \, d\theta$

Integrating this equation we have

$$U = -mB\cdot\cos\theta + constant$$

Usually we choose the potential energy equal to zero when $\theta = \pi/2$ with this initial condition, *constant* = 0, then

$$U = -mB\cdot\cos\theta = -\mathbf{m}\cdot\mathbf{B} \qquad \text{...(3.79)}$$

The energy given by eqn. (3.79) does not represent the total energy of the current loop. It represents that part of energy which is due to the existence of torque on the loop in the magnetic field. Nevertheless, U can be used to compute forces on steady current loop.

3.17. MAGNETIC SCALAR POTENTIAL

In a region occupied by current density **J**, the magnetic field **B** is given by $\nabla \times \mathbf{B} = \mu_0 \mathbf{J}$. Outside the current distribution, $\nabla \times \mathbf{B} = 0$. This permits us to write magnetic field as gradient of scalar potential ϕ_m which we shall call *magnetic scalar potential, i.e.,*

$$\mathbf{B} = -\nabla\phi_m \qquad \text{...(3.80)}$$

Since $\nabla\cdot\mathbf{B} = 0$, We have $\nabla^2\phi_m = 0$

Thus the magnetic scalar potential satisfies Laplace's equation. Now we shall find an explicit expression for potential ϕ_m due to a filamentary current distribution. The magnetic field due to a current loop is given by

$$\mathbf{B} = \frac{\mu_0}{4\pi}\oint\frac{d\mathbf{l}\times\mathbf{r}}{r^3}$$

If the point of observation is displaced by $d\mathbf{r}$ the change in potential is

$$d\phi_m = \nabla\phi_m\cdot d\mathbf{r} = -\mathbf{B}\cdot d\mathbf{r} \qquad \text{...(3.81)}$$

$$d\phi_m = \frac{\mu_0}{4\pi}\oint\frac{d\mathbf{l}\times\mathbf{r}}{r^3}dr \qquad \text{...(3.82)}$$

The same change in potential can be brought about by displacing the current loop rigidly by equal displacement $d\mathbf{r}'$ in opposite direction, $d\mathbf{r}' = -d\mathbf{r}$. Thus

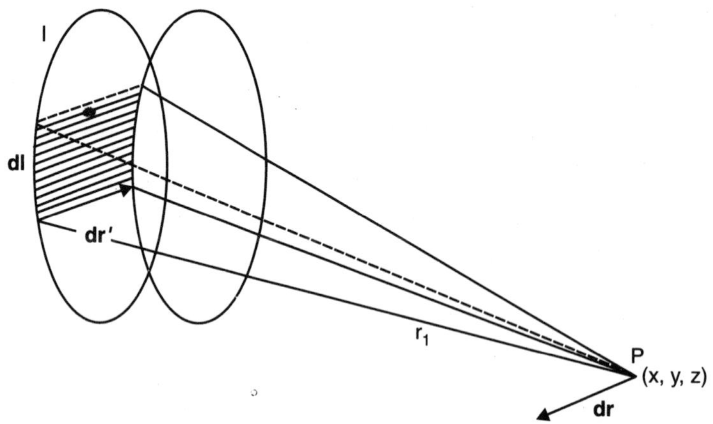

Fig. 3.18

$$d\phi_m = \frac{\mu_0 I}{4\pi}\oint\frac{d\mathbf{l}\times\mathbf{r}}{r^3}\cdot d\mathbf{r}' = \frac{\mu_0 I}{4\pi}\oint\frac{d\mathbf{r}'\cdot(d\mathbf{l}\times\mathbf{r})}{r^3} = \frac{\mu_0 I}{4\pi}\oint\frac{(d\mathbf{r}'\times d\mathbf{l})\cdot\mathbf{r}}{r^3}$$

$$d\phi_m = \frac{\mu_0 I}{4\pi}\oint\frac{d\mathbf{S}'\cdot\mathbf{r}}{r^3} \qquad \text{...(3.83)}$$

where $d\mathbf{S}' = d\mathbf{r}'\times d\mathbf{l}$ is the area swept by the current element $d\mathbf{l}$ when it is displaced by $d\mathbf{r}'$. Recalling that

$$\oint\frac{d\mathbf{S}'\cdot\mathbf{r}}{r^3} = d\Omega \qquad \text{...(3.84)}$$

is change in solid angle subtended at the field point when the loop is displaced by $d\mathbf{r}'$. thus

$$d\phi_m = \frac{\mu_0 I}{4\pi}\cdot d\Omega \qquad \text{...(3.85)}$$

where the constant of integration has been assumed to be zero.

In terms of Ω, the magnetic field is given by

$$\mathbf{B} = -\nabla\phi_m = -\frac{\mu_0}{4\pi}\nabla\Omega \qquad \text{...(3.86)}$$

It is worth to notice that the gradient of solid angle involves differentiation with respect to observer's coordinates (x, y, z) and Ω is positive if the area $\int d\mathbf{S}' = \mathbf{S}$ points towards the observer. From the view-point of an observer at P, if the current in the loop circulates counterclockwise, the direction of $d\mathbf{S}$ is positive.

3.18. VECTOR POTENTIAL

An electrostatic field is completely specified by equations

$$\nabla\cdot\mathbf{E} = \rho/\varepsilon_0\,;\ \nabla\times\mathbf{E} = 0$$

The equation $\nabla\times\mathbf{E} = 0$ permits us to represent $\mathbf{E}$ as the gradient of scalar potential ϕ

$$\mathbf{E} = -\nabla\phi$$

The scalar potential ϕ satisfies Poisson eqn.

$$\nabla^2\phi = -\rho/\varepsilon_0$$

When Poisson equation is solved for ϕ, we get

$$\phi = \frac{1}{4\pi\varepsilon_0}\int\frac{\rho\, d\tau}{r}$$

The introduction of scalar potential ϕ considerably facilitate the study of electrostatic phenomenon.

We have seen that the magnetic field of a steady current is specified by equations

$$\nabla\cdot\mathbf{B} = 0,\ \nabla\times\mathbf{B} = \mu_0\mathbf{J} \qquad \text{...(3.87)}$$

Consistent with these two equations, it is possible to represent a magnetic field as curl of some vector function $\mathbf{A}$ as

$$\mathbf{B} = curl\,\mathbf{A} \qquad \text{...(3.88)}$$

The vector function $\mathbf{A}$ defined by eqn. (3.88) is called the *vector potential* of the magnetic field and always satisfies the equation $\nabla\cdot\mathbf{B} = 0$. Equation 3.88 does not define the vector potential uniquely. If we add gradient of some scalar ψ to $\mathbf{A}$ then new vector potential also yields the same magnetic field.

If $\qquad \mathbf{A}' = \mathbf{A} + \nabla\psi \qquad \text{...(3.89)}$

then $\qquad \nabla\times\mathbf{A}' = \nabla\times(\mathbf{A} + \nabla\psi) = \nabla\times\mathbf{A} = \mathbf{B}$

In electrostatics, it was found convenient to choose the electrostatic potential ϕ equal to zero at large distance from the charge distribution. Likewise, great mathematical simplifications result if one imposes some suitable restriction on $\mathbf{A}$. In magnetostatics, the most convenient condition is to choose,

$$\nabla\cdot\mathbf{A} = 0 \qquad \text{Lorentz condition} \qquad \text{...(3.90)}$$

With this restriction on $\mathbf{A}$, the Ampere's law becomes

$$\nabla\times\mathbf{B} = \nabla\times(\nabla\times\mathbf{A}) = \nabla(\nabla\cdot\mathbf{A}) - \nabla^2\mathbf{A} = \mu_0\mathbf{J}$$

or $$\nabla^2 \mathbf{A} = -\mu_0 \mathbf{J} \qquad ...(3.91)$$

This vector equation is equivalent to three scalar equations:

$$\left.\begin{aligned} \nabla^2 A_x &= -\mu_0 J_x \\ \nabla^2 A_y &= -\mu_0 J_y \\ \nabla^2 A_z &= -\mu_0 J_z \end{aligned}\right] \qquad ...(3.92)$$

Equations (3.92) are similar to Poisson's equation in electrostatics. Making use of the correspondence,

$$\phi \to A_x$$

$$\rho/\varepsilon_0 \to \mu_0 J_x$$

we can write the solutions of eqs. 3.92 as:

$$\left.\begin{aligned} A_x &= \frac{\mu_0}{4\pi}\int \frac{J_x}{r}\,d\tau \\ A_y &= \frac{\mu_0}{4\pi}\int \frac{J_y}{r}\,d\tau \\ A_z &= \frac{\mu_0}{4\pi}\int \frac{J_z}{r}\,d\tau \end{aligned}\right] \qquad ...(3.93)$$

The three eqns. (3.93) can be combined into a single vector equation

$$\mathbf{A} = \frac{\mu_0}{4\pi}\int \frac{\mathbf{J}}{r}\,d\tau \quad \text{(volume)} \qquad ...(3.94)$$

Thus the problem of finding vector potential reduces to the problem of solving Poisson's equations. For linear and surface current distributions we have,

$$\mathbf{A} = \frac{\mu_0 I}{4\pi}\int \frac{d\mathbf{l}}{r} \quad \text{(linear)} \qquad ...(3.95)$$

$$\mathbf{A} = \frac{\mu_0}{4\pi}\int \frac{\mathbf{K}}{r}\,ds \quad \text{(surface)} \qquad ...(3.96)$$

This advantage of introduction of the concept of vector potential lies in the fact that the integrals (3.94–3.96) are easier to work with than the integrals appearing in Biot-Savart law.

The vector potential is a type of vector field for which we can draw field lines. The vanishing of divergence of **A** means that the field lines have no beginning or end. In general, the direction of lines of **A** is parallel to the current since **A** is proportional to the current element.

Once we know the vector potential of a given current distribution, the corresponding magnetic field is obtained from the equation,

$$\mathbf{B} = \nabla \times \mathbf{A}$$

or

$$\left.\begin{aligned} B_x &= \left(\frac{\partial A_z}{\partial y} - \frac{\partial A_y}{\partial z}\right) \\ B_y &= \left(\frac{\partial A_x}{\partial z} - \frac{\partial A_z}{\partial x}\right) \\ B_z &= \left(\frac{\partial A_y}{\partial x} - \frac{\partial A_x}{\partial y}\right) \end{aligned}\right] \qquad \text{...(3.97)}$$

$$\mathbf{B}(x, y, z) = \frac{\mu_0}{4\pi}\int \frac{\mathbf{J}(x', y', z') \times \mathbf{r}}{r^3} d\tau \qquad \text{...(3.98)}$$

where r is the magnitude of position vector of the point of observation relative to the source point and $d\tau = dx'dy'dz'$ is the volume element at the source point. The integration in eqn. (3.98) is performed over the primed coordinates (x', y', z').

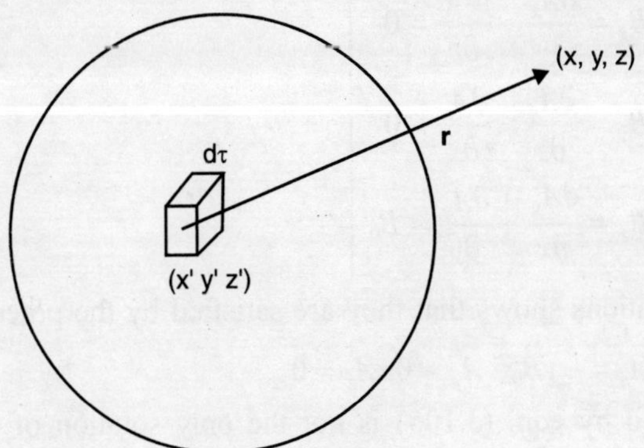

Fig. 3.19

Now

$$\begin{aligned} \nabla \times \frac{\mathbf{J}}{r} &= \nabla\left(\frac{1}{r}\right) \times \mathbf{J} + \frac{1}{r}\nabla \times \mathbf{J} \\ &= -\mathbf{J} \times \nabla\left(\frac{1}{r}\right) + \frac{1}{r}\nabla \times \mathbf{J} \end{aligned} \qquad \text{...(3.99)}$$

In eqn. (3.99), differentiation in operation with ∇ is performed over the unprimed coordinates x, y, z. Since $\mathbf{J}$ is independent of x, y, z we have $\nabla \times \mathbf{J} = 0$. Therefore

$$\nabla \times \frac{\mathbf{J}}{r} = -\mathbf{J} \times \nabla\left(\frac{1}{r}\right) = \mathbf{J} \times \frac{\mathbf{r}}{r^3} \qquad \text{...(3.100)}$$

Making use of the result expressed by eqn. (3.100), we can write eqn. (3.98) as,

$$\mathbf{B} = \frac{\mu_0}{4\pi}\int \nabla \times \frac{\mathbf{J}}{r} d\tau \qquad \text{...(3.101)}$$

In eqn. (3.101), integration is performed over x', y', z' and differentiation is performed over x,y,z. The change of the order of these operations does not affect the result. Consequently, we can write

$$\mathbf{B} = \nabla \times \left[\frac{\mu_0}{4\pi}\int \frac{\mathbf{J}}{r} d\tau\right] \qquad ...(3.102)$$

Comparison of this equation with the defining equation of vector potential $\mathbf{B} = \nabla \times \mathbf{A}$, we find

$$\mathbf{A} = \frac{\mu_0}{4\pi}\int \frac{\mathbf{J}}{r} d\tau \qquad ...(3.103)$$

3.19. VECTOR POTENTIAL OF A UNIFORM MAGNETIC FIELD

Let us calculate the vector potential of a uniform magnetic field $\mathbf{B}_0$ = constant. We direct z-axis along B_0. Hence $B_x = B_y = 0$, $B_z = B_0$

$$\left.\begin{aligned} B_x &= \frac{\partial A_z}{\partial y} - \frac{\partial A_y}{\partial z} = 0 \\ B_y &= \frac{\partial A_x}{\partial z} - \frac{\partial A_z}{\partial x} = 0 \\ B_z &= \frac{\partial A_y}{\partial x} - \frac{\partial A_x}{\partial y} = B_0 \end{aligned}\right] \qquad ...(3.104)$$

A glance at these equations shows that they are satisfied by the potential

$$A_x = -yB_0,\ A_y = 0,\ A_z = 0 \qquad ...(3.105)$$

The potential expressed by eqn. (3.105) is not the only solution of eqn. (3.104). The potential given by

$$A_x = 0,\ A_y = xB_0,\ A_z = 0 \qquad ...(3.106)$$

is also a solution. Not only these, but also a linear combination of following two potentials is also a solution.

$$A_x = -\frac{1}{2}yB_0,\ A_y = \frac{1}{2}xB_0,\ A_z = 0 \qquad ...(3.107)$$

Keeping in mind that $B_x = B_y = 0$, we can write the solution as,

$$\left.\begin{aligned} A_x &= \frac{1}{2}(zB_y - yB_z) \\ A_y &= \frac{1}{2}(xB_z - zB_x) \\ A_z &= \frac{1}{2}(yB_x - xB_y) \end{aligned}\right] \qquad ...(3.108)$$

or

$$A_x = \frac{1}{2}(\mathbf{B}_0 \times \mathbf{r}) \qquad ...(3.109)$$

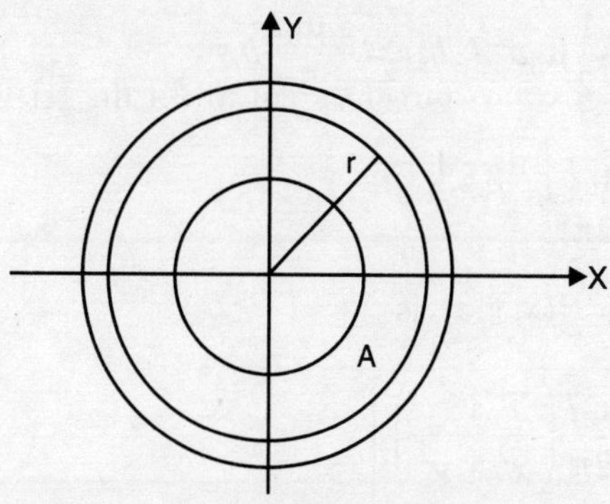

Fig. 3.20

Where **r** is position vector of point of observation relative to the origin.

3.20. VECTOR POTENTIAL OF AN INFINITELY LONG STRAIGHT WIRE

Consider an infinitely long wire carrying a current *I*. If ***a*** is the cross-sectional radius of the wire, the current density through it is $J = I/\pi a^2$. Let us take Z-axis along the wire.

Then $J_x = 0, J_y = 0, J_z = I/\pi a^2$. Since the vector potential is proportional to current density, we have $A_x = 0, A_y = 0$. Thus we have to find A_z only.

The determination of A_z for an infinitely long current carrying conductor is analogous to the problem of finding electrostatic potential of an infinite charged cylinder. The electrostatic potential at points outside an infinite charged cylinder is,

$$\phi = -\frac{\lambda}{2\pi\varepsilon_0} \ln r \qquad ...(3.110)$$

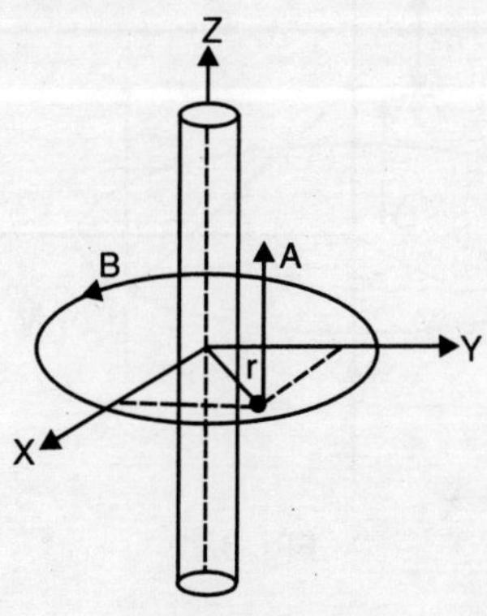

Fig. 3.21

where $\lambda = \pi a^2 \rho$ is the charge per unit length. Substituting $\mu_0 J_z$ for ρ/ε_0 in above equation, we get the vector potential A_z,

$$A_z = -\frac{1}{2}\mu_0 a^2 J_z \ln r = -\frac{\mu_0 I}{2\pi}\ln r \qquad ...(3.111)$$

or
$$A_z = \frac{\mu_0 I}{2\pi}\ln\sqrt{x^2+y^2}$$

The magnetic field at point $P(x, y, z)$ is

$$\left.\begin{aligned} B_x &= \frac{\mu_0 I}{2\pi}\left(\frac{y}{x^2+y^2}\right) \\ B_y &= \frac{\mu_0 I}{2\pi}\left(\frac{x}{x^2+y^2}\right) \\ B_z &= 0 \end{aligned}\right] \qquad ...(3.112)$$

or
$$B = \left(B_x^2 + B_y^2 + B_z^2\right)^{1/2} = \frac{\mu_0 I}{2\pi\sqrt{x^2+y^2}} = \frac{\mu_0 I}{2\pi r} \qquad ...(3.113)$$

***Aliter*:** The vector potential of a long straight wire may also be obtained by making use of eqn. (3.95). Let the point of observation be at a distance r from the wire. We choose origin at the foot of perpendicular drawn from the point of observation to the wire and direct the axes as shown in the Fig. 3.22. Consider a current element Idz at a distance z from the origin O. The vector potential of this current element is,

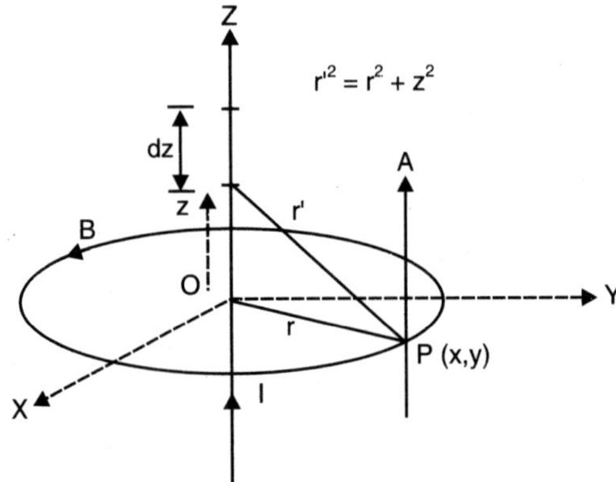

Fig. 3.22

$$d\mathbf{A} = \frac{\mu_0 I}{4\pi}\left(\frac{dz}{r'}\hat{\mathbf{z}}\right) = \frac{\mu_0 I\hat{\mathbf{z}}}{4\pi}\frac{dz}{\sqrt{r^2+z^2}}$$

Where $\hat{\mathbf{z}}$ is unit vector along z-direction. The vector potential of the entire wire is,

$$\mathbf{A} = \frac{\mu_0 I \hat{\mathbf{z}}}{4\pi} \int_{-\infty}^{\infty} \frac{dz}{\sqrt{r^2 + z^2}} = \frac{\mu_0 I \hat{\mathbf{z}}}{2\pi} \int_{0}^{\infty} \frac{dz}{\sqrt{r^2 + z^2}} = \frac{\mu_0 I \hat{\mathbf{z}}}{2\pi} \left[ln\left(z + \sqrt{r^2 + z^2}\right) \right]_0^{\infty}$$

$$= \frac{\mu_0 I \hat{\mathbf{z}}}{2\pi} [c_\infty - ln\, r]$$

where c_∞ is an infinitely great arising from the infinite extent of the wire over which the integration is performed. Since the magnetic field **B** involves the derivatives of **A**, the presence of this is not going to affect **B**. So without any loss of generality we can take

$$\mathbf{A} = -\frac{\mu_0 I \hat{\mathbf{z}}}{2\pi} ln\, r \qquad ...(3.114)$$

The surfaces of constant vector potential are coaxial cylinders surrounding the wire.

3.21. VECTOR POTENTIAL OF A LONG SOLENOID

Consider a long solenoid with n turns per unit length. Let I be the current in its windings. The field lines of **A** are concentric circles centred on the axis of the solenoid. Let us calculate the circulation of **A** around a circle of radius r (less than the radius of the solenoid) in a plane normal to the axis.

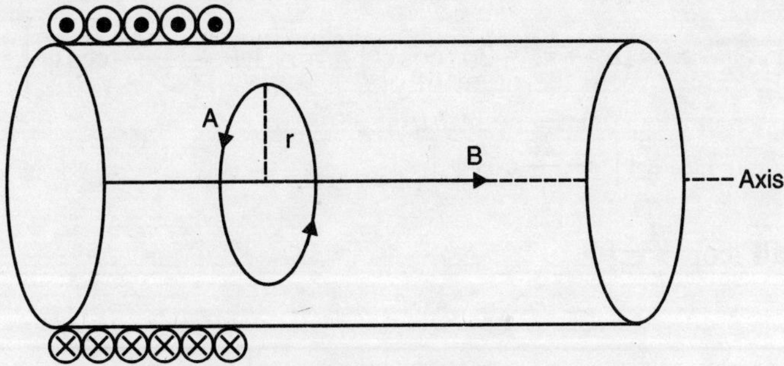

Fig. 3.23. Vector potential of a solenoid.

$$\oint \mathbf{A} \cdot d\mathbf{l} = \int_s \nabla \times \mathbf{A} \cdot d\mathbf{S} = \int_s \mathbf{B} \cdot d\mathbf{S} = \Phi \qquad ...(3.115)$$

where **S** is the surface bounded by the circle and Φ is the magnetic flux through this surface. The vector potential is constant in magnitude on this circle. Therefore

$$\oint \mathbf{A} \cdot d\mathbf{l} = (2\pi r) A$$

and the flux $\quad \Phi = \pi r^2 B = (\pi r^2)(\mu_0 n I)$

Substituting these values in eq. 3.115 we obtain

$$A = \frac{1}{2} \mu_0 n r I \qquad \text{(inside, } r < R\text{)} \qquad ...(3.116)$$

At points outside the solenoid, the vector potential can be calculated in the same way. The result comes out to be

$$A = \frac{1}{2}\mu_0 nI\left(\frac{R^2}{r}\right) \quad \text{(outside, } r > R) \qquad ...(3.117)$$

where R is radius of the solenoid.

3.22. VECTOR POTENTIAL OF A SMALL CURRENT LOOP

Consider a small current loop of radius $\boldsymbol{a}$. We choose $\boldsymbol{xy}$ plane in the plane of the loop, and origin at its center. Let the point of observation $\boldsymbol{P}$ lie in $\boldsymbol{xz}$ plane. $\mathbf{r}$ is the position vector of point $\boldsymbol{P}$ relative to origin and $\mathbf{r}'$ be that relative to a current element Idl ($= Iad\phi$). Angles θ, ϕ and ψ are defined in the Fig. 3.24.

Vector potential of a current Idl at point $\boldsymbol{P}$ is

$$dA = \left(\frac{\mu_0 I}{4\pi}\right)\frac{dl}{r'}$$

The x-component of $\boldsymbol{dA}$ due to current element Idl at angle ϕ cancel with that due to current element at angle $-\phi$. (on the other side of x-axis) whereas y-components add up. Thus the vector potential at point $\boldsymbol{P}$ is parallel to $\boldsymbol{y}$-axis.

For the loop,

$$A(r) = \int dA\cos\phi = \frac{\mu_0 Ia}{4\pi}\int\frac{\cos\phi\, d\phi}{r'}$$

Now
$$r' = \left(a^2 + r^2 - 2ar\cos\psi\right)^{1/2} = r\left(1 + \frac{a^2}{r^2} - \frac{2a}{r}\cos\psi\right)^{1/2}$$

$$\cong r\left(1 - \frac{2a}{r}\cos\psi\right)^{1/2}$$

because for a small loop $\frac{a}{r} \to 0$

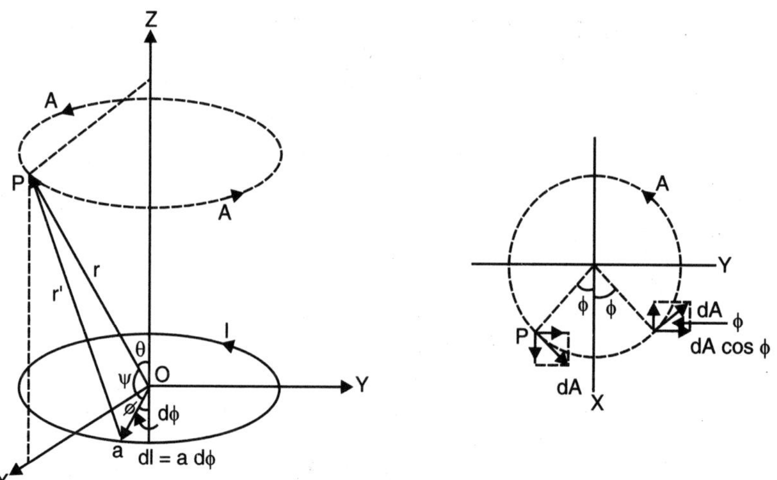

Fig. 3.24. Vector potential of a current loop. Point P lies on xz-plane. ψ is angle between vector **r** and **a.**

Now $$\frac{1}{r'} = \frac{1}{r}\left(1 - \frac{2a}{r}\cos\psi\right)^{-1/2}$$

$$= \frac{1}{r}\left(1 + \frac{a}{r}\cos\psi\right) \qquad \text{...(3.118)}$$

In component form, **r** and **a** can be written as

$$\mathbf{r} = (r\sin\theta)\,\mathbf{i} + (r\cos\theta)\,\mathbf{k}$$

$$\mathbf{a} = (a\cos\phi)\,\mathbf{i} + (a\sin\phi)\,\mathbf{j}$$

$\therefore$ $$\mathbf{r}\cdot\mathbf{a} = ar\cos\psi = ar\sin\theta\cos\phi$$

or $$\cos\psi = \sin\theta\cos\phi \qquad \text{...(3.119)}$$

$\therefore$ $$\frac{1}{r'} = \frac{1}{r}\left(1 + \frac{a}{r}\sin\theta\cos\phi\right) \qquad \text{...(3.120)}$$

$\therefore$ $$A = \frac{\mu_o I_a}{4\pi}\int_0^{2\pi}\cos\phi\cdot\frac{1}{r}\left(1 + \frac{a}{r}\sin\theta\cos\phi\right)d\phi$$

$$= \frac{\mu_0 \pi a^2 I\sin\theta}{4\pi r^2} = \frac{\mu_0}{4\pi}\cdot\frac{m\sin\theta}{r^2},\ m = \pi a^2 I$$

or $$\mathbf{A} = \frac{\mu_0}{4\pi}\cdot\frac{\mathbf{m}\times\mathbf{r}}{r^3} \qquad \text{...(3.121)}$$

The magnetic field of the current loop is

$$\mathbf{B} = \nabla\times\mathbf{A} = \nabla\times\left(\frac{\mu_0}{4\pi}\mathbf{m}\times\frac{\mathbf{r}}{r^3}\right)$$

Using the vector indentity

$$\nabla\times(\mathbf{A}\times\mathbf{B}) = (\mathbf{B}\cdot\nabla)\mathbf{A} + \mathbf{A}(\nabla\cdot\mathbf{B}) - (\mathbf{A}\cdot\nabla)\mathbf{B} - \mathbf{B}(\nabla\cdot\mathbf{A})$$

we have

$$\mathbf{B} = \frac{\mu_0}{4\pi}\left[\left(\frac{\mathbf{r}}{r^3}\cdot\nabla\right)\mathbf{m} + \mathbf{m}\left(\nabla\cdot\frac{\mathbf{r}}{r^3}\right) - (\mathbf{m}\cdot\nabla)\frac{\mathbf{r}}{r^3} - \frac{\mathbf{r}}{r^3}(\nabla\cdot\mathbf{m})\right]$$

Since m is independent of r, the first and the last term vanishes. Also $\nabla\cdot\mathbf{r}/r^3 = 0$, so we are left with

$$\mathbf{B} = \frac{\mu_0}{4\pi}\left[-(\mathbf{m}\cdot\nabla)\frac{\mathbf{r}}{r^3}\right] = -\frac{\mu_0}{4\pi}\left[\mathbf{m}\cdot\left(\frac{1}{r^3}\nabla\right)\mathbf{r} + \mathbf{m}\cdot\mathbf{r}\nabla\frac{1}{r^3}\right] = -\frac{\mu_0}{4\pi}\left[\frac{1}{r^3}(\mathbf{m}\cdot\nabla)\mathbf{r} - \mathbf{r}\left(\mathbf{m}\cdot\frac{3\mathbf{r}}{r^3}\right)\right]$$

$$= \frac{\mu_0}{4\pi}\left[\frac{1}{r^3}\mathbf{m} - \frac{3(\mathbf{m}\cdot\mathbf{r})\mathbf{r}}{r^5}\right] = -\frac{\mu_0}{4\pi}\left[\frac{\mathbf{m}}{r^3} - \frac{3(\mathbf{m}\hat{\mathbf{r}})\hat{\mathbf{r}}}{r^3}\right]$$

$$= \frac{\mu_0}{4\pi}\left[\frac{3(\mathbf{m}\cdot\hat{\mathbf{r}})\hat{\mathbf{r}} - \mathbf{m}}{r^3}\right] \qquad ...(3.122)$$

This expression for the magnetic field of a small current loop is identical to that of electric field of an electric dipole viz.

$$\mathbf{E} = \frac{1}{4\pi\varepsilon_0}\left[\frac{3(\mathbf{p}\cdot\hat{\mathbf{r}})\hat{\mathbf{r}} - \mathbf{p}}{r^3}\right] \qquad ...(3.123)$$

For this reason, a small current loop is called a magnetic dipole.

3.23. MAGNETIC FIELD IN MATTER

So far we confined our attention to the magnetic field in vacuum and learned few methods of computing magnetic fields produced by various current distributions, and also studied the properties of magnetic field. Now, we shall study the magnetic field in materials. At the outset, it is worth to mention that the understanding of magnetic behaviour of materials requires the knowledge of quantum mechanics, solid state physics, nuclear physics and spectroscopy. These disciplines are beyond the grasp of the readers for whom this subject matter is written. However, we shall try to explain magnetic behaviour of materials on classical principle.

It is experimental fact that when a material is placed in a magnetic field, say $\mathbf{B}_0$ the magnetic field inside the specimen is changed. In some cases, depending upon the nature of the specimen, the magnetic field inside the specimen is reduced and in other cases it is enhanced. A simple explanation of this phenomenon is like this: under the action of the external field $\mathbf{B}_0$ the specimen acquires magnetism and produces its own magnetic field $\mathbf{B}'$, which is superimposed on the external field.

$$\underset{\text{(resultant field)}}{\mathbf{B}} = \underset{\text{(external field)}}{\mathbf{B}_0} + \underset{\text{(field produced by specimen)}}{\mathbf{B}'} \qquad ...(3.124)$$

In materials which produce their own field in a direction opposite to the external field, the resultant field inside them is reduced. Such materials are called diamagnetic. In those materials which produce their own field in the same direction as the external one, the resultant field is increased. Such materials are either *para* or *ferromagnetic.*

Prior to the birth of quantum theory, the early workers tried to explain the magnetic behaviour of materials in terms of some kind of *microscopic currents* circulating within atoms and molecules of the materials. The exact nature and origin of these currents were not known. Now these currents are assumed to be associated with the orbital and spin motion of electrons within the atom. Due to these microscopic currents, an atom of a material may or may not have magnetic moment depending upon the complete or incomplete cancellations of these currents. Atoms and molecules possessing magnetic moments behave like small magnets and are called *atomic or molecular dipoles.* In materials, these dipoles are arranged in irregular fashion and hence the material in bulk shows no magnetic behaviour. When a material is placed in a magnetic field, the latter induces magnetic moment in its atoms and molecules either parallel or antiparallel to it; and the material in bulk exhibits magnetic behaviour. Such a material is said to be magnetized.

Magnetization Vector M: The state of magnetization of a material is described by *magnetization vector M* which is defined as follows: Consider a substance which has acquired magnetization under the action of some external field. Let an element of volume $d\tau$ contains dn number of diapoles. The magnetic moment associated with this elementary volume is,

$$d\boldsymbol{\mu} = \boldsymbol{\mu}\, dn$$

The magnetic moment per unit volume is called the magnetization vector *M*.

$$\mathbf{M} = \frac{d\boldsymbol{\mu}}{d\tau} \qquad ...(3.125)$$

The magnetization vector **M** is a vector field and obeys the usual laws of vector calculus.

3.24. MAGNETIC FIELD OF A MAGNETIZED BODY: BOUND CURRENT DENSITIES

A magnetized piece of material produces its own magnetic field. Consider a piece of magnetized matter having a non-uniform magnetization **M**. A volume element $d\tau$ of this material around a point (x', y', z') contains a dipole moment $d\boldsymbol{\mu} = \mathbf{M}d\tau$. The vector potential of this element at an external point (x, y, z) is

$$d\mathbf{A} = \frac{\mu_0}{4\pi}\cdot\frac{d\boldsymbol{\mu}\times\mathbf{r}}{r^3} = \frac{\mu_0}{4\pi}\cdot\frac{\mathbf{M}\times\mathbf{r}}{r^3}d\tau$$

where $\mathbf{r} = (x - x')\mathbf{i} + (y - y')\mathbf{j} + (z - z')\mathbf{k}$

The vector potential of the entire piece of material is given by,

$$\mathbf{A} = \frac{\mu_0}{4\pi}\int\frac{\mathbf{M}\times\mathbf{r}}{r^3}d\tau \qquad ...(3.126)$$

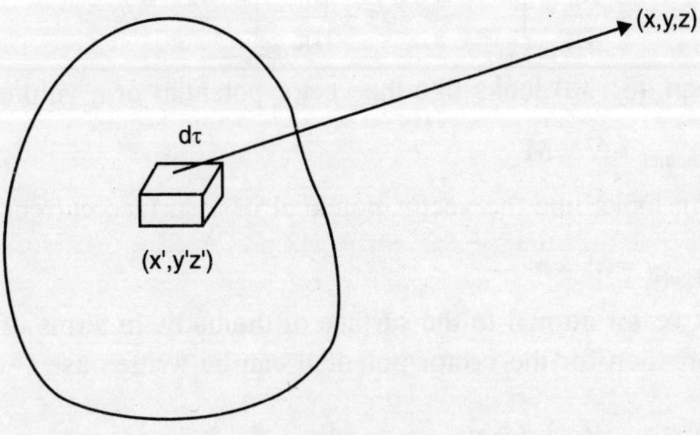

Fig. 3.25

Making use of the identity

$$\nabla\left(\frac{1}{r}\right)=\frac{\mathbf{r}}{r^3} \quad ...(3.127)$$

in which differentiation is performed with respect to source coordinates (x',y',z'), we can write eqn. (3.126) as

$$\mathbf{A}=\frac{\mu_0}{4\pi}\int \mathbf{M}\times\nabla\left(\frac{1}{r}\right)d\tau \quad ...(3.128)$$

In eqn. (3.128), the integration is carried over the volume occupied by the body.

With the help of the vector identity

$$\nabla\times(\phi\mathbf{A})=\nabla\phi\times\mathbf{A}+\phi\nabla\times\mathbf{A}$$

we can write

$$\nabla\left(\frac{1}{r}\mathbf{M}\right)=\nabla\left(\frac{1}{r}\right)\times\mathbf{M}+\frac{1}{r}\nabla\times\mathbf{M} \quad ...(3 .129)$$

In view of eqn. (3.129), we can write eqn. (3.128) as,

$$\mathbf{A}=\frac{\mu_0}{4\pi}\int\frac{\nabla\times\mathbf{M}}{r}d\tau-\frac{\mu_0}{4\pi}\int\nabla\times\left(\frac{\mathbf{M}}{r}\right)d\tau$$

The last integral in above equation can be transformed into surface integral with the help of identity,

$$\int_{\text{Volume}}\nabla\times\mathbf{A}d\tau=\int_{\text{Surface}}\mathbf{n}\times\mathbf{A}ds$$

Doing so we have

$$\mathbf{A}(x,y,z)=\frac{\mu_0}{4\pi}\int_{\text{Volume}}\frac{\nabla\times\mathbf{M}}{r}d\tau+\frac{\mu_0}{4\pi}\int_{\text{Surface}}\frac{\mathbf{M}\times\mathbf{n}}{r}ds \quad ...(3.130)$$

The first term in eqn. (3.130) looks like the vector potential of a volume current density.

$$\mathbf{J}_{\text{bound}}=\nabla\times\mathbf{M} \quad ...(3.131)$$

and the second term looks like the vector potential of a surface current density.

$$\mathbf{K}_{\text{bound}}=\mathbf{M}\times\mathbf{n} \quad ...(3.132)$$

where $\boldsymbol{n}$ is the unit vector normal to the surface of the body. In terms of bound current densities defined above, the expression for the vector potential can be written as

$$\mathbf{A}(x,y,z)=\frac{\mu_0}{4\pi}\int_{\text{Volume}}\frac{\mathbf{J}_{\text{bound}}}{r}d\tau+\frac{\mu_0}{4\pi}\int_{\text{Surface}}\frac{\mathbf{K}_{\text{bound}}}{r}ds \quad ...(3.133)$$

Taking curl of eqn. (3.133), the magnetic field can be evaluated. Here the differentiation in curl operation is to be performed with respect to the observer's coordinates (x,y,z). Equation (3.133) states that a magnetized body can be replaced by a region endowed with a volume distribution of current density $\mathbf{J}_{\text{bound}} = \nabla \times \mathbf{M}$ and a surface distribution of current density $\mathbf{K}_{\text{bound}} = \mathbf{M} \times \mathbf{n}$. Thus the problem of calculating the magnetic field of a magnetized object reduces to the problem of finding volume and surface current densities $\mathbf{J}_{\text{bound}}$ and $\mathbf{K}_{\text{bound}}$ respectively. It is worth to notice that these current densities are only mathematical abstractions; they do not transport charges on a macroscopic scale like free current. Recall that eq. 3.133 is similar to the corresponding equation of dielectrics.

3.25. ORIGIN OF BOUND CURRENTS

Let us try to understand the origin of bound currents. Consider a thin slab of uniformly magnetized material with magnetization vector M normal to its flat surfaces. In current-analysis method of describing a magnetized body, the atomic dipoles are represented by tiny current loops. These tiny current loops are shown on the surfaces of the specimen under consideration. Consider a tiny loop marked (1) in the interior of the specimen. This loop is all around surrounded by loops which carry equal and opposite currents and hence the current in the loop (1) is cancelled. This happens to all the loops which have their neighbours all around. For the loops lying on the boundary, the cancellation is not complete because there are no neighbours on the boundary site. Thus, if the magnetization M is uniform, all the currents circulating in the interior cancel each other; only the surface currents are left. The magnetized specimen is then equivalent to a single ribbon current flowing around the boundary. If A is the area of a tiny loop carrying a current i, then its magnetic moment is $\mu = iA$. If z is the thickness of the slab, then μ can also be written as $\mu = MAz$. These two ways of writing magnetic moment permits us to write $i = Mz$ or $M = i/z$. But i/z is the surface current density.

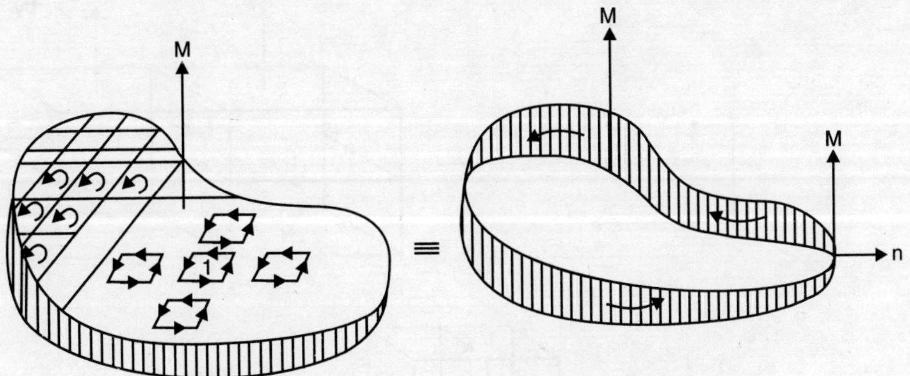

Fig. 3.26. A uniformly magnetized thin slab is equivalent to a ribbon of current flowing around the boundary.

Thus

$$K_b = M$$

or in terms of vectors notation,

$$\mathbf{K}_\mathbf{b} = \mathbf{M} \times \mathbf{n} \qquad \text{...(3.134)}$$

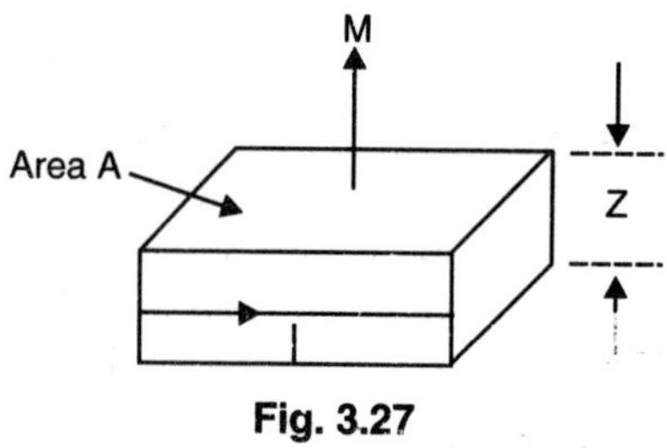

Fig. 3.27

On the flat surface, the unit vector $\boldsymbol{n}$ and $\mathbf{M}$ are parallel and hence $\mathbf{K}_b = 0$

Now consider a piece of magnetized material in which the magnetization M varies from point to point, *i.e.,* the magnetization is non-uniform. In this case, incomplete cancellation of microscopic currents in the interior of the substance gives rise to volume current. Imagine a small rectangular block of material of dimension dx, dy, dz. The block is so small that the magnetization is uniform within the block. Suppose that the block has magnetization parallel to z-axis.

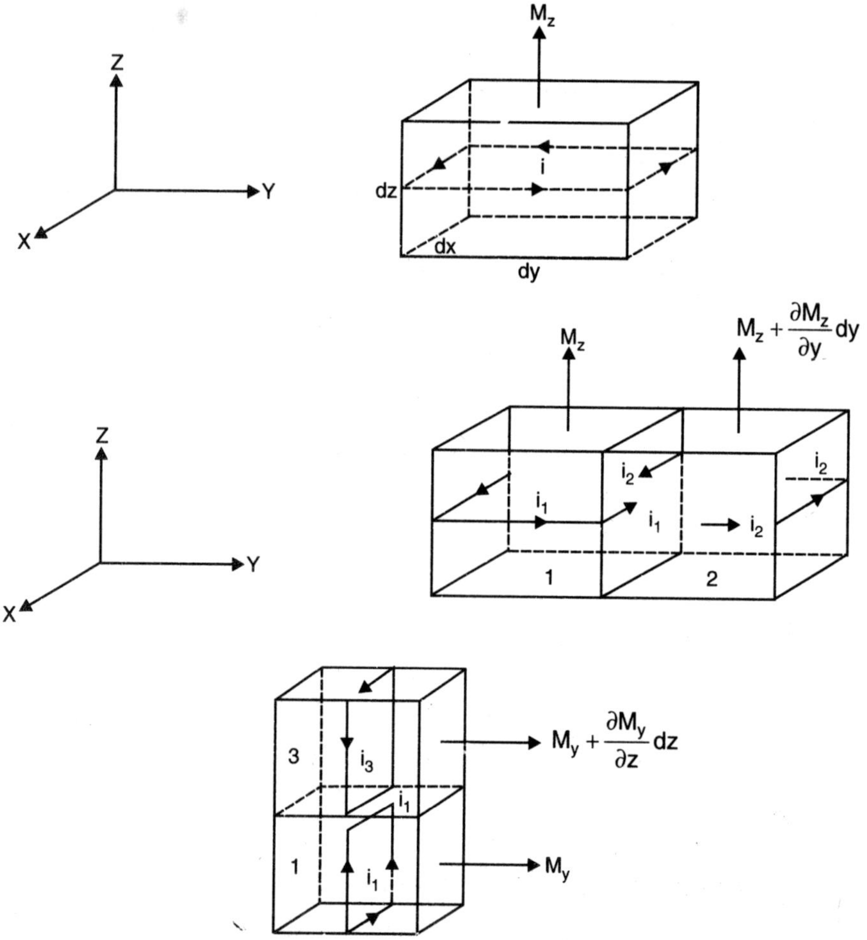

Fig. 3.28

The effect of this magnetized block is equivalent to that of a surface current $i_1\left(=M_z dz\right)$ circulating around the vertical faces as shown in the Fig. 3.28. Now imagine another identical block (2) touching the right face of the block (1). The *z*-component of magnetization of this block is $\left(M_z+\frac{\partial M_z}{\partial y}dy\right)$ and is equivalent to a surface current i_2 circulating around its vertical face, where

$$i_2=\left(M_z+\frac{\partial M_z}{\partial y}dy\right)dz$$

The common surface of the two blocks has two currents i_1 in –x direction and i_2 in +x direction. The net current in +x direction on the common surface is,

$$i_x=i_2-i_1=\left(M_z+\frac{\partial M_z}{\partial y}dy\right)dz-M_z dz=\frac{\partial M_z}{\partial y}dydz$$

The volume current density associated with i_x is

$$\left(J_b'\right)_x=\frac{i_x}{dydz}=\frac{\partial M_z}{\partial y} \qquad \text{...(3.135)}$$

The *y*-component of *M* also contribute to the current density in *x*-direction. In order to compute it, we imagine an identical rectangular block placed over the top of the block (1). The *y*-components of *M* in block (1) and (3) in Fig. 3.28 are M_y and $M_y+\frac{\partial M_y}{\partial z}dz$. Let i_1 and i_3 be the equivalent current in block (1) and (3), then

$$i_1=M_y dy$$

$$i_3=\left(M_y+\frac{\partial M_y}{\partial z}dz\right)dy$$

The net current flowing in +*x* direction over the common surface is,

$$i_x=i_1-i_3=M_y dy-\left(M_y+\frac{\partial M_y}{\partial z}dz\right)dy=-\frac{\partial M_y}{\partial z}dydz$$

and the corresponding current density is

$$\left(J_b''\right)_x=-\frac{\partial M_y}{\partial z} \qquad \text{...(3.136)}$$

Total current density in +***x*** direction is,

$$\left(J_b\right)_x=\left(J_b'\right)_x+\left(J_b''\right)_x=\left(\frac{\partial M_z}{\partial y}\right)-\frac{\partial M_y}{\partial z}=\left(\nabla\times M\right)_x \qquad \text{...(3.137a)}$$

The current densities in +*y* and +*z* directions can be calculated in the way described above. These come out to be

$$(J_b)_y = \left(\frac{\partial M_x}{\partial z} - \frac{\partial M_z}{\partial x}\right) = (\nabla \times M)_y \qquad ...(3.137b)$$

and
$$(J_b)_x = \left(\frac{\partial M_y}{\partial x} - \frac{\partial M_x}{\partial y}\right) = (\nabla \times M)_z \qquad ...(3.137c)$$

Combining eqns. 3.137(a), 3.137(b) and 3.137(c) we find

$$\mathbf{J}_{\text{bound}} = \nabla \times \mathbf{M} \qquad ...(3.138)$$

3.26. THE MAGNETIC FIELD STRENGTH VECTOR H

Consider a piece of matter which carries a free curent density $\mathbf{J}_{\text{free}}$ and a non-uniform magnetization $\mathbf{M}$. The effect of magnetization is to establish a bound current density $\mathbf{J}_{\text{bound}} = \nabla \times \mathbf{M}$ which circulates within the material. The macroscopic behaviour of current carrying magnetized material can be understood in terms of these two current densities $\mathbf{J}_{\text{free}}$ and $\mathbf{J}_{\text{bound}}$. The macroscopic magnetic field **B** inside the material is given by Ampere's law.

$$\nabla \times \mathbf{B} = \mu_\theta \mathbf{J}_{\text{total}} = \mu_0 (\mathbf{J}_{\text{free}} + \mathbf{J}_{\text{bound}})$$

$$= \mu_0 (\mathbf{J}_{\text{free}} + \nabla \times \mathbf{M})$$

$$\nabla \times \left(\frac{\mathbf{B}}{\mu_0} - \mathbf{M}\right) = \mathbf{J}_{\text{free}} \qquad ...(3.139)$$

We now introduce a new vector **H**, called the magnetic field strength vector defined by

$$\mathbf{H} = \frac{\mathbf{B}}{\mu_0} - \mathbf{M} \qquad ...(3.140)$$

or
$$\mathbf{B} = \mu_0 (\mathbf{H} + \mathbf{M})$$

In terms of **H**, Ampere's law becomes

$$\nabla \times \mathbf{H} = \mathbf{J}_{\text{free}} \qquad ...(3.141)$$

In vacuum $\mathbf{M} = 0$, and $\mathbf{B} = \mu_0 \mathbf{H}$. Equation (3.141) clearly states that the field **H** has nothing to do with the material.

Multiplying eqn. (3.141) by $d\mathbf{S}$ and integrating it over the surface S, we obtain

$$\int_s \nabla \times \mathbf{H} \cdot d\mathbf{S} = \int_s \mathbf{J}_{\text{free}} \cdot d\mathbf{S} \qquad ...(3.142)$$

$$\oint_C \mathbf{H} \cdot d\mathbf{l} = \Sigma \mathbf{J}_{\text{free}} \qquad ...(3.143)$$

Where C is the boundary of the surface S and $\mathbf{J}_{\text{free}}$ is the current threading the curve C. In writing eqn. (3.143), Stokes theorem has been used to transform the surface integral to line integral. Equation (3.143) is Ampere's Law in integral form which states that the circulation of the vector **H** around a closed curve equals the algebraic sum of the free currents enclosed by this curve.

The vector field **H** is associated with free currents only. It is worth to distinguish between the free current and the bound current. Free current involves actual transport of charge and can be started and stopped with a switch; it can be measured with an ammeter and controlled by rheostat. Bound current arises because of the magnetization of the material. It is associated with the orbital and the spin motion of electrons within the atom, and cannot be switched on or off . In magnetostatics, **H** plays the same role which the vector **D** plays in electrostatics. The way **D** is related to its source ρ_{free}, vector **H** is related to its source $\mathbf{J}_{free}$ through eqn. (3.143).

SOLVED EXAMPLES

***Example* 1:** *A regular polygon with n sides is inscribed in a circle of radius R. The polygon carries a current I. Show that the magnetic field at the centre of the circle is*

$$B = \frac{\mu_0 nI}{2\pi R}\tan\left(\frac{\pi}{n}\right)$$

***Solution*:** Each side of the polygon subtends an angle $2\pi/n$ at the centre of the circle. The distance of each side from the centre is $R\cos\pi/n$. The magnetic fields of all sides add up.

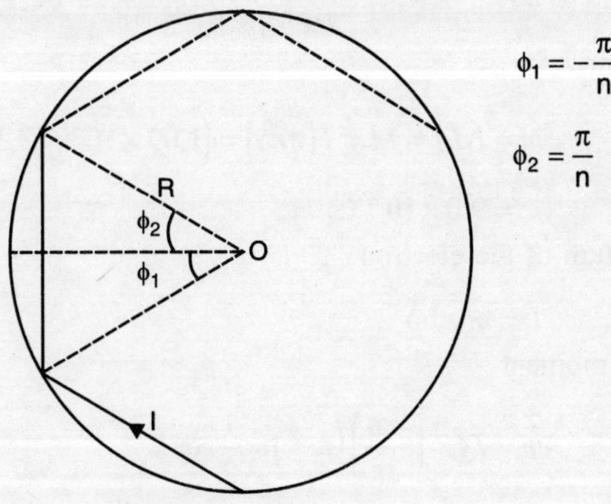

Fig. 3.29

The magnetic field of all sides is

$$B = \frac{\mu_0 nI}{4\pi a}(\sin\phi_2 - \sin\phi_1)$$

where $a = R\cos\pi/n, \phi_1 = -\pi/n, \phi_2 = \pi/n$

$$B = \frac{\mu_0 nI}{2\pi R}\tan(\pi/n) \qquad ...(3.144)$$

Note: Equation (3.144) may be written as,

$$B = \frac{\mu_0 I}{2R}\frac{\sin(\pi/n)}{\pi/n}\cdot\frac{1}{\cos(\pi/n)} \qquad ...(3.145)$$

In the limit $\lim n \to \infty$ eqn. (2) reduces to $B = \frac{\mu_0 I}{2R}$ which is the field of a circular loop at its centre.

***Example* 2:** *In hydrogen atom, electron revolves around the nucleus in a circular orbit of radius* $5.1 \times 10^{-11} m$ *at a frequency of* 6.8×10^{15} *revolutions per second. Calculate (i) the magnetic field at the centre, (ii) the magnetic moment of the orbit, (iii) the ratio of the magnetic moment to the angular momentum of the electron.*

Solution: (*i*) The electron rotating in circular orbit is equivalent to a current loop. The current in the loop is

$$I = (\text{charge})(\text{frequency}) = (e)(f)$$

$$= \left(1.6 \times 10^{-19}\right)\left(6.8 \times 10^{15}\right) = 1.09 \times 10^{-3} A$$

Magnetic field at the centre

$$B = \frac{\mu_0 I}{2r} = \frac{4\pi \times 10^{-7} \times 1.09 \times 10^{-3}}{2 \times 5.1 \times 10^{-11}} \cong 14 \text{ Tesla}$$

(*ii*) Magnetic moment

$$m = NIA = IA = I\left(\pi r^2\right) = \left(1.09 \times 10^{-3}\right)(3.14) \times \left(5.1 \times 10^{-11}\right)^2$$

$$= 9.0 \times 10^{-24} A\, m^2$$

(*iii*) Angular momentum of the electron

$$L = m_e r^2 \omega$$

and the magnetic moment

$$m = IA = \left(\frac{e\omega}{2\pi}\right)\left(\pi r^2\right) = \frac{1}{2} e\omega r^2$$

The ratio of magnetic moment to the angular momentum

$$\frac{m}{L} = \frac{e}{2m_e} \qquad \text{(gyromagnetic ratio)}$$

$$= \frac{1.6 \times 10^{-19}}{2 \times 9.1 \times 10^{-31}} \cong 9 \times 10^{10} \text{ A.s/kg.}$$

***Example* 3:** *A solenoid with radius 10 cm and length 20 cm has 1600 turns distributed uniformly over its entire length. A current of 2 ampere is made to flow in it. Calculate the magnetic field at an axial point situated at (i) one end, (ii) 10 cm inside from one end, (iii) at a distance of 10 cm outside from one end.*

Solution: The magnetic field inside a solenoid is

$$B = \frac{1}{2}\mu_0 nI\left[\cos\alpha - \cos\beta\right]$$

(*i*) If the point of observation lies at one end of the solenoid then

$$\cos\alpha = \frac{L}{\sqrt{R^2 + L^2}} = \frac{20}{\sqrt{10^2 + 20^2}} = \frac{2}{\sqrt{5}}$$

$$\cos\beta = 0, \beta = \pi/2$$

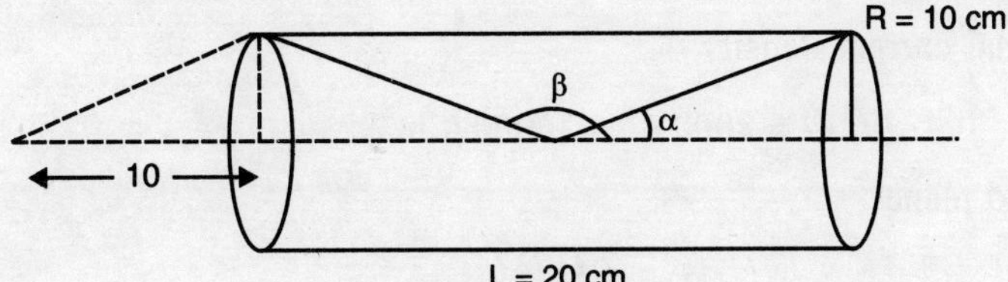

Fig. 3.30

$$B = \frac{1}{2}\mu_0 nI \frac{L}{\sqrt{R^2 + L^2}} = \frac{1}{2} \times 4\pi \times 10^{-7} \times 8000 \times 2 \times \frac{2}{\sqrt{5}}$$

$$= \frac{64\pi \times 10^{-4}}{\sqrt{5}} \text{ T}$$

(*ii*) At the middle point,

$$\cos\alpha = \frac{L/2}{\sqrt{R^2 + L^2/4}}, \cos\beta = \frac{L/2}{\sqrt{R^2 + L^2/4}}$$

$$B = \frac{1}{2}\mu_0 nI \frac{L}{\sqrt{R^2 + L^2/4}}$$

$$= \frac{1}{2} \times 4\pi \times 10^{-7} \times 8000 \times 2 \times \sqrt{2}$$

$$= 32\pi\sqrt{2} \times 10^{-4} \text{ T}$$

(*iii*) At a point outside the solenoid

$$\cos\alpha = \frac{L+10}{\sqrt{R^2 + (L+10)^2}} = \frac{3}{\sqrt{10}}$$

$$\cos\beta = \frac{10}{\sqrt{R^2 + 10^2}} = \frac{1}{\sqrt{2}}$$

$$B = \frac{1}{2} \times 4\pi \times 10^{-7} \times 8000 \times 2 \times \left(\frac{3}{\sqrt{10}} - \frac{1}{\sqrt{2}}\right)$$

$$= \frac{32\pi\left(3 - \sqrt{5}\right) \times 10^{-4}}{\sqrt{10}} \text{ T}$$

***Example* 4:** *From the data given in example 3 calculate,*

(*i*) *solenoidal current density.*

(*ii*) *flux of magnetic field through one end plane.*

(*iii*) *flux of magnetic field through the middle cross-section.*

(*iv*) *magnetic moment.*

***Solution*:** (*i*) Solenoidal current density

$$J = nI = 8000 \times 2 = 16000 \text{ A m}^{-1}$$

(*ii*) Flux through end plane

$$\Phi = B_{end}\left(\pi R^2\right) = \frac{64}{\sqrt{5}} \times 10^{-5} \text{ Weber}$$

(*iii*) Flux through the middle cross-section

$$\Phi = B_{middle}\left(\pi R^2\right) = 32\sqrt{2} \times 10^{-5} \text{ Weber}$$

(*iv*) Magnetic moment

$$m = NIA = 1600 \times 2 \times \pi \times (0.10)^2 = 32\pi \text{ A m}^{-2}$$

***Example* 5:** *A straight round conductor of cross-section radius R carries a current I. Find the magnetic field at a distace x from the axis of the conductor. The permeability of the conductor may be assumed to be equal to unity.*

Solution: The cross-section of the conductor is shown in the Fig. 3.31. Consider an Amperian loop of radius $x(> R)$. According to Ampere's law,

$$\oint \mathbf{B} \cdot d\mathbf{l} = \mu_0 I$$

$$B(2\pi x) = \mu_0 I$$

$$B = \frac{\mu_0 I}{2\pi x}; \qquad x > R \qquad \text{...(3.146)}$$

At the surface of the conductor, $x = R$

$$B = \frac{\mu_0 I}{2\pi R}; \qquad x = R \qquad \text{...(3.147)}$$

In order to calculate the magnetic field inside the conductor, we imagine an Amperian loop of radius $x(< R)$. Let I' be current through this loop, then

$$I' = \left(\frac{I}{\pi R^2}\right)\pi x^2 = \left(\frac{x^2}{R^2}\right) I$$

According to Ampere's law

$$\oint \mathbf{B} \cdot d\mathbf{l} = \mu_0 I'$$

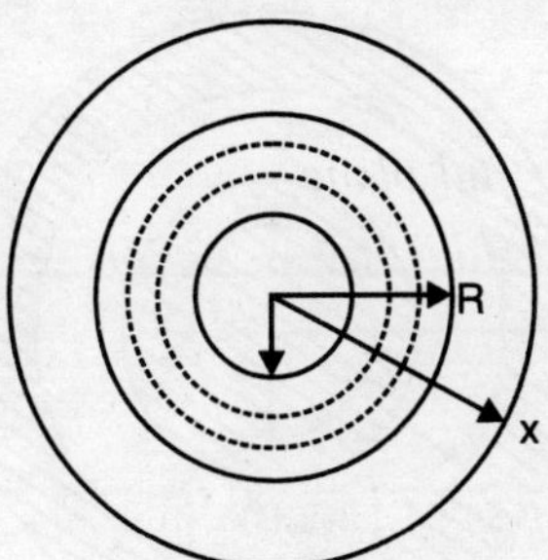

Fig. 3.31

$$B(2\pi x) = \mu_0 \left(\frac{x^2}{R^2} \right) I$$

$$B = \frac{\mu_0 I x}{2\pi R^2}$$

***Example* 6:** *A coaxial cable consists of two concentric cylindrical conductors, the inner one has radius a and the outer one has inner radius b and outer radius c. The two conductors carry equal and opposite current I. Find the magnetic field B at a distance r,*

(*i*) *within the inner conductor* ($r < a$)

(*ii*) *in the space between the two conductors* ($a < r < b$)

(*iii*) *within the outer conductor* ($b < r < c$)

(*iv*) *outside the cable* ($r > c$)

***Solution*:** (*i*) The cross-section of the cable is shown in the Fig. 3.32. Imagine an Amperian loop of radius $r > a$, lying wholly within the inner conductor. According to Ampere's law,

$$\oint \mathbf{B} \cdot d\mathbf{l} = \mu_0 I_1$$

$$B(2\pi r) = \mu_0 \left(\frac{\pi r^2}{\pi a^2} \right) I_1$$

$$B = \frac{\mu_0 I r}{2\pi a^2} \qquad r < a \qquad \text{...(3.148)}$$

(*ii*) If we imagine an Amperian loop $r > a$, then by Ampere's law we have

$$\oint \mathbf{B} \cdot d\mathbf{l} = \mu_0 I$$

$$B(2\pi r) = \mu_0 I$$

$$B = \frac{\mu_0 I}{2\pi r}$$

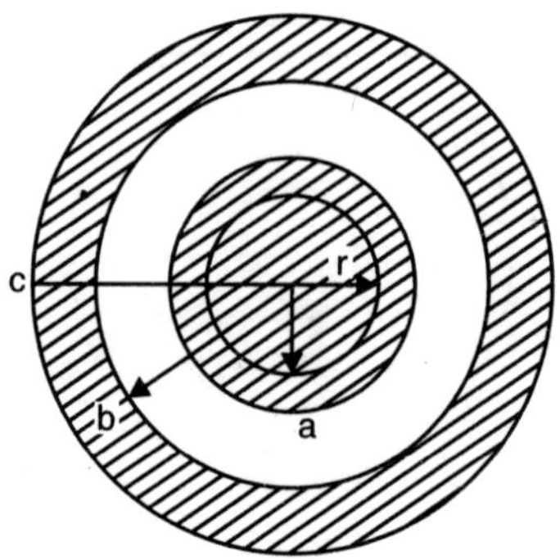

Fig. 3.32

(*iii*) If we imagine an Amperian loop of radius $r > b$, $r < c$

$$\oint \mathbf{B}\cdot d\mathbf{l} = \mu_0 I_2$$

where
$$I_2 = I - \frac{\pi\left(r^2 - b^2\right)}{\pi\left(c^2 - b^2\right)} I_1$$

After simplification we obtain

$$B = \frac{\mu_0 I}{2\pi r}\left(\frac{c^2 - r^2}{c^2 - b^2}\right)$$

(*iv*) Applying Ampere's law over a circular loop of radius $r > c$ we have

$$\oint \mathbf{B}\cdot d\mathbf{l} = 0$$

$$B = 0$$

because the net current through the Amperian loop is zero.

Example 7: *A thin insulated wire forms a plane spiral of N turns. It carries a current I. The inner and the outer radii of the spiral are a and b. Show that (i) the magnetic field at the centre of the coil is*

$$B = \frac{\mu_0 NI}{2(b-a)} ln\frac{b}{a}$$

(*ii*) *the magnetic moment of the coil is*

$$m = \frac{1}{3}\pi NI\left(a^2 + ab + b^2\right)$$

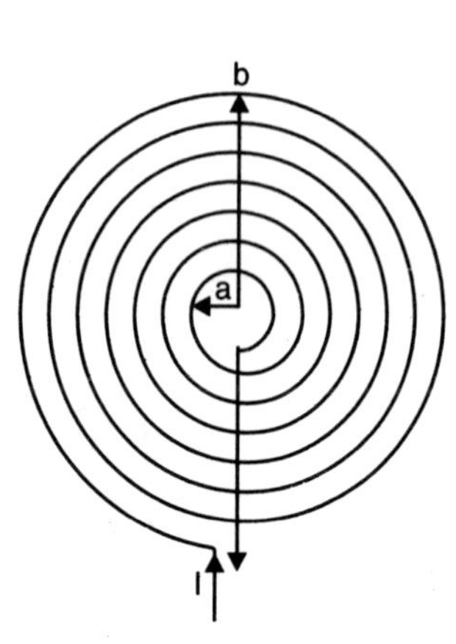

Solution:

(*i*) The number of turns between the radii r and $r + dr$ is

$$dn = \left(\frac{N}{b-a}\right) dr$$

The magnetic field of this part of the coil at the centre is

$$dB = \frac{\mu_0 I}{2r} dn = \frac{\mu_0 I}{2r}\left(\frac{N}{b-a}\right) dr$$

The magnetic field of the whole spiral

$$B = \frac{\mu_0 NI}{2(b-a)} \int_a^b \frac{dr}{r} = \frac{\mu_0 NI}{2(b-a)} ln\frac{b}{a}$$

(*ii*) Magnetic moment of the part of the coil within the radii r and $r + dr$ is,

$$dm = (dn) I \left(\pi r^2\right) = \left(\frac{\pi NI}{b-a}\right) r^2 dr$$

$$m = \int dm = \left(\frac{\pi NI}{b-a}\right) \int_a^b r^2 dr = \left(\frac{\pi NI}{b-a}\right)\left(\frac{b^3 - a^3}{3}\right)$$

$$= \frac{1}{3} \pi NI \left(b^2 + ab + a^2\right)$$

***Example* 8:** *A long thin conductor of width 'a' arries a current I. Calculate the magnetic field B at a point lying in the plane of the conductor at a distance d from its nearest edge.*

Solution:

Consider a current filament of width dx as shown in the Fig. 3.33. The magnetic field of this element at the point in question is

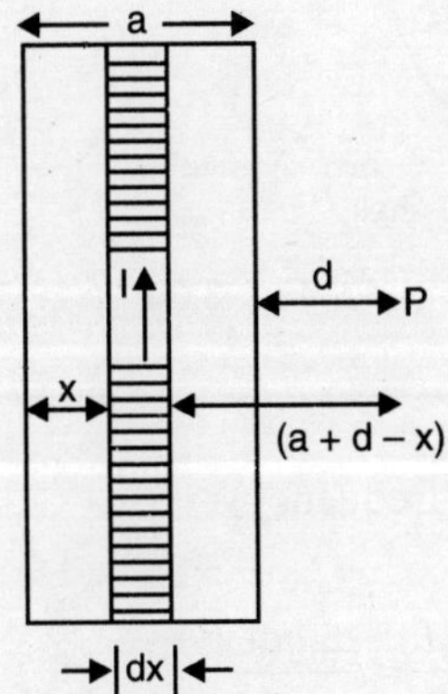

Fig. 3.33

$$dB = \frac{\mu_0 dI}{2\pi(a + d - x)}$$

where dI is the current in the filament.

$$dI = \frac{I}{a} dx$$

B due to the entire conductor is

$$B = \frac{\mu_0 I}{2\pi a}\int_0^a \frac{dx}{(a+d-x)} = \frac{\mu_0 I}{2\pi a}\ln\left(\frac{a+d}{d}\right)$$

Example 9: *In the following figures we have a ring, a circular disc. a spherical shell and a sphere each of radius R. Each of them carries a charge q and rotates about its axis of symmetry with angular velocity ω. Calculate (i) the magnetic field at the centre of the ring, disc and spherical shell, (ii) in each case the ratio of magnetic moment to the angular momentum.*

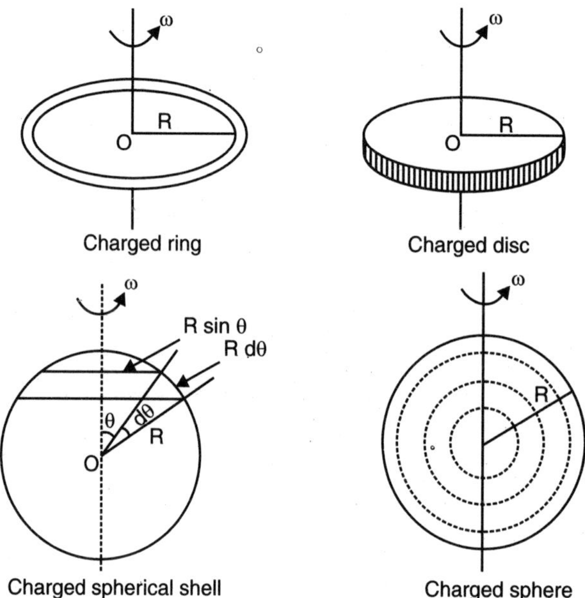

Fig. 3.34

Solution:

Ring. Current in the ring I = (charge) (frequency) $= \frac{q\omega}{2\pi}$

Magnetic field at the centre $B = \frac{\mu_0 I}{2R} = \frac{\mu_0 q\omega}{4\pi R}$

Magnetic moment $m = IA = \frac{1}{2} q\omega R^2$

Angular momentum $L = \mathscr{I}\omega = MR^2\omega$

where M = mass of ring.

$$\frac{m}{L} = \frac{q}{2M}$$

Disc. Consider an elemental ring of radius *r* and width *dr*. Charge over this ring is

$$dq = (2\pi r dr)\frac{q}{\pi R^2} = \frac{2qrdr}{R^2}$$

Current associated with this ring

$$dI = dq \cdot \frac{\omega}{2\pi} = \frac{q\omega r dr}{\pi R^2}$$

Magnetic field of this current at the centre

$$dB = \frac{\mu_0 dI}{2r} = \frac{\mu_0 q\omega}{2\pi R^2} dr$$

$$\therefore \qquad B = \frac{\mu_0 q\omega}{2\pi R^2}\int_0^R dr = \frac{\mu_0 \omega q}{2\pi R}$$

Magnetic moment of the elementary ring

$$dm = (dI)(A)\left(\frac{q\omega r dr}{\pi R^2}\right)(\pi r^2) = \frac{q\omega}{R^2} r^3 dr$$

$$\therefore \qquad m = \frac{q\omega}{R^2}\int_0^R r^3 dr = \frac{1}{4}\omega q R^2$$

Angular momentum of the disc

$$L = \mathscr{I}\omega = \frac{1}{2}MR^2\omega$$

$$\therefore \qquad \frac{m}{L} = \frac{q}{2M}$$

Spherical shell. Consider an elementary ring at angular position θ and of angular width *d*θ as shown in the Fig. 3.34. Area of this ring is $(2\pi R\sin\theta)\,(R\,d\theta)$. Charge on this ring is

$$dq = (2\pi R\sin\theta \cdot R d\theta) \times \left(\frac{q}{4\pi R^2}\right)$$

Current associated with the rotation of this ring

$$dI = (dq)\left(\frac{\omega}{2\pi}\right) = \frac{q\omega \sin\theta d\theta}{4\pi}$$

Magnetic field of this elementary current at the centre of the shell is

$$dB = \frac{\mu_0 (R\sin\theta)^2 .(dI)}{2R^3} = \frac{\mu_0 \omega q \sin^3\theta\, d\theta}{8\pi R}$$

Magnetic field of the spherical shell

$$B = \frac{\mu_0 \omega q}{8\pi R}\int_0^x \sin^3\theta d\theta = \frac{\mu_0 \omega q}{6\pi R}$$

Magnetic moment of the elementary ring

$$dm = (dI)(\pi R^2 \sin^2\theta) = \frac{1}{4} q\omega R^2 \sin^3\theta d\theta$$

$$m = q\omega R^2 \int_0^{\pi} \sin^3\theta d\theta = \frac{1}{3} q\omega R^2$$

Angular momentum of the shell

$$L = \mathscr{I}\omega = \frac{2}{3} MR^2\omega$$

$$\frac{m}{L} = \frac{q}{2M}$$

Sphere. Volume element in spherical polar coordinate is

$$d\tau = r^2 \sin\theta \, dr \, d\theta \, d\phi$$

Charge in this volume elements,

$$d\tau = (d\tau)\frac{q}{\frac{4}{3}\pi R^3} = \frac{3q}{4\pi R^3} r^2 \sin\theta \, dr \, d\theta \, d\phi$$

This elementary charge rotates in a circle of radius $r \sin\theta$ and is equivalent to a circular current element.

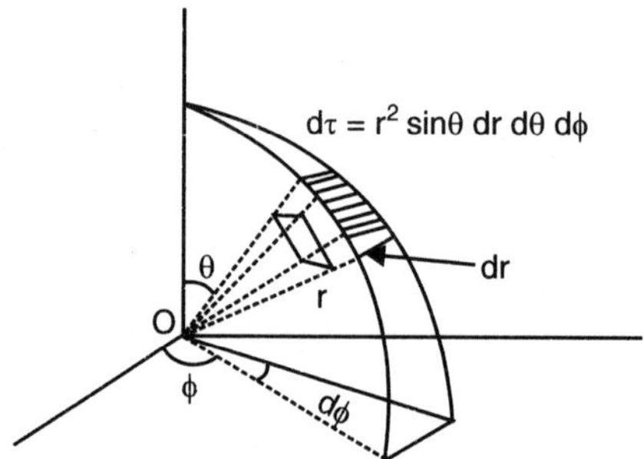

Fig. 3.35. A volume element in spherical polar coordinates.

$$dI = dq\frac{\omega}{2\pi} = \frac{3q\omega}{8\pi^2 R^3} r^2 \sin\theta \, dr \, d\theta \, d\phi$$

Magnetic moment associated with this current is

$$dm = A(dI) = \pi(r\sin\theta)^2 \left[\frac{3q\omega r^2 \sin\theta \, dr \, d\theta \, d\phi}{8\pi^2 R^3}\right]$$

$$= \frac{3q\omega}{8\pi R^3} r^4 \sin^3\theta \, dr \, d\theta \, d\phi$$

Magnetic moment of the sphere is

$$m = \frac{3q\omega}{8\pi R^3} \int_{r=0}^{R} \int_{\theta=0}^{\pi} \int_{\phi=0}^{2\pi} \left(r^4 dr\right)\left(\sin^3\theta d\theta\right) d\phi$$

$$= \frac{3q\omega}{8\pi R^3}\left[\frac{R^5}{5}\right]\left[\frac{4}{3}\right][2\pi]$$

$$= \frac{1}{5} q\omega R^2$$

Angular momentum of the sphere

$$L = \mathscr{I}\omega = \frac{2}{5} MR^2 \omega$$

$$\frac{m}{L} = \frac{q}{2M}$$

In all the examples, we have seen that the ratio of magnetic moment to angular momentum is the same. This ratio is called the gyromagnetic ratio.

***Example* 10:** *A toroidal solenoid of rectangular cross-section is shown in the Fig. 3.36. Internal and external radii are 10 cm and 20 cm respectively. Height of the toroid is 5 cm and the total number of turns are 1000. If the toroid carries a current of 2.0 ampere, find the magnetic flux through its cross-section.*

***Solution*:** Magnetic field at a distance r from the centre of the toroid is

$$B = \frac{\mu_0 NI}{2\pi r}$$

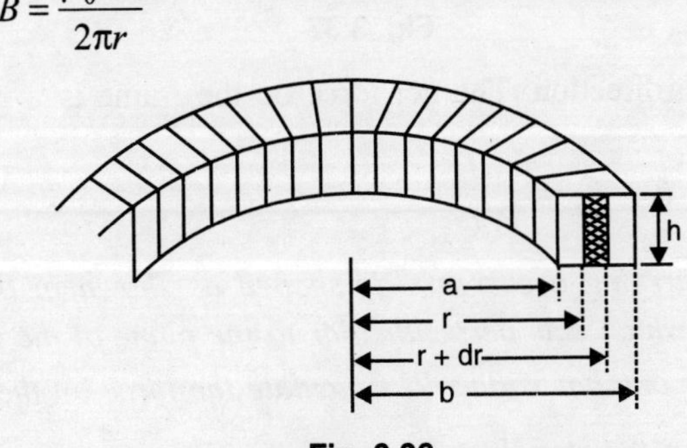

Fig. 3.36

Flux through the cross-section of toroid is

$$\Phi = N\int \mathbf{B}\cdot d\mathbf{S} = N\int_a^b B\,h\,dr = \frac{\mu_0 N^2 Ih}{2\pi}\int_a^b \frac{dr}{r} = \frac{\mu_0 N^2 Ih}{2\pi} ln\frac{b}{a}$$

$$= \left[\frac{4\pi\times 10^{-7}\times(1000)^2\times 2\times 0.05}{2\pi}\right]\ln 2$$

$= 13.9 \times 10^{-3}$ Weber

***Example* 11:** *A square frame of side 'a' carries a current I. A straight wire carrying a current I_0 is placed parallel to one side of the square in the same plane. The nearest side of the frame is at a distance 'a' from the wire. Find the net force acting on the frame.*

Solution: Magnetic field of the straight conductor at the location of the side marked 1 of the square frame is

$$B = \frac{\mu_0 I_0}{2\pi a}$$

Force on side 1 is

$$F_1 = IB_1 a = \frac{\mu_0 I I_0}{2\pi}$$

Forces on sides 2 and 4 are equal and opposite and hence cancel out. Force of the side 3 is

$$F_3 = IB_3 a = \frac{\mu_0 I I_0}{4\pi}$$

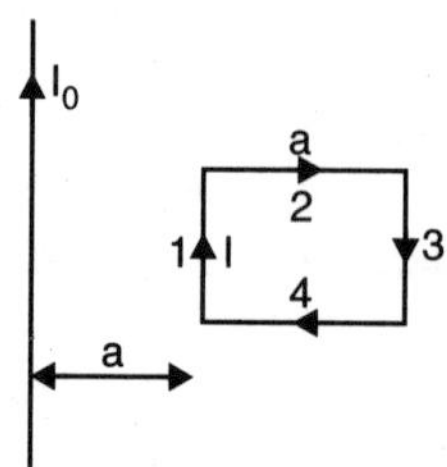

Fig. 3.37

F_1 and F_3 are opposite in direction. The net force on the frame is

$$F = F_1 - F_3 = \frac{\mu_0 I I_0}{4\pi}$$

***Example* 12:** *A conductor carrying a current I is shaped as shown in the Fig. 3.38. The wire is placed in a magnetic field B which acts perpendicular to the plane of the wire. The straight portion has lenght L and the circular one has radius R. Calculate the force on the wire.*

***Solution*:** Forces F_1 and F_3 on the straight portion are:

$$F_1 = IBL$$

$$F_3 = IBL$$

The force on a current element $I\,dl\left(= IR\,d\theta\right)$ is

$$dF = I\,B\,dl = I\,BR\,d\theta$$

where angles θ and $d\theta$ are defined in the Fig. 3.38

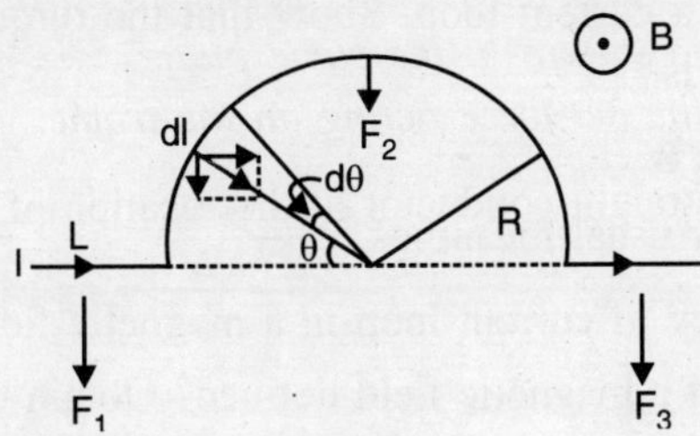

Fig. 3.38

Force dF acts along the inward radius. Horizontal and vertical components of dF are $dF\cos\theta$ and $dF\sin\theta$. Total force on the circular part is given by

$$\sum dF\cos\theta = 0 \qquad \text{(Horizontal)}$$

$$\sum dF\sin\theta = 0 \qquad \text{(Vertical)}$$

Force on the circular part is

$$F_2 = \int dF\sin\theta = IBR\int_0^\pi \sin\theta\, d\theta = 2\,IBR$$

Total force acting on the entire length of wire

$$F = F_1 + F_2 + F_3 = 2I\,B(L+R)$$

QUESTIONS AND PROBLEMS

1. State Bio-Savart law. Use this law to find the magnetic field of a straight current carrying conductor at an external point. Investigate the formula when the length of conductor becomes infinite.
2. Find the magnetic field of a circular coil at an axial point.
3. Explain how the variation of magnetic field along the axis of a circular current has been utilized to obtain a uniform field at considerable extent. Determine the field at the centre of coil.
4. Calculate the magnetic field of a solenoid at a point on the axis (*i*) at one end, (*ii*) at the centre, (*iii*) outside the solenoid. Investigate the formulae obtained in the limit $\frac{R}{L} \to 0$ where R is the radius and L is the length of solenoid.
5. Derive an expression for the magnetic field at the centre of a long solenoid. Show that the field at the ends of such a solenoid is one half that at the centre.
6. Prove the following relations :

$$\nabla\cdot\mathbf{B} = 0$$

$$\nabla\times\mathbf{B} = \mu_0\mathbf{J}$$

and explain their meaning.

7. Define magnetic moment of a current loop. Show that the torque acting on a current loop in a homogeneous magnetic field is

$$\boldsymbol{\tau} = \mathbf{m} \times \mathbf{B}$$

where the symbols have their usual meanings.

8. Show that the potential energy of current loop in a magnetic field is $U = -\mathbf{m}\cdot\mathbf{B}$.

9. How is the vector potential of a magnetic field defined? Obtain the vector potential of a uniform magnetic field.

10. Show that the vector potential of a current loop at a distance r is given by

$$\mathbf{A} = \frac{\mu_0}{4\pi} \cdot \frac{\mathbf{m} \times \mathbf{r}}{r^3}$$

11. Calculate the magnetic field of a following current distributions at point O. The straight part of the conductors shown without limit have infinite length.

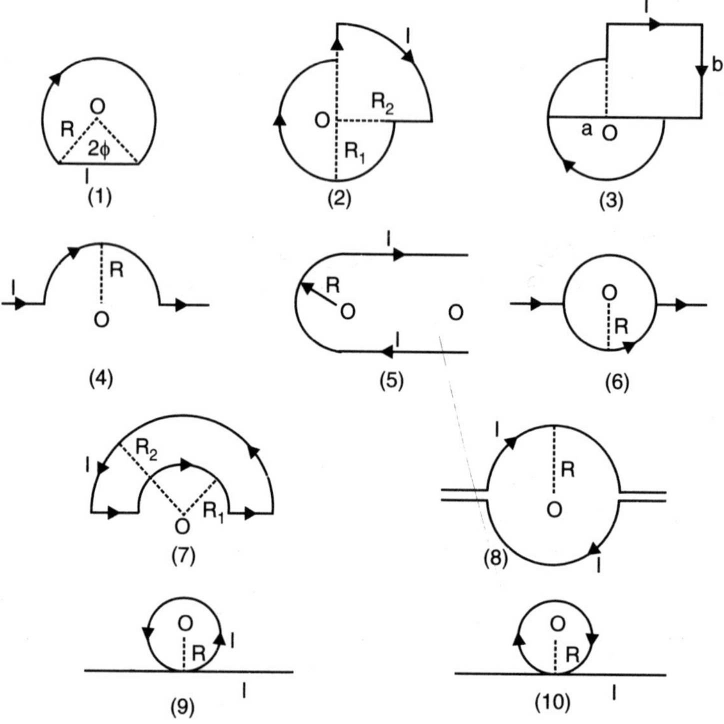

Fig. 3.39

Ans. (*i*) $\dfrac{\mu_0 I}{2\pi R}(\pi - \phi + \tan\phi)$

(*ii*) $\dfrac{\mu_0 I}{4\pi}\left(\dfrac{2\pi - \phi}{R_1} + \dfrac{\phi}{R_2}\right)$

(*iii*) $\frac{\mu_0 I}{4\pi}\left(\frac{3\pi}{4a}+\frac{\sqrt{2}}{b}\right)$

(*iv*) $\frac{\mu_0 I}{4\pi}\left(\frac{\pi}{R}\right)$

(*v*) $\frac{\mu_0 I}{4\pi}\left(\frac{\pi+2}{R}\right)$

(*vi*) Zero

(*vii*) $\frac{\mu_0 I}{4}\left(\frac{1}{R_1}-\frac{1}{R_2}\right)$

(*viii*) $\frac{\mu_0 I}{2\pi R}$ into the page.

(*ix*) $\frac{\mu_0 I}{2R}\left(1+\frac{1}{\pi}\right)$ out of page.

(*x*) $\frac{\mu_0 I}{2R}\left(1-\frac{1}{\pi}\right)$ into the page.

12. A straight conductor of length l subtends an angle 2α at a point lying at a distance R on the perpendicular bisector. Show that the magnetic field at this point is,

$$B=\frac{\mu_0 I\sin\alpha}{2\pi R}=\frac{\mu_0 Il}{2\pi R\sqrt{l^2+4R^2}}$$

where I is the current in the conductor.

13. A square frame of side a carries a current I. Show that the magnetic field at the centre of the frame is

$$B=\frac{2\sqrt{2}\mu_0 I}{\pi a}$$

14. A rectangle of length a and breadth b carries a current I. Show that the magnetic field at the centre is

$$B=\frac{2\mu_0 I\sqrt{a^2+b^2}}{\pi ab}$$

15. Two long parallel wires are at a distance d apart. They carry equal and opposite currents I. Show that the magnetic field at a point on the perpendicular bisector is

$$B=\frac{2\mu_0 Id}{\pi\left(d^2+4R^2\right)}$$

where R is the distance of point of observation from the line joining the wires.

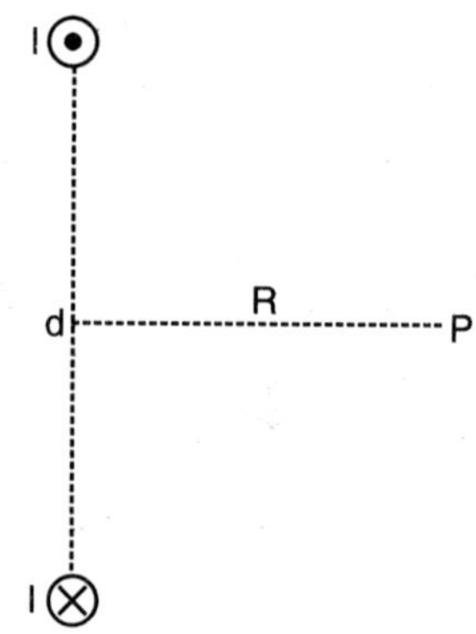

Fig. 3.40

16. Two long straight parallel wires carry equal and opposite currents. Their separation is d. Calculate

(*i*) the magnetic field at a point midway between them.

(*ii*) the magnetic flux through a rectangular frame of length l and breadth b symmetrically placed between the wires in such a way that the frame and the wires lie in a plane.

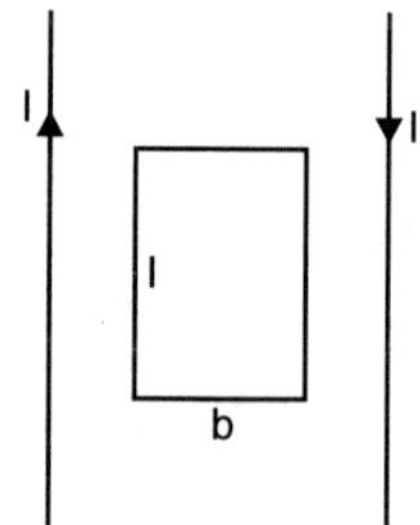

Fig. 3.41

17. A ring has internal radius a, external radius b and thickness h. A straight wire carrying a current I passes through the centre and at right angles to the plane of the ring.

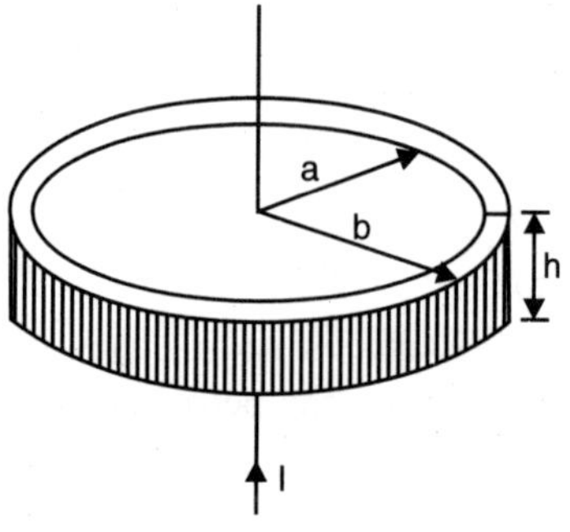

Fig. 3.42

Calculate the flux of magnetic field through the cross-section of the ring.

18. A wooden sphere is wrapped with closely spaced turns of fine wire in a single layer with planes of turns perpendicular to one of its diameter. A current I is made to flow in the windings. Show that the magnetic flux density B at the centre of the sphere is,

$$B = \frac{\mu_0 NI}{4R}$$

where N is the number of turns and R is the radius of the sphere.

19. A solenoid of length 50 cm and radius 5 cm has 1×10^4 turns of wire evenly wrapped on it. A current of 5A flows through it. Calculate

(*i*) the surface current density.

(*ii*) the magnetic field at the centre of the solenoid.

(*iii*) the magnetic moment.

(*iv*) flux through its end plane.

(*v*) flux through its cross-section at the middle point.

20. A toroid with rectangular cross-section carries a current of 10 A. The number of turns is 1000, the ratio of the outer diameter to the inner one is 3:2, and the width is 4 cm. Calculate the magnetic flux through its cross-section.

21. The parameter of a coaxial cable are: the radius of inner conductor $a = 2$ cm, the internal radius of outer conductor b = 3 cm, the external radius of the outer conductor $c = 4$ cm. The inner conductor carries a current of 10 A in one direction and the outer conductor the same current in opposite direction. Calculate the magnetic field at the following distances from the axis of the cable:

(*i*) 1.0 cm (*ii*) 2.5 cm (*iii*) 3.5 cm (*iv*) 5 cm

22. A long straight conductor and a rectangular frame lie in the same plane Fig. 3.43. Calculate the resultant force on the frame.

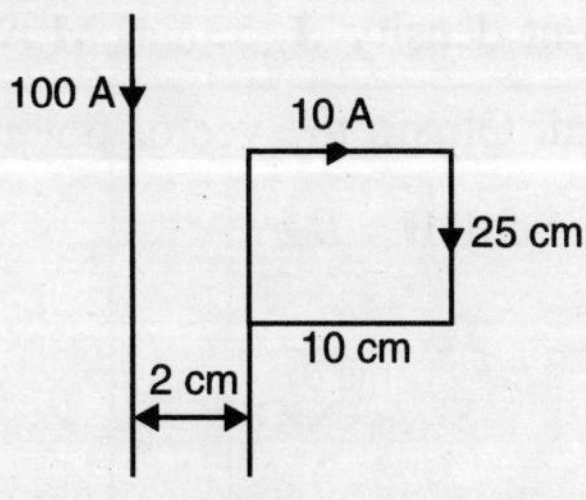

Fig. 3.43

23. A long straight copper tube having inner radius of 1 cm and outer radius 2 cm carries a current of 200 A. Compute the magnetic field at distances of 0.5 cm, 1.5 cm and 4.0 cm from the axis.

Ans: (*i*) 0 (*ii*) 1.1×10^{-3} Wb m^{-2} (*iii*) 1.0×10^{-3} Wb m^{-2}

24. Two protons move parallel to each other with equal velocity 5×10^5 m s^{-1}. Find the ratio of forces of magnetic and electrical interaction.

[**Hint.** $F_e = \dfrac{q^2}{4\pi\varepsilon_0 r^2}$

$$F_m = qvB = qv\left(\frac{\mu_0}{4\pi}\cdot\frac{qv}{r^2}\right)$$

$$F_m / F_e = \mu_0\varepsilon_0 v^2 = (v/c)^2$$

25. Making use of the definition of vector potential

$$\mathbf{A} = \frac{\mu_0}{4\pi}\int \frac{\mathbf{J}}{r}\, d\tau$$

obtain Biot-Savart law.

[**Hint.** $\mathbf{B} = \nabla \times \mathbf{A} = \dfrac{\mu_0}{4\pi} \cdot \displaystyle\int \nabla \times \frac{\mathbf{J}}{r}\, d\tau$

Now use the vector indentity

$$\nabla \times \phi\mathbf{A} = \nabla\phi \times \mathbf{A} + \phi\nabla \times \mathbf{A}$$

in which $\nabla \times \mathbf{J} = 0$, because **J** is independent of observer's coordinates (x, y, z).

26. Define current density vector. Derive the equation of continuity. Discuss the integral and differential forms of Ohm's law.

27. Define vector potential. Compare it with scalar potential. An infinite sheet of charge density σ is in the xy plane and is travelling with velocity $v\hat{y}$. Determine the vector potential and magnetic field at the point $(0,0,z)$.

28. State the Biot-Savart law. Derive the magnetic field at the axis of a circular loop.

29. Prove that the magnetisation current density $\mathbf{J}_m = \text{curl}\,\mathbf{M}$ where **M** is the magnetisation.

30. Define and discuss vector potential. Obtain the vector potential for a uniform magnetic field.

31. Obtain vector potential due to the field $\mathbf{B} = B\hat{\mathbf{z}}$.

OOO

CHAPTER 4 Electromagnetic Induction

4.1. FARADAY LAW OF ELECTROMAGNETIC INDUCTION

With the help of a series of experiments, Faraday showed that a current may be set up in a conducting loop by changing magnetic flux through it. The conclusions of his experiments may be stated as follows:

A time varying magnetic field produces an electric field. If a conducting loop is placed in this electric field, an electromotive force (emf), which is defined as the closed line integral of induced electric field around the loop is set up. The induced emf equals the negative time rate of change of magnetic flux passing through the loop. The direction of emf is such that it always opposes the cause that produces it (Lenz's law). In mathematical form, Faraday law is expressed as

$$\text{Induced } emf \quad \varepsilon = \oint \mathbf{E}\cdot d\mathbf{l} = -\frac{d\Phi}{dt} \qquad \text{...(4.1)}$$

Where **E** is the induced electric field and Φ is the magnetic flux through the loop. The electric field produced by time varying magnetic field is *non-conservative.*

4.2. FARADAY LAW IN INTEGRAL AND DIFFERENTIAL FORM

Suppose that a conducting loop enclosing an area S is placed in a time varying magnetic field **B** (t). If **E** is the induced electric field in the loop, then the induced *emf* is given by

$$\varepsilon = \oint_{\text{loop}} \mathbf{E}\cdot d\mathbf{l}$$

The magnetic flux passing through the coil is

$$\Phi = \int_S \mathbf{B}\cdot d\mathbf{S}$$

According to Faraday law

$$\oint_{\text{loop}} \mathbf{E}\cdot d\mathbf{l} = -\frac{\partial}{\partial t}\int_S \mathbf{B}\cdot d\mathbf{S}$$

or $$\oint_{\text{loop}} \mathbf{E}\cdot d\mathbf{l} = -\int_S \frac{\partial \mathbf{B}}{\partial t}\cdot d\mathbf{S} \qquad ...(4.2)$$

Equation (4.2) is known as the *integral form of Faraday's law*. This equation represents one of the fundamental law of electromagnetism and is called *fourth Maxwell's equation for electromagnetic field.*

Transforming the line integral of eqn. (4.2) into surface integral by Stokes' theorem we have

$$\int_S \nabla\times\mathbf{E}\cdot d\mathbf{S} = -\int_S \frac{\partial \mathbf{B}}{\partial t}\cdot d\mathbf{S}$$

Since surface enclosed by loop is arbitrary, we must have

$$\nabla\times\mathbf{E} = -\frac{\partial \mathbf{B}}{\partial t} \qquad ...(4.3)$$

This is *Faraday law of electromagnetic induction or fourth Maxwell's equation in differential form.*

The induced electric field E produced by time varying magnetic field is different from that produced by stationary charges in one respect. The field lines of electrostatic field can always be drawn to start on a positive charge and end on a negative charge and the closed line integral of electrostatic field is always zero and hence the electric field is conservative. This property of electric field permitted to define a scalar potential φ.

Electrostatic field : $\oint \mathbf{E}\cdot d\mathbf{l} = 0, \quad \Rightarrow \quad \nabla\times\mathbf{E} = 0 \quad \Rightarrow \quad \mathbf{E} = -\nabla\varphi$

The lines of force of induced electric field have neither beginning nor end i.e. they form closed loops. The closed line integral of the induced electric field is not zero and therefore it is not conservative.

Induced electric field : $\oint \mathbf{E}\cdot d\mathbf{l} = -\int \frac{\partial \mathbf{B}}{\partial t}\cdot d\mathbf{S} \quad \Rightarrow \quad \nabla\times\mathbf{E} = -\frac{\partial \mathbf{B}}{\partial t}, \quad \mathbf{E} \neq \nabla\varphi$

The magnetic field **B** can be expressed in terms of vector potential **A** as

$$\mathbf{B} = \nabla \times \mathbf{A}$$

In terms of potential **A** we can write eqn. (4.3) as

$$\nabla\times\mathbf{E} = -\frac{\partial}{\partial t}(\nabla\times\mathbf{A})$$

or $$\nabla\times\left(\mathbf{E} + \frac{\partial \mathbf{A}}{\partial t}\right) = 0 \qquad ...(4.4)$$

A solution to eqn. (4.4) is

$$\mathbf{E} + \frac{\partial \mathbf{A}}{\partial t} = -\nabla\psi$$

or $$\mathbf{E} = -\frac{\partial \mathbf{A}}{\partial t} - \nabla\psi \qquad ...(4.5)$$

Where ψ is a scalar function. This is the general relation giving the induced electric field in terms of vector potential and scalar potential.

***Example* 1:** *A circular conducting loop of radius r is placed in a uniform time varying magnetic field* **B**, *the plane of the loop being normal to magnetic field. What is the magnitude of the electric field in the loop?*

***Solution*:** According to Faraday law

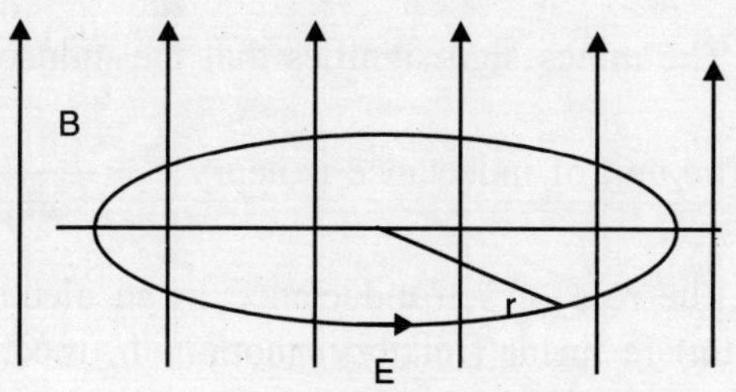

Fig. 4.1

$$\oint_{\text{loop}} \mathbf{E} \cdot d\mathbf{l} = -\int_S \frac{\partial \mathbf{B}}{\partial t} \cdot d\mathbf{S}$$

$$E(2\pi r) = -\frac{\partial B}{\partial t}(\pi r^2)$$

$$E = -\frac{1}{2} r \frac{\partial B}{\partial t}$$

The electric field has circumferential direction. If **B** is decreasing, **E** points in counter clockwise direction when viewed from above.

***Example* 2:** *The magnetic field inside a long solenoid varies as B = kt, where k is a constant. A ring of radius r is placed coaxially inside the solenoid. Find the electric field induced in the ring. If the resistance of the ring is R, what is the current in the ring?*

***Solution*:** The electric field in the ring is given by

$$\oint_{\text{ring}} \mathbf{E} \cdot d\mathbf{l} = -\int_S \frac{\partial B}{\partial t} . dS$$

$$\oint_{\text{ring}} E dr = -\int_S k dS$$

$$E(2\pi r) = -k(\pi r^2)$$

$$E = -\frac{1}{2} rk$$

Induced *emf* in the ring $\varepsilon = -\int_S \frac{\partial B}{\partial t} dS = -k \int_S dS = -k(\pi r^2)$

Current in the ring $i = \frac{\varepsilon}{R} = \frac{k\pi r^2}{R}$

4.3. SELF INDUCTION

When a current passes in a coil, the magnetic field produced by the current threads the coil itself. If the current in the coil varies with time, so does the magnetic flux passing through the coil. The changing flux produces an induced *emf* and hence an induced current in the coil. This phenomenon is called *self induction*. The magnetic flux Φ linked with the coil is proportional to the current *I* in it.

$$\Phi = LI \qquad ...(4.6)$$

Where L is proportionality constant and is called *coefficient of self-induction* or *self inductance* of the coil. It depends on the geometry (shape and size) and the permeability μ of the medium in which the coil is placed. The induced *emf* produced in the coil is

$$\varepsilon = -\frac{d\Phi}{dt} = -L\frac{dI}{dt} \qquad ...(4.7)$$

The minus sign signifies that the induced *emf* is directed so as to oppose the cause producing it. The unit of inductance is henry $\left(= \frac{\text{volt. sec}}{\text{amp}}\right)$.

The role of self-inductance in an electrical circuit is analogous to that of mass (moment of inertia) in linear (rotatory) motion. In mechanical system, the mass (moment of inertia) opposes any change in the state of motion, in the similar way the self-inductance opposes the change in current in electric circuit. This analogy is displayed in the following table.

Table 4.1

Mechanical system		**Electrical system**
Linear motion	Rotatory motion	
Equation of motion $m\ddot{x} = m\frac{dv}{dt} = F$	$I\ddot{\theta} = I\frac{d\omega}{dt} = \tau$	$L\ddot{q} = L\frac{dI}{dt} = V\text{(voltage)}$
Momentum $p = m\dot{x} = mv$	Angular momentum $J = I\dot{\theta} = I\omega$	flux $\Phi = L\dot{q} = LI$
Kinetic energy $T = \frac{1}{2}m\dot{x}^2$	Kinetic energy $T = \frac{1}{2}I\dot{\theta}^2$	Magnetic energy $U = \frac{1}{2}LI^2$

4.4. SELF-INDUCTANCE OF A SOLENOID

Consider a long solenoid of length l, cross-section A and number of turn per unit length n. Let I be the current in the solenoid. The magnetic field inside the solenoid is

$$B = \mu_0 nI$$

Flux through each turn of the solenoid is BA. Total flux through the solenoid is

$$\Phi = BAnl = \mu_0 Aln^2 I$$

Self-inductance of the solenoid is

$$L = \frac{\Phi}{I} = \mu_0 Aln^2$$

When a magnetic substance of relative permeability μ_r is inserted inside the solenoid, its self-inductance becomes

$$L = \mu_0\mu_r Aln^2 \qquad ...(4.8)$$

4.5. SELF-INDUCTANCE OF A TOROID

(a) Rectangular Cross-section

Let the parameters of the toroid be as follows:

N = number of turns, a = internal radius, b = external radius, h = thickness and I = current in the windings. The magnetic field inside a toroid at a distance r ($a < r < b$) from its centre is

$$B = \frac{\mu_0 NI}{2\pi\ r}$$

Magnetic flux through the cross-section of the toroid

$$\Phi = N\int \mathbf{B}\cdot d\mathbf{S} = N\int_a^b \left(\frac{\mu_0 NI}{2\pi r}\right)(hdr) = \frac{\mu_0 N^2 Ih}{2\pi}\ln\frac{b}{a}$$

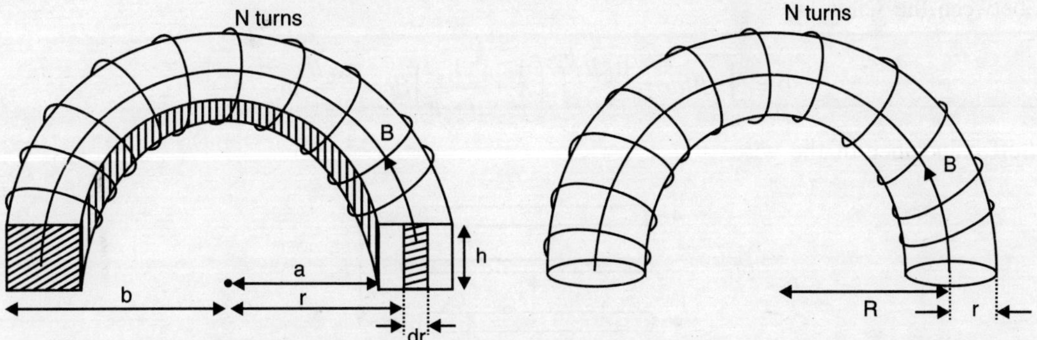

Fig. 4.2. A toroid (a) Rectangular cross-section (b) Circular cross-section.

Self inductance of toroid

$$L = \frac{\Phi}{I} = \frac{\mu_0 N^2 h}{2\pi}\ln\frac{b}{a} \qquad \text{...(4.9a)}$$

(b) Circular Cross-section

Let r be the radius cross-section of the coil and R be the mean radius of the toroid. N denote the total number of turns on it. If the toroid carries a current I, the magnetic field at a distance R from the centre of toroid is

$$B = \frac{\mu_0 NI}{2\pi R}$$

This field is along the circumferential direction as shown in the Fig. 4.2. Magnetic flux linked with coils of the toroid is

$$\Phi = BNA, \text{ where } A = \pi r^2$$

$$\therefore \qquad \Phi = \frac{\mu_0 NI}{2\pi R}\cdot N(\pi r^2)$$

Self-inductance of the toroid

$$L = \frac{\Phi}{I} = \frac{\mu_0 N^2 r^2}{2R} \qquad \text{...(4.9b)}$$

4.6. SELF-INDUCTANCE OF TWO THIN LONG PARALLEL WIRES

Let us calculate the self-inductance of two parallel wires each of length l and radius a. The wires, which are at distance d apart, carry equal and opposite currents. The magnetic field at a distance r from one of the wires is

$$B = \frac{\mu_0 I}{2\pi r} + \frac{\mu_0 I}{2\pi(d-r)}$$

Consider an element of area in the form of a rectangle of length l and width dr in the plane of the wires as shown in the figure. Magnetic flux through this area is $B(ldr)$. Flux through the entire area between the wires is

$$\Phi = \int_a^{d-a} Bldr = \frac{\mu_0 Il}{2\pi}\int_a^{d-a}\left(\frac{1}{r} + \frac{1}{d-r}\right)dr = \frac{\mu_0 Il}{\pi}\ln\frac{d-a}{a}$$

Self-inductance of the wires

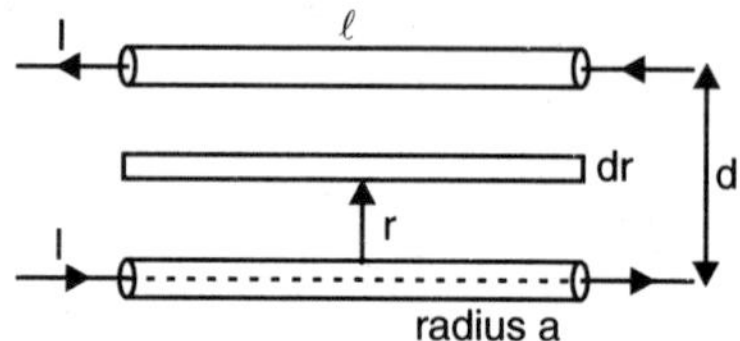

Fig. 4.3.

$$L = \frac{\Phi}{I} = \frac{\mu_0 l}{\pi}\ln\frac{d-a}{a} \qquad \text{...(4.10)}$$

4.7. MUTUAL INDUCTION

Suppose we have two coils 1 and 2 lying close together. When a current I_1 is switched on in coil 1, it sets up a magnetic flux Φ_1 through the coil 1 and a part of this flux is also linked with the coil 2. When the current I_1 is made to vary with time, the magnetic flux Φ_{21} linked with coil 2 also varies and this varying flux produces an induced *emf* and hence induced current in the coil 2. This phenomenon is called *mutual induction.* It is worth to notice that the coils 1 and 2 are not directly coupled still a varying current in one coil can produce a voltage and current in the other coil. The flux linked with the coil 2 is proportional to the current I_1. Thus,

$$\Phi_{21} = M_{21} I_1 \qquad \text{...(4.11)}$$

The constant of proportionality M_{21} is called the mutual inductance of the coils 1 and 2. Similarly, when a current I_2 is set up in the coil 2, the magnetic flux Φ_{12} linked with the coil 1 is proportional to the current I_2. That is,

$$\Phi_{12} = M_{12} I_2 \qquad ...(4.12)$$

Here the proportionality constant M_{12} is again called the mutual inductance of the pair of coils. It can be shown that

$$M_{12} = M_{21} = M, \quad \text{say}$$

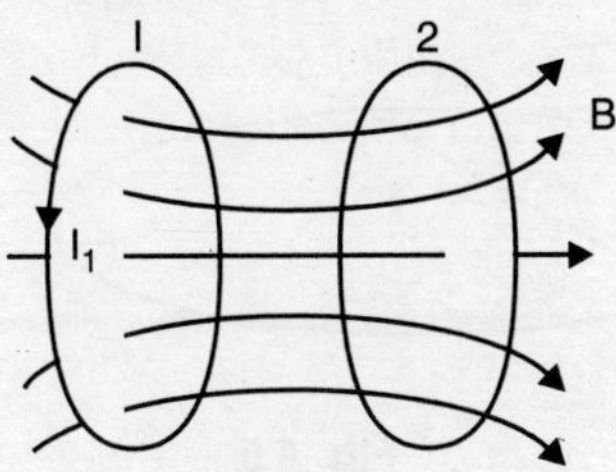

Fig. 4.4

Hereafter we shall use the symbol M for the mutual inductance. The induced *emf* in coil 2 due to varying current I_1 in coil 1 is

$$\varepsilon_{21} = -\frac{d\Phi_{21}}{dt} = -M_{21}\frac{dI_1}{dt} \qquad ...(4.13)$$

Similarly, the induced *emf* in coil 1 due to varying current I_2 in coil 2 is

$$\varepsilon_{12} = -\frac{d\Phi_{12}}{dt} = -M_{12}\frac{dI_2}{dt} \qquad ...(4.14)$$

Mutual inductance of a pair of coils depends on the geometry of coils and their orientation with respect to each other. If the coils are arranged in such a way that the larger fraction of flux produced by one coil is linked with the other coil, the mutual inductance is large. On the other hand, if a small fraction of flux produced by one coil is linked with the other coil, the mutual inductance is small. If the space between the coils is filled with magnetic material of high permeability, the mutual inductance is enhanced by a large factor. M is also measured in *henry.*

4.8. RECIPROCITY THEOREM

Suppose we have two loops C_1 and C_2 with current I_1 in the C_1. The magnetic flux linked with the loop C_2 is

$$\Phi_{21} = \int_{S_2} \mathbf{B}_1 \cdot d\mathbf{S}_2 = \int_{S_{21}} \nabla \times \mathbf{A}_1 \cdot d\mathbf{S}_2 = \oint_{C_2} \mathbf{A}_1 \cdot d\mathbf{l}_2 \qquad ...(4.15)$$

Where $\mathbf{B}_1$ is the magnetic field due to current I_1 in loop C_1 at the location of an element of area $d\mathbf{S}_2$ of the loop C_2 and $\mathbf{A}_1$ is the vector potential of $\mathbf{B}_1$. The vector potential $\mathbf{A}_1$ is given by

$$\mathbf{A}_1 = \frac{\mu_0 I_1}{4\pi} \oint_{C_1} \frac{dl_1}{r} \qquad ...(4.16)$$

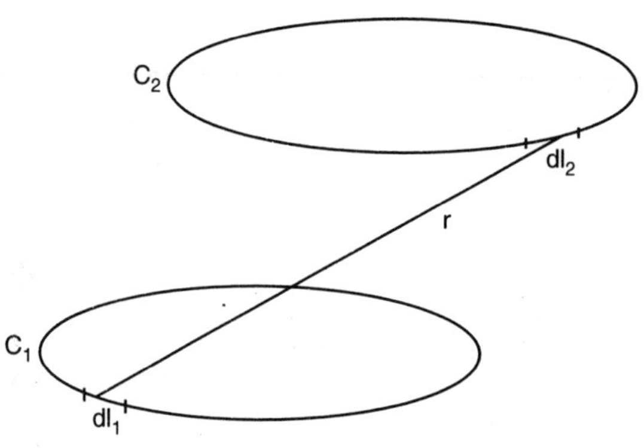

Fig. 4.5

Substituting the expression for $\mathbf{A}_1$ in eqn. (4.15) we have

$$\Phi_{21} = \oint_{C_2} \left(\frac{\mu_0 I_1}{4\pi} \oint_{C_1} \frac{d\mathbf{l}_1}{r} \right) \cdot d\mathbf{l}_2 = \frac{\mu_0 I_1}{4\pi} \oint_{C_2} \oint_{C_1} \frac{d\mathbf{l}_1 \cdot d\mathbf{l}_2}{r} \qquad ...(4.17)$$

By definition, the mutual inductance of the loops is

$$M_{21} = \frac{\mu_0}{4\pi} \oint_{C_2} \oint_{C_1} \frac{d\mathbf{l}_1 \cdot d\mathbf{l}_2}{r} \qquad ...(4.18)$$

This is the *Neumann formula* for the mutual inductance of a pair of coils.

If we run a current I_2 in loop 2, the flux linked with the loop 1 is

$$\Phi_{12} = \int_{S_1} \mathbf{B}_2 \cdot d\mathbf{S}_1 = \oint_{S_1} \nabla \times \mathbf{A}_2 \cdot d\mathbf{S}_1 = \oint_{C_1} \mathbf{A}_2 \cdot d\mathbf{l}_1$$

$$= \oint_{C_1} \left(\oint_{C_2} \frac{\mu_0 I_2}{4\pi} d\mathbf{l}_2 \right) \cdot d\mathbf{l}_1 = \frac{\mu_0 I_2}{4\pi} \oint_{C_1} \oint_{C_2} \frac{d\mathbf{l}_1 \cdot d\mathbf{l}_2}{r} \qquad ...(4.19)$$

Hence, $$M_{12} = \frac{\Phi_{12}}{I_2} = \frac{\mu_0}{4\pi} \oint_{C_1} \oint_{C_2} \frac{d\mathbf{l}_1 \cdot d\mathbf{l}_2}{r} \qquad ...(4.20)$$

From Eqns. (4.18) and (4.20)

$$M_{12} = M_{21} \qquad ...(4.21)$$

4.9. MUTUAL INDUCTANCE OF TWO CIRCULAR COILS

Consider two circular coils coaxially placed at a distance d apart. Let the larger coil has radius a_1 and the smaller coil a_2. The larger coil carries a current I. We assume that the magnetic field of larger coil 1 is uniform over the plane of the smaller coil 2. The magnetic field of larger coil at the position of smaller coil is

$$B = \frac{\mu_0 I a_1^2}{2(a_1^2 + d^2)^{3/2}} \quad ...(4.22)$$

The flux linked with the coil 2 is

$$\Phi_{21} = B(\pi a_2^2) = \frac{\mu_0 \pi I a_1^2 a_2^2}{2(a_1^2 + d^2)^{3/2}} \quad ...(4.23)$$

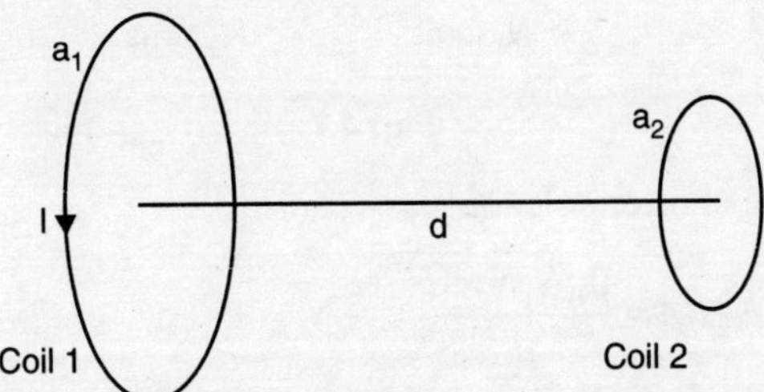

Fig. 4.6

The mutual inductance of the coils is

$$M = \frac{\Phi_{21}}{I} = \frac{\mu_0 \pi a_1^2 a_2^2}{2(a_1^2 + d^2)^{3/2}} \quad ...(4.24)$$

If the coils have very small dimensions, $a_1 << d$, $a_2 << d$ then, from eqn. (4.24)

$$M = \frac{\mu_0 \pi a_1^2 a_2^2}{2d^3} \quad ...(4.25)$$

If the smaller coil lies at the centre of larger coil, $d = 0$ then

$$M = \frac{\mu_0 \pi a_1^2 a_2^2}{2a_1^3} \quad ...(4.26)$$

4.10. MUTUAL INDUCTANCE OF TWO COAXIAL SOLENOIDS

Suppose we have a long solenoid of length l, cross-section A and the total number of turns being N_1. Outside it, we have another short solenoid having total number of turns N_2. The windings of shorter solenoid are wrapped over that of the larger solenoid so that both the solenoids have the same cross-section. When a current I is set up in the larger solenoid, it produces a magnetic field inside it whose magnitude is

$$B = \mu_0 n I = \frac{\mu_0 N_1 I}{l} \quad ...(4.27)$$

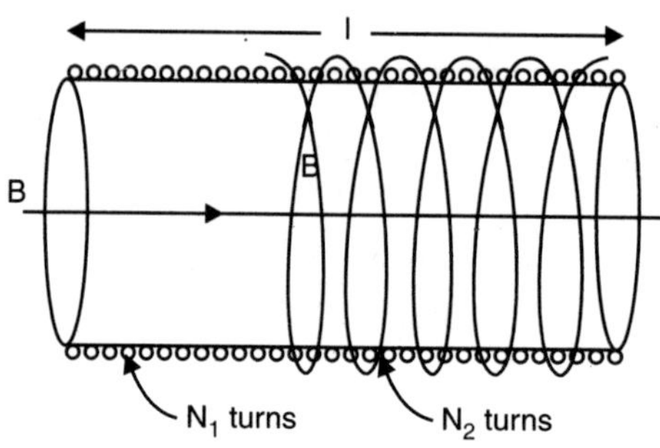

Fig. 4.7

Total flux linked with the shorter solenoid is

$$\Phi = N_2BA = \frac{\mu_0 N_1 N_2 AI}{l} \quad \text{...(4.28)}$$

Mutual inductance of the solenoids is

$$M = \frac{\mu_0 N_1 N_2 A}{l} \quad \text{...(4.29)}$$

4.11. COUPLED CIRCUITS

Two circuits are said to be coupled if current or voltages in one circuit alters by changing the current or voltage in the other circuit. Coupled circuits are of two types: (i) Directly coupled circuits (ii) Indirectly coupled circuits.

(*i*) **Directly Coupled Circuits:** Two circuits are said to be directly coupled if they are interconnected with the help of any circuit elements or their combination. A directly coupled circuit is shown in the Fig. 4.8.

(*ii*) **Indirectly Coupled Circuits:** If current or voltage of one circuit alters by changing the current or voltage in the other but the two circuits are not interconnected by means of any circuit elements or their combinations, then they are called indirectly coupled circuits. A magnetically coupled circuit is shown in the Fig. 4.9.

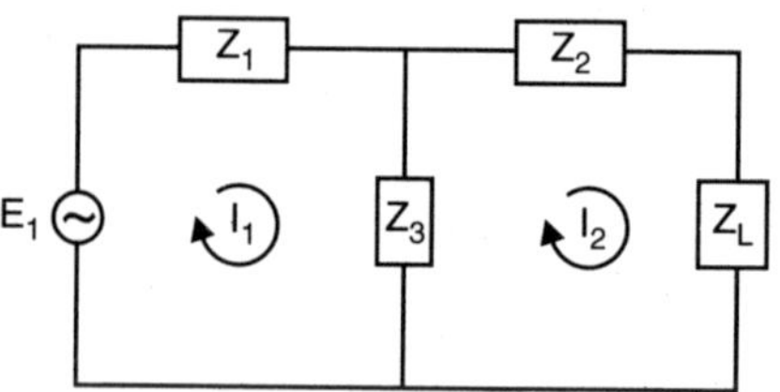

Fig. 4.8. Directly coupled circuit.

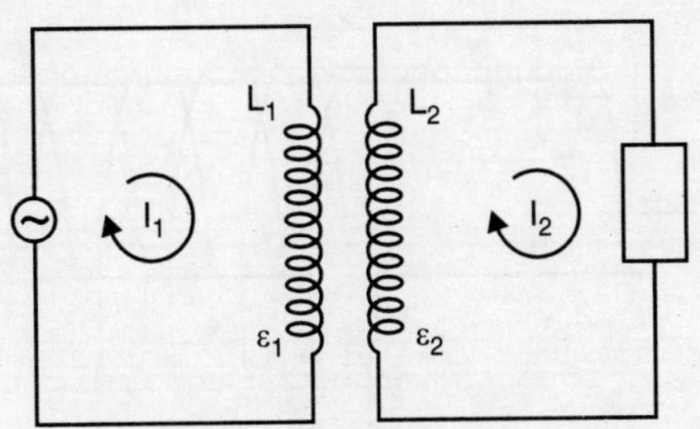

Fig. 4.9. Indirectly coupled circuit.

4.12. BASIC FEATURES OF MAGNETICALLY COUPLED CIRCUITS

Magnetically coupled circuit works on the principle of magnetic induction and in working obeys the Faraday's law of electromagnetic induction. In order to get basic features of magnetically coupled circuit, let us consider two magnetically coupled coils 1 and 2. Let N_1 and N_2 be the number of turns and L_1 and L_2 their self-inductances. Let us assume that a current I_1 flows in coil 1 and produces magnetic flux Φ_1 all around the space. A part of this flux, say Φ_{21} links with the coil 2. That is,

$$\Phi_{21} = k_1 \Phi_1 \qquad \text{...(4.30)}$$

Where k_1 is a constant and is called the coefficient of coupling between the coils 1 and 2. Now if the current I_1 varies with time, Φ_1 as well as Φ_{21} also vary with time. The varying flux Φ_1 will produce a self-induced voltage, say ε_1 in the coil 1 and varying flux Φ_{21} will induce a voltage ε_{21} in coil 2. Thus,

$$\varepsilon_1 = -L_1 \frac{dI_1}{dt} = -N_1 \frac{d\Phi_1}{dt} \qquad \text{...(4.31)}$$

From Eqn. (4.31) we have

$$L_1 = N_1 \frac{d\Phi_1}{dI_1} \qquad \text{...(4.32)}$$

and

$$\varepsilon_{21} = -M_{21} \frac{dI_1}{dt} = -N_2 \frac{d\Phi_{21}}{dt} \qquad \text{...(4.33)}$$

From Eqn. (4.33) we have

$$M_{21} = N_2 \frac{d\Phi_{21}}{dI_1} \qquad \text{...(4.34)}$$

Where M_{21} is mutual inductance between coils 1 and 2. Substituting $\Phi_{21} = k_1 \Phi_1$ in Eqn. (4.34), we have

$$M_{21} = N_2 k_1 \frac{d\Phi_1}{dI_1} \qquad \text{...(4.35)}$$

Combining eqn. (4.32) and (4.35) we get

$$M_{21} = k_1\left(\frac{N_2}{N_1}\right) L_1 \qquad ...(4.36)$$

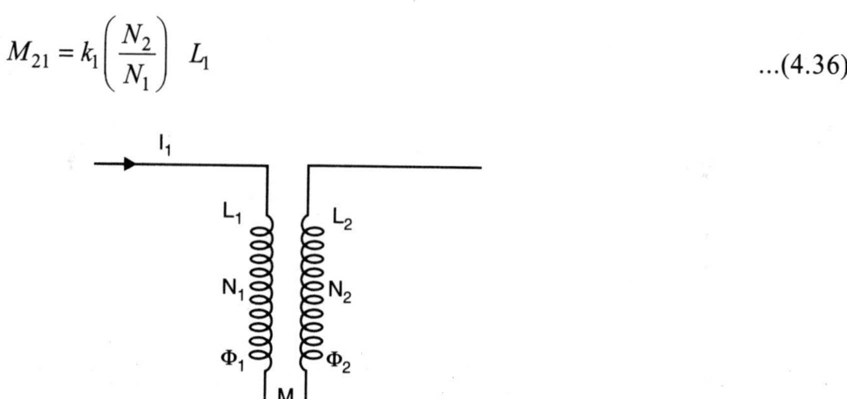

Fig. 4.10. Magnetically coupled circuit.

Similarly, if a current I_2 is made to flow in coil 2, a flux Φ_2 is produced all around the space, a part of which, say, Φ_{12} links with the coil 1. Change in I_2 will produce change in Φ_2 and Φ_{12} with time. This will induce self-voltage ε_2 in coil 2 and a mutual voltage ε_{12} in coil 1. As discussed above we can write similar equations in this case as follows.

$$\Phi_{12} = k_2\Phi_2 \qquad ...(4.37)$$

$$\varepsilon_2 = -L_2\frac{dI_2}{dt} = -N_2\frac{d\Phi_2}{dt} \qquad ...(4.38)$$

or $$L_2 = N_2\frac{d\Phi_2}{dI_2} \qquad ...(4.39)$$

$$\varepsilon_{12} = -M_{12}\frac{dI_2}{dt} = -N_1\frac{d\Phi_{12}}{dt} \qquad ...(4.40)$$

or $$M_{12} = N_1\frac{d\Phi_{12}}{dI_2} \qquad ...(4.41)$$

or $$M_{12} = N_1 k_2\frac{d\Phi_2}{dI_1} = k_2\left(\frac{N_1}{N_2}\right) L_2 \qquad ...(4.42)$$

where k_2 and M_{12} are the coefficients of coupling and mutual inductances between the coils 2 and 1.

Multiplying eqns. (4.36) and (4.42) we have

$$M_{12}M_{21} = k_1k_2L_1L_2 \qquad ...(4.43)$$

If the medium between the coils is isotropic then $M_{12} = M_{21} = M$. In most of the magnetically coupled coils $k_1 = k_2 = k$. Then

$$M = k\sqrt{L_1L_2} \qquad ...(4.44)$$

Also, $$\frac{M_{12}}{M_{21}} = \frac{k_2}{k_1}\left(\frac{N_1}{N_2}\right)^2 \frac{L_2}{L_1}$$

or $$\frac{L_1}{L_2} = \left(\frac{N_1}{N_2}\right)^2 = a^2 \qquad ...(4.45)$$

Where a is called turn ratio.

4.13. LEAKAGE FLUX AND LEAKAGE INDUCTANCE

Let Φ_1 be the magnetic flux produced by current I_1 flowing in coil 1 and Φ_{21} be that linked with coil 2. The remaining flux that does not link with the coil 2 is called *leakage flux* Φ_{11} and the corresponding inductance as *leakage inductance* L_{11} of coil 1. Thus

$$\Phi_{11} = \Phi_1 - \Phi_{21} = (1-k)\Phi_1 \qquad ...(4.46)$$

and $$L_{11} = N_1\frac{d\Phi_{11}}{dI_1} = N_1(1-k)\frac{d\Phi_1}{dI_1} = N_1(1-k)\frac{L_1}{N_1}$$

$$= (1-k)L_1 = L_1 - \frac{ML_1}{\sqrt{L_1L_2}} = L_1 - M\sqrt{\frac{L_1}{L_2}} \qquad ...(4.47)$$

Similarly, we can find an expression for secondary leakage flux Φ_{22} and leakage inductance L_{22}. The results are:

$$\Phi_{22} = (1-k)\Phi_2 \qquad ...(4.48)$$

$$L_{22} = (1-k)L_2 = L_2 - M\sqrt{\frac{L_2}{L_1}} \qquad ...(4.49)$$

4.14. INTERACTING COMBINATION OF INDUCTANCES

4.14.1 Series Combination of Inductances

If inductance coils are joined in such a way that the flux of one coil links with the other coil, they are said to be *interacting*. Suppose that we have two inductance coils L_1 and L_2 connected together in series. In series combination the same current passes through both the coils. Let Φ_1 and Φ_2 be the fluxes linked with coil 1 and 2 respectively. If the currents in the coils flow such that Φ_1 and Φ_2 have the same direction, a *positive coupling* is said to exist, see Fig. 4.11(a). On the other hand Φ_1 and Φ_2 have opposite directions, *negative coupling* is said to exist. In positive coupling the induced voltage in one coil due to mutual induction has the same sign as the induced voltage due to self induction. The induced voltages in coil 1 and 2 can be written as

$$\varepsilon_1 = -L_1\dot{I} - M\dot{I} \qquad ...(4.50)$$

$$\varepsilon_2 = -L_2\dot{I} - M\dot{I} \qquad ...(4.51)$$

where $\dot{I} = \frac{dI}{dt}$.

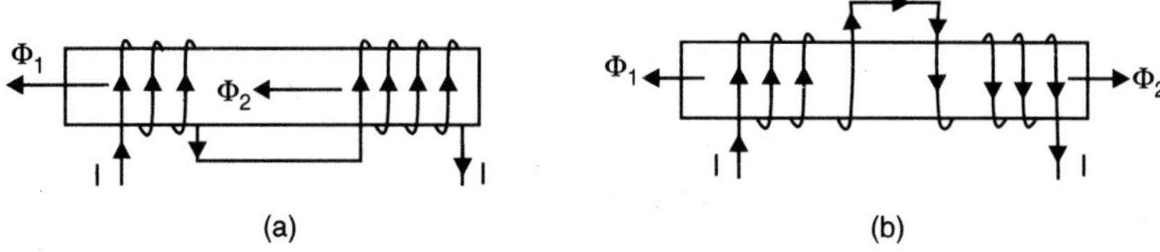

Fig. 4.11. (a) Positive coupling (b) Negative coupling.

Let L_+ be the equivalent self-inductance of the combination. Then the total induced voltage across the combination is given by

$$\varepsilon = \varepsilon_1 + \varepsilon_2$$

$$-L_+\dot{I} = -L_1\dot{I} - M\dot{I} - L_2\dot{I} - M\dot{I}$$

$$L_+ = L_1 + L_2 + 2M \qquad (\textit{positive coupling}) \qquad ...(4.52)$$

For negative coupling the equivalent self-inductance is given by

$$L_- = L_1 + L_2 - 2M \qquad (\textit{negative coupling}) \qquad ...(4.53)$$

For *non-interacting* coils M = 0. In this case equivalent self-inductance of the combination is

$$L = L_1 + L_2 \qquad ...(4.54)$$

4.14.2 Parallel Combination of Inductances

A parallel combination of two inductances is shown in the Fig. 4.12. A voltage source V is connected across the combination. Let I_1 and I_2 be the currents in the two branches. Applying *KVL* to the two loops we have

$$L_1\dot{I}_1 \pm M\dot{I}_2 = V \qquad ...(4.55)$$

$$L_2\dot{I}_2 \pm M\dot{I}_1 = V \qquad ...(4.56)$$

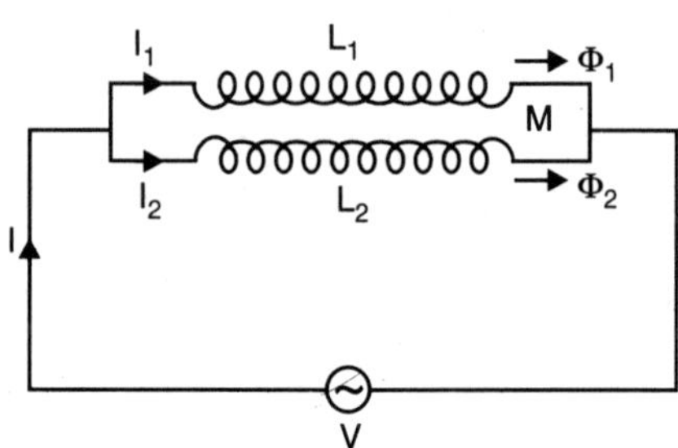

Fig. 4.12. Parallel combination of inductances.

Positive sign is to taken when the coupling is positive. From these equations we get

$$L_1\dot{I}_1 \pm M\dot{I}_2 = L_2\dot{I}_2 \pm M\dot{I}_1$$

Choosing the positive sign, we have

$$\dot{I}_2 = \frac{L_1 - M}{L_2 - M}\dot{I}_1 \quad ...(4.57)$$

Let L_+ be the equivalent self-inductance of the combination. Then

$$L_+(\dot{I}_1 + \dot{I}_2) = V \quad ...(4.58)$$

Substituting the expressions for V and $\dot{I}_2$ from eqns. (4.55) and (4.57) respectively in eqn. (4.58) we get

$$L_+\left(\dot{I}_1 + \frac{L_1 - M}{L_2 - M}\dot{I}_1\right) = \left(L_1\dot{I}_1 + M\frac{L_1 - M}{L_2 - M}\dot{I}_1\right)$$

$$L_+ = \frac{L_1L_2 - M^2}{L_1 + L_2 - 2M} \quad ...(4.59)$$

Similarly, for negative coupling the equivalent inductance is given by

$$L_- = \frac{L_1L_2 - M^2}{L_1 + L_2 + 2M} \quad ...(4.60)$$

For *non-interacting* combination $M = 0$, and

$$L = \frac{L_1L_2}{L_1 + L_2} \quad ...(4.61)$$

4.15. MAGNETIC ENERGY

When a current I is switched on in an inductance coil, an induced *emf* is set up which opposes the voltage source. In order to establish current in the inductance, the source does work against the back *emf*. The work done against the back *emf* when the current grows from 0 to I is

$$W = \int_0^I \left(L\frac{dI}{dt}\right) Idt = \frac{1}{2}LI^2 \quad ...(4.62)$$

This work is stored in the form of magnetic field in the space around the coil and is called magnetic energy associated with the current. Let us calculate the magnetic energy of long solenoid carrying a current I. Let l be the length, A the cross-section and N the total number of turns on the solenoid. The magnetic field inside the solenoid is

$$B = \mu_0 nI = \frac{\mu_0 NI}{l} \quad ...(4.63)$$

For a long solenoid, almost all the magnetic field is confined within its volume. The self-inductance of the solenoid is

$$L = \frac{\mu_0 A N^2}{l} \qquad ...(4.64)$$

The magnetic energy stored in the solenoid is

$$W = \frac{1}{2}LI^2 = \frac{1}{2}\left(\frac{\mu_0 A N^2}{l}\right)\left(\frac{Bl}{\mu_0 N I}\right)^2 = \frac{B^2}{2\mu_0}(Al) = \frac{B^2}{2\mu_0}(vol.\ of\ solenoid)$$

The volume density of magnetic energy is

$$u = \frac{W}{\text{volume}} = \frac{B^2}{2\mu_0} \qquad ...(4.65)$$

Thus the energy in magnetic field may be considered to be distributed with energy density u. The total energy in a volume V may be obtained by expression

$$W = \int_V u\,d\tau = \frac{1}{2\mu_0}\int_V B^2 d\tau \qquad ...(4.66)$$

Now we shall give general derivation for the expression for the magnetic energy. Consider a current loop with self-inductance L and carrying a current I. The flux linked with the loop is

$$\Phi = LI \qquad ...(4.67)$$

Also, $$\Phi = \int \mathbf{B}\cdot d\mathbf{S} = \nabla \times \mathbf{A}\cdot d\mathbf{S} = \oint_{\text{loop}} \mathbf{A}\cdot d\mathbf{l} \qquad ...(4.68)$$

From eqns. (4.67) and (4.68) we have

$$LI = \oint_{\text{loop}} \mathbf{A}\cdot d\mathbf{l} \qquad ...(4.69)$$

The magnetic energy associated with the loop is

$$W = \frac{1}{2}LI^2 = \frac{1}{2}I\oint_{\text{loop}} \mathbf{A}\cdot d\mathbf{l} = \frac{1}{2}\oint_{\text{loop}} \mathbf{A}\cdot \mathbf{I}\,dl \qquad ...(4.70)$$

For volume distribution of current the above equation becomes

$$W = \frac{1}{2}\int_{\text{volume}} \mathbf{A}\cdot\mathbf{J}\,d\tau \qquad ...(4.71)$$

In eqn. (4.71), the integration is to be performed over the region occupied by the current distribution. In the region not occupied by current $\mathbf{J} = \mathbf{0}$ and therefore, extending the region of integration to include all space does not alter the total energy.

$$W = \frac{1}{2}\int_{\text{all space}} \mathbf{A}\cdot\mathbf{J}\,d\tau \qquad ...(4.72)$$

Using the relation $\nabla \times \mathbf{B} = \mu_0 \mathbf{J}$ we eliminate $\mathbf{J}$ from above equation to get

$$W = \frac{1}{2\mu_0} \int_{\text{all space}} \mathbf{A} \cdot \nabla \times \mathbf{B}\, d\tau \qquad ...(4.73)$$

We now use the following vector identity to transform eqn. (4.73) in a more convenient form.

$$\nabla \cdot (\mathbf{A} \times \mathbf{B}) = \mathbf{B} \cdot \nabla \times \mathbf{A} - \mathbf{A} \cdot \nabla \times \mathbf{B}$$

$$\therefore \quad \mathbf{A} \cdot \nabla \times \mathbf{B} = \mathbf{B} \cdot \nabla \times \mathbf{A} - \nabla \cdot (\mathbf{A} \times \mathbf{B})$$

$$= \mathbf{B} \cdot \mathbf{B} - \nabla \cdot (\mathbf{A} \times \mathbf{B})$$

In view of this identity, eqn. (4.73) can be written as

$$W = \frac{1}{2\mu_0} \left[\int_{\text{all space}} \mathbf{B} \cdot \mathbf{B}\, d\tau - \int_{\text{all space}} \nabla \cdot (\mathbf{A} \times \mathbf{B})\, d\tau \right] \qquad ...(4.74)$$

Transforming the last integral into surface integral using divergence theorem we obtain

$$W = \frac{1}{2\mu_0} \int_{\text{all space}} B^2 d\tau - \frac{1}{2\mu_0} \int_{\text{surface}} \mathbf{A} \times \mathbf{B} \cdot d\mathbf{S} \qquad ...(4.75)$$

In eqn. (4.75) the surface bounding all space is far away from the current distribution and at this surface r goes to infinity and hence the integral vanishes. (The vector potential A goes as $1/r$, B goes as $1/r^2$ and element of area dS varies as r^2). So we are left with only one term

$$W = \int_{\text{all space}} \left(\frac{B^2}{2\mu_0} \right) d\tau \qquad ...(4.76)$$

Equation (4.76) permits us to interpret that the *magnetic energy of a current distribution is distributed over all space in the form of magnetic field with energy density* $u = \dfrac{B^2}{2\mu_0} = \dfrac{1}{2}\mu_0 H^2$.

SOLVED EXAMPLES

***Example* 1:** *Show that the charge transported by an induced current resulting from a change of flux* $d\Phi$ *is* $dq = \dfrac{|d\Phi|}{R}$.

Solution: Induced current in the loop $I = \dfrac{\varepsilon}{R} = -\dfrac{1}{R}\dfrac{d\Phi}{dt}$

Magnitude of charge transported $dq = Idt = \dfrac{d\Phi}{R}$

***Example* 2:** *A thin metal rod of length L rotates with constant angular velocity* ω *in a uniform magnetic field B. Show that the emf produced between its ends is* $\varepsilon = \dfrac{1}{2}\omega B L^2$.

Solution: If the rod rotates through an angle $d\theta$ in time dt, the magnetic flux threaded by it is

$$d\Phi = BdA = B\left(\frac{1}{2}L^2 d\theta\right)$$

Induced *emf* produced between the ends of the rod is

$$\varepsilon = \left|\frac{d\Phi}{dt}\right| = \frac{1}{2}BL^2\frac{d\theta}{dt} = \frac{1}{2}\omega BL^2 \qquad \left(\because \omega = \frac{d\theta}{dt}\right).$$

Example 3: *A metal disc of radius R rotates with constant angular velocity ω about an axis passing through its centre and at right angles to the disc. A uniform field B acts normal to the plane of the disc. Find the potential difference between the centre and the rim.*

***Solution*:** Consider a radial segment of length dr at a distance r from the axis of rotation. This element moves in a plane perpendicular to the magnetic field with velocity $v = r\omega$. The induced *emf* across this element is

$$d\varepsilon = vBdr = \omega Brdr$$

Total *emf* between the centre and the rim is

$$\varepsilon = \omega B\int_0^R rdr = \frac{1}{2}\omega BR^2$$

Example 4: *A straight wire slides over another parabolic wire frame as shown in the figure. A uniform magnetic field acts normal to the plane of the frame. At t = 0, the slider starts moving from the vertex with zero velocity and moves with constant acceleration α. Find the emf in the frame.*

Solution: Let x be the distance of the slider from origin at instant t. The length of the slider at this instant is

$$\ell = 2y = 2\sqrt{ax}$$

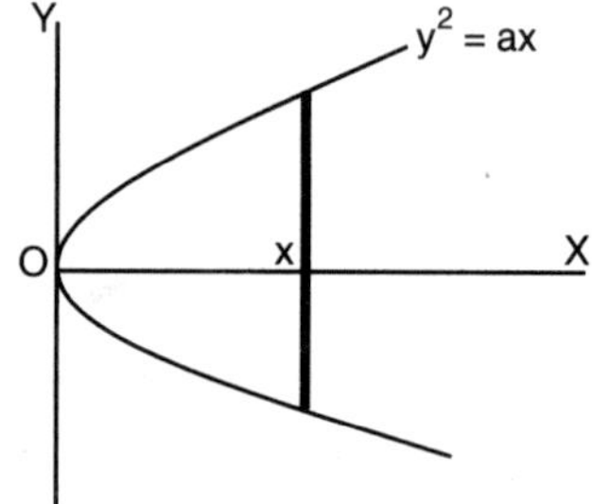

Fig. 4.13

The acceleration of the slider is

$$\frac{dv}{dt} = \alpha$$

Hence the velocity of slider at time t is

$$v = \alpha t$$

Its position at time is

$$x = \frac{1}{2}\alpha t^2$$

Induced *emf* in the loop is

$$\varepsilon = B\ell v = B(2y)(\alpha t) = B(2\sqrt{ax})(\alpha t) = \left(\sqrt{8\alpha a}\right)Bx$$

Example 5: *An infinite straight conductor carries a current I. In the vicinity of this conductor, there is a square frame of side a. The nearest side of the frame is at a distance b from the wire. The* *frame is rotated about the side of the frame which is parallel to the conductor and farthest to it. Calculate the charge that flows through the frame. The resistance of the frame is R.*

Solution: The magnetic field at a distance x (> b) from the wire is

$$B = \frac{\mu_0 I}{2\pi x}$$

The magnetic flux linked with the coil

$$\Phi_1 = \int \mathbf{B} \cdot d\mathbf{S} = \int_b^{b+a} \frac{\mu_0 I}{2\pi x} a dx = \frac{\mu_0 I a}{2\pi} \ln\left(\frac{a+b}{b}\right)$$

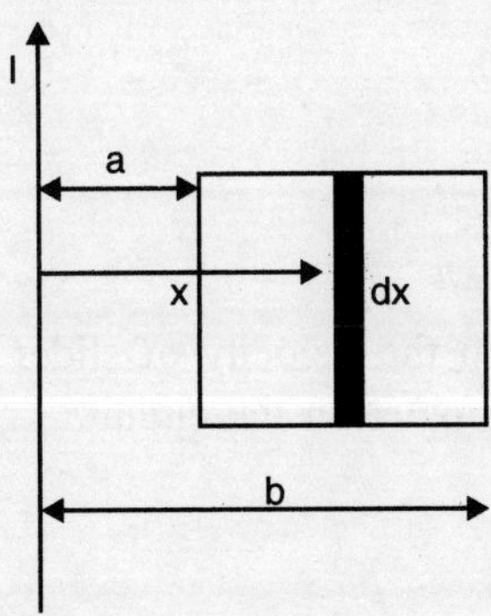

Fig. 4.14

The flux linked with the loop when the coil is rotated through angle 180°

$$\Phi_2 = \int_{a+b}^{b+2a} \frac{\mu_0 I}{2\pi x} a dx = \frac{\mu_0 I a}{2\pi} \ln\left(\frac{b+2a}{a+b}\right)$$

Change in flux $\quad \Delta\Phi = \Phi_2 - (-\Phi_1) = \Phi_1 + \Phi_2 = \frac{\mu_0 I}{2\pi} \ln \frac{2a+b}{b}$

Charge circulated in the frame

$$\Delta q = \frac{\Delta\Phi}{R} = \frac{\mu_0 I a}{2\pi R} \ln\left(1 + \frac{2a}{b}\right).$$

Example 6: *An infinite wire carries a current I. Two straight wires which run parallel to the current carrying conductor are connected by a resistance R. A straight conductor slides over the parallel wires with velocity v as shown in the figure. Calculate the (i) induced current (ii) force required to maintain the slider's velocity constant.*

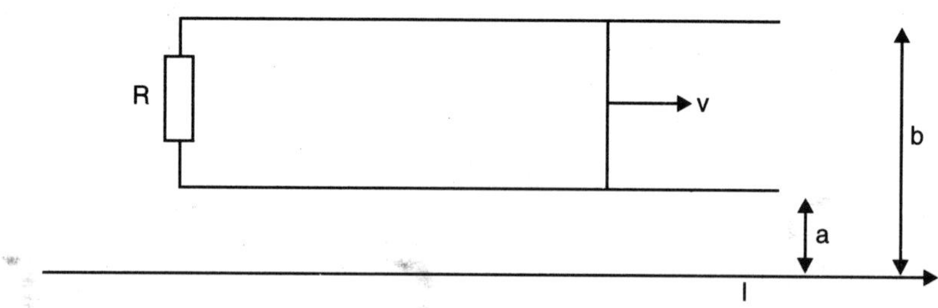

Fig. 4.15

Solution: (*i*) The magnetic field at a distance x from the wire is

$$B = \frac{\mu_0 I}{2\pi x} \quad \text{...(4.77)}$$

Induced *emf* across the slider

$$\varepsilon = \int_a^b Bv dx = \frac{\mu_0 I v}{2\pi}\int_a^b \frac{dx}{x} = \frac{\mu_0 I v}{2\pi}\ln\frac{b}{a} \quad \text{...(4.78)}$$

(*ii*) If F is the force required to keep the velocity of slider constant, the power delivered to the system must be equal to that dissipated in the circuit.

$$Fv = \frac{\varepsilon^2}{R}$$

$$\therefore \quad F = \frac{\varepsilon^2}{vR} = \frac{v}{R}\cdot\left(\frac{\mu_0 I}{2\pi}\ln\frac{b}{a}\right)^2 \quad \text{...(4.79)}$$

Example 7: *A long coaxial cable carries a current I. The current flows down along the central conductor and back along the outer conductor. (i) Find the energy stored per unit length of the cable (ii) making use of the expression for energy, obtain self inductance per unit length of the cable.*

Solution: (*i*) Let a and b be the radii of the central and the outer conductor respectively. The magnetic field at a distance r ($a < r < b$) from the axis of the wire is

$$B = \frac{\mu_0 I}{2\pi r} \quad \text{...(4.80)}$$

At points $r < a$ and $r > b$, the magnetic field is zero. It is wholly confined in the space between the inner and outer conductor. The magnetic energy lies in a cylindrical shell of internal radius a and external radius b. The energy in a thin cylindrical shell of radius r and thickness dr and of length l is

$$dW = \frac{B^2}{2\mu_0}d\tau = \frac{B^2}{2\mu_0}(2\pi r l dr) = \frac{\mu_0 I^2 l}{4\pi}\frac{dr}{r}$$

Total energy within the limit of the cable is

$$W = \frac{\mu_0 I^2 l}{4\pi}\int_a^b \frac{dr}{r} = \frac{\mu_0 I^2 l}{4\pi}\ln\frac{b}{a}$$

Energy per unit length is

$$U = \frac{W}{l} = \frac{\mu_0 I^2}{4\pi} \ln \frac{b}{a}$$

(*ii*) Equating the energy W to $\frac{1}{2} L I^2$ we obtain the self-inductance of the cable

$$L = \frac{\mu_0 l}{2\pi} \ln \frac{b}{a}$$

$$\text{Self-inductance per unit length} = \frac{\mu_0}{2\pi} \ln \frac{b}{a}$$

***Example* 8:** *A coil has self-inductance L_1. Another closed coil of self-inductance L_2 is brought in the vicinity of the first coil so that it has a mutual inductance M with the first coil. Show that the self-inductance of the first coil in the presence of the second is* $L_1 - \frac{M^2}{L_2}$.

***Solution*:** When a steady voltage E is applied across the first coil, the equation for potential during the growth of current is

$$L_1 \frac{dI_1}{dt} + M \frac{dI_2}{dt} = E$$

At the same time, the equation for the potential drops in the second coil is

$$L_2 \frac{dI_2}{dt} + M \frac{dI_1}{dt} = 0$$

Substituting dI_2/dt from second equation in the first equation we get

$$\left(L_1 - \frac{M^2}{L_2} \right) \frac{dI_1}{dt} = E$$

This equation shows that the effective self-inductance of the first coil is $L_1 - \frac{M^2}{L_2}$.

***Example* 9:** *Two identical coils when coupled in series in two ways, the self-inductances of the combination are found to be 100 mH and 80 mH. Find the self-inductances of individual coils, their mutual inductance and the coefficient of coupling.*

Solution: Given that

$$L_I = L_1 + L_2 + 2M = 100 \text{ mH}$$

$$L_{II} = L_1 + L_2 - 2M = 80 \text{ mH}$$

From these equations

$$M = \frac{L_I - L_{II}}{4} = 5 \text{ mH}$$

Since $L_1 = L_2 = L$(say), therefore, $L_1 = L_2 = L = 45\,\text{mH}$

Now the coefficient of coupling $$k = \frac{M}{\sqrt{L_1 L_2}} = \frac{5}{\sqrt{45 \times 45}} = \frac{1}{9}$$

***Example* 10:** *Two identical coils are joined in parallel in one way, the combination is found to have a self-inductance of 4 mH. When joined in parallel in another way, the combination has self-inductance of 36 mH. The mutual inductance in each arrangement remains the same. Calculate the self-inductance of the coils and the coefficient of coupling.*

Solution: $$L = \frac{L_1 L_2 - M^2}{L_1 + L_2 \pm 2M} \qquad L_1 = L_2 = L \text{ (say)}$$

Now $$4 = \frac{L^2 - M^2}{2(L+M)} \Rightarrow L - M = 8$$

and $$36 = \frac{L^2 - M^2}{2(L-M)} \Rightarrow L + M = 72$$

Solving (1) and (2) for L and M we get

$$L = 40 \text{ mH and } M = 32 \text{ mH}$$

Coefficient of coupling $$k = \frac{M}{\sqrt{L_1 L_2}} = \frac{32}{\sqrt{40 \times 40}} = 0.8$$

QUESTIONS AND PROBLEMS

1. Consider a circular conducting loop in the plane of the paper. A magnetic field B acts perpendicular to the plane of the loop pointing towards the reader. Indicate the direction of the induced current in the loop if (*i*) B grows (*ii*) B diminishes (*iii*) the loop is stretched (*iv*) the loop contracts.

Ans. (*i*) clockwise (*ii*) counter-clockwise (*iii*) clockwise (*iv*) counter-clockwise.

2. A rod of length 1.0 m rotates at a frequency of 500 rps about one of its end in a horizontal plane. A magnetic field of 10 mT acts vertically upwards. Calculate the potential difference between the ends of the rod.

3. A metal disc of radius 0.50 m rotates at a frequency of 1000 r.p.m. A magnetic field B = 0.02 *T* acts normal to the plane of the disc. Calculate the potential difference between the centre and the rim of the disc.

4. A magnetic flux through a coil varies with time according to the law $\varphi = 10t^2 + 5t + 1$ milli-weber where t is time in second. Calculate the *emf* in the coil at $t = 1$ sec.

5. A small coil with cross-sectional area 5 mm^2, number of turns 50 and resistance 2 ohm is placed between the poles of an electromagnet. The face of the coil is normal to the magnetic field. The coil is connected to a ballistic galvanometer of 48 ohms. The coil is suddenly rotated through an angle of 180°. The charge that passes through the galvanometer is 5 μC. Calculate the magnetic field of the electromagnet.

6. A long straight wire carries a current of 2 A. Near it a rectangular frame is placed whose one arm moves away from the wire at a constant speed v = 10 m/s. See Fig. 4.16. The resistance of the moving arm is 1 ohm, other arms have negligible resistance. Calculate the current induced in the loop at the instant the moveable arm is at a distance of 1 cm. The length of the moving arm is 10 cm.

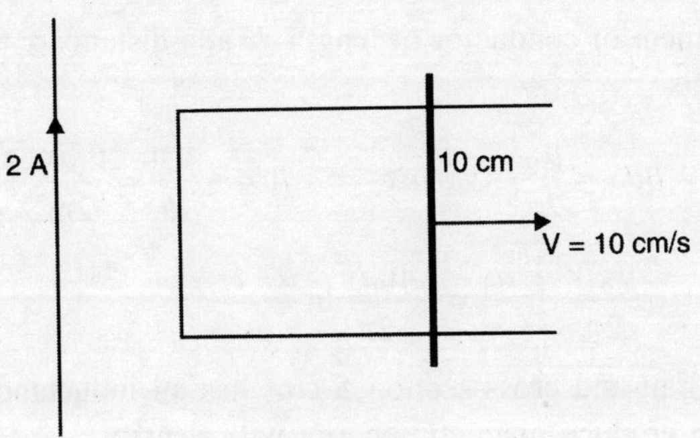

Fig. 4.16

Hint: $d\varphi = BdS = \frac{\mu_0 I}{2\pi x} l dx \Rightarrow \varepsilon = -\frac{d\varphi}{dt} = -\frac{\mu_0 I l\ v}{2\pi\ x}$

7. A wire is bent into the shape of a semi-circle rotates about is diameter with angular velocity ω in a uniform magnetic field B. The axis of rotation is at right angles to the magnetic field. See Fig. 4.17. The ends of the wire are connected to a resistance R. Calculate the mean power dissipated in the resistance

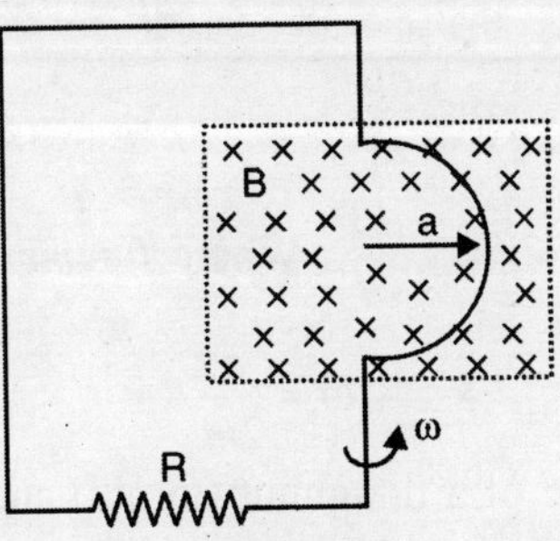

Fig. 4.17

8. A copper wire of length l = 20 cm moves with constant velocity v = 10 m/s parallel to a straight conductor carrying a current I = 150 A. The nearest end of the wire is at a distance of 2 cm from the wire. Calculate the potential difference between the end of moving wire.

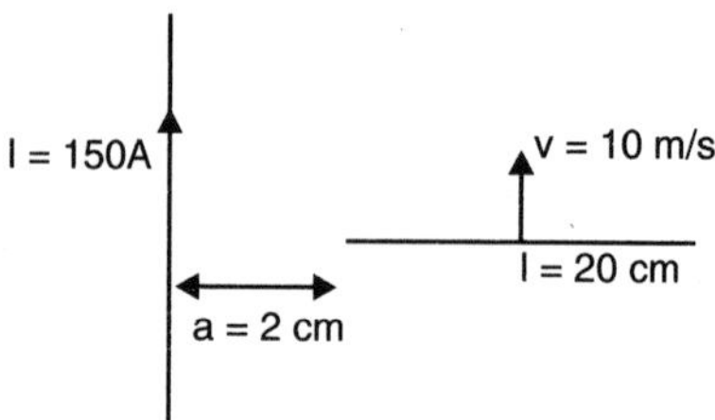

Fig. 4.18

Hint: Consider an element of conductor of length dx at a distance x from the wire. Flux threaded by this element is

$$d\varphi = BdS = \frac{\mu_0 I}{2\pi x}.(vdt)dx \Rightarrow d\varepsilon = -\frac{d\varphi}{dt} = \frac{\mu_0 Iv}{2\pi}.\frac{dx}{x}$$

$$\varepsilon = -\frac{\mu_0 Iv}{2\pi}\int_a^{a+l}\frac{dx}{x} = -\frac{\mu_0 Iv}{2\pi}\ln\frac{a+l}{a}$$

9. A solenoid of length 1 m and cross-section 5 cm^2 has an inductance 5×10^{-7} henry. Caculate the current required to produce magnetic energy with density 2×10^{-3} J/m^3.

Hint: $\textit{energy density } u = \frac{\textit{total energy}}{\textit{volume}} = \frac{(1/2)LI^2}{Al}$

10. A circular ring of mass m carries charge q and is free to rotate about an axis passing through its centre and at right angles to the plane of the ring. A time varying magnetic field **B** is switched on, which is normal to the plane of the ring. Show that the angular velocity of the ring is $\omega = \frac{q}{2m}B$.

Hint: Induced electric field in the ring $E = -\frac{1}{2}r\frac{dB}{dt}$.

Torque on the ring $\tau = qEr = -\frac{1}{2}qr^2\frac{dB}{dt}$

Equation of motion $I\frac{d\omega}{dt} = -\frac{1}{2}qr^2\frac{dB}{dt}$. Where $I = mr^2$

$\therefore$ $d\omega = \frac{q}{2m}dB \Rightarrow \omega = \frac{q}{2m}B$

11. Calculate the mutual inductance of a doughnut (toroid) and an infinite wire passing through the axis of the toroid. The cross-section of the toroid is rectangular (Fig. 4.19). The number of turns on the toroid is N.

Magnetic field of wire at a distance r

$$B = \frac{\mu_0 I}{2\pi r}$$

An element of area of toroid at a distance r

$$ds = h\, dr$$

Flux through the toroid

$$\Phi = N\int_a^b BdS = \frac{N\mu_0 Ih}{2\pi}\int_a^b \frac{dr}{r}$$

$$= \frac{\mu_o NIh}{2\pi}\ell n\frac{b}{a}$$

∴ Mutual inductance

$$M = \frac{\Phi}{I} = \frac{\mu_0 Nh}{2\pi}\cdot\ell n\frac{b}{a}$$

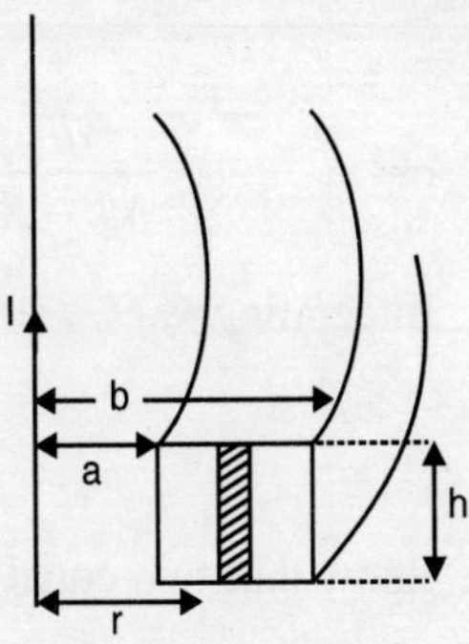

Fig. 4.19

12. Two concentric rings are placed in the same plane. The smaller ring has radius a and the larger one has radius b. Assuming $a << b$, find the mutual inductance of the rings. If the inner ring carries a current I, calculate the flux through the larger ring.

Ans. $M = \frac{1}{2}\mu_0\pi a^2/b,\qquad \Phi_2 = \frac{1}{2}\mu_0\pi a^2 I/b$

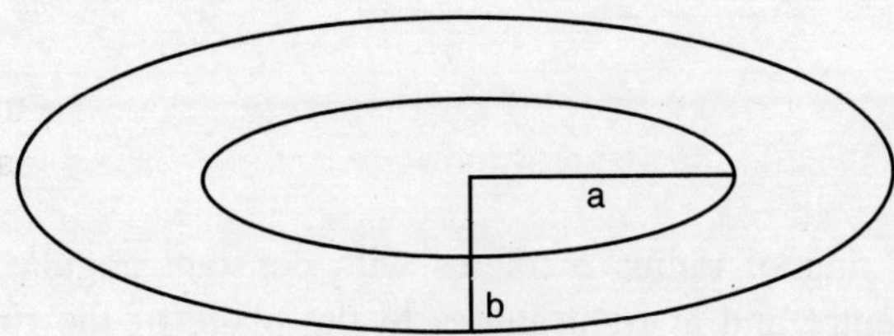

Fig. 4.20

13. An iron cored solenoid supports $N = 1000$ turns. A current of 2.0 A produces a magnetic flux $\Phi = 2 \times 10^{-3}$ weber over its cross-section. Calculate the energy of the magnetic field.

Hint: $W = \frac{1}{2}N\Phi I$

14. Two loops are magnetically coupled, the mutual inductance of the coils being M. The current in one varies according to the law $I_1 = kt$, where k is a constant and t is time. Find the current in the other coil if it has self-inductance L_2 and resistance R.

Hint: Equation of potential drops in the second loop is

$$RI_2 + L_2\frac{dI_2}{dt} - M\frac{dI_1}{dt} = 0$$

or

$$L_2\frac{dI_2}{dt} = Mk - RI_2$$

or $$\frac{dI_2}{Mk - RI_2} = \frac{1}{L_2} dt$$

Integrating w.r.t. t and using the condition $t = 0$, $I_2 = 0$, we get

$$I_2 = \frac{Mk}{R}\left(1 - e^{-Rt/L_2}\right)$$

15. Show that two equal circular coils of equal radii placed coaxially with their centres at a distance d apart have mutual inductance $M = \frac{\mu_0 \pi a^4}{2d^3}$, $d >> a$, where a is the radius of each coil.

16. In a certain region, the magnetic field in vacuum is $B = 2.0\ T$. What is the magnitude of electric field which has the same energy density as that of the magnetic field.

Hint: $\frac{1}{2}\varepsilon_0 E^2 = \frac{B^2}{2\mu_0} \Rightarrow E = \frac{B}{\sqrt{\mu_0 \varepsilon_0}} = cB,\ c = \textit{speed of light in vacuum.}$

17. A long hollow cylinder of radius r carries uniform charge distribution with surface density σ. It rotates with uniform angular velocity ω about its axis. Find the magnetic energy per unit length of the cylinder.

Ans. $\frac{1}{2}\pi\mu_0\sigma^2 r^4 \omega^2$

18. A uniformly charged ring of radius a rotates with constant angular velocity ω about an axis passing through its centre and at right angles to the plane of the ring. Show that the ratio of volume energy densities of magnetic and electric fields at an axial point at a distance $x = a$ from the centre is $\frac{U_m}{U_e} = \frac{\mu_0 \varepsilon_0 a^4 \omega^2}{x^4}$.

Hint: Electric field of a charged ring at a distance from its centre

$$E = \frac{1}{4\pi\varepsilon_0} \frac{qx}{(a^2 + x^2)^{3/2}}$$

Magnetic field of rotating ring

$$B = \frac{\mu_0}{2} \frac{Ia^2}{(a^2 + x^2)^{3/2}}, \text{ where } I = \lambda v = \frac{q}{2\pi a} \cdot \frac{\omega}{2\pi}$$

$$\therefore \quad \frac{U_m}{U_e} = \frac{B^2/2\mu_0}{\varepsilon_0 E^2/2} = \frac{1}{\mu_0 \varepsilon_0} \cdot \frac{B^2}{E^2}$$

19. An air cored toroid has a circular cross-section of radius 4 mm. Find the inductance if there are 2500 turns and the mean radius is 20 mm.

20. Explain the phenomenon of mutual induction. What is the theorem of reciprocity? Discuss giving necessary proof.

A 3 m long solenoid with diameter 4 cm and 2000 turns has a secondary of 100 turns wound closely near its middle point. Calculate the mutual inductance between the coils.

21. Derive an expression for the energy density associated with the magnetic field of current distribution.

A long coaxial cable carries current I (current flows down the surface of the inner cylinder of radius a and back along the outer cylinder of radius b). Determine the energy stored in the form of magnetic field per unit length of the cable.

22. The electron in hydrogen atom circulates in the orbit of radius 0.51 × 10^{-10} m. Calculate the change in magnetic moment of electron if a magnetic field of strength 2.0 T acts at right angles to the plane of the orbit.

Hint: $\Delta\mu = \frac{1}{2} er^2 \Delta\omega = \frac{1}{2} er^2 \left(\frac{eB}{2m}\right) = \frac{(1.6\times10^{-19})^2 (0.51\times10^{-10})^2 (2.0)}{4\times9.1\times10^{-31}} = 4 \times 10^{-29}$ A.m^2

23. For two coupled circuits prove that $M \le L_1 L_2$, symbols have their usual meaning.

5 CHAPTER

Magnetic Properties of Materials

5.1. INTRODUCTION

The understanding of magnetic behaviour of materials requires the knowledge of quantum mechanics, statistical mechanics, solid state physics etc. This approach is beyond the scope of this text. Here we shall present a brief discussion about the magnetic properties of materials making use of classical and semi-classical theories.

5.2. DIAMAGNETIC, PARAMAGNETIC AND FERROMAGNETIC SUBSTANCES

According to Bohr's classical picture of atom, electrons revolve in circular orbits around the nucleus. An electron revolving in a circle is equivalent to a tiny current loop, which behaves like a tiny bar magnet, called magnetic dipole. The magnetic moment of current loop (magnetic dipole) is defined as the product of the area of loop and the current in it. The magnetic moment is a vector quantity pointing in the direction perpendicular to the plane of the loop. In addition to the orbital motion, electron spins about its own axis. The spinning electron is again equivalent to a current loop and hence possesses intrinsic magnetic moment. In an atom, containing many electrons, the vector sum of the magnetic moments resulting from the orbital and spin motion of electron may have zero or non-zero value. In the former case the atom is magnetically neutral and in the latter case the atoms behaves like a permanent magnetic dipole. Substances whose atoms or molecules have no magnetic moment are called **diamagnetic substances** and those, whose atoms or molecules have magnetic moment are called **paramagnetic substances**. Ferromagnetism is a special case of paramagnetism.

The magnetic behaviour of materials is described by **magnetization vector M,** which is defined as follows. When a substance is placed in magnetic field, magnetic moment is induced in its constituent atoms or molecules. If $\Delta\mu$ is the magnetic moment induced in volume ΔV then **the magnetic moment per unit volume is defined as the magnetization M.**

$$\mathbf{M} = \lim_{\Delta V \to 0}\left(\frac{\Delta\mu}{\Delta V}\right) \qquad ...(5.1)$$

Like real currents, (which can be controlled by rheostats and measured by ammeters) the magnetization also produces magnetic field **B.** Thus the magnetic field **B** in a material is sum of the contributions from real currents and magnetization, the latter has origin in microscopic or *amperean* currents. In electromagnetism it is customary to introduce another auxiliary vector **H,** called the *intensity of magnetic field*, whose sources are real currents. The vector **H** is defined as

$$\mathbf{H} = \frac{\mathbf{B}}{\mu_0} - \mathbf{M} \text{ or } \mathbf{B} = \mu_0(\mathbf{M} + \mathbf{H}) \qquad ...(5.2)$$

μ_0 is permeability of free space.

In free space **M** is zero and $\mathbf{H} = \mathbf{B}/\mu_0$ or $\mathbf{B} = \mu_0 \mathbf{H}$.

Except ferromagnetic materials, for small **H** the magnetization **M** acquired by a substance is proportional to the *intensity of magnetic field* **H** *i.e.*

$$\mathbf{M} = \chi \mathbf{H} \qquad ...(5.3)$$

where χ is proportionality constant, called *magnetic susceptibility*.

Combining eqns. (5.2) and (5.3) we have

$$\mathbf{B} = \mu_0 (1 + \chi) \mathbf{H} = \mu_0 \mu_r \mathbf{H} \qquad ...(5.4)$$

where $\mu_r = 1 + \chi$.

The quantities μ_r is called *relative permeability* of the medium. From eqns. (5.2) and (5.3) we have

$$\mathbf{M} = \chi\left(\frac{\mathbf{B}}{\mu_0} - \mathbf{M}\right)$$

$$\therefore \qquad \mathbf{B} = \left(\frac{1+\chi}{\chi}\right)\mu_0 \mathbf{M}$$

For most of the materials (except ferromagnetic materials), $\chi << 1$ and hence the above relation can be written as

$$\mathbf{B} = \frac{\mu_0 \mathbf{M}}{\chi}$$

$$\text{or} \qquad \chi = \frac{\mu_0 \mathbf{M}}{\mathbf{B}} \qquad ...(5.5)$$

Magnetic susceptibility can be experimentally determined. For diamagnetic substances χ is negative and is of the order of 10^{-8} to 10^{-6}. For paramagnetic substances χ is positive, temperature dependent and is of the order of 10^{-3}. For ferromagnetic substances χ is positive and very high, for iron it may be as high as 10^5.

5.3. RELATION BETWEEN MAGNETIC MOMENT AND ANGULAR MOMENTUM

Consider an electron, mass *m*, charge *e*, revolving with velocity *v* round the nucleus in a circular orbit of radius *r*. The revolving electron in a circular orbit is equivalent to current loop. The magnetic moment associated with the current loop is

$$\mu = \text{(current in the loop) (area of the loop)}$$

$$= \left(-\frac{ev}{2\pi r}\right)\left(\pi r^2\right)$$

$$= -\left(\frac{e}{2m}\right)(mvr)$$

$$= -\left(\frac{e}{2m}\right)L_o \qquad \text{...(5.6)}$$

where $L_o = mvr$ is the orbital angular momentum of electron. It is remarkable to note that this classical result is identical with that obtained quantum mechanically. The ratio of magnetic moment to orbital angular momentum viz $(-e/2m)$ is called *gyromagnetic ratio.* The electron also spins about its own axis and possesses intrinsic or spin angular momentum. Like orbital magnetic moment, the spin magnetic moment is also related to spin angular momentum. For purely quantum mechanical reasons, the ratio of spin magnetic moment to spin angular momentum is twice as large as it is for orbital motion. That is

$$\mu = -2\left(\frac{e}{2m}\right)L_{\text{spin}} \qquad \text{...(5.7)}$$

Relation between angular momentum and magnetic moment of atomic system:

We have seen that the magnetic moments associated with orbital motion and spin motion of electron are given by

$$\boldsymbol{\mu}_o = -\left(\frac{e}{2m}\right)\mathbf{L}_o,\ \boldsymbol{\mu}_S = -\left(\frac{e}{m}\right)\mathbf{L}_S$$

These relations are also expressed as

$$\boldsymbol{\mu}_o = -g_l\left(\frac{e}{2m}\right)\mathbf{L}_o \quad \text{and} \quad \boldsymbol{\mu}_S = -g_S\left(\frac{e}{2m}\right)\mathbf{L}_S$$

Where for orbital motion $g_l = 1$ and for spin motion $g_S = 2$. The factor g is called *spectroscopic splitting factor* or *Lande g–factor.*

It should be emphasized that these relations between μ and L derived classically come out to be the same as those obtained quantum mechanically. The only difference is that the concept of angular momentum in quantum mechanics is different from that of classical mechanics.

In an atom containing several electrons, the total angular momentum of electrons is equal to the vector sum of orbital and spin angular momenta and the total magnetic moment of the atom is equal to the vector sum of magnetic moments of electrons. It is a quantum mechanical result that the direction of magnetic moment of an isolated atom is exactly opposite to the direction of angular momentum and the ratio of magnetic moment to angular momentum is neither $-e/2m$ nor $-e/m$ but somewhere in between the two. If **J** is the total angular momentum of atom then

$$\boldsymbol{\mu}_{\text{atom}} = -g\left(\frac{e}{2m}\right)\mathbf{J} \qquad \text{...(5.8)}$$

Where g is characteristic of the *state* of the atom and depends on orbital quantum numbers L, spin quantum number S and total angular momentum quantum number J.

The total angular momentum of closed sub-shell is zero and so is true for magnetic moment. Atoms or ions having closed sub-shells are therefore diamagnetic. Atoms with partly filled sub-shells *i.e.* those having unpaired electrons possess angular momentum and hence magnetic moment. Such atoms or ions are paramagnetic. Atoms or ions of transition and rare earth elements have unpaired electron in their $3d$ and $4f$ sub-shells and are paramagnetic.

5.4. MAGNETIC ENERGY OF ATOMS

When an atom with magnetic moment $\boldsymbol{\mu}$ is placed in magnetic field $\mathbf{B}$, it acquires extra energy given by

$$U = -\boldsymbol{\mu}\cdot\mathbf{B} \qquad \text{...(5.9)}$$

If $\mathbf{B}$ points along z-axis, we can write

$$U = -\mu_Z B = g\left(\frac{e}{2m}\right) J_Z B = g\left(\frac{e}{2m}\right) M_J \hbar B = g\left(\frac{e\hbar}{2m}\right) B M_J \qquad \text{...(5.10)}$$

where $J_Z = M_J \hbar$, M_J is magnetic quantum number.

The quantity $\dfrac{e\hbar}{2m}$ is called *Bohr magneton* and is usually denoted by μ_β.

$$\textit{Bohr magneton } \mu_\beta = \frac{e\hbar}{2m_e} = 9.28 \times 10^{-24} \text{ joule/tesla}$$

Bohr magneton is a natural unit of magnetic moment. Thus when an atomic system is placed in a magnetic field, its allowed energy levels split up more energy levels given by

$$U = M_J g \mu_\beta B \qquad \text{...(5.11)}$$

where quantum number M_J can take on values J, $J-1$, $J-2$, ... $-(J-2)$, $-(J-1)$, $-J$. The spliting up of energy levels of atomic system into $2J + 1$ levels, called Zeeman effect, and energy levels are called Zeeman levels.

The simplest atomic system is a single electron atom. The total angular momentum quantum number (which is equal to the spin quantum number of electron) of this atom is $J = s = ½$ and hence $M_J = ½, -½$. The L and $g-$factor for spin motion is 2. Hence the magnetic energy levels are given by

$$U = M_J g \mu_\beta B, \quad M_J = \frac{1}{2}, -\frac{1}{2}$$

The energy level of the atom is split into two levels U_+ and U_-.

$$U_+ = \tfrac{1}{2}.2.\mu_\beta B = \mu_\beta B$$

$$U_- = -\tfrac{1}{2}.2.\mu_\beta B = -\mu_\beta B$$

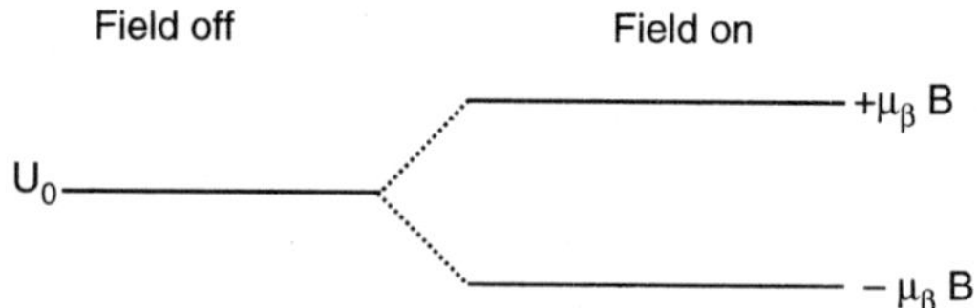

Fig. 5.1. Splitting of energy level of one electron atom in magnetic field.

5.5. DIAMAGNETISM (LANGEVIN'S CLASSICAL THEORY)

Diamagnetic atoms or molecules are magnetically neutral. However, when magnetic field is applied to such atoms or molecules, magnetic moment is induced in them in a direction opposite to the external magnetic field. In other words a diamagnetic substance in magnetic field acquires magnetization M opposite to the applied field. For this reason the diamagnetic susceptibility χ is negative.

Consider an electron revolving round the nucleus in a circular orbit of radius ρ. The magnetic moment associated with the orbital motion of electron is related to the corresponding angular momentum L through the relation

$$\mu = -\left(\frac{e}{2m}\right)L \qquad \text{...(5.12)}$$

This relation shows that a change in angular momentum will produce a change in magnetic moment. Now let us choose the Cartesian coordinate axes such that the xy-plane contains the plane of the orbit. We now switch on a magnetic field B in z-direction *i.e.* perpendicular to the plane of the orbit. According to Faraday law of electromagnetic induction, changing magnetic field produces changing electric field. Let E be the magnitude of induced electric field tangential to the electronic orbit. In accordance with the Faraday law "*the line integral of induced electric field around the electronic orbit equals the negative time rate of change of magnetic flux through the area enclosed by orbit*."

$$\oint_{\text{ORBIT}} \mathbf{E}\cdot\mathbf{dl} = -\frac{d}{dt}\int_{\text{ORBIT}} \mathbf{B}\cdot\mathbf{dS}$$

Fig. 5.2. Changing magnetic field produces changing electric field.

The above equation simplifies to

$$E(2\pi\rho) = -\frac{d}{dt}(B\cdot\pi\rho^2)$$

$$\therefore \qquad E = -\tfrac{1}{2}\rho\ \frac{dB}{dt} \qquad ...(5.13)$$

The induced electric field exerts a torque $-eE\rho$ on electron, which in turn produces a change in angular momentum in accordance with the equation

$$\tau = \frac{dL}{dt}$$

$$-eE\rho = \frac{dL}{dt}$$

$$-e\left(-\frac{1}{2}\rho\ \frac{dB}{dt}\right)\rho = \frac{dL}{dt} \qquad ...(5.14)$$

The change in angular momentum ΔL of electron during the magnetic field changes from 0 to B is obtained by integrating above equation. Thus

$$\Delta L = \frac{1}{2}e\rho^2 B \qquad ...(5.15)$$

This change in angular momentum produces change in magnetic moment given by

$$\Delta\mu = -\left(\frac{e}{2m}\right)\Delta L = -\frac{e^2 B}{4m}\rho^2 \qquad ...(5.16)$$

The electronic orbits in an atom have different radii and different orientations. If r_i represents the radius i^{th} orbits and θ_i the angle which the normal to the plane of ith orbit makes with B, the projection of r_i onto the plane perpendicular to B is $\rho_i = r_i \cos\theta_i$. The induced magnetic moment in atom is given by

$$\Delta\mu_{\text{ATOM}} = -\frac{e^2 B}{4m}\sum_{i=1}^{Z}\rho_i^2\,, \qquad Z \text{ being the atomic number.}$$

$$= -\frac{e^2 B}{4m} Z\langle\rho^2\rangle \qquad ...(5.17)$$

where $\langle\rho^2\rangle = \dfrac{\sum_{i=1}^{Z}\rho_i^2}{Z}$ and $\langle\rho^2\rangle = \langle x^2\rangle + \langle y^2\rangle$

The average of square of atomic radius r is given by

$$\langle r^2\rangle = \langle x^2\rangle + \langle y^2\rangle + \langle z^2\rangle \text{ where } \langle x^2\rangle = \langle y^2\rangle = \langle z^2\rangle = \frac{1}{3}\langle r^2\rangle$$

$$\therefore \qquad \langle\rho^2\rangle = \langle x^2\rangle + \langle y^2\rangle = \frac{2}{3}\langle r^2\rangle \qquad ...(5.18)$$

In view of eqn. (5.18), the expression for magnetic moment induced in atom becomes

$$\mu_{\text{ATOM}} = -\frac{Ze^2 B}{4m}\frac{2}{3}\langle r^2 \rangle$$

$$= -\frac{Ze^2 B}{6m}\langle r^2 \rangle \qquad \text{...(5.19)}$$

If there are N atoms per unit volume, the magnetization induced in the specimen is

$$M = N\mu_{\text{ATOM}} = -\frac{NZe^2 B}{6m}\langle r^2 \rangle \qquad \text{...(5.20)}$$

The diamagnetic susceptibility of the specimen is

$$\chi = \frac{\mu_0 M}{B} = -\frac{\mu_0 NZe^2}{6m}\langle r^2 \rangle \qquad \text{...(5.21)}$$

Thus the diamagnetic susceptibility is negative. This is due to the fact that the induced magnetic moment is opposite to the applied field. Since the motion of electrons and size of their orbits are not influenced by temperature, χ is independent of temperature. Whether the atom possesses magnetic moment or not, the applied field always induces magnetic moment and therefore all substances show diamagnetism. In paramagnetic substances the diamagnetism is masked by large magnetic moment produced by alignment of the atomic dipoles under the action of the applied field. Diamagnetism is not an intrinsic property of atoms but it is a temporarily induced effect. When the external magnetic field is removed, the diamagnetic effect vanishes. Diamagnetic effect is universal in the sense that it is induced in all kinds of molecules when they are subjected to magnetic field. Because of its small magnitude it is usually masked in paramagnetic substances.

5.6. PARAMAGNETISM (CLASSICAL LANGEVIN'S THEORY)

The classical theory of paramagnetism was developed by the French physicist Paul Langevin in 1905. The atoms or molecules of paramagnetic substances behave like permanent magnetic dipoles. The random orientation of these dipoles gives the matter in bulk no magnetization. When a paramagnetic substance is subjected to an external magnetic field, the magnetic dipoles tend to align parallel to the field but this tendency of alignment is opposed by thermal agitation of the molecules. At equilibrium the substance acquires net magnetic moment in the direction of the applied field. At low temperature the thermal agitation is small and hence a relatively weak field is capable of aligning a large number of dipoles parallel to the field. At high temperature the vigorous random motion of atomic dipoles strongly opposes the action of applied field and hence a relatively strong magnetic field is required to induce magnetization. It was discovered by Curie that the paramagnetic susceptibility χ is inversely proportional to the temperature T.

$$\chi = \frac{C}{T}, \text{ where } C \text{ is constant called Curie constant.}$$

Langevin, making use of *Boltzmann* classical statistics, gave a theoretical explanation of Curie law. In magnetic field B, an atomic dipole acquires extra energy U given by

$$U = -\mu B \cos\theta$$

where θ is the angle between the magnetic field and dipole axis. According to classical statistics the number of dipoles with energy U and having orientations between the angles θ and θ + $d\theta$, is given by

$$dn = c\,e^{-U/kT}\sin\theta\, d\theta, \qquad c \text{ is a constant.}$$

$$= c\,e^{\mu B\cos\theta/kT}\sin\theta\, d\theta \qquad ...(5.22)$$

where T is temperature of the specimen. The total number of dipoles in the specimen is given by

$$n = c\int_0^{\pi} e^{\mu B\cos\theta/kT}\sin\theta\, d\theta \qquad ...(5.23)$$

The component of magnetic moment of a dipole parallel to the magnetic field is $\mu\cos\theta$. The average magnetic moment is

$$\bar{\mu} = \frac{\text{total magnetic moment parallel to the field}}{\text{total number of dipoles}}$$

$$= \frac{\int \mu\cos\theta\, dn}{n}$$

$$= \frac{\int_0^{\pi} \mu\cos\theta\cdot e^{\mu B\cos\theta/kT}\sin\theta\, d\theta}{\int_0^{\pi} e^{\mu B\cos\theta/kT}\sin\theta\, d\theta}$$

Let us put $\frac{\mu B}{kT} = a$ and change variable θ to x through the substitution $\cos\theta = x$. Then

$$\bar{\mu} = \mu\frac{\int_{-1}^{1} x e^{ax}\, dx}{\int_{-1}^{1} e^{ax}\, dx}$$

$$= \mu\frac{d}{da}\left(\ell n\int_{-1}^{1} e^{ax} dx\right)$$

$$= \mu\frac{d}{da}\left(\ell n(e^{a} - e^{-a}) - \ell n\, a\right)$$

$$= \mu\left(\frac{e^{a} + e^{-a}}{e^{a} - e^{-a}} - \frac{1}{a}\right)$$

$$= \mu\left(\coth a - \frac{1}{a}\right) \qquad ...(5.24)$$

$$= \mu L(a) \qquad ...(5.25)$$

where

$$L(a) = \coth a - 1/a \qquad ...(5.26)$$

is called Langevin function. If N is the number of dipoles per unit volume, the magnetization is given by

$$M = N\,\bar{\mu} = N\mu\,L(a) \qquad ...(5.27)$$

The expression for paramagnetic susceptibility χ comes out to be

$$\chi = \frac{\mu_0 M}{B} = \frac{\mu_0 \mu\, N\,L(a)}{B} \qquad ...(5.28)$$

The Langevin function $L(a)$ is plotted as a function of a $(=\mu B/kT)$ in Fig. 5.3. For small values of a *i.e.* at high temperature the curve is linear and

$$L(a) = \frac{a}{3} = \frac{\mu B}{3kT} \qquad ...(5.29)$$

Under this approximation the susceptibility comes out to be

$$\chi = \frac{\mu_0 \mu^2 N}{3kT} = \frac{C}{T}$$

$$\text{where} \quad C = \frac{\mu_0 \mu^2 N}{3k} \qquad ...(5.30)$$

which is the Curie law.

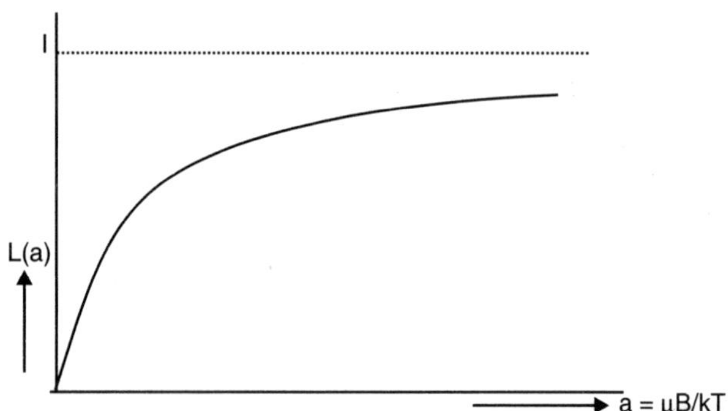

Fig. 5.3. Variation of Langevin's function $L(a)$ with a.

For large values of $a = \mu B/kT$ i.e. at low temperature, Langevin's function tends to unity. From eqn. (5.27) we see that under this condition the magnetization attains maximum value. This is because of the fact that at low temperatures the thermal motions of atoms are small and a weak field is capable of aligning most of the magnetic dipoles. This state is called the *saturation state.*

Langevin's theory as such can only be applied to gases where magnetic dipoles are sufficiently far apart and their mutual interactions are negligibly small. In case of solids and liquids, the interactions of magnetic dipoles are large and they must be taken into consideration. For solids and liquids the susceptibility is given by

$$\chi = \frac{C}{T - \Theta} \qquad ...(5.31)$$

where Θ is a constant, called Weiss constant.

5.7. QUANTUM THEORY OF PARAMAGNETISM

The atoms or ions of a paramagnetic substance have permanent magnetic moment. In absence of external magnetic field, the magnetic moments are randomly oriented and hence the substance shows no bulk magnetization. When magnetic field is switched on such a substance, each magnetic dipole experiences torque, which tends to align the dipoles parallel to the field. But this tendency of magnetic field is opposed by thermal energy of the dipoles. In equilibrium, the specimen acquires net magnetic moment in the direction of the magnetic field.

Let the specimen be subjected to a magnetic field in z-direction. If the atom has angular momentum **J**, the component of magnetic moment of atom in the direction of the magnetic field is

$$\mu_z = -g\left(\frac{e}{2m}\right)J_z = -g\left(\frac{e}{2m}\right)M_J\hbar = -g\left(\frac{e\hbar}{2m}\right)M_J = -g\mu_\beta M_J \qquad ...(5.32)$$

where the magnetic quantum number $M_J = -J, -J+1, ...0,.........+J$.

The magnetic interaction energy of the atom (dipole) in magnetic field is

$$U = -\vec{\mu}\cdot\mathbf{B} = \mu_z B = -(-g\mu_\beta M_J)B = g\mu_\beta BM_J \qquad ...(5.33)$$

Since M_J has $(2J+1)$ values, the magnetic field splits the energy level into $(2J+1)$ components, called *Zeeman* levels. In presence of magnetic field B, the atoms are distributed among these Zeeman levels according to Maxwell-Boltzmann statistics. The number of atoms per unit volume occupying the Zeeman level with energy $g\mu_\beta BM_J$ at temperature T is given by

$$dN = C\exp\left(-\frac{U}{kT}\right) = C\exp\left(-\frac{g\mu_\beta BM_J}{kT}\right), \; C \text{ is a constant.} \qquad ...(5.34)$$

The magnetic moment in the z-direction due dN atoms is

$$dM = \mu_z dN = -g\mu_\beta M_J.dN$$

The average value of magnetic moment in z-direction is

$$\bar{\mu}_z = \frac{\text{total magnetic moment in } z\text{-direction}}{\text{total number of atoms}} = \frac{\sum dM}{\sum dN}$$

$$= \frac{\sum_{M_J=-J}^{M_J=J}(-g\mu_\beta M_J)\exp\left(-\frac{g\mu_\beta BM_J}{kT}\right)}{\sum_{M_J=-J}^{M_J=J}\exp\left(-\frac{g\mu_\beta BM_J}{kT}\right)}$$

$$= \frac{g\mu_\beta \sum_{M_J=-J}^{J} -M_J \exp(-xM_J)}{\sum_{M_J=-J}^{J} \exp(-xM_J)}, \quad \text{where} \quad x = \frac{g\mu_\beta B}{kT} \qquad ...(5.35)$$

Let us simplify the expression under summation sign.

$$\frac{\sum_{M_J=-J}^{J} -M_J \exp(-xM_J)}{\sum_{M_J=-J}^{J} \exp(-xM_J)} = \frac{d}{dx}\left[\ln\left\{\sum_{M_J=-J}^{J} \exp(-xM_J)\right\}\right]$$

$$= \frac{d}{dx}\left[\ln\left\{e^{Jx} + e^{(J-1)x} + ...e^{1} + e^{0} + e^{-1} + ...e^{-Jx}\right\}\right]$$

$$= \frac{d}{dx}\left[\ln\left\{e^{Jx}\left(1 + e^{-x} + ...e^{-2Jx}\right)\right\}\right]$$

$$= \frac{d}{dx}\left[\ln\left\{e^{Jx}\left(\frac{1-e^{-(2J+1)x}}{1-e^{-x}}\right)\right\}\right]$$

$$= \frac{d}{dx}\left[\ln\left\{\frac{e^{Jx} - e^{-(J+1)x}}{1-e^{-x}}\right\}\right]$$

$$= \frac{d}{dx}\left[\ln\left\{\frac{e^{(2J+1)\,x/2} - e^{-(2J+1)\,x/2}}{e^{x/2} - e^{-x/2}}\right\}\right]$$

[*Numerator and denominator have been multiplied by exp(x/2)*]

$$= \frac{d}{dx}\left[\ln\frac{\sinh\left(\frac{2J+1}{2}\right)x}{\sinh\frac{x}{2}}\right]$$

$$= \frac{2J+1}{2}\coth\frac{2J+1}{2}x - \frac{1}{2}\coth\frac{x}{2}$$

Substituting $x = \frac{a}{J}$ or $a = Jx$, we get

$$= J\left[\left(\frac{2J+1}{2J}\right)\coth\left(\frac{2J+1}{2J}\right)a - \frac{1}{2J}\coth\frac{a}{2J}\right]$$

$$= J\,B_J(a) \qquad ...(5.36)$$

where $$B_J(a) = \left[\left(\frac{2J+1}{2J}\right)\coth\left(\frac{2J+1}{2J}\right)a - \frac{1}{2J}\coth\frac{a}{2J}\right] \qquad ...(5.37)$$

is called ***Brillouin Function.***

The average value of z-component of magnetic moment is

$$\bar{\mu}_z = g\mu_\beta J\, B_J(a) \quad ...(5.38)$$

The magnetic moment per unit volume or magnetization is given by

$$M = N\bar{\mu}_z = Ng\mu_\beta J B_J(a) \quad ...(5.39)$$

The susceptibility χ is given by

$$\chi = \frac{\mu_0 M}{B} = \frac{\mu_0 N g\mu_\beta J}{B} B_J(a) \quad ...(5.40)$$

(*i*) When the magnetic *field* is *weak* and *temperature* is *high,* the condition $a \ll 1$ is satisfied.

Under this condition, $B_J(a) \to \frac{J+1}{3} a$, the susceptibility becomes

$$\chi = \frac{\mu_0 N g^2 \mu_\beta^2 J(J+1)}{3kT} = \frac{C}{T} \quad ...(5.41)$$

which is Curie Law. The Curie constant is given by

$$C = \frac{\mu_0 N g^2 \mu_\beta^2 J(J+1)}{3} \quad ...(5.42)$$

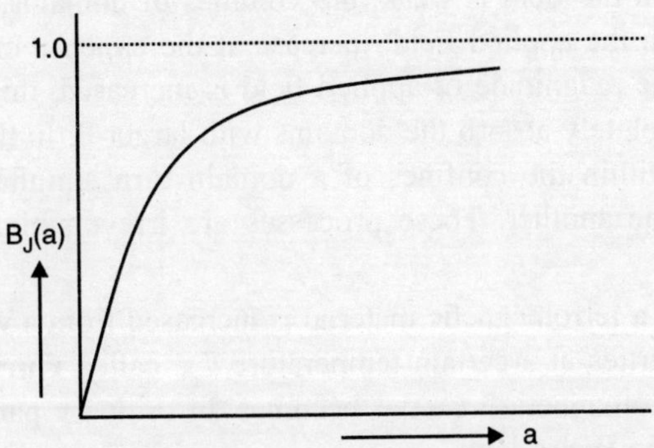

Fig. 5.4. Variation of Brillouin function with *a*

(*ii*) When magnetic field is very high and temperature is low, $a \gg 1$, under this condition, $B_J(a) \to 1$. The magnetization becomes

$$M = Ng\mu_\beta J$$

Since the maximum value of M_J is J, this value of magnetization represents the maximum (saturation) value of magnetization.

Thus $$M_S = Ng\mu_\beta J \quad ...(5.43)$$

In this state of magnetization, all the magnetic moments become parallel to the applied field. This can be understood as follows. When field B is very high, the separation of successive Zeeman levels ($\Delta E = g\mu_\beta B$) is very large. At low temperature, thermal energy kT is so small that none of the atoms (dipoles) are excited to higher Zeeman levels. Meaning thereby, all the atoms remain in the lowest energy state which corresponds to $M_J = -J$. In this state, each atom has magnetic moment $\mu_z = g\mu_\beta J$ and hence the magnetization is $M = Ng\mu_\beta J$.

5.8. FERROMAGNETISM

Substances, which are capable of having magnetization even in absence of external magnetic field are called *ferromagnetics*. Iron, nickel, cobalt, gadolinium, and some of their alloys fall in this class. *Ferromagnetics* are strongly magnetic substances. Their magnetization exceeds that of dia- and paramagnetics.

The study of *gyromagnetic* phenomena clearly indicates that the intrinsic (spin) magnetic moments of electrons are responsible for the magnetic properties of ferromagnetic materials. In specific conditions, *exchange forces*, (whose origin can be understood only by quantum mechanics), appear in *ferromagnetics*, and cause the magnetic moments of electrons to line up parallel to one another. This alignment of magnetic moments occurs in relatively small regions, called *domains*. Domains have dimensions of the order of 1 to 10 μm. Within the confines of each domain, a ferromagnetic material is spontaneously magnetized to saturation and has a definite magnetic moment. The directions of these moments are different for different domains. Because of random orientations of domains, the total magnetic moment of a piece of ferromagnetic material is zero in absence of external field.

Under the action of external magnetic field, the increase in magnetization takes place in two independent ways. First when the field is weak, the volumes of domains, whose magnetic moments make smaller angles (θ) with the applied field, increase at the expense of domains whose moments make larger angles. When the magnitude of applied field is increased, this process goes on until the domains with smaller θ completely absorb the domains with larger θ. In the next stage, the magnetic moments of the electrons within the confines of a domain turn simultaneously without violating their strict parallelism to one another. These processes are irreversible, and this is exactly what causes *hysteresis*.

When the temperature of a ferromagnetic material is increased from a very low value, the material loses its ferromagnetic properties at a certain temperature T_C, called **Curie point**. At a temperature above the Curie point, a ferromagnetic material becomes an ordinary paramagnetic material whose susceptibility obeys the **Curie-Weiss** law

$$\chi = \frac{C}{T - T_C}$$

5.9. WEISS THEORY OF FERROMAGNETISM

In 1907 Pierre Weiss formulated the theory of ferromagnetism. To explain the phenomenon of spontaneous magnetization he postulated the existence of *internal field*, which causes the alignment of magnetic dipoles even in the absence of external field. Weiss did not know the exact mechanism of internal field. Twenty years later Heisenberg presented the quantum mechanical explanation for the origin of *internal field*. The internal field H_I, also called Weiss molecular field, is proportional to the magnetization M. That is $H_I = \gamma M$ where γ is a constant and is of the order of 10^4.

The effective *magnetic field* H_m acting on a magnetic dipole is

$$H_m = H + \gamma M \quad \text{...(5.44)}$$

where H is external field.

Taking Weiss *internal field* into consideration and applying Brillouin's quantum theory of paramagnetism to ferromagnetic substances, the expression for magnetization comes out to be

$$M(T) = Ng\mu_\beta J B_J(a) \quad \text{...(5.45)}$$

$$\text{where } a = \frac{Jg\mu_\beta \mu_0 H_m}{kT} = \frac{g\mu_\beta \mu_0 (H + \gamma M) J}{kT} \quad \text{...(5.46)}$$

At very low temperature (*i.e.* $T \to 0$) $a >> 1$, *Brillouin's function* tends to unity and magnetization M assumes its saturation value

$$M_S(0) = Ng\mu_\beta J. \quad \text{...(5.47)}$$

In terms of saturation magnetization $M_S(0)$, the magnetizatiom M at temperature T is expressed as

$$M(T) = M_S(0) B_J(a)$$

$$\text{or} \quad \frac{M(T)}{M_S(0)} = B_J(a) \quad \text{...(5.48)}$$

Spontaneous Magnetization: Even in absence of external magnetic field ($H = 0$), the magnetization in a domain of ferromagnetic material has saturation value M_S. In zero external field ($H = 0$), let us denote the value of a by a'. That is,

$$a' = [a]_{H=0} = \frac{Jg\mu_\beta \mu_0 \gamma M(T)}{kT} \quad \text{...(5.49)}$$

Whence

$$M(T) = \left(\frac{kT}{Jg\mu_\beta \mu_0 \gamma} \right) a' \quad \text{...(5.50)}$$

$$\text{or} \quad \frac{M(T)}{M_S(0)} = \left(\frac{kT}{NJ^2 (g\mu_\beta)^2 \mu_0 \gamma} \right) a' \quad \text{...(5.51)}$$

The general behaviour of the magnetization can be found from graphical solution eqns. (5.48) and (5.51). To obtain a graphical solution we plot the two functions $M(T)/M_S(0)$ given by eqns. (5.48) and (5.51) against a' as shown in Fig. 5.5. Equation (5.51) gives a straight line, which passes through the origin and intersects the curve representing the Brillouin function at this point. Thus one possible value of the magnetization is always zero. From eqn. (5.51) we see that the slope of the line is proportional to the absolute temperature T. So at *high temperatures* we would have line like (*b*). The solution is $M(T)/M_S(0) = 0$. This means that the substance shows no spontaneous magnetization in zero external field ($H = 0$) at high temperatures. As the temperature falls, the slope of the line given by eqn. (5.51) decreases until at a certain temperature T_C at which it is tangential to the Brillouin curve (*a*) at origin. Thus at critical temperature T_C, called Curie temperature, we have

Slope of straight line = slope of tangent to Brillouin curve at origin

$$\frac{kT_C}{N(g\mu_\beta)^2 J^2 \mu_0 \gamma} = \frac{d}{da'}\left[B_J(a')\right]_{a'\to 0} = \frac{d}{da'}\left[\frac{J+1}{3J}a'\right] = \frac{J+1}{3J}$$

$$\left\{\because B_J(a') = \frac{J+1}{3J}a' \quad \text{for} \quad a' << 1\right\}$$

Whence
$$T_C = \frac{N(g\mu_\beta)^2 \mu_0 \gamma J(J+1)}{3k} \qquad \text{...(5.52)}$$

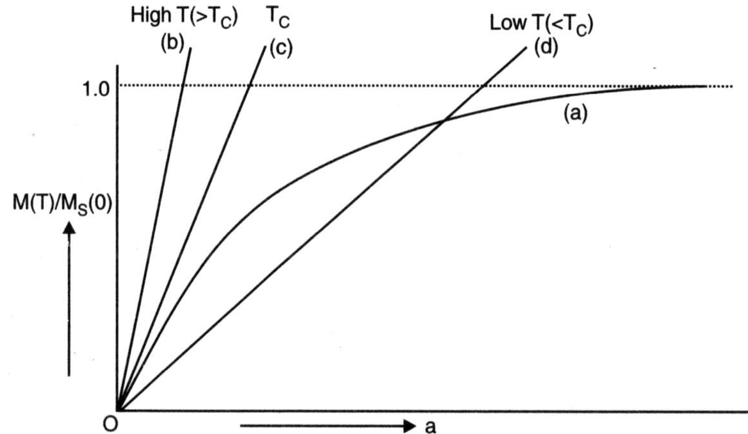

Fig. 5.5. Graphical solution of equation (5.48) and (5.51).

The quantity γ can be written in terms of measurable properties of material as

$$\gamma = \frac{3kT_C}{N(g\mu_\beta)^2 \mu_0 J(J+1)} \qquad \text{...(5.53)}$$

At still lower temperature ($T < T_C$), the slope of the line is less than the initial slope of the *Langevin* curve, and there will be two points of intersection, and two possible values of $M(T)/M_S(0)$ one with $M(T)/M_S(0) = 0$ and one with $M(T)/M_S(0) \simeq 1$. It can be seen that only upper solution is stable. This means that a magnetic material should magnetize itself spontaneously at sufficiently low temperatures. In other words, when the thermal motions are small enough, the coupling between atomic magnets causes them all to line up parallel to each other.

Temperature Dependence of Spontaneous Magnetization

Below Curie temperature T_C the spontaneous magnetization is given by the intersection of Brillouin curve (*a*) and the straight line (*d*). If we solve for M/M_0 for various temperatures – by varying the slope of the line (*d*) we get the theoretical curve shown below. This curve should be the same for all ferromagnetic materials for which atomic magnetic moment comes from a single electron. The curves for other materials are only slightly different.

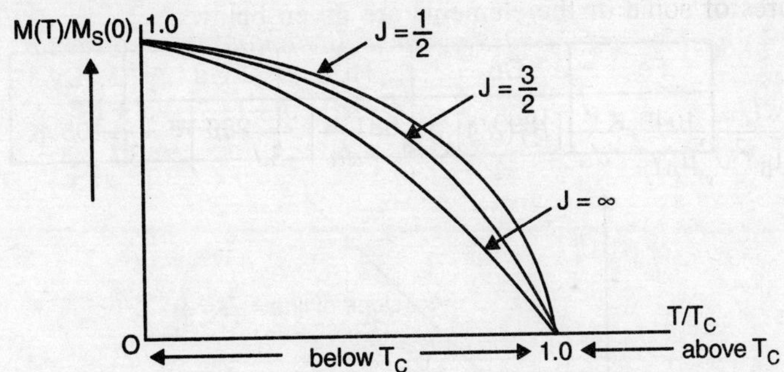

Fig. 5.6. Spontaneous magnetization as function of temperature.

From eqn. (5.48) the value of M/M_0 can be expressed as

$$\frac{M(T)}{M_S(0)} = \frac{a'(J+1)}{3J}\left(\frac{T}{T_C}\right) \qquad ...(5.54)$$

Curie-Weiss Law (paramagnetic region): At temperature $T > T_C$ and for weak field we have

$$a << 1 \text{ and } B_J(a) = \frac{J+1}{3J}a$$

The magnetization of the specimen is given by

$$M(T) = Ng\mu_\beta JB_J(a) = \frac{Ng\mu_\beta(J+1)a}{3} = \frac{Ng\mu_\beta(J+1)}{3}.\frac{g\mu_\beta\mu_0(H+\gamma M)J}{kT}$$

$$\Rightarrow \qquad = \left(\frac{H+\gamma M}{\gamma}\right)\frac{T_C}{T}$$

$$\Rightarrow \qquad M\left[1-\frac{T_C}{T}\right] = \frac{(T_C/\gamma)\ H}{T}$$

$$\Rightarrow \qquad M = \frac{CH}{T-T_C} \text{ where } C = T_C/\gamma$$

$$\chi = \frac{M}{H} = \frac{C}{T-T_C} \qquad ...(5.55)$$

Equation (5.55) is Curie-Weiss law. Constant C is called Curie constant and T_C the Curie temperature.

A plot of $1/\chi$ against T is a straight line. The slope of this line equals the reciprocal of Curie constant C. From the measurement of χ at different temperatures, the magnetic moment of atomic dipoles can be calculated.

Curie temperatures of some of the elements are given below.

Fe	Co	Ni	Gd	Dy
1043 K	1393 K	631 K	289 K	105 K

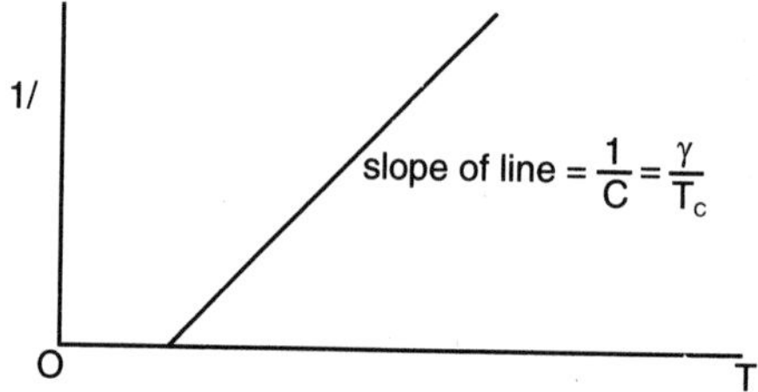

Fig. 5.7. Variation of $1/\chi$ with temperature.

5.10. HYSTERESIS

Consider a ferromagnetic material placed in a magnetizing field *H*. When the field *H* is increased, the magnetic field *B* in the specimen also increases. If the field *H* is increased to such a value, say H_{max}, that all the dipoles in the specimen are aligned, the specimen is said to have attained the state of saturation and in this state *B* is maximum. The state of magnetization of the specimen during this process is represented by the curve *OA*. If *H* is decreased, *B* is also decreased, and the state of magnetization during this process follows the curve *AB*. When $H = 0$, $B \neq 0$, it has value $B_R = OB$. Thus *B lags behind H.* This phenomenon is called hysteresis. The magnetic field *B* in the specimen is seen to depend not only on the field *H* but also on the past history of the specimen. Thus we see that when $H = 0$, the magnetic field *B* inside the specimen is B_R. This is called the *residual magnetization* or *remanence.* If *H* is reversed and increased to the value $-H_{max}$ the magnetization follows the curve *BCD*. Again we see that to erase the residual magnetization, a reverse *H* field equal to $-H_C$ is needed. This field (H_C) is called *coervice force.* The part of the curve for which *B* is positive and *H* is negative represents *demagnetization.* When the magnitude of *H* is decreased from the value at point *D* to zero, the state of magnetization follows the curve *DE*. On further increasing the field *H* we get the curve *EA*. The loop *ABCDEA* is called the hysteresis loop. A substance with large coercive force is called hard and that with small coercive force is called soft. The shapes of hysteresis loop differ from one substance to another. For permanent magnet, *coercivity OC* and *retentivity OB* must be large. For electromagnet area of hysteresis loop, *coercivity* and *retentivity* must be small.

Hysteresis Loss

When a ferromagnetic material is placed in an alternating magnetizing field, the specimen is taken through a cycle of magnetization during each cycle of magnetizing current and in each cycle some energy is lost. This energy goes into heating the material. The area of hysteresis loop represents the energy lost per unit volume of the material.

When magnetizing current I is made to change in the windings of an endless solenoid, an induced *emf* of magnitude $\varepsilon = N\dfrac{d\varphi}{dt}$ is set up. The rate at which the energy is delivered to the coil is given by

$$\text{Power} = \frac{dW}{dt} = \varepsilon I$$

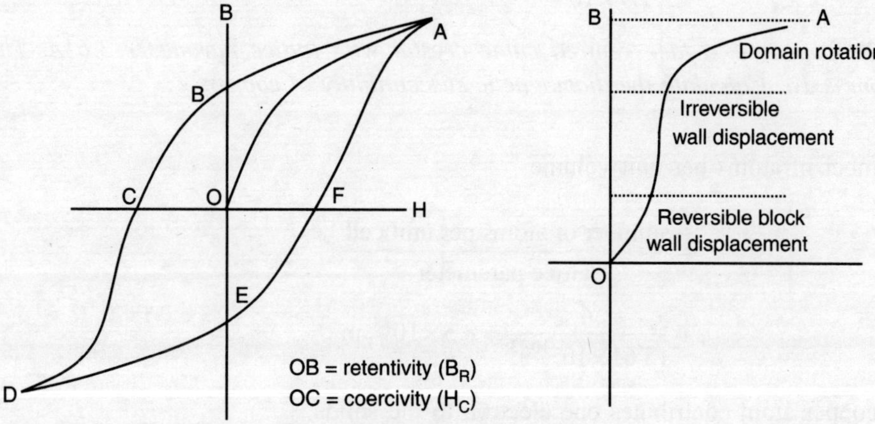

Fig. 5.8. Hysteresis loop.

This energy is expended in doing work against the back *emf*. The energy expended in one cycle is

$$W = \oint dW = \oint \varepsilon I\, dt = \oint N\frac{d\varphi}{dt} I\, dt = \oint NA\frac{dB}{dt}.Idt = \oint (NAdB)\left(\frac{HL}{N}\right)$$

Where A = cross-section of the solenoid, L = length of solenoid, N = number of turns wrapped on the solenoid. The volume of the solenoid is $V = AL$. Therefore

$$W = V\oint HdB$$

$$\frac{W}{V} = \oint HdB = \textit{area of } B - H \textit{ loop}. \qquad \text{...(5.56)}$$

Thus the area of B—H loop represents the energy dissipated per unit volume per cycle. In order to have minimum loss of energy, materials with narrow hysteresis loop are needed for the design of transformer cores.

SOLVED EXAMPLES

***Example* 1:** *The mean of square of radius* $< r^2 >$ *of atomic hydrogen is* $3a_0^2$, *where* $a_0 = 0.50 \times 10^{-10}$ m *is Bohr radius. Calculate the diamagnetic susceptibility of hydrogen.*

Solution: Number of atoms per unit volume

$$N = \frac{6.023\times 10^{26}}{22.4\times 10^{-3}}\,\text{m}^{-3} = 2.69\times 10^{28}\ \text{m}^{-3}$$

Diamagnetic susceptibility $\chi = -\dfrac{\mu_0 NZe^2}{6m} < r^2 > = -\dfrac{\mu_0 NZe^2 a_0^2}{2m}$

$$= -\frac{4\pi \times 10^{-7} \times 2.69 \times 10^{28} \times (1.6 \times 10^{-19})^2 (0.50 \times 10^{-10})^2}{2 \times 9.1 \times 10^{-31}}$$

$$= -1.9 \times 10^{-6}$$

***Example* 2:** *Copper is a face centred cubic crystal with lattice parameter 3.61Å. The radius of copper atom is 1Å. Calculate the diamagnetic susceptibility of copper.*

Solution:

Number of atoms per unit volume

$$= \frac{\text{number of atoms per unit cell}}{\text{lattice parameter}}$$

$$= \frac{4}{(3.61 \times 10^{-10})^3} = 8.5 \times 10^{28} \text{ m}^{-3}$$

Each copper atom contributes one electron to the solid.

Susceptibility $\chi = -\dfrac{\mu_0 NZe^2}{6m} < r^2 >$

$$= -\frac{4\pi \times 10^{-7} \times 8.5 \times 10^{28} \times (1.6 \times 10^{-19})^2 \times (1 \times 10^{-10})^2}{6 \times 9.1 \times 10^{-31}}$$

$$= -5.0 \times 10^{-6}$$

***Example* 3:** *A paramagnetic substance contains 1×10^{28} ions/m^3, each of which has magnetic moment of 2 Bohr magneton. It is placed in a magnetic field of strength 1.25 T at room temperature. Calculate the paramagnetic susceptibility and magnetization.*

Solution: $\mu = 2\mu_B = 2 \times 9.27 \times 10^{-24}$ A m^{-2}

Susceptibility $\chi = \dfrac{\mu_0 N \mu^2}{3kT} = \dfrac{4\pi \times 10^{-7} \times 10^{28} \times (2 \times 9.27 \times 10^{-24})^2}{3 \times 1.38 \times 10^{-23} \times 300}$

$$= 0.347 \times 10^{-4}$$

Magnetization $M = \chi H = \chi \dfrac{B}{\mu_0} = \dfrac{0.347 \times 10^{-4} \times 1.25}{4\pi \times 10^{-7}} = 34.55 \text{ A m}^{-2}$

QUESTIONS AND PROBLEMS

1. What do you mean by diamagnetic, paramagnetic and ferromagnetic substances? Define the terms: magnetization M, intensity of magnetic field H, magnetic susceptibility χ.
2. Derive an expression for the magnetic moment of an atom in terms of angular momentum. Show that the interaction energy of an atom in magnetic field is given by

$$U = M_J g \, \mu_B B$$

where the symbols have their usual meaning.
3. What do you mean by diamagnetism? Describe Langevin's theory of diamagnetism. Why is the diamagnetic susceptibility independent of temperature?
4. What do you mean by paramagnetism? Describe Langevin's theory of paramagnetism. Derive Curie law. Discuss the limitations of the theory.
5. Describe Weiss theory of ferromagnetism. Discuss the temperature dependence of spontaneous magnetization.

6

CHAPTER

Transient and Steady State Behaviour of Simple Circuits

6.1. INTRODUCTION

The basic circuit elements-resistor, capacitor and inductor have certain distinct characteristic features. A resistor in the circuit dissipates electrical energy in the form of heat when an electrical current is allowed to pass through it. Thus it does not store energy. The capacitor on the other hand stores energy and does not dissipates it. In charging process, it acquires positive charge on one plate and negative charge on the other. The charges are held by electrostatic forces. Thus a charged capacitor has storage of electrostatic energy. This energy can be taken back if charges on the plates are allowed to leak *i.e.* when capacitor is discharged. A perfect capacitor gives back all the stored electrostatic energy in appropriate condition. An inductor also opposes the growth (or decay) of current in it by producing a self induced voltage across it. In this process the inductor stores magnetic energy in the form of magnetic field produced by the moving charges. This magnetic energy can be given up by the inductor gradually after the current is stopped. The process of energy storage by the capacitor or inductor takes a finite time. Due to this reason, whenever a circuit containing capacitor or inductor is fed by a source of electrical energy, the process of energy storage by the capacitor or inductor begins and circuit voltage or current starts building up gradually. After sometime when elements have stored energy to their full capacity, voltage and current attain a value which is independent of time. In this situation it is said that circuit has attained a steady state. Now if at this stage the source is switched off, the energy stored in capacitor or inductor is released and the voltage and current of the circuit is not allowed to go to zero instantaneously. Thus it decreases gradually and after some time becomes zero and circuit attains no current steady state. Similar situation is encountered when the voltage of the source is increased or decreased. A charge in circuit elements will lead to similar situation.The circuit is said to be in transient state during the period the circuit voltage or current gradually builds up due to storage of energy by circuit elements or it gradually decays due to release of energy by circuit elements. During transient state, the voltage and current in the circuit are function of time whose exact nature depends upon the components of the circuit. In this chapter we shall discuss the transient and steady state of some simple circuit fed by d.c. source.

6.2. KIRCHHOFF'S CIRCUIT LAW

An *electrical circuit* or a *network* consists of many *active* and *passive* elements. *Active* elements are those which supply energy to the network, and those which either absorb or store energy from the source are called *passive* elements. The resistor, inductor and capacitor are passive elements. The cell and generator are the active elements. In order to predict the behaviour of the network as a whole, it is necessary to calculate the currents in the different branches of the circuit. The calculation of currents in the different branches is considerably simplified by the use of Kirchhoff's laws.

Kirchhoff's first law applies to a *junction* (*node or branch point*). A *junction* is defined as the point where three or more than three conductors meet. While applying the first rule at a junction, the incoming currents are assumed to have one sign (plus or minus) and the outgoing currents are assigned opposite signs (minus or plus)

1. **Kirchhoff's Current Law (KCL):** *The algebric sum of instantaneous currents meeting at a junction is zero,* $\sum I = 0$

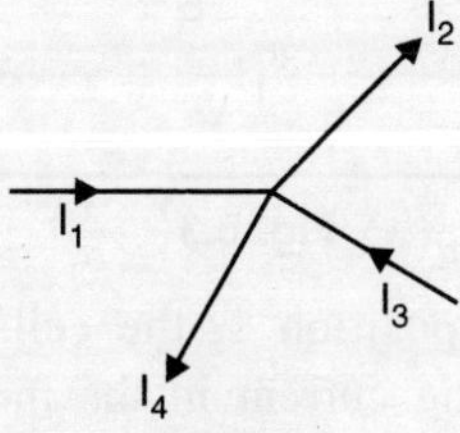

Fig. 6.1

Applying the law at the junction shown in the Fig. 6.1, we have

$$\sum I = I_1 - I_2 + I_3 - I_4 = 0 \qquad ...(6.1)$$

(Kirchhoff's first law is a direct consequence of the law of conservation of charge. At a junction, there is no accumulation of charges and hence the charge carried by the incoming currents must be equal to that carried by the outgoing currents).

2. **Kirchhoff's Voltage Law (KVL):** Kirchhoff's second law applies to a *closed circuit* (*or loop or mesh*) and involves voltages. A sign convention is necessary in order to specify voltage across an element. For this, we choose the direction of current arbitrarily around the loop. The end at which current enters an element is marked (+) and that at which the current leaves the elements is marked (–). A d.c. voltage source is assigned its own intrinsic polarity. The voltage across an element is written as the product of *current* and *resistance* in case of d.c. circuits and as the product of *current* and *impedance* in case of a.c.circuits. Kirchhoff's voltage law (KVL) is stated as follows:

   The algebraic sum of instantaneous voltage drops across the circuit elements around a loop is zero.

   The voltage drop across an element is positive if it is traversed from (+) end to (–) end and negative if it is traversed from (–) end to (+) end. Applying KVL to the circuit shown in the Fig. 6.2 we have

$$\left.\begin{array}{l} I_1R_1 + (I_1 - I_2)\,R_2 + I_1R_3 - V_1 = 0 \\ I_2R_4 + V_2 + I_2R_5 + (I_2 - I_1)R_2 = 0 \end{array}\right] \quad ...(6.2)$$

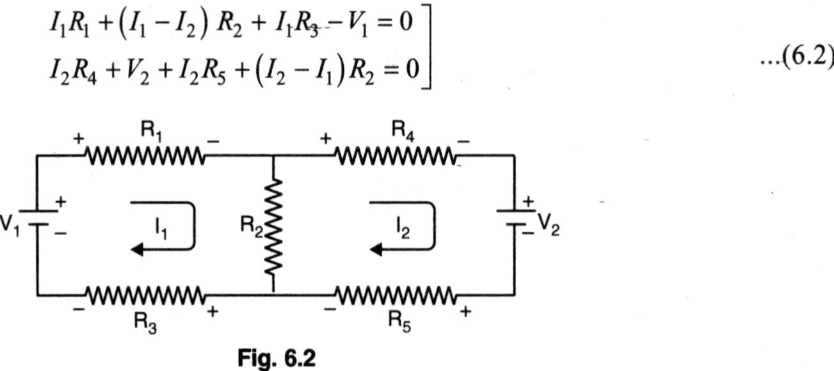

Fig. 6.2

Now we shall apply Kirchhoff's law to a circuit carrying a transient current. Consider a circuit arrangement shown in the Fig. 6.3.

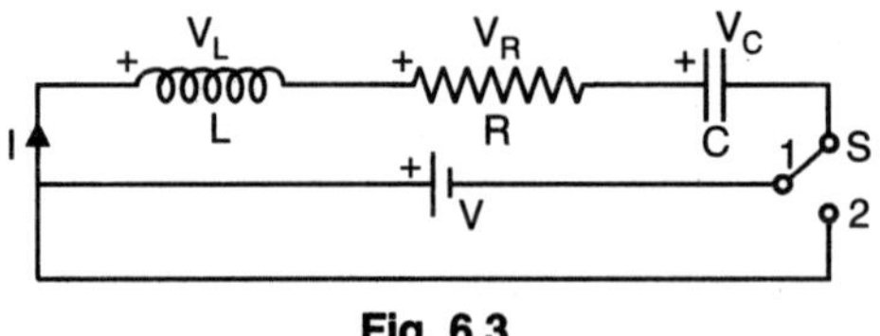

Fig. 6.3

When the switch S is thrown into position 1, the cell comes into the circuit and a current starts growing in the circuit. The growing current in the inductor produces an induced *emf* (back *emf*) which opposes the current. [Lenz's law]. The polarity of the back *emf* is shown in the figure and its magnitude is LdI/dt. Voltage across the resistor is RI. The flow of current in the circuit result an increases in charge on the capacitor. If at any instant t, charge on the capacitor is Q, then voltage across it is Q/C. The plate at which the current enters the capacitor is taken to be positive. Now KVL applied to the circuit gives

$$L\frac{dI}{dt} + RI + \frac{Q}{C} - V = 0 \quad ...(6.3)$$

The solution of this equation gives a *transient* current which exists only in the beginning and then it becomes zero.

Now let us take another situation. A capacitor is fully charged to a certain potential and then it is allowed to discharge through an inductor and a resistor. The discharge of the capacitor is accompanied by a growing current in the circuit (Fig. 6.4). At any instant t, the voltage across the elements are shown with polarity.

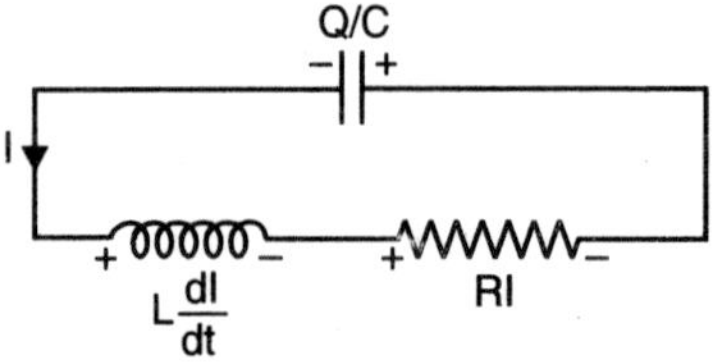

Fig. 6.4

KVL gives the equation

$$L\frac{dI}{dt} + RI + \frac{Q}{C} = 0; \qquad I = \frac{dQ}{dt}, \frac{dI}{dt} = \frac{d^2Q}{dt^2}$$

$$\therefore \qquad L\frac{d^2Q}{dt^2} + R\frac{dQ}{dt} + \frac{Q}{C} = 0 \qquad ...(6.4)$$

In a.c. circuits, the generator (source) is assigned its polarity arbitrarily and a current is assumed around the loop. The voltage across an element is IZ where Z is the impedance of the element. For inductor $Z = j\omega l$, for capacitor $Z = -j/\omega C$ and for resistor $Z = R$, where ω is the frequency of the source. KVL applied to the circuit shown in the Fig. 6.5 gives

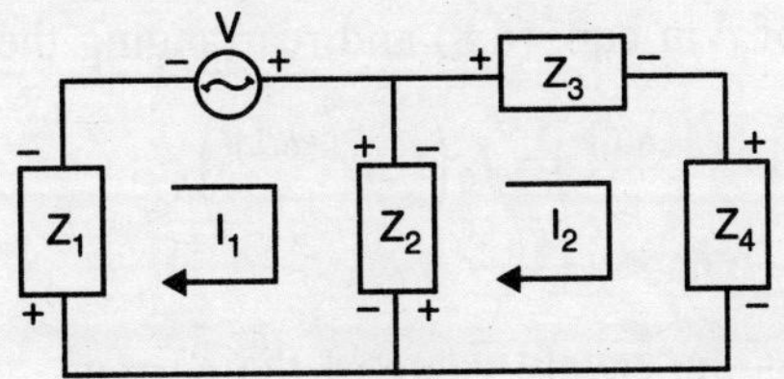

Fig. 6.5

$$\left.\begin{aligned} -V + (I_1 - I_2)Z_2 + I_1Z_1 = 0 \\ I_2Z_3 + I_2Z_4 + (I_2 - I_1)Z_2 = 0 \end{aligned}\right] \qquad ...(6.5)$$

6.3. GROWTH OF CURRENT IN LR CIRCUIT

Consider a circuit consisting of an inductance, resistance and a cell arranged as shown in the Fig. 6.6. Initially, the switch S is in position 2 and there is no current in the circuit. At time $t = 0$, the switch S is turned to the position 1. The current in the circuit grows and it takes

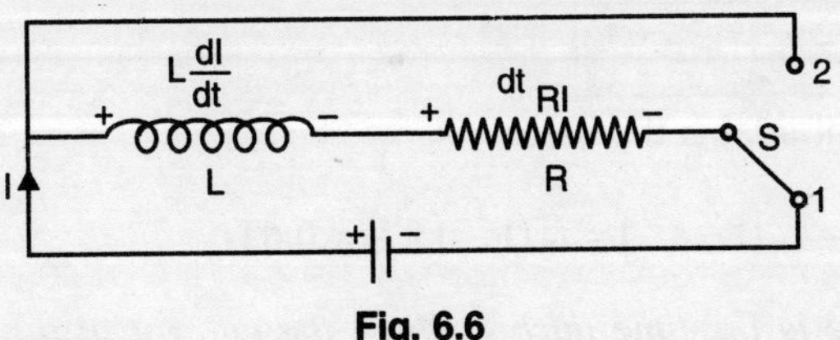

Fig. 6.6

certain time to attain its steady value. During the time the current grows, an induced *emf* $\left(= -L\frac{dI}{dt}\right)$ is set up in the inductance which opposes the growing current. The polarity of the induced voltage is such as to oppose the driving voltage of the cell. The magnitude voltage drop across L is $L\frac{dI}{dt}$. At any instant t, the equation of voltage is

$$L\frac{dI}{dt} + RI - V = 0 \qquad \text{KVL} \qquad ...(6.6)$$

The behaviour of the circuit is described by this equation. This equation can be solved by the method of separation of variables. It can be arranged in the form,

$$\frac{dI}{V - RI} = \frac{1}{L} dt \qquad \text{...(6.7)}$$

Integrating eqn. (6.7) we get

$$-\frac{1}{R} \ln (V - RI) = \frac{t}{L} + c \qquad \text{...(6.8)}$$

where c is the constant of integration. Using the initial condition $t = 0$, $I = 0$

we get $$c = -\frac{1}{R} \ln V$$

Substituting back the value of c in eqn. (6.8) and rearranging the resulting equation we have

$$I = \frac{V}{R}\left(1 - e^{(-R/L)t}\right) = I_0\left(1 - e^{(-R/L)t}\right) \qquad \text{...(6.9)}$$

where $I_0 = V/R$

As $t \to \infty$, $I \to I_0$. Thus I_0 is the steady value of the current.

The ratio L/R has the dimension of time.

$$\frac{L}{R} = \frac{\text{henry}}{\text{ohm}} = \frac{\text{volt}\cdot\text{sec}}{\text{Ampere}} \cdot \frac{\text{Ampere}}{\text{volt}} = \text{sec}$$

For this reason, the ratio L/R is called *the time constant* or *relaxation time* or *characteristic time* and is usually denoted by τ

$$\tau = \frac{L}{R} \qquad \text{...(6.10)}$$

In terms of time constant, eqn. (6.9) may be written as

$$\boxed{I = I_0\left(1 - e^{-t/\tau}\right)} \qquad \text{...(6.11)}$$

At time $t = \tau$, the current attains the value

$$I = I_0\left(1 - e^{-1}\right) = I_0 (1 - 0.37) = 0.63 I_0 \qquad \text{...(6.12)}$$

Thus the relaxation time is the time during which the current in the LR circuit builds up 63% of its steady value.

The rate at which the current grows in the circuit is given by

$$\frac{dI}{dt} = \frac{I_0}{\tau} e^{-t/\tau} = \frac{I_0 - I}{\tau} \qquad \text{...(6.13)}$$

Thus the rate of growth of current is inversly proportional to the time constant. As the time goes on, the rate of growth becomes less rapid and the current attains the steady state value asymptotically.

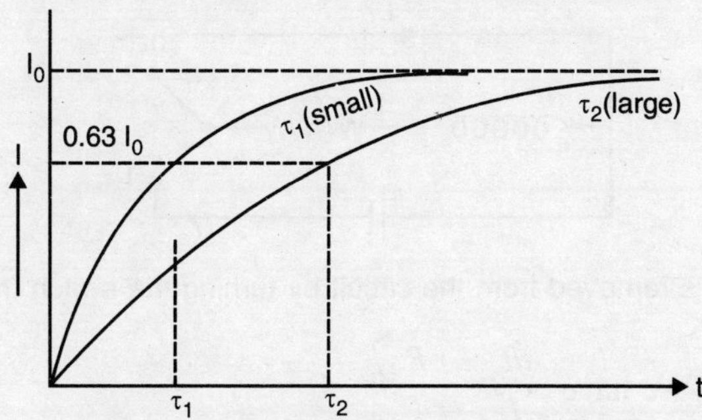

Fig. 6.7. Growth of current in LR circuit.

Voltage across the inductance is,

$$V_L = L\frac{dI}{dt} = L\frac{I_0}{\tau}e^{-t/\tau} = RI_0\,e^{-t/\tau} \qquad \text{...(6.14)}$$

and across the resistance is

$$V_R = IR = RI_0\left(1 - e^{-t/\tau}\right) \qquad \text{...(6.15)}$$

Notice that: $V_L + V_R = RI_0 = V$

The time dependance of V_R and V_L are shown in the Fig. 6.8.

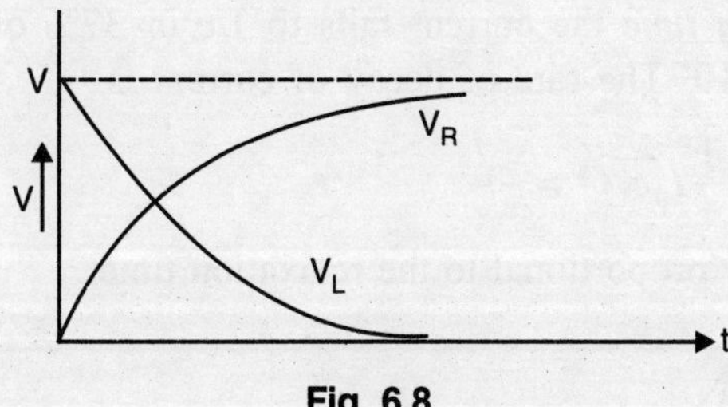

Fig. 6.8

6.4. DECAY OF CURRENT IN LR CIRCUIT

Suppose we have a *LR* circuit in which a constant current I_0 had been flowing. Now we remove the source suddenly. What will happen to the current? We shall consider this problem in what follows. When the source is removed from the circuit, the current decays, which in turn sets up an induced *emf*. The *emf* tries to maintain the current [Lenz Law] and thus the decay of current is delayed. The equation of voltage is

$$\left.\begin{aligned} V_L + V_R &= 0 \\ L\frac{dI}{dt} + RI &= 0 \end{aligned}\right] \quad \text{(KVL)} \qquad \text{...(6.16)}$$

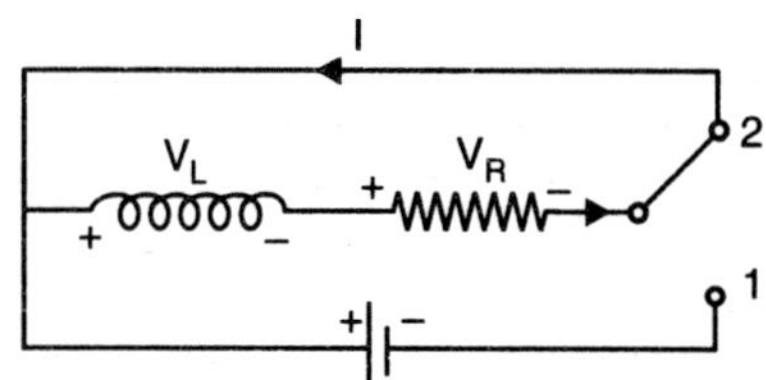

Fig. 6.9. The source is removed from the circuit by turning the switch from position 1 to 2.

Separating the variables we have $\dfrac{dI}{I} = -\dfrac{R}{L}dt$

which on integration gives, $\ln I = -\dfrac{R}{L}t + c$ ...(6.17)

where c is the constant of integration. Making use of the initial condition:

$$t = 0, \;\; I = I_0$$

we get $c = \ln I_0$. Substituting this value of of c in eqn. (6.17) we have

$$\boxed{I = I_0 e^{-(R/L)t} = I_0 e^{-t/\tau}} \qquad ...(6.18)$$

Thus the current falls exponentially with time.

At time $t = \tau$, $\quad I = I_0 e^{-1} = 0.37 I_0$ ...(6.19)

Thus during the *relaxation time* the current falls to $1/e$ or 37% of its initial value. The decay of current is shown in Fig. 6.10. The rate of decay of current is

$$\frac{dI}{dt} = -\frac{1}{\tau} I_0 e^{-t/\tau} = -\frac{I}{\tau} \qquad ...(6.20)$$

The decay rate is inversely proportional to the relaxation time.

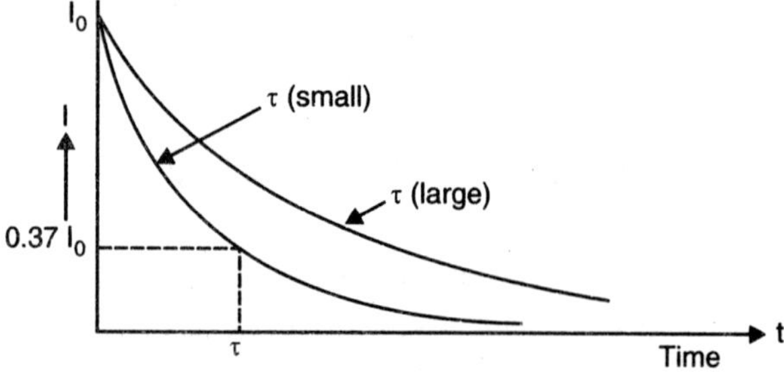

Fig. 6.10. Decay of current.

The voltage across the inductance and the resistance are given by

$$V_L = LI\frac{dI}{dt} = -\frac{LI}{\tau}e^{-t/\tau} = -RI_0 e^{-t/\tau} \qquad ...(6.21)$$

$$V_R = RI = RI_0 e^{-t/\tau} \qquad ...(6.22)$$

The time dependence of V_L and V_R is shown in the Fig. 6.11. The voltage across the inductance has polarity opposite to that shown in the Fig. 6.8.

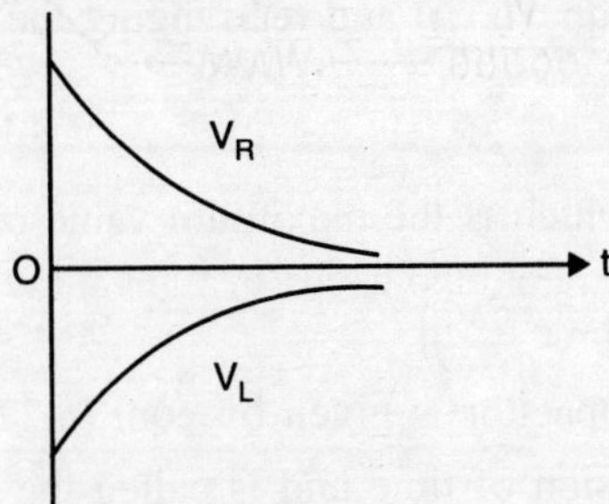

Fig. 6.11

6.5. CHARGING OF A CAPACITOR THROUGH A RESISTANCE

When a series combination of a resistor and a capacitor is connected across a cell, the capacitor is charged. During the charging process, a transient current flows in the circuit. When the capacitor is fully charged, the current in the circuit stops.

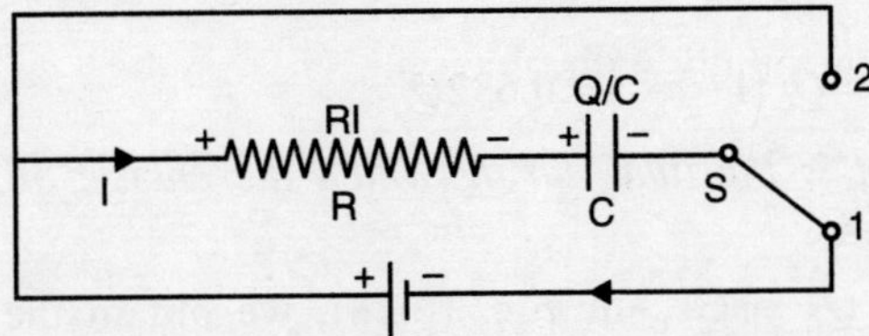

Fig. 6.12. Charging of a capacitor, Turning the switch to position 1, the capacitor is charged.

Let I be the current at some instant t and Q be the charge on the capacitor. The polarity of the voltages across the resistor and the capacitor is shown in the Fig. 6.12. Applying KVL to the circuit we have

$$RI + Q/C = V \qquad \text{...(6.23)}$$

where $$I = \frac{dQ}{dt}$$

In terms of charge on the capacitor, the equation for voltages becomes

$$R\frac{dQ}{dt} + \frac{Q}{C} = V \qquad \text{...(6.24)}$$

Separating the variables we obtain

$$\frac{dQ}{CV - Q} = \frac{1}{RC}dt$$

which on integration yields.

$$-\ln(CV - Q) = \frac{t}{RC} + K \qquad \text{...(6.25)}$$

where K is the constant of integration. Using the initial condition $t = 0$, $Q = 0$

we get $$K = -\ln CV$$

Substituting the value of K in eqn. (6.25) and rearranging the equation,we have

$$Q = CV\left(1 - e^{-t/RC}\right) \qquad ...(6.26)$$

At time $t \to \infty, Q \to CV_0 = Q_0$ which is the maximum value of charge on the capacitor. Thus

$$Q = Q_0\left(1 - e^{-t/RC}\right) \qquad ...(6.27)$$

The growth of charge on the capacitor is given by eqn. (6.27).

The quantity RC has the dimension of time and is called the *time constant* (or *relaxation time*) and is usually denoted by τ

$$\tau = RC = \text{Ohm}\cdot\text{Farad} = \frac{\text{Volt}}{\text{Ampere}}\cdot\frac{\text{Coulomb}}{\text{Volt}} = \text{sec.}$$

In terms of time constant, we can write the equation for the growth of charge as

$$Q = Q_0\left(1 - e^{-t/\tau}\right) \qquad ...(6.28)$$

At time $t = \tau = RC$

$$Q = Q_0\left(1 - e^{-1}\right) = 0.632Q_0$$

Thus the time constant is the time during which the charge on the capacitor builds up to 63.2% of its steady state value.

Writing $Q = CV$ and $Q_0 = CV_0$ in eqn. (6.28), we obtain the growth of *voltage on the capacitor.*

$$V = V_0\left(1 - e^{-t/\tau}\right) \qquad ...(6.29)$$

At any instant t, the current in the circuit is

$$I\frac{dQ}{dt} = \left(\frac{V}{R}\right)e^{-t/RC} = \frac{V}{R}e^{-t/\tau} \qquad ...(6.30)$$

The growth of charge and voltage on the capacitor are displayed in the Fig. 6.13. The current in the circuit decreases exponentially with time (Fig. 6.13).

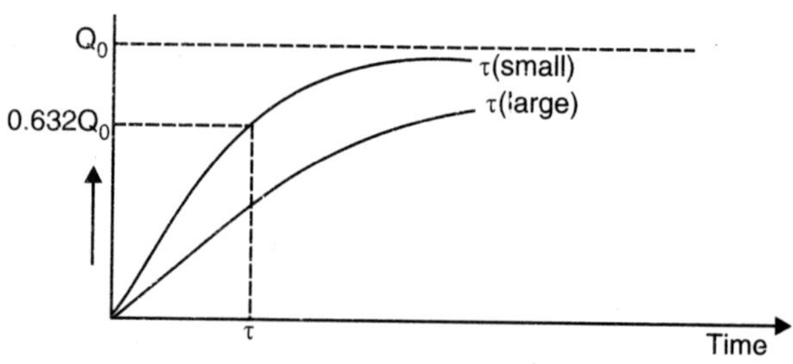

Contd...

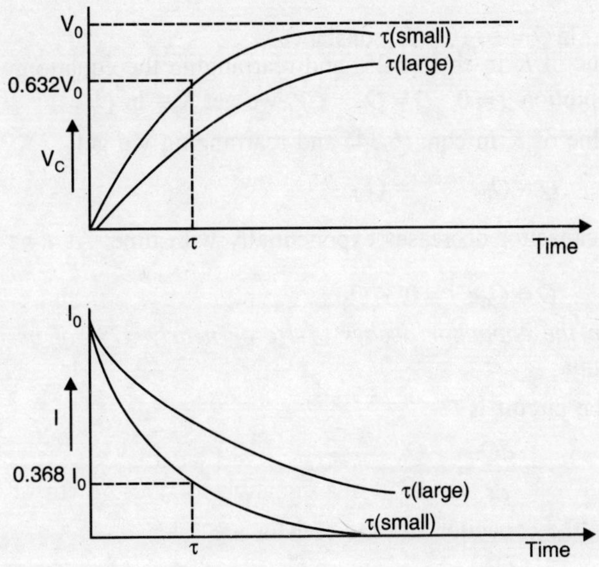

Fig. 6.13. Variation of charge, Voltage on the capacitor and the current in the circuit with time.

6.6. DISCHARGE OF A CAPACITOR THROUGH A RESISTANCE

Consider a capacitor charged to a potential V_0. It is then discharged through a resistance R. The discharge of the capacitor is accompanied by a transient current in the circuit. Applying KVL to the circuit we have

$$RI + \frac{Q}{C} = 0, \quad I = \frac{dQ}{dt} \qquad \text{...(6.31)}$$

Fig. 6.14. A charged capacitor is discharged through a resistance by turning the switch from position 1 to 2.

or $$R\frac{dQ}{dt} + \frac{Q}{C} = 0 \qquad \text{...(6.32)}$$

Separating the variables,we obtain

$$\frac{dQ}{Q} = -\frac{1}{RC}dt \qquad \text{...(6.33)}$$

Integrating (6.33), we get

$$\ln Q = -\frac{t}{RC} + K(\text{constant}) \qquad ...(6.34)$$

Using the initial condition $t = 0,\ Q = Q_0 = CV_0$ we get $K = \ln Q_0$

Substituting the value of K in eqn. (6.34) and rearranging we get,

$$Q = Q_0 e^{-t/RC} = Q_0 e^{-t/\tau} \qquad ...(6.35)$$

The charge on the capacitor decreases exponentially with time. At $t = \tau\,(= RC)$

$$Q = Q_0 e^{-1} \cong 0.37 Q_0$$

Thus *the charge on the capacitor decays to 1/e or nearly 37% of its initial value in the time equal to the time constant.*

The current in the circuit is

$$I = \frac{dQ}{dt} = -\frac{Q_0}{RC} e^{-t/RC} = -\left(\frac{V_0}{R}\right) e^{-t/RC} \qquad ...(6.36)$$

The voltages across the capacitor and the resistor are :

$$V_c = \frac{Q}{C} = V_0 e^{-t/RC} \qquad ...(6.37)$$

$$V_R = IR = -V_0 e^{-t/\tau} \qquad ...(6.38)$$

The variation of Q, I, V_c and V_R with time are shown in the Fig. 6.15.

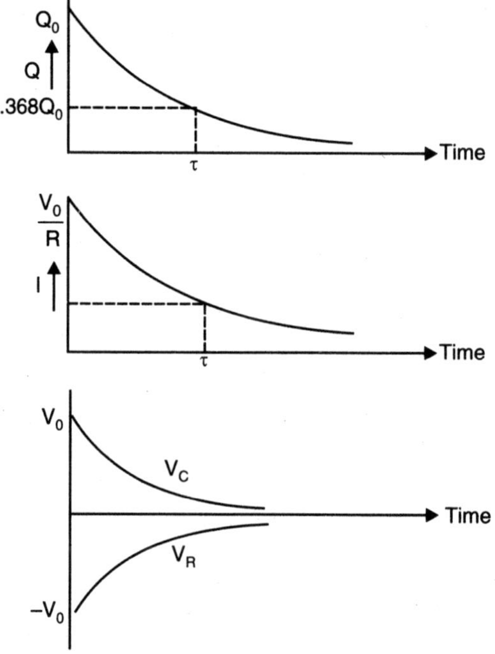

Fig. 6.15

6.7. DISCHARGE OF A CAPACITOR THROUGH AN INDUCTOR—ELECTRICAL OSCILLATIONS

Suppose we have a capacitor which is charged to a certain potential. It is then discharged through an inductor. The charge on the capacitor flows through the inductor giving rise to a current. The growing current in the inductor sets up an induced *emf* (–*LI*/*dt*) which opposes the current. The polarity of the voltages across the capacitor and the inductor are shown in the Fig. 6.16. KVL gives the voltage equation.

$$L\frac{dI}{dt}+\frac{Q}{C}=0,\ I=\frac{dQ}{dt}$$

Fig. 6.16

$$L\frac{d^2Q}{dt^2}+\frac{Q}{C}=0 \qquad ...(6.39)$$

or

$$\frac{d^2Q}{dt^2}+\omega_0{}^2Q=0,\ \omega_0=\frac{1}{\sqrt{LC}} \qquad ...(6.40)$$

The growth of charge on the capacitor follows this equation. The solution of eqn. (6.40) is of the form

$$Q=Q_0\left(\cos\omega_0 t+\theta\right) \qquad ...(6.41)$$

where Q_0 is the initial charge on the capacitor and θ is constant to be determined from the initial condition.

The current in the circuit is given by

$$I\frac{dQ}{dt}=Q_0\omega_0\sin\left(\omega_0 t+\theta\right) \qquad ...(6.42)$$

The frequency of the current in the circuit is

$$\omega_0=\frac{1}{\sqrt{LC}} \qquad ...(6.43)$$

Physically, the oscillations in a *LC* circuit can be understood as follows:

Initially, when the capacitor is fully charged, the current in the inductance is zero. The total energy of the circuit in the form of electrostatic field confined between the plates of the capacitor. The charged capacitor now begins to discharge as a result of which current starts growing in the inductance. The growing current in the inductance sets up a magnetic field. Thus during the discharge process, the electrostatic field collapses and the magnetic field builds up. At the instant capacitor is fully discharged, the current in the inductance is maximum, and the total energy of the circuit is in the form of magnetic field.

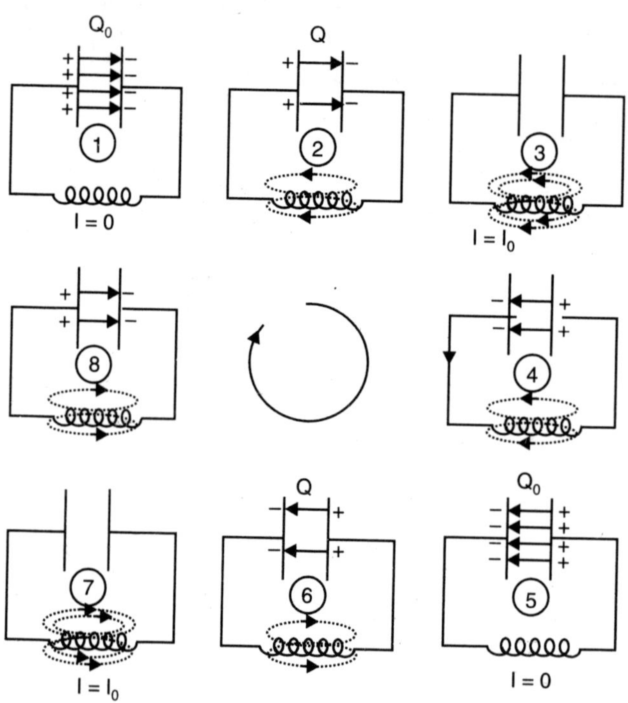

Fig. 6.17

Now there is no agency to increase the current and therefore it begins to decrease in the same direction. The magnetic field starts collapsing and the charge on the capacitor begins to grow but in opposite sense. At the instant the current in the inductance is zero, the capacitor is fully charged. Now the magnetic energy is zero and the total energy is again electrostatic.

The fully charged capacitor again begins to discharge and sets up a current in the inductance in opposite direction. The process goes on repeating as shown in the Fig. 6.17. The energy of the circuit oscillates between two forms—the electrostatic and the magnetic. In the absence of any resistance, the oscillations continue forever with constant magnitude.

If V is potential across the capacitor at any instant and I is the current in the inductance, then the total energy is given by,

$$\frac{1}{2}CV^2 + \frac{1}{2}LI^2 = \frac{1}{2}LI_0^2 = \text{constant} \qquad ...(6.44)$$

6.8. DISCHARGE OF A CAPACITOR THROUGH AN INDUCTOR AND A RESISTOR-DAMPED ELECTRICAL OSCILLATIONS

When a charge capacitor is discharged through an inductor and a resistor, the nature of discharge depends on the relative magnitudes of the resistance, capacitance and inductance. If the resistance of the circuit is small, the discharge is oscillatory and the amplitude of the oscillatory current decreases in each cycle because a part of energy of the circuit drains away in the form of Joule heat. These oscillations of decreasing amplitude are callled the *damped electrical oscillations.* If the resistance of the circuit is too large, the discharge is *non-oscillatory.*

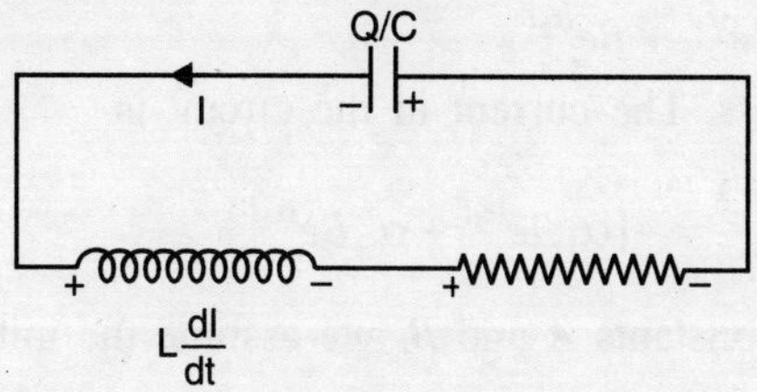

Fig. 6.18

At any instant t, let the charge on the capacitor be Q and $I\left(=\frac{dQ}{dt}\right)$ be the current in the circuit. KVL gives the equation of voltage

$$L\frac{dI}{dt}+RI+\frac{Q}{C}=0,\ I=+\frac{dQ}{dt} \quad ...(6.45)$$

or, $$L\frac{d^2Q}{dt^2}+R\frac{dQ}{dt}+\frac{Q}{C}=0 \quad ...(6.46)$$

Let us try the solution of eqn. (6.46) in the form

$$Q=e^{\alpha t} \quad ...(6.47)$$

where the value of α is obtained by substituting eqn. (6.47) in eqn. (6.46). Doing so, we obtain

$$L\alpha^2+R\alpha+\frac{1}{C}=0 \quad ...(6.48)$$

Equation (6.48) is known as the auxiliary equation of eqn. (6.46). It is obtained by replacing

$$\frac{d^2}{dt^2}\to\alpha^2$$

$$\frac{d}{dt}\to\alpha$$

Equation (6.48) is quadratic in α. Its roots are

$$\alpha_1=-\frac{R}{2L}+\left[\left(\frac{R}{2L}\right)^2-\frac{1}{LC}\right]^{1/2}=-\frac{R}{2L}+\beta \quad ...(6.49)$$

$$\alpha_2 = -\frac{R}{2L} - \left[\left(\frac{R}{2L}\right)^2 - \frac{1}{LC}\right]^{1/2} = -\frac{R}{2L} - \beta \quad ...(6.50)$$

where $$\beta = \left[\left(\frac{R}{2L}\right)^2 - \frac{1}{LC}\right]^{1/2} \quad ...(6.51)$$

The complete solution of the differential eqn. (6.46) is written in terms of two arbitrary constants as

$$Q = Ae^{\alpha_1 t} + Be^{\alpha_2 t} \quad ...(6.52)$$

where A and B are constants. The current in the circuit is

$$I = \frac{dQ}{dt} = -\left(\alpha_1 Ae^{\alpha_1 t} + \alpha_2 Be^{\alpha_2 t}\right) \quad ...(6.53)$$

In order to determine the constants A and B, we assume the initial conditions as

$$\left.\begin{aligned} t = 0,\ Q = Q_0 \\ t = 0,\ I = -\frac{dQ}{dt} = 0 \end{aligned}\right] \quad ...(6.54)$$

Making use of these conditions in eqns. (6.52) and (6.53), we have

$$\left.\begin{aligned} A + B = Q_0 \\ \alpha_1 A + \alpha_2 B = 0 \end{aligned}\right] \quad ...(6.55)$$

These equation can be solved for A and B.

$$\left.\begin{aligned} A &= -\left(\frac{\alpha_2}{\alpha_1 - \alpha_2}\right) Q_0 = -\frac{\alpha_2}{2\beta} Q_0 \\ B &= \left(\frac{\alpha_1}{\alpha_1 - \alpha_2}\right) Q_0 = \frac{\alpha_1}{2\beta} Q_0 \end{aligned}\right] \quad ...(6.56)$$

Substituting the values of A and B in eqn. (6.52), we have

$$Q = \frac{Q_0}{2\beta} e^{-Rt/2L} \left(\alpha_1 e^{-\beta t} + \alpha_2 e^{+\beta t}\right) \quad ...(6.57)$$

Nature of Discharge

***Case* 1:** If the resistance of the circuit is very high so that the condition

$$\left(\frac{R}{2L}\right)^2 >> \frac{1}{LC}$$

is satisfied, then the terms β defined by eqn. (6.51) is positive. In this case, the charge on the capacitor decays with time as shown in the Fig. 6.19. The current in the circuit is *non-oscillatory*.

***Case* 2:** If the resistance of the circuit is such that the condition

$$\left(\frac{R}{2L}\right)^2 = \frac{1}{LC} \quad \text{or} \quad R = 2\sqrt{\frac{L}{C}} \qquad \text{...(6.58)}$$

is satisfied, the charge on the capacitor quickly disappears. In this case, the circuit is said to be critically damped.

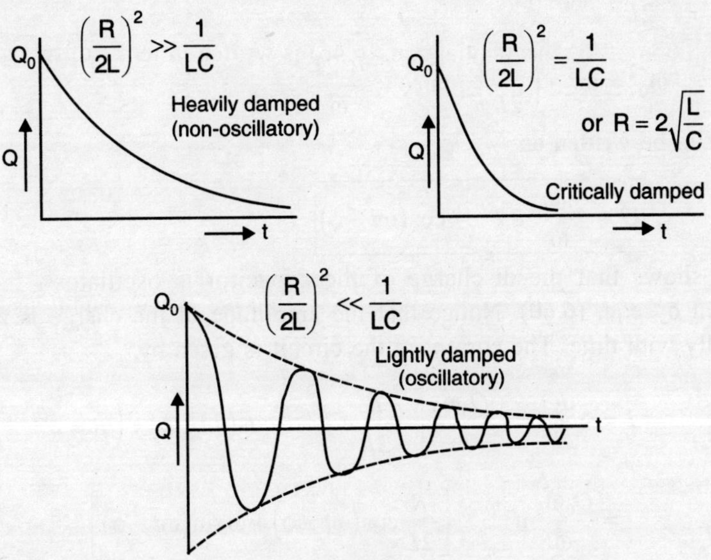

Fig. 6.19

***Case* 3:** If the resistance of the circuit is small and the condition

$$\left(\frac{R}{2L}\right)^2 < \frac{1}{LC} \qquad \text{...(6.59)}$$

is satisfied, then the term β is imaginary and we can write

$$\beta = \sqrt{\left(\frac{R}{2L}\right)^2 - \frac{1}{LC}} = j\omega$$

or

$$\boxed{\omega = \sqrt{\frac{1}{LC} - \left(\frac{R}{2L}\right)^2} = \sqrt{\omega_0^{\,2} - \left(\frac{R}{2L}\right)^2}} \qquad \text{...(6.60)}$$

In this case, the solution of the differential equation can be written as

$$Q = \frac{Q_0}{2j\omega} e^{-Rt/2L}\left[\alpha_1 e^{-j\omega t} - \alpha_2 e^{j\omega t}\right]$$

$$= \frac{Q_0}{2j\omega} e^{-Rt/2L}\left[(\alpha_1 - \alpha_2)\cos\omega t - j(\alpha_1 + \alpha_2)\sin\omega t\right]$$

$$= \frac{Q_0}{2j\omega} e^{-Rt/2L} \left[2j\omega \cos \omega t + j\frac{R}{L} \sin \omega t \right] \qquad ...(6.61)$$

Making use of substitution $\omega = \omega_0 \cos \phi$

$$\frac{R}{2L} = \omega_0 \sin \phi$$

where $\omega_0^2 = \omega^2 + \left(\frac{R}{2L}\right)^2, \ \tan \phi = \frac{R/2L}{\omega}$

Equation (6.61) can be written as

$$\boxed{Q = \frac{Q_0 \omega_0}{\omega} e^{-Rt/2L} \cos(\omega t - \phi)} \qquad ...(6.62)$$

Equation (6.62) shows that the discharge of the capacitor is oscillatory, the frequency of oscillations ω is given by eqn. (6.60). Notice that the amplitude of the charge is not constant but decreases exponentially with time. The current in the circuit is given by,

$$I = -\frac{dQ}{dt} = -\frac{Q_0 \omega_0}{\omega} \left[-\frac{R}{2L} e^{-Rt/2L} \cos(\omega t - \phi) + \left(-\omega e^{-Rt/2L}\right) \sin(\omega t - \phi) \right]$$

$$= \frac{Q_0 \omega_0}{\omega} e^{-Rt/2L} \left[\frac{R}{2L} \cos(\omega t - \phi) + \omega \sin(\omega t - \phi) \right]$$

$$= \frac{Q_0 \omega_0^2}{\omega} e^{-Rt/2L} [\sin \omega t] \qquad ...(6.63)$$

$$= I_0 e^{-Rt/2L} \sin \omega t$$

where $I_0 = \frac{Q_0 \omega_0^2}{\omega}$ ...(6.64)

The amplitude of the current decreases with time. The voltage across the capacitor is given by

$$V = V_0 e^{-Rt/2L} \cos(\omega t - \phi) \qquad ...(6.65)$$

6.9. Q-FACTOR OR FIGURE OF MERIT

The Q-factor of an oscillatory circuit is defined by the ratio

$$\boxed{Q = 2\pi \frac{\textit{Energy stored in the circuit}}{\textit{Energy dissipated per cycle}}} \qquad ...(6.66)$$

$$= 2\pi \left(\frac{U}{-\Delta U} \right) \qquad ...(6.67)$$

The energy of a *LCR* circuit consists of magnetic energy $\frac{1}{2}LI^2$ in the inductor and electrostatic energy $\frac{1}{2}CV^2$ in the capacitor. When the current in the circuit is maximum, the entire energy of the circuit is magnetic. Thus, the total energy of the circuit is

$$U = \frac{1}{2}LI_0^2\, e^{-Rt/L} = U_0 e^{-Rt/L} \qquad \text{...(6.68)}$$

where $U_0 = \frac{1}{2}LI_0{}^2$ is the initial energy. The rate of loss of energy is given by,

$$-\frac{dU}{dt} = \frac{R}{L}U_0 e^{-Rt/L} = \frac{R}{L}U \qquad \text{...(6.69)}$$

Loss of energy per cycle

$$-\Delta U = -\frac{dU}{dt}T = \left(\frac{R}{L}U\right)T \qquad \text{...(6.70)}$$

$$\therefore \qquad -\frac{\Delta U}{U} = \frac{RT}{L} = \frac{2\pi R}{\omega L} \qquad \text{...(6.71)}$$

$$\therefore \qquad Q = \frac{\omega L}{R} \qquad \text{...(6.72)}$$

Thus the quality factor of a circuit is proportional to the time constant *L*/*R* of the circuit. In terms of *Q*, the dependence of energy of the circuit on time can be written as,

$$U = U_0 e^{-\omega t/Q} \qquad \text{...(6.73)}$$

If the resistance *R* of the circuit is very small, $\omega \to \omega_0 = \frac{1}{\sqrt{LC}}$ then

$$Q \cong \frac{\omega_0 L}{R} = \frac{1}{R}\sqrt{\frac{L}{C}} \qquad \text{...(6.74)}$$

If the resistance *R* of the circuit is small, the rate of energy loss is small and then *Q* is high. Consequently, the oscillations in the circuit will continue for a longer time. If the resistance *R* is large, the rate of energy loss is high and then *Q* is small and therefore, the oscillations in the circuit will die out very soon. The *Q*-factor of a circuit is measure of damping.

6.10. BALLISTIC GALVANOMETER

The ballistic galvanometer is usually employed to measure the quantity of charge flowing in a given circuit due to transient currents. It consists of a coil of copper wire wound on a non-conducting frame which is suspended by a phospher bronze strip between the pole-pieces of a strong permanent magnet. A mirror is attached to the phospher bronze strip. The whole apparatus is covered in a shell to avoid disturbance from outside. The deflection of the coil is measured by lamp and scale arrangement.

Let N be the number of turns in the coil, A its area and B the magnetic field of the pole-pieces. When a current i passes through the coil of the galvanometer, it experiences a deflecting couple

$$\tau = NABi \qquad ...(6.75)$$

If a momentary current i passes for a time interval Δt the coil gets angular impulse given by

$$\text{Angular Impulse} \int_0^{\Delta t} \tau dt = \int_0^{\Delta t} NABidt = NABq \qquad ...(6.76)$$

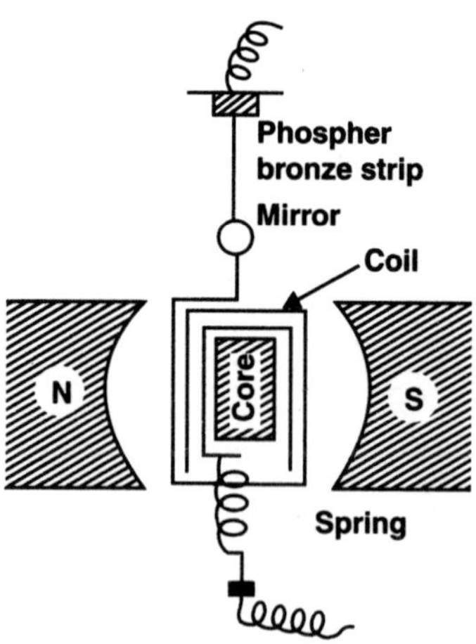

Fig. 6.20. Ballistic Galvanometer.

where $q = \int idt$ is the charge associated with the momentary current i.

Suppose that the moment of inertia of the coil is so large that it starts moving after the whole charge has passed through it. If the coil acquires initial angular velocity $\hat{\omega}$, then using the result of mechanics

(*Angular Impulse*) = (*Change in Angular Momentum*)

We have

$$NABq = I\hat{\omega} \qquad ...(6.77)$$

Initial kinetic energy of the coil is $\frac{1}{2}I\hat{\omega}^2$. If there were no damping, its entire kinetic energy would be used in twisting the suspension fibre. If θ_0 is the twist in the suspension fibre (or the deflection of the coil), then the elastic potential energy of the suspension fibre equals $\frac{1}{2}c\theta_0^2$ where c is the torsional rigidity of the material of the fibre. In the absence of damping, the entire initial kinetic energy of the coil is used up in twisting the suspension fibre. Thus

$$\frac{1}{2}I\hat{\omega}^2 = \frac{1}{2}c\theta_0^2 \qquad \text{...(6.78)}$$

Eliminating $\hat{\omega}$ from eqns. (6.77) and (6.78) we get

$$q^2 = \left(\frac{c}{NAB}\right)^2 \frac{I}{c}\cdot\theta_0^2 \qquad \text{...(6.79)}$$

If the coil is free from damping forces, it begins to oscillate with time period

$$T = 2\pi\sqrt{I/c} \qquad \text{...(6.80)}$$

Making use of eqn. (6.80) we can write eqn. (6.79) as

$$q = \left(\frac{c}{NAB}\right)\frac{T}{2\pi}\cdot\theta_0 = K\theta_0 \qquad \text{...(6.81)}$$

where $K = \frac{c}{NAB}\cdot\frac{T}{2\pi}$ is constant for a particular galvanometer and is called the *ballistic Galvanometer constant* .

In eqn. (6.81), θ_0 is the deflection of the coil in the absence of damping. Damping forces are always present as a result of which the actual deflection is always less than θ_0 and therefore a correction term must accompany the term θ_0.

Effect of Damping

The moving coil of the ballistic galvanometer is subject to two types of damping :

(*i*) *Air or mechanical damping*: It is proportional to the angular velocity of the coil.

Air damping $= r_1\frac{d\theta}{dt}$ where r_1 is constant.

(*ii*) *Electromagnetic damping*: When the coil circuit is closed, the motion of the coil in the magnetic field causes a change in flux linking it and therefore an induced current is produced in it which opposes the motion of the coil. This type of damping is called the electromagnetic damping and is proportional to the angular velocity of the coil and inversely proportional to the resistance R of the coil circuit.

Electromagnetic damping $= \frac{r_2}{R}\cdot\frac{d\theta}{dt}$ where r_2 is a constant.

The equation of motion of the coil is

$$I\frac{d^2\theta}{dt^2} = -c\theta - r\frac{d\theta}{dt} - \frac{r^2}{R}\cdot\frac{d\theta}{dt}$$

or,

$$\frac{d^2\theta}{dt^2} + \frac{1}{I}\left(r_1 + \frac{r_2}{R}\right) + \frac{c}{I}\theta = 0$$

$$\frac{d^2\theta}{dt^2}+\Gamma\frac{d\theta}{dt}+\omega_0{}^2\theta=0 \qquad ...(6.82)$$

where $$\Gamma=\frac{1}{I}\left(r_1+\frac{r_2}{R}\right) \qquad ...(6.83)$$

$$\omega_0{}^2=\frac{c}{I} \qquad ...(6.84)$$

Let us try the solution of eqn. (6.82) in the form

$$\theta=e^{\alpha t} \qquad ...(6.85)$$

Substituting this solution in eqn. (6.82) we get $\alpha^2+\Gamma\alpha+\omega_0{}^2=0$ which gives

$$\alpha=-\frac{1}{2}\Gamma\pm\frac{1}{2}\left(\Gamma^2-4\omega_0{}^2\right)^{1/2}$$

$$=-\frac{1}{2}\Gamma\pm\beta \qquad ...(6.86)$$

where $$\beta=\frac{1}{2}\left(\Gamma^2-4\omega_0^2\right)^{1/2} \qquad ...(6.87)$$

The solution of eqn. (6.82) is then

$$\theta=Ae^{-\left(\frac{1}{2}\Gamma+\beta\right)t}+Be^{\left(-\frac{1}{2}\Gamma-\beta\right)t} \qquad ...(6.88)$$

where A and B are constants to be determined from initial conditions. Let us assume the initial conditions as follow: $t=0,\ \theta=0$

$$t=0,\ \frac{d\theta}{dt}=\hat{\omega}$$

Making use of the condition in eqn. (6.88) we get

$$A=\frac{\hat{\omega}}{2\beta},\ B=-\frac{\hat{\omega}}{2\beta} \qquad ...(6.89)$$

Substituting the values of A and B in eqn. (6.88) we get

$$\theta=\frac{1}{2}\cdot\frac{\hat{\omega}}{\beta}\left[e^{\left(-\frac{1}{2}\Gamma+\beta\right)t}-e^{\left(-\frac{1}{2}\Gamma-\beta\right)t}\right]=\frac{1}{2}\cdot\frac{\hat{\omega}}{\beta}e^{-\frac{1}{2}\Gamma t}\left[e^{\beta t}-e^{-\beta t}\right]$$

$$\theta=\frac{\hat{\omega}}{\beta}e^{-\frac{1}{2}\Gamma t}\sinh\beta t \qquad ...(6.90)$$

***Case* I:** If the damping is very high, β is positive and eqn. (6.90) represents *non-oscillatory* motion.The galvanometer is said to be *dead beat.*

***Case* II:** If the damping is such that the condition $\Gamma^2 = 4\omega_0^2$ is satisfied, β is zero. The motion is said to be *critically damped* and is again *non-oscillatory.*

***Case* III:** When the damping is small and the condition.

$$\Gamma^2 << 4\omega_0^2$$

is satisfied, β is imaginary.

Let

$$\beta = \frac{1}{2}\left(\Gamma^2 - 4\omega_0^2\right)^{1/2} = j\omega_1$$

$$\omega_1^2 = \omega_0^2 - \frac{1}{4}\Gamma^2 \qquad ...(6.91)$$

Under this condition, the solution eqn. (6.90) becomes

$$\theta = \frac{\hat{\omega}}{j\omega_1} e^{-\frac{1}{2}\Gamma t} . \sinh j\omega_1 t$$

$$\theta = \frac{\hat{\omega}}{\omega_1} e^{-\frac{1}{2}\Gamma t} \sin \omega_1 t \qquad ...(6.92)$$

Equation (6.92) represents damped harmonic oscillations with frequency ω_1 given by eqn. (6.91) and amplitude

$$a(t) = \frac{\hat{\omega}}{\omega_1} e^{-\frac{1}{2}\Gamma t} \qquad ...(6.93)$$

The presence of factor $e^{-\frac{1}{2}\Gamma t}$ shows that the amplitude of the oscillator decays with time. In case of very low damping $(\Gamma \to 0)$, the amplitude would be $\hat{\omega}/\omega_0$ which is θ_0, the undamped amplitude. We can thus write

$$a(t) = \theta_0 e^{-\frac{1}{2}\Gamma t} \qquad ...(6.94)$$

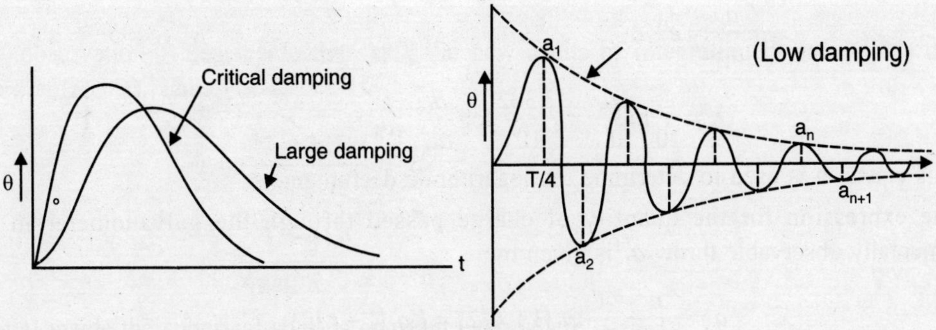

Fig. 6.21

Logarithmic Decrement λ. The logarithmic decrement of a damped oscillator is defined as the ratio of two successive amplitudes separated by half time period. It is a measure of degree of damping. For large damping, the logarithmic decrement is large.

$$\lambda = \ln \frac{a_n}{a_{n+1}} \qquad \text{...(6.95)}$$

$$= \ln \frac{\theta_0 e^{-\frac{1}{2}\Gamma t_n}}{\theta_0 e^{-\frac{1}{2}\Gamma t_{n+1}}}$$

$$= \ln e^{\frac{1}{2}\Gamma(t_{n+1}-t_n)} = \ln e^{\frac{1}{2}\Gamma T/2}$$

$$\lambda = \frac{1}{4}\Gamma T \qquad \text{...(6.96)}$$

Damping Correction. In the case of small damping, the first amplitude is obtained after time $T/4$.

$$a_1 = \theta_0 e^{-\frac{1}{2}\Gamma T/4} = \theta_0 e^{-\lambda/2}$$

$$\theta_0 = a_1 e^{\lambda/2} = a_1\left(1+\frac{\lambda}{2}+.........\right)$$

$$\theta_0 = a_1(1+\lambda/2) \qquad \text{...(6.97)}$$

This eqn. (6.97) gives the undamped throw θ_0 in terms of first throw a_1 which is observed.

Determination of λ. From the defining eqnuation of logarithmic decrement λ we have

$$\frac{a_n}{a_{n+1}} = e^{\lambda}$$

which is independent of n, and hence holds for any two successive amplitudes. Thus, we have

$$\frac{a_1}{a_2} = e^{\lambda}, \frac{a_2}{a_3} = e^{\lambda}, ... \frac{a_{10}}{a_{11}} = e^{\lambda}$$

Multiplying these equations together we get

$$\frac{a_1}{a_{11}} = e^{10\lambda}$$

$$\lambda = \frac{1}{10}\ln\frac{a_1}{a_{11}} = \frac{2.302}{10}\log\frac{a_1}{a_{11}} \qquad \text{...(6.98)}$$

This equation is used to determine the logarithmic decrement.

The expression for the quantity of charge passed through the galvanometer in terms of experimentally observable throw a_1 is given by

$$q = \frac{c}{NAB}\cdot\frac{T}{2\pi}.a_1(1+\lambda/2) = Ka_1(1+\lambda/2) \qquad \text{...(6.99)}$$

Current Sensitivity, c_s. When a steady current i passes through a ballistic galvanometer, a steady deflection ϕ is produced.The current i is given by $i = \frac{c}{NAB}\phi = c_s\phi$ where $c_s = \frac{c}{NAB} = \frac{i}{\phi}$ is called the current sensitivity of the galvanometer. It is *defined as the current required to produce a deflection of 1 mm on a scale placed at a distance of 1 meter from the mirror.*

Charge Sensitivity, q_s. The quantity of charge passing through a ballistic galvanometer in terms of deflection is given by,

$$q = \frac{c}{NAB}\frac{I}{2\pi}\theta_1(1+\lambda/2) = c_s.\frac{T}{2\pi}.\theta_1(1+\lambda/2)$$

The quantity q_s defined by $q_s = c_s\frac{T}{2\pi}$

is called the charge sensitivity of the galvanometer and is constant for a given galvanometer. It is *defined as the quantity of charge required to produce a deflection of 1 mm on a scale placed at a distance of 1meter from the galvanometer.*

6.11. SOME ELECTRICAL MEASUREMENTS

6.11.1 Determination of Ballistic Constant of Ballistic Galvanometer

Condenser Method: To determine the ballistic constant of a ballistic galvanometer a cell and a condensor of known capacity are connected to morse key as shown in the Fig. 6.22.

By pressing the morse key the condenser is charged to a known potential V (which is measured by a voltmeter connected across the condenser), and then discharged through a ballistic galvanometer. The first and the eleventh throw of the coil are measured. The charge $q = CV$ that passes through the galvanometer is related to the first throw θ_1 and the logarithmic decrement λ by the relationship

$$q = CV = K\theta_1(1+\lambda/2) \quad ...(6.100)$$

$$K = \frac{CV}{\theta_1(1+\lambda/2)} \quad ...(6.101)$$

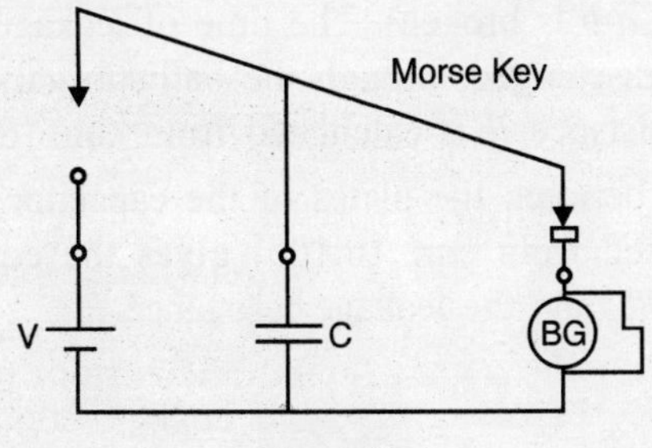

Fig. 6.22

where λ is calculated from the relation,

$$\lambda = \frac{1}{10}\times 2.3026\ \log_{10}\frac{\theta_1}{\theta_{11}} \quad ...(6.102)$$

6.11.2 Measurement of High Resistance by Method of Leakage

When a capacitor is fully charged and then immediately discharged through a ballistic galvanonmeter, the charge q_0 on the capacitor is related to the first throw θ_0 of the galvanometer as

$$q_0 = K\theta_0(1+\lambda/2) \qquad ...(6.103)$$

Now, the charge on the capacitor is allowed to leak through the high resistance R to be determined for a known time t, and then discharged through the ballistic galvanometer. If the first throw in the galvanometer is θ_1, then the charge on the capacitor at time is given by

$$q = q_0 e^{-t/CR} = K\theta_1(1+\lambda/2) \qquad ...(6.104)$$

Dividing eqn. (6.103) by (6.104) we get

$$e^{t/CR} = \frac{\theta_0}{\theta_1}; \quad R = \frac{t}{\ln \theta_0/\theta_1}$$

$$R = \frac{t}{2.3026 \log \theta_0/\theta_1} \qquad ...(6.105)$$

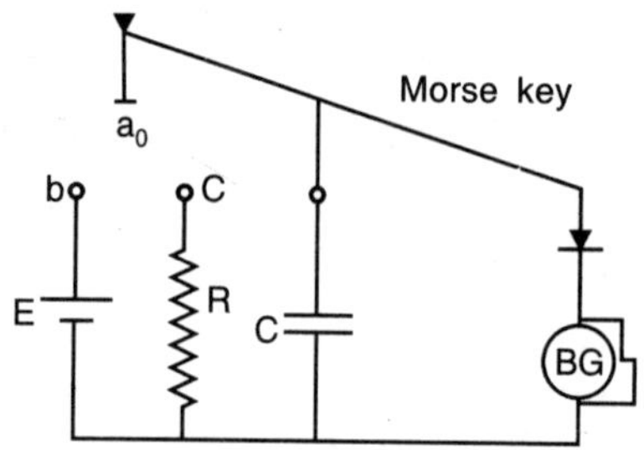

Fig. 6.23

This equation is used to determine the unknown resistance. To perform the experiment, electrical connections are made as shown in the Fig. 6.23 and the following procedure is followed (*i*) *a* and *b* are connected and then the Morse key is pressed; the capacitor is charged. It is then discharged through the ballistic galvanometer and the first thrown θ_0 is observed. (*ii*) As above, the capacitor is charged and the capacitor is allowed to leak through the unknown high resistance R by connecting *a-c* (connection *a-b* is broken). The time of leakage is noted by stop watch. After a few seconds, the capacitor is discharged through the ballistic galvanometer and the first thrown θ_1 is measured.The unknown resistance R is calculated from eqn. (6.105).

Usually, the dielectric filled between the plates of the capacitor show some leakage resistance R' (say). The resistance calculated from eqn. (6.105) gives the equivalent resistance of parallel combination of actual resistance R_0 and the leakage resistance R'.

$$\frac{1}{R} = \frac{1}{R'} + \frac{1}{R_0} \qquad ...(6.106)$$

To measure the leakage resistance R', the capacitor is charged and is allowed to leak through its own dielectric (without the high resistance R_0) for known time t' and then discharged through the ballistic galvanometer and the corresponding deflection q_1' is noted. R' is calculated from equation.

$$R' = \frac{t}{2.3026\ \log\theta_0/\theta_1'} \qquad ...(6.107)$$

Measuring R and R', the actual value of high resistance R_0 is calculated from eqn. (6.106).

6.11.3 Measurement of Magnetic Field B

When the magnetic flux linking through a coil changes, an induced *emf* is set up in the coil. If the circuit is complete, a momentary current exists so long as the change of flux takes place. Measuring the charge transported by the momentary current, the strength of the magnetic field can be computed. Suppose, we have a small coil of N turns, each of area A placed in a magnetic field B with its face normal to the field direction. The ends of the coil are connected to a *ballistic galvanometer.* The magnetic flux linking the coil is

$$\Phi = N\int B\cdot dS = NBA \qquad ...(6.108)$$

If the coil is suddenly removed from field, the induced *emf* in the coil is

$$e = -\frac{d\Phi}{dt}$$

and the induced current is

$$I = \frac{dq}{dt} = \frac{e}{R} = -\frac{1}{R}\cdot\frac{d\Phi}{dt} \qquad ...(6.109)$$

The total charge transported by the induced current is

$$q = \int Idt = -\frac{1}{R}\int\frac{d\Phi}{dt}dt = -\frac{1}{R}\int d\Phi$$

$$q = \frac{\Delta\Phi}{R} \qquad ...(6.110)$$

Thus, the charge that flows through the coil (and hence through the ballsitic galvanometer) during the time, the magnetic flux change equals the ratio of the change in flux to the resistance of the coil-galvanometer circuit.

If the coil is moved from the field to the region of zero field, the change in the magnetic flux is $\Delta\Phi = NAB$ and hence

$$q = \frac{NAB}{R} \qquad ...(6.111)$$

If the coil is rotated through an angle of 180° in the magnetic field, change in magnetic flux is $\Delta\Phi = NAB - (-NAB) = 2NAB$. Hence

$$q = \frac{2NAB}{R} \qquad ...(6.112)$$

Measuring the quantity of charge q associated with the flux change, the magnetic field B can be determined.

6.11.4 Earth Inductor: Measurement of Earth Magnetic Field and Angle of Dip.

The earth inductor consists of a large number of turns of copper wire wound on a circular wooden or ebonite frame. It is capable of rotating about its diameter. It is used to measure the Earth's magnetic field.

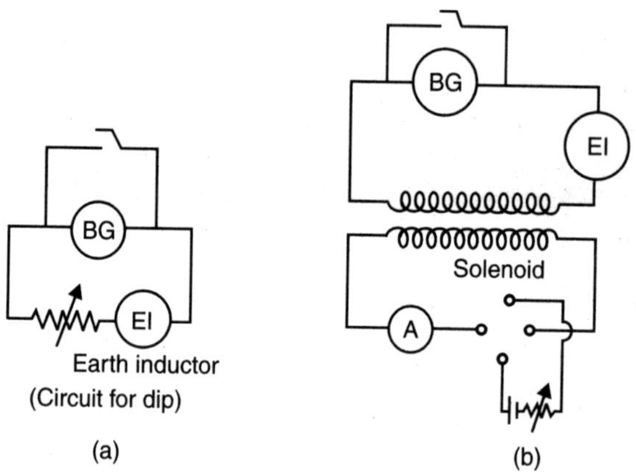

Fig. 6.24

To determine the horizontal and vertical components of the earth's magnetic field, the circuit shown in the Fig. 6.24 is employed. Let

N = number of turns in earth inductor.

A = area of the earth inductor.

n_1 = number of turns per unit length in the primary of the solenoid.

n_2 = total number of turns in the secondary.

a_s = cross-section of the solenoid.

R = resistance of the secondary circuit (BG, earth inductor and the secondary coil of the solenoid).

Now, the earth inductor is placed with its axis of rotation vertical and its plane normal to the horizontal component H of the earth's field. The coil is quickly rotated through an angle of 180°. The flux linking the coil is changed by amount $2NAH$ and the charge passing through the ballistic galvanometer is given in terms of the first throw θ_H as

$$\frac{2NAH}{R} = K\theta_H (1 + \lambda/2) \quad ...(6.113)$$

where K is ballistic galvanometer constant.

Next, the earth inductor is placed in such a way that its axis of rotation is parallel to the magnetic meridian and its plane normal to the vertical complement V of earth's magnetic field. The earth inductor is then rotated through 180°. The flux linking the coil is $2NAV$ and the charge passing through the ballistic galvanometer in terms of the first throw θ_V is given by

$$\frac{2NAV}{R} = K\theta_V (1 + \lambda/2) \quad ...(6.114)$$

From eqns. (6.113) and (6.114) we get

$$\frac{V}{H} = \frac{\theta_V}{\theta_H}$$

If ϕ is the angle of dip then $\tan\phi = \frac{V}{H} = \frac{\theta_V}{\theta_H}$ ...(6.115)

A known current i is made to flow in the primary of the solenoid. The magnetic field inside the solenoid $(\mu_0 n_1 i)$. The flux linked through the secondary of the solenoid is $(\mu_0 n_1 i)(n_2 a_s)$. If the current in the primary is reversed, the change in flux in the secondary is $2\mu_0 n_1 n_2 a_s i$. If the first throw in the ballistic galvanometer is θ_s, then

$$\frac{2\mu_0 n_1 n_2 a_s i}{R} = K\theta_s(1+\lambda/2) \qquad ...(6.116)$$

From eqns. (6.113) and (6.116),we get

$$\frac{NAH}{\mu_0 n_1 n_2 a_s i} = \frac{\theta_H}{\theta_S} \qquad ...(6.117)$$

$$H = \frac{\mu_0 n_1 n_2 a_s i}{NA} \cdot \frac{\theta_H}{\theta_S}$$

Similarly eqns. (6.114) and (6.116) give

$$V = \frac{\mu_0 n_1 n_2 a_s i}{NA} \cdot \frac{\theta_V}{\theta_S} \qquad ...(6.118)$$

6.11.5 Measurement of Strong Magnetic Field

Search Coil: A search coil is small circular coil containing about 20–50 turns. It is used to determine strong magnetic field such as the field of an electromagnet. To find the field between the pole pieces of an electromagnet, connections are made as shown in Fig. 6.25.

Let

n = number of turns in the search coil.

a = area of the search coil.

N = number of turns in the earth inductor.

A = face-area of the earth inductor.

R = resistance of the galvanometer circuit.

The search coil is placed between the pole-pieces of the electromagnet with its face area

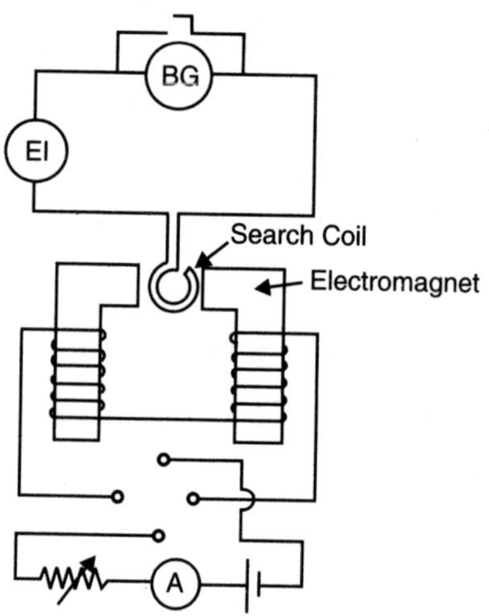

Fig. 6.25

normal to the magnetic field. A current is fed to the electromagnet. If B is the strength of the magnetic field, the flux threading the search coil is naB. If the current in the electromagnet is reversed, the change in flux linking the search coil is $2naB$. The change in flux in the search coil causes a charge $q = 2naB/R$ to flow in the galvanometer giving a throw θ_1 in it. Thus,

$$\frac{2naB}{R} = K\theta_1(1+\lambda/2) \qquad ...(6.119)$$

Now, the electromagnet circuit is removed. The earth inductor is placed with its axis vertical and face area normal to the horizontal component of the earth's magnetic field. The earth inductor is rotated through an angle of 180°. The flux through it changes by amount $2NAH$, and the charge passing through the ballistic galvanometer is $2NAH/R$. If θ_H is the first throw in the galvanometer, then

$$\frac{2NAH}{R} = K\theta_H(1+\lambda/2) \qquad ...(6.120)$$

From eqns. (6.119) and (6.120) we get

$$\frac{2naB}{2NAH} = \frac{\theta_1}{\theta_H}$$

$$B = \frac{NAH}{na} \cdot \frac{\theta_1}{\theta_H} \qquad ...(6.121)$$

This equation may be used to determine the strength of the magnetic field of the electromagnet. In place of earth inductor, we can also use a solenoid in the galvanometer circuit. This method employs the circuit as shown in Fig. 6.26.

With search coil placed between the pole-pieces of the electromagnet, the current in the electromagnet is reversed and the first throw θ_1 is measured.

n_1 = number of turns per unit length of the solenoid.

n_2 = number of turns in the secondary.

a_s = cross-section of the solenoid.

The charge passed through the galvanometer when the current in the electromagnet is reversed is $2naB/R$, where R is the resistance of the galvanometer circuit.

$$\frac{2naB}{R} = K\theta_1(1+\lambda/2) \quad ...(6.122)$$

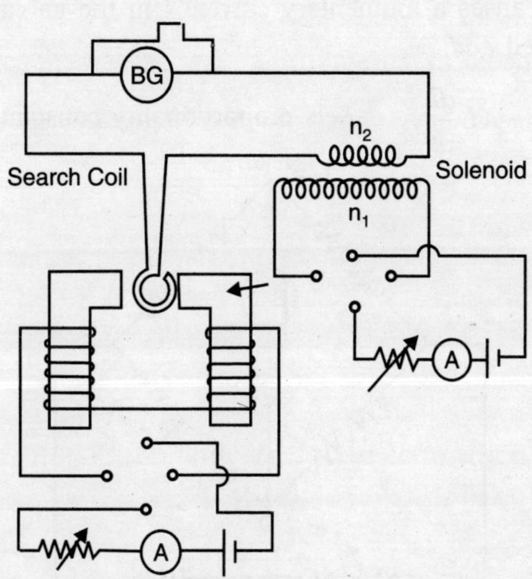

Fig. 6.26

The electromagnet circuit is removed. A known current i is passed in the primary of the solenoid. The magnetic field inside the solenoid is $\mu_0 n_1 i$ and the flux through the secondary of the solenoid is $(n_2 a_s)(\mu_0 n_1 i)$. If the current in the primary is reversed, the change in flux linking the secondary of the solenoid is $2\mu_0 n_1 n_2 a_s i$. If the charge corresponding to this change of flux gives rise to a throw θ_2 in the galvanometer then,

$$\frac{2\mu_0 n_1 n_2 a_s i}{R} = K\theta_2(1+\lambda/2) \quad ...(6.123)$$

From eqns. (6.122) and (6.123) we get

$$\frac{naB}{2\mu_0 n_1 n_2 a_s i} = \frac{\theta_1}{\theta_2}$$

$$B = \frac{2\mu_0 n_1 n_2 a_s i}{na} \cdot \frac{\theta_1}{\theta_2} \quad ...(6.124)$$

6.11.6 Determination of Self-Inductance: Rayliegh's Method

In Rayleigh method of determining self-inductance of a coil, Wheatstones bridge circuit is employed.

The unknown inductance L together with a standard resistance r of very low value is introduced in the fourth arm DC of the bridge. In the first part of the experiment, the standard resistance r is kept out of circuit by closing the key K_3. The bridge is balanced for steady currents in a usual way by adjusting the resistances in the various arms.

Now keeping the galvanometer key K_2 pressed, the battery key is released. The current in the inductance decays and gives rise to an induced *emf* of $-L\frac{dI}{dt}$ where I is the current in the inductance at time t. This induced *emf* causes a momentary current i in the galvanometer branch. The current i is proportional to the induced *emf.*

$$i = -KL\frac{dI}{dt}, \quad K \text{ is proportionality constant.}$$

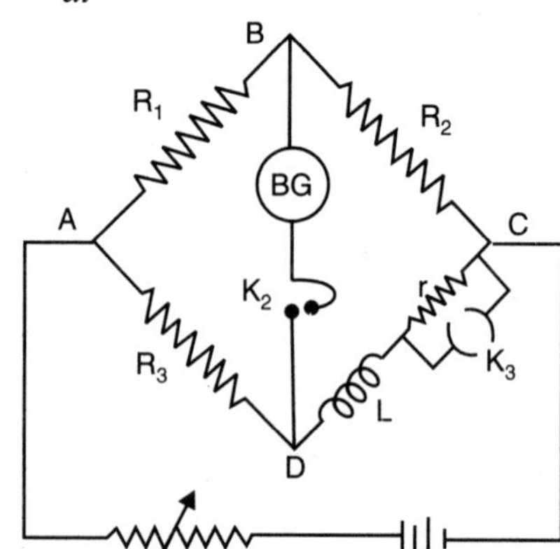

Fig. 6.27. Self-inductance by Rayleigh method

The charge q transported by this current passes through the galvanometer and a kick in its coil is observed.

$$q = \int_0^t idt = -KL\int_{I_0}^{0} \frac{dI}{dt}\cdot dt = KLI_0$$

where I_0 is the steady current flowing in the arm CD in the balanced condition of the bridge. If θ_1 is the first throw observed in the galvanometer, then

$$KLI_0 = \left(\frac{c}{NAB}\right)\frac{T}{2\pi}\cdot\theta_1(1+\lambda/2) \quad ...(6.125)$$

Now the standard resistance r in the arm CD is introduced by opening the key K_2. The resistance r is taken so small that it does not produce any appreciable change in the current I_0. The effect of r is to develop an additional potential difference equal to $I_0 r$ in the arm CD. This potential difference produces a steady current $KI_0 r$ in the galvanometer branch and a steady deflection ϕ is observed. Thus

$$KI_0 r = \left(\frac{c}{NAB}\right)\phi \quad ...(6.126)$$

Eliminating KI_0 from eqns. (6.125) and (6.126) we get

$$L = \frac{T}{2\pi}\left(\frac{r}{\phi}\right)\theta_1(1+\lambda/2) \qquad ...(6.127)$$

Measuring the time period T, θ_1 and ϕ, the self-inductance can be calculated from eqn. (6.127).

6.11.7 Determination of Mutual Inductance

To determine mutual inductance M of a pair of coils, the connections are made according to the circuit diagram (6.28). P is the primary and S is the secondary coil. 1, 2, 3 and 4 are the terminals of a commutator. A cell, a variable resistance R_1 and a small standard resistance $r(\cong 0.01\,\text{ohm})$ are connected in series with the primary coil P. The secondary coil is connected to a ballistic galvanometer through the terminals 1 and 2 of the commutator.

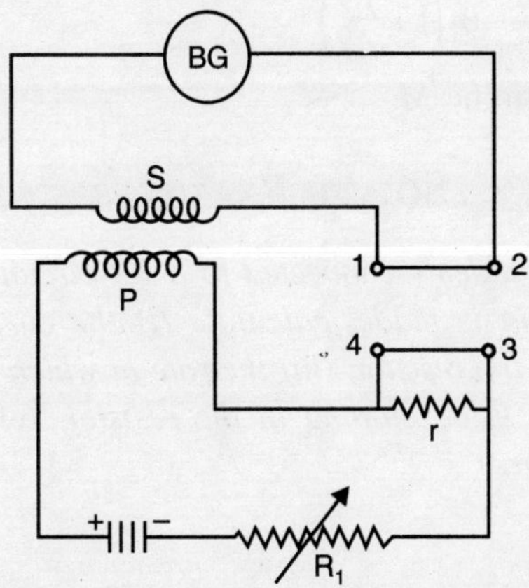

Fig. 6.28. Determination of mutual inductance.

First of all the secondary circuit is made complete by connecting terminals 1 and 2 together and in the primary, the standard resistance r is kept out of circuit by connecting the terminals 3 and 4 together. Now a current I_1 is switch on in the primary circuit. The growing current in the primary causes an induced *emf* $e = M\frac{dI_1}{dt}$ in the secondary circuit. If R_2 is the resistance of the entire secondary circuit, the current in the secondary is $I_2 = \frac{M}{R_2}.\frac{dI_1}{dt}$. The charge transported by this current through the ballistic galvanometer is

$$q = \int_0^t I_2 dt = \frac{M}{R_2}\int_0^{I_0} \frac{dI_1}{dt}\cdot dt = \frac{MI_0}{R_2} \qquad ...(6.128)$$

where I_0 is the steady current in the primary. If θ_1 is the first throw in the galvanometer due to passage of this charge then

$$\frac{MI_0}{R_2} = \frac{c}{NAB}\cdot\frac{T}{2\pi}\cdot\theta_1(1+\lambda/2) \qquad ...(6.129)$$

Now the terminals 1, 2 and 3, 4 are disconnected. The terminals 1, 4 and 2, 3 are connected together. Doing so, the standard resistance r comes into the primary circuit. The small value of r does not change appreciably the current in the primary. A potential difference $I_0 r$ develops across the resistance r and is applied to the secondary circuit and a steady current $i = \frac{I_0 r}{R}$ flows in the galvanometer circuit giving rise to a steady deflection ϕ in the galvanometer. Thus

$$\frac{I_0 r}{R_2} = \frac{c}{NAB} \cdot \phi \qquad ...(6.130)$$

Eliminating $\frac{I_0}{R}$ from eqns. (6.129) and (6.130) we get

$$M = r\phi \cdot \frac{T}{2\pi} \cdot \theta_1 \left(1 + \lambda/2\right) \qquad ...(6.131)$$

This equation is used to determine M.

SOLVED EXAMPLES

***Example* 1:** *A 20 volt battery is suddenly connected to a LR circuit with L = 5H and R = 10 ohms. At time 1.0 s after the connection is made, calculate (i) the current in the circuit, (ii) potential difference across the inductor and the resistor, (iii) the rate at which power is delivered by the battery, (iv) the rate at which Joule heat is developing in the resistor, (v) the rate at which the magnetic energy is appearing in the inductor.*

Solution:

Time constant $\tau = \frac{L}{R} = \frac{5}{10} = 0.5 \text{ s}$

Steady current $I_0 = \frac{V}{R} = \frac{20}{10} = 2 \text{ Amp}$

(*i*) At time t, the current in the circuit is given by

$$I = I_0\left(1 - e^{-t/\tau}\right)$$

At t = 1.0 s, the current in the circuit is

$$I = 2\left(1 - e^{-2}\right) = 2(1 - 0.1353) = 1.73 \text{ A}$$

Now $\frac{dI}{dt} = \frac{I_0}{\tau} e^{-t/\tau} = \frac{2}{0.5}\left(e^{-2}\right) = 0.54 \text{ A s}^{-1}$

(*ii*) Potential difference across the inductor

$$V_L = L\frac{dI}{dt} = 5 \times 0.54 = 2.70 \text{ V}$$

Potential difference across the resistor

$$V_R = IR = 1.73 \times 10 = 17.30 \text{ V}$$

Notice that

$$V_L + V_R = 2.70 + 17.30 \cong 20 \text{ V}$$

(*iii*) The rate at which power is delivered by the battery

$$VI = 20 \times 1.73 = 34.6 \text{ W}$$

(*iv*) The rate at which Joule heat is appearing

$$P_{\text{heat}} = I^2 R = (1.73)^2 \times 10 = 30.23 \text{ W}$$

(*v*) The rate at which the magnetic energy is appearing

$$P_{\text{magnetic}} = LI\frac{dI}{dt} = 5 \times 1.73 \times 0.54 = 4.67 \text{ W}$$

Notice that: $VI = I^2 R + LI\dfrac{dI}{dt}$ is satisfied.

***Example* 2:** *A 3 meg-ohm resistor and 1 μ F capacitor are connected in series with a battery of 5.0 volt emf and negligible internal resistance. After 1.0 s from the start, what are rates at which*

(*i*) *the charge on the capacitor is increasing,*

(*ii*) *the energy is being stored in the capacitor,*

(*iii*) *the heat is generated in the resistance,*

(*iv*) *the energy is being delivered by battery.*

Solution:

(*i*) At any instant *t*, the charge on the capacitor is given by

$$Q = Q_0\left(1 - e^{-t/\tau}\right)$$

where $Q_0 = CV = 1 \times 10^{-6} \times 5 = 5 \times 10^{-6}$ coulomb

and $\tau = RC = 3 \times 10^6 \times 1 \times 10^{-6} = 3 \text{ s}$

The rate of growth of charge at t = 1.0 s

$$I = \frac{dQ}{dt} = \frac{Q_0}{\tau}e^{-t/\tau} = \frac{5 \times 10^{-6} \times e^{-1/3}}{3} = 1.2 \times 10^{-6} \text{ A}$$

(*ii*) Rate of increase of energy stored in the capacitor

$$\frac{dU_c}{dt} = \frac{d}{dt}\left(\frac{1}{2}.\frac{Q^2}{C}\right) = \frac{Q}{C}.\frac{dQ}{dt}$$

Now $Q = Q_0\left(1 - e^{-t/\tau}\right) = 5 \times 10^{-6}\left(1 - e^{-1/3}\right) = 1.40 \times 10^{-6}$ coulomb

$$\therefore \quad \frac{dU_c}{dt} = \frac{1.40 \times 10^{-6}}{1 \times 10^6}\left(1.2 \times 10^{-6}\right) = 1.68 \times 10^{-6} \text{ watt}$$

(*iii*) The rate at which energy is dissipated in the resistor is

$$I^2R = \left(1.20\times10^{-6}\right)^2 \times 3\times10^6 = 4.32\times10^{-6}\text{ watt}$$

(*iv*) The rate at which energy is being delivered by the battery

$$VI = 5.0\times1.20\times10^{-6} = 6.0\times10^{-6}\text{ watt}$$

Notice that: $$VI = I^2R + \frac{dU_c}{dt}$$

***Example* 3:** *After how many time constants will the energy stored in the capacitor reach one-half its equilibrium value (i) during the charging and (ii) during the discharging process of a capacitor through a resistor.*

Solution: (*i*) During the charging process, the growth of charge is given by equation.

$$Q = Q_0\left(1 - e^{-t/\tau}\right)$$

and the stored energy in the capacitor is given by

$$U = \frac{1}{2}.\frac{Q^2}{C} = \frac{Q_0^{\ 2}}{2C}\left(1 - e^{-t/\tau}\right)^2$$

or $$U = U_0\left(1 - e^{-t/\tau}\right)^2$$

where U_0 is the maximum energy. Putting $U = \frac{1}{2}U_0$ we have

$$\frac{1}{2} = \left(1 - e^{-t/\tau}\right)^2$$

∴ $$\left[\frac{t}{\tau} = \ln\frac{141}{41} \Rightarrow t = \tau\ \ln\ \frac{141}{41} = \tau\left(2.30\log\frac{141}{41}\right) = 1.22\tau\right]$$

(*ii*) During the discharge, the charge on the capacitor is given by $Q = Q_0e^{-t/\tau}$ and the stored energy is given by

$$U = \frac{1}{2}.\frac{Q^2}{C} = \frac{Q_0^{\ 2}}{2C}e^{-2t/\tau} = U_0e^{-2t/\tau}$$

Putting $U = \frac{1}{2}U_0$ we have

$$\frac{1}{2} = e^{-2t/\tau}$$

$$\tau = \left(\frac{1}{2}\ln 2\right)\tau = 0.346\tau$$

***Example* 4:** *A capacitor of 2μF is charged by a 200 V power supply through a resistance. If a neon tube operating on 120 V is connected across the capacitor, calculate the value of resistance so that the tube glows after 5 second of the circuit being switched on.*

Solution: The potential difference across the capacitor as a function of time is given by,

$$V = V_0\left(1 - e^{-t/\tau}\right),$$

$$\tau = RC$$

From this equation we get $R = \dfrac{t}{C\ln\left(\dfrac{V_0}{V_0 - V}\right)} = \dfrac{t}{2.302C\log\left(\dfrac{V_0}{V_0 - V}\right)}$

Substituting $t = 5\,\text{s}, C = 2\times10^{-6}\,\text{F}$, $V_0 = 200$ V and $V = 120$ V we get

$$R = 2.7\times10^{6}\,\Omega$$

***Example* 5:** *A capacitor of capacitance C = 20 μf is charged to a potential of 100 volts and is then connected to a coil of inductance L = 20 mH. What is the amplitude of the oscillatory current? Neglect the resistance of the circuit.*

Solution: Maximum electrostatic energy

$$U_0 = \frac{1}{2}CV_0^{\,2}$$

When the capacitor is fully discharged, the electrostatic energy is converted into magnetic energy. Maximum value of magnetic energy is

$$U_m = \frac{1}{2}LI_0^{\,2}$$

Using the principle of conservation of energy we have

$$\frac{1}{2}LI_0^{\,2} = \frac{1}{2}CV_0^{\,2}$$

$$I_0 = \sqrt{\frac{C}{L}}V_0 = \sqrt{\left(\frac{2\times10^{-6}}{20\times10^{-3}}\right)}\times(100) = 1.0\text{ Amp}$$

***Example* 6:** *An oscillatory LC circuit consists of an inductance L = 10 mH and a capacitance C =10 nF. The capacitor is fully charged at the instant t = 0. When the energy is equally shared between the electric and the magnetic field, calculate (i) the charge on the capacitor, (ii) the time elapsed.*

Solution: (*i*) When the total energy is equally shared between the electric and the magnetic field, the charge on the capacitor is given by

$$\frac{1}{2}\cdot\frac{Q^2}{C} = \frac{1}{2}\left(\frac{Q_0^{\,2}}{2C}\right)$$

or $$Q = \frac{Q_0}{\sqrt{2}}$$

(*ii*) The angular frequency of the current is

$$\omega_0 = \frac{1}{\sqrt{LC}} = \frac{1}{\sqrt{10\times10^{-3}\times10\times10^{-9}}} = 1.0\times10^5 \text{ rad s}^{-1}.$$

At any instant t, the charge on the capacitor is $Q = Q_0 \cos\omega_0 t$.

The required time is given by putting $Q = \frac{Q_0}{\sqrt{2}}$ in the above equation.

$$\frac{Q_0}{\sqrt{2}} = Q_0 \cos\omega_0 t$$

$$\omega_0 t = \frac{\pi}{4}$$

$$t = \frac{\pi}{4\omega_0} = 7.85\times10^{-6}\text{s}$$

***Example* 7:** *In a LCR circuit, L = 20 mH, C = 2.0* μF. *Calculate the maximum value of the resistance R to make it oscillatory.*

Solution: The required value of R is given by

$$\frac{R^2}{4L^2} = \frac{1}{LC}$$

$$R = \sqrt{\frac{4L}{C}} = \sqrt{\frac{4\times20\times10^{-3}}{2\times10^{-6}}} = 200 \text{ ohms}$$

***Example* 8:** *In a LCR circuit, L = 2 mH, C = 4.0* μF *and R = 10 ohm. Calculate the time during which the oscillation amplitude (charge or current) is reduced to half of its initial value.*

Solution: The time dependence of the oscillation amplitude is given by

$$Q = Q_0 \exp(-Rt/2L)$$

Putting $Q = Q_0/2$ and solving for t we get

$$t = \frac{2L}{R}\ln 2 = \frac{2\times2\times10^{-3}\times0.693}{10}$$

$$= 2.77\times10^{-4}\text{ s}$$

***Example* 9:** *In an oscillatory LCR circuit, L = 0.1 mH, C=4*μF *and R = 1.0 ohm. What is the quality factor of the circuit? What relative error do we make in calculating the quality factor by the approximate formula,*

$$Q = \frac{1}{R}\sqrt{\frac{L}{C}}$$

Solution: Angular frequency of the circuit

$$\omega = \left[\frac{1}{LC} - \frac{R^2}{4L^2}\right]^{1/2}$$

$$Q = \frac{\omega L}{R} = \frac{L}{R}\left[\frac{1}{LC} - \frac{R^2}{4L^2}\right]^{1/2} = \sqrt{\frac{L}{CR^2} - \frac{1}{4}}$$

$$= \sqrt{\frac{0.1\times10^{-3}}{4\times10^{-6}\times1} - \frac{1}{4}} \cong 4.975$$

Using the formula $Q = \frac{1}{R}\sqrt{\frac{L}{C}} = 5.0$

Relative error $\frac{\Delta Q}{Q} = \frac{0.025}{4.975} \cong 0.5\ \%$

***Example* 10:** *What mean power must be supplied to a LCR circuit to maintain undamped oscillations with voltage amplitude across the capacitor of 10 volt. Given that: $L = 5\mu H$, $C = 4.0\ nF$, $R = 10$ ohms.*

Solution: In order to maintain oscillations with constant amplitude, the mean power supplied must be equal to the mean power dissipated in the resistance.

Mean power dissipated $= \frac{1}{2} I_0^2 R$

$$= \frac{1}{2}.\frac{CRV_0^2}{L} \qquad \left\{\frac{1}{2}LI_0^2 = \frac{1}{2}CV_0^2\right\}$$

$$= \frac{1\times10^{-9}\times100\times10}{2\times5\times10^{-6}}$$

$$= 100\times10^{-3}\text{ watt}$$

***Example* 11:** *A circuit has Q = 50 and ω_0 = 5 KHz. How much time will it take to diminish its energy half its original value?*

Solution: Energy of a *LCR* circuit decays according to the equation

$$U = U_0 e^{-\omega_0 t/Q}$$

Required time is obtained by putting $U = \frac{1}{2}U_0$ in above equation.

$$\frac{1}{2} = e^{-\omega_0 t/Q}$$

$$t = \frac{Q}{\omega_0} \ln 2$$

$$= \frac{50 \times 2.30 \times 0.3010}{5 \times 10^3} = 6.9 \times 10^{-3} \text{s}$$

QUESTIONS AND PROBLEMS

1. What are transients? Explain the growth and decay of current in a *LR* circuit. What is time constant?

2. Discuss the growth and decay of charge in a *RC* circuit. What is time constant?

3. Calculate the time during which (*i*) the current in a *LR* circuit reduces to half its steady state value, (*ii*) the voltage across the inductor equals that across the resistor, (*iii*) the energy dissipated in the resistor equals half the original value.

4. A capacitor is fully charged to a certain voltage. At time $t = 0$, it is connected across a resistor. At what time t (*i*) the charge reduces to half its original value, (*ii*) the voltage across the capacitor equals that across the resistor, (*iii*) the electrostatic energy of the capacitor reduces to 1/2 its original value.

5. Obtain the equations of voltages in growth and decay of current in *LR* circuit and charge in *RC* circuit using the law of conservation of energy.

Hint: The power supplied by the battery equals the rate at which the magnetic energy is building up in the inductor plus the rate at which energy is dissipated in the resistance.

$$VI = \left(L\frac{dI}{dt} \right) I + I^2 R$$

$$V = L\frac{dI}{dt} + IR$$

6. Discuss the discharge of capacitor through an inductor and a resistor. Under what condition the discharge is oscillatory? Obtain the frequency of the current.

7. What do you mean by quality factor of a circuit? Show that: $Q = \dfrac{\omega L}{R}$

8. Show that the amplitude and the energy of oscillations in *LCR* circuit can be expressed as,

$$I(t) = I_0 e^{-\omega t/2Q} = I_0 e^{-n\pi/Q}$$

and

$$U(t) = U_0 e^{-\omega t/2Q} = U_0 e^{-2\pi/Q}$$

where I_0 and U_0 are the current and energy amplitude at $t = 0$, Q = quality factor and n is the number of oscillations performed in time t.

9. Derive a relation between current sensitivity and charge sensitivity of a ballistic galvanometer.

10. The time constant of an inductive coil was found to be 2.5×10^{-3} s. With a resistance of 80 ohms added in series, a new time constant of 0.5×10^{-3} s was obtained. Find the inductance of the coil.

Ans. R = 20 ohms, L = 50 mH.

11. A coil of inductance L = 300 mH and a resistance R = 140 m-ohm is connected to a constant voltage source. How soon will the coil current reach 50% of the steady state value?

Ans. 1.5 sec

12. A coil with an inductance L = 200 mH and a resistance R = 200 mΩ is connected to a source of constant voltage. In what time will the current in the coil reach (i) half its steady value, (ii) two third of its steady value, (iii) $1/e$ of steady value, (iv) $1/e^3$ of its steady value.

13. A coil with L = 4H and R = 10 ohms is suddenly connected to battery of 10 volts. At 0.8s after the connection is made, what are the rates at which (i) energy is being stored in the magnetic field, (ii) Joule heat is appearing, (iii) energy is being delivered by the battery, $\left(e^{-2}=0.1353\right)$

Ans. (i) 1.170 watt (ii) 7.477 watt (iii) 8.647 watt

14. A capacitor of C = 0.1 μF is first charged and then discharged through a resistance of 10 mega-ohm. Find the time the potential will take to half its orginal value.

Ans. t = ln 2 sec

15. The time constant of a RC circuit is 5 s. How much time the capacitor will take to discharge to $1/e^3$ of its maximum charge?

Ans. 15 s

16. A capacitor of 0.22 μF charged to a potential of 100 V is discharged through a resistance of 10 mega-ohms. What is the charge on it after 1.1 s.

Ans. 13.34×10^{-6} coulomb

17. A capacitor with C = 4 μF carries charge $Q_0=2\times10^{-3}$ coulomb. It is then discharged through a resistance of 10 mega-ohms. Find

(*i*) the charge flowing through the resistance during a time interval of 2 s.

(*ii*) the amount of heat generated during the same time.

Hint:

(*i*) $\Delta Q=\int I\,dt=\dfrac{-Q_0}{RC}\int_0^2 e^{-t/RC}\,dt$

(*ii*) Heat generated $=\int_0^2 I^2 R\,dt$

18. A *LCR* circuit is critically damped with $L = 0.2$ H and $R = 100$ ohms. What is the value of L?

19. What is Q-factor of the circuit with $R = 1\,\Omega$, $L = 2.5$ mH, $C = 1\mu$F?

$$\left[Q = \frac{1}{R}\sqrt{\frac{L}{C}} = 50\right]$$

20. In a *LCR* circuit with $L = 0.1$ H, $C = 5\,\mu$F, $R = 200$ ohms, the capacitor is charged to a potential $V_0 = 200$ volt. What is the transient current?

[**Hint:** $\omega_0^2 = 2\times10^6, \omega^2 = 1\times10^6, Q_o = CV_0 = 1\times10^{-3}$ coul.]

$$\text{Current } I = \left(\frac{Q_0\omega_0^{\ 2}}{\omega}\right)e^{-Rt/2L}\sin\omega t$$

$$= 2 \exp(-1000\, t)\ [\sin 1000\, t] \text{ Ampere}$$

21. A capacitor $C = 0.2\ \mu$F is charged by a source of 6 volt through a resistance of 100 Ω. If the resistance is increased to 500 Ω, by what factor will the steady state charge on the capacitor change?

22. A capacitor $C = 0.2\ \mu$F is charged by a source of 5 V through a resistance of 5 MΩ. Calculate the charge on the capacitor in 10 s.

23. A circuit contains $L = 1$ henry, $C = 1\mu$F and $R = 400\ \Omega$ all connected in series. The capacitor is first charged by d.c. source of 10 V *emf.* After the capacitor is fully charged, it is discharged through the source R and L. Calculate the maximum potential difference across the capacitor in the second cycle.

24. A battery of *emf* 100 volt is connected in series with an inductance of 10 mH, a capacitor of 0.05 μF and a resistance of 100 ohm. Is the circuit oscillatory? What is the frequency of oscillatory current if such a current flows?

25. Give the theory of oscillatory discharge of a condenser through an inductance. Give a method for the measurement of high resistance of the order of megaohm based on the theory of discharge of a condenser, through a resistance.

26. In a *L-R* circuit, the inductance has a value 1 henry and resistance has value 10 Ω. In what time the current will fall to 36.8% of its steady state value?

27. In a series *LCR* circuit, $L = 2$ mH and $C = 2\ \mu$F. Calculate the maximum value of the resistance to make it oscillatory and also the frequency of oscillations.

28. Obtain the equation of motion of the coil in galvanometer. When does it become oscillatory? What is the value of critical damping in a ballistic galvanometer?

29. Differentiate between steady state and transient response of *LCR* circuit. Obtain condition for critical damping in a *LCR* circuit and illustrate its practical application.

Examine when would a *LCR* circuit with $L = 0.2$ H and $R = 100\ \Omega$ would be critically damped.

ooo

7 CHAPTER

Analysis of A.C. Circuits

7.1. A.C. SIGNALS AND ITS PARAMETERS

A current which changes its direction as well as magnitude periodically with time is referred to as *alternating current* (*a.c.*) and the *voltage* corresponding to it as alternating voltage or *a.c. signal*. The instrument generating it may be called an *a.c. source*. The number of times *a.c. current* changes its direction per second is called its *frequency* (f). Its unit is Hertz (Hz). 2π times f is called its *angular frequency* (ω) and $2\pi/\omega$ its *time period* (T). It is the time taken by *a.c.* to complete its one cycle. An *a.c.* signal may have different forms of variation with time. Few of these are shown in Fig. 7.1.

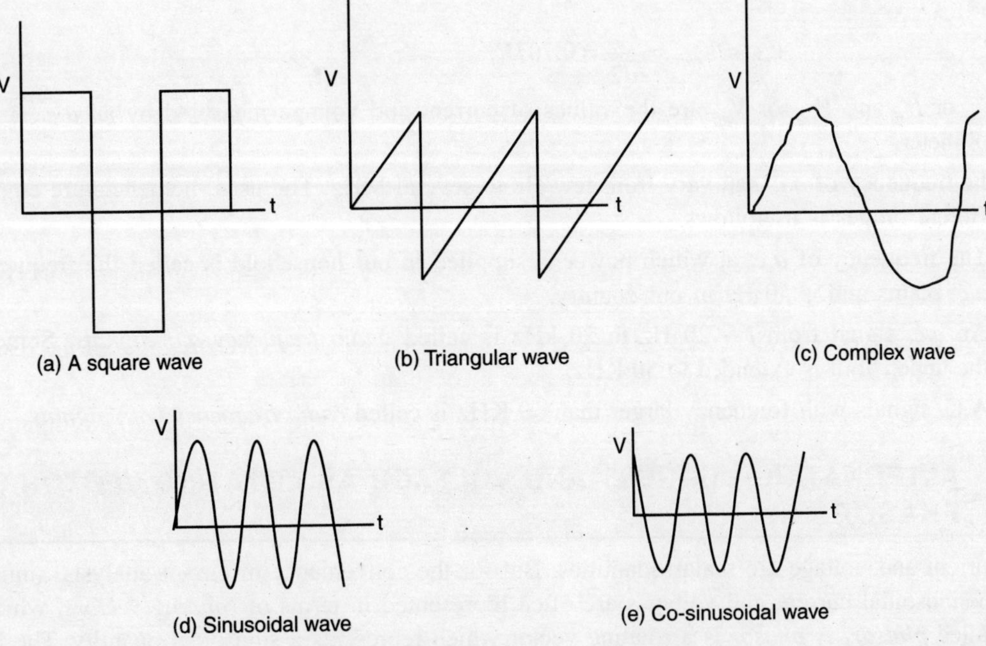

Fig. 7.1. Different kinds of a.c. signals.

Out of these signals, the signal (*d*) can be represented by sine function ($v = V_m \sin\omega t$) and the signal (*e*) by cosine function ($v = V_m \cos\omega t$) and therefore are called *sinusoidal* and *co-sinusoidal* signal respectively. In the present chapter, we shall be concerned with sinusoidal and co-sinusoidal signals. A typical sinusoidal signal is represented by the equation

$$v(t) = V_m \sin\omega t \quad \text{...(7.1)}$$

And corresponding current by

$$i(t) = I_m \sin(\omega t + \varphi) \quad \text{...(7.2)}$$

$v(t)$ and $i(t)$ are the *instantaneous values* of voltage and current respectively. V_m and I_m are the maximum value of voltage and current and are called amplitudes or peak values of voltage and current respectively, φ is the phase difference between voltage and current and may vary from $-\pi/2$ to $+\pi/2$.

Alternating current and voltage are measured in terms of their *root mean square* (*rms*) or *effective values* which are often referred to as *virtual current* and *virtual voltage*. Thus for a sinusoidal current and voltage, the virtual current I_{rms} and virtual voltage V_{rms} are given by

$$I_{eff}^2 = I_{rms}^2 = \frac{1}{T}\int_0^T i^2 dt = \frac{1}{T}\int_0^T I_m^2 \sin^2(\omega t + \varphi) dt = \frac{I_m^2}{2}$$

$$\therefore \quad I_{eff} = I_{rms} = \frac{I_m}{\sqrt{2}} = 0.707 I_m \quad \text{...(7.3)}$$

Similarly,

$$V_{eff}^2 = V_{rms}^2 = \frac{1}{T}\int_0^T v^2 dt = \frac{1}{T}\int_0^T V_m^2 \sin^2\omega t dt = \frac{V_m^2}{2}$$

$$\therefore \quad V_{eff} = V_{rms} = \frac{V_m}{\sqrt{2}} = 0.707 V_m \quad \text{...(7.4)}$$

I_{rms} or I_{eff} and V_{rms} or V_{eff} are the values of current and voltage measured by an *a.c.* ammeter and voltmeter.

The frequency of *a.c.* can vary from few Hz to several MHz. The usual nomenclature employed for different ranges is as follows.

(*i*) The frequency of *a.c.* at which power is supplied in our household is called the frequency of *a.c.* mains and is 50 Hz in our country.

(*ii*) An *a.c.* signal from $f = 20$ Hz to 20 kHz is called *audio frequency a.c. signals*. Sometimes the upper limit is extended to 50 KHz.

(*iii*) A.C. signals with frequency larger than 50 KHz is called *radio frequency* (*r.f.*) *signals*.

7.2. ALTERNATING CURRENT AND VOLTAGE AS ROTATING VECTOR OR PHASOR

The current and voltage are scalar quantities. But for the convenience of circuit analysis, sinusoidal and co-sinusoidal current and voltages are often represented in terms of *rotating vectors*, which are also called **phasor.** A *phasor* is a rotating vector which represents a sinusoidal quantity. The length of the vector represents the amplitude of the quantity. It is supposed to be rotating with angular velocity equal to the angular frequency of the quantity. The projection of the *phasor* onto a fixed direction gives the instantaneous value of the quantity. A *phasor* is also represented as a complex number with real and imaginary parts. In representing a complex number, we make use of symbol $\sqrt{-1}$ to be equal to j, which in general sense can be taken as an operator. It is appropriate to explain briefly the meaning of complex number, the operator j and *phasor* before presenting alternating current and voltage as a *phasor*.

(a) Complex Number: A number of the form $\gamma = x + jy$, where x and y are real numbers and $j = \sqrt{-1}$, is called complex number. Here x and jy are the real and imaginary parts of the complex number respectively. To represent a complex number geometrically on a plane, we take two orthogonal lines OX and OY and measure a distance $OA = x$ along OX and a distance $OB = y$ along OY. The rectangle $OAPB$ is completed. The diagonal OP represents the complex number γ. We see that the real and imaginary parts of a complex number add like the components of a vector. The length of the vector OP is called the *modulus* (*amplitude*) and the angle which it makes with x-axis is called the *argument* or *phase* of the complex number.

$$|\gamma| = \sqrt{x^2 + y^2} \quad \text{and} \quad \tan\theta = \frac{y}{x} \qquad ...(7.5)$$

The addition and subtraction of two complex numbers $\gamma_1 = x_1 + jy_1$ *and* $\gamma_2 = x_2 + jy_2$, follows the following rules.

$$\gamma_1 + \gamma_2 = (x_1 + jy_1) + (x_2 + jy_2) = (x_1 + x_2) + j(y_1 + y_2) \qquad ...(7.6)$$

$$\gamma_1 - \gamma_2 = (x_1 + jy_1) - (x_2 + jy_2) = (x_1 - x_2) + j(y_1 - y_2) \qquad ...(7.7)$$

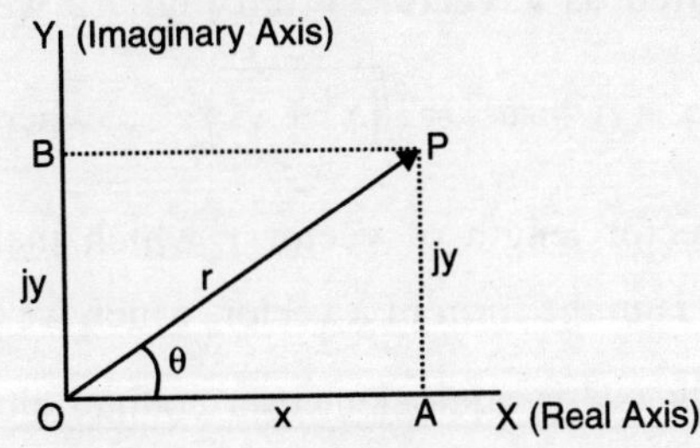

Fig. 7.2

From Fig. 7.2, we can write

$$x = r\cos\theta \text{ and } y = r\sin\theta, \ |\gamma| = r \qquad ...(7.8)$$

Therefore, the complex number γ can be written as

$$\gamma = x + jy = r(\cos\theta + j\sin\theta) = re^{j\theta} \qquad ...(7.9)$$

The complex number γ represented as $re^{j\theta}$ is called exponential form of the complex number. The polar form of complex number γ is often written as $r\angle\theta$. Thus,

$$\gamma = re^{j\theta} = r\angle\theta \qquad ...(7.10)$$

(b) Operator j: The quantity $\sqrt{-1}$ is represented by symbol j. The representation of the imaginary part of complex number along y-axis permits us to broaden the interpretation of the symbol j. The symbol j may be regarded as an operator which has following properties.

(*i*) The symbol j read as instruction to perform a counter-clockwise rotation of 90° of the vector representing the quantity before which it appears. In other words, a quantity multiplied by j is ahead in phase by 90°. Similarly, $-j$ is to be regarded as an instruction to perform a clockwise rotation by 90° of the vector representing the quantity before which it appears. Thus, the quantity multiplied by $-j$ lags in phase by 90°.

(*ii*) The quantity j^2x is to be identified with $j\,(jx)$, which is equivalent to two successive operations with j. Two successive rotation, each of 90° in the same direction, transforms a vector x into $-x$. Thus, $j^2x = -x$, hence $j^2 = -1$. We further observe that

$$j^3x = j(j^2x) = -jx \qquad ...(7.11)$$

$$\frac{1}{j}x = \frac{j}{j^2}x = \frac{j}{-1}x = -jx \qquad ...(7.12)$$

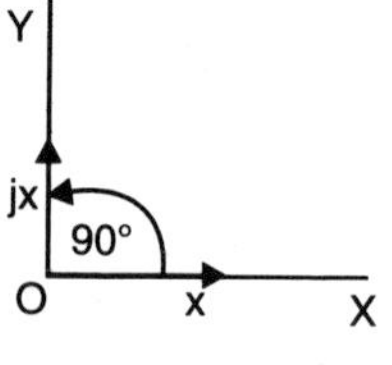

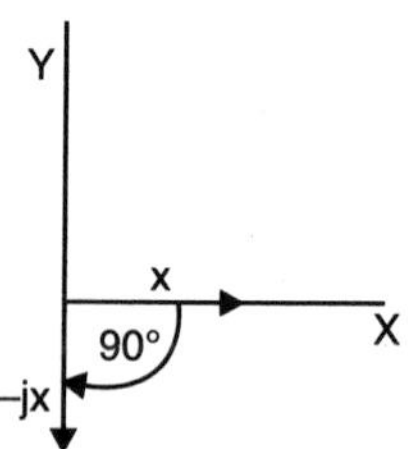

Fig. 7.3

(*c*) Complex Number represented as a Vector: From Fig. 7.2 we can write

$$\gamma = x + jy = re^{j\theta} = \sqrt{(x^2 + y^2)}\,e^{j\theta}, \text{ where } \theta = \tan^{-1}\frac{y}{x} \qquad ...(7.13)$$

The quantity $\sqrt{x^2 + y^2}$ is vector length of vector **r** which makes angle θ with x-axis. Thus representation of γ by eqn. (7.13) is in the form of a vector, which we call *rotating vector*. Multiplying a vector **r** of length $\sqrt{x^2 + y^2}$ by $e^{j\theta}$ is equivalent to a counter-clockwise rotation of vector **r** by angle θ. It is obvious that in this representation only direction of the vector is changing but its magnitude remains the same. Thus a rotating $re^{-j\theta}$ is regarded as a vector rotated through angle θ in clockwise direction. Obviously, it will make angle $-\theta$ with x-axis. Angle θ is called the phase of the rotating vector.

Now suppose we have a vector in which θ is changing with time *i.e.* $\theta = \omega t$ where θ is a real quantity and may be called angular velocity. Thus the rotating vector $\gamma = re^{j\omega t}$ is changing its phase with time which means it is rotating with angular velocity ω. Such a rotating vector is called a *phasor*. Since a complex number can be represented in following different forms, so is the case a *phasor*. The three forms of *phasor* representation are:

Exponential form $\gamma = re^{j\omega t} = re^{j\theta}$

Polar form $\gamma = r\angle\omega t = r\angle\theta$ ...(7.14)

Rectangular form $\gamma = r\cos\theta + jr\,sin\theta$

The addition of two *phasors* is usually performed in rectangular form. Thus, if we have

$$\gamma_1 = r_1 e^{j\theta_1} \text{ and } \gamma_2 = r_2 e^{j\theta_2}$$

Then we write

$$\gamma_1 \pm \gamma_2 = (r_1 \cos\theta_1 \pm r_2 \cos\theta_2) + j(r_1 \sin\theta_1 \pm r_2 \sin\theta_2) \quad ...(7.15)$$

Multiplication and division of *phasor* are usually performed by expressing them in exponential or polar forms. Thus

$$\gamma_1\gamma_2 = r_1 r_2 e^{j(\theta_1+\theta_2)} = r_1 r_2 \angle(\theta_1+\theta_2) \quad ...(7.16)$$

$$\frac{\gamma_1}{\gamma_2} = \frac{r_1}{r_2} e^{j(\theta_1-\theta_2)} = \frac{r_1}{r_2} \angle(\theta_1-\theta_2) \quad ...(7.17)$$

(*d*) **Phasor of Alternating Voltage and Current:** For simplifying the mathematical analysis of circuits, alternating voltage *v*(*t*) is often represented by a vector **V** as

$$\mathbf{V} = V_m e^{j\omega t} \quad ...(7.18)$$

Where V_m is the peak value of the voltage and ωt is its phase angle. The phase ωt is changing with time while V_m remains constant. The symbol $V_m e^{j\omega t}$ is referred to as *phasor* or rotating vector of the alternating voltage. If we depict this vector on complex plane, we see that at $t = 0$, this vector coincides with *x*-axis and it has magnitude V_m. At any instant *t* its phase becomes ωt and hence the vector representing the voltage makes an angle ωt with *x*-axis and has the same magnitude V_m. The projection of voltage *phasor* along *x*-axis is $V_m \cos \omega t$ and along *y*-axis is $V_m \sin \omega t$. These are referred to as the real and imaginary parts of the voltage. The real part is the actual form of voltage and is used whenever calculation of power is required.

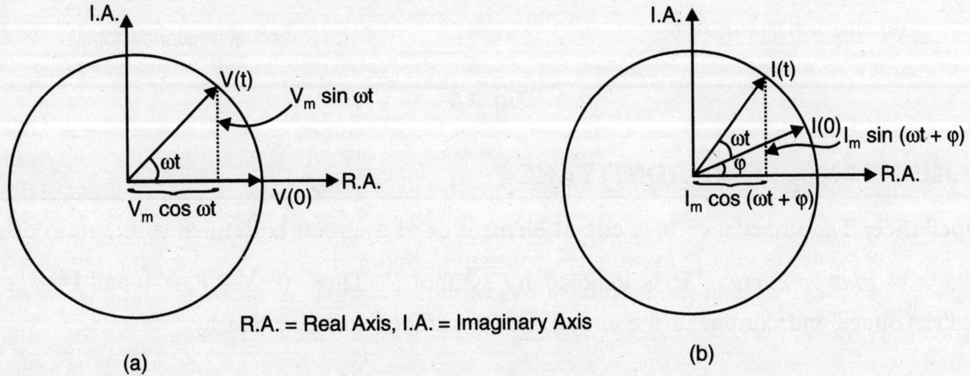

Fig. 7.4. (a) Phasor of alternating voltage $\mathbf{V} = V_m e^{j\omega t}$ (b) Phasor of alternating current $\mathbf{I} = I_m e^{j(\omega t+\varphi)}$.

The current vector **I** resulting from the voltage vector **V** is expressed by relation

$$\mathbf{I} = I_m e^{j(\omega t+\varphi)} \quad ...(7.19)$$

Where I_m is the peak value of current, $(\omega t + \varphi)$ the phase angle of the current and φ is the phase difference between the current and voltage. The quantity φ may be negative, zero or positive. If φ is negative, the current is said to be lagging behind the voltage and if φ is positive, the current is said to be leading the voltage. If φ is zero, the current is said to be in phase with the voltage. The expression $\mathbf{I} = I_m e^{j(\omega t+\varphi)}$ is referred to as the *phasor* current or *rotating current vector*. At $t = 0$, this vector makes an angle φ with x-axis. However, its magnitude remains I_m and at instant t, it makes an angle $(\omega t + \varphi)$ with x-axis without changing its magnitude. The projections of *phasor* current on real and imaginary axes are: $I_m \cos(\omega t + \varphi)$ and $I_m \sin(\omega t + \varphi)$.

There are two ways of representing a sinusoidal quantity as a rotating vector (*phasor*). If the sinusoidal quantity is represented as a rotating vector which contains time explicitly, it is said to in *time domain*. If the sinusoidal quantity is expressed in terms of its effective value and its phase and time does not occur, it is said to be in *frequency domain*. For example, the phasor representation of a sinusoidal voltage $v(t) = 200\sqrt{2}\cos\left(1000t + \frac{\pi}{3}\right)$ in time domain is $\mathbf{V} = 200\, e^{j(\omega t+\pi/3)}$. In frequency domain it is represented as $\mathbf{V} = 200 \angle 60°$.

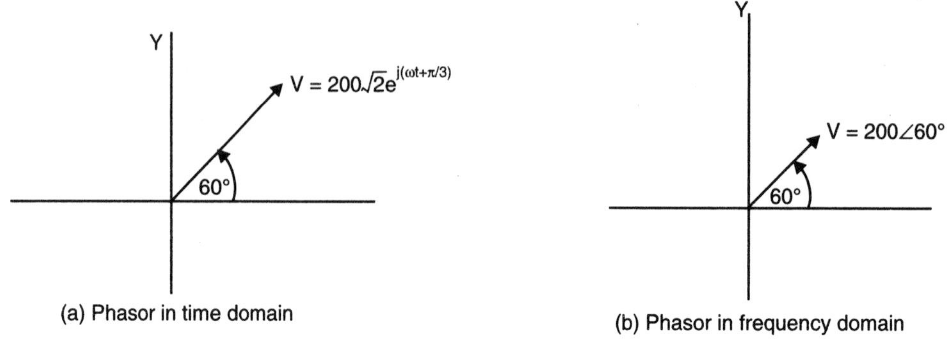

(a) Phasor in time domain

(b) Phasor in frequency domain

Fig. 7.5

7.3. IMPEDANCE AND ADMITTANCE

(*a*) Impedance: The impedance of a circuit element or of a circuit is defined as the ratio of *phasor voltage* to *phasor current*. It is denoted by symbol Z. Thus, if $\mathbf{V} = V_m e^{j\omega t}$ and $\mathbf{I} = I_m e^{j(\omega t+\varphi)}$ are the voltage and current in the circuit then the impedance is given by

$$Z = \frac{\mathbf{V}}{\mathbf{I}} = \frac{V_m e^{j\omega t}}{I_m e^{j(\omega t+\varphi)}} = \frac{V_m}{I_m} e^{-j\varphi} = |Z|\, e^{-j\varphi} = |Z| \angle -\varphi \qquad ...(7.20)$$

Where $|Z|$ is the magnitude of impedance and $(-\varphi)$ its phase angle. The magnitude and phase are independent of time. It is evident from eqn. (7.20) that the impedance is a complex quantity and can be represented in exponential, polar and rectangular forms. In rectangular form we can write

$$Z = R + jX \qquad ...(7.21)$$

Where the real part R is referred to as *resistive* part and imaginary part X as *reactive* part. We can write impedance Z as

$$|Z| = \sqrt{R^2 + X^2} \text{ and } \varphi = \tan^{-1}(X/R) \qquad ...(7.22)$$

The imaginary (reactive) part of impedance does not consume power whereas the real part does. The average power consumed in the circuit is

$$P = \frac{1}{T}\int_0^T V_{\text{real}} I_{\text{real}}\, dt = \frac{1}{T}\int_0^T V_m \cos\omega t \cdot I_m \cos(\omega t + \varphi)\, dt$$

$$= \frac{1}{2} V_m I_m \cos\varphi \qquad ...(7.23)$$

The laws of combination of impedances are similar to those of resistances. Thus, if several impedances Z_1, Z_2, Z_3, ...Z_n are connected in series, the resultant impedance Z of the combination is

$$Z = Z_1 + Z_2 + Z_3 + ...Z_n \qquad ...(7.24)$$

If these impedances are connected in parallel, the resultant impedance Z of combination is given by

$$\frac{1}{Z} = \frac{1}{Z_1} + \frac{1}{Z_2} + \frac{1}{Z_3} + ...\frac{1}{Z_n} \qquad ...(7.25)$$

(*b*) Admittance: The *admittance* of a circuit element or of a circuit is defined as the ratio of *phasor* current to *phasor* voltage. It is denoted by symbol Y. Thus,

$$Y = \frac{\mathbf{I}}{\mathbf{V}} = \frac{I_m e^{j(\omega t + \varphi)}}{V_m e^{j\omega t}} = |Y| e^{j\varphi} = |Y| \angle \varphi \qquad ...(7.26)$$

Where $|Y|$ is the magnitude of the admittance and φ its phase angle. In general, Y is a complex quantity and may be written as

$$Y = G + jS \qquad ...(7.27)$$

The real part G of Y is called *conductance* and the imaginary part S *susceptance* of the circuit. The magnitude $|Y|$ and phase φ of admittance can be written as

$$|Y| = \sqrt{G^2 + S^2} \text{ and } \varphi = \tan^{-1}(S/G) \qquad ...(7.28)$$

From the definition of Z and Y, it is evident that

$$Y = \frac{1}{Z}$$

or

$$G + jS = \frac{1}{R + jX} = \frac{R - jX}{R^2 + X^2} = \frac{R - jX}{|Z|^2} \qquad ...(7.29)$$

Therefore,

$$G = \frac{R}{|Z|^2} \text{ and } S = -\frac{X}{|Z|^2} \qquad ...(7.30)$$

The laws of combination of admittances are similar to those of capacitances. Thus, when admittance Y_1, Y_2, Y_3,....Y_n are connected in parallel, the resultant admittance Y is given by

$$Y = Y_1 + Y_2 + Y_3 + ...Y_n \qquad ...(7.31)$$

If the admittances are connected in series the resultant admittance Y is given by

$$\frac{1}{Y} = \frac{1}{Y_1} + \frac{1}{Y_2} + \frac{1}{Y_3} .... \frac{1}{Y_n} \qquad ...(7.32)$$

7.4. OHM'S LAW IN VECTOR FORM

When a voltage vector **V** is applied to a resistor of resistance R, the resulting current vector **I** is given by

$$\mathbf{I} = \frac{\mathbf{V}}{R} \quad \text{or} \quad \mathbf{V} = R\mathbf{I} \qquad ....(7.33)$$

This is the vector form of Ohm's law.

If vector voltage **V** is applied across an inductor of self-inductance L and **I** is the resulting vector current in it then voltage across the inductor is given by

$$\mathbf{V} = \mathbf{V}_L = L\frac{d\mathbf{I}}{dt} \qquad ...(7.34)$$

Let the current vector be

$$\mathbf{I} = I_m e^{j(\omega t + \varphi)} \qquad ...(7.35)$$

Substituting (7.35) in (7.34) we find

$$\mathbf{V} = \mathbf{V}_L = j\omega L\mathbf{I} \qquad ...(7.36)$$

Similarly, when a voltage vector **V** is applied across a capacitor of capacitance C, the charge q on the plates of the capacitor is given by

$$\mathbf{V} = \mathbf{V}_C = \frac{q}{C} = \frac{1}{C}\int \mathbf{I}dt = \frac{1}{C}\int I_0 e^{j(\omega t + \varphi)} dt = \frac{\mathbf{I}}{j\omega C} \qquad ...(7.37)$$

Equation (7.36) and (7.37) express Ohm's law and give voltages across the inductor and capacitor respectively. The ratio **V/I** in case of inductor is $j\omega L$ and in case of capacitor is $\frac{1}{j\omega C}$ or $-\frac{j}{\omega C}$ which are called inductive reactance and capacitive reactance and denoted by X_L and X_C respectively. Thus,

$$\mathbf{X}_L = j\omega L = \omega L e^{j\pi/2} = \omega L \angle 90°,$$

$$\text{and } \mathbf{X}_C = \frac{1}{j\omega C} = \frac{-j}{\omega C} = \frac{1}{\omega C} e^{-j\pi/2} = \frac{1}{\omega C} \angle -90° \qquad ...(7.38)$$

7.5. PURE RESISTIVE CIRCUIT SUBJECTED TO ALTERNATING VOLTAGE

A circuit is said to be resistive if it is composed of only pure resistor. All the resistors connected in any form can be replaced by a pure resistance R. Thus, a pure resistive circuit subjected to an alternating voltage can be represented by Fig. 7.6.

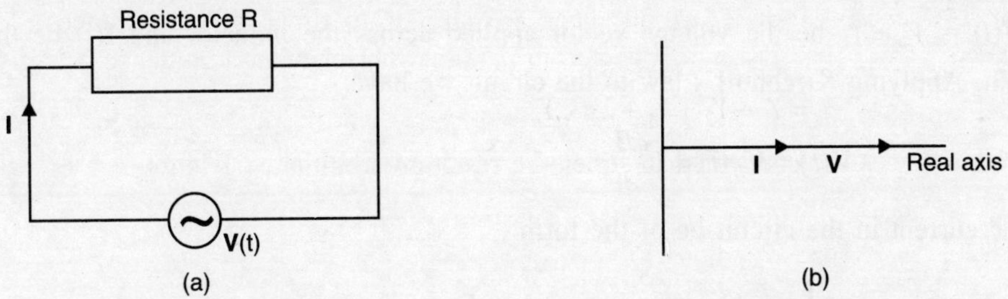

Fig. 7.6. (a) Resistive circuit (b) Voltage and current in resistive circuit.

Let an alternating voltage $\mathbf{V}(t) = V_m e^{j\omega t}$ be applied to the circuit. According to Ohm's law, the current **I** in the circuit is given by

$$\mathbf{I} = \frac{\mathbf{V}}{R} \qquad \text{...(7.39)}$$

Since R is real, the current in the resistor is in phase with the voltage and can be represented by

$$\mathbf{I} = I_m e^{j\omega t}, \quad \text{where } I_m = \frac{V_m}{R} \qquad \text{...(7.40)}$$

The impedance **Z** of the circuit is real and is independent of frequency of the voltage. In pure resistive circuit $Z = R$.

The average power consumed per cycle in the circuit is

$$P = \frac{1}{T}\int_0^T V_{\text{real}} I_{\text{real}} dt = V_m I_m \left(\frac{1}{T}\int_0^T \cos^2 \omega t dt\right) = \frac{1}{2} V_m I_m = V_{rms} I_{rms} \qquad \text{...(7.41)}$$

7.6. PURE INDUCTIVE CIRCUIT

A circuit is called inductive if all the elements of the circuit are pure inductors or the circuit as a whole behaves as a pure inductor. In both cases, it can be replaced by an inductor of effective inductance L. The inductive circuit subjected to alternating voltage can be represented by Fig. 7.7.

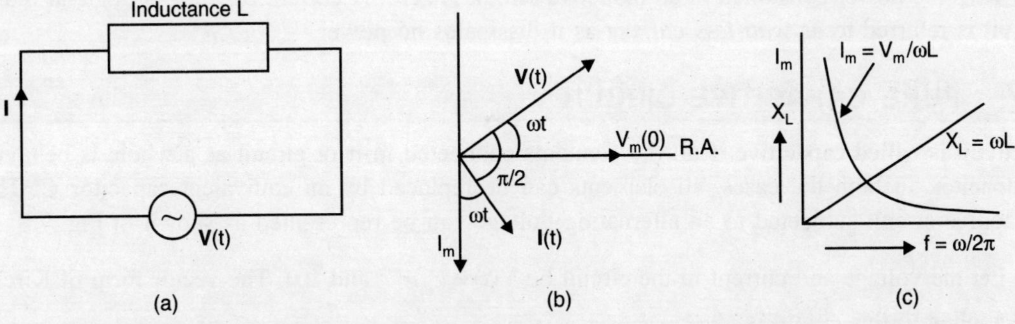

Fig. 7.7. (a) Inductive circuit (b) Voltage and current vectors (c) Variation of impedance (reactance) and I_m with frequency of a.c. signal.

Let $\mathbf{V}(t) = V_m e^{j\omega t}$ be the voltage vector applied across the inductor and $\mathbf{I}(t)$ be the resulting current in it. Applying Kirchhoff's law to the circuit we have

$$\mathbf{V}(t) = \mathbf{V}_L(t) = L\frac{d\mathbf{I}}{dt} \qquad \text{...(7.42)}$$

Let the current in the circuit be of the form

$$\mathbf{I} = I_m e^{j(\omega t+\varphi)} \qquad \text{...(7.43)}$$

Substituting this form of current in eqn. (7.42) we have

$$\mathbf{V}(t) = \mathbf{V}_L(t) = j\omega L\mathbf{I}$$

or

$$\mathbf{I} = \frac{\mathbf{V}(t)}{j\omega L} = -j\frac{V_m e^{j\omega t}}{\omega L} = \frac{V_m}{\omega L}e^{j(\omega t-\pi/2)} = I_m e^{j(\omega t-\pi/2)} \qquad \text{...(7.44)}$$

Comparison of eqns. (7.43) and (7.44) shows that

$$I_m = \frac{V_m}{\omega L} \quad \text{and} \quad \varphi = -\pi/2 \qquad \text{...(7.45)}$$

Thus the peak value of current is frequency dependent and it lags behind the voltage by $\pi/2$. Equation (7.44) shows that an inductor offers an impedance Z given by

$$Z = \frac{\mathbf{V}}{\mathbf{I}} = j\omega L \qquad \text{...(7.46)}$$

The impedance of inductor is pure reactive in nature and usually denoted by X_L. Thus

$$X_L = j\omega L, \ |X_L| = \omega L = 2\pi fL, \ X_L = \omega L \angle 90^\circ \qquad \text{...(7.47)}$$

The average power consumed per cycle in a purely inductive circuit is

$$P = \frac{1}{T}\int_0^T V_{\text{real}} I_{\text{real}} dt = \frac{1}{T}\int_0^T V_m \cos\omega t \cdot I_m \cos(\omega t - \pi/2)dt = 0 \qquad \text{...(7.48)}$$

Thus the power consumed in an inductive circuit is zero. A current flowing through an inductive circuit is referred to as *watt-less current* as it dissipates no power.

7.7. PURE CAPACITIVE CIRCUIT

A circuit is called capacitive if all the elements connected in it or circuit as a whole is behaving as a capacitor. In both the cases, all elements can be replaced by an equivalent capacitor C. Thus, a capacitive circuit subjected to an alternating voltage can be represented as shown in Fig. 7.8.

Let the voltage and current in the circuit be $\mathbf{V}(t) = V_m e^{j\omega t}$ and $\mathbf{I}(t)$. The vector form of Kirchoff's law applied to this circuit is

$$\mathbf{V}(t) = \mathbf{V}_C = \frac{1}{C}\int \mathbf{I}dt = \frac{\mathbf{I}}{j\omega C} = -j\frac{\mathbf{I}}{\omega C} \qquad \text{...(7.49)}$$

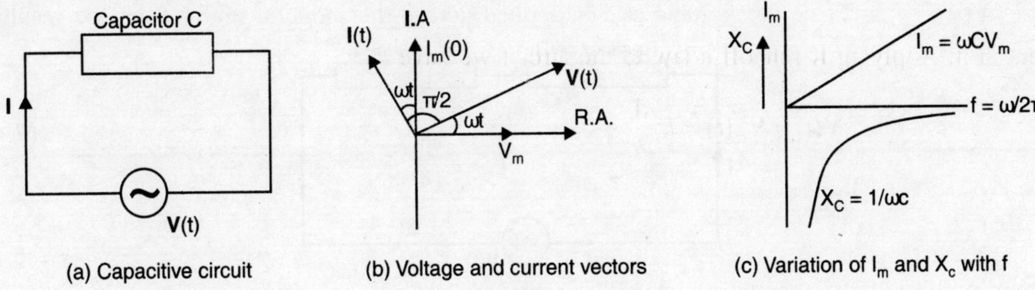

(a) Capacitive circuit (b) Voltage and current vectors (c) Variation of I_m and X_c with f

Fig. 7.8

The current in the circuit is

$$\mathbf{I}(t) = j\omega C\mathbf{V}(t) = \omega C V_m e^{j(\omega t+\pi/2)} = \frac{V_m}{\left(\frac{1}{\omega C}\right)} e^{j(\omega t+\pi/2)} = I_m e^{j(\omega t+\pi/2)} \quad \text{...(7.50)}$$

Where peak value of current I_m is given by

$$I_m = \omega C V_m \quad \text{...(7.51)}$$

Evidently the current increases with increasing frequency of the applied voltage.

Equation (7.50) shows that the current leads the voltage by π/2. The impedance Z of the circuit is

$$Z = \frac{\mathbf{V}(t)}{\mathbf{I}(t)} = \frac{1}{j\omega C} = -\frac{j}{\omega C} \quad \text{...(7.52)}$$

The impedance Z is purely reactive in nature and is usually denoted by X_C. Thus

$$X_C = \frac{1}{j\omega C} = -\frac{j}{\omega C}, \quad |X_C| = \frac{1}{\omega C}, \; X_C = \frac{1}{\omega C}\angle -90° \quad \text{...(7.53)}$$

The average power per cycle consumed in the capacitive circuit is

$$P = \frac{1}{T}\int_0^T V_{\text{real}} I_{\text{real}}\, dt = \frac{1}{T}\int_0^T (V_m \cos\omega t)\cdot[I_m \cos(\omega t + \pi/2)]dt = 0 \quad \text{...(7.54)}$$

Thus the capacitive circuit does not consume power and hence the current flowing in such circuit is said to be *watt-less*.

7.8. RESISTOR-INDUCTOR (R-L) CIRCUIT

The circuit containing resistor and inductor is shown in the Fig. 7.9. An alternating voltage $\mathbf{V}(t) = V_m e^{jwt}$ is applied to the circuit. Let **I** be the resulting current. Applying vector form of Kirchhoff's law to the circuit we have

$$R\mathbf{I} + L\frac{d\mathbf{I}}{dt} = \mathbf{V}(t)$$

$$R\mathbf{I} + j\omega L\mathbf{I} = V$$

$$Z\mathbf{I} = \mathbf{V} \quad \text{...(7.55)}$$

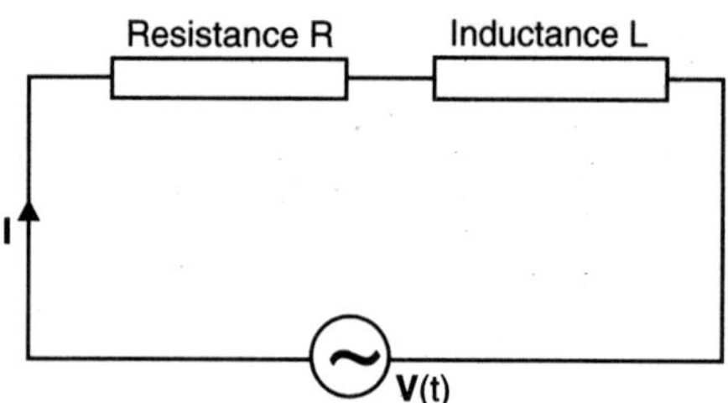

Fig. 7.9. R-L circuit.

Where

$$Z = R + j\omega L = \sqrt{R^2 + \omega^2 L^2}\, e^{j\varphi} = |Z|\; e^{j\varphi} = |Z|\angle\varphi,\ \varphi = \tan^{-1}\frac{\omega L}{R} \qquad ...(7.56)$$

Z is called complex impedance of the circuit. Its magnitude is Z_0. In view of eqn. (7.56) we can write eqn. (7.55) as

$$\mathbf{I} = \frac{\mathbf{V}}{Z} = \frac{V_m e^{j\omega t}}{|Z| e^{j\varphi}} = \frac{V_m}{|Z|} e^{j(\omega t - \varphi)} = I_m e^{j(\omega t - \varphi)} \qquad ...(7.57)$$

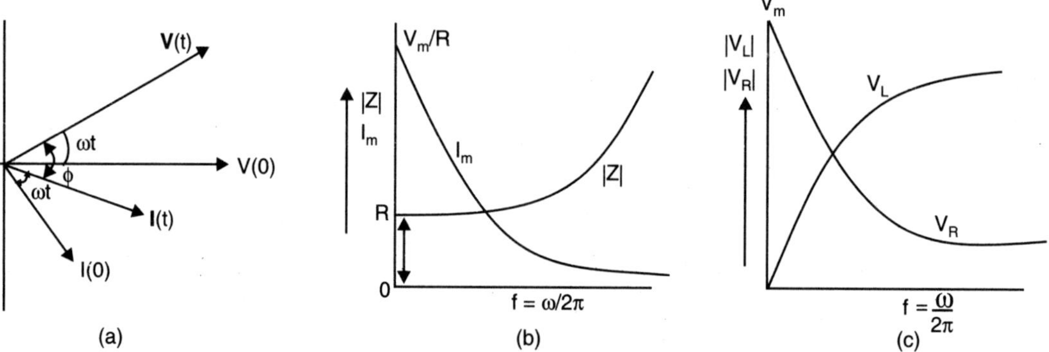

Fig. 7.10. (a) Vector voltage and vector current diagram
(b) Variation of |Z| and I_m with frequency
(c) Variation of $|V_L|$ and $|V_R|$ with frequency.

Where the peak value of current is

$$I_m = \frac{V_m}{|Z|} = \frac{V_m}{\sqrt{R^2 + \omega^2 L^2}} \qquad ...(7.58)$$

Thus the current in R-L circuit lags behind the voltage by angle $\varphi = \tan^{-1}\dfrac{\omega L}{R}$. The vector diagram of **I, V** and variation of $|Z|$ and I_m with frequency is shown in Fig. 7.10.

7.9. RESISTOR-CAPACITOR (R-C) CIRCUIT

Such a circuit subjected to an alternating voltage $\mathbf{V}(t) = V_m e^{j\omega t}$ is shown in Fig. 7.11. Let **I** be the current in the circuit. Applying vector form of Kirchhoff's law to this circuit we have

$$R\mathbf{I} + \frac{\mathbf{I}}{j\omega C} = \mathbf{V} \quad ...(7.59)$$

or $$\left(R + \frac{1}{j\omega C}\right)\mathbf{I} = \mathbf{V}$$

or $$Z\mathbf{I} = \mathbf{V} \quad ...(7.60)$$

Where $$Z = R + \frac{1}{j\omega C} = R - jX_C = |Z|\ e^{-j\varphi} \quad ...(7.61)$$

$$|Z| = \sqrt{R^2 + X_C^2} = \sqrt{R^2 + \frac{1}{\omega^2 C^2}} \text{ and } \varphi = \tan^{-1}\frac{1}{\omega CR} \quad ...(7.62)$$

From eqn. (7.60), the current in the circuit is

$$\mathbf{I} = \frac{\mathbf{V}}{Z} = \frac{V_m e^{j\omega t}}{|Z|\ e^{-j\varphi}} = \left(\frac{V_m}{|Z|}\right) e^{j(\omega t + \varphi)} = I_m e^{j\left(\omega t + \frac{1}{\omega CR}\right)} \quad ...(7.63)$$

Where $$I_m = \frac{V_m}{|Z|} = \frac{V_m}{\sqrt{R^2 + \frac{1}{\omega^2 C^2}}} \quad ...(7.64)$$

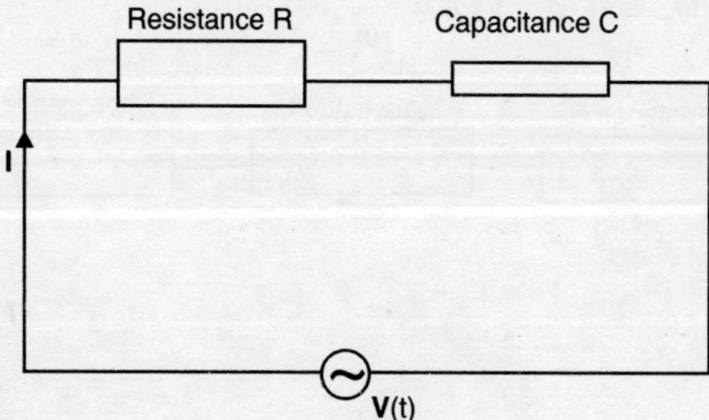

Fig. 7.11

It is evident from eqn. (7.63) that the current leads the voltage by angle φ, with varies with frequency. The vector diagram of **V** and **I** is shown in Fig. 7.12(a) and variation of $|Z|$, I_m and φ with frequency in Fig. 7.12(b).

The voltage across resistor and capacitor are given by

$$\mathbf{V}_R = R\mathbf{I} = R\frac{\mathbf{V}}{Z} = \frac{RV_m e^{j\omega t}}{|Z|\ e^{-j\varphi}} = \frac{RV_m}{|Z|} e^{j(\omega t + \varphi)} \quad ...(7.65)$$

$$\mathbf{V}_C = -jX_C\mathbf{I} = -\frac{jX_C\mathbf{V}}{Z} = -\frac{X_C V_m e^{j\omega t}}{|Z|\ e^{-j\varphi}} = \frac{X_C V_m}{|Z|} e^{j(\omega t+\varphi-\pi/2)} \quad ...(7.66)$$

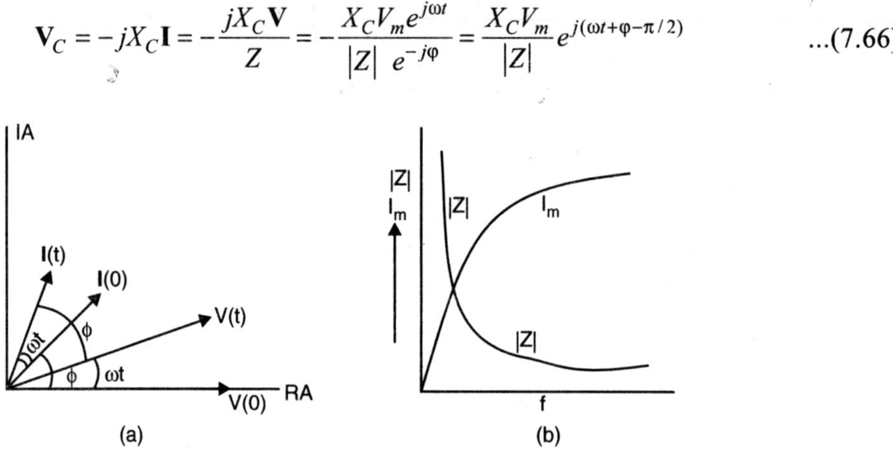

Fig. 7.12. (a) Voltage and current vectors (b) Variation of |Z| and I_m with frequency.

7.10. L-C-R ALTERNATING CURRENT CIRCUIT

(*a*) Series L-C-R circuit: An *LCR* circuit subjected to an alternating voltage $\mathbf{V}(t) = V_m e^{j\omega t}$ is shown in the Fig. 7.13. Let **I** be the current vector in the circuit. Applying Kirchhoff's law in vector form we have

$$R\mathbf{I} + L\frac{d\mathbf{I}}{dt} + \frac{q}{C} = \mathbf{V},$$

$$\text{with } \frac{d\mathbf{I}}{dt} = j\omega, \text{ and } q = \int \mathbf{I}dt = \frac{\mathbf{I}}{j\omega} \quad ...(7.67)$$

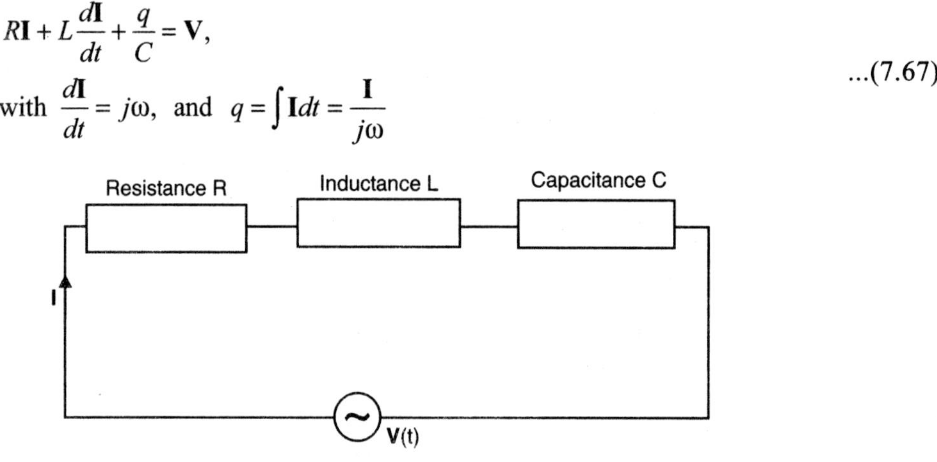

Fig. 7.13

Equation (7.67) can be expressed as follows.

$$R\mathbf{I} + j\omega L\mathbf{I} + \frac{\mathbf{I}}{j\omega C} = \mathbf{V}$$

$$\left(R + j\omega L + \frac{1}{j\omega C}\right)\mathbf{I} = \mathbf{V}$$

$$Z\,\mathbf{I} = \mathbf{V} \qquad ...(7.68)$$

Where
$$Z = R + j\left(\omega L - \frac{1}{\omega C}\right) = R + jX = \sqrt{R^2 + X^2}\; e^{j\varphi} = |Z|\; e^{j\varphi} \qquad ...(7.69)$$

With
$$X = \left(\omega L - \frac{1}{\omega C}\right),\ |Z| = \sqrt{R^2 + \left(\omega L - \frac{1}{\omega C}\right)^2}\ ,\quad \varphi = \tan^{-1}\frac{\omega L - \dfrac{1}{\omega C}}{R} \qquad ...(7.70)$$

The quantity $Z = R + j\,(\omega L - 1/\omega C)$ is called complex impedance of the circuit and $|Z|$ is its magnitude. R is resistive part of impedance and X is the reactive part. The quantity φ is the phase of the impedance.

The current vector in the circuit is given by

$$\mathbf{I} = \frac{\mathbf{V}}{Z} = \frac{V_m e^{j\omega t}}{|Z|\; e^{j\varphi}} = \frac{V}{|Z|} e^{j(\omega t - \varphi)} = I_m e^{j(\omega t - \varphi)} \qquad ...(7.71)$$

And
$$I_m = \frac{V_m}{|Z|} = \frac{V_m}{\sqrt{R^2 + \left(\omega L - \dfrac{1}{\omega C}\right)^2}} \qquad ...(7.72)$$

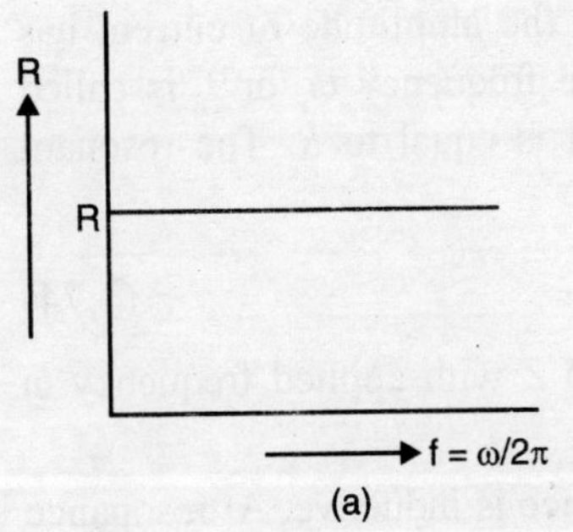

(a)

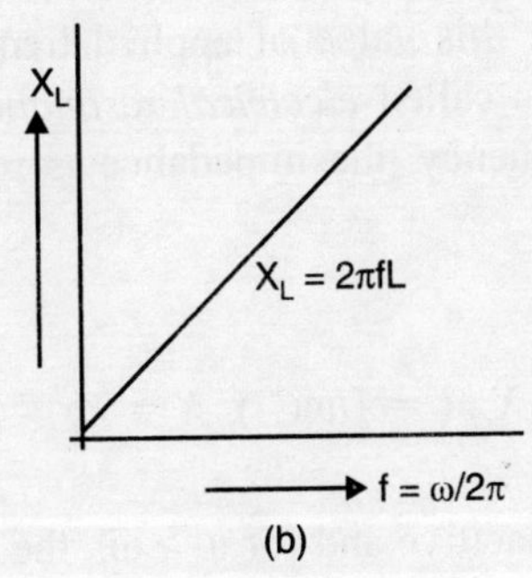

(b)

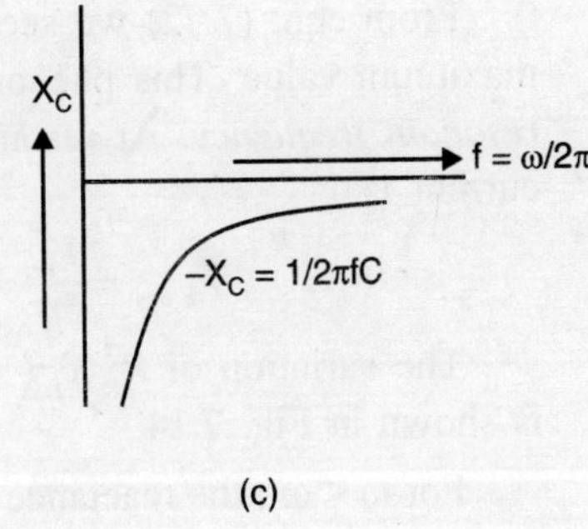

(c)

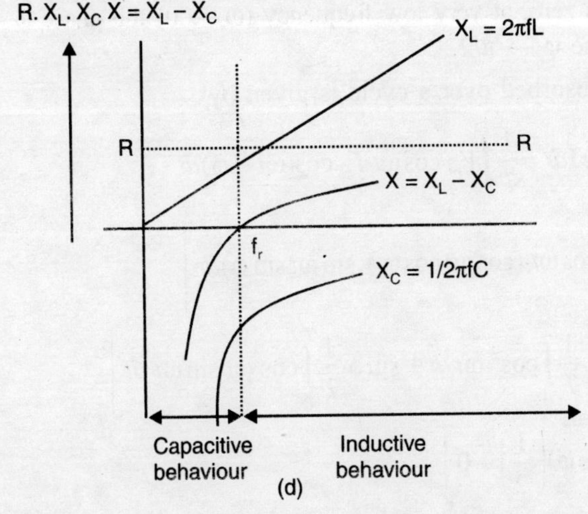

(d)

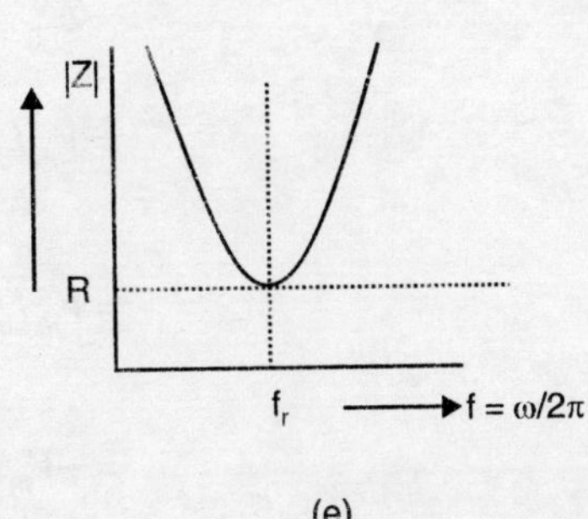

(e)

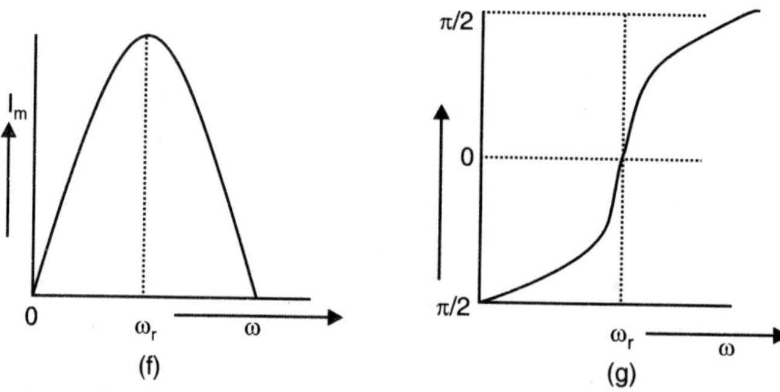

Fig. 7.14. Variation of R, X_L, X_C, X (= $X_L - X_C$), |Z|, I_m and φ with applied frequency ω = 2πfC.

Obviously, the impedance $|Z|$, peak value of current $|I|$ and phase difference φ between voltage and current are frequency dependent. The frequency dependence of these quantities are shown in Fig. 7.14. From eqn. (7.70) it is evident that $|Z|$ is *minimum* when

$$\omega L - \frac{1}{\omega C} = 0 \quad \text{or} \quad \omega L = \frac{1}{\omega C}$$

$$\text{or} \qquad \omega = \frac{1}{\sqrt{LC}} = \omega_r \quad \text{or} \quad f = \frac{1}{2\pi\sqrt{LC}} = f_r \qquad \text{...(7.73)}$$

From eqn. (7.72) we see that for this value of applied frequency, the amplitude of current has maximum value. This phenomenon is called *electrical resonance*. The frequency ω_r or f_r is called *resonant frequency*. At resonant frequency, the impedance is real and is equal to R. The resonant current is

$$I_{m,res} = \frac{V_m}{R} \qquad \text{...(7.74)}$$

The variation of R, X_L (= ωL), X_C (= $1/\omega C$), $X = X_L - X_C$ and Z with applied frequency ω is shown in Fig. 7.14.

For $\omega < \omega_r$, the reactance X is capacitive and for $\omega > \omega_r$, the reactance is inductive. At resonance the impedance is purely resistive ($Z = R$).

At resonance, the phase difference φ is zero, at very low frequency ($\omega \to 0$) the phase $\varphi \to -\pi/2$. At very high frequency ($\omega \to \infty$) the phase $\varphi \to \pi/2$.

Power Absorption: The average power absorbed over a cycle is given by

$$P = \frac{1}{T}\int_0^T \text{Re}\,\mathbf{V}\cdot\text{Re}\,\mathbf{I}dt = \frac{1}{T}\int_0^T V_m \cos\omega t \cdot I_m \cos(\omega t - \varphi)dt$$

$$= V_m I_m \left[\frac{1}{T}\int_0^T \cos\omega t\cdot(\cos\omega t\cos\varphi + \sin\omega t \sin\varphi)dt\right]$$

$$= V_m I_m \left[\cos\phi\cdot\frac{1}{T}\int_0^T \cos^2\omega t\, dt + \sin\phi\cdot\frac{1}{T}\int_0^T \cos\omega t \sin\omega t\, dt\right]$$

$$= -V_m I_m\left[(\cos\varphi)\left(\frac{1}{2}\right) + 0\right]$$

$$= \frac{1}{2} V_m I_m \cos\varphi = V_{rms} I_{rms} \cos\varphi \qquad ...(7.75)$$

The term $\cos\varphi$ appearing in the expression of average power is called *power factor*. Since $\tan\varphi = X/R$, we must have

$$\cos\varphi = \frac{R}{Z} = \frac{R}{\sqrt{R^2 + \left(\omega L - \frac{1}{\omega C}\right)^2}} \qquad ...(7.76)$$

Substituting $I_m = \frac{V_m}{|Z|} = \frac{V_m}{\sqrt{R^2 + \left(\omega L - \frac{1}{\omega C}\right)^2}}$ and $\cos\varphi$ from eqn. (7.76) in eqn. (7.75) we have

$$P = \frac{V_m^2 R}{2\left[R^2 + \left(\omega L - \frac{1}{\omega C}\right)^2\right]} \qquad ...(7.77)$$

From this equation we see that the average power consumed varies with frequency. It is maximum at resonant frequency $\omega = \omega_r$, the maximum power being

$$P_0 = \frac{V_m^2}{2R} \qquad ...(7.78)$$

In terms of P_0, the expression for average power consumed becomes

$$P = P_0 \frac{R^2}{\left[R^2 + \left(\omega L - \frac{1}{\omega C}\right)^2\right]} \qquad ...(7.79)$$

The dependence of P on frequency ω is shown in Fig. 7.15. P is maximum at resonant frequency $\omega = \omega_r$.

Sharpness of Resonance

The average power consumed in the circuit decreases on both lower and higher frequency sides of the resonant frequency. If the power absorption falls rapidly on both sides of the resonant frequency, the resonance is said to be sharp. Let ω_1 and ω_2 be respectively the frequencies on the lower and higher sides of resonant frequency at which power absorption is half of the maximum power P_0. These frequencies are called *half power frequencies* (*cut-off frequencies*). The frequency difference $\Delta\omega = \omega_2 - \omega_1$ is called *bandwidth*. The sharpness of resonance is defined in terms of this bandwidth. That is,

$$SR = \frac{\omega_r}{\omega_2 - \omega_1}$$

The resonance is said to be *sharp* if *bandwidth* is small and *flat* if *bandwidth* is large.

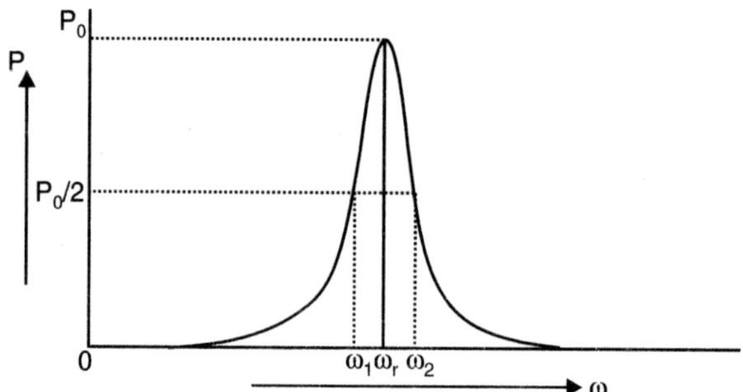

Fig. 7.15. Variation of average power absorption with applied frequency ω.

The half power frequencies can be obtained by substituting $P = P_0/2$ in eqn. (7.79) and solving the resulting equation for ω. Thus

$$\frac{1}{2}P_0 = P_0 \frac{R^2}{R^2 + \left(\omega L - \frac{1}{\omega C}\right)^2}$$

or $$\omega L - \frac{1}{\omega C} = \pm R$$

or $$\omega^2 - \frac{1}{LC} = \pm \frac{R}{L}\omega$$

or $$\omega^2 - \omega_r^2 = \pm \frac{R}{L}\omega \qquad ...(7.80)$$

Since ω_1 and ω_2 are the roots of eqn. (7.80) we must have

$$\omega_2^2 - \omega_r^2 = +\frac{R}{L}\omega_2 \qquad ...(7.81)$$

And $$\omega_1^2 - \omega_r^2 = -\frac{R}{L}\omega_1 \qquad ...(7.82)$$

From these equations we get

$$\omega_2^2 - \omega_1^2 = \frac{R}{L}(\omega_2 + \omega_1)$$

or $$\omega_2 - \omega_1 = \frac{R}{L} \qquad ...(7.83)$$

This is the expression for bandwidth in terms of R and L. Eliminating R/L from eqns. (7.81) and (7.82) we get

$$\omega_r = \sqrt{\omega_1 \omega_2} \qquad ...(7.84)$$

Thus, the resonant frequency is geometric mean of half-power frequencies.

Now, in view of eqn. (7.83) the expression for sharpness of resonance becomes

$$SR = \frac{\omega_r}{\omega_2 - \omega_1} = \frac{\omega_r L}{R} \qquad ...(7.85)$$

Thus the ratio L/R determines the sharpness of resonance. If R is small resonance is sharp otherwise it is flat.

It is customary to express the sharpness of resonance in terms of *quality factor* Q of the circuit at resonant frequency. Q is defined as follows.

$$Q = \frac{2\pi \times \text{maximum energy stored in the circuit at } \omega_r}{\text{Energy dissipated per cycle at } \omega_r} \qquad ...(7.86)$$

The inductor and capacitor store energy and resistor dissipates energy. The energy stored in inductor and capacitor is

$$W = \frac{1}{2}L[\text{Re}\,\mathbf{I}]^2 + \frac{1}{2}\frac{q^2}{C} = \frac{1}{2}L\left[I_m \cos(\omega t - \varphi)\right]^2 + \frac{1}{2C}\left[\text{Re}\int \mathbf{I}dt\right]^2$$

$$= \frac{1}{2}LI_m^2 \cos^2(\omega t - \varphi) + \frac{1}{2C}\left[\text{Re}\frac{-j\mathbf{I}}{\omega}\right]^2$$

$$= \frac{1}{2}LI_m^2 \cos^2(\omega t - \varphi) + \frac{1}{2C}\left[\text{Re}\frac{I_m e^{j(\omega t - \varphi)}\, e^{-j\pi/2}}{\omega}\right]^2$$

$$= \frac{1}{2}LI_m^2 \cos^2(\omega t - \varphi) + \frac{1}{2\omega^2 C} I_m^2 \cos^2(\omega t - \varphi - \pi/2)$$

$$= \frac{1}{2}LI_m^2 \cos^2(\omega t - \varphi) + \frac{1}{2\omega^2 C} I_m^2 \sin^2(\omega t - \varphi),$$

At resonance $\omega_r^2 = \dfrac{1}{LC}$, $\therefore \dfrac{1}{\omega_r^2 C} = L$, whence

$$W = \frac{1}{2}LI_m^2 \cos^2(\omega t - \varphi) + \frac{1}{2}LI_m^2 \sin^2(\omega t - \varphi)$$

$$= \frac{1}{2}LI_m^2 \qquad \left(\text{at resonance } I_m = \frac{V_m}{R}\right)$$

$$= \frac{V_m^2 L}{2R} \qquad ...(7.87)$$

The energy dissipated per cycle in resistor is

$$\Delta E = P_0 T = \frac{V_m^2}{2R} \cdot \frac{2\pi}{\omega_r} \qquad ...(7.88)$$

Therefore, Q-factor

$$Q = 2\pi \frac{W_r}{\Delta W_r} = 2\pi \left(\frac{V_m^2 L}{2R}\right)\left(\frac{2\omega_r R}{2\pi V_m^2}\right)$$

or
$$Q = \frac{\omega_r L}{R} = \frac{1}{\omega_r CR} \qquad ...(7.89)$$

Evidently, a circuit with high inductance and low resistance will have high quality factor and will exhibit sharp resonance.

At resonance, the vector voltage across inductor and capacitor are

$$\mathbf{V}_L = j\omega_r L\mathbf{I} \quad \text{and} \quad \mathbf{V}_C = -\frac{j\mathbf{I}}{\omega_r C} \qquad ...(7.90)$$

At resonance $\mathbf{I} = \frac{\mathbf{V}}{Z} = \frac{\mathbf{V}}{R}$, therefore,

$$\mathbf{V}_L = \frac{j\omega_r L\mathbf{V}}{R} = jQ\mathbf{V} \qquad ...(7.91)$$

And
$$\mathbf{V}_C = -\frac{j\mathbf{V}}{\omega_r RC} = -jQ\mathbf{V} \qquad ...(7.92)$$

Equations (7.91) and (7.92) can be written as

$$\mathbf{V}_L = QV_m e^{j(\omega t + \pi/2)} \qquad ...(7.93)$$

And
$$\mathbf{V}_C = QV_m e^{j(\omega t - \pi/2)} \qquad ...(7.94)$$

Hence,
$$\frac{|\mathbf{V}_L|}{V_0} = Q \quad \text{and} \quad \frac{|\mathbf{V}_C|}{V_0} = Q \qquad ...(7.95)$$

Thus, at resonance, the ratio of magnitude of voltages across inductor or capacitor to that of the source equals the quality factor Q. The circuit, therefore, behaves like a *voltage amplification unit*.

Series L-C-R Circuit as a Selector or acceptor: We have seen that maximum current in LCR series circuit flows at resonance ($\omega = \omega_r$). If an alternating signal consisting of a large number of alternating voltage is fed to the LCR series circuit with high value of Q, then current corresponding to a narrow band of frequencies of width $\Delta\omega = \omega_2 - \omega_1$ is appreciable in the circuit and is very small for frequencies lying outside this band. Thus circuit can accept signals with frequency within range $\omega_2 - \omega_1$ and will reject other. Due to this reason, LCR series circuit is also called *selector* or *acceptor* circuit. A circuit is said to have large selectivity if its response for this frequency range is very large in comparison to other. For high selectivity the circuit must have high value of Q. The resonant frequency of *LCR* series circuit can be altered by changing the value of *C*. The process of picking up signal of desired frequency by changing the resonant frequency of *LCR* circuit is called *tuning*.

Selectivity: The term *selectivity* of a series *R-L-C* resonant circuit is used to describe its ability to pick up a narrow band of frequencies about the resonant frequency. The narrower the band the greater is the selectivity. The sharpness of resonance, selectivity and *Q*-factor are all related to the bandwidth ($\Delta\omega = \omega_2 - \omega_1 = R/L$). Thus,

$$\begin{bmatrix} \text{Sharpness of resonance} \\ \text{Selectivity} \\ Q\text{-factor} \end{bmatrix} = \frac{\omega_r}{BW} = \frac{\omega_r}{\omega_2 - \omega_1} = \frac{\omega_r L}{R} = \frac{1}{R}\sqrt{\frac{L}{C}} \quad ...(7.96)$$

For a given value of *L* and *C*, if *R* decreases, the bandwidth decreases and hence sharpness of resonance, selectivity and *Q*-factor increases. For a given value *R*, if the ratio *L*/*C* is increased, sharpness of resonance, selectivity and *Q*-factor increases.

Variation of V_L and V_C with Frequency

The voltage across inductor is

$$V_L = IX_L = \frac{V\omega L}{\sqrt{R^2 + (\omega L - 1/\omega C)^2}}$$

$$\therefore \quad V_L^2 = \frac{V^2\omega^2 L^2}{R^2 + \left(\omega L - \dfrac{1}{\omega C}\right)^2} = \frac{V^2\omega^4 L^2 C^2}{\omega^2 C^2 R^2 + (\omega^2 LC - 1)^2}$$

The frequency f_L at which V_L will be maximum is obtained by solving the equation $\left(\dfrac{dV_L^2}{d\omega}\right)_{\omega=\omega_L} = 0$. The resulting equation gives

$$\omega_L = \frac{1}{\sqrt{LC - \dfrac{1}{2}C^2R^2}}$$

or

$$f_L = \frac{1}{2\pi\sqrt{LC}\sqrt{1 - \dfrac{CR^2}{2L}}} \quad ...(7.97)$$

Equation (7.97) shows that the maximum voltage across inductor occurs at a frequency which is higher than the resonant frequency.

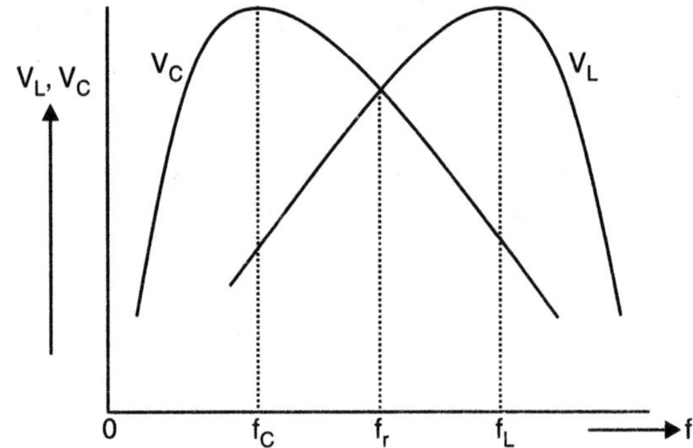

Fig. 7.16. Variation of voltages across inductor and capacitor with frequency.

The voltage across capacitor is

$$V_C = IX_C = \frac{V}{\omega C\sqrt{R^2 + \left(\omega L - \frac{1}{\omega C}\right)^2}}$$

$$V_C^2 = \frac{V^2}{\omega^2 C^2 R^2 + (\omega^2 LC - 1)^2}$$

The frequency f_C at which V_C will be maximum is obtained by solving the equation $\left(\frac{dV_C^2}{d\omega}\right)_{\omega=\omega_C} = 0$. The resulting equation gives

$$\omega_C = \frac{1}{LC} - \frac{R^2}{2L^2} \quad f_C = \frac{1}{2\pi\sqrt{LC}}\left(1 - \frac{CR^2}{2L}\right) \qquad \text{...(7.98)}$$

Equation (7.99) shows that the maximum voltage across capacitor occurs at a frequency which is lower than the resonant frequency.

(*b*) Inductor-Capacitor-Resistor (LCR) Parallel Circuit: A parallel *LCR* circuit fed by an alternating voltage $\mathbf{V} = V_m e^{j\omega t}$ is shown in the Fig. 7.17. Let the current vector be $\mathbf{I} = I_m e^{j(\omega t + \varphi)}$.

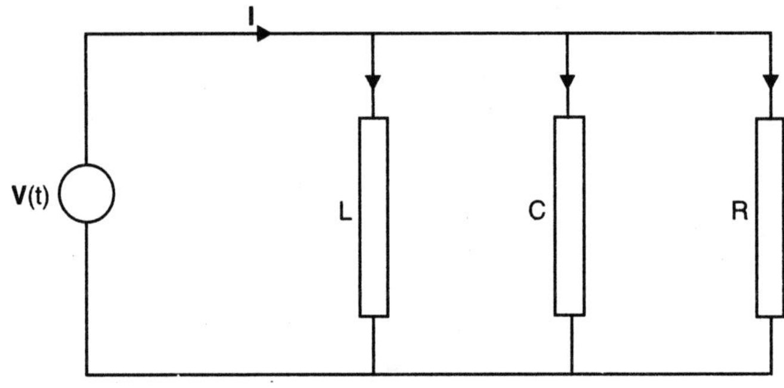

Fig. 7.17. A parallel LCR circuit.

The vector current **I** entering the circuit is given by

$$\mathbf{V} = Z\,\mathbf{I} \quad ...(7.99)$$

Where Z is the impedance of the circuit. In parallel circuit, the analysis becomes much simpler if we employ admittance of the circuit rather than its impedance. In terms of admittance Y the current is given by

$$\mathbf{I} = Y\mathbf{V}, \quad Y = \frac{1}{Z} \quad ...(7.100)$$

If Z_1, Z_2 and Z_3 are the impedances and Y_1, Y_2 and Y_3 the corresponding admittances respectively, then

$$\frac{1}{Z} = \frac{1}{Z_1} + \frac{1}{Z_2} + \frac{1}{Z_3} \quad ...(7.101)$$

$$Y = Y_1 + Y_2 + Y_3 \quad ...(7.102)$$

Since $Y_1 = \frac{1}{R}$, $Y_2 = \frac{1}{j\omega L}$, $Y_3 = j\omega C$, we have

$$Y = \frac{1}{R} + j\left(\omega C - \frac{1}{\omega L}\right) \quad ...(7.103)$$

$$= |Y|\, e^{j\varphi} \quad ...(7.104)$$

The magnitude $|Y|$ and phase φ of admittance are

$$|Y| = \sqrt{\frac{1}{R^2} + \left(\omega C - \frac{1}{\omega L}\right)^2}, \quad \varphi = \tan^{-1}\left(\frac{\omega C - 1/\omega L}{1/R}\right) \quad ...(7.105)$$

The vector current is

$$\mathbf{I} = Y\mathbf{V} = |Y|\, V_m e^{j(\omega t + \varphi)} = I_m e^{j(\omega t + \varphi)} \quad ...(7.106)$$

Where $I_m = |Y|\, V_m = \sqrt{\frac{1}{R^2} + \left(\omega C - \frac{1}{\omega L}\right)^2} \cdot V_m$

From eqn. (7.106) it is evident that there is a phase difference of φ between the current and voltage. From the expressions of $|Y|$, I_m and φ are frequency dependent. From eqn. (7.105) we see that $|Y|$ is minimum at a frequency $\omega = \omega_r$ given by

$$\omega_r C - \frac{1}{\omega_r L} = 0 \text{ or } \omega_r = \frac{1}{\sqrt{LC}} \quad ...(7.107)$$

At resonant frequency (ω_r), $|Y| = \frac{1}{R} =$ minimum, therefore the current in the circuit is minimum.

The frequency $\omega_r = \frac{1}{\sqrt{LC}}$ is called resonant frequency. The frequency dependence of $|Y|$, $|Z|$, I_m and phase φ are shown in Fig. 7.17 (a, b, c, d).

At frequencies $\omega < \omega_r$, the *susceptance* of the circuit is negative, therefore, the circuit behaves as inductive. At resonant frequency *susceptance* becomes zero and the circuit becomes pure resistive. Finally, at frequencies $\omega > \omega_r$ the *susceptance* becomes positive and the circuit behaves as capacitive.

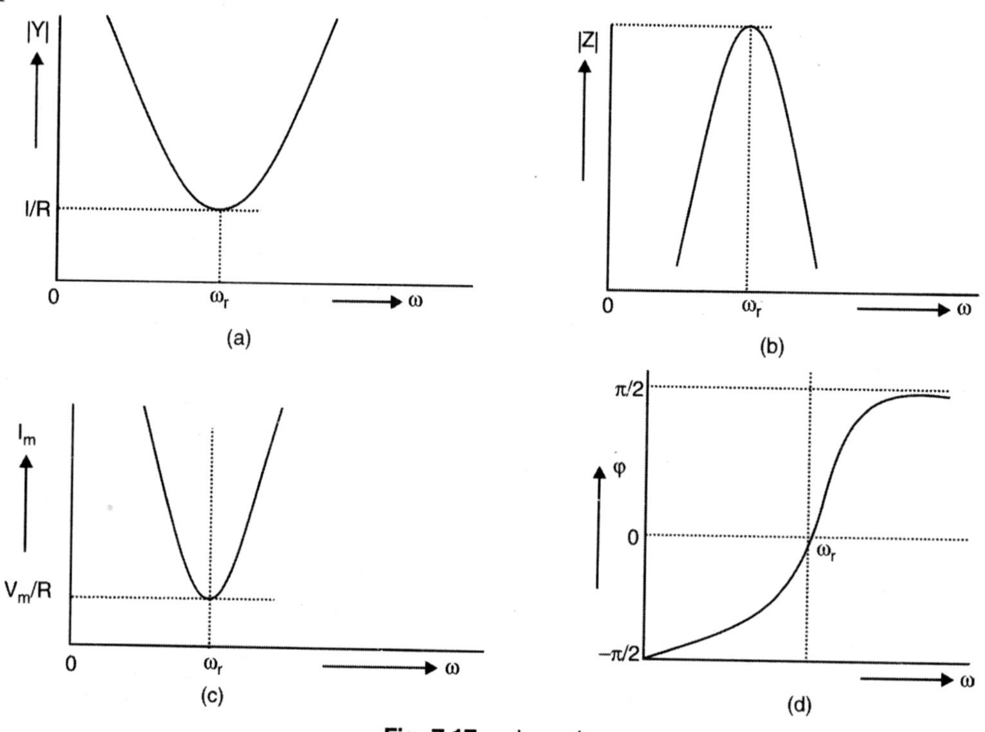

Fig. 7.17. a, b, c, d.

The parallel *LCR* circuit allows minimum current through it at resonant frequency. Thus it is a rejector circuit. It can reject voltage corresponding to ω_r. This rejection is more effective if |Z| vs ω plot is sharp. We call this plot as resonance curve of parallel *LCR* circuit. The sharpness of this curve is measured in terms of its bandwidth $\Delta\omega = \omega_2 - \omega_1$, where ω_2 and ω_1 are the angular frequencies on either side of ω_r at which the value of $|Z|$ falls to $\frac{1}{\sqrt{2}}$ of its maximum value ($|Z|_{max} = R$). These frequencies are the roots of the equation

$$\frac{1}{|Z|^2} = \frac{1}{\left(R/\sqrt{2}\right)^2}$$

$$\frac{1}{R^2} + \left(\omega C - \frac{1}{\omega L}\right)^2 = \frac{2}{R^2}$$

$$\omega^2 - \frac{1}{LC} = \pm\frac{\omega}{RC}$$

$$\omega^2 - \omega_r^2 = \pm \frac{\omega}{RC} \qquad ...(7.108)$$

Since ω_1 and ω_2 are the roots of this equation we must have

$$\omega_2^2 - \omega_r^2 = +\frac{\omega_2}{RC} \qquad ...(7.109)$$

And
$$\omega_1^2 - \omega_r^2 = -\frac{\omega_1}{RC} \qquad ...(7.110)$$

From eqn. (7.109) and (7.110) we have

$$\omega_2 - \omega_1 = \frac{1}{RC} \qquad ...(7.111)$$

And
$$\omega_r = \sqrt{\omega_1 \omega_2} \qquad ...(7.112)$$

Thus the resonant frequency is geometric mean of ω_1 and ω_2. The sharpness of resonance curve is

$$SR = \frac{\omega_r}{\omega_2 - \omega_1} = \omega_r RC = \frac{R}{\omega_r L} \qquad ...(7.113)$$

Q-factor: It is customary to express the sharpness of resonance curve in terms of quality factor Q of the circuit at resonance. Q is defined as

$$Q = 2\pi \frac{\textit{energy stored in the circuit}}{\textit{energy dissipated per cycle at resonance}} \qquad ...(7.114)$$

We know that inductor and capacitor store energy whereas resistor dissipates energy. The energy stored in inductor is

$$W_L = \frac{1}{2}L[\text{Re}\,\mathbf{I}_L]^2 = \frac{1}{2}L\left[\text{Re}\frac{\mathbf{V}}{j\omega L}\right]^2 = \frac{1}{2}L\left[\text{Re}\frac{-jV_m e^{j\omega t}}{\omega L}\right]^2 = \frac{1}{2}L\frac{V_m^2}{\omega^2 L^2}\left[\text{Re}\,e^{j(\omega t - \pi/2)}\right]^2$$

$$= \frac{1}{2}\frac{V_m^2}{\omega^2 L}\sin^2 \omega t$$

$$= \frac{1}{2}CV_m^2 \sin^2 \omega t \qquad \left(\text{at resonance } \omega_r^2 = \frac{1}{LC}\right) \qquad ...(7.115)$$

Similarly, the energy stored in capacitor is

$$W_C = \frac{1}{2}C[\text{Re}\,V_C]^2 = \frac{1}{2}C[\text{Re}\,V]^2 = \frac{1}{2}C[V_m \cos \omega t]^2 = \frac{1}{2}CV_m^2 \cos^2 \omega t \qquad ...(7.116)$$

Therefore,

$$W_r = W_L + W_C = \frac{1}{2}CV_m^2 \qquad ...(7.117)$$

Average power dissipated in resistor is

$$P = \int_0^T V_m \cos \omega t . \frac{V_m}{R} \cos \omega t dt = \frac{1}{2}\frac{V_m^2}{R}$$

Energy dissipated per cycle is

$$\Delta W = \frac{V_m^2}{2R}T = \frac{V_m^2}{2R}.\frac{2\pi}{\omega_r} = \frac{\pi V_m^2}{\omega_r R} \qquad ...(7.118)$$

Hence,
$$Q = 2\pi\frac{W_r}{\Delta W} = \omega_r CR \qquad ...(7.119)$$

Thus, a circuit having high value of Q will exhibit sharp resonance. The sharpness of resonance is determined by factor RC.

It can be shown that

$$Q = \frac{|\mathbf{I}_L|}{I_m} = \frac{|\mathbf{I}_C|}{I_m} = \text{current magnification of the circuit.} \qquad ...(7.120)$$

(c) Inductor-Capacitor Parallel Circuit: This circuit is shown in Fig. 7.18. Since an inductor is made of wires, which has small but finite resistance, therefore a small resistor is shown in series with inductor.

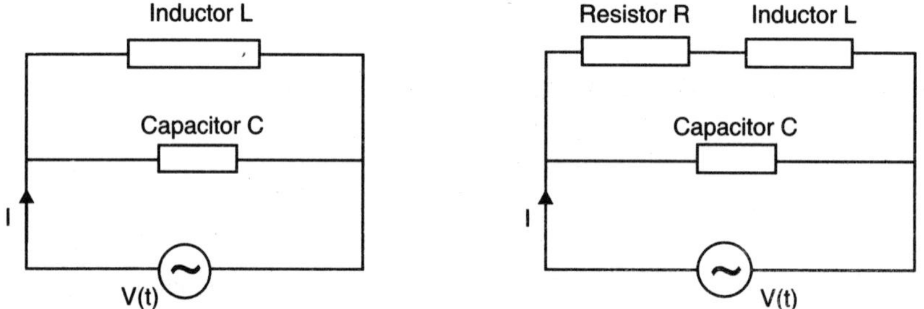

Fig. 7.18. Inductor-capacitor parallel circuit and its equivalent one.

Let $\mathbf{V} = V_m e^{jwt}$ be the *phasor* voltage applied to the circuit and $\mathbf{I}$ be the *phasor* current. The Ohm's law applied to the circuit gives

$$\mathbf{I} = Y\mathbf{V} \quad \text{or} \quad \mathbf{V} = Z\mathbf{I} \qquad ...(7.121)$$

The admittance of the circuit is

$$Y = \frac{1}{Z} = \frac{1}{R + j\omega L} + j\omega C = \frac{R}{R^2 + \omega^2 L^2} + j\left(\omega C - \frac{\omega L}{R^2 + \omega^2 L^2}\right) \qquad ...(7.122)$$

In *phasor* notation the admittance can be written as

$$Y = |Y| e^{j\varphi} \qquad ...(7.123)$$

Where
$$|Y| = \left[\left(\frac{R}{R^2 + \omega^2 L^2}\right)^2 + \left(\omega C - \frac{\omega L}{R^2 + \omega^2 L^2}\right)^2\right]^{1/2} \qquad ...(7.124)$$

And
$$\tan\varphi = \frac{\omega C - \left(\dfrac{\omega L}{R^2 + \omega^2 L^2}\right)}{\left(\dfrac{R}{R^2 + \omega^2 L^2}\right)} = \frac{\omega C\left(R^2 + \omega^2 L^2\right) - \omega L}{R} \qquad ...(7.125)$$

The resulting current in the circuit is

$$\mathbf{I} = Y\mathbf{V} = |Y|e^{j\varphi}V_m e^{j\omega t} = I_m e^{j(\omega t+\varphi)} \quad ...(7.126)$$

$$I_m = V_m|Y| = V_m\left[\left(\frac{R}{R^2+\omega^2L^2}\right)^2 + \left(\omega C - \frac{\omega L}{R^2+\omega^2L^2}\right)^2\right]^{1/2} \quad ...(7.127)$$

From above equations it is evident that $|Y|$, I_m and φ are frequency dependent. In parallel circuit the *resonance* is defined as the condition when admittance is real or minimum. (In series *L-C-R* circuit impedance is real or minimum at resonance). Let this happen at frequency $\omega = \omega_r$. Then from eqn. (7.122) we have

$$\omega_r C = \frac{\omega_r L}{R^2 + \omega_r^{\,2} L^2}$$

This equation yields

$$\omega_r = \left[\frac{1}{LC}\left(1 - \frac{CR^2}{L}\right)\right]$$

or

$$f_r = \frac{1}{2\pi\sqrt{LC}}\left(1 - \frac{CR^2}{L}\right) \quad ...(7.128)$$

This frequency is called *resonant frequency*. The minimum value of admittance is then

$$|Y|_{\min} = \frac{R}{R^2 + \omega_r^{\,2}L^2} = \frac{RC}{L} \quad ...(7.129)$$

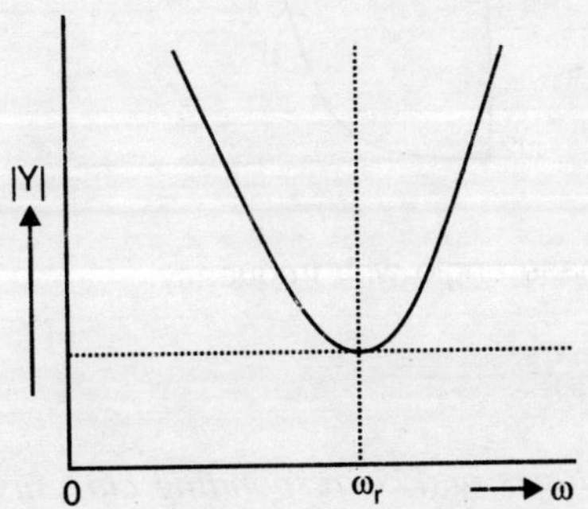

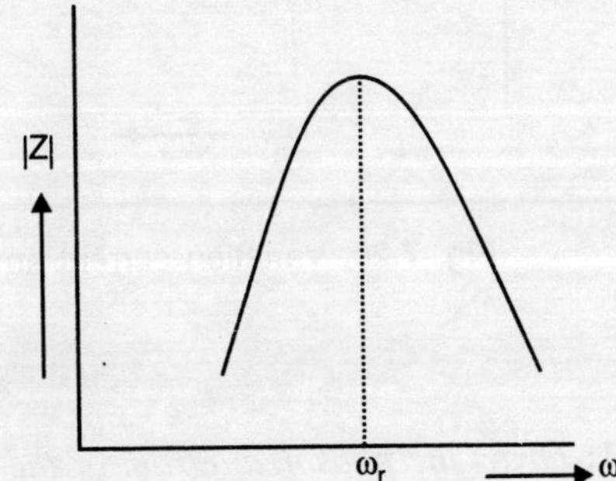

Fig. 7.19. Variation |Y| and |Z| with frequency.

When ω decreases from ω_r, the *susceptance* term becomes negative but its square term increases and hence $|Y|$ increases. Similarly, when ω increases from ω_r, the susceptance becomes positive and its square increases, hence $|Y|$ increases. Thus $|Y|$ increases both on decreasing and increasing ω from ω_r as shown in Fig. 7.19.

For $\omega < \omega_r$ the *susceptance* of the circuit is negative, therefore the circuit behaves as an inductive circuit. For $\omega > \omega_r$, the *susceptance* becomes positive and the circuit behaves as a capacitive circuit.

The magnitude of vector current $\mathbf{I}_m$ equals the product of $\mathbf{V}_m$ and $|Y|$. Since $\mathbf{V}_m$ is independent of frequency, the variation of $\mathbf{I}_m$ with ω is similar to that of $|Y|$. The phase angle φ becomes zero at $\omega = \omega_r$. For $\omega < \omega_r$, the phase angle φ is negative. In the extreme case when $\omega \to 0$, $\varphi \to -\pi/2$. Similarly, when $\omega > \omega_r$, the phase angle becomes positive and increases with increasing frequency. In the extreme case, when $\omega \to \infty$, $\varphi \to \pi/2$.

The anti-resonant circuit offers very high impedance to *a.c.* signals whose frequencies are close to resonant frequency and hence allows minimum current to flow through it at this frequency. Thus it is a *rejector* circuit for frequencies close to ω_r. The rejection will be more effective if $|Z|$ vs. ω plot is sharp. This property of anti-resonant circuit can be used to pick up the voltage corresponding to frequencies very close to ω_r. The anti-resonant circuit offers very low impedance to all other *a.c.* signals whose frequencies are either much below resonant frequency or much above the resonant frequency. Thus, only voltage corresponding to resonant frequency is developed across the circuit, other frequencies are short circuited. This makes possible to select an *a.c.* voltage of desired frequency. The selectivity of the circuit will depend upon the sharpness of anti-resonance curve ($|Z|$ vs. ω curve).

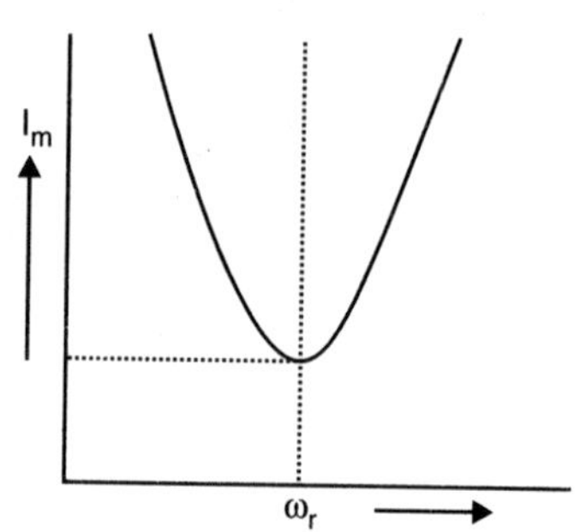

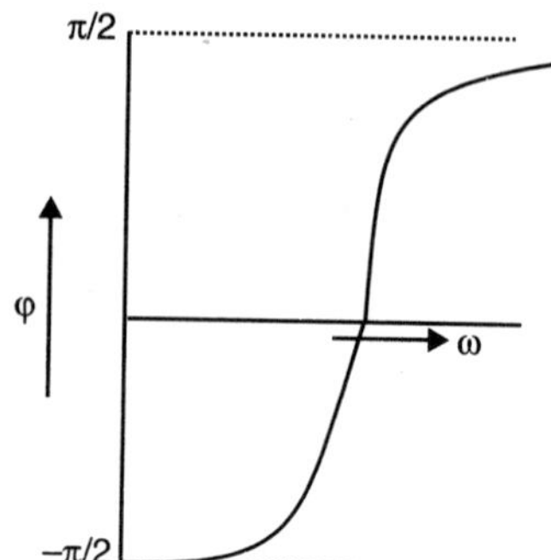

Fig. 7.20. Variation current amplitude and phase angle with frequency.

Solved Examples

***Example* 1:** *Draw the phasor diagram of the following voltages and corresponding currents.*

(*i*) $v_1 = 14.14 \cos(\omega t + 30°)$, $i_1 = 1.414 \cos(\omega t + 60°)$

(*ii*) $v_2 = 28.28 \cos(100t + 45°)$, $i_2 = 4.24 \cos(100t + 90°)$

(*iii*) $v_3 = 70.70 \sin(\omega t + 60°)$, $i_3 = 2.82 \cos(\omega t + 60°)$

(*iv*) $v_4 = 113.12 \cos(\omega t - 150°)$, $i_4 = 8.484 \cos(\omega t + 30°)$

Solution: (*i*)

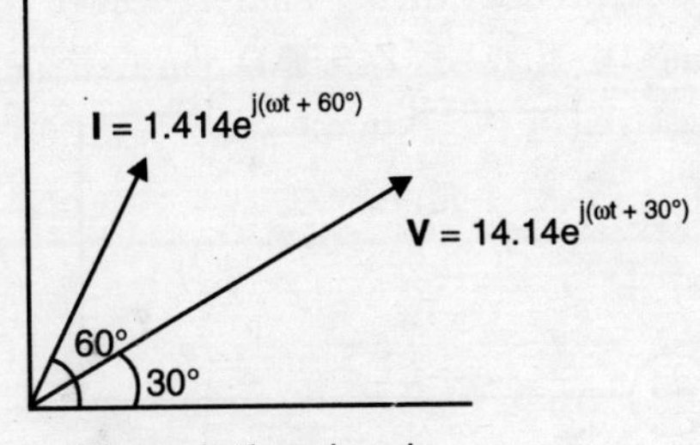

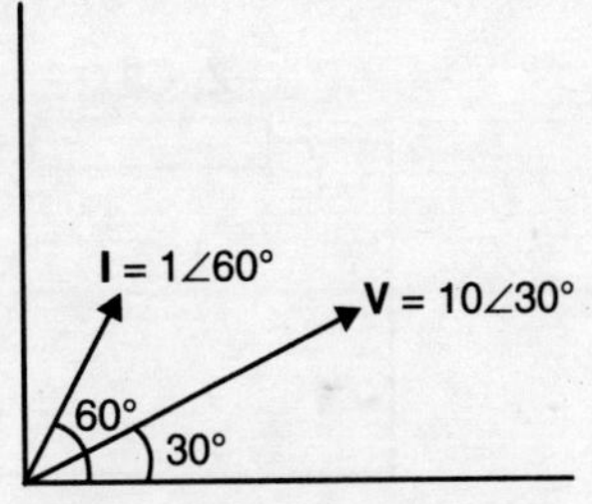

(*ii*)

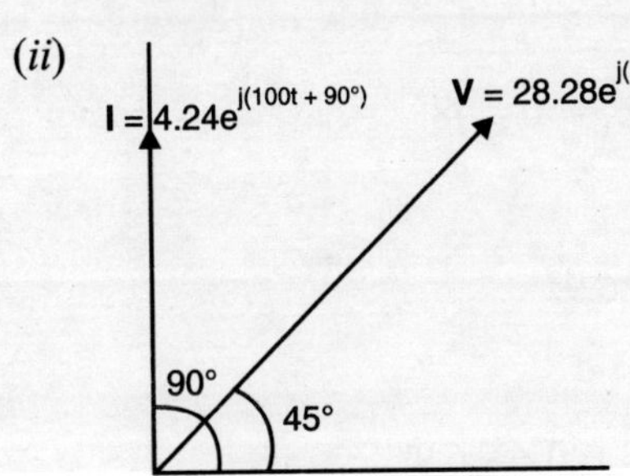

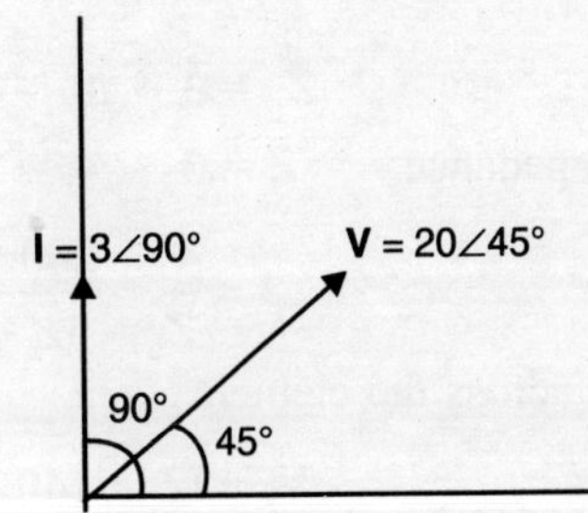

(*iii*)

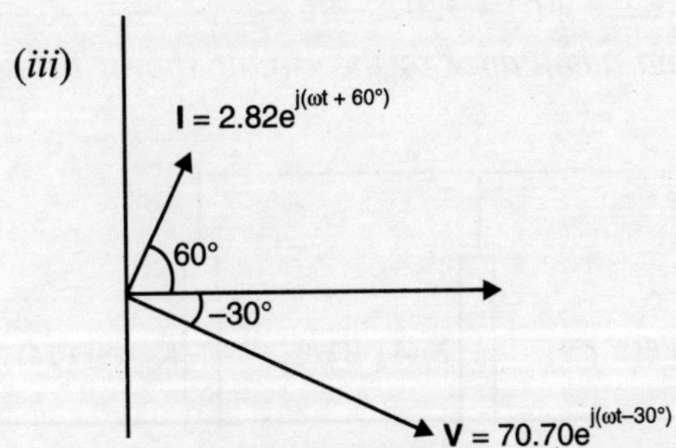

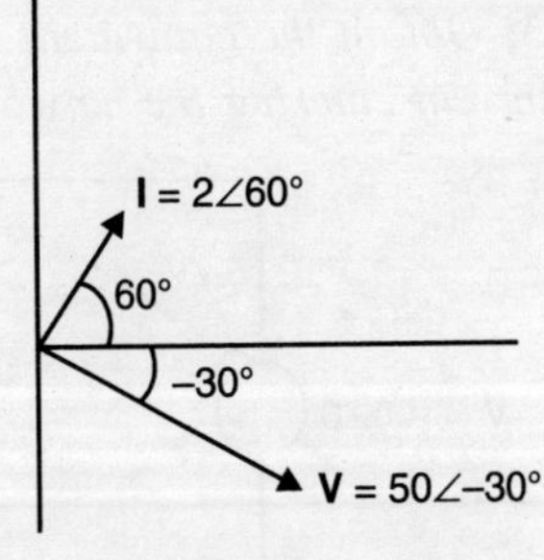

(*iv*)

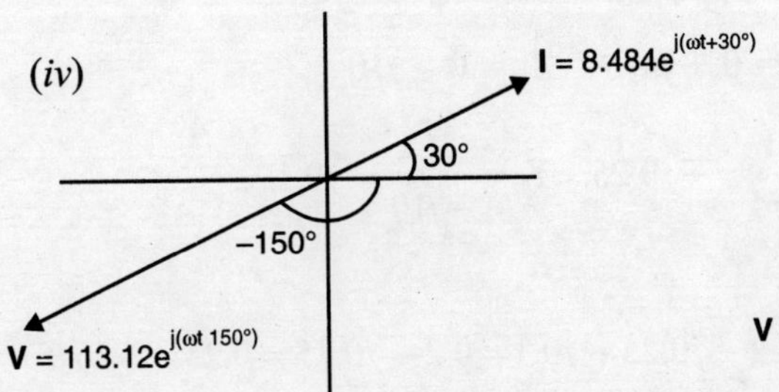

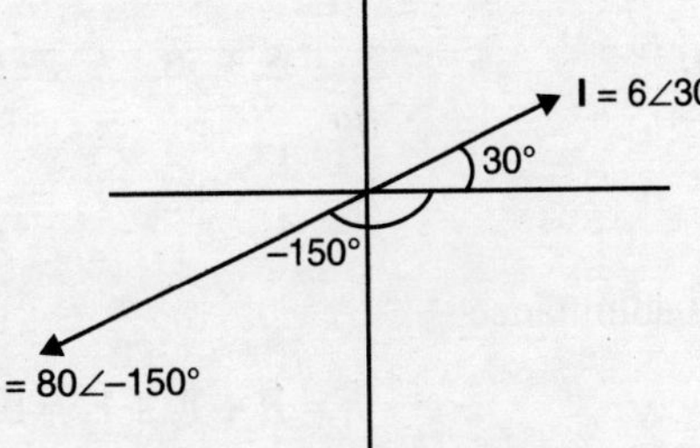

Fig. 7.21

***Example* 2:** *Calculate the voltage across each element in the circuit given below.*

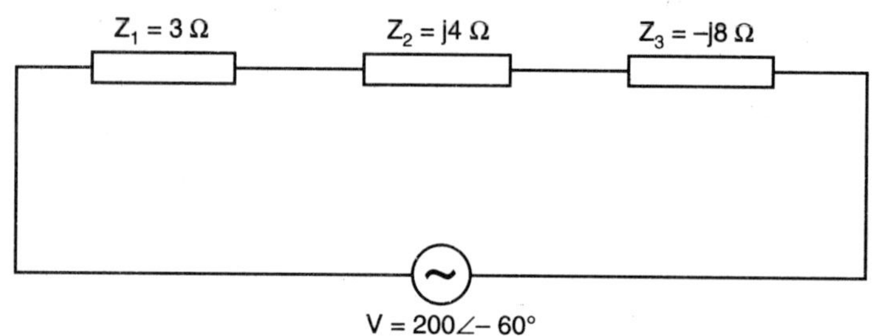

Fig. 7.22

Solution: $Z_1 = 3 + j0, \quad Z_2 = 0 + j4, \quad Z_3 = 0 - j8$

Total impedance $Z = 3 - j4 = 5\angle 53.1°$

Current $\mathbf{I} = \dfrac{\mathbf{V}}{Z} = \dfrac{200\angle -60°}{5\angle -53.1°} = 40\angle -6.9°$

Voltage across the elements

$$\mathbf{V}_1 = \mathbf{I}Z_1 = (40\angle -6.9°)(3\angle 0) = 120\angle -6.9°$$

$$\mathbf{V}_2 = \mathbf{I}Z_2 = (40\angle -6.9°)(4\angle 90°) = 160\angle 83.1°$$

$$\mathbf{V}_3 = \mathbf{I}Z_3 = (40\angle -6.9°)(8\angle -90°) = 320\angle -96.9°$$

***Example* 3:** *Obtain the equivalent impedance and admittance of the circuit shown below. Compute the total current entering the network.*

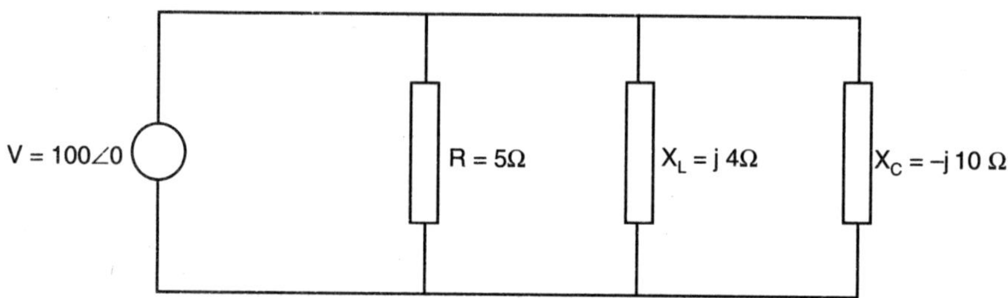

Fig. 7.23

Solution: $Z_1 = 5 + j0, \quad Z_2 = 0 + j4, \quad Z_3 = 0 - j10$

$$Y_1 = \frac{1}{5} = 0.2, \quad Y_2 = \frac{1}{j4} = -j0.25, \quad Y_3 = \frac{1}{-j10} = j0.1$$

Total admittance

$$Y = Y_1 + Y_2 + Y_3 = 0.2 - j0.25 + j0.1 = 0.2 - j0.15 = 0.25\angle -36.9°$$

Total current entering the network

$$\mathbf{I} = Y\mathbf{V} = (0.25\angle -36.9°)(100\angle 0) = 25\angle -36.9$$

***Example* 4:** *Find the sum of currents* $\mathbf{I}_1 = 10 \angle 45°$ and $\mathbf{I}_2 = 5 \angle 120°$ *at the frequency of 100 Hz in a circuit.*

Solution:

$$\mathbf{I}_1 = 10e^{j45} = 10(\cos 45 + j\sin 45) = 7.07 + j7.07$$

$$\mathbf{I}_2 = 5e^{i120} = 5(\cos 120 + j\sin 120) = -2.5 + j4.33$$

$$\mathbf{I} = \mathbf{I}_1 + \mathbf{I}_2 = 4.57 + j11.4 = 15.8e^{j\varphi}, \quad \text{where } \tan\varphi = 2.49$$

$$= 15.8\angle\varphi$$

***Example* 5:** *The quality factor of a LCR circuit is 20 and the resonant frequency is 1.0 KHz. If R = 100 ohm, calculate L, C and lower and upper cut-off frequencies.*

Solution:

$$Q = 20,\ \omega_r = 2\pi f_r = 2\pi \times 10^3 \text{ rad s}^{-1}$$

$$Q = \frac{\omega_r L}{R} \Rightarrow L = \frac{QR}{\omega_r} = \frac{20 \times 100}{2 \times 3.14 \times 10^3} = \frac{1}{\pi} = 0.318 \text{ H}$$

From relation $\omega_r^2 = \frac{1}{LC}$ we have $C = \frac{1}{\omega_r^2 L} = \frac{1}{4\pi}\mu\text{F} = 0.08\mu\text{F}$

The cut-off frequencies are given by

$$\omega = \pm\frac{R}{2L} + \sqrt{\omega_r^2 + \left(\frac{R}{2L}\right)^2} = \pm\frac{R}{2L} + \omega_r \qquad \left(\because \frac{R}{2L} \ll \omega_r\right)$$

$$\therefore \quad \omega = \pm\frac{R}{2L} + \omega_r = \pm 50\pi + 2\pi \times 10^3 = 1950\pi,\ 2050\pi \text{ rad s}^{-1}$$

***Example* 6:** *Calculate the band-width of a series LCR circuit with R = 10Ω, L = 25 mH and C = 0.4 μF. Find the quality factor using the formula* (*i*) $Q = \frac{\omega L}{R}$, (*ii*) $Q = \frac{1}{\omega CR}$, (*iii*) $Q = \frac{\omega}{Bandwidth}$.

Solution: Half-power frequencies are

$$\omega = \pm\frac{R}{2L} + \sqrt{\left(\frac{R}{2L}\right)^2 + \frac{1}{LC}}$$

Upper half power frequency

$$\omega_2 = \frac{R}{2L} + \sqrt{\left(\frac{R}{2L}\right)^2 + \frac{1}{LC}} = 1.02 \times 10^4 \text{ rad s}^{-1}$$

Lower half power frequency

$$\omega_1 = -\frac{R}{2L} + \sqrt{\left(\frac{R}{2L}\right)^2 + \frac{1}{LC}} = 0.98 \times 10^4 \text{ rad s}^{-1}$$

Bandwidth $\omega_2 - \omega_1 = 400 \text{ rad s}^{-1}$

Resonant frequency $\omega = \dfrac{1}{\sqrt{LC}} = 1\times10^4 \text{ rad s}^{-1}$

Therefore, (*i*) $Q = \dfrac{\omega L}{R} = \dfrac{1\times10^4\times25\times10^{-3}}{10} = 25$

(*ii*) $Q = \dfrac{1}{\omega CR} = \dfrac{1}{1\times10^4\times0.4\times10^{-6}\times10} = 25$

(*iii*) $Q = \dfrac{\omega}{\text{bandwidth}} = \dfrac{1\times10^4}{400} = 25$

Example 7: *An inductor with L = 0.2 H and R = 100 ohm is in parallel with a capacitor of C = 5μF. An a.c. source with 200 volt is applied to the circuit. Calculate (i) resonant frequency, (ii) the impedance at resonance, (iii) current drawn from the source at resonance, (iv) current magnification at resonance.*

Solution: Resonant frequency

$$\omega = \frac{1}{\sqrt{LC}}\sqrt{1-\frac{CR^2}{L}} = \frac{1}{\sqrt{0.2\times5\times10^{-6}}}\sqrt{1-\frac{5\times10^{-6}\times10^4}{0.2}} = 867 \text{ rad/s}$$

Impedance at resonance $Z = \dfrac{L}{CR} = \dfrac{0.2}{5\times10^{-6}\times100} = 400 \text{ ohm}$

Main current at resonance $I = \dfrac{V}{Z} = \dfrac{200}{400} = 0.5 \text{ A}$

Current in capacitive branch $I_C = \dfrac{V}{1/\omega C} = \omega CV = 867\times5\times10^{-6}\times200 = 0.867 \text{ A}$

Current magnification $\dfrac{I_C}{I} = \dfrac{0.867}{0.5} = 1.73$

QUESTIONS AND PROBLEMS

1. An alternating voltage is applied to a circuit containing series combination of resistor, inductor and a capacitor. Obtain an expression for current in the circuit and deduce the condition under which resonance occurs.

2. A circuit containing a resistor, an inductor and a capacitor in series is fed with an a.c. generator of variable frequency while its voltage remains constant. Show that

(*i*) the voltage across the capacitor is maximum at frequency $\omega = \omega_r\left(1-\dfrac{1}{2Q^2}\right)^{1/2}$

(*ii*) the voltage across the inductor is maximum at frequency $\omega = \omega_r\left(1-\dfrac{1}{2Q^2}\right)^{-1/2}$

3. Derive an expression for mean power delivered by an alternating source of *emf* to a series *LCR* circuit. Obtain the frequency at which power is maximum. Define bandwidth and obtain expression for it. Explain what do you mean by sharpness of resonance? How is sharpness of resonance related to bandwidth.

4. What do you mean by electrical resonance? Explain sharpness of resonance. How is it related to the bandwidth and quality factor of the circuit?

5. Obtain an expression for the amplitude of current in a series *LCR* circuit driven by an *a.c.* voltage source. Draw a graph showing the variation of current amplitude and applied frequency. Calculate

(*i*) the frequency at which the current amplitude is maximum.

(*ii*) the frequencies ω_1 and ω_2 at which the current amplitude falls to $\frac{1}{\sqrt{2}}$ of its maximum value.

(*iii*) show that $\omega_2 - \omega_1 = \frac{R}{L}$ and $\omega_r = \sqrt{\omega_1 \omega_2}$.

6. In a series *LCR a.c.* circuit show that

(*i*) voltage across the capacitor equals the voltage across the inductor and the two voltages differ in phase by 180°.

(*ii*) the ratio of voltage across the capacitor to the applied voltage equals the Q-factor of the circuit.

7. Show that the resonant frequency of an *LCR* series circuit is geometric mean of the lower and upper half power frequencies.

8. Prove that the *Q*-factor of *R-L-C* series resonant circuit is inversely proportional to the bandwidth. The quality factor of the circuit is 30 and the resonant frequency is 3000 rad s^{-1}. The value of *L* is 0.3 H. What is the peak value of potential drop across *L* if a voltage $V(t) = 5 \sin 3000t$ volt is applied? What is the phase difference between the p.d. across *L* and the applied *emf* ?

9. A generator having *emf* $v(t) = 282 \sin 100\pi t$ and internal resistance 2 kΩ is connected to a series combination of inductance $L = 40/\pi$ henry, capacitance $C = 10/\pi$ μF and resistance 2 kΩ. Calculate

(*i*) the rms value of current flowing in the circuit.

(*ii*) the rms value of voltage across the inductor

(*iii*) the frequency at which the impedance of the circuit is purely resistive.

10. A series *LCR* circuit with $R = 10.0$ ohm, $L = 1$ mH, $C = 1000$ *p*F is connected to an alternating *emf* of amplitude 200 volts and frequency $\omega = 314$ rad s^{-1}. Find

(*i*) the current amplitude in the circuit.

(*ii*) the phase difference between the current and the applied voltage.

(*iii*) the amplitude of voltages across the inductor and capacitor.

11. Find the sum of currents

$$i_1 = 14.14 \sin(\omega t + 13.2°),\ i_2 = 8.95 \sin(\omega t + 121.6°)$$

12. A circuit having impedance 30 + j30 is connected to a voltage source of *emf* $200\angle 30°$. Find the current in the circuit.

13. In a circuit a voltage $V(t) = 25\angle 20°$ is applied. The current in the circuit is $I(t) = 0.5\angle 50°$. Calculate the resistive and reactive part of impedance.

Hint: $Z = \dfrac{V}{I} = \dfrac{25\angle 20}{0.5\angle 50} = 50\angle -30 = 50(\cos 30 - j\sin 30) = 25\sqrt{3} - j25$

14. In a L-R circuit R = 100 Ω, L = 80 mH and current lags behind the voltage by 60°. Calculate the frequency of the applied voltage.

Hint: $\tan\varphi = \dfrac{\omega L}{R}$

15. A 2.5 μF capacitor is connected in series with a resistor of 10 Ω. At what frequency does the resulting current lead the voltage by 45°?

Hint: $\tan\varphi = \dfrac{\omega C}{R}$

16. Find the Q of a circuit having an inductor L = 1 H connected in parallel to a resistor R = 10 kΩ at angular frequency $\omega = 1 \times 10^3$ rad s^{-1}.

17. Two voltages represented by v_1 = 10 sin ωt and v_2 = 8 sin (ωt + 90) are connected in series. Find the equivalent voltage source.

Hint: $\mathbf{V}_1 = 7.07\angle 0 = 7.07(\cos 0 + j\sin 0) = 7.07 + j\,0$

$$\mathbf{V}_2 = 5.66\angle 90° = 5.66\,(\cos 90 + j\sin 90) = 0 + j\,5.66$$

$$\mathbf{V} = \mathbf{V}_1 + \mathbf{V}_2 = 7.07 + j\,5.66 = 9.056\angle 38.67$$

$$\mathbf{V} = 12.80\cos(\omega t + 38.67)$$

18. An $a.c.$ voltage v = 141.4 sin ωt applied to a series combination of R, L and C. If R = 3 Ω, X_L = 8 Ω and X_C = 4 Ω, calculate impedance, V_R, V_L and V_C.

Hint: $Z = R + j(X_L - X_C) = 3 + j(8-4) = 3 + j4 = 5\angle 53.1$

Since $X_L > X_C$, current will lag behind the source voltage. Current in the circuit is

$$\mathbf{I} = \frac{\mathbf{V}}{Z} = \frac{10\angle 0}{5\angle 53.1} = 20\angle -53.1$$

$$\mathbf{V}_R = \mathbf{I}R = 60\angle -53.1,\quad \mathbf{V}_L = \mathbf{I}X_L = (20\angle -53.1)(8\angle 90) = 160\angle 36.9$$

$$\mathbf{V}_C = \mathbf{I}X_C = (20\angle -53.1)(4\angle -90) = 80\angle -143.1$$

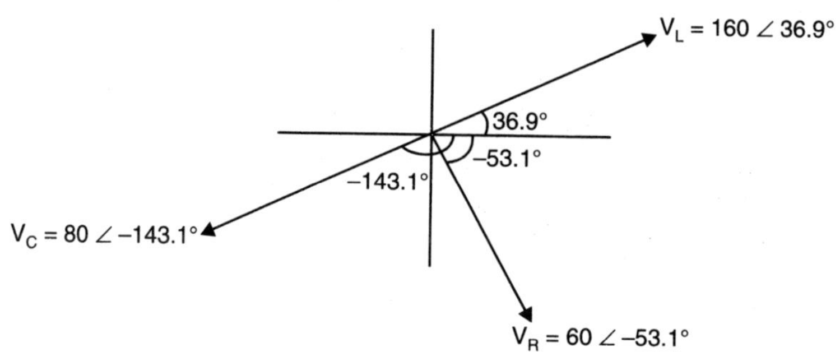

Fig. 7.24

OOO

8 CHAPTER Basic Circuit Elements

An electrical circuit consists of one or more than one of the following components: resistors, capacitors, inductors, batteries (or other energy sources), switches, meters, transformers, transistors, vacuum tubes etc. These components are called circuit elements. All these elements can be subdivided into two classes: (*i*) *passive circuit elements* and (*ii*) *active circuit elements*. The components which never act as a source of energy, such as resistors, capacitors, inductors, meters, switches, connecting wires belong to the first class viz. passive elements and those which act as source of energy (generators) such as transformers, transistors, vacuum tubes etc. come under the second class viz. active elements. Resistors, capacitors and inductors are the integral parts of all electrical circuits and are called *basic circuit elements.*

8.1. RESISTOR

Resistor is a basic circuit element, which is used to limit the current in both a.c. and d.c. circuits. For an ideal resistor, the voltage V across it is always in phase with the current I passing through it. The ratio of V and I is called its resistance and is usually denoted by R.

$$R = \frac{V}{I} \qquad \text{...(8.1)}$$

In circuit it is represented as

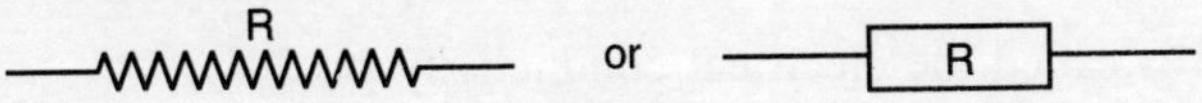

Fig. 8.1

8.1.1. Characteristics of a Resistor

A typical resistor has three basic characteristics:

(*i*) **Magnitude of its resistance:** The value of R is the magnitude of the resistance of a resistor. Its unit is ohm (Ω). Larger units are Kilo-ohm $\left(10^3\,\Omega = 1\,\text{K}\Omega\right)$, mega-ohm $\left(10^6\,\Omega = 1\,\text{M}\Omega\right)$, giga-ohm $\left(10^9\,\Omega = 1\,\text{G}\Omega\right)$.

(*ii*) **Wattage and current carrying capacity:** When a current I is passed through a resistor, a voltage V is developed across its ends. The amount of work done per unit time is $VI = I^2R$. This work done is converted into heat. A part of this heat is dissipated into the surrounding while the other part is retained by the resistor and raises its temperature. A steady state is reached when the temperature of the resistor becomes such that the heat generated per second equals the heat dissipated per second. If the current is high, the steady state temperature becomes high. If this temperature is large enough to melt or burn the materials used for making the resistor, the resistor can not be used to carry such high currents. Thus for every resistor, there exists a maximum current that can safely be passed through it. This optimum value of current is called the *allowable current* through the resistor. It depends upon the material, shape and size of the resistor. The product of the square of the maximum allowable current and the resistance is called the Wattage (P) of the resistor. Thus

$$P = I_m^2 R = V_m I_m \qquad ...(8.2)$$

and

$$I_m = \sqrt{\frac{P}{R}} \qquad ...(8.3)$$

To be on safe side, it is advisable that in a circuit where the current has to be passed for a longer time, the resistance should be used in such a way that it should consume only two-third of its rated power.

(*iii*) **Tolerance:** It is difficult to have the exact value of resistance specified on the resistor. The variation in the resistance from its exact value occurs due to temperature variation, humidity or due to inherent manufacturing limitations. The percentage change which can be expected from the written value of the resistance is known as tolerance. It varies from 0.1 for a very good resistor to 20% for an ordinary resistor.

8.1.2. Resistor Materials

The property of materials which is used for making a resistor is its *conductivity* or *resistivity*. The resistivity ρ of a material in cylindrical or parallelopiped form with cross-section A and length l and resistance R is defined by the equation,

$$\rho = \frac{RA}{l} \text{ ohm. metre} \qquad ...(8.4)$$

The reciprocal of ρ is called the electrical conductivity σ

$$\sigma = \frac{l}{RA} = \frac{lG}{A} \qquad ...(8.5)$$

where G is known as the *conductance* of the specimen. Thus the resistance of a body depends upon the conductivity of its material, shape and size. The material normally used for making resistors are:

(*i*) carbon with doped impurities.

(*ii*) composite materials.

(*iii*) wires of metal and alloys.

(*iv*) thin films of metals, carbon as well as composite materials.

8.1.3. Common Resistor

The resistors available in the market are of several types. Some common types of resistors are:

(*a*) **Carbon resistor:** The common resistor from few ohms to 10^8 ohms and 0.25 to 30 watts are usually made using carbon with doped impurities. They are cheap. From design consideration, they can be sub-divided into two categories:

(*i*) *Axial lead resistor,*

(*ii*) *Radial lead resistor.*

(i) Axial lead resistor: The connecting leads in this type of resistor are along the axis. The cross-sectional diagram of this type of resistor is shown in Fig. 8.2. The figure is self-explanatory.

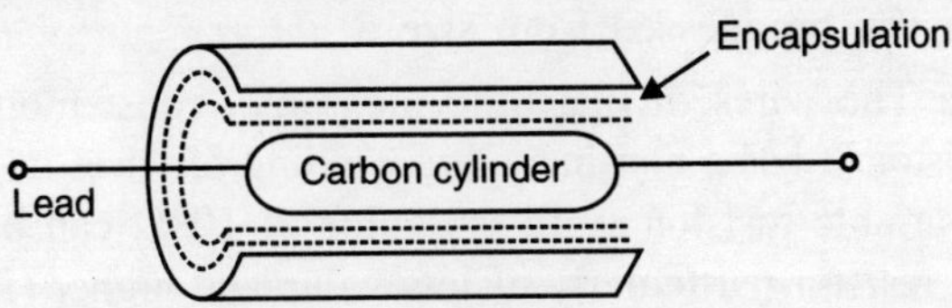

Fig. 8.2

(ii) Radial lead resistor: In this type of resistor, the leads are along the diameter. The cross-sectional diagram is shown in Fig. 8.3.

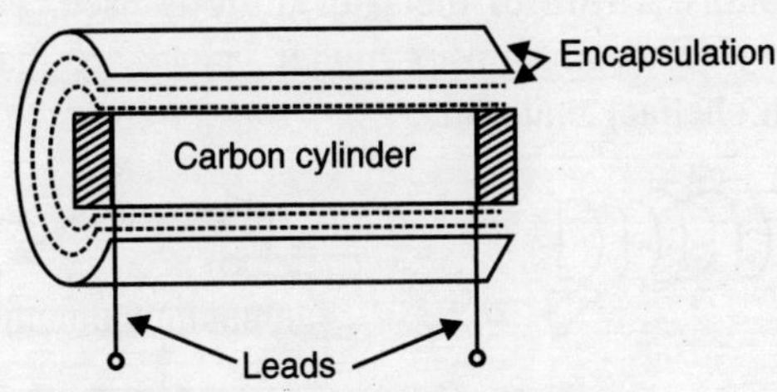

Fig. 8.3

Two types of nomenclature are used for carbon resistors:

(*i*) In the first type of nomenclature, the value, wattage and tolerance etc. of resistor is directly written on the body of the resistor.

(*ii*) The second way of specifying the parameters of a resistor is colour coding. In this method, the value, wattage and tolerance of a resistor are expressed in terms of colour on the body of the resistor.

Table 8.1: Colour code

Brown	Red	Orange	Yellow	Green	Blue	Violet	Grey	White	Black
1	2	3	4	5	6	7	8	9	0

In axial type of resistor, colour strips are made to give information about the parameters of the resistor. In radial type of resistor, the body colour and dots at specific positions give these informations. Each coloured strip on the body of the resistor is assigned a number according to the convention given in the Table 8.1. Four coloured strips are made on the resistor. The number corresponding to the colour of the first strip gives the first significant figure of the magnitude of the resistor, and that of the second strip second significant figure. The third strip gives the number of zeros following the first two figures. The fourth strip gives the tolerance. If the third strip is gold, the multiplying factor becomes 10^{-2}. The tolerance (given by the fourth strip) is estimated according to the following rule

no colour 20%, silver 10%, gold 5%.

The wattage of resistor can be guessed from size.

(*b*) **Wire bound resistors:** The wires of maganin, nichrome, constanton, eureka etc. are used for making this type of resistor. It has a non-inductive winding of wires on a non-metallic (insulating) base. Both fixed and variable resistor up to the value of $10^6\,\Omega$ can be made using these wires. It is easy to make such resistor particularly of low value and higher (few hundred watt) wattage. The disadvantage with these resistors are: (*i*) they are costly, (*ii*) it is difficult to avoid inductance, (*iii*) it becomes extremely difficult to make a resistor of more than $10^6\,\Omega$ value.

(*c*) **Thin film resistor:** Thin films of metal, alloys, carbon and composite materials are used for making this type of resistor. Films of 10 nm or less thickness are usually convenient. In a resistor of few thousand ohms, a film of metal or alloy is used. For still higher values, carbon films are used. The resistor of mega ohm or higher values are made using films of composite (usually mixture of carbon shellac) materials.

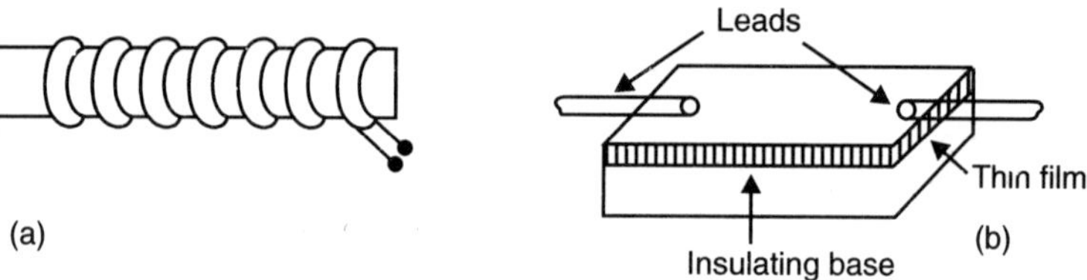

Fig. 8.4. (a) Non-inducting winding on wire bound resistor (b) Thin film resistor.

8.1.4. Symbols Employed for Resistor

Following symbols are usually employed for different uses of resistors:

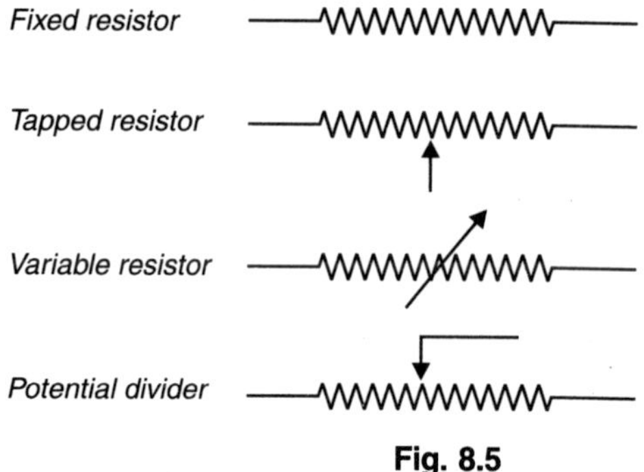

Fig. 8.5

8.2. CAPACITOR

A capacitor is formed whenever a dielectric separates two conductors between which a potential difference can exist. Sandwitched mica between two conduction plates is an excellent example of a capacitor. A capacitor is also formed between wires of a co-axial cable and between the plates of a vacuum tubes but they can not be used as circuit elements.

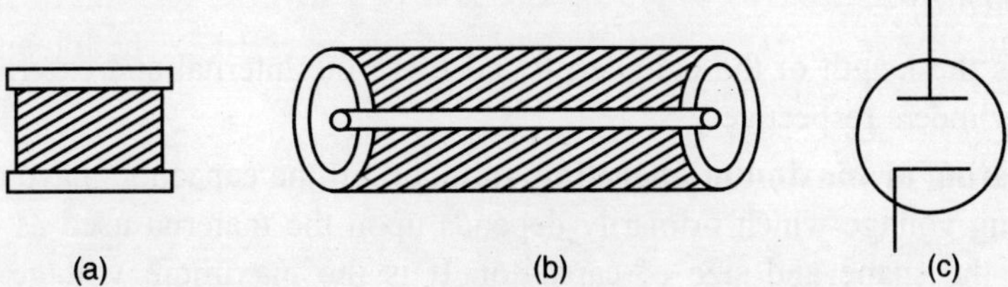

Fig. 8.6. Different forms of capacity formation: (a) Parallel plate capacitor, (b), (c) capacitor formed between wires of a coaxial cable and plates of vacuum tube.

Out of these, only first can be used as circuit element and is ordinarily termed as a capacitor. In an ideal capacitor, the charging current always leads the voltage by $\pi/2$. It is well known that a conductor has capacity to retain charges. By placing a second conductor near to it, the charge retaining capacity of the former can be increased. Thus, a capacitor is also defined as an arrangement by which the capacity of a conductor can be increased. A capacitor has three main parts: (*a*) dielectric material, (*b*) electrode plates, (*c*) leads for external connection.

For convenience, the conductors separating dielectric material in a capacitor have standard geometrical shape. Thus, there are three forms of capacitors, namely (*i*) parallel plate (*ii*) cylindrical and (*iii*) spherical. Out of these, the first two are practically used.

8.2.1. Characteristics of a Capacitor

(*a*) Capacity of a capacitor: The principal property of a capacitor is to store charge. Thus when a capacitor is charged, it stores positive charges on its one plate and negative charges on other. In putting these charges on the plates of capacitor, work is done and energy is used. The charges can be made to flow in the form of current through a resistor and the electrical energy can be taken back. Thus a capacitor is an electrical energy storing device. A perfect capacitor gives back all the energy stored in it when discharged. If a quantity of charge $+q$ is given to one plate of a capacitor, $-q$ charge is induced on the other plate and thereby a potential difference V is produced between the plates. The capacity C of the capacitor is given by,

$$C = \frac{q}{V} \frac{\text{coulomb}}{\text{volt}} = \text{Farad}$$

and is expressed in **farad.** Smaller units of capacitance are microfarad $\left(\mu\text{f} = 10^{-6}\,\text{f}\right)$ and pico-farad $\text{pf} = \mu\mu\text{f} = 10^{-12}\,\text{f}$.

The capacity of a capacitor depends upon the geometry of plate and dielectric constant of the material used as dielectric. It can be calculated from the formulae:

(*i*) $C = \frac{\varepsilon_0 KA}{t}$ (parallel plate capacitor)

where K = dielectric constant of the material filled between the plates, t = plate separation, A = area of each plate.

(*ii*) $C = \frac{2\pi\varepsilon_0 L}{ln(b/a)}$ (cylindrical capacitor)

where L is the length of the cylinder, a and b are the internal and external radii of the co-axial metallic cylinders respectively.

(*b*) Voltage rating or maximum operating voltage: All the capacitors have certain maximum value of operating voltage which primarily depends upon the material used as dielectric, and to some extent on the shape and size of capacitor. It is the maximum voltage which can be applied between the plates of the capacitor without causing any damage to it. This happens because of the phenomenon known as *dielectric breakdown.* When we apply voltage across the plates of the capacitor, the dielectric between them gets polarized. When the voltage becomes very high, some of the electrons of the dielectric atoms get detached from their parent atoms. These free electrons cause a current and the dielectric no longer remains insulator. This phenomeon is known as dielectric breakdown, and once it takes place, the capacitor action is destroyed. This sets a maximum limit on the voltage which can be applied across the capacitor.

8.2.2. Lossy Capacitor—Equivalent Circuit and Quality Factor

An ideal capacitor returns all the energy which is given to it during charging process. A real capacitor always dissipates some energy and hence all of its stored energy is not available. To account the loss of energy in a capacitor, the latter is represented in two models. In one model, the capacitor is represented as a series combination of a resistance R_s and a capacitance C_s and in the other model it is represented as a parallel combination of a resistance R_p and a capacitor C_p.

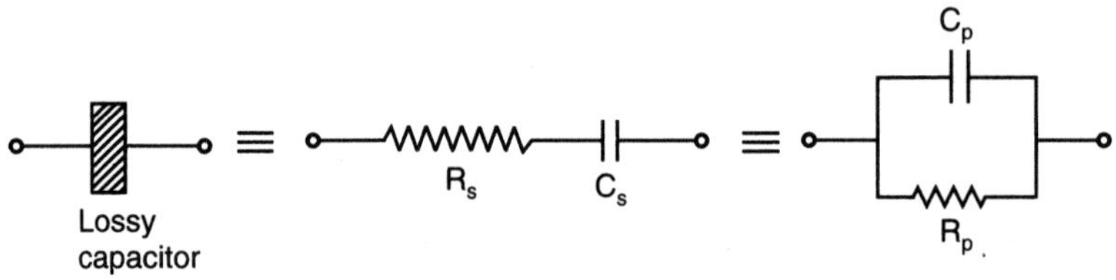

Fig. 8.7

Let us consider the series resistance-capacitance model of a lossy capacitor. If a voltage $V = V_0 \cos\omega t$ is applied across it, the current is given by $I = I_0 \cos(\omega t + \theta)$ where $\tan\theta = \frac{(1/\omega C_s)}{R_s}$.

The average power dissipated in the lossy capacitor is given by,

$$\langle P \rangle = \frac{1}{T}\int_0^T VI\,dt = \frac{1}{T}V_0 I_0 \int_0^T \cos\omega t \cdot \cos(\omega t + \theta)\,dt$$

$$= \frac{1}{2} V_0 I_0 \cos\theta = V_{rms} \; I_{rms} \cos\theta \qquad ...(8.8)$$

where $$\cos\theta = \frac{R_s}{\sqrt{R_s^2 + \left(\frac{1}{\omega C_s}\right)^2}} = \frac{1}{\sqrt{1 + \left(\frac{1}{\omega C_s R_s}\right)^2}} \qquad ...(8.9)$$

is known as the *power factor* of the capacitor.

The merit of a capacitor is expressed in terms of *quality factor* Q which is defined as,

$$Q = 2\pi \frac{\textit{Maximum energy stored}}{\textit{Energy dissipated per cycle}} \qquad ...(8.10)$$

$$= 2\pi \frac{U}{\Delta U}$$

Now maximum energy stored in a capacitor is

$$U = \frac{1}{2} C_s V_0^2 = C_s V^2{}_{rms} = C_s \left(\frac{I_{rms}}{\omega C_s}\right)^2 = \frac{I^2{}_{rms}}{C_s \omega^2} \qquad ...(8.11)$$

and energy dissipated per cycle,

$$\Delta U = \langle P \rangle T = V_{rms} \cdot I_{rms} \cdot \cos\theta \cdot T$$

$$= Z I^2{}_{rms} \frac{R_s}{Z} \cdot T$$

$$= I^2{}_{rms} R_s \frac{2\pi}{\omega}$$

$\therefore$ $$Q = \frac{\left(I_{rms}^2 / C_s \omega^2\right)}{I_{rms}^2 \; R_s 2\pi / \omega} \qquad ...(8.12)$$

or, $$Q = \frac{1}{\omega C_s R_s} \qquad ...(8.13)$$

and power factor

$$P_f = \cos\theta = \frac{1}{\sqrt{1 + \left(\frac{1}{\omega C_s R_s}\right)^2}} = \frac{1}{\sqrt{1 + Q_s^2}} \qquad ...(8.14)$$

For a capacitor with high $Q_s (>>1)$

$$P_f = \frac{1}{Q_s} = \omega C_s R_s \qquad ...(8.15)$$

and the equivalent resistance R_s is given by

$$R_s = \frac{1}{\omega C_s Q_s} = \frac{P_f}{\omega C_s} \qquad ...(8.16)$$

In parallel resistance-capacitance model of a lossy capacitor, the maximum energy stored in it is

$$U = \frac{1}{2} C_p V_0^2 = C_p V_{rms}^2 \quad \text{...(8.17a)}$$

and the energy dissipated in the resistanced R_p is given by,

$$\Delta U = I^2_{rms} R_p \cdot \frac{2\pi}{\omega}$$

$$= \frac{V^2_{rms}}{R_p} \cdot \frac{2\pi}{\omega} \quad \text{...(8.17b)}$$

∴ Quality factor

$$Q_p = 2\pi \cdot \frac{U}{\Delta U} = 2\pi \frac{C_p V^2_{rms}}{\left(\frac{V_{rms}^2}{R_p} \cdot \frac{2\pi}{\omega}\right)}$$

or $$Q_p = \omega C_p R_p \quad \text{...(8.18)}$$

and power factor

$$P_f = \cos\theta = \frac{1}{\sqrt{1+Q_p^2}} = \frac{1}{\sqrt{1+(\omega C_p R_p)^2}} \quad \text{...(8.19)}$$

Often $Q_p >> 1$, then $$P_f = \frac{1}{Q_p} = \frac{1}{\omega C_p R_p} \quad \text{...(8.20)}$$

$$R_p \cong \frac{Q_p}{\omega C_p} = \frac{1}{\omega C_p P_f} \quad \text{...(8.21)}$$

8.2.3. Types of Capacitors

Depending upon the dielectric used in the design of capacitors, they are of the following types;

Paper Capacitors: In this type of capacitor, a thin sheet of paraffined paper (dielectric constant = 2) or a thin plastic film is inserted between two long thin foils.The whole thing is flexible and is rolled up in the form of a cylinder to give it a compact shape. Paper capacitors are made in the range 0.01 μf to 10μf and can be used up to 1000 volts.

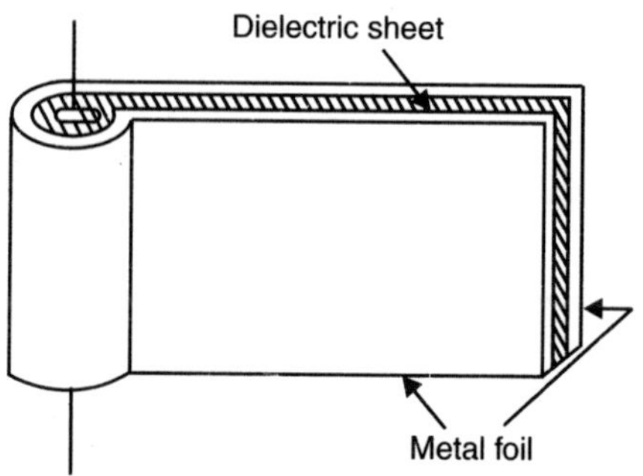

Fig. 8.8

Mica capacitors: A mica capacitor consists of a number of copper sheets separated by thin mica sheets (dielectric constant 6): the alternate copper sheets are connected together. Such capacitors are made in the range of 0.0001 μf to 0.05 μf and can be used up to 500 volts. The power loss in mica is very small. They are used in radio and electronic sets. Some ceramics (such as titanates) with very high dielectric constant have been developed. Making use of these ceramics, capacitors of large capacitance are made.

Electrolytic capacitors: When two aluminium electrodes are dipped in a solution of boric acid and a current is passed through it, a thin layer of aluminium oxide is deposited at the anode as a result of electrolysis. This thin layer of Al_2O_3 is non-conducting and acts as a dielectric. Thus the whole system can be used as a capacitor. Capacitors of such types are called *electrolytic capacitors.* These are of two types: wet and dry. In the former type, an aluminium cylinder (anode) rests in an electrolyte (usually borates) contained in a metallic can which works as cathode. In the latter type, two aluminium strips, one of which is coated with Al_2O_3, are separated by a cotton or paper gauge soaked with electrolyte. The whole thing is rolled up in the form of a cylinder. Such capacitors are marked with polarity and therefore they can be used in unidirectional supplies. When current is reversed in such capacitors, the dielectric layer (Al_2O_3) is reduced to Al and O_2 and the capacitor action is lost. The release of O_2 results in an increase in pressure which may cause damage to the capacitor.

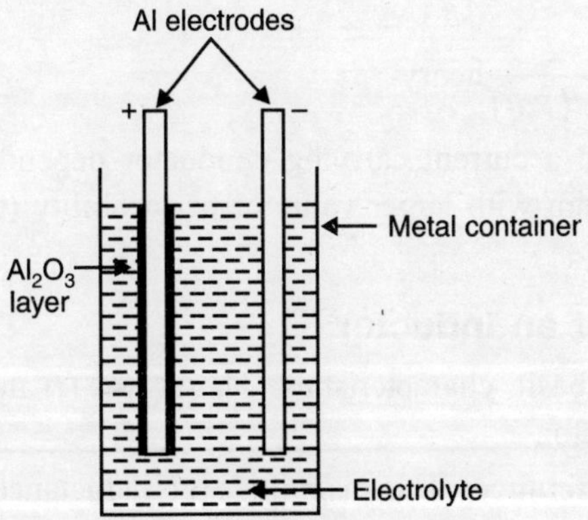

Fig. 8.9

Variable capacitors: In such capacitors, air is used as dielectric. A variable capacitor consists of a series of fixed circular metallic plates and a series of movable circular plates attached on a shaft. By rotating the shaft, the movable plates can be inserted into the gaps between the fixed plates. The capacitance of the capacitor depends on the area overlapping between the fixed and the movable plates. Since the dielectric constant of air is small ($\cong 1$) and the plate separation is kept large to avoid short circuit, the capacitance of such capacitors is very small.

8.3. INDUCTOR

Broadly speaking, an inductor is formed whenever the magnetic flux generated by a current flowing in a conductor links any part of the conductor. A straight wire has negligible inductance because the chances of encircling different parts of the wire by the generated magnetic flux by current in it is almost negligible but a conductor in the form of coil has high inductance because in such cases the chances of encircling by magnetic flux becomes fairly large as shown in the Fig. 8.10.

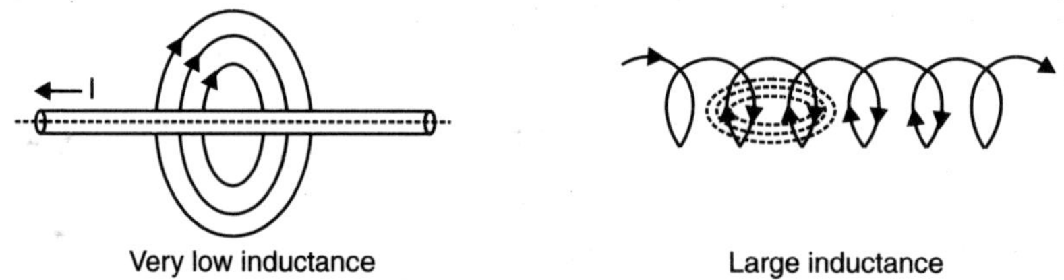

Fig. 8.10

If a varying current is set up in such a coil, an induced voltage is produced in the coil itself which oppose the driving current. Obviously, there will be no inductor action in d.c. All such conducting wires (or inductors) have the property to limit the current in a.c. circuits but they can not be used as a circuit element. An inductor used as a circuit element is usually a conducting wire wound on a simple frame. The basic purpose of such an element is to limit the alternating current in a circuit without consuming any power within itself. The basic property of an inductor is its inductance which is usually denoted by L. The inductance L of a coil is numerically equal to the induced voltage when a current varies in it at the rate of 1 ampere/sec

$$L = \frac{e}{(dI/dt)} \text{henry} \qquad ...(8.22)$$

The magnetic flux around a current carrying conductor depends upon the permeability of the surrounding medium. A medium with larger value of permeability (μ) as a core of an inductor will increase its *inductance.*

8.3.1. Characteristics of an Inductor

A typical inductor has three basic characteristics. These are: (*i*) magnitude of its inductance, (*ii*) current rating, (*iii*) quality factor.

(*i*) **The magnitude of inductance:** The magnitude of inductance of an inductor depends upon shape, size of its frame, number of turns of its winding, medium used as core and to some extent upon the diameter of the winding wires. If the values of above parameters are known, the inductance of the inductor can be calculated. For a long single layered solenoid

$$L = \mu n^2 Al \qquad ...(8.23)$$

where n = number of turns per unit length, l = length of the solenoid, A = area of cross-section of the solenoid and μ = permeability of the core.

(*ii*) **Current rating of an inductor:** Metal wires used for making inductor are usually painted (enamelled) by organic paints for insulation. The metal wires have small but finite resistance. When a current is passed through these wires, a finite amount of heat is generated, a part of which is radiated to the surrounding and the rest is retained within the windings and raises its temperature. As the current in the winding is increased, the temparature of the inductor is also increased. To keep the insulation intact, this temperature cannot be allowed to go high.

Thus a limit to current is set for every inductor. This current besides depending to some extent on the material of the wire, largely depends upon the cross-sectional area of the wire. The maximum value of current which is allowed to flow through the inductor is termed as the current rating. Usually it is two third of the maximum value of the current which can be allowed to flow without causing any damage to it or its insulation.

(iii) **Quality factor of an inductor:** Inductor is primarily an energy storing device which stores energy when current through the coil is increasing and releases it when the current is decreasing. When the stored energy is the same as that delivered afterwards, the inductor is said to be an *ideal inductor*. Practically, this never happens. A part of energy given to a inductor always dissipates in it. This property of an inductor is expressed by its *quality factor* Q which is defined by eqn. (8.10).

Lossy inductor ≡ Ideal inductor (L) — Resistance (R)

Fig. 8.11

The loss of energy in an inductor is explained on the basis of assumption that a resistance R is present in series with the inductor.

When a voltage $V = V_0 \cos \omega t$ is applied across an inductor, the current in it is given by $I = I_0 \cos(\omega t - \theta)$ where $\tan \theta = \omega L/R$. The average power dissipated in the resistance is

$$<P> = \frac{1}{2} V_0 I_0 \cos\theta = V_{rms} I_{rms} \cos\theta \qquad ...(8.24)$$

where $$\cos\theta = \frac{R}{\sqrt{R^2 + \omega^2 L^2}} = \frac{1}{\sqrt{1 + (\omega L/R)^2}} \qquad ...(8.25)$$

is called the power factor of the inductor.

Maximum energy stored in the inductor is

$$U = \frac{1}{2} L I_0^2 = L I_{rms}^2 \qquad ...(8.26)$$

and the energy dissipated per cycle is

$$\Delta U = I_{rms}^2 R \cdot T = I_{rms}^2 R \cdot \left(\frac{2\pi}{\omega}\right)$$

Hence $$Q = 2\pi \frac{U}{\Delta U} = \frac{\omega L}{R} \qquad ...(8.27)$$

The power factor in terms of Q factor is given by

$$P_f = \cos\theta = \frac{1}{\sqrt{1 + Q^2}} \qquad ...(8.28)$$

At moderate frequencies, the reactance of the inductor is much larger than its resistance ($\omega L >> R$). Hence we can write,

$$P_f = \frac{R}{\omega L} = \frac{1}{Q} \qquad ...(8.29)$$

Thus Q of an inductor is approximately equal to the reciprocal of its power factor.

8.3.2. Principal Causes of Energy Loss in an Inductor

The factors responsible for loss in an inductor are:

(*i*) Skin-effect.

(*ii*) Proximity effect resulting from interaction between nearby turns.

(*iii*) Dielectric loss associated with distributed capacitance of coils.

(*iv*) Eddy current loss in the shields and other neighouring metallic objects.

(*v*) Hysteresis loss.

The first four factors are important for air core inductors, the last one dominates in magnetic core coils.

Skin effect: It has been observed that at radio and higher frequencies, the resistance offered by a conductor is considerably greater than the d.c. ohmic resistance. This is because of the skin effect. Due to this effect, the current tends to concentrate in certain part of the conductor and leaves the remaining part. Let us explain it with an example. Consider a wire carrying a high frequencey current. The magnetic field lines associated with the current are in the form of concentric circles as shown in the Fig. 8.12.

Some of the magnetic flux exists within the conductor. It is evident from the Fig. 8.12 that the central part of the conductor is encircled by greater number of magnetic field lines than the outer part. Thus the central part of the conductor has larger inductance than the outer part and so is true of the inductive reactance. In other words, the part of the conductor near its surface offers less impedance than that at the centre and hence, the current tends to concetrate in the outer part. For this reason, the current density is maximum at the surface and is minimum at the centre.

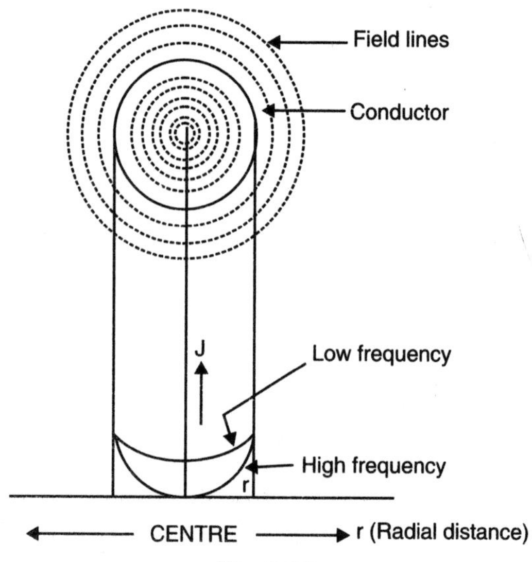

Fig. 8.12

Skin depth δ: When the frequency of current flowing in a conductor is very high, the current tends to confine to the region very close to the surface. The current density falls with depth z from the surface in accordance with the relation

$$J = J_s e^{-z/\delta} \qquad \text{...(8.30)}$$

where J_s is the current density at the surface and δ is a parameter called skin depth and is very small ($\delta << r$) compared to the radius of the wire. It depends upon the frequency (f) of the current, d.c. resistivity (ρ) and magnetic permeability (μ) of the material of the wire.

$$\delta = K\left(\frac{\rho}{\mu f}\right)^{1/2} \qquad \text{...(8.31)}$$

where K is a constant.

This equation is valid only when the radius of curvature of the conducting surface is at least several than the skin depth and the effective thickness of the conductor at the same time at least three or four times the skin depth. The power loss associated with the current flowing in any particular portion of the conducting surface is same as though this current were uniformly distributed down to a depth δ. Thus in an isolated round wire where the current is uniformly distributed over the surface, the effective resistance at high frequencies is the d.c. resistance of a hollow cylindrical shell having the same outer diameter as the wire possessing thickness δ. The d.c resistance of a strip of surface one skin depth thick, one metre long and one metre wide is some times called the "*surface resistivity*". It is the actual resistivity that is operative to the current at very high frequencies.

Proximity effect: When two or more adjacent conductors carry currents, the current distribution in any one conductor is affected by the magnetic flux produced by the other. This is called the proximity effect. Due to this effect, the true or effective resistance of the conductor is greater than that due to simple skin effect and is particularly important in radio frequency inductive coils. The current distribution due to proximity effect follows the same law as for the simple skin effect.

Dielectric losses: The dielectric loss results due to presence of distributed capacitance in the coils of the inductor. The origin of distributed capacitance can be understood in the following ways. In inductor, the windings are closely spaced. When a current passes throught it, a finite potential difference exists between two adjacent turns as shown in the Fig. 8.13. This capacitance is known as distributed capacitance. The medium acts as a dielectric. Due to this capacitance and dielectric loss, some energy is lost and the effective current throught the coils becomes less. The dielectric loss is comparatively larger in magnetic core (ferrite or garnet) coils than in air core coils.

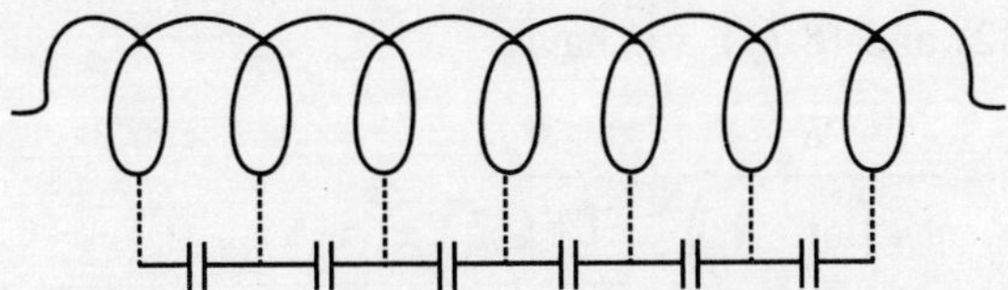

Fig. 8.13. Distributed capacitance across windings.

Eddy current losses: Whenever a conductor is placed in a varying magnetic field, an induced current is set up which circulates throughout the volume of the conductor. Due to their circulatory nature, they are called *eddy currents.* In the inductor which uses conducting core such as iron, eddy currents are generated within the core whenever an alternating current is switched on in it. These eddy currents not only consume power but also produce undesirable magnetic flux. Eddy current losses become important even at moderate audio frequencies. This type of loss in an inductor can be minimized by use of laminated cores instead of a single solid piece of iron. Thin sheets of iron are stacked together keeping them electrically insulated to form the core. Thus the *eddy current*, instead of spreading over the whole volume, are restricted to within the thin lamina.

SOLVED EXAMPLES

***Example* 1:** *A real capacitor is represented in two equivalent modes as shown in the Fig. 8.14. Express R_s and C_s in terms of R_p and C_p and viceversa.*

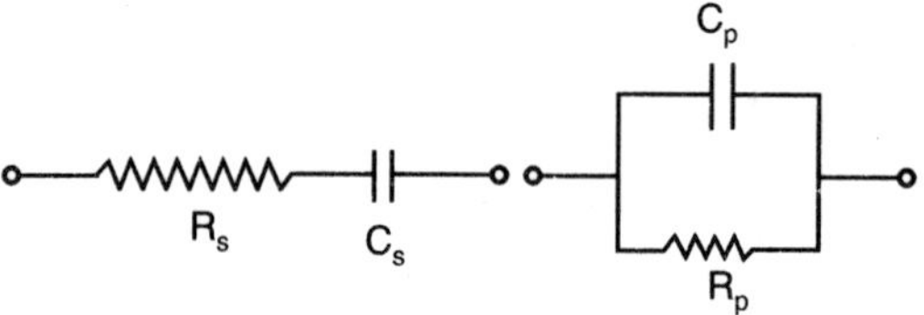

Fig. 8.14

Solution: The two modes of representation are equivalent if their impedances are equal.

In the series mode, the impedance is given by,

$$Z_s = R_s + \frac{1}{j\omega C_s}$$

$$= R_s - \frac{j}{\omega C_s} \qquad \text{...(8.32)}$$

In parallel mode, the impedance is given by,

$$\frac{1}{Z_p} = \frac{1}{R_p} + j\omega C_p = \frac{1 + j\omega C_p R_p}{R_p}$$

$$Z_p = \frac{R_p}{1 + j\omega C_p R_p} = \frac{R_p}{1 + (\omega C_p R_p)^2} - \frac{j\omega C_p R_p^2}{1 + (\omega C_p R_p)^2} \qquad \text{...(8.33)}$$

Comparing eqns. (8.32) and (8.33), we have,

$$R_s = \frac{R_p}{1 + (\omega C_p R_p)^2} = \frac{R_p}{1 + Q_p^2} \qquad \text{...(8.34)}$$

$$C_s = \frac{1 + (\omega C_p R_p)^2}{\omega^2 C_p R_p^2} = C_p \left[1 + \frac{1}{(\omega C_p R_p)^2}\right] = C_p \left(1 + \frac{1}{Q_p^2}\right) \qquad \text{...(8.35)}$$

In order to compute R_p and C_p in terms of R_s and C_s it is convenient to equate the admittances in the two modes.

$$Y_s = \frac{1}{Z_s} = \frac{j\omega C_s}{1 + j\omega C_s R_s} = \frac{\omega^2 C_s^2 R_s}{1+(\omega C_s R_s)^2} + \frac{j\omega C_s}{1+(\omega C_s R_s)^2} \quad ...(8.36)$$

$$Y_p = j\omega C_p + \frac{1}{R_p} \quad ...(8.37)$$

Comparing (8.36) and (8.37) we obtian

$$R_p = R_s\left(1 + \frac{1}{(\omega C_s R_s)^2}\right) = R_s\left(1 + Q_s^2\right) \quad ...(8.38)$$

and
$$C_p = \frac{C_s}{1+(\omega C_s R_s)^2} = \frac{C_s}{\left(1+1/Q_s^2\right)} \quad ...(8.39)$$

***Example* 2:** *A real inductor is represented in two equivalent modes as shown in the Fig. 8.15. Express R_s and L_s in terms of R_p and L_p and vice-versa.*

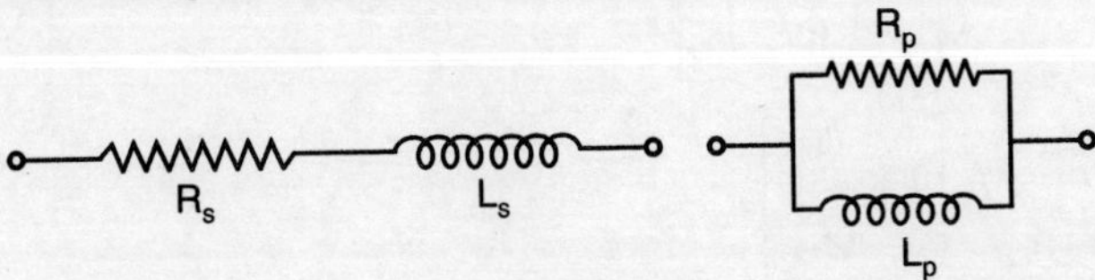

Fig. 8.15

Solution: Impedance of the inductor in series

$$Z_s = R_s + j\omega L_s \quad ...(8.40)$$

and in parallel mode is

$$\frac{1}{Z_p} = \frac{1}{R_p} + \frac{1}{j\omega L_p} = \frac{R_p + j\omega L_p}{j\omega L_p R_p}$$

$$Z_p = \frac{j\omega L_p R_p}{R_p + j\omega L_p} = \frac{\omega^2 L_p^2 R_p + j\omega L_p R_p^2}{R_p^2 + \omega^2 L_p^2} \quad ...(8.41)$$

Comparing eqns. (8.40) and (8.41), we have

$$R_s = \frac{\omega^2 L_p^2 R_p}{R_p^2 + \omega^2 L_p^2} = \frac{R_p}{1+\left(R_p/\omega L_p\right)^2} = \frac{R_p}{1+Q_p^2} \quad ...(8.42)$$

$$L_s = \frac{L_p R_p^2}{R_p^2 + \omega^2 L_p^2} = \frac{L_p}{1+\left(\dfrac{\omega L_p}{R_p}\right)^2} = \frac{L_p}{1+1/Q_p^2} \quad ...(8.43)$$

In order to calculate R_p and L_p in terms of R_s and L_s, we equate the admittances in the two modes of representations.

$$Y_p = \frac{1}{R_p} + \frac{1}{j\omega L_p} = \frac{1}{R_p} - \frac{j}{\omega L_p} \quad ...(8.44)$$

$$Y_s = \frac{1}{R_s + j\omega L_s} = \frac{R_s - j\omega L_s}{R_s^2 + \omega^2 L_s^2} \quad ...(8.45)$$

$\therefore$
$$R_p = \frac{R_s^2 + \omega^2 L_s^2}{R_s} = R_s\left[1 + \left(\frac{\omega L_s}{R_s}\right)^2\right] \quad ...(8.46)$$

or
$$R_p = R_s\left(1 + Q_s^2\right)$$

and
$$L_p = \frac{R_s^2 + \omega^2 L_s^2}{\omega^2 L_s} = L_s \frac{R_s^2 + \omega^2 L_s^2}{\omega^2 L_s^2}$$

$$= L_s\left[1 + \left(\frac{R_s}{\omega L_s}\right)^2\right]$$

$$= L_s\left[1 + \frac{1}{Q_s^2}\right] \quad ...(8.47)$$

For high $Q_s (\geq 10)$

$$\left.\begin{array}{l} R_p \cong R_s Q_s^2 \\ L_p \cong L_s \end{array}\right]$$

***Example* 3:** *A lossy capacitor, in series combination, is represented by R =100 Ω,* $C = \frac{10}{\pi}$ *pF. Obtain the equivalent parallel model at frequency 100 kHz.*

Solution:

$$Q_s = \frac{1}{\omega C_s R_s} = \frac{1}{2\pi \times 10^5 \times \frac{10}{\pi} \times 10^{-12} \times 100^4}$$

$$= \frac{1}{2 \times 10^{-4}} = 5000$$

$$R_s = R_s\left(1 + Q_s^2\right)$$

$$\cong R_s Q_s^2 = 100 \times 25 \times 10^6 = 2500 \text{ M}\Omega$$

$$C_p = \frac{C_s}{\left(1 + 1/Q_s^2\right)} \cong C_s = \frac{10}{\pi}\text{pF}$$

Example 4: *A real inductor is represented by a series combination of L = 20 mH and R = 3.14 Ω. Obtain an equivalent parallel combination of L and R at frequencies (i) 10 KHz (ii) 100 Hz.*

Solution:

$$L_s = 20 \times 10^{-3}\,\text{H}$$

$$R_s = 3.14\Omega$$

(*i*) At $f = 10 \times 10^3\,\text{Hz};\ Q_s = \dfrac{\omega L_s}{R_s}$

$$Q_s = \frac{2 \times 3.14 \times 10 \times 10^3 \times 20 \times 10^{-3}}{3.14}$$

$$= 400$$

The resistance and inductance in parallel combination are given by,

$$R_p = R_s\left[1 + Q_s^{\ 2}\right] = 3.14\left[1 + 400^2\right] \cong 5 \times 10^4\,\Omega$$

$$L_p = L_s\left[1 + \frac{1}{Q_s^{\ 2}}\right]$$

$$= 20 \times 10^{-9}\left[1 + \frac{1}{400^2}\right] \cong 20\text{ mH}$$

(*ii*) At $f = 100\text{ Hz},\ Q_s = \dfrac{\omega L_s}{R_s}$

$$Q_s = \frac{2 \times 3.14 \times 100 \times 20 \times 10^{-3}}{4.14}$$

$$= 4$$

$$R_p = R_s\left[1 + Q_s^{\ 2}\right] = 3.14[1 + 16] = 53.4\Omega$$

$$L_p = L_s\left[1 + \frac{1}{Q_s^{\ 2}}\right] = 20 \times 10^{-3}\,[1 + 0.06] \cong 21.2\text{ mH}$$

QUESTIONS AND PROBLEMS

1. Describe the various types of resistors and state their characteristics.
2. Give the equivalent circuits of a lossy capacitor and obtain expressions for quality factors and power factors in each mode of representation.
3. Describe the characteristics of an inductor. Obtain expressions for quality factor and power factor of a real inductor.
4. What are the principal causes of energy loss in an inductor?

5. Find the parallel equivalent of a series *RC* circuit with $R = 10\Omega$, $C = \frac{1}{\pi}\mu f$ at frequencies (*i*) 50 Hz (*ii*) 10 KHz.

6. Find the series equivalent of a parallel *RC* circuit with $R = 50\Omega$ and $C = \frac{0.1}{\pi}\mu f$ at a frequency of 10 KHz.

7. A real inductor in its series representation has $R = \frac{10}{\pi}\Omega$ and $L = 50\text{mH}$. Design its parallel equivalent at a frequency of 10 KHz.

8. What is the maximum safe current that can be passed in a 10 kΩ, 4 watt resistor?

9 CHAPTER

Network Transformation and Analysis

9.1. INTRODUCTION

An electrical circuit or network is an interconnection of circuit elements in a form which results in a closed path. Often they are connected in complicated manner which makes it difficult to predict their behaviour in relation to other circuits and to evaluate current through and potential difference across any circuit element. To do that, such networks are often transformed into equivalent simple network. The process used for this is called network transformation. The network analysis, on the other hand, is a theoretical process by which the current and potential distribution in various circuit elements is evaluated. This is usually done by Kirchhoff's laws. Several methods have been developed for transforming a network into simple network. Some of these methods will be discussed in this chapter.

9.2. NETWORK DEFINITIONS

Before proceeding to network analysis, let us explain some basic terms which very often come across in this process.

(*i*) **Circuit elements:** The elements like resistors, inductors, capacitors, transformers, diodes, transistors, energy sources (batteries, generators) etc. which constitute an electrical circuit or network are called circuit elements.

(*ii*) **Branch:** A group of circuit elements connected in series and having two terminals for connection is called a branch.

(*iii*) **Node:** The junction of three or more branches is known as a node or vertex.

(*iv*) **Mesh:** A set of branches forming a closed path in an electrical network is called a mesh.

(*v*) **Loop:** A mesh which cannot be sub-divided further into smaller meshes is called a loop.

(*vi*) **Passive network:** An electrical network containing only passive circuit elements i.e. resistor, inductor, capacitor is called a passive network.

(*vii*) **Active network:** An electrical network containing circuit elements and energy sources is called active network.

(*viii*) **Linear network:** An electrical network, in which the equations relating the current and voltage, whether they are algebraic, differential, integral etc. are linear, is called a linear network.

9.3. COMMON IMPEDANCES OF NETWORKS

1. **Loop Impedance Z_{11}, Z_{22}:** The loop impedance Z_{11} is the sum of impedance through which current I_1 flows. Similarly, loop impedance Z_{22} is the sum of impedances through which current I_2 flows. The loop impedance of any loop may also be defined as the sum of impedances with all other loop open circuited. For a two loop network of Fig. 9.1, the loop impedances of loops 1 and 2 are

$$Z_{11} = Z_1 + Z_3, \qquad Z_{22} = Z_2 + Z_3 + Z_L \qquad ...(9.1)$$

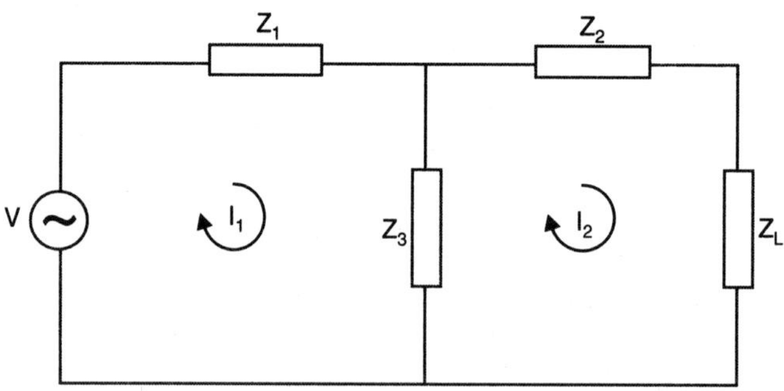

Fig. 9.1

2. **Mutual Impedance Z_{12} and Z_{21}:** It is equal to the sum of impedances through which currents I_1 and I_2 both pass. It is assigned positive (+) sign if I_1 and I_2 have the same direction and negative (–) sign if I_1 and I_2 are in opposite direction. It may also defined as the ratio of voltage induced in the second loop by the current flowing in the first loop with all other loops kept open circuited. The mutual impedance between loops 1 and 2 of Fig. 9.1 is

$$Z_{12} = Z_{21} = -Z_3 \qquad ...(9.2)$$

or

$$Z_{12} = -\frac{I_1 Z_3}{I_1} = -Z_3 \quad \text{and} \quad Z_{21} = -\frac{I_2 Z_3}{I_2} \qquad ...(9.3)$$

3. **Input or Driving Point Impedance:** It is the impedance measured between the input terminals of a network with all energy sources in the network replaced by their impedances. The input impedance of the network of Fig. 9.1 is

$$Z_{in} = Z_1 + \frac{Z_3(Z_2 + Z_L)}{Z_2 + Z_3 + Z_L} = \frac{Z_1(Z_2 + Z_3 + Z_L) + Z_3(Z_2 + Z_3 + Z_L) - Z_3^2}{Z_2 + Z_3 + Z_L}$$

$$= \frac{(Z_1 + Z_3)(Z_2 + Z_3 + Z_L) - Z_3^2}{Z_2 + Z_3 + Z_L}$$

$$= \frac{Z_{11}Z_{22} - Z_{12}^2}{Z_{22}} \qquad ...(9.4)$$

4. **Transfer Impedance:** The ratio of voltage applied to any (say j^{th}) mesh of the network to the current flowing in another (say k^{th}) mesh is called the transfer impedance of jth mesh to k^{th} mesh and is denoted by $Z_{T,jk}$. Thus,

$$Z_{T,jk} = \frac{E_j}{I_k}. \qquad ...(9.5)$$

For a network containing bilateral impedance

$$Z_{T,jk} = Z_{T,kj}. \qquad ...(9.6)$$

The transfer impedance between meshes 1 and 2 of Fig. 9.1 is

$$Z_{T,12} = \frac{E_1}{I_2} = \frac{-I_2 Z_3 + I_1(Z_1 + Z_3)}{I_2} \qquad ...(9.7)$$

$$I_2 = \frac{Z_3 I_1}{Z_2 + Z_3 + Z_L} \qquad ...(9.8)$$

Putting the value of I_2 from eqns. (9.8) in (9.7) we get

$$Z_{T,12} = \frac{(Z_1 + Z_3)(Z_2 + Z_3 + Z_L)}{Z_3} - Z_3 = Z_{12} - \frac{Z_{11}Z_{22}}{Z_{12}} \qquad ...(9.9)$$

5. **Open and Short Circuited Impedances:** Every network has two input and two output terminals as shown in the Fig. 9.2.

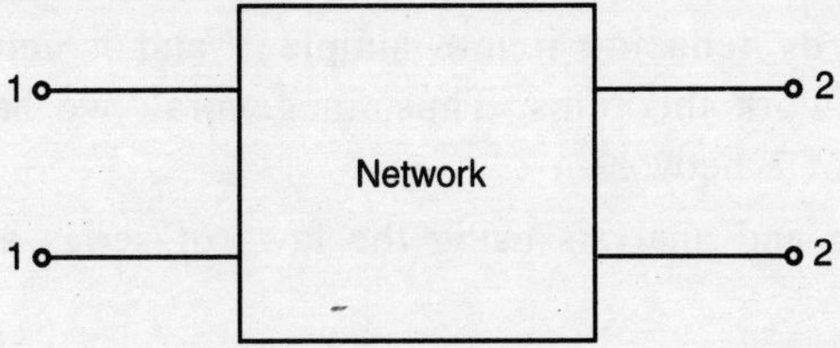

Fig. 9.2. A network with two input terminals 1,1 and two output terminals 2,2.

There are two open and two short circuited impedances of a network which are very helpful in determining its behaviour. These are:

Z_{1oc} = the impedance measured across the terminals 1,1 with terminals 2,2 open circuited
Z_{1sc} = the impedance measured across the terminals 1,1 with terminals 2,2 short circuited
Z_{2oc} = the impedance measured across the terminals 2,2 with terminals 1,1 open circuited
Z_{2sc} = the impedance measured across the terminals 2,2 with terminals 1,1 short circuited.

9.4. EQUIVALENT AND SYMMETRIC NETWORK

1. **Equivalent Networks:** Two electrical networks, each with two input terminals 1,1 and two output terminals 2,2 are said to be equivalent if Z_{1oc}, Z_{2oc}, Z_{1sc}, and Z_{2sc} of one network are the same as that of the second network. Thus,

$$(Z_{1oc})_1 = (Z_{1oc})_2, \quad (Z_{2oc})_1 = (Z_{2oc})_2, \quad (Z_{1sc})_1 = (Z_{1sc})_2, \quad (Z_{2sc})_1 = (Z_{2sc})_2 \qquad ...(9.10)$$

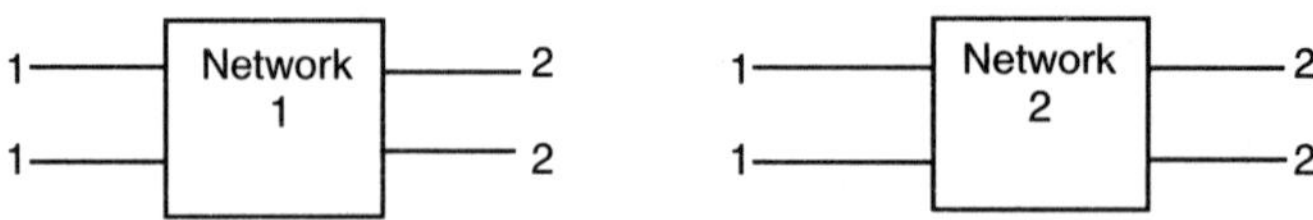

Fig. 9.3

Equivalent networks are not identical internally but have identical values of external voltage and current.

2. **Symmetrical Networks:** A network with two input and two output terminals is said to be symmetrical if

$$Z_{1oc} = Z_{2oc}, \qquad Z_{1sc} = Z_{2sc}.$$

9.5. METHODS OF NETWORK TRANSFORMATION AND ANALYSIS

An electrical network consists of a large number of meshes and loops, each of which contains active and passive circuit elements. The process of determination of the current and potential distribution in various branches of the network is called circuit analysis. This is usually done using Kirchhoff's laws or the laws of series and parallel combination of impedances. Often we are not interested in detailed analysis of the network but want to know its external behaviour. In such cases, we prefer to reduce it into simpler equivalent network. The laws of series and parallel impedances are often used to reduce and to find the impedances of network. Proceeding systematically backward, it becomes sometimes possible to analyse the network. Its external behaviour is often analysed by reducing it into simple T and π network. Active networks are often transformed using network theorems. Thus, in general, we have following methods for transformation and analysis of a network.

(*i*) Network transformation and analysis using the laws of series and parallel combination of impedances.

(*ii*) Network analysis using Kirchhoff's laws

(*iii*) Network analysis by transforming it into T and π networks

(*iv*) Network transformation and analysis using Network theorems

9.6. NETWORK ANALYSIS USING KIRCHHOFF'S LAWS

Kirchhoff's Current Law (KCL): According to this law:

The algebraic sum of instantaneous currents meeting at a junction is zero.

$$\sum I = 0$$

While applylling KCL to a junction, the incoming currents are assumed to have one sign (plus or minus) and the outgoing currents are assigned opposite sign (minus or plus). This law is a direct consequence of law of conservation of charge.

Kirchhoff's Voltage Law (KVL): This law states that:

The algebraic sum of instantaneous voltage drops across the circuit elements around a loop is zero.

As regards the sign for the voltage drops we adopt the following convention. We choose the direction arbitrarily around the loop. In passive elements, the end at which current enters is marked plus and that at which it leaves is marked minus. A d.c. source has its own intrinsic polarity. Next we choose a direction of circumvention. The voltage drop across a circuit element is equal to the product of current and resistance and is assigned plus sign if it is traversed from positive end to negative end. The same convention is adopted for voltage source i.e. if it is traversed from positive terminal to negative terminal it is taken as positive voltage drop otherwise negative.

In a.c. circuit, the voltage source is arbitrarily assigned its instantaneous polarity and accordingly instantaneous current is assumed around the loop. The voltage drop across an element is product of current I and impedance Z, (For resistance $Z = R$, for inductor $Z = j\omega L$, for capacitor $Z = -j/\omega C$). Applying KVL to the two loops of the circuit given in Fig. 9.4(a), we have the following equations.

$$I_1R_1 + (I_1 - I_2)R_2 + I_1R_3 - V_1 = 0 \quad ...(9.11)$$

$$I_2(R_4 + R_5) + (I_2 - I_1)R_2 + V_2 = 0 \quad ...(9.12)$$

In terms of loop impedances Z_{11} $(= R_1 + R_2 + R_3)$, Z_{22} $(= R_2 + R_4 + R_5)$ and mutual impedance $Z_{12} = Z_{21}$ $(= -R_2)$, the above equations become

$$Z_{11}I_1 + Z_{12}I_2 = V_1 \quad ...(9.13)$$

$$Z_{21}I_1 + Z_{22}I_2 = -V_2 \quad ...(9.14)$$

Applying KVL to the circuit given in Fig. (9.4b) gives following equations

$$-V + (I_1 - I_2)Z_2 + I_1Z_1 = 0 \quad ...(9.15)$$

$$I_2Z_3 + I_2Z_4 + (I_2 - I_1)Z_2 = 0 \quad ...(9.16)$$

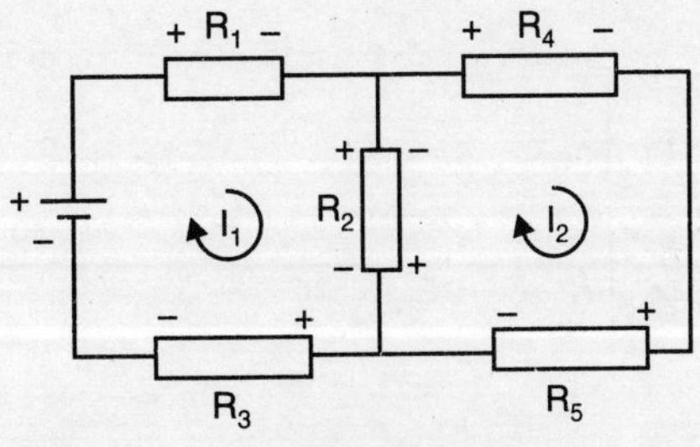

Fig. 9.4(a)

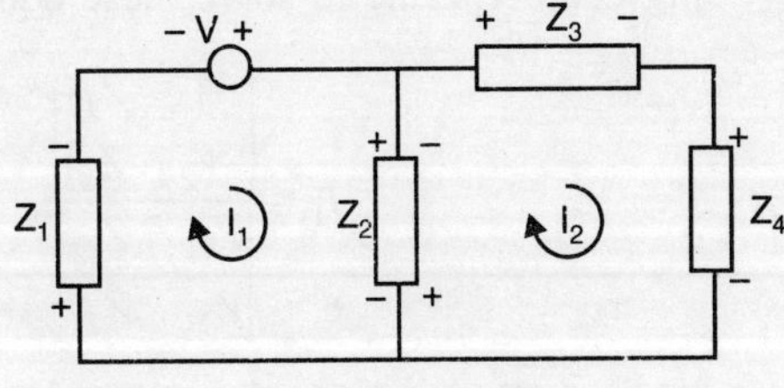

Fig. 9.4(b)

In terms of loop impedance Z_{11} $(= Z_1 + Z_2)$, Z_{22} $(= Z_2 + Z_3 + Z_4)$, and mutual impedance $Z_{12} = Z_{21} = -Z_2$ we can write above equations as

$$Z_{11}I_1 + Z_{12}I_2 = V$$

$$Z_{21}I_1 + Z_{22}I_2 = 0$$

Analysis of Two Meshes Network

The general circuit of a two loops network is shown in the Fig. 9.5. Both the loops contain voltage sources V_1 and V_2 with their impedances Z_{1S} and Z_{2S} respectively. At any instant the polarity of sources and the direction of currents in the two loops have been shown. Applying KVL to the two loops we get following equations.

$$(Z_{1S} + Z_1 + Z_3) + (-Z_3)I_2 = V_1 \qquad ...(9.17)$$

$$(-Z_3)I_1 + (Z_2 + Z_4 + Z_{2S} + Z_3)I_2 = -V_2 \qquad ...(9.18)$$

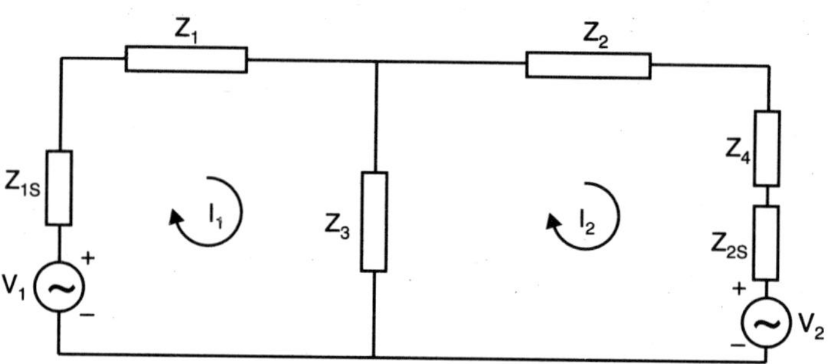

Fig. 9.5. Two loops network.

The loop impedances of the two loops are: $Z_{11} = Z_{1S} + Z_1 + Z_3$, $Z_{22} = Z_{2S} + Z_2 + Z_3 + Z_4$), and mutual impedance is $Z_{12} = Z_{21} = -Z_3$. Above equations can be written as

$$Z_{11}I_1 + Z_{12}I_2 = V_1 \qquad ...(9.19)$$

$$Z_{21}I_1 + Z_{22}I_2 = -V_2 \qquad ...(9.20)$$

In matrix form these equations are

$$\begin{bmatrix} Z_{11} & Z_{12} \\ Z_{21} & Z_{22} \end{bmatrix} \begin{bmatrix} I_1 \\ I_2 \end{bmatrix} = \begin{bmatrix} V_1 \\ -V_2 \end{bmatrix} \qquad ...(9.21)$$

Using Cramer's rule to solve these equations we get

$$I_1 = \frac{\begin{vmatrix} V_1 & Z_{12} \\ -V_2 & Z_{22} \end{vmatrix}}{\begin{vmatrix} Z_{11} & Z_{12} \\ Z_{21} & Z_{22} \end{vmatrix}}, \qquad I_2 = \frac{\begin{vmatrix} Z_{11} & V_1 \\ Z_{21} & -V_2 \end{vmatrix}}{\begin{vmatrix} Z_{11} & Z_{12} \\ Z_{21} & Z_{22} \end{vmatrix}} \qquad ...(9.22)$$

Analysis of Three Loops Network

The method of analysis described above can be extended to three or n loop network. Let the equations of voltage drops for a three loops network, each containing a voltage source be of the form

$$Z_{11}I_1 + Z_{12}I_2 + Z_{13}I_3 = V_1 \qquad ...(9.23)$$

$$Z_{21}I_1 + Z_{22}I_2 + Z_{23}I_3 = V_2 \qquad ...(9.24)$$

$$Z_{31}I_1 + Z_{32}I_2 + Z_{33}I_3 = V_3 \qquad ...(9.25)$$

In matrix form

$$\begin{bmatrix} Z_{11} & Z_{12} & Z_{13} \\ Z_{21} & Z_{22} & Z_{23} \\ Z_{31} & Z_{32} & Z_{33} \end{bmatrix} \begin{bmatrix} I_1 \\ I_2 \\ I_3 \end{bmatrix} = \begin{bmatrix} V_1 \\ V_2 \\ V_3 \end{bmatrix} \qquad ...(9.26)$$

From Cramers's rule

$$I_1 = \frac{\begin{vmatrix} V_1 & Z_{12} & Z_{13} \\ V_2 & Z_{22} & Z_{23} \\ V_3 & Z_{32} & Z_{33} \end{vmatrix}}{\begin{vmatrix} Z_{11} & Z_{12} & Z_{13} \\ Z_{21} & Z_{22} & Z_{23} \\ Z_{31} & Z_{32} & Z_{33} \end{vmatrix}}, \quad I_2 = \frac{\begin{vmatrix} Z_{11} & V_1 & Z_{13} \\ Z_{21} & V_2 & Z_{23} \\ Z_{31} & V_3 & Z_{33} \end{vmatrix}}{\begin{vmatrix} Z_{11} & Z_{12} & Z_{13} \\ Z_{21} & Z_{22} & Z_{23} \\ Z_{31} & Z_{32} & Z_{33} \end{vmatrix}}, \quad I_3 = \frac{\begin{bmatrix} Z_{11} & Z_{12} & V_1 \\ Z_{21} & Z_{22} & V_2 \\ Z_{31} & Z_{32} & V_3 \end{bmatrix}}{\begin{vmatrix} Z_{11} & Z_{12} & Z_{13} \\ Z_{21} & Z_{22} & Z_{23} \\ Z_{31} & Z_{32} & Z_{33} \end{vmatrix}} \quad \text{...(9.27)}$$

***Example* 1:** *Obtain the currents I_1, I_2 and I_3 in the following network.*

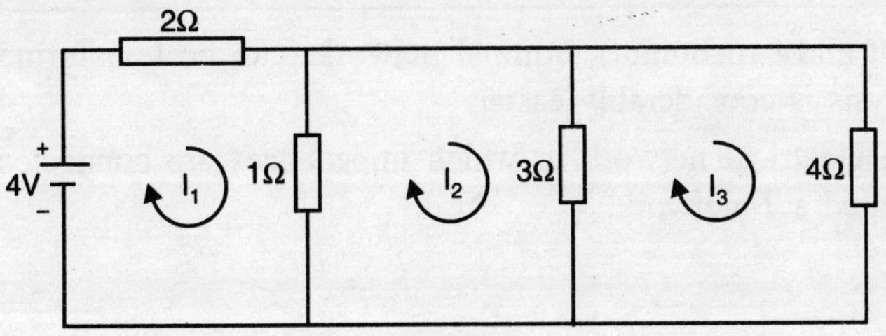

Fig. 9.6

Solution:

Loop impedances $Z_{11} = 2 + 1 = 3\ \Omega$, $Z_{22} = 3 + 1 = 4\ \Omega$, $Z_{33} = 4 + 3 = 7\ \Omega$

Mutual impedances $Z_{12} = -1\ \Omega = Z_{21}$, $Z_{23} = -3\ \Omega = Z_{32}$, $Z_{13} = 0 = Z_{31}$

KVL gives following equations:

$$3I_1 + (-1)I_2 + 0I_3 = 4$$

$$-I_1 + 4I_2 + (-3)I_3 = 0$$

$$0I_1 + (-3)I_2 + 7I_3 = 0$$

In matrix form above equations can be written as

$$\begin{bmatrix} 3 & -1 & 0 \\ -1 & 4 & -3 \\ 0 & -3 & 7 \end{bmatrix} \begin{bmatrix} I_1 \\ I_2 \\ I_3 \end{bmatrix} = \begin{bmatrix} 4 \\ 0 \\ 0 \end{bmatrix}$$

$$|Z| = \begin{vmatrix} 3 & -1 & 0 \\ -1 & 4 & -3 \\ 0 & -3 & 7 \end{vmatrix} = 50$$

From Cramer's rule

$$I_1 = \frac{1}{50} \begin{vmatrix} 4 & -1 & 0 \\ 0 & 4 & -3 \\ 0 & -3 & 7 \end{vmatrix} = 1.52\text{A}$$

$$I_2 = \frac{1}{50}\begin{vmatrix} 3 & 4 & 0 \\ -1 & 0 & -3 \\ 0 & 0 & 7 \end{vmatrix} = 0.56A$$

$$I_3 = \frac{1}{50}\begin{vmatrix} 3 & -1 & 4 \\ -1 & 4 & 0 \\ 0 & -3 & 0 \end{vmatrix} = 0.24A$$

9.7. NETWORK ANALYSIS BY TRANSFORMING IT INTO 'T' AND 'π' NETWORK

Many four (two input and two output) terminal networks can be transformed into simple T and π networks whose analysis is considerably easier.

(i) T-network: An electrical network in which impedances are connected in T shape as shown in Fig. 9.7 is called a T-network.

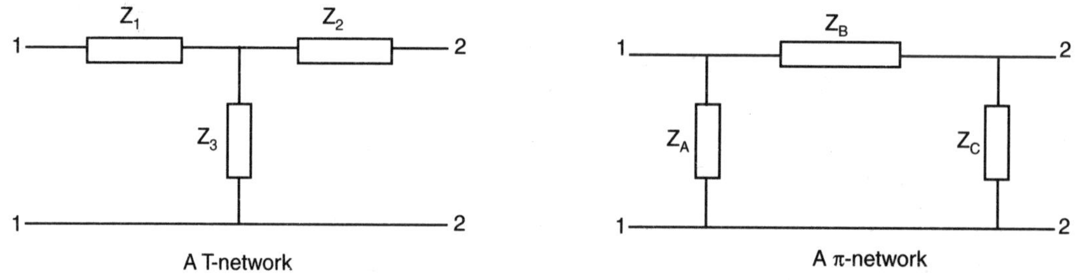

Fig. 9.7. T and π network.

Here Z_1, Z_2 and Z_3 are impedances, which may be combination of resistor, inductor and capacitor.

(ii) π-network: An electrical network in which impedances are arranged in π shape as shown in Fig. 9.7 is called a π-network.

(iii) Common impedances of T and π network: There are four impedances which are very useful in circuit analysis. We shall calculate them for T and π networks. These are:

Z_{1oc} = the impedance measured across the terminals 1,1 with terminals 2,2 open circuited

Z_{2oc} = the impedance measured across the terminals 2,2 with terminals 1,1 open circuited

Z_{1sc} = the impedance measured across the terminals 1,1 with terminals 2,2 short circuited

Z_{2sc} = the impedance measured across the terminals 2,2 with terminals 1,1 short circuited

For T network these impedances become

$$Z_{1oc} = Z_1 + Z_3 \quad ...(9.28)$$

$$Z_{2oc} = Z_2 + Z_3 \quad ...(9.29)$$

$$Z_{1sc} = Z_1 + \frac{Z_2 Z_3}{Z_2 + Z_3} \quad \text{...(9.30)}$$

$$Z_{2sc} = Z_2 + \frac{Z_1 Z_3}{Z_1 + Z_3} \quad \text{...(9.31)}$$

For a π-network these impedances are:

$$Z_{1oc} = \frac{Z_A(Z_B + Z_C)}{Z_A + Z_B + Z_C} \quad \text{...(9.32)}$$

$$Z_{2oc} = \frac{Z_C(Z_A + Z_B)}{Z_A + Z_B + Z_C} \quad \text{...(9.33)}$$

$$Z_{1sc} = \frac{Z_A Z_B}{Z_A + Z_B} \quad \text{...(9.34)}$$

$$Z_{2sc} = \frac{Z_B Z_C}{Z_B + Z_C} \quad \text{...(9.35)}$$

9.8. CONVERSION OF T-NETWORK INTO π-NETWORK AND VICE-VERSA

A *T*-network can be replaced by an equivalent network and vice-versa. We shall discuss how impedances of equivalent *T*-network are related with the impedances of π-network.

(*i*) **Conversion of a π-network into an equivalent T-network:** Let us assume that we know the impedances Z_A, Z_B and Z_C of π-network. The problem is to find the impedances of an equivalent *T*-network. Let them be Z_1, Z_2 and Z_3. If the two networks are equivalent then

$$(Z_{1oc})_T = (Z_{1oc})_\pi$$

or
$$Z_1 + Z_3 = \frac{Z_A(Z_B + Z_C)}{Z_A + Z_B + Z_C} \quad \text{...(9.36)}$$

and
$$(Z_{2oc})_T = (Z_{2oc})_\pi$$

or
$$Z_2 + Z_3 = \frac{Z_C(Z_A + Z_B)}{Z_A + Z_B + Z_C} \quad \text{...(9.37)}$$

and
$$(Z_{1sc})_T = (Z_{1sc})_\pi$$

or
$$Z_1 + \frac{Z_2 Z_3}{Z_2 + Z_3} = \frac{Z_A Z_B}{Z_A + Z_B} \quad \text{...(9.38)}$$

and
$$(Z_{2sc})_T = (Z_{2sc})_\pi$$

or
$$Z_2 + \frac{Z_1 Z_3}{Z_1 + Z_3} = \frac{Z_B Z_C}{Z_B + Z_C} \quad \text{...(9.39)}$$

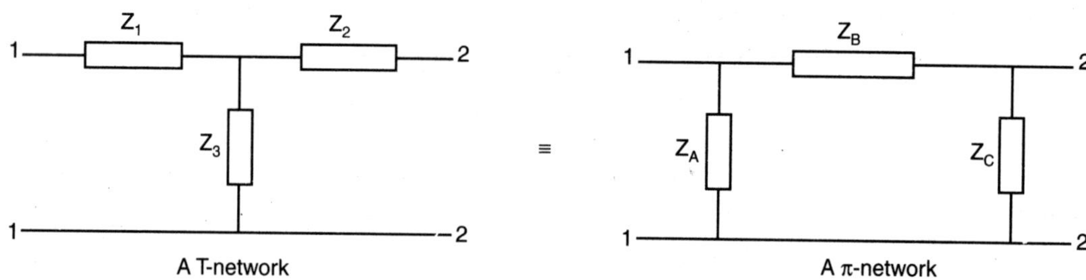

Fig. 9.8

Subtracting eqns. (9.38) from (9.36) we get

$$Z_3 - \frac{Z_2 Z_3}{Z_2 + Z_3} = \frac{Z_A(Z_B + Z_C)}{Z_A + Z_B + Z_C} - \frac{Z_A Z_B}{Z_A + Z_B}$$

$$\frac{Z_3^2}{Z_2 + Z_3} = \frac{Z_A^2 Z_C}{(Z_A + Z_B)(Z_A + Z_B + Z_C)} \quad \text{...(9.40)}$$

Multiplying eqns. (9.37) and (9.40) we get

$$Z_3^2 = \left(\frac{Z_C Z_A}{Z_A + Z_B + Z_C}\right)^2$$

$$\therefore \quad Z_3 = \frac{Z_C Z_A}{Z_A + Z_B + Z_C} \quad \text{...(9.41)}$$

Substituting the expression for Z_3 in eqns. (9.36) and (9.37) we get

$$Z_1 = \frac{Z_A Z_B}{Z_A + Z_B + Z_C} \quad \text{...(9.42)}$$

and

$$Z_2 = \frac{Z_B Z_C}{Z_A + Z_B + Z_C} \quad \text{...(9.43)}$$

Determination of Impedances of π-network

Multiplying eqns. (9.37) and (9.38) we have

$$(Z_2 + Z_3)\left(Z_1 + \frac{Z_2 Z_3}{Z_2 + Z_3}\right) = \frac{Z_A Z_B Z_C}{Z_A + Z_B + Z_C}$$

or

$$Z_1 Z_2 + Z_2 Z_3 + Z_3 Z_1 = \frac{Z_A Z_B Z_C}{Z_A + Z_B + Z_C} \quad \text{...(9.44)}$$

Dividing eqns. (9.44) by (9.43), (9.41) and (9.42) one by one we get

$$Z_A = \frac{Z_1 Z_2 + Z_2 Z_3 + Z_3 Z_1}{Z_2} \quad \text{...(9.45)}$$

$$Z_B = \frac{Z_1 Z_2 + Z_2 Z_3 + Z_3 Z_1}{Z_3} \quad \text{...(9.46)}$$

$$Z_C = \frac{Z_1Z_2 + Z_2Z_3 + Z_3Z_1}{Z_1} \qquad ...(9.47)$$

9.9. REDUCTION OF A COMPLICATED NETWORK INTO 'T' AND π NETWORK

Many circuits are so complicated that it is often difficult to analyse their external behaviour by simple procedure. Great simplification results when it is reduced to an equivalent T or π network. We have a general theorem in this connection which states that "*any linear bilateral passive network can be represented at a single frequency by a T or π network.*"

A complicated network, with 1, 1, as two input and 2, 2. two output terminals is shown in Fig. 9.9 by a closed box.

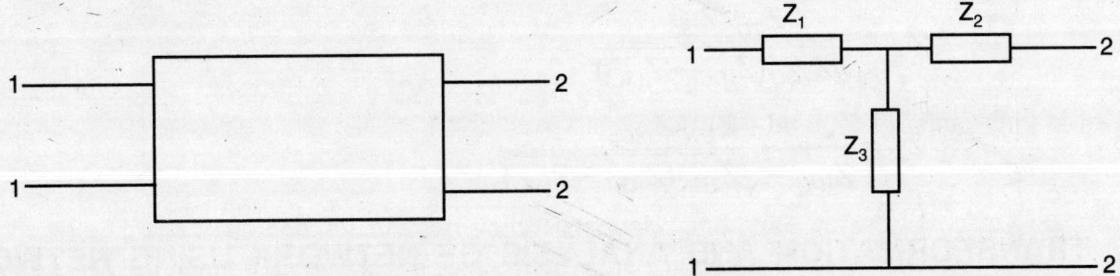

Fig. 9.9

Let Z_{1OC}, Z_{2OC}, Z_{1SC} and Z_{2SC} be the impedances of the complicated network. Let the impedances of equivalent T network be Z_1, Z_2 and Z_3. Then we have

$$(Z_{1OC})_T = Z_{1OC}, \quad (Z_{2OC})_T = Z_{2OC}, \quad (Z_{1SC})_T = Z_{1SC}, \quad (Z_{2SC})_T = Z_{2SC}$$

These conditions lead to the following equations.

$$Z_1 + Z_3 = Z_{1OC} \qquad ...(9.48)$$

$$Z_2 + Z_3 = Z_{2OC} \qquad ...(9.49)$$

$$Z_1 + \frac{Z_2Z_3}{Z_2 + Z_3} = Z_{1SC} \qquad ...(9.50)$$

$$Z_2 + \frac{Z_1Z_3}{Z_1 + Z_3} = Z_{2SC} \qquad ...(9.51)$$

Subtracting eqns. (9.50) from (9.48) we get

$$Z_3 - \frac{Z_2Z_3}{Z_2 + Z_3} = Z_{1OC} - Z_{1SC} \qquad ...(9.52)$$

$$\frac{Z_3^2}{Z_2 + Z_3} = Z_{1OC} - Z_{1SC}$$

$$Z_3^2 = (Z_{1OC} - Z_{1SC})(Z_2 + Z_3)$$

$$= (Z_{1OC} - Z_{1SC})Z_{2OC}$$

$$\therefore \qquad Z_3 = \pm\sqrt{Z_{2OC}(Z_{1OC} - Z_{1SC})} \qquad ...(9.53)$$

Substituting the expression for Z_3 in eqns. (9.48) and (9.49) we get

$$Z_1 = Z_{1OC} \pm \sqrt{Z_{2OC}(Z_{1OC} - Z_{1SC})} \qquad ...(9.54)$$

$$Z_2 = Z_{2OC} \pm \sqrt{Z_{2OC}(Z_{1OC} - Z_{1SC})} \qquad ...(9.55)$$

Thus the impedance of a T network equivalent to a complicated network can be calculated from eqns. (9.53), (9.54), (9.55).

Using similar procedure, one can obtain the impedance Z_A, Z_B and Z_C of an equivalent π network as,

$$Z_A = \frac{Z_{2OC}Z_{1SC}}{Z_{2OC} - \sqrt{Z_{2OC}(Z_{1OC} - Z_{1SC})}} \qquad ...(9.56)$$

$$Z_B = \frac{Z_{2OC}Z_{1SC}}{\sqrt{Z_{2OC}(Z_{1OC} - Z_{1SC})}} \qquad ...(9.57)$$

$$Z_C = \frac{Z_{2OC}Z_{1SC}}{Z_{1OC} - \sqrt{Z_{2OC}(Z_{1OC} - Z_{1SC})}} \qquad ...(9.58)$$

9.10. TRANSFORMATION AND ANALYSIS OF NETWORK USING NETWORK THEOREMS

Network theorems are powerful tools for solving complicated network problems. Through these theorems, we directly analyse some network and can look at the external behaviour of others by transforming it into other network. Some important theorems frequently used in circuit analysis are described in this section.

9.10.1 Superposition Theorem

This theorem states that "*in any linear network containing bilateral linear impedances and current sources, the current flowing in any element is the algebraic sum of currents that are separately caused to flow in the element by each energy source.*"

To prove this theorem let us consider a *T*-network containing two energy sources E_1 and E_2 as shown in the Fig. 9.10(a).

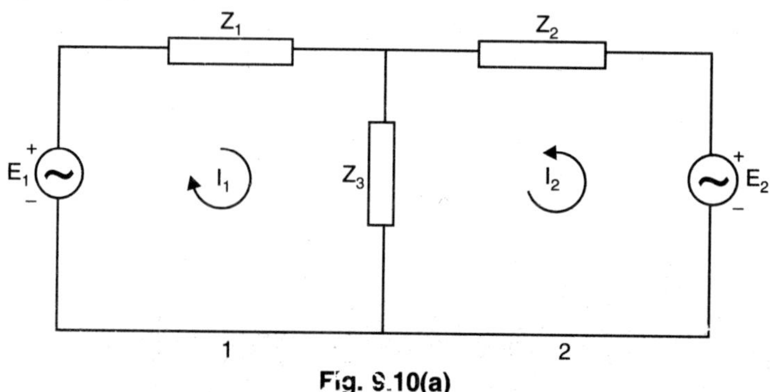

Fig. 9.10(a)

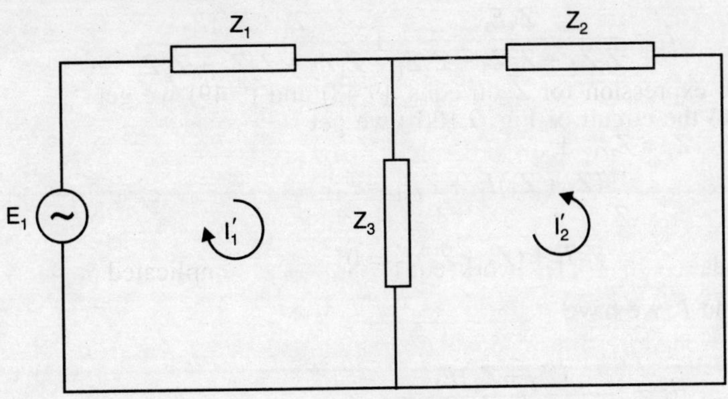

Fig. 9.10(b)

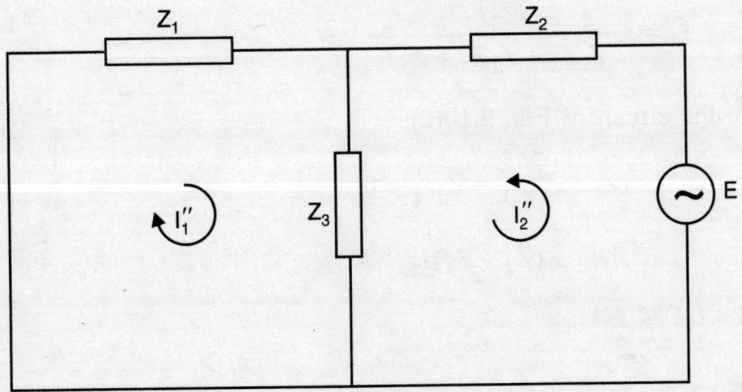

Fig. 9.10(c)

Let I_1 and I_2 be the cyclic current in meshes 1 and 2 respectively. Let I_1' and I_2' be the currents in meshes 1 and 2 caused by source E_1 alone and I_1'' and I_2'' be those in the two meshes caused by source E_2 alone. Then according to theorem,

$$I_1 = I_1'' + I_1'' \qquad \ldots(9.59)$$

$$I_2 = I_2' + I_2''$$

Let us establish current voltage equations for different meshes and find out the values of current I_1 and I_2, I_1' and I_2', I_1'' and I_2''. From Fig. 9.10(a)

$$(Z_1 + Z_3)I_1 + Z_3 I_2 = E_1 \qquad \ldots(9.60)$$

$$Z_3 I_1 + (Z_2 + Z_3)I_2 = E_2 \qquad \ldots(9.61)$$

Solving for I_1 and I_2 we get

$$I_1 = \frac{(Z_1 + Z_3)E_1}{Z_1 Z_2 + Z_2 Z_3 + Z_3 Z_1} - \frac{Z_3 E_2}{Z_1 Z_2 + Z_2 Z_3 + Z_3 Z_1} \qquad \ldots(9.62)$$

$$I_1 = \frac{Z_3 E_1}{Z_1 Z_2 + Z_2 Z_3 + Z_3 Z_1} + \frac{(Z_1 + Z_3) E_2}{Z_1 Z_2 + Z_2 Z_3 + Z_3 Z_1} \quad \text{...(9.63)}$$

Applying *KVL* to the circuit of Fig. 9.10(b) we get

$$(Z_1 + Z_3) I_1' + Z_3 I_1' = E_1 \quad \text{...(9.64)}$$

$$Z_3 I_1' + (Z_2 + Z_3) I_2' = 0 \quad \text{...(9.65)}$$

Solving for I_1' and I_2' we have

$$I_1' = \frac{(Z_2 + Z_3) E_1}{Z_1 Z_2 + Z_2 Z_3 + Z_3 Z_1} \quad \text{...(9.66)}$$

$$I_2' = -\frac{Z_3 E_1}{Z_1 Z_2 + Z_2 Z_3 + Z_3 Z_1} \quad \text{...(9.67)}$$

Applying *KVL* to the circuit of Fig. 9.10(c)

$$(Z_1 + Z_3) I_1'' + Z_3 I_2'' = 0 \quad \text{...(9.68)}$$

$$Z_3 I_1'' + (Z_2 + Z_3) I_2'' = E_2 \quad \text{...(9.69)}$$

Solving for I_1'' and I_2'' we get

$$I_1'' = -\frac{Z_3 E_2}{Z_1 Z_2 + Z_2 Z_3 + Z_3 Z_1} \quad \text{...(9.70)}$$

$$I_2'' = \frac{(Z_1 + Z_3) E_1}{Z_1 Z_2 + Z_2 Z_3 + Z_3 Z_1} \quad \text{...(9.71)}$$

It can easily be seen that

$$I_1' + I_1'' = I_1 \quad \text{and} \quad I_2' + I_2'' = I_2 \quad \text{...(9.72)}$$

This proves the superposition theorem.

9.10.2 Reciprocity Theorem

The theorem states that "*in any linear network, containing bilateral and linear impedances and energy sources, the ratio of voltages E introduced in one mesh to the current I in any other mesh is the same if the position of E and I are interchanged with other energy sources removed*". This ratio is referred to as the transfer impedance Z_{Tij} between the two loops i and j.

To prove this theorem, let us consider a network containing two loops as shown in Fig. 9.11(a). Let the voltage in loop 1 be E_1 and the corresponding current in loop 2 be I_2. Then

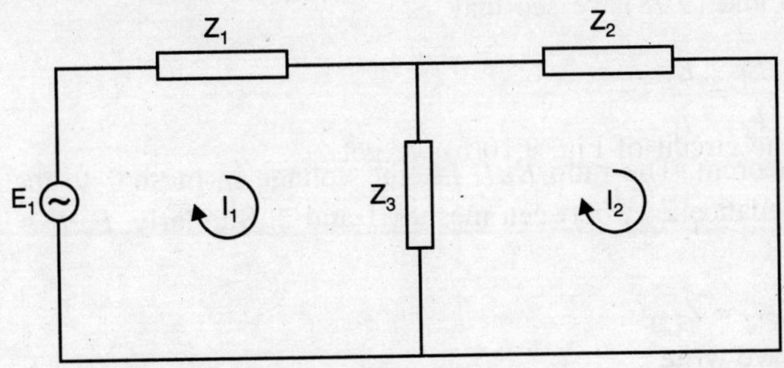

Fig. 9.11(a)

$$(Z_1 + Z_3)I_1 - Z_3 I_2 = E_1 \quad \text{...(9.73)}$$

$$-Z_3 I_1 + (Z_2 + Z_3)I_2 = 0 \quad \text{...(9.74)}$$

Substituting the value of I_1 from eqns. (9.74) in (9.73) and solving for E_1 we get

$$E_1 = \frac{(Z_1 + Z_3)(Z_2 + Z_3)I_2}{Z_3} - Z_3 I_2$$

$$\frac{E_1}{I_2} = \frac{Z_1 Z_2 + Z_2 Z_3 + Z_3 Z_1}{Z_3} \quad \text{...(9.75)}$$

Now let us change the position of source and current. Let a source E_2' in loop 2 causes a current I_1' in loop 1 and I_2' in loop 2 as shown in Fig. 9.11(b).

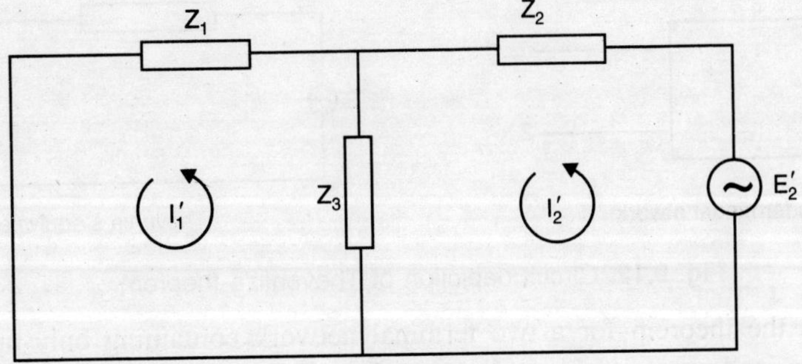

Fig. 9.11(b)

The current voltage equations for the circuit are

$$(Z_1 + Z_3)I_1' - Z_3 I_2' = 0 \quad \text{...(9.76)}$$

$$-Z_3 I_1' + (Z_2 + Z_3)I_2' = E_2' \quad \text{...(9.77)}$$

Substituting I_2' from eqns. (9.76) in (9.77) and solving for E_2' we get

$$\frac{E_2'}{I_1'} = \frac{Z_1 Z_2 + Z_2 Z_3 + Z_3 Z_1}{Z_3} \quad \text{...(9.78)}$$

From eqns. (9.75) and (9.78) we see that

$$\frac{E_1}{I_2} = \frac{E_2'}{I_1'}$$

This proves the theorem. The ratio E_1/I_2 *i.e.* the voltage in mesh 1 to the current in mesh 2 is termed as transfer impedance Z_{T12} between meshes 1 and 2. Similarly, $E_2'/I_1' = Z_{T21}$. Thus according to this theorem

$$Z_{T12} = Z_{T21}$$

On generalization, we write

$$Z_{Tij} = Z_{Tji} \qquad \text{...(9.79)}$$

9.10.3 Thevenin's Theorem

The theorem states that:

"*any two terminal linear network containing energy sources and impedances is equivalent to a circuit consisting of a voltage source E′ having a series impedance Z′, where E′ is the open circuit voltage between the terminals of the network and Z′ is the impedance measured between the terminal with all energy sources removed and replaced by their internal impedances*".

Since this theorem reduces a network containing energy sources into voltage source equivalent circuit, hence it is often referred to as "*theorem for voltage source equivalent circuit*".

We can depict this theorem diagrammatically as follows:

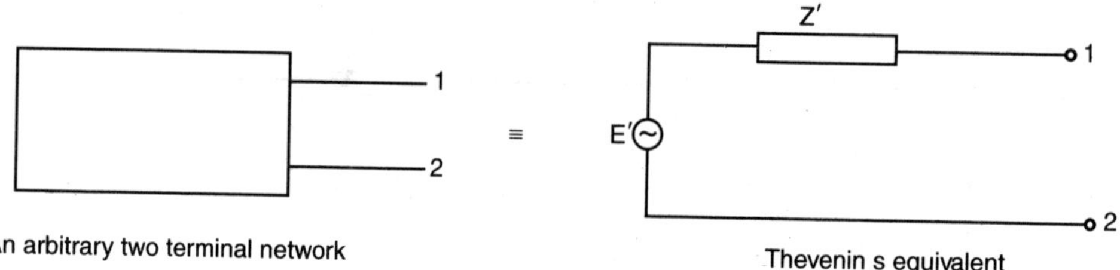

Fig. 9.12. Circuit depiction of Thevenin's theorem.

Proof: Let us prove the theorem for a two terminal network containing only one energy source. For analysis we put a load across the output terminals of this network as shown in the figure.

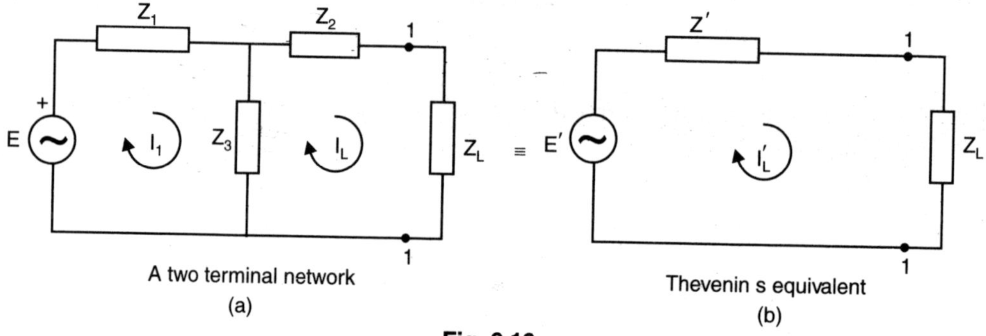

Fig. 9.13

We know that a particular linear network can always be replaced by a T network at a single frequency. Let the impedances of this equivalent T network be Z_1, Z_2 and Z_3. Then the given network is equivalent to that shown in Fig. 9.13(a). Let I_1 and I_L be the currents in the two loops of the T network. Applying KVL to these loops, we get

$$(Z_1 + Z_3)I_1 - Z_3I_L = E \quad \text{...(9.80)}$$

$$-Z_3I_1 + (Z_2 + Z_3 + Z_L)I_L = 0 \quad \text{...(9.81)}$$

Substituting I_1 from eqns. (9.81) in (9.80) and solving for I_L we get

$$I_L = \frac{Z_3E}{(Z_1 + Z_3)(Z_2 + Z_L) + Z_1Z_3} \quad \text{...(9.82)}$$

By definition of E' and Z' we have

$$E' = \left(\frac{E}{Z_1 + Z_3}\right)Z_3, \text{ and } Z' = Z_2 + \frac{Z_1Z_3}{Z_1 + Z_3} = \frac{Z_1Z_2 + Z_2Z_3 + Z_3Z_1}{Z_1 + Z_3}$$

From Thevenin's equivalent, the current in the load impedance is

$$I_L' = \frac{E'}{Z' + Z_L} = \frac{EZ_3}{Z_1Z_2 + Z_2Z_3 + Z_3Z_1 + (Z_1 + Z_3)Z_L} \quad \text{...(9.83)}$$

From eqns. (9.82) and (9.83)

$$I_L = I_L'$$

This proves the theorem.

9.10.4 Norton's Theorem

The theorem states that "*any two terminal linear network containing energy sources and impedances is equivalent to circuit consisting of a current source I_{SC} with an impedance Z' in parallel with it, where I_{SC} is the short circuited current between the terminals of the network and Z' is the impedance measured between the terminals with all energy sources replaced by their impedances*". The equivalent circuit so obtained is termed as "*current equivalent circuit*".

Taking above meanings of I_{SC} and Z', we can depict this theorem diagrammatically as shown in Fig. 9.14.

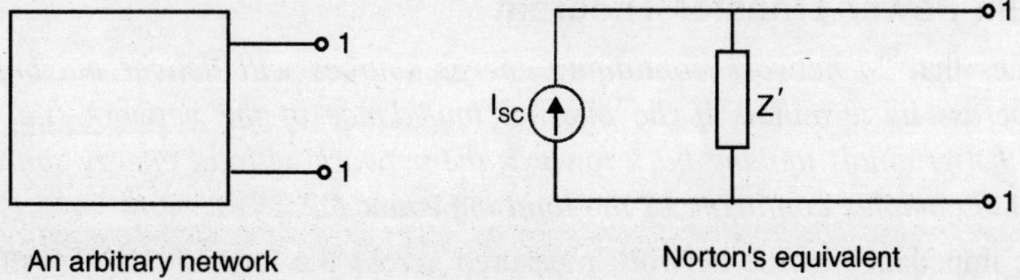

Fig. 9.14

Proof: Let the terminals of the network 1, 1, be connected to a load Z_L as shown in the Fig. 9.15(a). According to Thevenin's theorem, the circuit left to terminals 1, 1 is equivalent to a voltage source E' with an impedance Z' in series with it, where E' is the open circuit voltage across the terminals 1, 1 and Z' is the impedance measured across the terminals 1, 1 with source of the network replaced by its impedance. The equivalent circuit of the network becomes as shown in Fig. 9.15(b). The load current in this circuit is

$$I_L = \frac{E'}{Z' + Z_L} \qquad ...(9.84)$$

By definition, $$I_{SC} = \frac{E'}{Z'} \qquad ...(9.85)$$

In the Norton's equivalent Fig. 9.15(c), the short circuit current I_{SC} is divided into two branches one containing load impedance Z_L and the other containing impedance Z'.

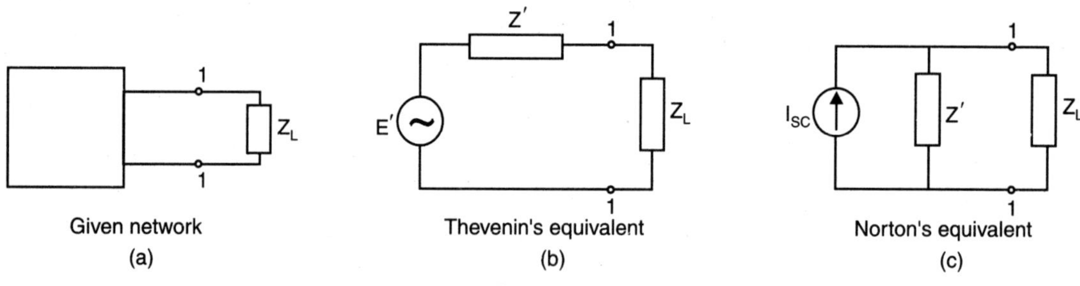

Fig. 9.15

The load current in Norton's equivalent is

$$I'_L = I_{SC} \frac{Z'}{Z' + Z_L}$$

$$= \frac{E'}{Z'} \cdot \frac{Z'}{Z' + Z_L}$$

$$= \frac{E'}{Z' + Z_L}$$

$$= I_L$$

This proves the Norton's theorem.

9.10.5 Maximum Power Transfer Theorem

This theorem states that "*a network containing energy sources will deliver maximum power to a load connected across its terminals if the internal impedance of the network (i.e. the impedance measured across the terminals looking back towards the network with all energy sources replaced by their impedances) is complex conjugate of the load impedance*".

Let Z' be the impedance of the network measured across the terminals 1, 1 with load removed and all energy sources removed by their impedances. According to Thevenin's theorem the network left of terminal 1, 1 is equivalent to a source of e.m.f. E' and a series impedance Z', where E' is open circuit voltage across terminals 1, 1 and Z' is the impedance as described. Thus the given network is equivalent to a network shown in Fig. 9.16(b).

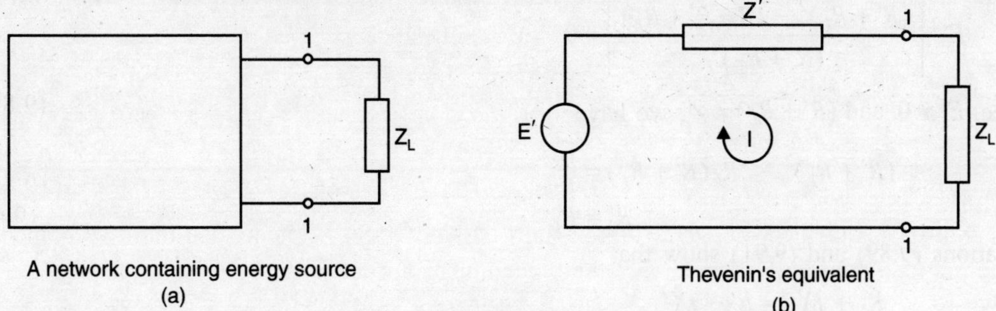

Fig. 9.16

We have to prove that $Z_L = Z^{*\prime}$. The current I flowing through the load in the circuit of Fig. 9.16(b) is

$$I = \frac{E'}{Z' + Z_L} = \frac{E'}{(R' + jX') + (R_L + jX_L)} = \frac{E'}{(R' + R_L) + j(X' + X_L)} \quad ...(9.86)$$

Where $Z' = R' + jX'$ and $Z_L = R_L + jX_L$, R' and R_L being the resistive and X' and X_L the reactive parts of the impedances Z' and Z_L respectively. Since the reactive part of impedance does not consume power, the power delivered to the load is

$$P = I^2 R_L = \left[\frac{E'^2}{(R' + R_L)^2 + (X' + X_L)^2}\right] R_L \quad ...(9.87)$$

If maximum power is delivered to a particular value of the load, then at this load,

$$\frac{\partial P}{\partial X_L} = 0 \quad \text{and} \quad \frac{\partial P}{\partial R_L} = 0 \quad ...(9.88)$$

Applying the condition $\frac{\partial P}{\partial X_L} = 0$ to eqn. (9.88) we get

$$\frac{2E'^2 R_L (X' + X_L)}{\left[(R' + R_L)^2 + (X' + X_L)^2\right]^2} = 0$$

Since E' and R_L are not zero and denominator is finite we must have

$$X' = -X_L \quad ...(9.89)$$

In view of eqns. (9.89) and (9.87) becomes

$$P = \frac{E'^2 R_L}{(R' + R_L)^2} \quad ...(9.90)$$

Applying the condition $\frac{\partial P}{\partial R_L} = 0$ to eqn. (9.90) we get

$$E'^2\left[\frac{(R'+R_L)^2-2R_L(R'+R_L)}{(R'+R_L)^4}\right]=0$$

Since $E' \neq 0$, and $(R'+R_L) \neq \infty$, we have

$$(R'+R_L)^2-2R_L(R'+R_L)=0$$

$$R'=R_L \quad ...(9.91)$$

Equations (9.89) and (9.91) show that

$$R_L + jX_L = R' - jX'$$

or

$$Z_L = Z'^* \quad ...(9.92)$$

This proves the theorem.

The maximum power delivered to the load is

$$P_{max}=\frac{E'^2}{4R_L}=\frac{E'^2}{4R'} \quad ...(9.93)$$

Solved Examples

***Example* 1:** *Calculate the current flowing through the 3Ω resistor in the network given below. Also obtain the power supplied by the tow voltage sources.*

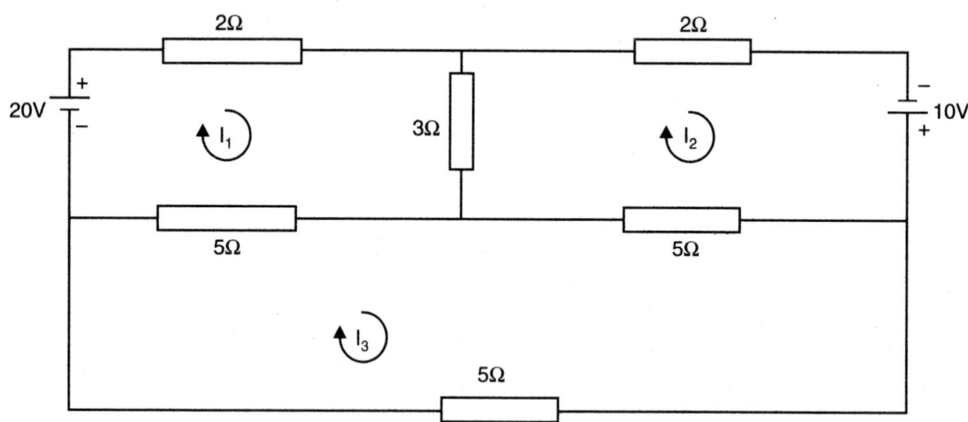

Fig. 9.17

Solution: Let currents I_1, I_2 and I_3 flow through loops 1, 2, and 3 respectively. Applying *KVL* to these loops we get

$$10I_1-3I_2-5I_3 = 20 \quad ...(1)$$

$$-3I_1 + 10I_2 - 5I_3 = 10 \quad ...(2)$$

$$-5I_1 - 5I_2 + 15I_3 = 0 \quad ...(3)$$

Solving these equations we get

$$I_1 = \frac{640}{143}A,\ I_2 = \frac{530}{143}A,\ I_3 = \frac{1070}{429}A$$

Current through 3Ω resistor

$$I_1 - I_2 = \frac{110}{143} = 0.77A$$

Power supplied by source 1

$$P_1 = VI = 20 \times \frac{640}{143} = 89.5 \text{ W}$$

Power supplied by source 2

$$P_2 = 10 \times \frac{530}{143} = 37 \text{ W}$$

***Example* 2:** *Obtain the equivalent π-network of the following T-network.*

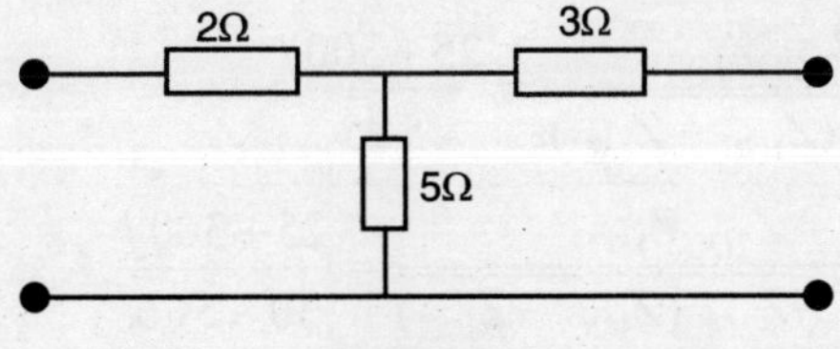

Fig. 9.18

Solution: The impedances of π-network are given by

$$R_A = \frac{R_1R_2 + R_2R_3 + R_3R_1}{R_2} = \frac{2\times3+3\times5+5\times2}{3} = \frac{31}{3}\Omega$$

$$R_B = \frac{R_1R_2 + R_2R_3 + R_3R_1}{R_3} = \frac{31}{5}\Omega$$

$$R_C = \frac{R_1R_2 + R_2R_3 + R_3R_1}{R_1} = \frac{31}{2}\Omega$$

***Example* 3:** *Obtain the impedance of equivalent T-network given below.*

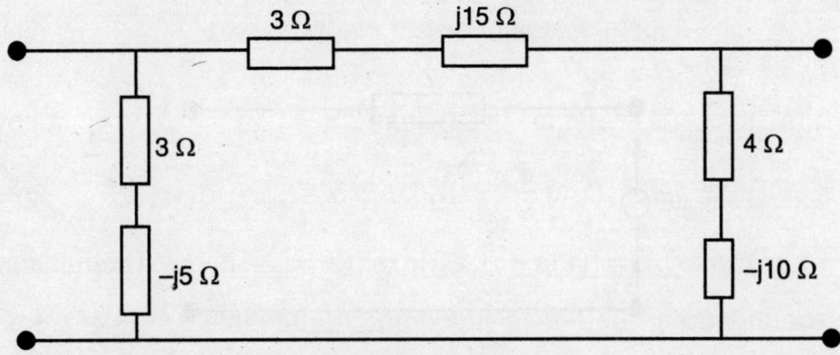

Fig. 9.19

Solution: $Z_A = 3 - j5, \quad Z_B = 3 + j15, \quad Z_C = 4 - j10$

$$Z_1 = \frac{Z_A Z_B}{Z_A + Z_B + Z_C} = \frac{(3-j5)(3+j15)}{10} = 8.4 + j3$$

$$Z_2 = \frac{Z_B Z_C}{Z_A + Z_B + Z_C} = 16.2 + j3$$

$$Z_3 = \frac{Z_C Z_A}{Z_A + Z_B + Z_C} = 3.8 - j5$$

Example 4: *A box consisting of impedances gave following measurements at frequency 50Hz.* $Z_{1OC} = 30 + 0j$, $Z_{2OC} = 5 + 10j$, $Z_{1SC} = 25 + 10j$. *Construct the equivalent π-network.*

Solution: Let the impedances of equivalent π-network be Z_A, Z_B and Z_C.

$$Z_A = \frac{Z_{2OC} Z_{1SC}}{Z_{2OC} - \sqrt{Z_{2OC}(Z_{OC} - Z_{1SC})}} = \frac{25 + 300j}{5(1+\sqrt{5}) + 10j}$$

$$Z_B = \frac{Z_{2OC} Z_{1SC}}{\sqrt{Z_{2OC}(Z_{1OC} - Z_{1SC})}} = \frac{25 + 300j}{5\sqrt{5}}$$

$$Z_C = \frac{Z_{2OC} Z_{1SC}}{Z_{1OC} - \sqrt{Z_{2OC}(Z_{1OC} - Z_{1SC})}} = \frac{25 + 300j}{30 - 5\sqrt{5}}$$

Example 5: *Find the voltage source equivalent circuit of the following network.*

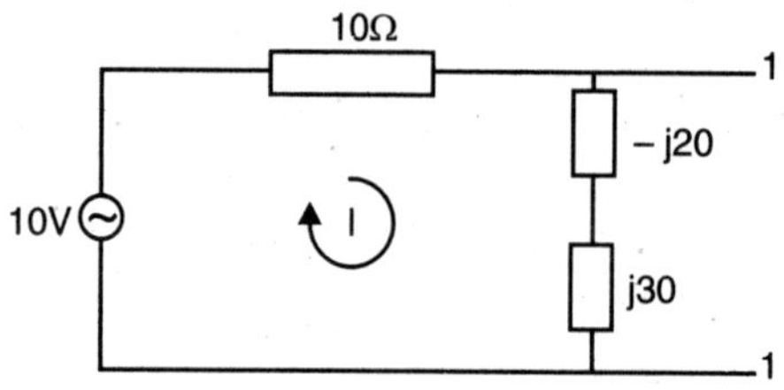

Fig. 9.20(a)

Solution: Let the voltage source equivalent (Thevenin's equivalent) of the given circuit be as shown below.

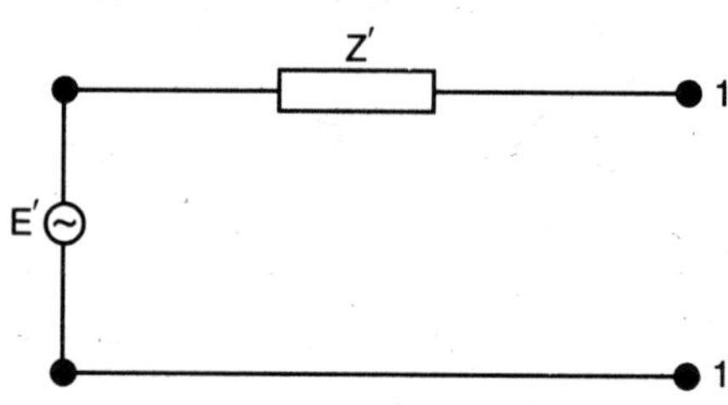

Fig. 9.20(b)

Impedance across terminals 1,1 is

$$Z' = \frac{10(j30 - j20)}{10 + (j30 - j20)} = \frac{j100}{10 + j10} = 5 + j5 = 5\sqrt{2}\angle 45$$

Thevenin's voltage $E' = \left(\frac{10}{10 + j10}\right)(j10) = 5 + j5 = 5\sqrt{2}\angle 45$

***Example* 6:** *Use Norton's theorem to find the current through the load.*

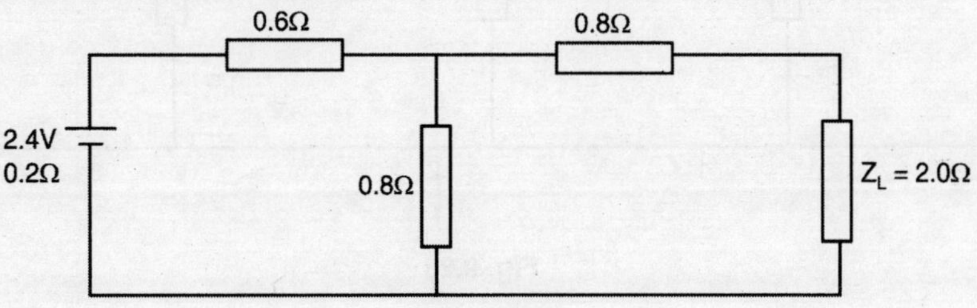

Fig. 9.21

Solution: Thevenin's voltage $E' = \left(\frac{2.4}{0.2 + 0.6 + 0.8}\right)(0.8) = 1.2\text{ V}$

Impedance $Z' = 0.8 + \frac{0.8 \times 0.8}{0.8 + 0.8} = 1.2\ \Omega$

Thevenin's equivalent is shown below in Fig. 9.22(a).

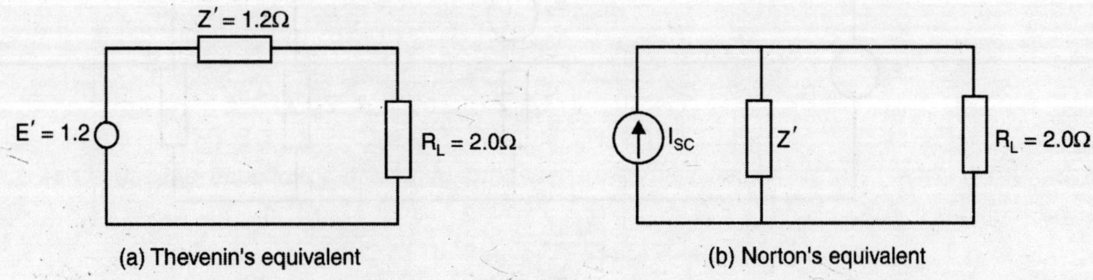

(a) Thevenin's equivalent (b) Norton's equivalent

Fig. 9.22

Short circuit current $I_{SC} = \frac{1.2}{1.2} = 1A$

Norton's equivalent is shown in Fig. 9.22(b). The current through the load is

$$I_L = I_{SC}\frac{Z'}{Z' + Z_L} = 1.0\left(\frac{1.2}{1.2 + 2.0}\right) = \frac{3}{8} = 0.375A$$

***Example* 6:** *Find the voltage source equivalent circuit for the network shown below.*

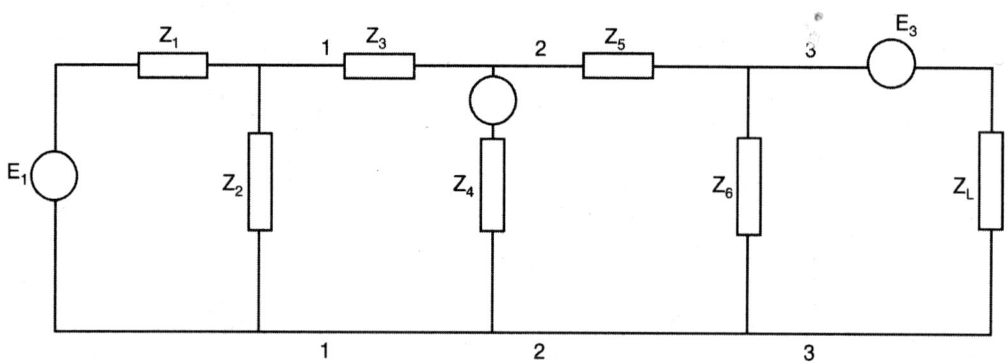

Fig. 9.23

Solution: First of all let us consider the circuit left to the terminal 1, 1. This can be replaced by a source E' with a series impedance Z' such that

$$E' = \left(\frac{E_1}{Z_1 + Z_2}\right) Z_2 \text{ and } Z' = \frac{Z_1 Z_2}{Z_1 + Z_2} \quad ...(9.94)$$

The equivalent circuit then becomes as shown in Fig. 9.24.

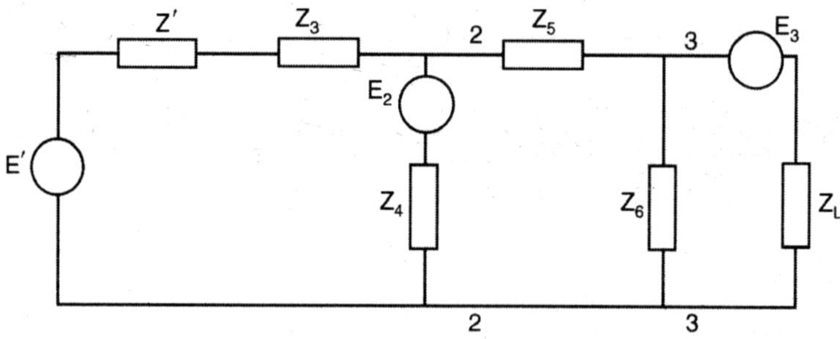

Fig. 9.24

Now consider the circuit left to terminals 2, 2. This can be replaced by a source E'' with a series impedance Z'' such that

$$E'' = E_2 + \left(\frac{E' - E_2}{Z' + Z_3 + Z_4}\right) Z_4 \quad ...(9.95)$$

and
$$Z'' = \frac{(Z' + Z_3)Z_4}{Z' + Z_3 + Z_4} \quad ...(9.96)$$

The equivalent circuit then becomes as shown in Fig. 9.25.

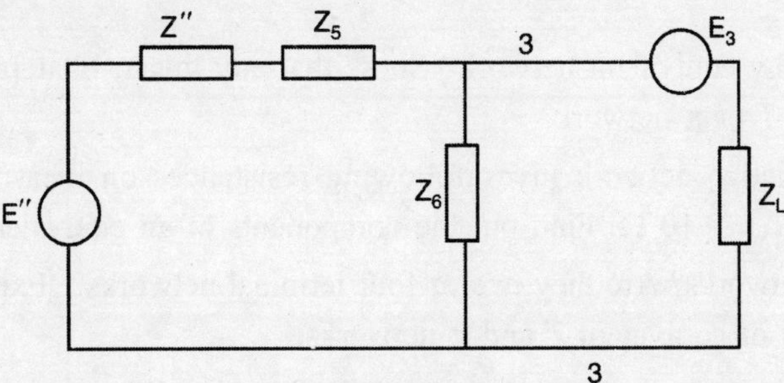

Fig. 9.25

Now let us consider the loop left to the terminals 3, 3. This can be replaced by a source E''' with a series impedance Z''' such that

$$E''' = \left(\frac{E''}{Z'' + Z_5 + Z_6}\right) Z_6 \quad \text{...(9.97)}$$

$$Z''' = \frac{(Z'' + Z_5)Z_6}{Z''' + Z_5 + Z_6} \quad \text{...(9.98)}$$

Now the equivalent circuit becomes as shown in the Fig. 9.26, which in turn can be represented by the circuit shown in Fig. 9.27 in which $E_4 = E''' + E_3$.

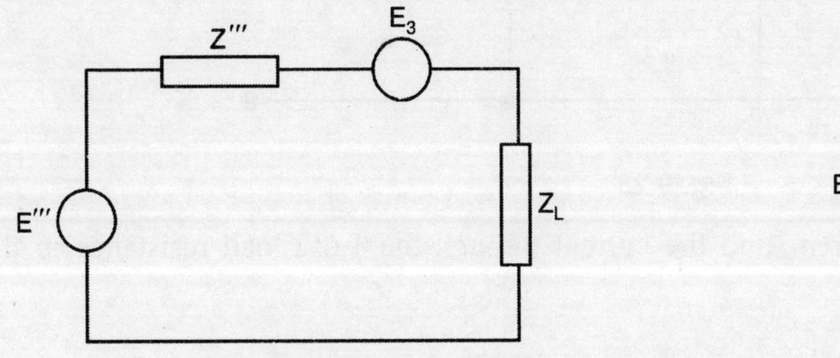

Fig. 9.26

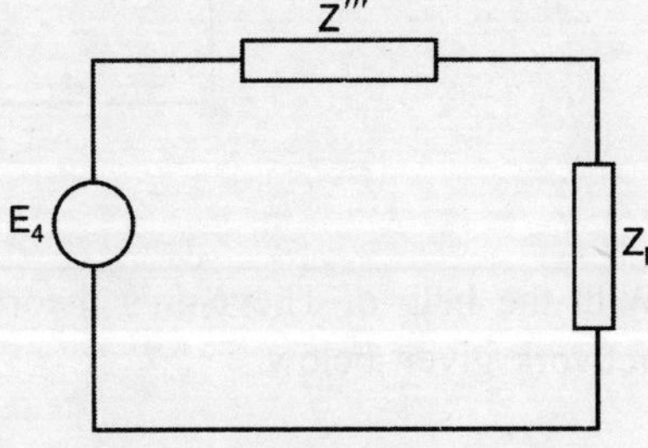

Fig. 9.27

QUESTIONS AND PROBLEMS

1. Explain clearly what is meant by network analysis and network transformation. Discuss briefly the common methods used for this purpose.
2. Explain the terms in the context of network analysis: *network, branch, node, mesh and loop.* What is meant by *active* and *passive* and *linear network?*
3. Explain *mesh, mutual, input and transfer impedance* in a network. What is meant by *equivalent* and *symmetrical networks?*

4. What do you mean by circuit analysis? How are the Kirchoff's laws employed in circuit analysis?

5. What do you mean by equivalent network? Show that any linear, bilateral passive network can T or π network.

6. A four terminal resistive network gives following resistances on measurement: $Z_{1OC} = 20\Omega$, $Z_{2OC} = 20\ \Omega$, and $Z_{1SC} = 10\ \Omega$. Find out the components of an equivalent T-network.

7. What are T and π networks? Are they two or four terminal networks? Explain and find relations between impedances of equivalent T and π networks.

8. A transformer has two input and two output terminals with following measurements:

   $Z_{1OC} = 400 + j4000$, $Z_{2OC} = 100 + j1000$, $Z_{1SC} = 38 + j380$

   Determine the T equivalent network.

9. State and prove Thevenin's theorem. Find out the voltage equivalent circuit of the following two terminals network.

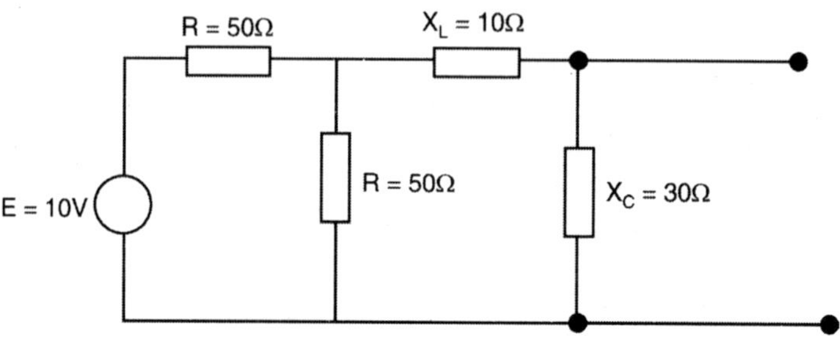

Fig. 9.28

10. With the help of Thevenin's theorem find the current through the 1.6Ω load resistance in the network given below.

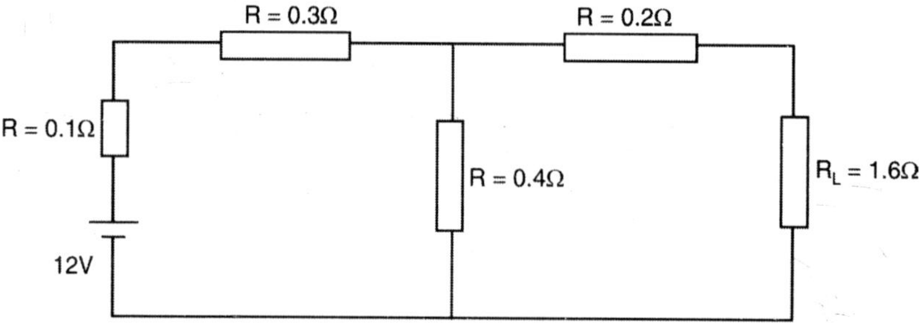

Fig. 9.29

11. Using Thevenin's theorem, calculate the current through the load impedance Z_L in the following network.

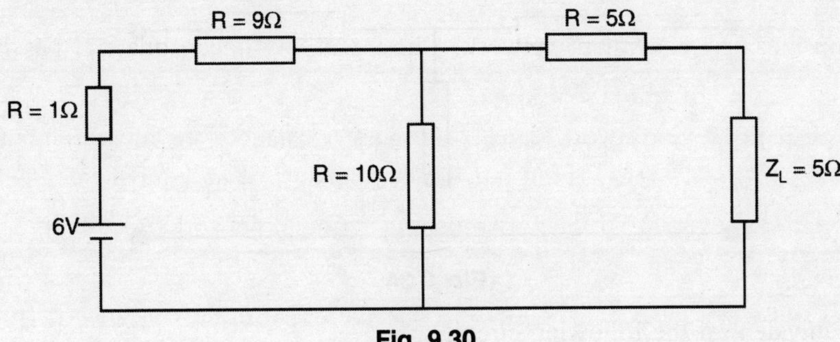

Fig. 9.30

12. Apply Norton's theorem to the circuit shown below to calculate the output potential drop.

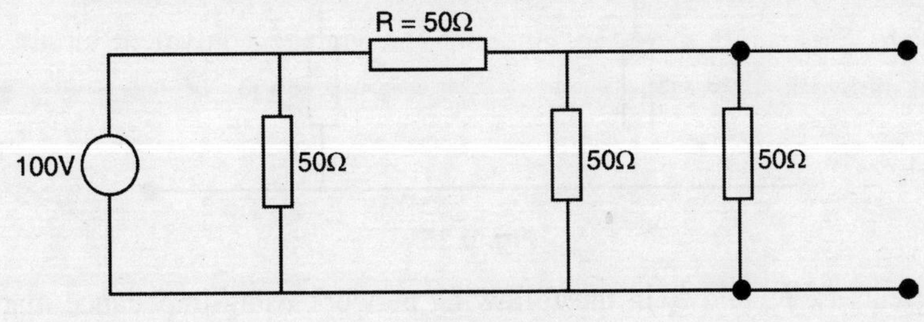

Fig. 9.31

13. Use Thevenin's theorem to find the current through the load impedance R_L.

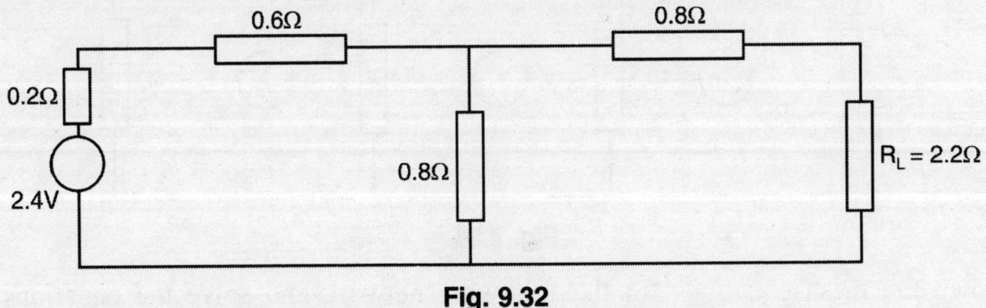

Fig. 9.32

14. State and prove maximum power transfer theorem. Find out the impedance and maximum power delivered to load in the following circuit.

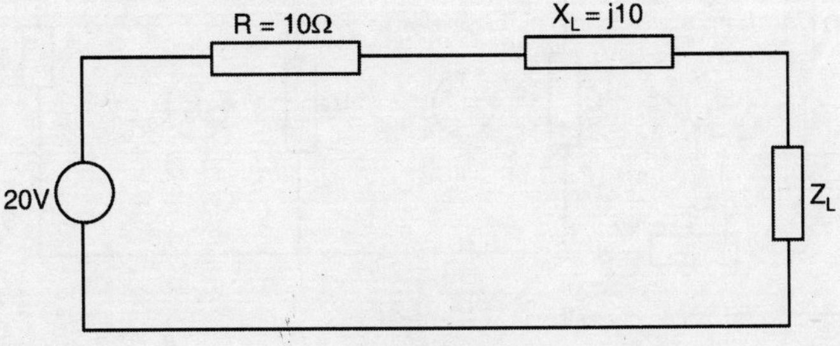

Fig. 9.33

15. What are T and π networks? Design a π-network equivalent to the following T-network.

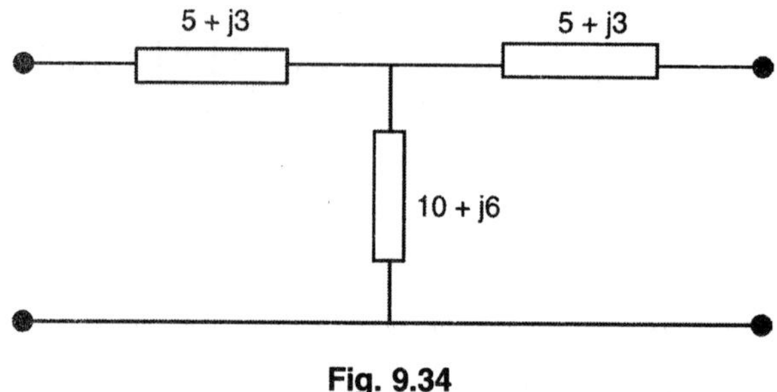

Fig. 9.34

16. Find the T equivalent of the following circuit.

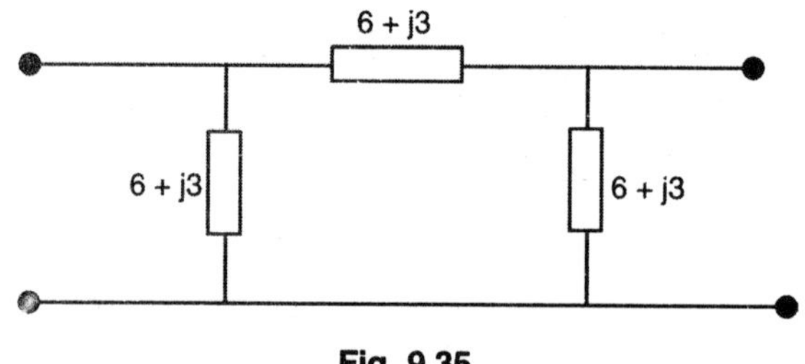

Fig. 9.35

17. Obtain the currents I_1, I_2, and I_3 in the following network using impedance matrix method.

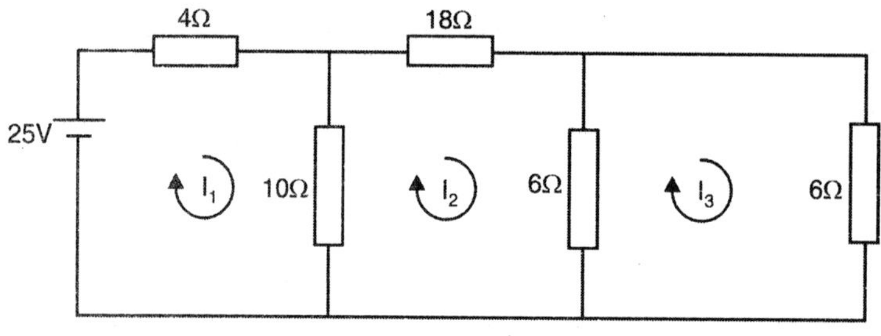

Fig. 9.36

18. Write down the mesh equations for the following network and solve the equations for I_1, I_2 and I_3.

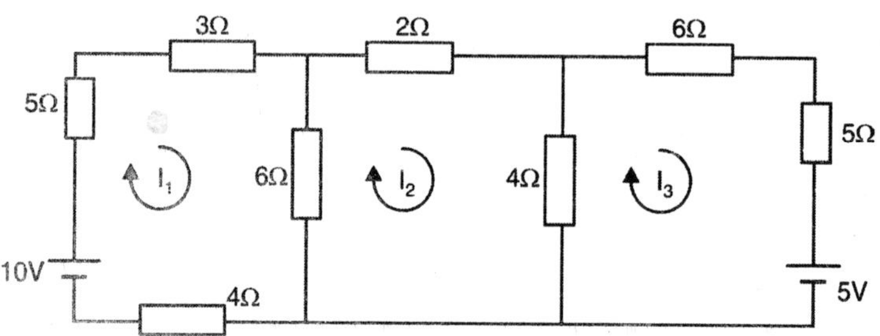

Fig. 9.37

10 CHAPTER

Coupled Circuits, Transformer and Electrical Filters

10.1. MAGNETICALLY COUPLED CIRCUITS

Consider two magnetically coupled circuits, one of which is fed with a voltage source $V_1 = V_{01}e^{j\omega t}$ and the other with $V_2 = V_{02}e^{j\omega t}$. Let $I_1 = I_{01}e^{j\omega t}$ and $I_2 = I_{02}e^{j\omega t}$ be the currents driven by these sources in their respective circuits. In order to apply the *KVL* in the two circuits, we have to assign proper sign to the mutual voltage. The sign of mutual voltage depends on the winding sense of the coupling coils. The polarity of the mutual voltage is determined by right hand flux rule.

"*Wrap the fingers of the right hand in the direction of the current, the thumb points in the direction of the flux. If the fluxes in the two coils aid each other, the sign of mutual voltage is the same as the self-induced voltage in the coil. On the other hand, if the fluxes in the coils oppose each other, the sign of mutual voltage is opposite to that of the self-induced voltage.*"

Let R_1 and L_1 be the resistance and inductance of the first coil respectively and the corresponding quantities for the second coil be R_2 and L_2. The mutual inductance of the couple coils is *M*.

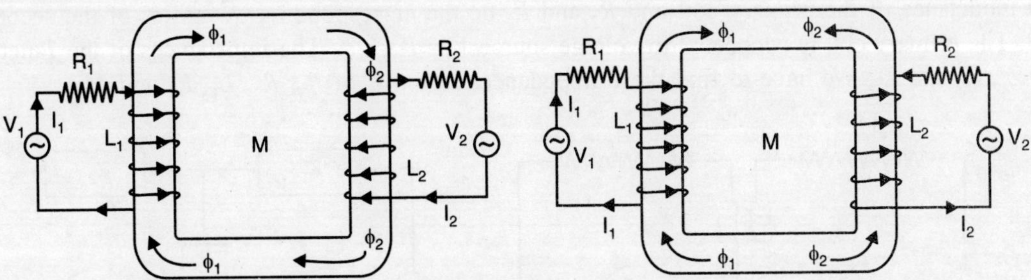

Fig. 10.1. Determination of sign of mutual voltage in positive and negative coupling.

Applying *KVL* to the first and second coils, we have

$$R_1I_1 + L_1\dot{I}_1 + M\dot{I}_2 = V_1 \quad \text{...(10.1)}$$

$$R_2I_2 + L_2\dot{I}_2 + M\dot{I}_1 = V_2 \quad \text{...(10.2)}$$

Substituting $I_1 = I_{01}\, e^{j\omega t}$ and $I_2 = I_{02}\, e^{j\omega t}$ in above equations we get

$$R_1 I_1 + j\omega L_1 + j\omega M I_2 = V_1 \qquad ...(10.3)$$

$$R_2 I_2 + j\omega L_2 + j\omega M I_1 = V_2 \qquad ...(10.4)$$

To simplify our analysis we assume that $V_2 = 0$. Then, from eqn. (10.4) we get

$$I_2 = \frac{j\omega M}{R_2 + j\omega L_2} I_1 \qquad ...(10.5)$$

Substituting this expression for I_2 in eqn. (10.3) we obtain

$$V_1 = I_1 \left[R_1 + j\omega L_1 + \frac{\omega^2 M^2}{R_2 + j\omega L_2} \right] \qquad ...(10.6)$$

Equation (10.6) shows that the coupling has increased the impedance of the first (primary) coil by amount $\frac{\omega^2 M^2}{R_2 + j\omega L_2}$. The increment in impedance of primary coil is called *reflected impedance.*

The modified impedance of the primary is

$$Z_p' = \left(R_1 + \frac{\omega^2 M^2 R_2}{R_2^2 + \omega^2 L_2^2} \right) + j\omega \left(L_1 - \frac{\omega^2 M^2 L_2}{R_2^2 + \omega^2 L_2^2} \right) \qquad ...(10.7)$$

Thus, we see that the effect of coupling is to increase the resistance of the primary coil by amount $\frac{\omega^2 M^2 R_2}{R_2^2 + \omega^2 L_2^2}$ and to decrease the inductance by amount $\frac{\omega^2 M^2 L_2}{R_2^2 + \omega^2 L_2^2}$.

10.2. T–EQUIVALENT NETWORK OF A MAGNETICALLY COUPLED CIRCUIT

A coupled circuit may be converted into its equivalent *T*-network. Let R_1 and L_1 be the resistance and inductance of the primary coil and R_2 and L_2 be the corresponding quantities of the secondary coil. The primary coil is connected to voltage source $V_1 = V_{01}\, e^{j\omega t}$. The impedances of the *T*-network are Z_1, Z_2 and Z_3. We have to find these impedances in terms of R_1, R_2, L_1, L_2 and M.

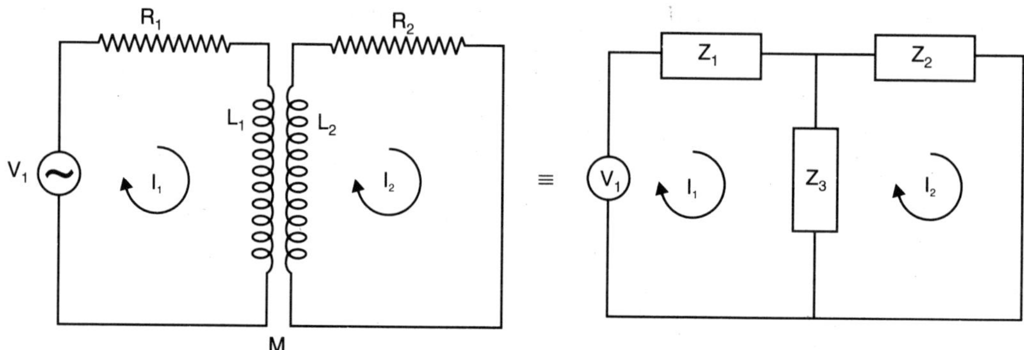

Fig. 10.2. A magnetically coupled circuit and its *T*-equivalent network.

Let I_1 and I_2 be the currents in the primary and the secondary circuits. Applying *KVL* to these circuits we have

$$V_1 = \left(R_1 + j\omega L_1\right) I_1 \pm j\omega M I_2 \quad ...(10.8)$$

$$0 = \left(R_2 + j\omega L_2\right) I_2 \pm j\omega M I_1 \quad ...(10.9)$$

We can choose any one of ± sign before the mutual inductance.

Applying *KVL* to the equivalent *T*-network we have

$$V_1 = (Z_1 + Z_3) I_1 - Z_3 I_2 \quad ...(10.10)$$

$$0 = -Z_3 I_1 + (Z_2 + Z_3)\ I_2 \quad ...(10.11)$$

Comparing the pair of eqns. (10.8) and (10.9) with the pair (10.10) and (10.11.) we obtain

$$Z_1 + Z_3 = R_1 + j\omega L_1 \quad ...(10.12)$$

$$Z_2 + Z_3 = R_2 + j\omega L_2 \quad ...(10.13)$$

$$Z_3 = j\omega M \quad ...(10.14)$$

From these equations we get

$$Z_1 = R_1 + j\omega(L_1 - M) \quad ...(10.15)$$

$$Z_2 = R_2 + j\omega(L_2 - M) \quad ...(10.16)$$

$$Z_3 = j\omega M \quad ...(10.17)$$

With these impedances we can design the equivalent *T*-network as shown in Fig. 10.3.

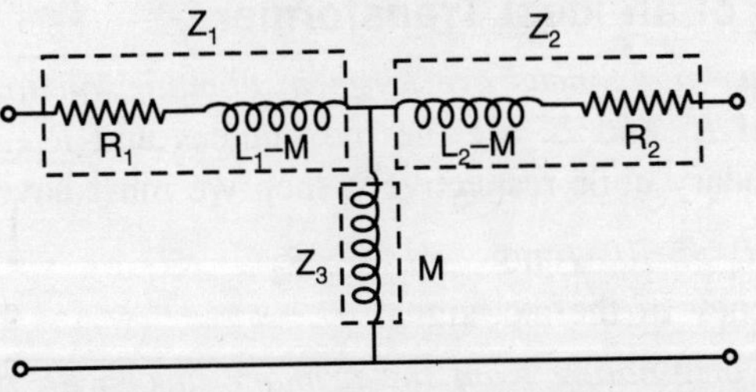

Fig. 10.3. Equivalent *T*-network of a magnetically coupled circuit.

10.3. TRANSFORMER

A transformer is a device which transforms a.c. power and impedance between two magnetically coupled circuits. It is used to perform following functions.

(*i*) *To transform an a.c. power from one circuit to another without interconnecting them directly*: A transformer can convert a high a.c. voltage of a low current into a low voltage of high current and vice versa. It should be remembered that transformer is not a power generating source and hence, in the process of transformation some power is always lost. For an ideal transformer, input power is equal to output power.

(*ii*) *To produce matching between an unmatched source and load*: We know that from maximum power transfer theorem that maximum power from a source is delivered to load when the internal impedance of the source is equal to the conjugate of load impedance. When this condition is not satisfied, a transformer is used between the source and the load for matching.

(*iii*) *To reverse the polarity of the voltage between the two circuits:* This is done by proper winding of coils.

(*iv*) *To isolate two circuits from d.c. voltage without disturbing the coupling of a.c. between them:* This automatically achieved as transformer does not work in d.c. circuits.

A transformer consists of two coils magnetically coupled with each other by suitable design. The working of transformer is based on the principle of magnetically coupled circuits. The coil to which power is fed from the source is called primary coil and the coil which delivers power to load is called secondary coil.

Transformer is an active circuit element in electronic circuitary. Like other elements, typical symbols are used for different classes of transformer. A few of these are shown in the figure.

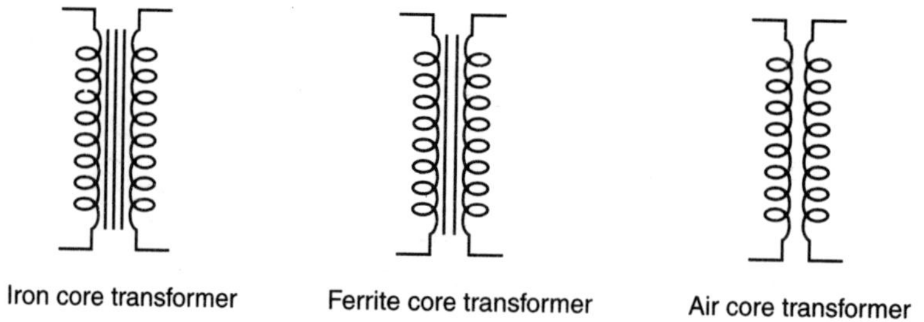

Fig. 10.4. Symbols for different kinds of transformers.

10.3.1 Characteristics of an Ideal Transformer

(*i*) *Primary and secondary reactances are large in comparison to any impedance connected in their circuits.* Thus, if L_1 and L_2 are the inductances and R_1 and R_2 are d.c. resistances of the primary and secondary coils respectively, then we must have

$$\omega L_1 >> R_1 \quad \text{and} \quad \omega L_2 >> R_2$$

where ω is the frequency of the a.c. signal.

(*ii*) *All the magnetic flux originating from the primary links with the secondary and vice versa.* This means that there is no leakage of magnetic flux *i.e.* coupling coefficient k is unity.

(*iii*) *There is no loss of energy in the transformer by any means.*

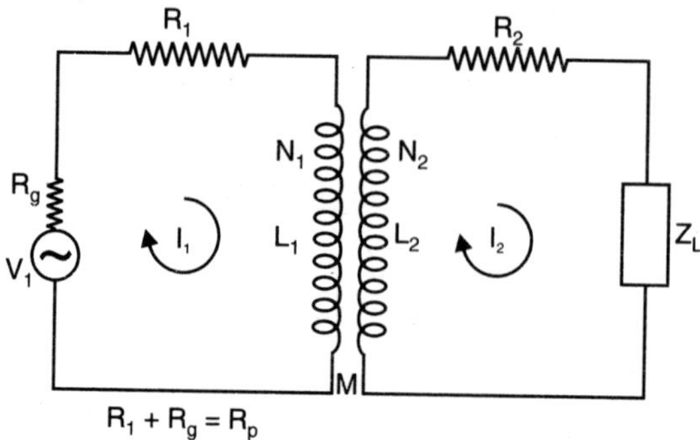

Fig. 10.5. An ideal transformer.

Let the primary of the transformer be connected to an a.c. source if internal impedance R_g and e.m.f. V operating at frequency ω. The primary coil has number of turns N_1, resistance R_1 and reactance ωL_1. The secondary circuit consists of secondary coil having number of turns N_2, resistance R_2, reactance ωL_2 and a load of impedance Z_L. The mutual inductance of the primary and secondary coils is M. To make the analysis simple, we shall denote the resistive part of impedance of primary by R_p. Thus,

$$Z_p = R_p + j\omega L_1 \qquad \text{and} \qquad Z_s = Z_2 + Z_L = (R_2 + j\omega L_2) + Z_L$$

Let I_1 and I_2 be the currents in the primary and the secondary circuits. Applying *KVL* to the primary and secondary circuits we have

$$Z_p I_1 - j\omega M I_2 = V_1 \qquad \text{...(10.18)}$$

$$(Z_2 + Z_L) I_2 - j\omega M I_1 = 0 \qquad \text{...(10.19)}$$

From eqn. (10.19)

$$\frac{I_1}{I_2} = \frac{Z_2 + Z_L}{j\omega M} \qquad \text{...(10.20)}$$

Since $Z_L << Z_2$ and $R_2 << \omega L_2$, and $M = \sqrt{L_1 L_2}$ eqn. (10.20) can be simplified as follows.

$$\frac{I_1}{I_2} = \frac{Z_2}{j\omega M} = \frac{R_2 + j\omega L_2}{j\omega M} = \frac{j\omega L_2}{j\omega M} = \frac{L_2}{\sqrt{L_1 L_2}} = \sqrt{\frac{L_2}{L_1}} = \frac{N_2}{N_1} \qquad \text{...(10.21)}$$

Eliminating I_2 from eqn. (10.18) with the help of eqn. (10.20) we get

$$Z_p I_1 - j\omega M \left(\frac{j\omega M}{Z_2 + Z_L} \right) I_1 = V_1$$

or
$$\left(Z_p + \frac{\omega^2 M^2}{Z_2 + Z_L} \right) I_1 = V_1$$

or
$$\frac{V_1}{I_1} = Z_p + \frac{\omega^2 M^2}{Z_2 + Z_L} \qquad \text{...(10.22)}$$

The ratio V_1/I_1 is the *effective impedance* Z_{in} of the *primary circuit* (also called *input impedance*). Thus the effect of magnetic coupling of two circuit is to increase the impedance of the primary circuit by amount $\dfrac{\omega^2 M^2}{Z_2 + Z_L}$, called *reflected impedance.*

$$\textit{Reflected impedance } Z_r = \frac{\omega^2 M^2}{Z_2 + Z_L} \cong \frac{\omega^2 M^2}{Z_2} = \frac{\omega^2 M^2}{R_2 + j\omega L_2} \qquad (\because Z_L << Z_2) \qquad \text{...(10.23)}$$

Separating the real and imaginary parts of reflected impedance we can write the effective impedance of the primary circuit as

$$Z_{in} = Z_p + \frac{\omega^2 M^2}{R_2 + j\omega L_2} = R_1 + j\omega L_1 + \frac{\omega^2 M^2 R_2}{R_2^2 + \omega^2 L_2^2} - j\omega \frac{\omega^2 M^2 L_2}{R_2^2 + \omega^2 L_2^2}$$

or $$Z_{in} = \left(R_1 + \frac{\omega^2 M^2 R_2}{R_2^2 + \omega^2 L_2^2}\right) - j\omega\left(L_1 - \frac{\omega^2 M^2 L_2}{R_2^2 + \omega^2 L_2^2}\right) \qquad ...(10.24)$$

Thus, the magnetic coupling increases the resistance of the primary by $\frac{\omega^2 M^2 R_2}{R_2^2 + \omega^2 L_2^2}$ and decreases the inductance by $\frac{\omega^2 M^2 L_2}{R_2^2 + \omega^2 L_2^2}$.

For ideal transformer, voltage across the load is

$$V_2 = I_2 Z_L = \frac{j\omega M}{Z_2 + Z_L} I_1 Z_L = \left(\frac{j\omega M}{Z_2 + Z_L}\right)\left(\frac{V_1}{Z_p + Z_r}\right) Z_L$$

$$\therefore \quad \frac{V_2}{V_1} = \frac{j\omega M Z_L}{\left(Z_p + \frac{\omega^2 M^2}{Z_2 + Z_L}\right)(Z_2 + Z_L)} = \frac{j\omega M Z_L}{Z_p(Z_2 + Z_L) + \omega^2 M^2}$$

$$= \frac{j\omega M Z_L}{j\omega L_1(j\omega L_2 + Z_L) + \omega^2 M^2} \qquad (\because Z_p \approx j\omega L_1, Z_2 \approx j\omega L_2)$$

$$= \frac{j\omega M Z_L}{-\omega^2 L_1 L_2 + j\omega L_1 Z_L + \omega^2 L_1 L_2}$$

$$= \frac{M}{L_1} = \sqrt{\frac{L_2}{L_1}} = \frac{N_2}{N_1} \qquad ...(10.25)$$

Combining eqns. (10.21) and (10.25) we obtain

$$\frac{V_2}{V_1} = \frac{I_1}{I_2} = \frac{N_2}{N_1} = \frac{1}{a}, \qquad ...(10.26)$$

where a is turn ratio.

10.3.2 Efficiency of Transformer

The transformer is used to transfer a.c. power from one circuit to the other. The ratio of output power delivered to the input power fed is termed as the efficiency (η) of the transformer. It is defined as

$$\eta = \frac{\text{Output power delivered}}{\text{Input power fed}}$$

It is usually expressed in per cent. For ideal transformer, the value of η should be one. However, it is never realized in practice as large amount of input power is lost within the transformer in various type of losses. The efficiency of practical transformer varies from 5 percent in case of radio frequency transformer to 9 per cent in case of mains frequency power transformer.

Principal Causes of Energy Loss in a Transformer

No transformer behaves as an ideal transformer. The output power obtained is always less than the input power fed. There are several causes within the transformer for the loss of this power. Important of these are, (*i*) *Power loss due to leakage of magnetic flux*: In practice, it is not possible to make a design transformer in which all the magnetic flux produced in primary coil links with the secondary. The unlinked magnetic flux does not generate any voltage in the secondary. This causes a loss of power. The leakage of flux can be reduced by using core material of high permeability. However, in air core transformer, the power loss due to leakage of magnetic flux is very large. The power loss due to leakage of magnetic flux for a particularly designed transformer does not depend upon the frequency of a.c. signal.

(*ii*) *Power loss due to heating produced in coils*: Transformer is made using copper wires or other conducting materials. They have finite resistance. When current flows through these coils, heat is produced because of finite resistance. Thus, some power is lost both from primary and secondary coils due to heating. This loss does not depend upon frequency. However, at very high frequency skin-effect comes in, which increases the effective resistance of the coils and hence, power loss due to heating.

(*iii*) *Power loss due to dielectric between the windings*: In both primary and secondary coils, each winding is separated but lies close to each other. When current passes through a coil, the potential of successive coils decreases. This results in formation of distributed capacitance across the adjacent turns. Through these capacitances, dielectric loss automatically comes in. This power loss generally increases with increase of frequency.

(*iv*) *Power loss due to eddy currents in conducting core*: If the core of the transformer is of conducting material, eddy currents are produced in it. When current flows through the primary and secondary coils, it results in power loss which increases with increase of signal frequency. In air core transformer, this loss is zero.

(*v*) *Power loss due to hysteresis*: If the core material of a transformer is ferro or ferrimagnetic, they undergo hysteresis during each cycle. In taking them through hysteresis, power is consumed, which is taken from the input fed power. This type of loss is not present in air core transformer. Hysteresis loss becomes larger with increase of signal frequency.

10.3.3 Classification of Transformers

Transformers can be classified according to their construction or purpose or the range of frequencies they are used. According to the range of frequencies we have three main classes of transformer:

(*i*) Mains frequency transformer

(*ii*) Audio frequency transformer

(*iii*) Radio frequency transformer

(*i*) ***Mains frequency transformer:*** The transformer falling in this category is most common and range in size from laboratory transformer used in power supply to giant transformer used at power stations. Such transformer is used for the transfer of power at mains frequency which is 50 Hz in our country and 60 Hz in some other. It employs, normally, laminated iron core. Due to high permeability of iron, the leakage of magnetic flux is often very low and coupling constant approaches unity. The k value of 0.97 is reached in a typical transformer. Due to low frequency of operation, power losses such as hysteresis, eddy current and dielectric are generally very low. If operated within the rating of winding wires, the heating loss is very low. Thus, in general, there is small loss of power in such type of transformer. In good designed transformer, power efficiency of 90% is achieved. Thus, power transformer is very close to an ideal transformer and following relations are usually fulfilled.

Voltage ratio across the coils = Turn ratio of the coils

$$\frac{V_2}{V_1} = \frac{N_2}{N_1}$$

And the impedance seen by the generator is a^2 times that of load

$$Z_{1,in} = a^2 Z_L$$

The transformer which is used in power supply has central tapping of the secondary which is normally earthed. This increases the output voltage. Generally, it has also few other secondary windings which are used for heating of valves in electronic circuits. Some step down transformers with several secondary windings specially designed for heating of filament are also common. They are termed as filament transformers.

(*ii*) ***Audio frequency transformer:*** Audio transformer is used in communication system and operates over frequency range of 2 to 20 KHz. Following categories of audio transformer are more common: (*i*) *Output transformer* (*ii*) *Input transformer* (*iii*) *Interstage transformer.*

(*iii*) ***Radio frequency transformer:*** The transformer used at radiofrequency is called radio frequency transformer (RFT). At radio frequency ($f \sim 100$ KHz), iron or any other ferro or ferromagnetic material cannot be used as core material because of hysteresis and other losses become very high. These losses become large compared to loss due to leakage of flux which they save. A high permeability low conducting material as *ferrite* or *garnet* etc. can be tolerated up to very high frequencies. However, most of the radio frequency transformers use air as core material. In air core transformer, the leakage flux becomes very large making $k << 1$. The RFT is basically used for two purposes:

(*a*) To obtain maximum transfer of power from a source to load *i.e.* to produce matching between source and load.

(*b*) To obtain largest possible value of voltage across the secondary.

10.4. SYMMETRICAL T AND π NETWORK

A filter circuit is designed by connecting together either T or π networks. So we start with some useful characteristics of these networks.

A network containing two input and two output terminals is said to be symmetrical if

$$Z_{1OC} = Z_{2OC}$$

$$Z_{1SC} = Z_{2SC} \quad ...(10.27)$$

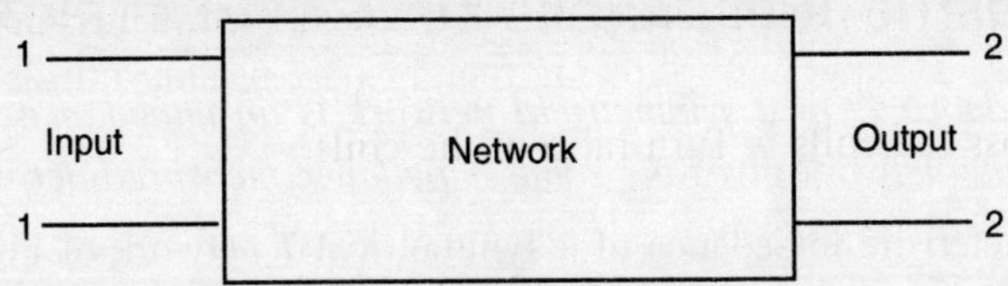

Fig. 10.6

In case of *T*-network with impedances Z_1, Z_2 and Z_3 we have

$$Z_{1OC} = Z_1 + Z_3 \quad \text{and} \quad Z_{2OC} = Z_2 + Z_3 \qquad ...(10.28)$$

Hence, for this network the symmetry requirement $Z_{1OC} = Z_{2OC}$ gives $Z_1 = Z_2$.

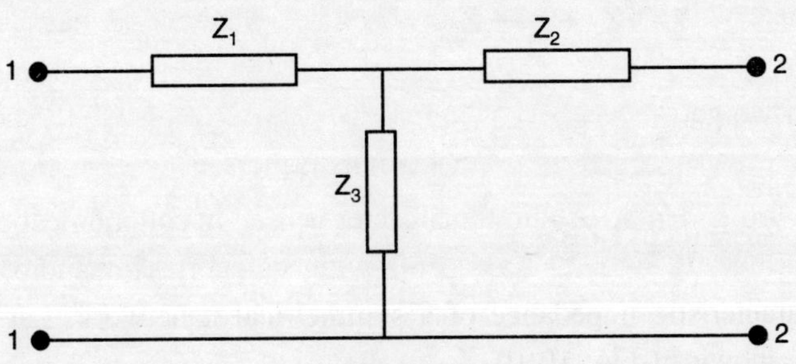

Fig. 10.7

Thus a *T*-network with $Z_1 = Z_2$ is a symmetrical network. Similarly, for a π-network with impedances Z_A, Z_B and Z_C, the symmetry requirement gives $Z_A = Z_C$.

It is customary to represent a symmetrical *T* network by impedances $Z_1/2$, and Z_2. Thus, a symmetrical network can be thought of as made up of two *L*-sections consisting of impedances $Z_1/2$ and $2Z_2$ as shown in the Fig. 10.8.

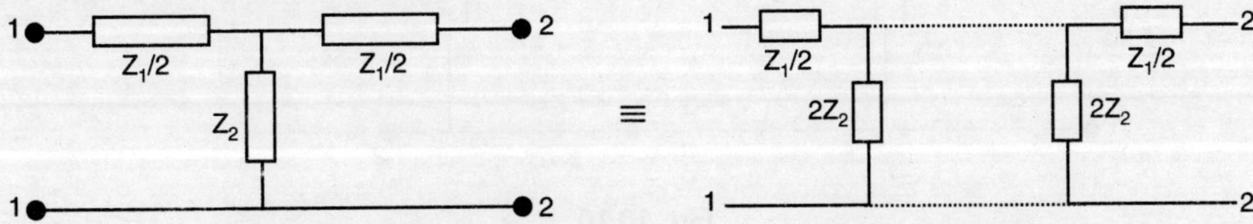

Fig. 10.8. A symmetrical T-network as a sum of two L-sections.

Similarly, a symmetrical π-network can be represented by two impedances Z_1 and $2Z_2$, which in turn can be thought of as sum of inverted *L*-sections as shown in the Fig. 10.9.

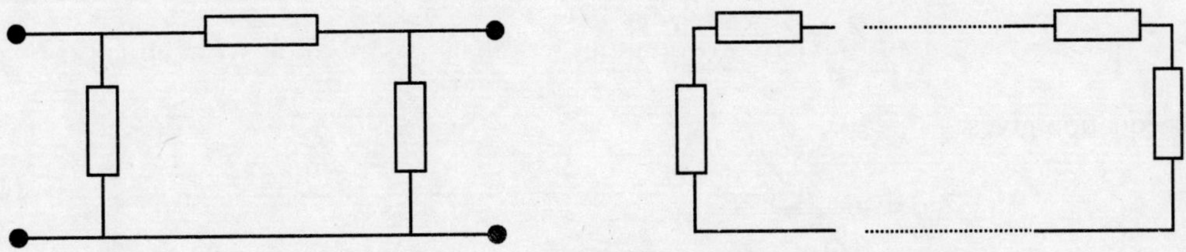

Fig. 10.9

10.5. CHARACTERISTIC IMPEDANCES OF A SYMMETRICAL T-NETWORK

The characteristic impedance Z_0 of a symmetrical network is an impedance which, when connected across the terminals of the network gives the same impedance measured across its terminals.

Let Z_{0T} be the characteristic impedance of a symmetrical T network of Fig. 10.8. Let its terminal 2, 2 be terminated with this impedance. Then according to the definition of characteristic impedance, the impedance measured across 1, 1 is

$$Z_{0T} = \frac{Z_1}{2} + \frac{Z_2\left(\frac{Z_1}{2} + Z_{0T}\right)}{Z_2 + \frac{Z_1}{2} + Z_{0T}} \qquad ...(10.29)$$

From this equation we get

$$Z_{0T} = \sqrt{\frac{Z_1^2}{4} + Z_1 Z_2} \qquad ...(10.30)$$

Let $Z_{0\pi}$ be the characteristic impedance of a symmetrical π network. Let its terminals 2, 2 be terminated with $Z_{0\pi}$ as shown in Fig. 10.10.

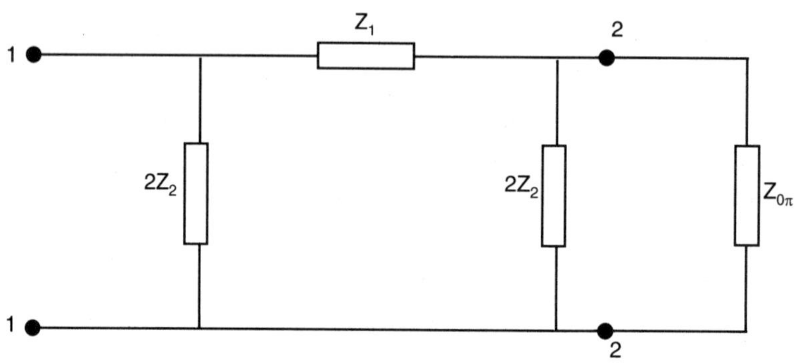

Fig. 10.10

Then
$$Z_{0\pi} = \frac{2Z_2\left(Z_1 + \frac{2Z_2 Z_{0\pi}}{2Z_2 + Z_{0\pi}}\right)}{2Z_2 + Z_1 + \frac{2Z_2 Z_{0\pi}}{2Z_2 + Z_{0\pi}}} \qquad ...(10.31)$$

This equation gives

$$Z_{0\pi} = \frac{Z_1 Z_2}{\sqrt{\frac{Z_1^2}{4} + Z_1 Z_2}} \qquad ...(10.32)$$

10.6. PROPAGATION CONSTANT OF A SYMMETRICAL T-NETWORK TERMINATED THROUGH ITS CHARACTERISTIC IMPEDANCE

Let a symmetrical *T*-network with branch impedances $Z_1/2$ and Z_2 be terminated through its characteristic impedance $Z_{0T} = Z_0$ as shown in the Fig. 10.11.

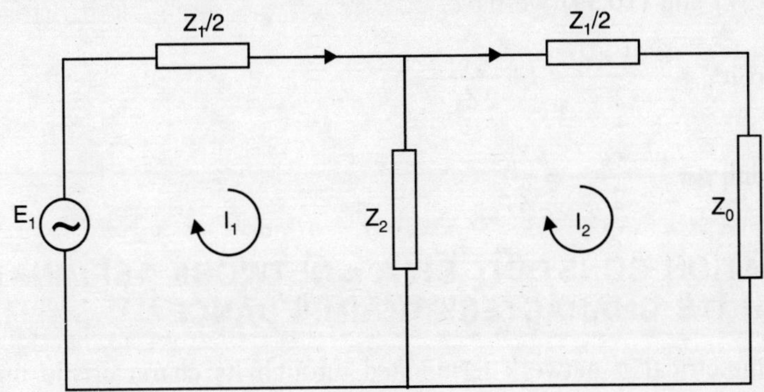

Fig. 10.11

Let I_1 and I_2 be the currents in the two loops of the circuit of Fig. 10.11. Using Kirchhoff's voltage law in the two loops we have

$$\left(\frac{Z_1}{2} + Z_2\right) I_1 - Z_2 I_2 = E_1 \qquad \text{...(10.33)}$$

$$Z_2 I_1 - \left(Z_2 + \frac{Z_1}{2} + Z_0\right) I_2 = 0 \qquad \text{...(10.34)}$$

From eqn. (10.34) we have

$$\frac{I_1}{I_2} = \frac{\dfrac{Z_1}{2} + Z_2 + Z_0}{Z_2} \qquad \text{...(10.35)}$$

The propagation constant γ is defined in terms of ratio of input current (voltage) to output current (voltage) and is given by

$$\frac{I_1}{I_2} = \frac{E_1}{E_2} = e^{\gamma} \qquad \text{...(10.36)}$$

For the *T*-network under investigation we have

$$e^{\gamma} = 1 + \frac{Z_1}{2Z_2} + \frac{Z_0}{Z_2} \qquad \text{...(10.37)}$$

or

$$\gamma = \ln\left[1 + \frac{Z_1}{2Z_2} + \frac{Z_0}{Z_2}\right], \quad \text{with } Z_0 = \sqrt{\frac{Z_1^2}{4} + Z_1 Z_2} \qquad \text{...(10.38)}$$

From eqn. (10.34) it can easily be shown that

$$e^{-\gamma} = \frac{1}{1+\dfrac{Z_1}{2Z_2}+\dfrac{Z_0}{Z_2}} = 1+\frac{Z_1}{2Z_2}-\frac{Z_0}{Z_2} \quad \text{...(10.39)}$$

From eqns. (10.37) and (10.39) we have

$$\cosh\gamma = \frac{e^{\gamma}+e^{-\gamma}}{2} = 1+\frac{Z_1}{2Z_2} \quad \text{...(10.40)}$$

And

$$\sinh\gamma = \frac{e^{\gamma}-e^{-\gamma}}{2} = \frac{Z_0}{Z_2} \quad \text{...(10.41)}$$

10.7. PROPAGATION CONSTANT OF A π-NETWORK TERMINATED THROUGH ITS CHARACTERISTIC IMPEDANCE

Now consider a symmetrical π network terminated through its characteristic impedance $Z_{0\pi}$. The current distribution resulting from the source voltage E_1 is shown in the Fig. 10.12. Applying *KVL* to the three loops we get following equations.

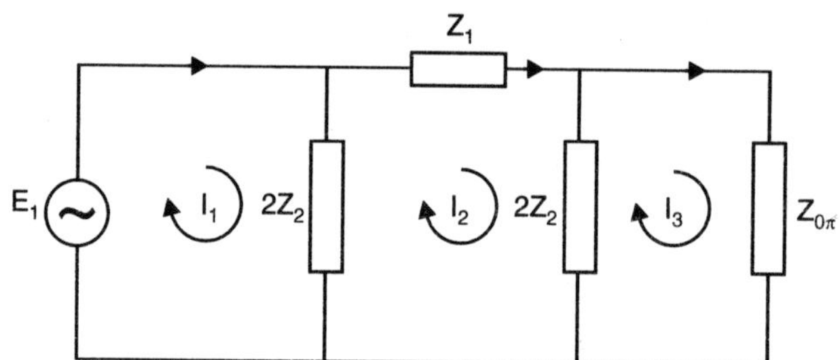

Fig. 10.12

$$2Z_1(I_1 - I_2) = E_1 \quad \text{...(10.42)}$$

$$Z_1I_2 + 2Z_2(I_2 - I_3) + 2Z_2(I_2 - I_1) = 0 \quad \text{...(10.43)}$$

$$Z_{0\pi}I_3 + 2Z_2(I_3 - I_2) = 0 \quad \text{...(10.44)}$$

From eqn. (10.44)

$$I_2 = \frac{2Z_2 + Z_{0\pi}}{2Z_2} I_3 \quad \text{...(10.45)}$$

Substituting the expression for I_2 from eqn. (10.45) in eqn. (10.43) and solving for I_1 we get

$$\frac{I_1}{I_3} = 1+\frac{Z_1}{2Z_2}+\left(\frac{Z_1+4Z_2}{4Z_2^2}\right)Z_{0\pi}, \text{ where } Z_{0\pi} = \frac{Z_1Z_2}{\sqrt{\dfrac{Z_1^2}{4}+Z_1Z_2}}$$

$$= 1+\frac{Z_1}{2Z_2}+\frac{\sqrt{\dfrac{Z_1^2}{4}+Z_1Z_2}}{Z_2} \quad \text{...(10.46)}$$

Therefore, $$e^{\gamma} = 1 + \frac{Z_1}{2Z_2} + \frac{Z_0}{Z_2} \qquad ...(10.47)$$

or $$\gamma = \ln\left[1 + \frac{Z_1}{2Z_2} + \frac{Z_0}{Z_2}\right] \qquad ...(10.48)$$

10.8. ELECTRICAL FILTERS

An electric filter is a passive network which allows the current and voltages of desired frequency to pass through without attenuation and completely stops the others. The desired group of frequencies which a filter passes is called ***pass band*** *and the group of frequencies which the filter stops is known as* ***stop band****.*

A network shown in Fig. 10.13 represents a uniform filter, which consists of a chain of similar sections. This chain may be thought of as composed of symmetrical T or π sections. The behaviour of a filter circuit made up of infinite chain of T or π networks is identical with that of a single section of T or π network terminated with its *characteristic impedance* Z_0. The frequency characteristic of T or π network terminated with its characteristic impedance is determined by *propagation constant* γ which defined in terms of the ratio of input current (voltage) *i.e.* current entering the network to output current (voltage) *i.e.* the current leaving the network. By definition,

$$\frac{I_1}{I_2} = \frac{E_1}{E_2} = e^{\gamma} \qquad ...(10.49)$$

In general, γ is a complex number and may be expressed as

$$\gamma = \alpha + j\beta$$

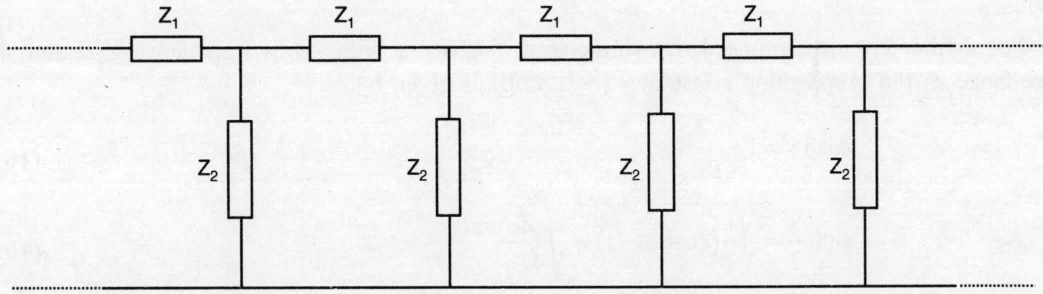

Fig. 10.13. A filter circuit consisting of an infinite chain of symmetrical networks.

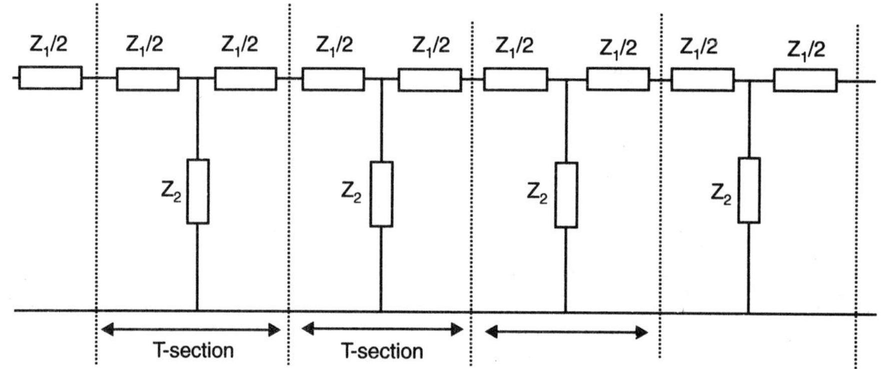

Fig. 10.14. A filter may thought of as composed of symmetrical *T*-networks.

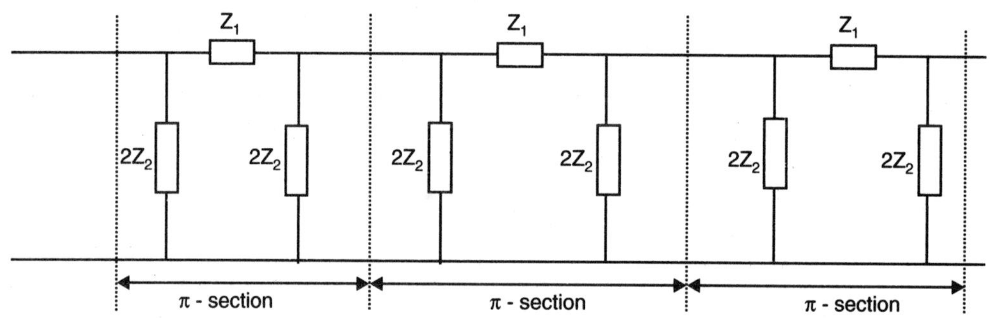

Fig. 10.15. A filter may thought of as composed of symmetrical π-networks.

Where α is called attenuation constant and β is phase shift. When $\alpha = 0$, the current (voltage) passes without attenuation from one section to another in the filter circuit. When $\alpha \neq 0$ the amplitude of the current (voltage) attenuates while passing from one section to another section. Thus, the essential requirement for a filter is that $\alpha = 0$ *in the pass band* and $\alpha = \infty$ *in the stop band.* The attenuation constant should rise abruptly where the limit of pass band ends and that of stop band begins.

For a filter circuit composed of symmetrical *T*-network with series impedance $Z_1/2$ and shunt impedance Z_2 the propagation constant γ (= $\alpha + j\beta$) is given by

$$\cosh\gamma = 1 + \frac{Z_1}{2Z_2} \qquad ...(10.50)$$

or

$$\sinh\frac{\gamma}{2} = \sqrt{\frac{1}{2}(\cosh\gamma - 1)} = \sqrt{\frac{Z_1}{4Z_2}} \qquad ...(10.51)$$

Therefore,

$$\sinh\left(\frac{\alpha}{2} + j\frac{\beta}{2}\right) = \sinh\frac{\alpha}{2}\cos\frac{\beta}{2} + j\cosh\frac{\alpha}{2}\sin\frac{\beta}{2} = \sqrt{\frac{Z_1}{4Z_2}} \qquad ...(10.52)$$

It is obvious from above expression that if any of the two impedances Z_1 and/or Z_2 are resistive, then in no case $\alpha = 0$ and hence attenuation of current or voltage will take place. Hence, for electric filters, only inductor and capacitor can be used as circuit elements. Under this situation, we can have two conditions:

(*i*) Z_1 and Z_2 are of the same type.

(*ii*) Z_1 and Z_2 are of different types.

Let us discuss both situations separately.

(*i*) If Z_1 and Z_2 are of the same type of reactance (either both inductor or both capacitor), then $Z_1/4Z_2$ is *real* and *positive*. This makes sinh $\gamma/2$ real. Then from eqn. (10.52) we have

$$\cosh\frac{\alpha}{2}\sin\frac{\beta}{2} = 0 \qquad ...(10.53)$$

And $$\sinh\frac{\alpha}{2}\cos\frac{\beta}{2} = \sqrt{\frac{Z_1}{4Z_2}} \text{ (a real positive number)} \qquad ...(10.54)$$

Both these conditions must be simultaneously satisfied. Now $\cosh\alpha/2$ cannot be zero for any value α, so we have

$$\sin\frac{\beta}{2} = 0 \Rightarrow \cos\frac{\beta}{2} = 1 \Rightarrow \beta = n\pi,\ n = 0, 2, 4...... \qquad ...(10.55)$$

For these values of β, eqn. (10.54) becomes

$$\sinh\frac{\alpha}{2} = \sqrt{\frac{Z_1}{4Z_2}} \quad \text{or} \quad \alpha = 2\sinh^{-1}\left(\frac{Z_1}{4Z_2}\right)^{1/2} \qquad ...(10.56)$$

Since $\sqrt{\frac{Z_1}{4Z_2}} > 0,\ \alpha \neq 0$. That is, attenuation of current or voltage will take place in passing from one section to another in the filter circuit. This is the requirement of *stop band filter.* Thus, for *stop band* we must have

$$\frac{Z_1}{4Z_2} \geq 0 \qquad ...(10.57)$$

(*ii*) If Z_1 and Z_2 are of opposite sign (for instance $Z_1 = j\omega L$ and $Z_2 = 1/j\omega C$ and vice-versa), then $Z_1/4Z_2 < 0$. Then from eqn. (10.51) we see that sinh $(\gamma/2) = \sqrt{\frac{Z_1}{4Z_2}}$ will be imaginary and eqn. (10.52) gives

$$\sinh\frac{\alpha}{2}\cos\frac{\beta}{2} = 0 \qquad ...(10.58)$$

And $$j\cosh\frac{\alpha}{2}\sin\frac{\beta}{2} = j\sqrt{\left|\frac{Z_1}{4Z_2}\right|} \qquad ...(10.59)$$

Equation (10.58) holds under two conditions.

(*a*) $$\sinh\frac{\alpha}{2} = 0 \quad \Rightarrow \quad \alpha = 0 \qquad ...(10.60)$$

(*b*) $$\cos\frac{\beta}{2} = 0, \Rightarrow \beta = (2n-1)\pi, \; n = 0,1,2,3.... \quad ...(10.61)$$

The first condition viz. $\alpha = 0$ is the condition for *pass band*. For $\alpha = 0$, the transmission of unattenuated current or voltage takes place. This frequency range, over which $\alpha = 0$, is defined as the *pass band.*

Now, for $\alpha = 0$, cosh $(\alpha/2) = 1$, eqn. (10.59) gives

$$j\sin\frac{\beta}{2} = j\sqrt{\left|\frac{Z_1}{4Z_2}\right|}$$

or $$\beta = 2\sin^{-1}\sqrt{\left|\frac{Z_1}{4Z_2}\right|} \quad ...(10.62)$$

$$\sin\frac{\beta}{2} \leq 1, \Rightarrow \left|\frac{Z_1}{4Z_2}\right| \leq 1 \Rightarrow -1 \leq \frac{Z_1}{4Z_2} \quad ...(10.63)$$

Let us come to the condition (*b*) expressed in eqn. (10.62). For $\beta = (2n - 1)\pi$, $\sin \beta/2 = 1$. For these values of β, eqn. (10.59) becomes

$$\cosh\frac{\alpha}{2} = \sqrt{\left|\frac{Z_1}{4Z_2}\right|} \quad ...(10.64)$$

Since cosh $(\alpha/2)$ is always greater than 1, $(\cosh x = 1 + \frac{x^2}{\underline{|2}} + \frac{x^4}{\underline{|4}} + ...)$, we have

$$\left|\frac{Z_1}{4Z_2}\right| > 1 \;\; i.e. \;\; \frac{Z_1}{4Z_2} < -1 \quad ...(10.65)$$

Equation (10.65) insures that $\alpha \neq 0$, which is the condition for *stop band.*

The conclusions from the above analysis can be stated as follows.

(*i*) For electric filter, both the impedances Z_1 and Z_2 must be reactive in nature.

(*ii*) For pass band these impedances must satisfy the condition

$$-1 \leq \frac{Z_1}{4Z_2} \leq 0 \quad (pass\ band) \quad ...(10.66)$$

(*iii*) For stop band the conditions are:

$\left|\frac{Z_1}{4Z_2}\right| \geq 0$, if Z_1 and Z_2 are of the same type.

And $\frac{Z_1}{4Z_2} \leq -1$, if Z_1 and Z_2 are of opposite type.

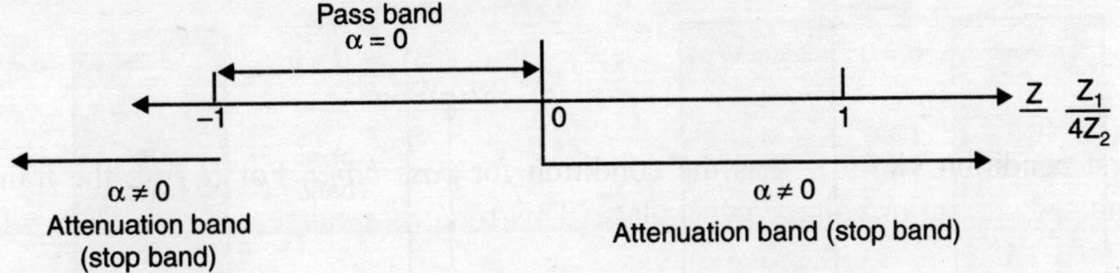

Fig. 10.16

10.8.1 Classification of Filters and their Ideal Requirement

Filters are classified into four categories.

(a) Low Pass Filter: The ideal requirement for a low pass filter is that it transmits all frequencies below a critical value f_c and stops those above it. Thus, for a low pass filter we must have

$$\alpha = 0 \text{ for } 0 < f \leq f_c$$
$$\alpha = \infty \text{ for } f > f_c$$

(b) High Pass Filter: The ideal requirement for a high pass filter is that it should pass all frequencies greater than certain critical frequency f_c and stop those below it. For this type of filter we must have

$$\alpha = 0 \text{ for } f \geq f_c$$
$$\alpha = \infty \text{ for } f \leq f_c$$

(c) Band Pass Filter: It passes a band of frequencies say from f_1 to f_2 and stops all other frequencies. Thus, for band pass filter, we must have

$$\alpha = 0 \text{ for } f_1 \leq f \leq f_2$$
$$\alpha = \infty \text{ for } f \leq f_1 \text{ and } f \geq f_2$$

(d) Band Stop Filter: This filter stops frequencies lying within a certain range, say f_1' to f_2' and allows to pass all other frequencies. Thus for a band stop filter we must have

$$\alpha = 0 \text{ for } f \leq f_1' \text{ and } f \geq f_2'$$
$$\alpha = \infty \text{ for } f_1' \leq f \leq f_2'$$

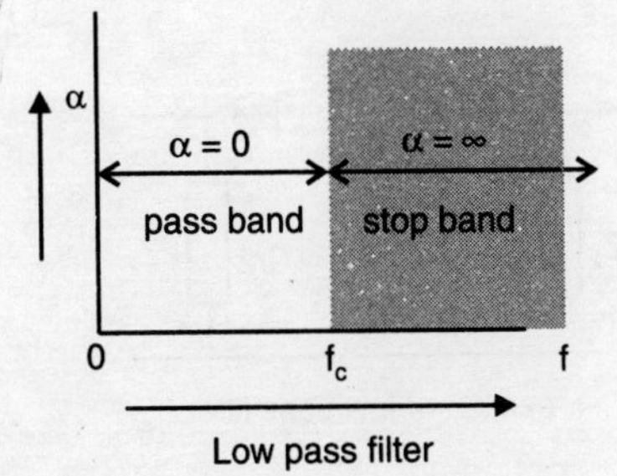

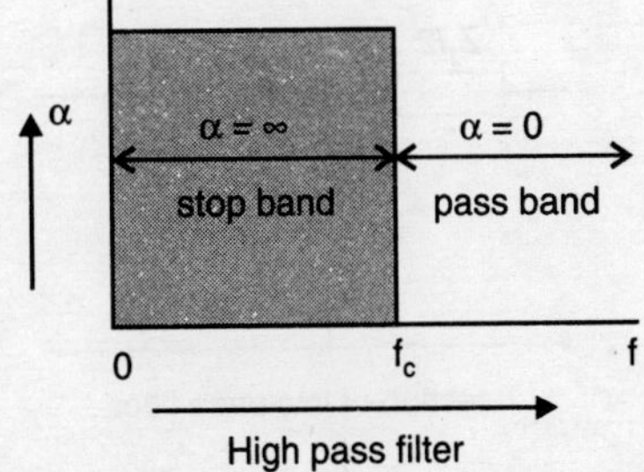

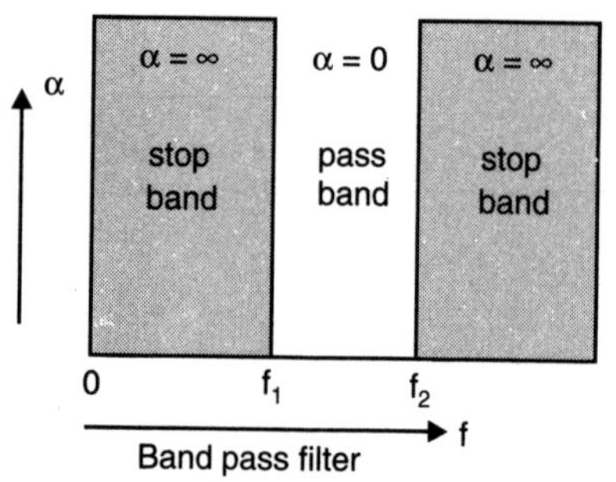

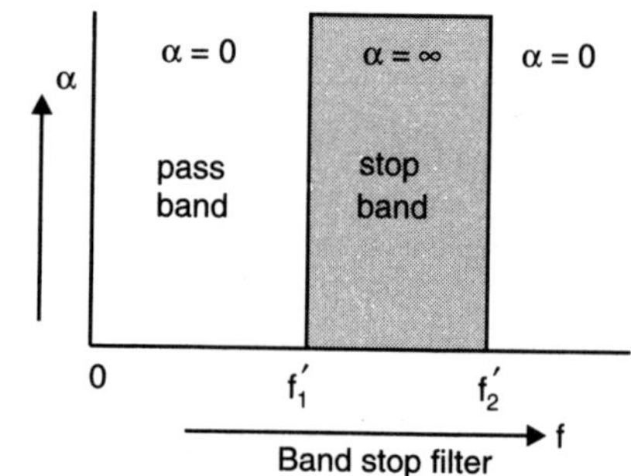

Fig. 10.17. Ideal characteristics of different kinds of filters.

The requirements described above are graphically shown in Fig. 10.17. The other common requirement for all these filters is that their characteristic impedance should not change with frequency. A filter is always used between a source and a load, hence to get maximum power from the source, its input impedance must match with the output impedance.

Low Pass Filter

The T or π sections used in the design of low pass filter are shown in the Fig. 10.18. If the series and shunt impedances Z_1 and Z_2 are such that Z_1Z_2 = a numerical constant = R_k^2 (say), then the filter is said to be constant K or prototype filter. Here, total series impedance $Z_1 = j\omega L$ and total shunt impedance is $Z_2 = 1/j\omega C$. The pass band is given by

$$-1 \leq \frac{Z_1}{4Z_2} \leq 0$$

$$0 \leq \frac{\omega^2 LC}{4} \leq 0$$

$$0 \leq \omega \leq \frac{2}{\sqrt{LC}}$$

$$0 \leq f_c \leq \frac{1}{\pi\sqrt{LC}} \qquad ...(10.67)$$

The cut-off frequency is $f_c = \dfrac{1}{\pi\sqrt{LC}}$. The pass band comprises of frequencies lying in the range $0 < f < f_c$.

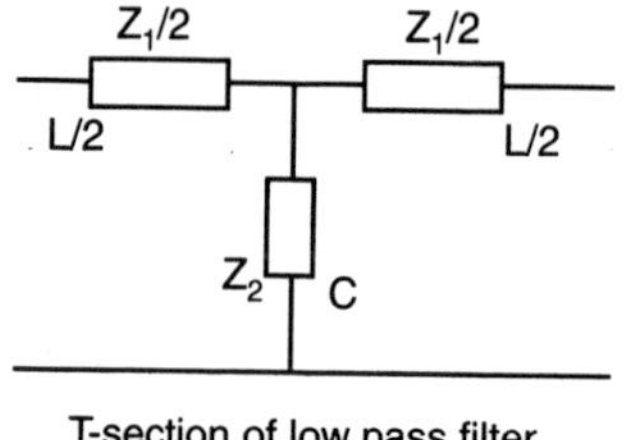

T-section of low pass filter

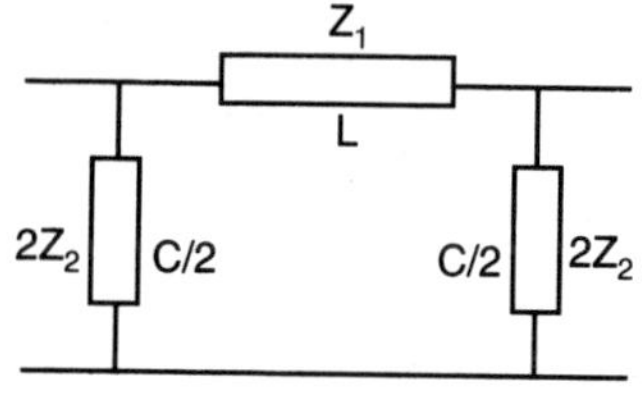

π-section of low pass filter

Fig. 10.18

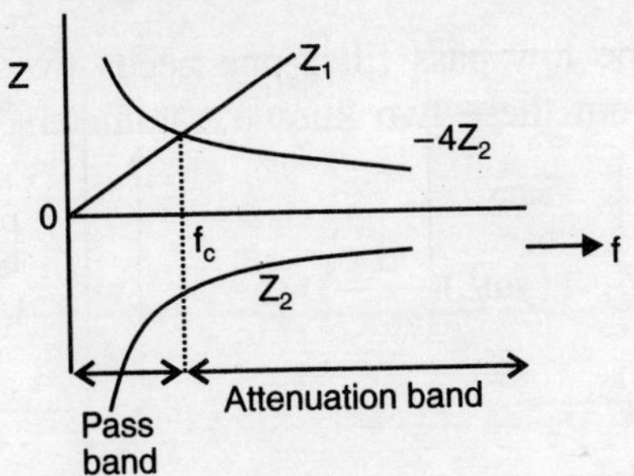

Fig. 10.19

In the pass band $\alpha = 0$ and the phase angle is

$$\beta = 2\sin^{-1}\sqrt{\frac{Z_1}{4Z_2}} = 2\sin^{-1}\left(\frac{4\pi^2 fLC}{4}\right) = 2\sin^{-1}\left(\frac{f}{f_c}\right) \quad \text{...(10.68)}$$

In the stop band the attenuation constant is

$$\alpha = 2\cosh^{-1}\sqrt{\frac{Z_1}{4Z_2}} = 2\cosh^{-1}\left(\frac{f}{f_c}\right) \quad \text{...(10.69)}$$

And phase shift $\beta = \pi$

Characteristic impedance of *T*-section is

$$Z_{0T} = \sqrt{\frac{Z_1^2}{4} + Z_1Z_2} = \sqrt{Z_1Z_2\left(1+\frac{Z_1}{4Z_2}\right)} = \sqrt{\frac{L}{C}\left(1-\frac{\omega^2 LC}{4}\right)} = R_k\sqrt{1-\left(\frac{f}{f_c}\right)^2} \quad \text{...(10.70)}$$

Characteristic impedance of π-section is

$$Z_{0\pi} = \frac{Z_1Z_2}{Z_{0T}} = \frac{R_k^2}{Z_{0T}} = \frac{R_k}{\sqrt{1-\left(\frac{f}{f_c}\right)^2}} \quad \text{...(10.71)}$$

The variation of α, β, Z_{0T} and $Z_{0\pi}$ with frequency is shown in the Fig. 10.20.

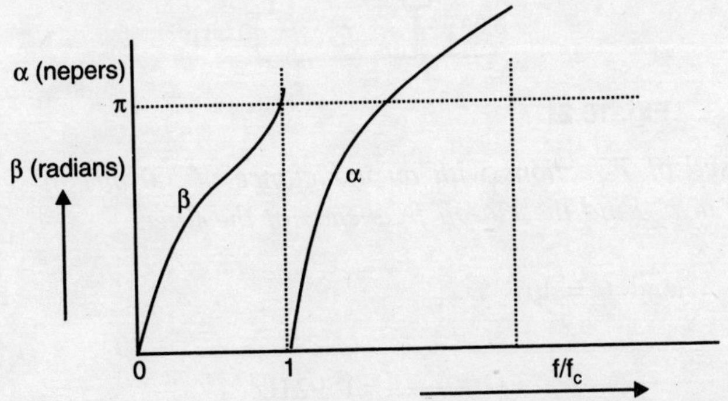

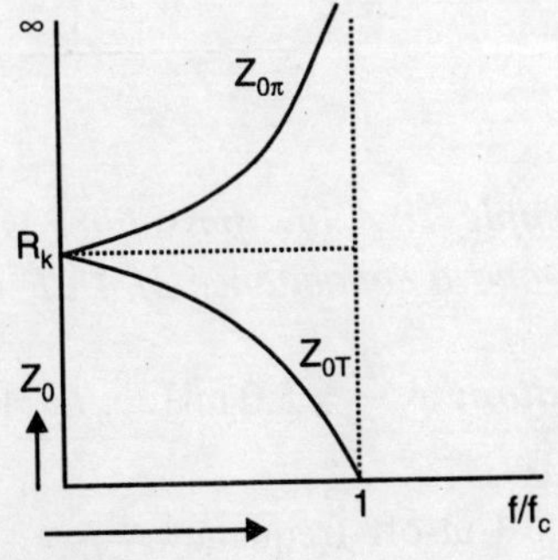

Fig. 10.20. Variation of α, β, Z_{0T} and $Z_{0\pi}$ with frequency.

Design of low pass filter

For the design of constant k type low pass filter one needs two parameters (*i*) cut-off frequency and (*ii*) constant $R_k^2 = Z_1Z_2$. From these two known parameters, one can calculate the values of components L and C. Now,

$$R_k^2 = Z_1Z_2 = (j\omega L)(\frac{1}{j\omega C}) = \frac{L}{C}$$

$$\therefore \qquad L = CR_k^2$$

And $$f_c = \frac{1}{\pi\sqrt{LC}} \qquad \therefore LC = \frac{1}{\pi^2 f_c^2}$$

From these two relations we have

$$L = \frac{R_k}{\pi f_c} \quad \text{and} \quad C = \frac{1}{\pi f_c R_k} \qquad ...(10.72)$$

Solved Examples

Example 1: *Design a low pass T-section and π-section filter with cut-off frequency 2 KHz and design impedance R_k = 1000 ohm.*

Solution: $$R_k = 1000\,\Omega \text{ and } f_c = 2000\,\text{Hz}$$

Now, $$L = \frac{R_k}{\pi f_c} = \frac{1000}{3.14 \times 2000} = 0.16 \text{ henry} = 160 \text{ mH}$$

$$C = \frac{1}{\pi f_c R_k} = \frac{1}{3.14 \times 2000 \times 1000} = 0.16 \times 10^{-6}\,\text{F} = 0.16\,\mu\text{F}$$

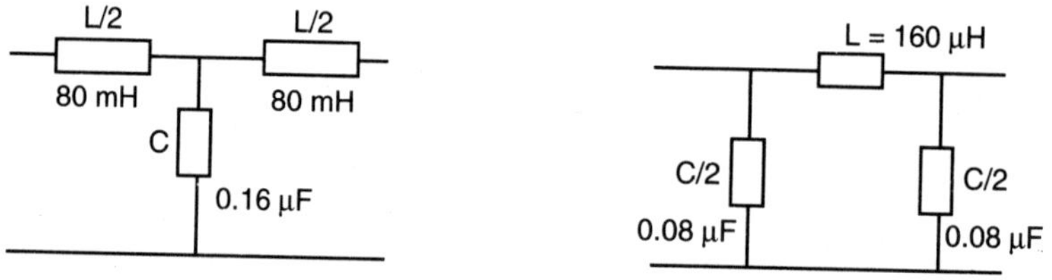

Fig. 10.21

Example 2: *A low pass filter is composed of T-sections with an inductance of 5.0 mH in series arm and a capacitance of 4 μF in shunt arm. Find the cut-off frequency of the filter.*

Solution: $$\frac{L}{2} = 5.0\text{ mH} \;\therefore L = 10.0\text{ mH} \quad \text{and } C = 4\mu\text{F}$$

Cut-off frequency $$f_c = \frac{1}{\pi\sqrt{LC}} = \frac{1}{3.14\sqrt{10 \times 10^{-3} \times 4 \times 10^{-6}}} = 1592\,\text{Hz}$$

***Example* 3:** *A low pass filter is composed of π-sections with an inductance of 6.4 mH in series arm and capacitance of 18 μF in each shunt arm. Calculate the cut-off frequency.*

***Solution*:** $\frac{C}{2} = 18\,\mu\text{F} \;\therefore\; C = 36\,\mu\text{F}$ and $L = 6.4$ mH

Cut-off frequency $f_c = \frac{1}{\pi\sqrt{LC}} = \frac{1}{3.14\sqrt{6.4\times10^{-3}\times 36\times10^{-6}}} = 663$ Hz.

High pass filter

The T and π sections of a constant K high pass filter are shown in the Fig. 10.22. Here $Z_1 = \frac{1}{j\omega C}$ and $Z_2 = j\omega L$, so that $Z_1 Z_2 = \frac{L}{C} = R_k^2$. The condition for pass band is

$$-1 \le \frac{Z_1}{4Z_2} \le 0$$

The lower cut-off frequency is given by

$$\frac{Z_1}{4Z_2} = -1 \text{ or } -\frac{1}{\omega^2 LC} = -1$$

This gives $$f = \frac{1}{4\pi\sqrt{LC}} = f_c$$

The upper cut-off frequency is given by

$$Z_1 = 0 \;\Rightarrow\; \frac{1}{j\omega C} = 0 \;\Rightarrow\; f = f_c = \infty$$

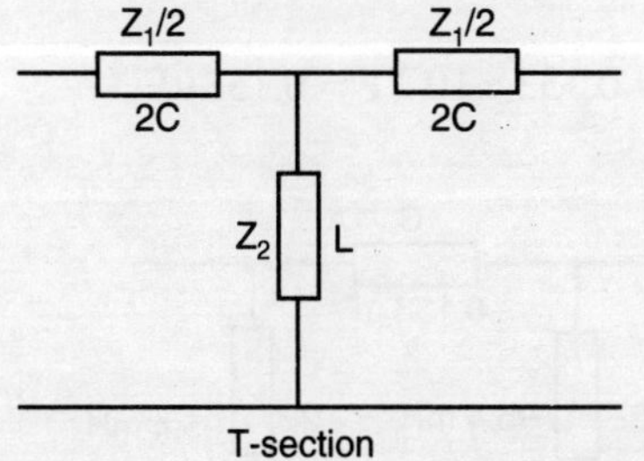

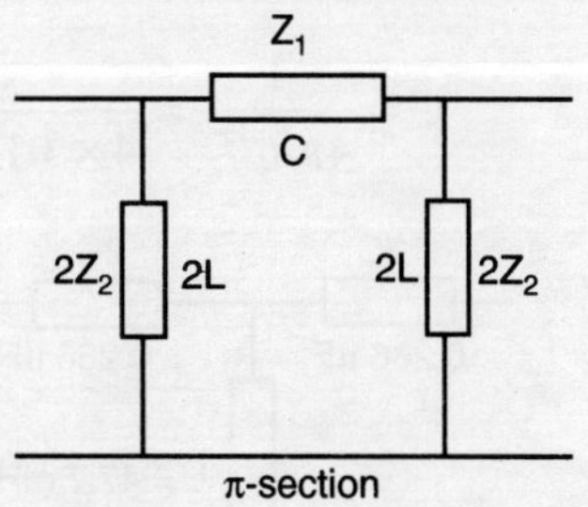

Fig. 10.22. High pass filter.

The range of pass band is from f_c to ∞. The stop band is obviously from 0 to f_c.

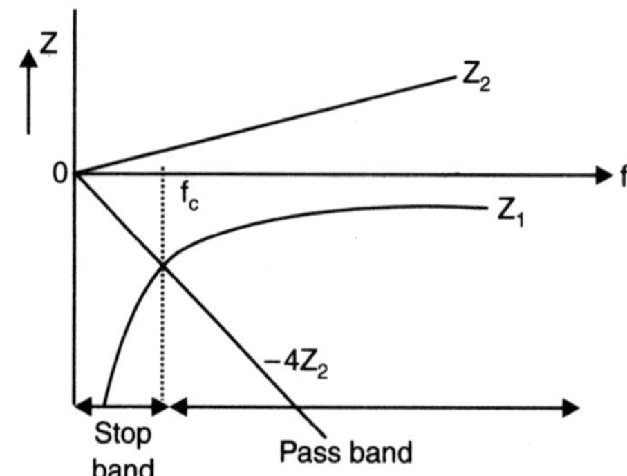

Fig. 10.23. Determination of pass band, stop band and cut-off frequency f_c.

Design of Constant–*K* High Pass Filter

The components of high pass filter can be determined from the knowledge of cut-off frequency and design impedance R_k. We know that

$$f_c = \frac{1}{4\pi\sqrt{LC}} \quad \text{and} \quad R_k = \sqrt{\frac{L}{C}}$$

From these equations we get

$$L = \frac{R_k}{4\pi f_c} \quad \text{and} \quad C = \frac{1}{4\pi f_c R_k} \qquad \text{...(10.76)}$$

***Example* 4:** *Determine the components of T and π sections used in the design of a high pass constant K filter with following data:*

Cut-off frequency f_c = 10 KHz, Design impedance R_k = 600 Ohm.

***Solution*:**

$$L = \frac{R_k}{4\pi f_c} = \frac{600}{4 \times 3.14 \times 1000} = 47.7 \times 10^{-3}\,\text{H} = 47.7 \text{ mH}$$

$$C = \frac{1}{4\pi R_k f_c} = \frac{1}{4 \times 3.14 \times 600 \times 1000} = 0.133 \times 10^{-6}\,\text{F} = 0.133\,\mu\text{F}$$

Fig. 10.24

***Example* 5:** *The components of a high pass constant K filter are C = 0.01 μF and L = 10 mH. Find out the cut-off frequency. Also calculate the characteristic impedance at frequency 10 KHz.*

Solution: $f_c = \dfrac{1}{4\pi\sqrt{LC}} = \dfrac{1}{4\times 3.14\times\sqrt{10\times 10^{-3}\times 0.01\times 10^{-6}}} = 7.96\times 10^{3}\text{ Hz} = 7.96\text{ KHz}$

Characteristic impedance

$$Z_0 = \frac{L}{C}\sqrt{1-\left(\frac{f_c}{f}\right)^2} = \frac{10\times 10^{-3}}{0.01\times 10^{-6}}\sqrt{1-\left(\frac{7.96}{10.0}\right)^2} = 6.05\times 10^{5}\,\Omega$$

QUESTIONS AND PROBLEMS

1. What do you mean by coupled circuits? Define input and transfer impedances. Discuss the basic features of two magnetically coupled coils.
2. Explain the meaning of reflected impedance in context of magnetically coupled circuits. Derive expressions for reflected resistance and reflected reactance.
3. What is a transformer? What work can it perform in an electrical circuit? State and explain the properties of an ideal transformer.
4. Enunciate basic features of a coupled circuit. In a transformer derive an expression for reflected impedance. Assuming that the impedance in series with primary and the load connected across the secondary are both pure resistive, find the reflected resistance and reflected reactance of the circuit. Discuss its behaviour.
5. Define symmetrical T and π network. Find expression for the characteristic impedance of symmetrical T and π network.
6. What do you mean by propagation constant? What are the physical significances of real and imaginary parts of propagation constant? Derive expression for propagation constant of T and π networks terminated through their characteristic impedance.
7. What do you mean by an electrical filter? Obtain conditions of pass and stop bands for a symmetrical T network having reactive components.
8. What are the basic requirements of an electrical filter? How can one achieve it practically? Discuss the general work which each section of the composite filter does.
9. What is an electric filter? Obtain conditions for pass band and attenuation band.
10. Using the conditions for pass band and stop band obtain the formulae for the critical frequencies of low pass filter and high pass filter. What are the values of α and β in these bands? Show the variation of α, β and characteristic impedance with frequency.
11. Calculate the elements of a high pass filter, whose cut-off frequency is 1000Hz and the product of their reactances is 600 Ohms.

OOO

Electromagnetic Waves

11.1. MAXWELL'S EQUATIONS

The four basic laws of electromagnetism: (*i*) Gauss's law for electrostatics, (*ii*) Gauss's law for magnetic field, (*iii*) Generalised form of Ampere's law and (*iv*) Faraday's law of electromagnetic induction, expressed in mathematical forms are called Maxwell's electromagnetic field equations. For the sake of convenience we restate them.

Gauss's Law for Electrostatics: Maxwell's First Equation

The law states that the electric flux over a closed surface equals $1/\varepsilon_0$ times the total net charge enclosed within the surface.

$$\oint_S \mathbf{E}\cdot d\mathbf{S} = \frac{1}{\varepsilon_0}\int_V \rho\, d\tau \quad \text{(Integral form)} \qquad ...(11.1)$$

$$\nabla\cdot\mathbf{E} = \frac{\rho}{\varepsilon_0} \quad \text{(Differential form)} \qquad ...(11.2)$$

Gauss's Law for Magnetic Field: Maxwell's Second Equation

The magnetic flux over a closed surface is always zero. In other words, magnetic lines of force are always closed i.e., free magnetic monopoles do not exist.

$$\oint_S \mathbf{B}\cdot d\mathbf{S} = 0 \quad \text{(Integral form)} \qquad ...(11.3)$$

$$\nabla\cdot\mathbf{B} = 0 \quad \text{(Differential form)} \qquad ...(11.4)$$

Generalised Form of Ampere's Law: Maxwell's Third Equation

Ampere's law for steady currents states that the circulation of magnetic field around a closed loop equals μ_0 times the total net current threading the loop. The integral and differential forms of the law is

$$\oint_C \mathbf{B}\cdot d\mathbf{l} = \mu_0 I = \mu_0 \oint_S \mathbf{J}\cdot d\mathbf{S} \quad \text{(Integral form)} \qquad ...(11.5)$$

$$\nabla \times \mathbf{B} = \mu_0 \mathbf{J} \qquad ...(11.6)$$

Taking divergence of eqn. (11.6) we have

$$\nabla \cdot \nabla \times \mathbf{B} = \mu_0 \nabla \cdot \mathbf{J} \qquad ...(11.7)$$

The left hand side of eqn. (11.7) is identically zero but the right hand is zero only for steady currents and not for non-steady currents. So Ampere's law in this form is not, in general, true. For non-steady current, the equation of continuity (which is a statement of law of conservation of charge) states that $\nabla \cdot \mathbf{J} = -\frac{\partial \rho}{\partial t}$. Thus, the Ampere's law in the form (11.6) is incompatible with the equation of continuity and hence, needs correction. It was James Clerk Maxwell who for the first time tried to remove the inconsistency between the Ampere's law and the equation of continuity. For non-steady current, the equation of continuity reads

$$\nabla \cdot \mathbf{J} = -\frac{\partial \rho}{\partial t} \qquad ...(11.8)$$

Substituting for ρ in above equation from Gauss's law (11.2) we have

$$\nabla \cdot \mathbf{J} = -\frac{\partial (\nabla \cdot \varepsilon_0 \mathbf{E})}{\partial t}$$

or

$$\nabla \cdot \left(\mathbf{J} + \varepsilon_0 \frac{\partial \mathbf{E}}{\partial t} \right) = 0 \qquad ...(11.9)$$

This equation shows that the quantity $\left(\mathbf{J} + \varepsilon_0 \frac{\partial \mathbf{E}}{\partial t} \right)$ and not simply $\mathbf{J}$ satisfies the equation of continuity. The quantity $\varepsilon_0 \frac{\partial \mathbf{E}}{\partial t}$ has the dimensions of current density. Maxwell called it *displacement current density.* Thus

$$\mathbf{J}_d = \varepsilon_0 \frac{\partial \mathbf{E}}{\partial t} \qquad ...(11.10)$$

This equation shows that a time–varying electric field constitutes a current which in turn will produce a magnetic field. Thus, a time varying electric field sets up a time varying magnetic field and vice-versa.

Taking the displacement current into consideration, the generalised form of Ampere's law becomes

$$\oint \mathbf{B} \cdot d\mathbf{l} = \mu_0 \int \left(\mathbf{J} + \varepsilon_0 \frac{\partial \mathbf{E}}{\partial t} \right) \cdot d\mathbf{S} \qquad ...(11.11)$$

In differential form this equation is written as

$$\nabla \times \mathbf{B} = \mu_0 \left(\mathbf{J} + \varepsilon_0 \frac{\partial \mathbf{E}}{\partial t} \right) \qquad ...(11.12)$$

Example of displacement current

Consider a parallel plate capacitor connected to a battery through a key. When the key is pressed, the charges begin to accumulate on the plates of the capacitor. During the growth of charge, conduction current flows through the connecting wire. At any instant, during the charging process, the electric field between the plates is related to the charge q on the plate through the relation

$$E = \frac{q}{\varepsilon_0 A}$$

The growth of electric field with time is given by

$$\frac{dE}{dt} = \frac{1}{\varepsilon_0 A}\frac{dq}{dt} = \frac{1}{\varepsilon_0 A} I_C$$

Where I_C is the conduction current in the connecting wire.

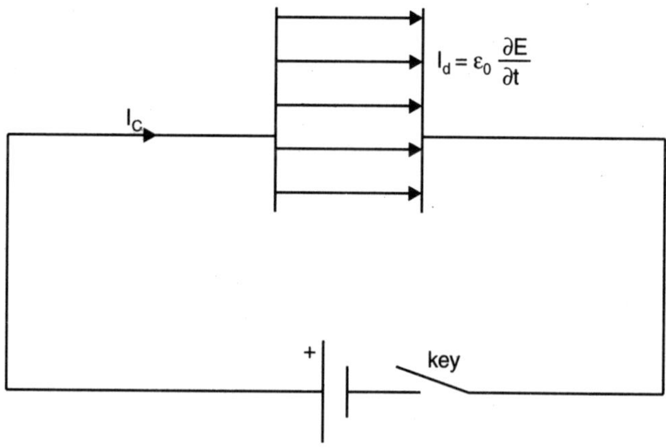

Fig. 11.1. Conduction current I_C flows in connecting wire whereas displacement current I_d flows between the capacitor plates. $I_d = I_C$.

Displacement current

$$I_d = \varepsilon_0 A \frac{\partial E}{\partial t} = \frac{dq}{dt} = I_C$$

Thus, the conduction current density J_C flowing through the connecting wire equals the displacement density J_d flowing between the plates. The introduction of displacement current maintains the idea of continuous current.

Faraday Law of Electromagnetic Induction: Maxwell's Fourth Equation

A time varying magnetic field sets up an electric field. The circulation of this induced electric field around a loop equals the negative time rate of change of magnetic flux linked with the loop.

$$\oint \mathbf{E}\cdot d\mathbf{l} = -\int \frac{\partial \mathbf{B}}{\partial t}\cdot d\mathbf{S} \quad \text{(Integral form)} \qquad ...(11.13)$$

$$\nabla \times \mathbf{E} = -\frac{\partial \mathbf{B}}{\partial t} \quad \text{(Differential form)} \qquad ...(11.14)$$

11.2. MAXWELL'S EQUATIONS IN VACUUM (FREE SPACE)

In free space the charge density ρ and conduction current density J_C associated with free charges are zero. Maxwell's equations in free space become

$$\nabla \cdot \mathbf{E} = 0 \qquad \text{...(11.15)}$$

$$\nabla \cdot \mathbf{B} = 0 \qquad \text{...(11.16)}$$

$$\nabla \times \mathbf{B} = \mu_0 \varepsilon_0 \frac{\partial \mathbf{E}}{\partial t} \qquad \text{...(11.17)}$$

$$\nabla \times \mathbf{E} = -\frac{\partial \mathbf{B}}{\partial t} \qquad \text{...(11.18)}$$

11.3. ELECTROMAGNETIC WAVE EQUATION IN FREE SPACE

Taking curl of eqn. (11.18) we obtain

$$\nabla \times \nabla \times \mathbf{E} = -\frac{\partial}{\partial t}(\nabla \times \mathbf{B})$$

$$-\nabla^2 \mathbf{E} + \nabla(\nabla \cdot \mathbf{E}) = -\frac{\partial}{\partial t}(\nabla \times \mathbf{B}) \qquad \text{...(11.19)}$$

Making use of equations $\nabla \cdot \mathbf{E} = 0$ and $\nabla \times \mathbf{B} = \mu_0 \varepsilon_0 \frac{\partial \mathbf{E}}{\partial t}$ in above equation we have

$$\nabla^2 \mathbf{E} = \mu_0 \varepsilon_0 \frac{\partial^2 \mathbf{E}}{\partial t^2} \qquad \text{...(11.20)}$$

Similarly, starting with eqn. (11.17) we can arrive at the equation

$$\nabla^2 \mathbf{B} = \mu_0 \varepsilon_0 \frac{\partial^2 \mathbf{B}}{\partial t^2} \qquad \text{...(11.21)}$$

Equations (11.20) and (11.21) are of the form of general *wave equation*. These equations state that the variations in **E** and **B** propagate with speed $\frac{1}{\sqrt{\mu_0 \varepsilon_0}}$ in free space. The constants μ_0 and ε_0 can be determined from purely electrical measurements and the value of $\frac{1}{\sqrt{\mu_0 \varepsilon_0}}$ comes out to be 3×10^8 m/s, which is the same as the speed of light c in vacuum. This accidental coincidence led Maxwell to suggest that *light is an electromagnetic wave.*

If the electric and magnetic fields do not vary with time, Maxwell's equations become

(*i*) $\nabla \cdot \mathbf{E} = 0$ (*ii*) $\nabla \cdot \mathbf{B} = 0$ (*iii*) $\nabla \times \mathbf{B} = \mu_0 \mathbf{J}$ (*iv*) $\nabla \times \mathbf{E} = 0$

Of these, (*i*) and (*iv*) equations describe the electrostatic phenomena, (*ii*) and (*iii*) describe the magnetostatic phenomena associated with steady currents. If **E** and **B** vary slowly, the displacement current is negligible, the first three equations remain the same, but the fourth equation becomes $\nabla \times \mathbf{E} = -\frac{\partial \mathbf{B}}{\partial t}$. In this case too, the variations in **E** and **B** do not move out far away from the source. On the other hand, if **E** and **B** vary rapidly with frequency greater than 10^5 Hz, the displacement current is not negligible and the Maxwell's equations predict new time varying **E** and **B** fields which propagate in free space with speed $c = \frac{1}{\sqrt{\mu_0 \varepsilon_0}} = 3 \times 10^8$ m/s. These rapidly varying fields are called *electromagnetic waves.*

Experiments show that the physiological, photochemical, photoelectrical and other actions of light are due to the oscillations of the **electric vector**, therefore, electric vector is considered to be the **light vector.**

11.4. PLANE WAVES

Far away from the source, the wave fronts of the electromagnetic waves are plane. A plane wave consists of parallel wave fronts which are perpendicular to the direction of propagation. The simplest type of wave that is solution of the wave equation is the plane sinusoidal waves. The sinusoidal waves are not only the simplest solutions of the wave equation but they are good approximations to many real problems. Moreover, the Fourier analysis enables us to represent any complex wave as a superposition of sinusoidal waves. For these reasons, we consider the sinusoidal waves as the solution to the wave equation.

A sinusoidal electromagnetic wave travelling in an arbitrary direction is represented as

$$\mathbf{E} = \mathbf{E}_0 e^{i(\mathbf{k}\cdot\mathbf{r}-\omega t)} \qquad ...(11.22)$$

$$\mathbf{B} = \mathbf{B}_0 e^{i(\mathbf{k}\cdot\mathbf{r}-\omega t)} \qquad ...(11.23)$$

The phase velocity of the wave is

$$c = \frac{\omega}{k} \qquad ...(11.24)$$

In eqns. (11.22) and (11.23) $\mathbf{E}_0$ and $\mathbf{B}_0$ represent the amplitudes of electric and magnetic fields and **k** is wave vector pointing in the direction of propagation of wave, $|\mathbf{k}| = \frac{2\pi}{\lambda}$. Vector **r** is the position vector of a point on the plane wave front. Obviously, $\mathbf{k}\cdot\mathbf{r} = k_x x + k_y y + k_z z$.

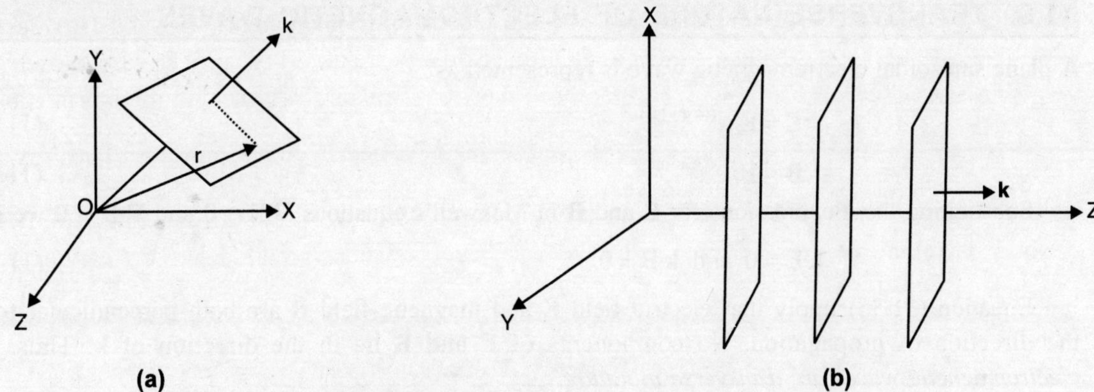

Fig. 11.2. (a) A plane wave propagating in an arbitrary direction.
(b) A plane wave propagating in z-direction.

Representing a sinusoidal wave in complex exponential form has an advantage. It is very convenient to perform mathematical manipulations with exponential functions. For instance, if

$$\mathbf{E} = \mathbf{E}_0 e^{i(k_x x + k_y y + k_z z - \omega t)} \qquad \text{...(11.25)}$$

Then
$$\frac{\partial \mathbf{E}}{\partial t} = -i\omega \mathbf{E} \qquad \text{...(11.26)}$$

And
$$\frac{\partial \mathbf{E}}{\partial x} = ik_x \mathbf{E}, \quad \frac{\partial \mathbf{E}}{\partial y} = ik_y \mathbf{E}, \quad \frac{\partial \mathbf{E}}{\partial z} = ik_z \mathbf{E}, \qquad \text{...(11.27)}$$

A careful examination of these relations reveals that the differentiation of **E** with respect to time is equivalent to multiplication of **E** by $-i\omega$, the differentiation of **E** with respect to x is equivalent to multiplication of **E** by ik_x and so on. For convenience we write the correspondence below.

$$\frac{\partial}{\partial t} \equiv -i\omega, \quad \frac{\partial}{\partial x} \equiv ik_x, \quad \frac{\partial}{\partial y} \equiv ik_y, \quad \frac{\partial}{\partial z} \equiv ik_z, \quad \nabla \equiv i\mathbf{k}, \quad \nabla\cdot\mathbf{E} \equiv i\mathbf{k}\cdot\mathbf{E}, \quad \nabla\times\mathbf{E} \equiv i\mathbf{k}\times\mathbf{E} \qquad \text{...(11.28)}$$

In view of these relations, the Maxwell's equations in free space assume the following *algebraic forms.*

$$\nabla\cdot\mathbf{E} = 0 \quad \Leftrightarrow \quad \mathbf{k}\cdot\mathbf{E} = 0 \qquad \text{...(11.29)}$$

$$\nabla\cdot\mathbf{B} = 0 \quad \Leftrightarrow \quad \mathbf{k}\cdot\mathbf{B} = 0 \qquad \text{...(11.30)}$$

$$\nabla\times\mathbf{B} = \mu_0\varepsilon_0 \frac{\partial \mathbf{E}}{\partial t} \quad \Leftrightarrow \quad \mathbf{k}\times\mathbf{B} = -\mu_0\varepsilon_0\omega\mathbf{E} \qquad \text{...(11.31)}$$

$$\nabla\times\mathbf{E} = -\frac{\partial \mathbf{B}}{\partial t} \quad \Leftrightarrow \quad \mathbf{k}\times\mathbf{E} = \omega\mathbf{B} \qquad \text{...(11.32)}$$

11.5. TRANSVERSE NATURE OF ELECTROMAGNETIC WAVES

A plane sinusoidal electromagnetic wave is represented as

$$\mathbf{E} = \mathbf{E}_0 e^{i(\mathbf{k}\cdot\mathbf{r}-\omega t)} \quad ...(11.33)$$

$$\mathbf{B} = \mathbf{B}_0 e^{i(\mathbf{k}\cdot\mathbf{r}-\omega t)} \quad ...(11.34)$$

Substituting these expressions for **E** and **B** in Maxwell's equations $\nabla\cdot\mathbf{E} = 0$ and $\nabla\cdot\mathbf{B} = 0$ we get

$$\mathbf{k}\cdot\mathbf{E} = 0 \text{ and } \mathbf{k}\cdot\mathbf{B} = 0 \quad ...(11.35)$$

Equation (11.35) imply that electric field **E** and magnetic field **B** are both perpendicular to **k,** the direction of propagation. No components of **E** and **B** lie in the direction of **k**. Thus, the *electromagnetic waves are transverse in nature.*

11.6. DISPERSION RELATION FOR ELECTROMAGNETIC WAVES IN VACUUM

The algebraic forms of Maxwell's equations $\nabla\times\mathbf{B} = \mu_0\varepsilon_0 \frac{\partial \mathbf{E}}{\partial t}$ and $\nabla\times\mathbf{E} = -\frac{\partial \mathbf{B}}{\partial t}$ are

$$\mathbf{k}\times\mathbf{B} = -\mu_0\varepsilon_0\omega\mathbf{E} \quad ...(11.36a)$$

and

$$\mathbf{k}\times\mathbf{E} = \omega\mathbf{B} \quad ...(11.36b)$$

Substituting **B** from (11.36a) in (11.36b) we have

$$\mathbf{k}\times(\mathbf{k}\times\mathbf{E}) = -\mu_0\varepsilon_0\omega^2\mathbf{E}$$

or
$$-(\mathbf{k}\cdot\mathbf{k})\mathbf{E} + (\bar{\mathbf{k}}\cdot\bar{\mathbf{E}})\bar{\mathbf{k}} = -\mu_0\varepsilon_0\omega^2\mathbf{E}$$

or
$$k^2 = \mu_0\varepsilon_0\omega^2 \text{ or } \omega = ck \quad ...(11.37)$$

This is the dispersion relation for electromagnetic waves in vacuum. The phase velocity of the wave is

$$\text{phase velocity } v_\varphi = \frac{\omega}{k} = c$$

Since the phase velocity is independent of frequency, vacuum is a *non-dispersive* medium to electromagnetic waves.

11.7. INTRINSIC IMPEDANCE OF VACUUM

The algebraic form of Maxwell's equation $\nabla\times\mathbf{B} = \mu_0\varepsilon_0 \frac{\partial \mathbf{E}}{\partial t}$ is

$$\mathbf{k}\times\mathbf{B} = -\mu_0\varepsilon_0\omega\mathbf{E}$$

This equation gives

$$\mathbf{E} = -\frac{\mathbf{k}\times\mathbf{B}}{\mu_0\varepsilon_0\omega}$$

The magnitude of electric field is

$$E = \frac{kB}{\mu_0 \varepsilon_0 \omega} = cB = \mu_0 cH \quad (\mathbf{k} \text{ and } \mathbf{B} \text{ are mutually perpendicular}) \quad ...(11.38)$$

The ratio E/H has units of impedance (ohm) and is called *intrinsic impedance* Z of vacuum.

$$Z = \frac{E}{H} = \mu_0 c = \frac{1}{\varepsilon_0 c} = \sqrt{\frac{\mu_0}{\varepsilon_0}} = \sqrt{4\pi \times 10^{-7} \times 4\pi \times 9 \times 10^9} = 120\pi = 376 \text{ ohm}$$

Since the ratio E/H or Z is a real number, the electric field **E** and magnetic field **H** are in phase.

11.8. E AND B ARE MUTUALLY PERPENDICULAR

Dotting eqn. (11.36b) with **E** we have

$$\mathbf{E}\cdot(\mathbf{k} \times \mathbf{E}) = \omega \mathbf{E}\cdot\mathbf{B}$$

Left hand side is zero (property of scalar triple product). Hence

$$\mathbf{E}\cdot\mathbf{B} = 0$$

Thus **E** and **B** are mutually perpendicular. Equations (11.36a) and (11.36b) show that **E, B** and **k** form a right-handed orthogonal triad of vectors.

11.9. RELATION BETWEEN E AND B

The geometrical form **k** × **E** = ω**B** of Faraday law $\nabla \times \mathbf{E} = -\frac{\partial \mathbf{B}}{\partial t}$ gives the relation between the magnitudes of **E** and **B.**

$$kE = \omega B \quad \text{or} \quad E = cB \quad ...(11.39)$$

A plane electromagnetic wave travelling in z-direction has $k_x = k_y = 0$ and $E_x = B_z = 0$. Making use of these results in equation **k** × **E** = ω**B** we obtain

$$E_x = cB_y \quad \text{and} \quad E_y = -cB_x \quad ...(11.40)$$

Equation (11.36) also gives the same results. Equation (11.40) show that E_x is coupled to B_y and E_y is coupled to B_x. This means that if E_x is set up, it produces B_y which in turn produces E_x and so on. In this case neither E_y nor B_x is produced. Also we see that if E_y is produced then B_x also appears which in turn sets up E_y. In this case E_x and B_y are not produced. Thus the components E_x and B_y are independent of E_y and B_x. It is then possible to produce an electromagnetic wave in which E_x and B_y are only present. Such a wave is called *linear* (*plane*) *polarized* along x-direction and is represented as

$$\mathbf{E}_x = \hat{\mathbf{x}} E_{0x} e^{i(k_z z - \omega t)} \quad ...(11.41)$$

$$\mathbf{B}_y = \hat{\mathbf{y}} B_{0y} e^{i(k_z z - \omega t)} \quad ...(11.42)$$

Here $\hat{\mathbf{x}}$ and $\hat{\mathbf{y}}$ are unit vectors in x- and y-directions.

If the wave contains E_y and B_x components only, it is said to be linearly polarized along y-direction and is represented as

$$\mathbf{E}_y = \hat{\mathbf{y}} E_{0y} e^{i(k_z z - \omega t)} \quad ...(11.43)$$

$$\mathbf{B}_x = \hat{\mathbf{x}} B_{0x} e^{i(k_z z - \omega t)} \quad ...(11.44)$$

11.10. INTENSITY OF ELECTROMAGNETIC WAVE

Electromagnetic waves transport energy and momentum with them. The amount of energy that is transported in unit time through unit area held normal to the direction of propagation is called *intensity* of wave. It is the product of energy density and the speed of the wave. The energy density of electromagnetic field in vacuum is

$$\textit{energy density } u = u_E + u_M = \frac{1}{2}\varepsilon_0 E^2 + \frac{1}{2}\frac{B^2}{\mu} \quad ...(11.45)$$

Since $E = cB, \ u_E = u_M$

Therefore, $u = \varepsilon_0 E^2$

The average value of energy density over one period is

$$\langle u \rangle = \varepsilon_0 \langle E^2 \rangle \quad ...(11.46)$$

Energy density is a real quantity. To calculate $\langle E^2 \rangle$ we must take real part of E. So

$$\langle E^2 \rangle = \langle [E_0 \cos(\mathbf{k}\cdot\mathbf{r} - \omega t)]^2 \rangle$$

$$= E_0^2 \left[\frac{1}{T} \int_0^T \cos^2(\mathbf{k}\cdot\mathbf{r} - \omega t) dt \right]$$

$$= \frac{1}{2} E_0^2$$

Therefore, $\langle u \rangle = \frac{1}{2}\varepsilon_0 E_0^2$ ...(11.47)

The intensity of wave is

$$I = c\langle u \rangle = \frac{1}{2}\varepsilon_0 E_0^2 \quad ...(11.48)$$

11.11. MAXWELL'S EQUATIONS INSIDE MATTER

Maxwell's equations with $\rho = 0$, $\mathbf{J} = \mathbf{0}$ describe the behaviour of field vectors **E** and **B** in vacuum. The propagation of electromagnetic waves in material media greatly affected by properties of media because there are other sources of field vectors **E** and **B**. In dielectric, the electric field of wave produces polarization as a result of which polarization charges with charge density $\rho_b = -\nabla\cdot\mathbf{P}$ appear where **P** is polarization vector. The time variation of **P** causes polarization current. If there are N charges per unit volume, each carrying a charge q and having average drift velocity **v**, the polarization current density $\mathbf{J}_p$ given by

$$\mathbf{J}_p = Nq\mathbf{v} = N\frac{d}{dt}(q\mathbf{x}) = N\frac{d}{dt}\mathbf{p} = \frac{d\mathbf{P}}{dt}$$

This polarization current is also a source of magnetic field.

When dealing with magnetic materials, the magnetization vector **M** also presents itself as a source of magnetic field. The sources of **M** are the atomic currents which result from the spin and orbital motion of electrons. These microscopic currents give rise to an equivalent average current density $\mathbf{J}_m = \nabla \times \mathbf{M}$. Notice that the current densities $\mathbf{J}_p$ and $\mathbf{J}_m$ are entirely different in their origin. Sources of $\mathbf{J}_p$ are the linear motion of charges whereas the sources of $\mathbf{J}_m$ are rotatory motion of electrons. Keeping in view of these new sources of **E** and **B** we shall obtain Maxwell's equations with appropriate modifications.

The Gauss's law in a polarized matter is

$$\nabla\cdot\mathbf{E} = \frac{\rho_{\text{total}}}{\varepsilon_0} = \frac{\rho_f + \rho_b}{\varepsilon_0} = \frac{\rho_f - \nabla\cdot\mathbf{P}}{\varepsilon_0}$$

or $$\nabla\cdot(\varepsilon_0\mathbf{E} + \mathbf{P}) = \rho_f$$

or $$\nabla\cdot\mathbf{D} = \rho_f \quad \text{where} \quad \mathbf{D} = \varepsilon_0\mathbf{E} + \mathbf{P} \qquad ...(11.49)$$

The equation expressing the Gauss's law for magnetic field viz

$$\nabla\cdot\mathbf{B} = 0 \qquad ...(11.50)$$

remains unchanged.

The Ampere's law inside matter is

$$\nabla\times\mathbf{B} = \mu_0\mathbf{J}_{\text{total}} = \mu_0\left(\mathbf{J}_{\text{free}} + \varepsilon_0\frac{\partial\mathbf{E}}{\partial t} + \mathbf{J}_p + \mathbf{J}_m\right)$$

or $$= \mu_0\left(\mathbf{J}_{\text{free}} + \varepsilon_0\frac{\partial\mathbf{E}}{\partial t} + \frac{\partial\mathbf{P}}{\partial t} + \nabla\times\mathbf{M}\right)$$

or $$\nabla\times\left(\frac{\mathbf{B}}{\mu_0} - \mathbf{M}\right) = \mathbf{J}_{\text{free}} + \frac{\partial}{\partial t}(\varepsilon_0\mathbf{E} + \mathbf{P})$$

or $$\nabla\times\mathbf{H} = \mathbf{J}_{\text{free}} + \frac{\partial\mathbf{D}}{\partial t} \quad \text{where} \quad \mathbf{H} = \frac{\mathbf{B}}{\mu_0} - \mathbf{M} \qquad ...(11.51)$$

This is the generalized form of Ampere's law in a material and represents Maxwell's third equation.

The Maxwell's fourth equation expressing Faraday law of electromagnetic induction remains unchanged in a material medium

$$\nabla\times\mathbf{E} = -\frac{\partial\mathbf{B}}{\partial t} \qquad ...(11.52)$$

We now rewrite all the Maxwell's equations inside matter together for convenience.

$$\boxed{\nabla\cdot\mathbf{B} = 0, \qquad \nabla\cdot\mathbf{D} = \rho_f, \qquad \nabla\times\mathbf{H} = \mathbf{J}_{free} + \frac{\partial\mathbf{D}}{\partial t}, \qquad \nabla\times\mathbf{E} = -\frac{\partial\mathbf{B}}{\partial t}}$$

Where $\mathbf{D} = \varepsilon_0 \mathbf{E} + \mathbf{P}$, and $\mathbf{H} = \dfrac{\mathbf{B}}{\mu_0} - \mathbf{M}$

In order to specify the polarization vector **P** and the magnetization vector **M,** which describe the properties of material medium we need two more equations, often called *constitutive relations.*

$$\mathbf{P} = \varepsilon_0 (\varepsilon_r - 1)\mathbf{E}, \quad \mathbf{D} = \varepsilon_0 \varepsilon_r \mathbf{E} = \varepsilon \mathbf{E} \qquad ...(11.53)$$

$$\mathbf{M} = \chi \mathbf{H}, \quad \mathbf{B} = \mu_0 \mu_r \mathbf{H} = \mu \mathbf{H} \qquad ...(11.54)$$

11.12. ELECTROMAGNETIC WAVES IN A DIELECTRIC MEDIUM

In a dielectric medium there are no external free charges and free currents. Maxwell's equations in such a medium are:

$$\nabla \cdot \mathbf{E} = 0, \ \nabla \cdot \mathbf{B} = 0, \ \nabla \times \mathbf{H} = \frac{\partial \mathbf{D}}{\partial t}, \nabla \times \mathbf{E} = -\frac{\partial \mathbf{B}}{\partial t}$$

We assume that the medium is linear in which the following *constitutive relations* hold.

$$\mathbf{D} = \varepsilon \mathbf{E} \ \text{ and } \ \mathbf{B} = \mu \mathbf{H} \qquad ...(11.55)$$

In view of constitutive relations the Maxwell's equations become

$$\nabla \cdot \mathbf{E} = 0, \ \nabla \cdot \mathbf{B} = 0, \ \nabla \times \mathbf{B} = \mu\varepsilon \frac{\partial \mathbf{E}}{\partial t}, \ \nabla \times \mathbf{E} = -\frac{\partial \mathbf{B}}{\partial t} \qquad ...(11.56)$$

These equations lead to the following wave equation

$$\nabla^2 \mathbf{E} = \mu\varepsilon \frac{\partial^2 \mathbf{E}}{\partial t^2} \ \text{ and } \ \nabla^2 \mathbf{B} = \mu\varepsilon \frac{\partial^2 \mathbf{B}}{\partial t^2} \qquad ...(11.57)$$

The velocity of the electromagnetic wave in the dielectric medium is

$$v = \frac{1}{\sqrt{\mu\varepsilon}} = \frac{1}{\sqrt{\mu_0 \varepsilon_0 \mu_r \varepsilon_r}} = \frac{c}{\sqrt{\mu_r \varepsilon_r}} \qquad ...(11.58)$$

The index of refraction of the medium is

$$n = \frac{c}{v} = \sqrt{\mu_r \varepsilon_r} \qquad ...(11.59)$$

For most of the materials (particularly non-magnetic ones) $\mu = \mu_0$ *i.e.* $\mu_r = 1$ and therefore the index of refraction is given by

$$n = \sqrt{\varepsilon_r} \qquad ...(11.60)$$

Sinusoidal plane wave solution of wave equation is

$$\mathbf{E} = \mathbf{E}_0 e^{i(\mathbf{k}\cdot\mathbf{r} - \omega t)}, \quad \mathbf{B} = \mathbf{B}_0 e^{i(\mathbf{k}\cdot\mathbf{r} - \omega t)} \qquad ...(11.61)$$

The vectors **E, B** and **k** form a set of orthogonal vectors and make a right-handed coordinate system.

The algebraic form of Maxwell equation $\nabla \times \mathbf{E} = -\dfrac{\partial \mathbf{B}}{\partial t}$ is $\mathbf{k} \times \mathbf{E} = \omega \mathbf{B} = \omega\mu \mathbf{H}$. This equation can be written as

$$\mathbf{H} = \frac{1}{\mu\omega}\mathbf{k} \times \mathbf{E} = \frac{k}{\mu\omega}\hat{\mathbf{k}} \times \mathbf{E} = \frac{1}{\mu v}\hat{\mathbf{k}} \times \mathbf{E}$$

Therefore, $$\frac{|\mathbf{E}|}{|\mathbf{H}|} = \frac{|\mathbf{E}_0|}{|\mathbf{H}_0|} = \sqrt{\frac{\mu}{\varepsilon}} \qquad \text{...(11.62)}$$

The ratio $|\mathbf{E}|/|\mathbf{H}|$ is called the *intrinsic impedance* Z of the medium. Since Z is real, **E**-field and **B**-field are in *phase*.

11.13. POYNTING THEOREM

Experiments show that an electromagnetic field has an energy that propagates in space with a certain energy density u and can flow from one place to another. This energy can also be transformed into other kinds of energy. For example, the field energy can do work on the charged particles of a substance through which it travels.

Let us consider a region of volume V enclosed by a surface Σ. We assume that there exists an electromagnetic field along with some charge and current configuration in the region. Now let us compute the work dw done by the electromagnetic field on a charged particle.

$$dw_i = \mathbf{F}\cdot d\mathbf{l} = q_i(\mathbf{E} + \mathbf{v}_i \times \mathbf{B})\cdot\mathbf{v}_i dt = q_i \mathbf{E}\cdot\mathbf{v}_i dt$$

The work done in unit time is

$$\frac{dw_i}{dt} = \mathbf{E}\cdot q_i \mathbf{v}_i$$

The rate of work done on all particles confined in unit volume is

$$\frac{dw}{dt} = \mathbf{E}\cdot(nq_i\mathbf{v}_i) = \mathbf{E}\cdot\mathbf{J}, \qquad n = \text{number of density of charged particles.}$$

Where **J** is current density in the region. The rate of work done by the electromagnetic field on all the particles confined to the volume V is

$$\frac{dW}{dt} = \int_V \mathbf{E}\cdot\mathbf{J}\, d\tau \qquad \text{...(11.63)}$$

Now we shall express $\mathbf{E}\cdot\mathbf{J}$ in terms of field vectors **E** and **B**. In doing so we shall make use of Maxwell equations

$$\nabla \times \mathbf{E} = -\frac{\partial \mathbf{B}}{\partial t} \quad (i) \text{ and } \quad \nabla \times \mathbf{H} = \mathbf{J} + \frac{\partial \mathbf{D}}{\partial t} \quad (ii)$$

The expression for $\mathbf{E}\cdot\mathbf{J}$ then becomes

$$\mathbf{E}\cdot\mathbf{J} = \mathbf{E}\cdot\left(\nabla \times \mathbf{H} - \frac{\partial \mathbf{D}}{\partial t}\right)$$

$$= \mathbf{E}\cdot\nabla \times \mathbf{H} - \mathbf{E}\cdot\frac{\partial \mathbf{D}}{\partial t}$$

The first term on the right hand side of above equation is transformed using the vector identity.

$$\nabla\cdot(\mathbf{a}\times\mathbf{b}) = \mathbf{b}\cdot\nabla\times\mathbf{a} - \mathbf{a}\cdot\nabla\times\mathbf{b}$$

$\therefore$ $$\mathbf{a}\cdot\nabla\times\mathbf{b} = \mathbf{b}\cdot\nabla\times\mathbf{a} - \nabla\cdot(\mathbf{a}\times\mathbf{b}), \quad \text{here } \mathbf{a}=\mathbf{E} \text{ and } \mathbf{b}=\mathbf{H}$$

Therefore, $$\mathbf{E}\cdot\mathbf{J} = -\nabla\cdot(\mathbf{E}\times\mathbf{H}) + \mathbf{H}\cdot\nabla\times\mathbf{E} - \mathbf{E}\cdot\frac{\partial\mathbf{D}}{\partial t}$$

Using Maxwell equation $\nabla\times\mathbf{E} = -\partial\mathbf{B}/\partial t$ we have

$$\mathbf{E}\cdot\mathbf{J} = -\nabla\cdot(\mathbf{E}\times\mathbf{H}) - \mathbf{H}\cdot\frac{\partial\mathbf{B}}{\partial t} - \mathbf{E}\cdot\frac{\partial\mathbf{D}}{\partial t}$$

or $$\mathbf{E}\cdot\mathbf{J} = -\nabla\cdot(\mathbf{E}\times\mathbf{H}) - \left[\mathbf{H}\cdot\frac{\partial\mathbf{B}}{\partial t} + \mathbf{E}\cdot\frac{\partial\mathbf{D}}{\partial t}\right] \qquad ...(11.64)$$

Now we shall show that the terms in the square bracket in above equation represents the time rate of change of energy density of electromagnetic field.

$$\mathbf{H}\cdot\frac{\partial\mathbf{B}}{\partial t} + \mathbf{E}\cdot\frac{\partial\mathbf{D}}{\partial t} = \mu\mathbf{H}\cdot\frac{\partial\mathbf{H}}{\partial t} + \varepsilon\mathbf{E}\cdot\frac{\partial\mathbf{E}}{\partial t}, \qquad \text{(in linear media } \mathbf{B}=\mu\mathbf{H},\ \mathbf{D}=\varepsilon\mathbf{E})$$

$$= \frac{\partial}{\partial t}\left(\frac{1}{2}\mu\mathbf{H}^2 + \frac{1}{2}\varepsilon\mathbf{E}^2\right)$$

$$= \frac{\partial}{\partial t}(u_e + u_m)$$

$$= \frac{\partial u}{\partial t} \qquad ...(11.65)$$

Where $u = u_e + u_m$ is the sum of electric and magnetic part of energy density and represents the total electromagnetic energy density.

So

$$\mathbf{E}\cdot\mathbf{J} = -\nabla\cdot(\mathbf{E}\times\mathbf{H}) - \frac{\partial u}{\partial t}$$

or $$-\frac{\partial u}{\partial t} = \nabla\cdot(\mathbf{E}\times\mathbf{H}) + \mathbf{E}\cdot\mathbf{J} \qquad ...(11.66)$$

Integrating both sides over the volume V we have

$$-\frac{\partial}{\partial t}\int_V u\,d\tau = \int_V \nabla\cdot(\mathbf{E}\times\mathbf{H})d\tau + \int_V \mathbf{E}\cdot\mathbf{J}d\tau \qquad ...(11.67)$$

When the volume integral in the first term of right hand side is transformed into surface integral with the help of divergence theorem, the above equation becomes

$$-\frac{\partial U}{\partial t} = \int_\Sigma (\mathbf{E}\times\mathbf{H})\cdot\mathbf{n}d\sigma + \int_V \mathbf{E}\cdot\mathbf{J}d\tau \qquad ...(11.68)$$

Let us interpret each term of this equation. The quantity (**E** × **H**) has the dimensions of $\frac{\text{enery}}{\text{time.area}} = \frac{\text{power}}{\text{area}}$ and represents power crossing unit area. The vector **E** × **H** is called ***Poynting Vector or energy flux density*** and is denoted by **S**.

$$\mathbf{S} = \mathbf{E} \times \mathbf{H} = \frac{\mathbf{E} \times \mathbf{B}}{\mu} \qquad \text{...(11.69)}$$

So the term $\int_{\Sigma} (\mathbf{E} \times \mathbf{H}) \cdot \mathbf{n} d\sigma$ or $\int_{\Sigma} \mathbf{S} \cdot \mathbf{n} d\sigma$ represents the power transported by the electromagnetic field through the surface Σ confining the volume V. The second term on the right hand side viz. $\int_V \mathbf{E} \cdot \mathbf{J}\, d\tau$ represents the rate at which electromagnetic energy is transforming into mechanical energy (kinetic + potential). The term on the left hand side is the rate of decrease of total electromagnetic energy. Therefore, the above equation states that the rate of diminution of total electromagnetic energy in volume V equals the sum of (*i*) energy flowing out per unit time through the surface Σ and (*ii*) the rate at which electromagnetic energy is being transformed into mechanical energy of particle. This statement is known as Poynting theorem and is nothing but the law of conservation of energy.

11.14. MOMENTUM OF ELECTROMAGNETIC FIELD

The electromagnetic waves exert pressure when they fall on a surface. This indicates that they carry momentum along with them. Consider a volume V enclosed by a surface Σ. Let there be electromagnetic field, charge and current configurations with the volume V. The force exerted by electromagnetic field on the charges and currents in unit volume is

$$\mathbf{f} = \rho(\mathbf{E} + \mathbf{v} \times \mathbf{B}) = \rho\mathbf{E} + \mathbf{J} \times \mathbf{B}, \qquad \mathbf{J} = \rho\mathbf{v} \qquad \text{...(11.70)}$$

On eliminating charge density ρ and current density **J** using Maxwell equations $\nabla \cdot \mathbf{E} = \rho/\varepsilon$ and $\nabla \times \mathbf{B} = \mu(\mathbf{J} + \varepsilon \frac{\partial \mathbf{E}}{\partial t})$ we have

$$\mathbf{f} = \varepsilon(\nabla \cdot \mathbf{E})\mathbf{E} + \frac{1}{\mu}(\nabla \times \mathbf{B}) \times \mathbf{B} - \varepsilon \frac{\partial \mathbf{E}}{\partial t} \times \mathbf{B} \qquad \text{...(11.71)}$$

We know that

$$\frac{\partial}{\partial t}(\mathbf{E} \times \mathbf{B}) = \frac{\partial \mathbf{E}}{\partial t} \times \mathbf{B} + \mathbf{E} \times \frac{\partial \mathbf{B}}{\partial t}$$

Substituting the expression for $\frac{\partial \mathbf{E}}{\partial t} \times \mathbf{B}$ from this formula in eqn. (11.71) we have

$$\mathbf{f} = \frac{\partial \mathbf{p}}{\partial t} = \varepsilon(\nabla \cdot \mathbf{E})\mathbf{E} - \frac{1}{\mu}\mathbf{B} \times (\nabla \times \mathbf{B}) + \varepsilon\mathbf{E} \times \frac{\partial \mathbf{B}}{\partial t} - \varepsilon \frac{\partial}{\partial t}(\mathbf{E} \times \mathbf{B})$$

In above equation **p** is momentum of particles per unit volume. To make the above equation more symmetric with respect to terms, we add $(\nabla \cdot \mathbf{B})\mathbf{B}$ to the right hand side. The addition of this term makes no change because $\nabla \cdot \mathbf{B} = 0$. Using Maxwell equation we also replace $\frac{\partial \mathbf{B}}{\partial t}$ by $-\nabla \times \mathbf{E}$. Performing these operations we get

$$\mathbf{f} = \frac{\partial \mathbf{p}}{\partial t} = \varepsilon(\nabla\cdot\mathbf{E})\mathbf{E} + (\nabla\cdot\mathbf{B})\mathbf{B} - \varepsilon\mathbf{E}\times(\nabla\times\mathbf{E}) - \frac{1}{\mu}\mathbf{B}\times(\nabla\times\mathbf{B}) - \varepsilon\frac{\partial}{\partial t}(\mathbf{E}\times\mathbf{B}) \qquad ...(11.72)$$

Transposing the last term to the left hand side we have

$$\frac{\partial \mathbf{p}}{\partial t} + \frac{\partial}{\partial t}(\varepsilon\mathbf{E}\times\mathbf{B}) = \varepsilon(\nabla\cdot\mathbf{E})\mathbf{E} + (\nabla\cdot\mathbf{B})\mathbf{B} - \varepsilon\mathbf{E}\times(\nabla\times\mathbf{E}) - \frac{1}{\mu}\mathbf{B}\times(\nabla\times\mathbf{B}) \qquad ...(11.73)$$

Integrating this equation over the volume V we get

$$\frac{\partial}{\partial t}\int_V \mathbf{p}\,d\tau + \frac{\partial}{\partial t}\int_V (\varepsilon\mathbf{E}\times\mathbf{B})\,d\tau = \int_V [\varepsilon(\nabla\cdot\mathbf{E})\mathbf{E} + (\nabla\cdot\mathbf{B})\mathbf{B} - \varepsilon\mathbf{E}\times(\nabla\times\mathbf{E}) - \frac{1}{\mu}\mathbf{B}\times(\nabla\times\mathbf{B})]\,d\tau \qquad ...(11.74)$$

The first term on left hand side represents the rate of change of *total mechanical momentum of particles*, say mechanical momentum $\mathbf{P}_{\text{mech}}$, the second term represents the rate of change of *total momentum of electromagnetic field.* Obviously, the quantity $\varepsilon(\mathbf{E} \times \mathbf{B}) = \varepsilon\mu(\mathbf{E} \times \mathbf{H})$ represents the momentum per unit volume of electromagnetic field or *electromagnetic momentum flux density.* Let it be denoted by $\mathbf{p}_{\text{field}}$. Thus

$$\mathbf{p}_{\text{field}} = \varepsilon\mu(\mathbf{E}\times\mathbf{H}) = \frac{\mathbf{E}\times\mathbf{H}}{v^2} = \frac{\mathbf{S}}{v^2} \qquad ...(11.75a)$$

The total momentum of field in volume V is

$$\mathbf{P}_{\text{field}} = \int_V \mathbf{p}_{\text{field}}\,d\tau = \int_V \varepsilon\mu(\mathbf{E}\times\mathbf{H})\,d\tau \qquad ...(11.75b)$$

In terms of total momentum (mechanical + electromagnetic) the force acting on the system is given by

$$\mathbf{F} = \frac{\partial}{\partial t}\left[\mathbf{P}_{\text{mech}} + \mathbf{P}_{\text{field}}\right] = \int_V [\varepsilon(\nabla\cdot\mathbf{E})\mathbf{E} + (\nabla\cdot\mathbf{B})\mathbf{B} - \varepsilon\mathbf{E}\times(\nabla\times\mathbf{E}) - \mu\mathbf{H}\times(\nabla\times\mathbf{H})]\,d\tau \qquad ...(11.76)$$

This equation is the statement of law of conservation of momentum in mathematical form.

11.15. MAXWELL STRESS TENSOR

The expression for the force per unit volume is

$$\mathbf{f}_{\text{mech + field}} = \frac{\partial}{\partial t}\left[\mathbf{p}_{\text{mech}} + \mathbf{p}_{\text{field}}\right] = \varepsilon\{(\nabla\cdot\mathbf{E})\mathbf{E} - \mathbf{E}\times(\nabla\times\mathbf{E})\} + \frac{1}{\mu}\{(\nabla\cdot\mathbf{B})\mathbf{B} - \mathbf{B}\times(\nabla\times\mathbf{B})\} \qquad ...(11.77)$$

Making use of the vector identities

$$\nabla(\mathbf{E}\cdot\mathbf{E}) = \nabla E^2 = 2(\mathbf{E}\cdot\nabla) + 2\mathbf{E}\times(\nabla\times\mathbf{E})$$

$$\nabla(\mathbf{B}\cdot\mathbf{B}) = \nabla B^2 = 2(\mathbf{B}\cdot\nabla) + 2\mathbf{E}\times(\nabla\times\mathbf{B})$$

we can transform the eqn. (11.77) into the following form

$$\mathbf{f}_{\text{mech + field}} = \varepsilon\left[(\nabla\cdot\mathbf{E})\mathbf{E} + (\mathbf{E}\cdot\nabla)\mathbf{E} - \frac{1}{2}\nabla E^2\right] + \frac{1}{\mu}\left[(\nabla\cdot\mathbf{B})\mathbf{B} + (\mathbf{B}\cdot\nabla)\mathbf{B} - \frac{1}{2}\nabla B^2\right] \qquad ...(11.78)$$

The expression on the right hand side of eqn. (11.78) is equal to the divergence of a quantity which has the dimensions of *stress* and is called **Maxwell stress tensor** and is denoted by $\vec{T}$. The *j*-th component of div $\vec{T}$ is given by

$$(\nabla\cdot\vec{\mathbf{T}})_j = \varepsilon\left[(\nabla\cdot\mathbf{E})E_j + (\mathbf{E}\cdot\nabla)E_j - \frac{1}{2}\nabla_j E^2\right] + \frac{1}{\mu}\left[(\nabla\cdot\mathbf{B})B_j + (\mathbf{B}\cdot\nabla)B_j - \frac{1}{2}\nabla_j B^2\right] \quad ...(11.79)$$

The nine elements of tensor $\vec{T} = \begin{pmatrix} T_{xx} & T_{xy} & T_{xz} \\ T_{yx} & T_{yy} & T_{yz} \\ T_{zx} & T_{zy} & T_{zz} \end{pmatrix}$ can be calculated from the formula

$$T_{ij} = \varepsilon\left[E_i E_j - \frac{1}{2}\delta_{ij}E^2\right] + \frac{1}{\mu}\left[B_i B_j - \frac{1}{2}\delta_{ij}B^2\right] \quad ...(11.80)$$

Where, $i, j = x, y, z$, and Kronecker delta $\delta_{ij} = 1$ for $i = j$ and $\delta_{ij} = 0$ for $i \neq j$. For example,

$$T_{xx} = \frac{1}{2}\varepsilon\left(E_x^2 - E_y^2 - E_z^2\right) + \frac{1}{2\mu}\left(B_x^2 - B_y^2 - B_z^2\right) \quad ...(11.81)$$

$$T_{xy} = \varepsilon E_x E_y + \frac{1}{\mu}B_x B_y \quad \text{etc.} \quad ...(11.82)$$

Physically, T_{ij} represents force per unit area in *i-th* direction acting on a surface element oriented in *j-th* direction. The diagonal elements of tensor $\vec{\mathbf{T}}$ viz. T_{xx}, T_{yy} and T_{zz} represent pressure and the off-diagonal elements T_{xy}, T_{xz}, etc. are shear.

In terms of $\vec{\mathbf{T}}$ we can write eqn. (11.78) as

$$\mathbf{f}_{\text{mech + field}} = \nabla\cdot\vec{\mathbf{T}} \quad ...(11.83)$$

Integrating both sides of this equation over the volume V we get

$$\mathbf{F} = \frac{\partial}{\partial t}\left(\mathbf{P}_{\text{mech}} + \mathbf{P}_{\text{field}}\right) = \int_V \nabla\cdot\vec{\mathbf{T}}\, d\tau$$

Transforming the volume integral on the right hand side into surface integral using divergence theorem we have

$$\frac{\partial}{\partial t}\left(\mathbf{P}_{\text{mech}} + \mathbf{P}_{\text{field}}\right) = \int_\Sigma \vec{\mathbf{T}}\cdot\mathbf{n}\, d\sigma \quad ...(11.84)$$

The left hand side represents the rate of growth of total momentum (mechanical + field) contained in the volume and the right hand side represents the flux of momentum of the field flowing into the volume V through the surface Σ confining it.

11.16. RELATION BETWEEN INTENSITY AND POYNTING VECTOR

In vacuum the Poynting vector **S** is

$$\mathbf{S} = \frac{\mathbf{E}\times\mathbf{B}}{\mu_0} = \frac{1}{\mu_0\omega}\mathbf{E}\times(\mathbf{k}\times\mathbf{E}) = \frac{1}{\mu_0\omega}\left[(\mathbf{E}\cdot\mathbf{E})\mathbf{k} - (\mathbf{E}\cdot\mathbf{k})\mathbf{E}\right]$$

$$= \left(\frac{E^2}{\mu_0\omega}\right)\mathbf{k} = \left(\frac{kE^2}{\mu_0\omega}\right)\hat{\mathbf{k}} = \varepsilon_0 cE^2\hat{\mathbf{k}}$$

$$|\mathbf{S}| = \varepsilon_0 cE^2 \qquad ...(11.85)$$

Time average of poynting vector is

$$< S > = \varepsilon_0 c < E^2 > = \frac{1}{2}\varepsilon_0 cE_0^2 \qquad ...(11.86)$$

Therefore

$$I = < S > = \frac{1}{2}\varepsilon_0 cE_0^2 \qquad ...(11.87)$$

11.17. ELECTROMAGNETIC WAVES IN A CONDUCTING MEDIUM

The propagation of electromagnetic wave in a conducting medium is greatly modified by its conductivity and permittivity. A conducting medium has no surplus charge *i.e.* $\rho_f = 0$. The motion of free charge carriers under the action of electric field of the incident electromagnetic wave constitutes a conduction current which in turn produces Joule heat. Thus the energy of the wave decreases as it progresses into the medium. For a homogeneous isotropic linear medium, the conduction current is given by $\mathbf{J_f} = \sigma\mathbf{E}$ where σ is conductivity of the medium. The Maxwell's equations in a simple conducting medium with $\mathbf{D} = \varepsilon\mathbf{E}$ and $\mathbf{B} = \mu\mathbf{H}$ are:

$$\nabla\cdot\mathbf{E} = 0 \qquad ...(11.88)$$

$$\nabla\cdot\mathbf{B} = 0 \qquad ...(11.89)$$

$$\nabla\times\mathbf{B} = \mu\sigma\mathbf{E} + \mu\varepsilon\frac{\partial\mathbf{E}}{\partial t} \qquad ...(11.90)$$

$$\nabla\times\mathbf{E} = -\frac{\partial\mathbf{B}}{\partial t} \qquad ...(11.91)$$

Taking curl of eqn. (11.91) and making use of eqn. (11.90) in the resulting equation we have

$$\nabla\times(\nabla\times\mathbf{E}) = -\frac{\partial(\nabla\times\mathbf{B})}{\partial t}$$

$$= -\frac{\partial}{\partial t}\left(\mu\sigma\mathbf{E} + \mu\varepsilon\frac{\partial\mathbf{E}}{\partial t}\right)$$

$$\nabla(\nabla\cdot\mathbf{E}) - \nabla^2\mathbf{E} = -\mu\sigma\frac{\partial\mathbf{E}}{\partial t} - \mu\varepsilon\frac{\partial^2\mathbf{E}}{\partial t^2}$$

$$\nabla^2 \mathbf{E} = \mu\sigma \frac{\partial \mathbf{E}}{\partial t} + \mu\varepsilon \frac{\partial^2 \mathbf{E}}{\partial t^2} \qquad ...(11.92)$$

A similar equation for field **B** can also be obtained.

$$\nabla^2 \mathbf{B} = \mu\sigma \frac{\partial \mathbf{B}}{\partial t} + \mu\varepsilon \frac{\partial^2 \mathbf{B}}{\partial t^2} \qquad ...(11.93)$$

This equation is called a generalized wave equation. We see that the wave eqns. (11.92 & 11.93) differ from that obtained in a dielectric medium in an additional term containing the first time derivative of **E** (or **B**). When $\sigma = 0$ this term vanishes and this equation terms into the corresponding equation of dielectric medium. The term $\frac{\partial \mathbf{E}}{\partial t}$ is called *damping term* and causes the energy of the electromagnetic wave to decrease as it propagates into the medium. The conducting medium is thus a *lossy* medium.

A plane wave of the following form may be taken as a solution of above wave equation

$$\mathbf{E} = \mathbf{E}_0 e^{i(\mathbf{k}\cdot\mathbf{r}-\omega t)} \qquad ...(11.94)$$

$$\mathbf{B} = \mathbf{B}_0 e^{i(\mathbf{k}\cdot\mathbf{r}-\omega t)} \qquad ...(11.95)$$

Substituting eqns. (11.94) in (11.88) and eqns. (11.95) in (11.89) we get

$$\mathbf{k}\cdot\mathbf{E} = \mathbf{k}\cdot\mathbf{B} = 0$$

This shows the transverse nature of electromagnetic wave.

When (11.94) is substituted in eqn. (11.90) we obtain

$$\mathbf{k}\times\mathbf{B} = -\mu\varepsilon\omega\left(1 + i\frac{\sigma}{\varepsilon\omega}\right)\mathbf{E} \qquad ...(11.96)$$

or

$$\mathbf{k}\times\mathbf{B} = -\mu\varepsilon\omega(1 + i\tau)\mathbf{E} \qquad ...(11.97)$$

Where

$$\tau = \frac{\sigma}{\varepsilon\omega} \qquad ...(11.98)$$

Similarly, when (11.95) is substituted in (11.91) we obtain

$$\mathbf{k}\times\mathbf{E} = \omega\mathbf{B} = \mu\omega\mathbf{H} \qquad ...(11.99)$$

Equations (11.96 or 11.97) and (11.99) are the algebraic form of Maxwell eqns. (11.90) and (11.91). Substituting **B** from eqns. (11.99) in (11.97) we have

$$\mathbf{k}\times(\mathbf{k}\times\mathbf{E}) = -\mu\varepsilon\omega^2(1 + i\tau)\mathbf{E}$$

$$(\mathbf{k}\cdot\mathbf{E})\mathbf{E} - (\mathbf{k}\cdot\mathbf{k})\mathbf{E} = -\mu\varepsilon\omega^2(1 + i\tau)\mathbf{E}$$

$$\tilde{k}^2 = \mu\varepsilon\omega^2(1 + i\tau) \qquad ...(11.100)$$

The symbol ~ over k indicates that it is a complex number. Equation (11.100) is the *dispersion relation* for an electromagnetic wave in a conducting medium. It is worth to notice that the propagation vector **k** is now a complex number and so are the phase velocity ($\tilde{v} = \frac{\omega}{k}$) and index of refraction ($\tilde{n} = \frac{c}{\tilde{v}} = \frac{c\tilde{k}}{\omega}$). Let us write $\tilde{k}$ in the form

$$\tilde{k} = k_1 + ik_2 \qquad ...(11.101)$$

Where k_1 and k_2 are real numbers.

Comparing (11.100) and (11.101) we have

$$k_1^2 - k_2^2 = \mu\varepsilon\omega^2 \qquad ...(11.102)$$

$$2k_1k_2 = \mu\sigma\omega \qquad ...(11.103)$$

Solving for k_1 *and* k_2 we get

$$k_1 = \omega\sqrt{\frac{\mu\varepsilon}{2}}\left[1 + \sqrt{1+\tau^2}\right]^{1/2} \qquad ...(11.104)$$

$$k_2 = \omega\sqrt{\frac{\mu\varepsilon}{2}}\left[-1 + \sqrt{1+\tau^2}\right]^{1/2} \qquad ...(11.105)$$

$$\therefore \qquad k^2 = k_1^2 + k_2^2 = \omega^2\left(\frac{\mu\varepsilon}{2}\right)\left(1+\tau^2\right)^{1/2}$$

or

$$k = \omega\sqrt{\frac{\mu\varepsilon}{2}}(1+\tau^2)^{1/4} \qquad ...(11.106)$$

Substituting $\mathbf{k} = \mathbf{k}_1 + i\mathbf{k}_2$ in eqns. (11.94) and (11.95) we get the equation of electromagnetic wave in conducting medium as

$$\mathbf{E} = \mathbf{E}_0 e^{-\mathbf{k}_2\cdot\mathbf{r}} e^{i(\mathbf{k}_1\cdot\mathbf{r} - \omega t)} \qquad ...(11.107)$$

$$\mathbf{B} = \mathbf{B}_0 e^{-\mathbf{k}_2\cdot\mathbf{r}} e^{i(\mathbf{k}_1\cdot\mathbf{r} - \omega t)} \qquad ...(11.108)$$

Equations (11.106) and (11.107) represent *damped wave* whose amplitudes attenuates exponentially as it progresses into the conducting medium. Notice that it is the imaginary part of the propagation constant that is responsible for the attenuation. Let $\mathbf{k}_2\cdot\mathbf{r} = ks$ where s is distance traversed along the direction of propagation. Equations (11.107) and (11.108) may be expressed as

$$\mathbf{E} = \mathbf{E}_0 e^{-k_2 s} e^{i(\mathbf{k}_1\cdot\mathbf{r} - \omega t)}$$

$$\mathbf{B} = \mathbf{B}_0 e^{-k_2 s} e^{i(\mathbf{k}_1\cdot\mathbf{r} - \omega t)}$$

Let the amplitude of the wave falls to $1/e$ its initial value after travelling a distance $s = \delta$ in the direction of propagation. The distance δ is called *skin depth* and is given by

$$E_0 e^{-k_2\delta} = E_0 e^{-1}$$

or

$$\delta = \frac{1}{k_2} \qquad ...(11.109)$$

Thus the imaginary part of k determines the attenuation of the wave and the real part of k determines the phase velocity and hence the conventional refractive index of the conductive medium.

Criterion for a Medium to be a Conductor or a Dielectric

Conductors are those materials in which conduction current dominates over the displacement current and converse is true for dielectrics (insulators). The ratio of the conduction current density to the displacement current density gives a criterion for dividing the substances into good conductors and dielectrics.

$$\frac{\mathbf{J}_{\text{conduction}}}{\mathbf{J}_{\text{displacement}}} = \frac{\sigma E}{\varepsilon \dfrac{\partial E}{\partial t}} = \frac{\sigma E}{-i\omega\varepsilon E} = i\frac{\sigma}{\omega\varepsilon} = i\tau \quad \text{...(11.110)}$$

A material for which $\tau = \dfrac{\sigma}{\omega\varepsilon} >> 1$ is called a *good conductor* and that for which $\tau = \dfrac{\sigma}{\omega\varepsilon} << 1$ is called a *good dielectric*. Notice that this criterion for classifying materials in two categories is frequency dependent. A material which is conductor at one frequency may be dielectric at the other.

For copper, $\sigma = 5.8\times10^{7}\,(\text{ohm.metre})^{-1}$ or Sm^{-1}

$$\varepsilon = \varepsilon_0 = 9\times10^{-12}\ \text{F/m}$$

$$\tau = \frac{\sigma}{\omega\varepsilon} = \frac{10^{18}}{\omega}$$

For frequencies up to, $\omega \approx 10^{16}$ rad/s (ultraviolet radiation), $\tau >> 1$ copper is a conductor. For frequencies greater than $\omega \approx 10^{20}$ rad/s (X-rays), $\tau << 1$, copper is a dielectric. For a typical insulator $\sigma \approx 10^{-15}$ $(\text{ohm.metre})^{-1}$ and $\varepsilon = 10^{-11}$ F/m we have $\tau = \dfrac{10^{-4}}{\omega}$. Thus for all frequencies $\tau << 1$, the displacement current dominates over conduction current hence the material is a good dielectric.

Skin Depth in a Good Conductor

For a good conductor, $\tau = \dfrac{\sigma}{\omega\varepsilon} >> 1$ we have

$$k_1 = k_2 = \omega\sqrt{\frac{\mu\varepsilon}{2}}\,\tau^{1/2} = \sqrt{\frac{\omega\mu\sigma}{2}} \quad \text{...(11.111)}$$

The *skin depth* in a good conductor is

$$\delta = \frac{1}{k_2} = \sqrt{\frac{2}{\omega\mu\sigma}} \quad \text{...(11.112)}$$

The *skin depth* is a measure of the distance to which an electromagnetic wave penetrates a conductor. For copper at frequency 50 Hz, skin depth δ = 9 mm and at frequency 1 MHz, δ = 0.007 mm. Thus *at very high frequency electromagnetic wave penetrates a very small distance in a conductor.*

Skin Depth at different wavelengths

Wavelength λ (m)	Skin depth δ (m)
10^{-7}	6.2×10^{-10}
10^{-5}	6.2×10^{-9}
10^{-1}	6.2×10^{-7}
10^{3}	6.2×10^{-5}

Refractive Index of Conducting Medium

In a conducting medium the propagation constant $\tilde{k}$ is complex and so will be the refracting index $\tilde{n}$. It is customary to write $\tilde{n}$ as $\tilde{n} = n + i\kappa$. Here the real part of $\tilde{n}$ viz. n is interpreted as the conventional refractive index and the imaginary part as attenuation constant. By definition

$$\tilde{n} = \frac{c}{\tilde{v}} = \frac{c}{\omega}\tilde{k}$$

$$\therefore \qquad n + i\kappa = \frac{c}{\omega}(k_1 + ik_2)$$

Thus, $$n = \frac{c}{\omega}k_1 \quad \text{and} \quad \kappa = \frac{c}{\omega}k_2$$

The propagation vector in a good conductor ($\tau = \frac{\sigma}{\omega\varepsilon} >> 1$)

$$k_1 = k_2 = \sqrt{\frac{\omega\mu\sigma}{2}}$$

And the phase velocity of the wave in a good conductor is

$$\tilde{v} = \frac{\omega}{k_1} = \sqrt{\frac{2\omega}{\mu\sigma}} \qquad ...(11.113)$$

The refractive index of a good conductor is therefore,

$$n = \frac{c}{\omega}k_1 = c\sqrt{\frac{\mu\sigma}{2\omega}} \qquad ...(11.114)$$

Since the refractive index of a conductor is frequency dependent, a conductor is thus a *dispersive medium* to electromagnetic waves.

Characteristic Impedance and Phase Difference between E and H or B

The algebraic form of Maxwell equation $\nabla \times \mathbf{B} = \mu\sigma\mathbf{E} + \mu\varepsilon\frac{\partial \mathbf{E}}{\partial t}$ is

$$\mathbf{k} \times \mathbf{B} = \mu\sigma\mathbf{E} + \mu\varepsilon\frac{\partial \mathbf{E}}{\partial t}$$

From this equation we have

$$\mathbf{E} = -\frac{\mathbf{k}\times\mathbf{B}}{\mu\varepsilon\omega(1+i\tau)} = -\frac{\tilde{k}}{\mu\varepsilon\omega(1+i\tau)}(\hat{\mathbf{k}}\times\mathbf{B}) = -\frac{\tilde{k}}{\omega\varepsilon(1+i\tau)}(\hat{\mathbf{k}}\times\mathbf{H}) \qquad ...(11.115)$$

The proportionality constant in above equation is called *characteristic (intrinsic) complex impedance* $\tilde{Z}$ of the medium.

$$\tilde{Z} = \frac{\tilde{k}}{\omega\varepsilon(1+i\tau)}, \qquad \text{where } \tilde{k} = \omega\sqrt{\mu\varepsilon(1+i\tau)}$$

In polar form $\tilde{Z}$ can be expressed as

$$\tilde{Z} = \frac{\sqrt{\mu/\varepsilon}}{(1+i\tau)^{1/2}} = \frac{\sqrt{\mu/\varepsilon}}{\left[(1+\tau^2)^{1/2}e^{i\varphi}\right]^{1/2}} = \frac{\sqrt{\mu/\varepsilon}}{(1+\tau^2)^{1/4}}e^{-i\varphi/2}, \quad \text{where } \tan\varphi = \tau = \frac{\sigma}{\omega\varepsilon}$$

The magnitude and phase of characteristic impedance are

$$|Z| = \frac{\sqrt{\mu/\varepsilon}}{\left[1+(\sigma/\varepsilon\omega)^2\right]^{1/4}} \quad \text{and} \quad \tan\varphi = \frac{\sigma}{\varepsilon\omega} \qquad ...(11.116)$$

Since the ratio E/H *i.e.* Z is complex, **E** and **H** are out of phase. In a conductor the phase difference between E and H is $\varphi/2$ where $\tan\varphi = \frac{\sigma}{\omega\varepsilon}$. For a perfect conductor $\sigma \to \infty \Rightarrow \phi \to \pi/2$. Therefore, $\varphi/2 = \pi/4$. If φ is small, then $\varphi \approx \tan\varphi = \frac{\sigma}{\omega\varepsilon}$. Hence phase difference between E and H is

$$\frac{\varphi}{2} = \frac{\sigma}{2\omega\varepsilon} \qquad ...(11.117)$$

11.18. ENERGY DENSITY IN A CONDUCTING MEDIUM

In a conducting medium electric field and magnetic field are given by

$$\mathbf{E} = \mathbf{E}_0 e^{-\mathbf{k}_2\cdot\mathbf{r}} e^{i(\mathbf{k}_1\cdot\mathbf{r}-\omega t)} \qquad ...(11.118)$$

$$\mathbf{B} = \mathbf{B}_0 e^{-\mathbf{k}_2\cdot\mathbf{r}} e^{i(\mathbf{k}_1\cdot\mathbf{r}-\omega t)} \qquad ...(11.119)$$

Instantaneous electric energy density is

$$u_e = \frac{1}{2}\varepsilon E^2 = \frac{1}{2}\varepsilon E_0^2 e^{-2\mathbf{k}_2\cdot\mathbf{r}}\cos^2(\mathbf{k}_1\cdot\mathbf{r}-\omega t) \qquad ...(11.120)$$

Time average of u_e over one period is

$$\langle u_e\rangle = \frac{1}{4}\varepsilon E_0^2 e^{-2\mathbf{k}_2\cdot\mathbf{r}} \qquad ...(11.121)$$

Instantaneous magnetic energy density is given by

$$u_m = \frac{B^2}{2\mu} = \frac{\mathbf{B}\cdot\mathbf{B}}{2\mu} = \frac{\mathbf{B}\cdot\mathbf{k}\times\mathbf{E}}{2\mu\omega} = \frac{\mathbf{B}\times\mathbf{k}\cdot\mathbf{E}}{2\mu\omega} = \frac{\varepsilon(1+i\tau)E^2}{2} = (1+i\tau)u_e \qquad ...(11.122)$$

Average value of magnetic energy is

$$\langle u_m \rangle = \sqrt{1+\tau^2}\,\langle u_e \rangle \qquad ...(11.123)$$

Evidently, the electric and magnetic energies are not equal in a conducting medium. The time average of total electromagnetic energy density is

$$\langle u \rangle = \langle u_e \rangle + \langle u_m \rangle = [1+\sqrt{1+\tau^2}]\langle u_e \rangle = \frac{1}{4}\left[1+\sqrt{1+\tau^2}\right]\varepsilon E_0^2 e^{-2\mathbf{k}_2\cdot\mathbf{r}} \qquad ...(11.124)$$

In a good conductor $\tau >> 1$, the energy density is

$$\langle u \rangle = \frac{1}{4}\cdot\frac{\sigma}{\omega} E_0^2 e^{-2\mathbf{k}_2\cdot\mathbf{r}} \quad \text{where} \quad k_2 = \sqrt{\frac{\mu\omega\sigma}{2}} \qquad ...(11.125)$$

The ratio of magnetic energy to electric energy is

$$\frac{\langle u_m \rangle}{\langle u_e \rangle} = \sqrt{1+\tau^2} \qquad ...(11.126)$$

It is evident that time averaged magnetic energy is greater than the time averaged electric energy and in a highly conducting medium such as metals ($\tau >> 1$), the energy is almost magnetic.

11.19. POYNTING VECTOR IN A CONDUCTING MEDIUM

The Poynting vector is given by

$$\mathbf{S} = \frac{\mathbf{E}\times\mathbf{B}}{\mu} = \frac{\mathbf{E}\times(\mathbf{k}\times\mathbf{E})}{\mu\omega} = \frac{(\mathbf{E}\cdot\mathbf{E})\mathbf{k} - (\mathbf{E}\cdot\mathbf{k})\mathbf{E}}{\mu\omega} = \frac{kE^2}{\mu\omega}\hat{\mathbf{k}} = \frac{|k|\,E^2 e^{i\varphi}}{\mu\omega}\hat{\mathbf{k}}, \quad \tan\varphi = \frac{k_2}{k_1}$$

Real part of S is

$$\mathbf{S} = \left[\frac{|k|}{\mu\omega} E_0^2 e^{-2\mathbf{k}_2\cdot\mathbf{r}} \cos^2(\mathbf{k}_1\cdot\mathbf{r} - \omega t)\cos\varphi\right]\hat{\mathbf{k}}$$

Time average of S is

$$\langle \mathbf{S} \rangle = \left[\frac{1}{2}\frac{|k|}{\mu\omega} E_0^2 e^{-2\mathbf{k}_2\cdot\mathbf{r}} \cos\varphi\right]\hat{\mathbf{k}}$$

For good conductor $k_2 = k_1 = \sqrt{\frac{\mu\omega\sigma}{2}}$, $\tan\varphi = 1$, $\varphi = 45°$. Therefore,

$$\langle \mathbf{S} \rangle = \left[\frac{1}{2}\sqrt{\frac{\sigma}{2\mu\omega}}\right] E_0^2 e^{-2\mathbf{k}_2\cdot r} \qquad ...(11.127)$$

SOLVED EXAMPLES

***Example* 1:** *A parallel plate capacitor consists of plane circular plates of radii 10 cm each. It is connected to a time varying voltage source. The electric field between the plates varies with time at the rate of 10^{10} V/s. What is the displacement current?*

***Solution*:**

Displacement current

$$I_d = J_d(plate\ area) = \left(\varepsilon_0 \frac{\partial E}{\partial t}\right)(\pi R^2) = \left(8.85\times10^{-12}\times10^{10}\right)(3.14\times10^{-2}) = 2.7\times10^{-3}\text{ A}$$

***Example* 2:** *A parallel plate capacitor with circular plates of radius R is being charged. During charging process, calculate the induced magnetic field between the plates at a distance (i) r < R, (ii) r > R from the axis of symmetry.*

***Solution*:**

During the charging process, the displacement current produces magnetic field whose field lines are concentric circles as shown in the figure. The circulation of magnetic field is

$$\oint \mathbf{B}\cdot\mathbf{dl} = \mu_0 I_d = \mu_0 \int \mathbf{J}\cdot\mathbf{d}A$$

Let us calculate the circulation around a circle of radius r.

$$B(2\pi r) = \mu_0\varepsilon_0 \frac{\partial E}{\partial t}(\pi r^2)$$

$$\therefore \quad B = \frac{1}{2}\mu_0\varepsilon_0 r\frac{\partial E}{\partial t} \quad \text{for} \quad r < R$$

For $r >$ R we have

$$B(2\pi r) = \mu_0\varepsilon_0 \frac{\partial E}{\partial t}(\pi R^2)$$

$$\therefore \quad B = \frac{1}{2}\mu_0\varepsilon_0 \frac{R^2}{r}\frac{\partial E}{\partial t}$$

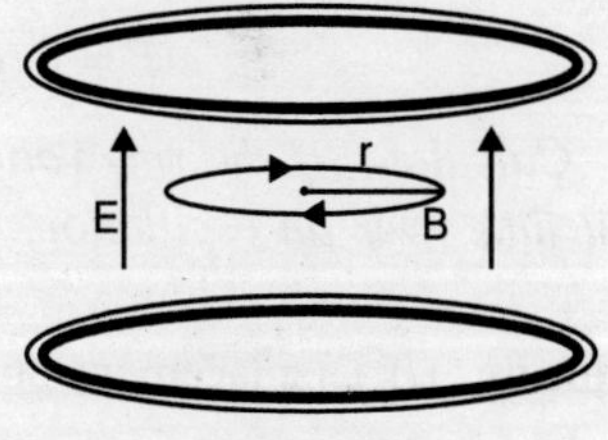

Fig. 11.3

***Example* 3:** *A 60 Watt point light source radiates equally in all directions. Calculate the magnitudes of the peak values of electric and magnetic fields at a distance 10 m from the source.*

***Solution*:**

The power radiated by the source is uniformly distributed in all directions. If $< S >$ is the mean value of Poynting vector at a distance r then,

$$P = 4\pi r^2 <S> = 4\pi r^2\left(\frac{1}{2}\varepsilon_0 c E_0^2\right)$$

$$\therefore \quad E_0 = \sqrt{\frac{2P}{4\pi\varepsilon_0 c r^2}} = \sqrt{\frac{2\times60}{(9\times10^9)^{-1}\times3\times10^8\times(10)^2}} = 6\text{ V/m}$$

And $$B_0 = \frac{E_0}{c} = \frac{6}{3\times10^8} = 2\times10^{-8}\text{ Wb m}^{-2}$$

***Example* 4:** *Outside the earth's atmosphere the intensity of sun light (solar constant) is 2.0 cal.cm^{-2}. min^{-1}(1.40 × 10^3 watt/m^2). Calculate*

(*i*) *the value of amplitudes of electric and magnetic field assuming light to be a plane wave.*

(*ii*) *the radiation pressure on the earth at normal incidence if it absorbs all the light.*

(*iii*) *the radiation pressure on the earth if it acts like a perfect mirror.*

***Solution*:**

(*i*) Amplitude of electric field $$E_0 = \sqrt{\frac{2I}{\varepsilon_0 c}} = \sqrt{\frac{2\times1.40\times10^3}{8.85\times10^{-12}\times3\times10^8}} = 1020\text{ Vm}^{-1}$$

Amplitude of magnetic field $$B_0 = \frac{E_0}{c} = \frac{1020}{3\times10^8} = 3.4\times10^{-6}\text{ Wb m}^{-2}$$

(*ii*) Radiation pressure on the earth $$p = \frac{I}{c} = \frac{1.4\times10^3}{3\times10^8} = 4.67\times10^{-6}\text{ N m}^{-2}$$

(*iii*) Radiation pressure $$p = \frac{2I}{c} = 9.34\times10^{-6}\text{ N m}^{-2}$$

***Example* 5:** *A plane polarized electromagnetic wave propagating in z-direction is represented by*

$$E = E_0\cos(kz - \omega t),\quad E_0 = 50\,mV\,m^{-1},\quad \nu = 100\,MHz.$$

Calculate (i) the rms value of displacement current (ii) mean energy flowing per unit area per unit time over an oscillation.

Solution. (*i*) Displacement current density $J_d = \varepsilon_0\dfrac{\partial E}{\partial t} = \varepsilon_0\omega E_0\sin(kz - \omega t)$

$$\therefore\quad <J_d{}^2> = \frac{1}{2}\varepsilon_0^2\omega^2 E_0^2$$

$$\left[<J_d{}^2>\right]^{1/2} = \frac{1}{\sqrt{2}}\varepsilon_0\omega E_0^2 = \frac{8.85\times10^{-12}\times(2\pi\times10^8)\times50\times10^{-3}}{1.414} = 1.98\times10^{-4}\text{ A m}^{-2}$$

(*ii*) Mean energy flowing per unit area per unit time

$$I = <S> = \frac{1}{2}\varepsilon_0 c E_0^2 = \frac{8.85\times10^{-12}\times3\times10^8\times(50\times10^{-3})^2}{2} = 3.4\times10^{-6}\text{ W m}^{-2}$$

***Example* 6:** *A round straight conductor having resistance R carries a current I. Show that the flux of Poynting vector across the lateral surface is I^{2}R.*

***Solution*:** The electric field within the conductor is $E = V/L$ where V is the potential difference across its ends and L is its length. The magnetic field at the surface of the conductor is

$$B = \frac{\mu_0 I}{2\pi a}, \; a \text{ is radius of conductor.}$$

The electric field points in the direction of current, **B** points in the circumferential direction. The Poynting vector is directed along the inward radius at all points on the surface of the conductor

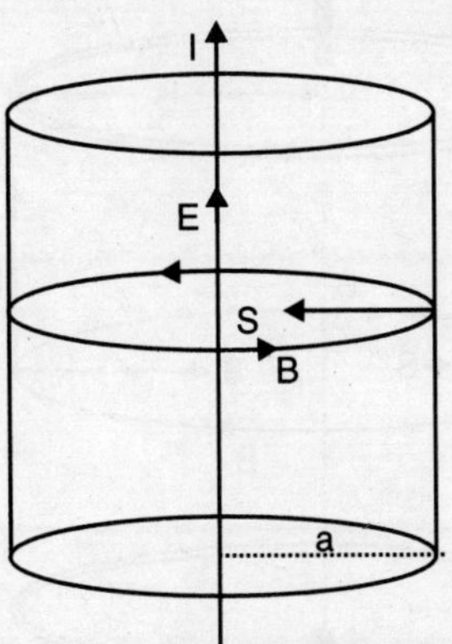

Fig. 11.4

The magnitude of Poynting vector is

$$S = \frac{EB}{\mu_0} = \frac{1}{\mu_0}\left(\frac{V}{L}\right)\left(\frac{\mu_0 I}{2\pi a}\right)$$

The contribution to the flux of Poynting vector comes only from the lateral surface of the conductor.

The flux of Poynting vector

$$\Phi = (S)(lateral\ area) = \left(\frac{VI}{2\pi aL}\right)(2\pi aL) = VI = I^2 R$$

***Example 7**: A parallel plate capacitor whose electrodes are shaped as round discs is charged by means of a battery. The radius of each plate is R and plate-separation is d.*

(i) *What is the direction of the Poynting vector in the space between the electrodes of the capacitor?*

(ii) *Show that the flux of Poynting vector between the electrodes is equal to the rate at which energy increases between them.*

Solution: In the space between the electrodes, **E** points in the direction of current, the lines of **B** are concentric circles in planes perpendicular to the direction of current, the centres of circles lie on the axis of symmetry of electrodes. The Poynting vector $\mathbf{S} = \frac{\mathbf{E}\times\mathbf{B}}{\mu_0}$ points radially towards the axis of symmetry. The magnitude of B at a distance R from the axis is

$$B = \frac{1}{2}\mu_0\varepsilon_0 R\frac{dE}{dt} \qquad \text{(see example 2)}$$

The magnitude of S is

$$S = \frac{EB}{\mu_0} = \frac{1}{2}\varepsilon_0 RE\frac{dE}{dt}$$

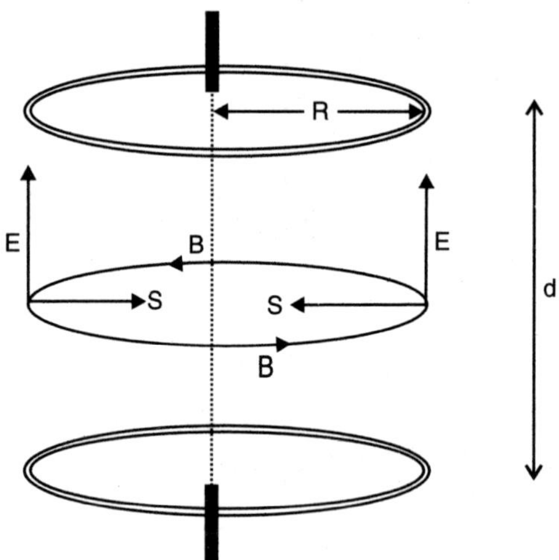

Fig. 11.5

The flux of Poynting vector is

$$\Phi = (S)(area) = \left(\frac{1}{2}\varepsilon_0 RE\frac{dE}{dt}\right)(2\pi Rd) = (\pi R^2 d)\frac{d}{dt}\left(\frac{1}{2}\varepsilon_0 E^2\right) = V\frac{du}{dt} = \frac{d}{dt}(uV) = \frac{dU}{dt}$$

Where u is energy density and $U = uV$ is total energy of the capacitor or field energy.

***Example* 8:** *A current is made to increase in the windings of a long straight solenoid at a very slow rate. Show that the flux of Poynting vector through the lateral surface of the solenoid is equal to the rate of increase of magnetic energy stored in it.*

***Solution*:**

At any instant, the energy stored in the solenoid is

$$U = \left(\frac{B^2}{2\mu_0}\right)(\pi R^2 L) = \frac{(\mu_0 nI)^2}{2\mu_0}(\pi R^2 L)$$

Where n = number of turns per unit length on the solenoid, R = radius, L = length, I = current. The rate of increase of energy is

$$\frac{dU}{dt} = \mu_0(\pi R^2 L)n^2 I\frac{dI}{dt}$$

The time varying current in the solenoid produces a time varying magnetic field which in turn induces an electric field. The field lines of **E** at the surface of the solenoid are in circumferential direction. Faraday law gives the value of the induced electric field.

$$\oint \mathbf{E} \cdot d\mathbf{l} = -\frac{d}{dt}\int \mathbf{B} \cdot d\mathbf{A}$$

$$E(2\pi R) = -\frac{d}{dt} B \cdot \pi R^2$$

$$\therefore \quad E = -\frac{1}{2} R \frac{dB}{dt} = -\frac{1}{2} \mu_0 n R \frac{dI}{dt}$$

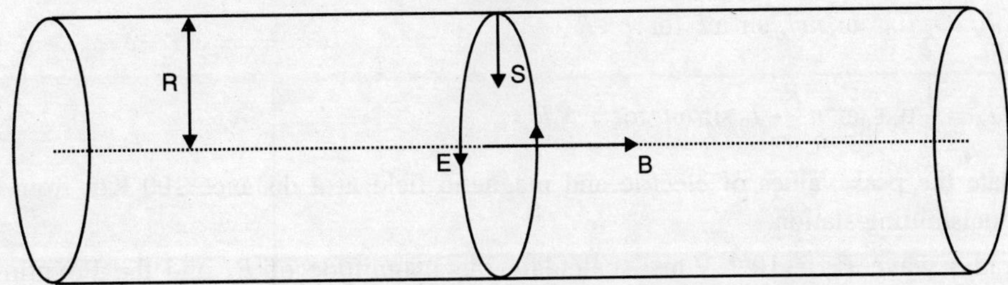

Fig. 11.6

Poynting vector $\mathbf{S} = \dfrac{\mathbf{E} \times \mathbf{B}}{\mu_0}$ points radially inward. The flux of S is given by

$$Flux\ \Phi = (S)(area) = \left(\frac{EB}{\mu_0}\right)(2\pi RL) = \frac{1}{\mu_0}\left(\frac{1}{2}\mu_0 nR \frac{dI}{dt} . \mu_0 nI\right)(2\pi RL)$$

$$= \mu_0 (\pi R^2 L) n^2 I \frac{dI}{dt}$$

$$= \frac{dU}{dt}$$

QUESTIONS AND PROBLEMS

1. Write Maxwell's equations in vacuum and state their meanings. Obtain electromagnetic wave equation from them. What is the velocity of electromagnetic waves?
2. Show that Maxwell's equations predict the existence of electromagnetic waves. Show that these waves are transverse.
3. Obtain the dispersion relation for electromagnetic waves in vacuum. Is vacuum a dispersive medium for e.m. waves? What is the intrinsic impedance of vacuum? Show that its value is 377 ohms.
4. Explain the meaning of linearly polarized electromagnetic wave. Show that the intensity of an electromagnetic wave is given by $I = \frac{1}{2} \varepsilon_0 c E_0^{\,2}$.

5. State Poynting theorem. Show the Poynting vector is given by $\mathbf{S} = \mathbf{E} \times \mathbf{H}$. Also show that time average of Poynting vector is given by $\langle S \rangle = \frac{1}{2}\varepsilon_0 c E_0^2$.

6. A long solenoid with n turns per unit length carries an alternating current $I = I_0 \sin \omega t$. Calculate the displacement current density as a function of distance r from the axis of the solenoid. The radius of cross-section of solenoid is R.

Ans. $J_d = \frac{1}{2}\mu_0\varepsilon_0\omega^2 n r I_0 \sin\omega t$ for $r < R$

$J_d = \frac{1}{2}\mu_0\varepsilon_0\omega^2 n \frac{R^2}{r} I_0 \sin\omega t$ for $r > R$

7. Calculate the peak values of electric and magnetic field at a distance 100 Km from a 100 W radio transmitting station.

8. In a radio wave $E_0 = 10^{-4}$ V m^{-1}, calculate the magnitude of B_0 and the Poynting vector. **Ans.** $B_0 = 3.3 \times 10^{-13}$ W m^{-2} and $S_0 = 1.3 \times 10^{-11}$ W m^{-2}.

9. The intensity of solar radiation striking the earth surface is 1.4×10^{-3} W/m^2. Assuming the earth to be a disc of radius 6.4×10^4 m and perfect black body, calculate the force exerted on the earth due to radiation pressure.

Hint. Radiation pressure = $\frac{\langle S \rangle}{c} = 4.7 \times 10^{-6}\,\text{N m}^{-2}$, Force = (pressure) (area).

10. How do Maxwell equations modify in matter? Obtain dispersion relation for electromagnetic waves in a conducting medium.

11. Show that Maxwell equations admit a damped wave in a conducting medium. Obtain expression for skin depth in a good conductor.

12. Discuss the propagation of electromagnetic wave in a conducting medium.

13. Obtain an expression for energy density of an electromagnetic wave in a conducting medium. Show that in a good conductor, the energy is almost magnetic.

14. Derive an expression for the Poynting vector in a good conductor.

15. Give an account of Maxwell equations explaining clearly the significance of the displacement current. Solve them to obtain the velocity of e.m. waves in free space.

16. Show that in a uniform plane wave in an isotropic and non-conductive medium, the electric and magnetic field and the direction of propagation are mutually perpendicular.

17. State Maxwell equations and solve them to obtain the velocity of the electromagnetic waves in a homogeneous isotropic dielectric medium. Calculate the velocity of e.m. waves in a simple non-magnetic dielectric medium having permittivity 2×10^{11} F m^{-1}.

18. Derive energy conservation theorem in electromagnetic waves and discuss the significance of Poynting vector.

19. Obtain an expression for momentum density in an electromagnetic wave.

OOO

12 CHAPTER Reflection, Refraction and Dispersion of Electromagnetic Waves

12.1. BOUNDARY CONDITIONS AT THE INTERFACE OF TWO MEDIA

When an electromagnetic wave is incident at the interface between two different media having different electromagnetic properties, some of the incident energy of the incident wave is reflected and the rest is transmitted. The determination of coefficients of amplitude of reflection and amplitude of transmission requires knowledge about how the different values of the field vectors **E, D, B** and **H** on the two sides of the boundary are connected. We shall assume that on one side of the interface there is a medium 1 and on the other side a medium 2. The field vectors in the medium will be labelled with subscript 1 and those in medium 2 with subscript 2. Also, we shall assume that the vectors are finite on the both sides of the boundary and their time derivatives change continuously. At the boundary of two media, the field vectors satisfy certain conditions, called boundary conditions, which can be obtained using integral form of Maxwell's equations

1. $\oint_S \mathbf{D}\cdot\mathbf{n}dS = \rho_f$

2. $\oint_S \mathbf{B}\cdot\mathbf{n}dS = 0$

3. $\oint_C \mathbf{E}\cdot d\mathbf{l} = -\frac{\partial}{\partial t}\int_S \mathbf{B}\cdot\mathbf{n}dS$

4. $\oint_C \mathbf{H}\cdot d\mathbf{l} = \int_S\left(\mathbf{J}_f + \frac{\partial \mathbf{D}}{\partial t}\right)\cdot\mathbf{n}dS$

1. ***Boundary Condition for Normal component of field D***

Consider a small cylindrical surface of height h with each base area ΔS_1 and ΔS_2 (= ΔS_1) and lateral surface ΔS_3 such that one half of its height is immersed in medium 1 and the remaining half in medium 2 as shown in the figure. The bases of the cylinder are parallel to the interface and are so small that the vector $\mathbf{D}_1$ in medium 1 is uniform over ΔS_1 and $\mathbf{D}_2$ in medium 2 over ΔS_2. The free electric charge enclosed within the cylinder is $\rho_f \Delta S_1 h$, ρ_f being the volume density of free charges.

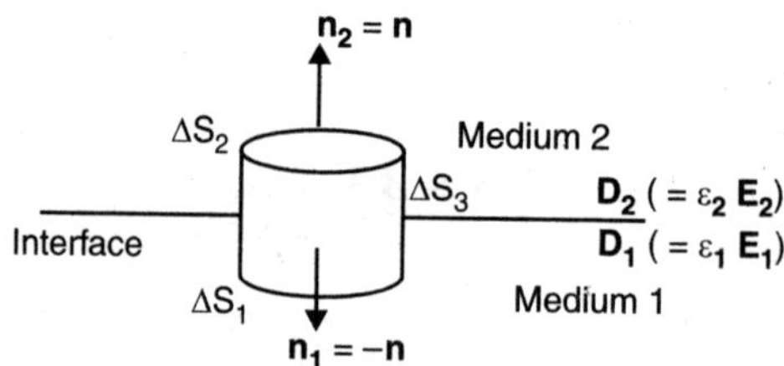

Fig. 12.1. Boundary condition for normal components of field **D** and **E.**

Applying Maxwell's equation $\oint_S \mathbf{D}\cdot\mathbf{n}dS = \rho_f$ to this surface, we get

$$\mathbf{D}_2\cdot\mathbf{n}_2\text{D}S_2 + \mathbf{D}_1\cdot\mathbf{n}_1\text{D}S_1, (\text{D}S_1 = \text{D}S_2 = \text{D}S_3)\cdot\mathbf{n}_1\text{D}S_1 + \langle \text{D}\rangle \text{D}S_3 = r_f h\text{D}S_1$$

$$(\mathbf{D}_2\cdot\mathbf{n} - \mathbf{D}_1\cdot\mathbf{n})\,\text{D}S + \langle \text{D}\rangle \text{D}S_3 = r_f h\text{D}S$$

Where $\langle D\rangle$ is the value of D averaged over the entire lateral surface of the cylinder.

Now we make h to tend to zero. In this limit $\Delta S_3 \to 0$ and so the term $\langle D\rangle > \Delta S_3 \to 0$. The volume density ρ_f of charge now become surface charge density σ_f. Keeping all this in mind we arrive at the result

$$(\mathbf{D}_2 - \mathbf{D}_1)\cdot\mathbf{n} = \sigma_f \qquad \text{...(12.1)}$$

or

$$D_{2n} - D_{1n} = \sigma_f \qquad \text{...(12.2)}$$

or

$$\varepsilon_2 E_{2n} - \varepsilon_1 E_{1n} = \sigma_f \qquad \text{...(12.3)}$$

Thus the normal components of field vector **D** or **E** are discontinuous across the boundary of two media by surface density of charge.

If the interface between the two media carries no surface charge, the normal components of **D** across the interface are continuous.

$$D_{2n} = D_{1n}$$

$$\varepsilon_2 E_{2n} = \varepsilon_1 E_{1n} \qquad \text{...(12.4)}$$

2. *Boundary Condition for Normal Component of Magnetic Field B*

Let us consider a cylindrical surface of height h with bases ΔS_1 and ΔS_2 parallel to the interface such that ΔS_1 lies in the medium 1 and ΔS_2 in medium 2. The lateral surface of the cylinder is ΔS_3. Applying Maxwell's equation to this cylindrical surface we have

$$\mathbf{B}_1\cdot\mathbf{n}_1\text{D}S_1 + \mathbf{B}_2\cdot\mathbf{n}_2\text{D}S_2 + \langle B\rangle \text{D}S_3 = 0$$

Where $\Delta S_1 = \Delta S_2 = \Delta S(\text{say}), \mathbf{n}_1 = -\mathbf{n}_2 = \mathbf{n}(\text{say}), \mathbf{n}$ is unit vector normal to the interface pointing from medium 1 to medium 2. $\langle B\rangle$ is the mean value of magnetic field over the lateral surface of the cylinder. We now make $h \to 0$. In this limit, $\Delta S_3 \to 0$ and hence, the term $\langle D\rangle\,\Delta S_3$ vanishes.

Then

$$(\mathbf{B}_1 - \mathbf{B}_2)\cdot\mathbf{n} = 0$$

or $$B_{2\perp} = B_{1\perp} \qquad ...(12.5)$$

Thus the normal component of magnetic field **B** is continuous across the interface of two media.

3. *Boundary Condition for Tangential Component of Electric Field*

Consider a rectangular loop ABCD with length Δl and breadth Δb. The sides AB is in medium 2 and CD is in medium 1 and both are parallel to the interface. The sides BC and AD are perpendicular to the interface. $\mathbf{E}_1$ and $\mathbf{E}_2$ are the electric field vectors in medium 1 and 2 respectively in the direct proximity of the interface.

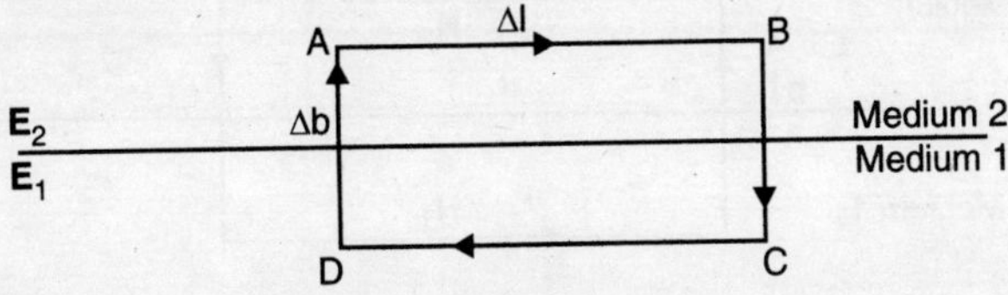

Fig. 12.2. Boundary condition for the tangential components of electric field.

Applying Maxwell's equation $\oint_C \mathbf{E}\cdot d\mathbf{l} = -\frac{\partial}{\partial t}\oint_S \mathbf{B}\cdot\mathbf{n}dS$ to this rectangular contour *ABCD* with direction of circumvention shown in the figure we have

$$\mathbf{E}_2\cdot\Delta\mathbf{l} - \mathbf{E}_1\cdot\Delta\mathbf{l} + 2\langle \mathrm{E}\rangle \Delta \mathrm{b} = -\frac{\partial}{\partial t}\oint_S \mathbf{B}\cdot d\mathrm{S}$$

Here *S* is the surface area enclosed by the contour *C i.e., ABCD* $\langle B\rangle$ is the average electric field over the width Δb of the rectangular loop. In the limit, $\Delta b \to 0$, the term $\langle E\rangle$ Δb vanishes. Hence,

$$\mathbf{E}_2\cdot\Delta\mathbf{l} - \mathbf{E}_1\cdot\Delta\mathbf{l} = 0$$

or $$E_{2\parallel} = E_{1\parallel} \qquad ...(12.6)$$

Thus, the components of electric field parallel to the interface between the two media are continuous.

4. *The tangential Components of Magnetic Field Intensity H*

The Maxwell's equation $\oint_C \mathbf{H}\cdot d\mathbf{l} = \int_S \left(\mathbf{j} + \frac{\partial \mathbf{D}}{\partial t}\right)\cdot\mathbf{n}dS$ is used to obtain the boundary condition for the tangential components of magnetic field intensity **H** or magnetic field **B** (= μ**H**). $\mathbf{H}_1$ and $\mathbf{H}_2$ denote the magnetic field intensity on the two sides of the boundary. Let us choose the path of integration on the left hand side of this equation in the form of an infinitely small rectangle whose upper side is in medium 2 and lower side in medium 1. These two sides are parallel to the tangent to the surface *S*. We denote the length of each of these sides by Δl and the length of each of the other two sides by Δb. Now, we take the width Δb of the rectangle to be infinitesimally small. In this limit the contribution to the line integral from the sides normal to the boundary vanishes. Also, since the field **D** and its derivatives are everywhere finite and $S \to 0$, surface integral $\int_S \frac{\partial \mathbf{D}}{\partial t} \cdot \mathbf{n} dS$ vanishes.

In the limit of infinitesimal width of rectangle, the volume current density becomes surface current density **K.** The direction of surface current density **K** is connected with the direction of circumvention of the integration path according to right hand screw rule *i.e.*, **K** is perpendicular to the plane of the rectangular loop *ABCD*. Let $\hat{\mathbf{n}}$ be the unit vector normal to the interface pointing from medium 1 to 2. Keeping all these in mind we have

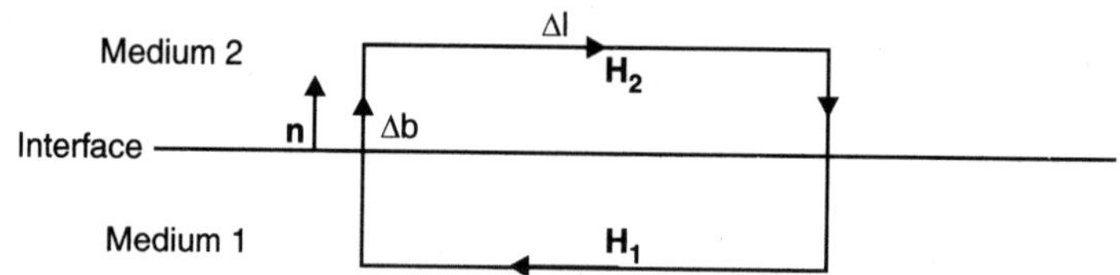

Fig. 12.3. Boundary condition for the tangential components of magnetic field.

$$\mathbf{H}_2 \cdot \Delta \mathbf{l} - \mathbf{H}_1 \cdot \Delta \mathbf{l} = \lim_{\Delta b \to 0} \mathbf{j} \cdot \Delta \mathbf{S} = (\mathbf{K} \times \hat{\mathbf{n}}) \cdot \Delta \mathbf{l}$$

or, $$H_{2\|} - H_{1\|} = K \qquad ...(12.7)$$

Thus the field **H** is discontinuous across the boundary by surface current.

For media of finite electric conductivity σ, the limit $\lim_{\Delta b \to 0} \mathbf{j} \cdot \Delta \mathbf{S} = \lim_{\Delta b \to 0} j \Delta l \cdot \Delta b \to 0$, since current density j cannot be infinite in real media containing finite charges. Thus for finite conductivity of the two media, we have

$$\mathbf{H}_2 \cdot \Delta \mathbf{l} - \mathbf{H}_1 \cdot \Delta \mathbf{l} = 0$$

or, $$H_{2\|} = H_{1\|} \qquad ...(12.8)$$

The tangential components of the magnetic intensity are continuous across the interface between two media.

12.2. REFLECTION AND REFRACTION OF ELECTROMAGNETIC WAVES AT THE INTERFACE OF TWO DIELECTRIC MEDIA

1. *Normal Incidence*

A plane electromagnetic wave propagating in a dielectric medium 1 with refractive index n_1 in normally incident at the interface of another dielectric medium 2 with refractive index n_2. We take *X* and *Y*–axes of the coordinate system at the interface and *Z*-axis along the direction of propagation $\mathbf{k}_i$. Experiments show that a fraction of incident energy is reflected at the interface and the rest is transmitted. Let the incident wave be polarized with *E*-vector along *X*-axis. The **E-fields, B-**fields and the propagation vectors of the incident wave, reflected wave and transmitted wave are shown in the Fig. 12.4. We assume that the frequency of electromagnetic wave remains unaltered while passing from one medium to another.

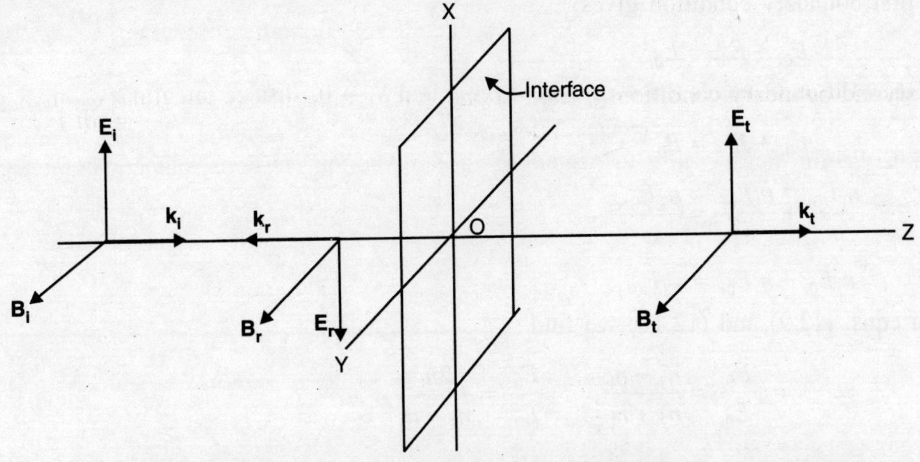

Fig. 12.4. Reflection and refraction of electromagnetic wave in normal incidence at dielectric-dielectric interface.

The electric and magnetic fields in the incident wave, reflected wave and transmitted wave are:

$$\mathbf{E}_i = \hat{\mathbf{x}}E_{0i} \exp[i(k_i z - \omega t)]$$

$$\mathbf{B}_i = \hat{\mathbf{y}}B_{0i} \exp[i(k_i z - \omega t)]$$

$$\mathbf{E}_r = -\hat{\mathbf{x}}E_{0r} \exp[i(k_r z - \omega t)] = -\hat{\mathbf{x}}E_{0r} \exp[i(-k_i z - \omega t)]$$

$$\mathbf{B}_r = \hat{\mathbf{y}}B_{0r} \exp[i(k_r z - \omega t)] = \hat{\mathbf{y}}B_{0r} \exp[i(-k_i z - \omega t)]$$

$$\mathbf{E}_t = \hat{\mathbf{x}}E_{0t} \exp[i(k_t z - \omega t)]$$

$$\mathbf{B}_t = \hat{\mathbf{y}}B_{0t} \exp[i(k_t z - \omega t)]$$

Where $\hat{\mathbf{x}}, \hat{\mathbf{y}}, \hat{\mathbf{z}}$ are unit vectors along the coordinate axes. The subscript 0 indicates the amplitudes of E and B fields. The amplitudes of E and B fields are mutually related through the relation

$$B_0 = \frac{E_0}{v} = \frac{nE_0}{c}$$

The magnitude of the propagation vector is related to index of refraction n of the medium through the relation

$$k = \frac{n\omega}{c}$$

We are interested in finding the fraction of incident amplitude that are reflected and transmitted.

To find $\frac{E_{0r}}{E_{0i}}$ and $\frac{E_{0t}}{E_{0i}}$ we apply the following boundary conditions at the interface $z = 0$.

(*i*) *The tangential component of electric field is continuous*

(*ii*) *The tangential component of magnetic field is continuous.*

The first boundary condition gives,

$$E_{0i} - E_{0r} = E_{0t} \quad ...(12.9)$$

The second boundary condition gives,

$$B_{0i} + B_{0r} = B_{0t}$$

or $$\frac{n_1 E_{0i}}{c} + \frac{n_1 E_{0r}}{c} = \frac{n_2 E_{0t}}{c}$$

or $$n_1 E_{0i} + n_1 E_{0r} = n_2 E_{0t} \quad ...(12.10)$$

From eqns. (12.9) and (12.10) we find

$$\frac{E_{0r}}{E_{0i}} = \frac{n_2 - n_1}{n_2 + n_1}, \qquad \frac{E_{0t}}{E_{0i}} = \frac{2n_1}{n_2 + n_1}$$

The ratios $\frac{E_{0r}}{E_{0i}}$ and $\frac{E_{0t}}{E_{0i}}$ are called *Fresnel's reflection coefficient(r) and transmission coefficient(t)* respectively. Thus

$$r = \frac{n_2 - n_1}{n_2 + n_1}, \qquad t = \frac{2n_1}{n_2 + n_1} \quad ...(12.11)$$

In terms of intensities of the reflected and transmitted waves, we define *reflectance R* and *transmittance T* as follows.

$$R = \frac{\langle S_r \rangle}{\langle S_i \rangle} \text{ and } T = \frac{\langle S_t \rangle}{\langle S_i \rangle} \quad ...(12.12)$$

The symbol $< S >$ represents the time average of Poynting vector **S**. The intensity of a wave is given by

$$I = \langle S \rangle = \frac{1}{2} \varepsilon v E_0^2 \quad ...(12.13)$$

Therefore, $$R = \frac{I_r}{I_i} = \frac{E_{0r}^2}{E_{0i}^2} = \left(\frac{n_2 - n_1}{n_2 + n_1}\right)^2 \quad ...(12.14)$$

$$T = \frac{I_t}{I_i} = \frac{\varepsilon_2 v_2 E_{0t}^2}{\varepsilon_1 v_1 E_{0i}^2} = \left(\frac{n_2}{n_1}\right)^2 \left(\frac{n_1}{n_2}\right)\left(\frac{2n_1}{n_2 + n_1}\right)^2 = \frac{4n_1 n_2}{(n_2 + n_1)^2} \quad ...(12.15)$$

From eqns. (12.14) and (12.15) we can see that $R + T = 1$, which is the law of conservation of energy.

2. *Oblique Incidence*

Parallel Polarization (Electric field of Incident Wave Parallel to the Plane of Incidence)

Consider two linear dielectric media 1 and 2 separated by a plane boundary (interface), which we take normal to the plane of the page. The permittivity and permeability of medium 1 are ε_1 and μ_1 respectively and those of medium 2 are ε_2 and μ_2. For most materials (non-magnetic substances)

$\mu_1 = \mu_2 = \mu_0$. Now consider a plane harmonic wave having direction of propagation $\mathbf{k}_i$ is incident on the interface from medium 1. We take the unit vector $\mathbf{n}$ normal to the interface at the point where vector $\mathbf{k}_i$ intersects the interface. The direction of $\mathbf{n}$ is taken from medium 1 to 2. The vectors $\mathbf{k}_i$ and $\mathbf{n}$ determine the plane of incidence which we take in the plane of drawing. The origin of Cartesian coordinate system is taken at the point of intersection of vector $\mathbf{k}_i$ with the interface. The x-axis is taken along the line of intersection of the plane of incidence and the interface. Y-axis is chosen along the normal to the plane of incidence. Obviously, the XY-plane coincides with the interface. We direct the z-axis along the normal to the interface such that the coordinate axes X, Y, Z form a right handed system. The ZX-plane coincides with the plane of incidence. Let propagation vectors of reflected and refracted wave be $\mathbf{k}_r$ and $\mathbf{k}_t$ respectively and the angles of reflection and refraction be θ_r and θ_t. Since the propagation vector $\mathbf{k}_i$ of incident wave lies in ZX-plane, we have $k_{iy} = 0$. Projections of $\mathbf{k}$*'s* onto the coordinate axes are:

$$\mathbf{k}_i = (k_i \sin\theta_i, 0, k_i \cos\theta_i),\quad \mathbf{k}_r = (k_r \sin\theta_r, 0, -k_r \cos\theta_r),\quad \mathbf{k}_t = (k_t \sin\theta_t, 0, k_t \cos\theta_t)$$

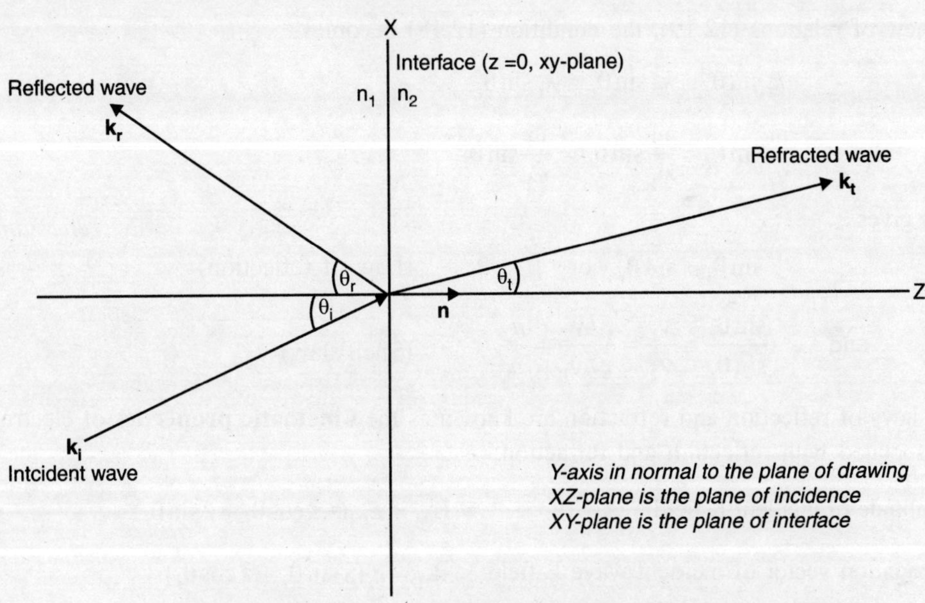

Fig. 12.5. Reflection and refraction of electromagnetic wave at the interface of two dielectric media.

Incident wave: $\mathbf{E}_i = \mathbf{E}_{0i} \exp[i(\mathbf{k}_i \cdot \mathbf{r} - \omega_i t)] = \mathbf{E}_{0i} \exp[i(k_{ix}x + k_{iz}z - \omega_i t)]$

Reflected wave: $\mathbf{E}_r = \mathbf{E}_{0r} \exp[i(\mathbf{k}_r \cdot \mathbf{r} - \omega_r t)] = \mathbf{E}_{0r} \exp[i(k_{rx}x + k_{rz}z - \omega_r t)]$

Refracted (transmitted) wave: $\mathbf{E}_t = \mathbf{E}_{0t} \exp[i(\mathbf{k}_t \cdot \mathbf{r} - \omega_t t)] = \mathbf{E}_{0t} \exp[i(k_{tx}x + k_{tz}z - \omega_t t)$

At the interface $z = 0$, the tangential component of $\mathbf{E}$-field is continuous. Use of this condition yields.

$$\mathbf{E}_{0i} \exp[i(k_{ix}x - \omega_i t) = \mathbf{E}_{0r} \exp[i(k_{rx}x - \omega_r t) = \mathbf{E}_{0t} \exp[i(k_{tx}x - \omega_t t) \qquad ...(12.16)$$

This condition must hold for all values of x and t. In particular, for $x = 0$ the above condition becomes

$$\mathbf{E}_{0i} \exp(i\omega_i t) = \mathbf{E}_{0r} \exp(i\omega_r t) = \mathbf{E}_{0t} \exp(i\omega_t t)$$

The sum of two harmonic functions will also be a harmonic function only if all of them will have the same frequency. Thus

$$\omega_i = \omega_r = \omega_t = \omega \qquad \text{...(12.17)}$$

In order that the condition (a) be satisfied for any value x, we must have

$$k_{ix} = k_{rx} = k_{tx} \qquad \text{...(12.18)}$$

This shows that the incident wave, reflected wave and refracted wave lie in the same plane. From the geometry of figure

$$k_{ix} = k_i \sin\theta_i, \quad k_{rx} = k_r \sin\theta_r, \quad k_{tx} = k_t \sin\theta_t \qquad \text{...(12.19)}$$

In view of relations (12.19), the condition (12.18) becomes

$$k_i \sin\theta_i = k_r \sin\theta_r = k_t \sin\theta_t$$

or

$$\frac{\omega}{v_1}\sin\theta_i = \frac{\omega}{v_1}\sin\theta_r = \frac{\omega}{v_2}\sin\theta_t$$

This gives

$$\sin\theta_i = \sin\theta_r \quad \text{or} \quad \theta_i = \theta_r \qquad \text{(Law of reflection)} \qquad \text{...(12.20)}$$

and

$$\frac{\sin\theta_i}{\sin\theta_t} = \frac{v_1}{v_2} = \frac{c/v_2}{c/v_1} = \frac{n_2}{n_1} \qquad \text{(Snell'slaw)} \qquad \text{...(12.21)}$$

The laws of reflection and refraction are known as the **kinematic properties** of electromagnetic wave associated with reflection and refraction.

Amplitude of incident E-field: $\mathbf{E}^i_{0\parallel} = E^i_{0\parallel}(-\hat{\mathbf{x}}\cos\theta_i + \hat{\mathbf{z}}\sin\theta_i)$

Propagation vector of incident wave E-field: $\mathbf{k}_i = k_i(\hat{\mathbf{x}}\sin\theta_i + \hat{\mathbf{z}}\cos\theta_i)$

Amplitude of reflected E-field: $\mathbf{E}^r_{0\parallel} = E^r_{0\parallel}(\hat{\mathbf{x}}\cos\theta_r + \hat{\mathbf{z}}\sin\theta_r)$, $\theta_r = \theta_i$

Propagation vector of reflected E-field: $\mathbf{k}_r = k_r(\hat{\mathbf{x}}\sin\theta_r - \hat{\mathbf{z}}\cos\theta_r)$, $\theta_r = \theta_i$

Amplitude of refracted E-field: $\mathbf{E}^t_{0\parallel} = E^t_{0\parallel}(-\hat{\mathbf{x}}\cos\theta_t + \hat{\mathbf{z}}\sin\theta_t)$

Propagation vector of refracted wave: $\mathbf{k}_t = k_t(\hat{\mathbf{x}}\sin\theta_t + \hat{\mathbf{z}}\cos\theta_t)$

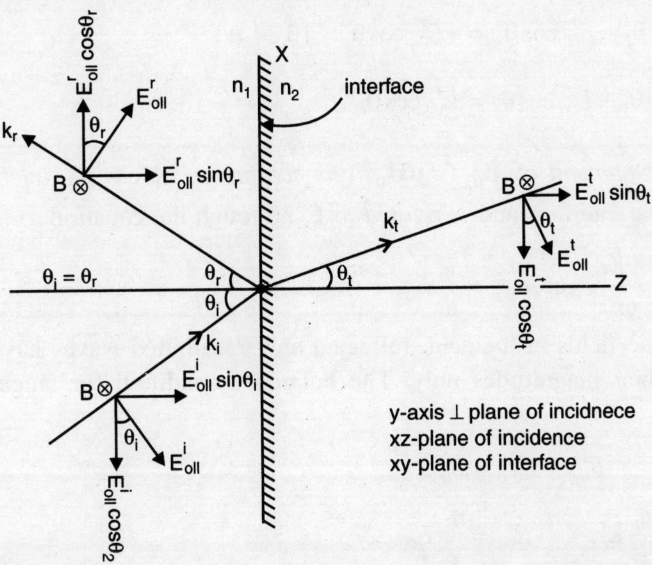

Fig. 12.6. E is || to the plane of incidence (parallel polarization).

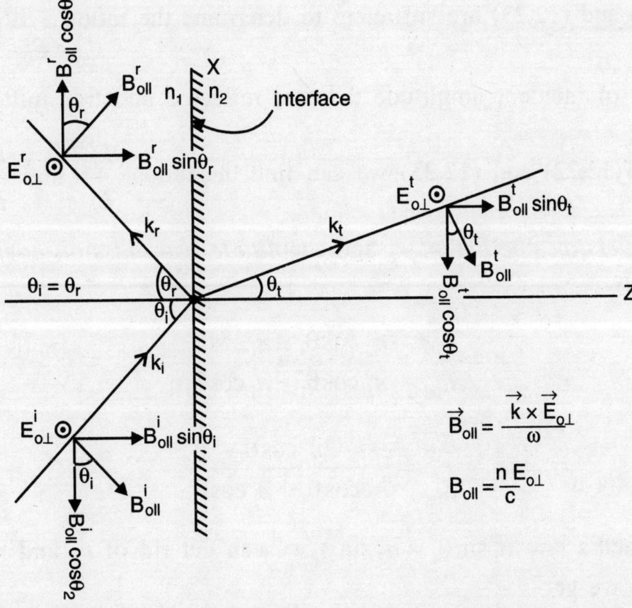

Fig. 12.7. E is ⊥ to the plane of incidence (perpendicular polarization).

Now we shall use the boundary condition: *the tangential component of electric field across the boundary is continuous.*

$$-E^i_{0\|}\cos\theta_i + E^r_{0\|}\cos\theta_r = -E^t_{0\|}\cos\theta_t \quad (\theta_r = \theta_i)$$

or
$$E^i_{0\|}\cos\theta_i - E^r_{0\|}\cos\theta_i = E^t_{0\|}\cos\theta_t \qquad ...(12.22)$$

The *tangential component of* $\mathbf{B}_{0\perp}(=\mu\mathbf{H}_{0\perp})$ *is continuous across the interface*. Remember that $\mathbf{B}_{0\perp}$ is tangential to the interface and *is related to* $\mathbf{E}_{0\|}$ through the equation

$$\mathbf{B}_{0\perp} = \frac{\mathbf{k}\times\mathbf{E}_{0\|}}{\omega} \text{ or } B_{0\perp} = \frac{k}{\omega}E_{0\|} = \frac{n}{c}E_{0\|}$$

Since the magnetic fields in incident, refracted and transmitted waves have the same direction, we can work with their magnitudes only. The boundary condition for tangential components of magnetic field gives

$$B^i_{0\perp} + B^r_{0\perp} = B^t_{0\perp}$$

or
$$\frac{n_1}{c}E^i_{0\|} + \frac{n_1}{c}E^r_{0\|} = \frac{n_2}{c}E^t_{0\|}$$

or
$$n_1E^i_{0\|} + n_1E^r_{0\|} = n_2E^t_{0\|} \qquad ...(12.23)$$

Equations (12.22) and (12.23) are sufficient to determine the ratios $\frac{E^r_{0\|}}{E^i_{0\|}}$ and $\frac{E^t_{0\|}}{E^i_{0\|}}$. These ratios represent the fraction of incident amplitude that are reflected and transmitted respectively at the interface. From eqns. (12.22) and (12.23) we can find the ratios $\frac{E^r_{0\|}}{E^i_{0\|}}$ and $\frac{E^t_{0\|}}{E^i_{0\|}}$, which are called *Fresnel amplitude reflection coefficient* $r_\|$ and *amplitude transmission coefficient* $t_\|$ for parallel polarization respectively.

$$r_\| = \frac{E^r_{0\|}}{E^i_{0\|}} = \frac{n_2\cos\theta_i - n_1\cos\theta_t}{n_2\cos\theta_i + n_1\cos\theta_t} \qquad ...(12.24)$$

$$t_\| = \frac{E^t_{0\|}}{E^i_{0\|}} = \frac{2n_1\cos\theta_i}{n_2\cos\theta_i + n_1\cos\theta_t} \qquad ...(12.25)$$

Making use of Snell's law $n_1\sin\theta_i = n_2\sin\theta_t$ we can get rid of n_1 and n_2 from eqns. (12.24) and (12.25). Doing so we get

$$r_\| = \frac{E^r_{0\|}}{E^i_{0\|}} = \frac{\tan(\theta_i - \theta_t)}{\tan(\theta_i + \theta_t)} \qquad ...(12.26)$$

$$t_\| = \frac{E^t_{0\|}}{E^i_{0\|}} = \frac{2\cos\theta_i\sin\theta_t}{\sin(\theta_i + \theta_t)\cos(\theta_i - \theta_t)} \qquad ...(12.27)$$

Perpendicular Polarization (Electric field of Incident Wave Normal to the Plane of Incidence)

In this case **E**-field of the incident wave is perpendicular to the plane of incidence (or tangential to the interface) and **B**-field is in the plane of incidence (or perpendicular to the interface). The polarization of the magnetic field changes upon reflection and transmission. The boundary condition viz. *the tangential component of E-field is continuous* gives

$$E^i_{0\perp} + E^r_{0\perp} = E^t_{0\perp} \quad \text{...(12.28)}$$

The tangential component of magnetic field is continuous. Use of this boundary condition gives

$$-B^i_{0\|}\cos\theta_i + B^r_{0\|}\cos\theta_r = -B^t_{0\|}\cos\theta_t, \qquad \theta_r = \theta_i$$

or, $$n_1 E^i_{0\perp}\cos\theta_i - n_1 E^r_{0\perp}\cos\theta_i = n_2 E^t_{0\perp}\cos\theta_t \quad \text{...(12.29)}$$

Fresnel's amplitude reflection coefficient $r_\perp$ *and transmission coefficient* $t_\perp$ can be obtained by solving eqns. (12.28) and (12.29). Thus

$$r_\perp = \frac{E^r_{0\perp}}{E^i_{0\perp}} = \frac{n_1\cos\theta_i - n_2\cos\theta_t}{n_1\cos\theta_i + n_2\cos\theta_t} \quad \text{...(12.30)}$$

$$t_\perp = \frac{2n_1\cos\theta_i}{n_1\cos\theta_i + n_2\cos\theta_t} \quad \text{...(12.31)}$$

Eliminating n_1 and n_2 with the help of Snell's law we have

$$r_\perp = -\frac{\sin(\theta_i - \theta_t)}{\sin(\theta_i + \theta_t)} \quad \text{...(12.32)}$$

$$t_\perp = \frac{2\cos\theta_i \sin\theta_t}{\sin(\theta_i + \theta_t)} \quad \text{...(12.33)}$$

For normal incidence $\theta_i = 0$ and $\theta_t = 0$ and there is no distinction between parallel and perpendicular polarization. Therefore, we have

$$r_\| = -r_\perp = \frac{n_2 - n_1}{n_2 + n_1} \quad \text{...(12.34)}$$

And $$t_\| = t_\perp = \frac{2n_1}{n_2 + n_1} \quad \text{...(12.35)}$$

Grazing Angle of Incidence

For grazing incidence $\theta_i = \pi/2$. In this case

$$r_\| = r_\perp = -1 \text{ and } t_\| = t_\perp = 0 \quad \text{...(12.36)}$$

Thus the incident electromagnetic wave undergoes total reflection without any transmission regardless of parallel or perpendicular polarization.

Relative Phase of Reflected and Transmitted Wave (E-vector || to plane of incidence)

The *Fresnel amplitude reflection coefficient* is

$$r_{\parallel} = \frac{E^r_{0\parallel}}{E^i_{0\parallel}} = \frac{\tan(\theta_i - \theta_t)}{\tan(\theta_i + \theta_t)}$$

From this equation we see that $r_{\parallel}$ is positive in two cases (*i*) when $\theta_i > \theta_t$ and $\theta_i + \theta_t < 90°$ and (*ii*) when $\theta_i < \theta_t$ and $\theta_i + \theta_t > \pi/2$. In all other cases $r_{\parallel}$ is negative. This means that when the conditions (*i*) and (*ii*) are satisfied, the reflected and incident waves are in the same phase. When the above two conditions are not satisfied, $r_{\parallel}$ is negative and then the reflected wave suffers a phase change of π.

The *Fresnel amplitude transmission coefficient* is

$$t_{\parallel} = \frac{E^t_{0\parallel}}{E^i_{0\parallel}} = \frac{2\cos\theta_i \sin\theta_t}{\sin(\theta_i + \theta_t)\cos(\theta_i - \theta_t)}$$

We can see that $t_{\parallel}$ is positive in both cases: (*i*) when $n_1 > n_2$ *i.e.* $\theta_i < \theta_t$ and (*ii*) when $n_1 < n_2$ *i.e.* $\theta_i > \theta_t$. Thus in all cases the *transmitted wave suffers no change of phase.*

E-vector ⊥ to plane of incidence

(*i*) $n_2 > n_1$ *i.e.* the light is incident at the interface from rarer medium to denser medium. The Snell's law gives

$$\frac{\sin\theta_i}{\sin\theta_t} = \frac{n_2}{n_1} > 1$$

$$\theta_t < \theta_i$$

The refracted wave deviates towards the normal to the interface. The *amplitude reflection coefficient* is

$$r_{\perp} = -\frac{\sin(\theta_i - \theta_t)}{\sin(\theta_i + \theta_t)} = \textit{negative number}$$

Thus the reflected wave undergoes a phase change of π.

(*ii*) $n_1 > n_2$ *i.e.* the light is incident at the interface from denser medium to rarer medium. In this case,

Snell's law gives

$$\frac{\sin\theta_i}{\sin\theta_t} = \frac{n_2}{n_1} < 1$$

$$\theta_t > \theta_i$$

That is, the refracted wave bends towards the normal. The *amplitude reflection* and *transmission coefficients* are

$$r_\perp = -\frac{\sin(\theta_i - \theta_t)}{\sin(\theta_i + \theta_t)} = \textit{positive number}$$

$$t_\perp = \frac{2\cos\theta_i \sin\theta_t}{\sin(\theta_i + \theta_t)} = \textit{positive number}$$

Thus the reflected wave and the transmitted wave in this polarization do not suffer any phase change.

(*iii*) In both cases $n_2 > n_1$ and $n_1 > n_2$, the Fresnel coefficient $t_\perp$ is always positive. Therefore, the transmitted wave suffers no phase change.

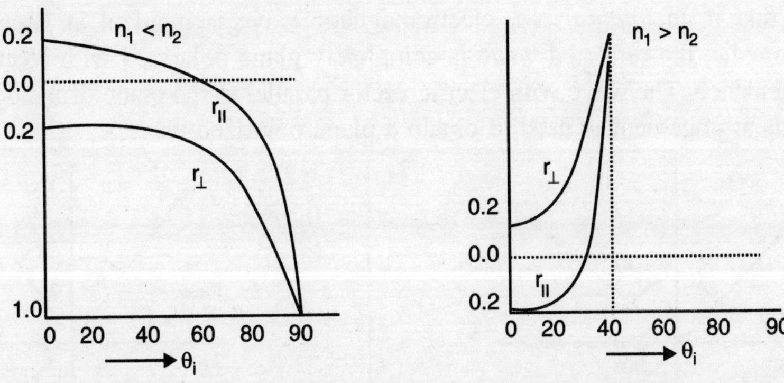

Fig. 12.8. Variation of $r_\parallel$ and $r_\perp$ with angle of incidence when $n_1 < n_2$ and $n_1 > n_2$.

Polarization by Reflection: Brewster's Angle

Fresnel amplitude reflection coefficients for both polarizations are

$$r_\parallel = \frac{E^r_{0\parallel}}{E^i_{0\parallel}} = \frac{\tan(\theta_i - \theta_t)}{\tan(\theta_i + \theta_t)}, \qquad r_\perp = \frac{E^r_{0\perp}}{E^i_{0\perp}} = -\frac{\sin(\theta_i - \theta_t)}{\sin(\theta_i + \theta_t)}$$

The expression for the $r_\parallel$ shows that an electromagnetic wave polarized in the plane of incidence, the amplitude of the reflected wave is zero when the angle of incidence θ_i is such that $\theta_i + \theta_t = \frac{\pi}{2}$ or $\theta_i = \frac{\pi}{2} - \theta_t$. This angle of incidence is called **Brewster angle** or the **angle of polarization** θ_B.

To calculate θ_B we use Snell's law

$$\frac{n_2}{n_1} = \frac{\sin\theta_i}{\sin\theta_t} = \frac{\sin\theta_B}{\sin\left(\frac{\pi}{2} - \theta_B\right)} = \frac{\sin\theta_B}{\cos\theta_B} = \tan\theta_B$$

or
$$\theta_B = \tan^{-1}\left(\frac{n_2}{n_1}\right) \qquad ...(12.37)$$

For *air-glass interface,* $n_1 < n_2$, the Brewster angle $\theta_B = \tan^{-1}\left(\frac{1.5}{1.0}\right) = 56.3°$.

For *glass-air interface,* $n_1 > n_2$, the Brewster angle $\theta_B = \tan^{-1}\left(\frac{1.0}{1.5}\right) = 33.7°$.

When the wave is incident at the interface at angle of incidence equal to Brewster angle ($\theta_i = \theta_B$), the *amplitude reflection coefficient* for polarization perpendicular to the plane of incidence is not zero. In fact it is given by

$$r_\perp = \frac{E^r_{0\perp}}{E^i_{0\perp}} = -\frac{\sin(\theta_i - \theta_t)}{\sin(\theta_i + \theta_t)} = \cos 2\theta_B$$

This means that if an *unpolarized,* electromagnetic wave is incident at Brewster angle at the interface of two media, the reflected wave is completely plane polarized with electric vector normal to the plane of incidence. The wave with electric vector parallel to the plane of incidence is completely extinguished. This arrangement is used to obtain a plane polarized wave.

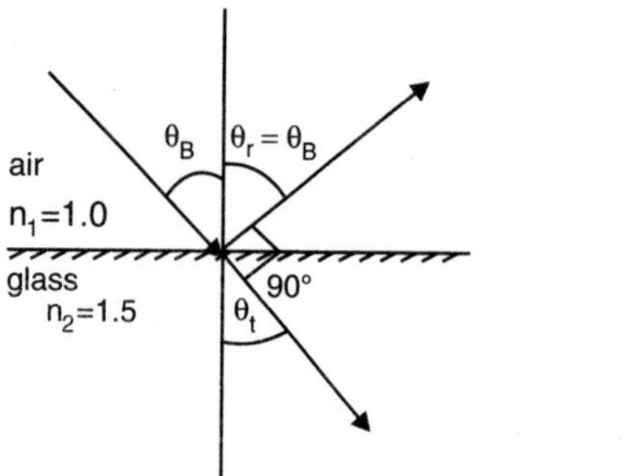

Fig. 12.9: Brewster angle for $n_1 < n_2$.

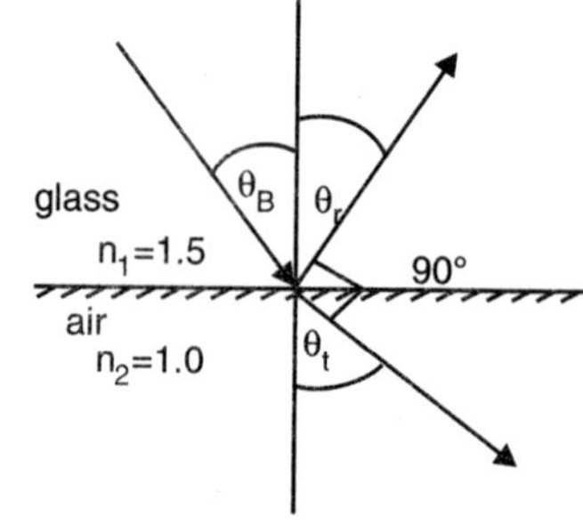

Fig. 12.10: Brewster angle for $n_1 > n_2$.

The variation of amplitude reflection coefficient and transmission coefficient with angle of incidence is shown in the Fig. 12.11.

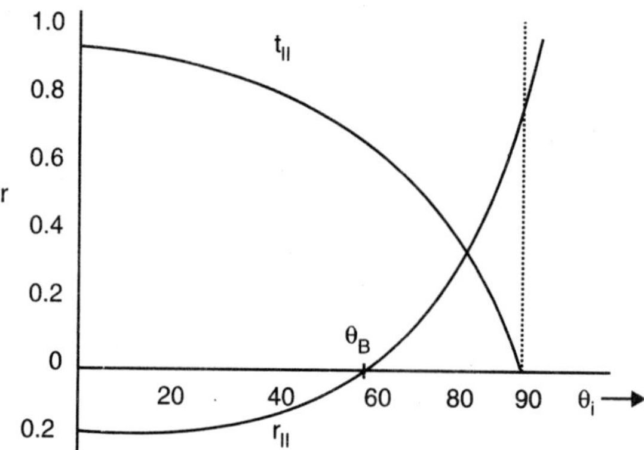

Fig. 12.11. Variation of amplitude reflection coefficient ($r_{||}$) and transmission coefficient ($t_{||}$) for air-glass interface. Notice that $r_{||}$ is zero at Brewster angle.

Total Internal Reflection

Inspection of Snell's law $\dfrac{\sin\theta_t}{\sin\theta_i} = \dfrac{n_1}{n_2}$ shows that when light passes from optically denser medium to an optically less dense one (*i.e.* $n_1 > n_2$), $\theta_t > \theta_i$. That is, the refracted wave moves away from the normal to the interface of the media. Thus, the increase in angle of incidence θ_i is attended with a more rapid increase in angle of refraction θ_t. The maximum possible value of θ_t is $\pi/2$. There exists an angle of incidence θ_i, for which the angle of refraction is just equal to $\pi/2$. This angle of incidence is called *critical angle* θ_C. For $\theta_i = \theta_C$, Snell's law becomes

$$n_1 \sin\theta_C = n_2 \sin 90°$$

This gives
$$\theta_C = \sin^{-1}\left(\frac{n_2}{n_1}\right) \qquad ...(12.38)$$

For glass-air interface, $\theta_C = \sin^{-1}\dfrac{1.0}{1.5} = 41.83°$

For water-air interface, $\theta_C = \sin^{1}\left(\dfrac{1.0}{4/3}\right) = 48.59°$

For glass-water interface $\theta_C = \sin^{-1}\left(\dfrac{1.33}{1.50}\right) = 62.46°$

When the light in incident at critical angle, $\theta_i = \theta_C$ and $\theta_C = \pi/2$, the Fresnel amplitude reflection coefficients are

$$r_{\parallel} = \frac{\tan(\theta_i - \theta_t)}{\tan(\theta_i + \theta_t)} = 1 \quad \text{and} \quad r_{\perp} = \frac{\sin(\theta_t - \theta_i)}{\sin(\theta_t + \theta_i)} = 1$$

$$R_{\parallel} = R_{\perp} = 1$$

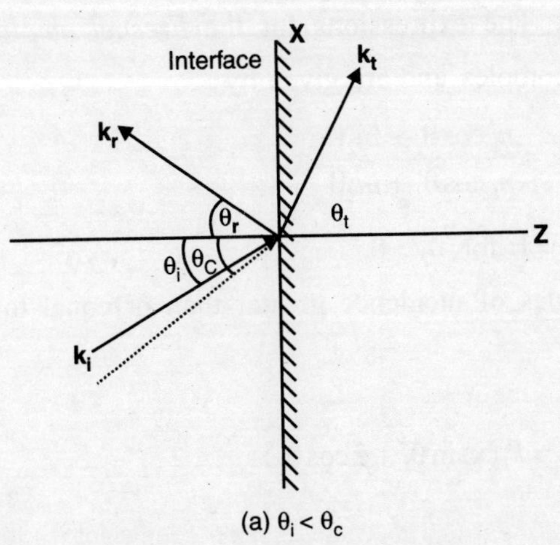

(a) $\theta_i < \theta_c$

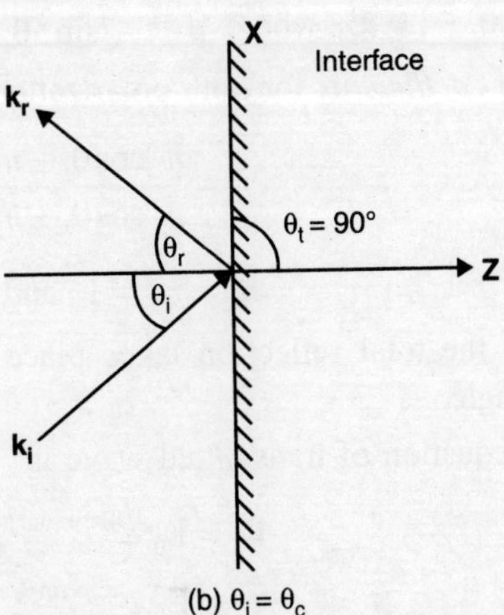

(b) $\theta_i = \theta_c$

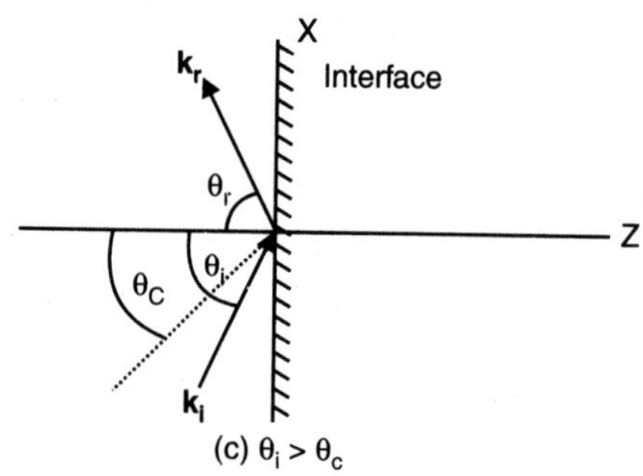

(c) $\theta_i > \theta_c$

Fig. 12.12. (a) Normal reflection and refraction when $\theta_i < \theta_c$
(b) Total internal reflection when $\theta_i = \theta_c$
(c) Total internal reflection when $\theta_i > \theta_c$.

Since the Fresnel amplitude reflection coefficients for both polarizations are unity, total light is reflected. As the angle of incidence increases, the intensity of reflected wave increases and that of refracted wave diminishes. The intensity of refracted wave vanishes when $\theta_i = \theta_c$, For angles of incidence between θ_C and $\pi/2$, the light penetrates into the second medium to a distance of the order of a wavelength λ and then returns to the first medium. This phenomenon is called **total internal reflection.**

For angle of incidence greater than critical angle, *i.e.* $\theta_i > \theta_c$, the Snell's law can be written as

$$\frac{\sin\theta_i}{\sin\theta_t} = \frac{n_2}{n_1} = \sin\theta_c$$

or
$$\sin\theta_t = \frac{\sin\theta_i}{\sin\theta_c} > 1 \qquad (\because \theta_i > \theta_c) \qquad ...(12.39)$$

This equation cannot be satisfied for real values of θ_t. For $\sin\theta_t > 1$, we have $\cos\theta_t = \sqrt{1-\sin^2\theta_t}$ $= i\sqrt{\sin^2\theta_t - 1} = i\beta$, where $\beta = \sqrt{\sin^2\theta_t - 1}$ is real. The expressions for the *Fresnel amplitude reflection coefficients* for both polarizations become complex and are given by

$$\tilde{r}_{\parallel} = \frac{n_2\cos\theta_i - in_1\beta}{n_2\cos\theta_i + in_1\beta} \quad \text{and} \quad \tilde{r}_{\perp} = \frac{n_1\cos\theta_i - in_2\beta}{n_1\cos\theta_i + in_2\beta}$$

And
$$R_{\parallel} = |r_{\parallel}|^2 = 1 \quad \text{and} \quad R_{\perp} = |r_{\perp}|^2 = 1 \quad \text{for } \theta_i > \theta_t$$

Thus the total reflection takes place for all angles of incidence greater than or equal to the critical angle.

The equation of transmitted wave is

$$\mathbf{E}_t = \mathbf{E}_{0t}e^{i[\mathbf{k}_t\cdot r - \omega t]}, \quad \text{where } \mathbf{k}_t = k_t(\hat{\mathbf{x}}\sin\theta_t + \hat{\mathbf{z}}\cos\theta_t)$$

$$= \mathbf{E}_{0t}e^{ik_t[x\sin\theta_t + z\cos\theta_t] - i\omega t}$$

$$= \mathbf{E}_{0t}e^{ik_t[x\sqrt{1-\cos^2\theta_t} + i\beta z] - i\omega t}$$

$$= \mathbf{E}_{0t} e^{-\beta k_t z} \, e^{i[k_t \sqrt{(1+\beta^2)}\, x] - i\omega t} \quad \text{...(12.40)}$$

Thus the transmitted wave propagates parallel to the surface (*i.e.* along x-axis) and its amplitude decays exponentially in the z-direction. This type of plane wave is not transverse but has a component of field parallel to **k**. It is called *evanescent wave.* We define a penetration depth δ along z-direction as the distance where the amplitude drops to $1/e$ of its initial value. Thus

$$e^{-ik_t z} = e^{-1} \quad \text{or} \quad z = \delta = \frac{1}{\beta k_t} \quad \text{...(12.41)}$$

12.3. PROPAGATION OF ELECTROMAGNETIC WAVE ACROSS A PLANE INTERFACE OF A CONDUCTOR DIELECTRIC

Normal Incidence

In this section we consider the reflection and transmission of electromagnetic wave at the interface of a dielectric and conductor. The first medium is a dielectric characterized by permittivity ε_1 (refractive index n_1) and second medium (a conductor or a metal) characterized by permittivity ε_2 (refractive index $\tilde{n}_2$), conductivity σ_2. While analysing the propagation electromagnetic wave in a conducting medium we have seen the propagation vector ($\tilde{k}$) and refractive index ($\tilde{n}$) come out to be complex. So we can apply the expressions for Fresnel's coefficients obtained for dielectric-dielectric interface to the dielectric-conductor interface with one modification: replacing the permittivity ε_2 and refractive index n_2 and propagation constant k_2 by complex numbers. The *Fresnel's reflection and transmission coefficients* for normal incidence at dielectric-metal interface then become

$$\tilde{r} = \frac{\tilde{n}_2 - n_1}{\tilde{n}_2 + n_1}, \qquad \tilde{t} = \frac{2n_1}{\tilde{n}_2 + n_1} \quad \text{...(12.42)}$$

Let us write

$$\tilde{n}_2 = n_2 + i\kappa_2 \quad \text{...(12.43)}$$

Here n_2 is conventional refractive index of the conductor and κ_2 is attenuation constant. In terms of n_2 and κ_2 the expressions for $\tilde{r}$ and $\tilde{t}$ become

$$\tilde{r} = \frac{(n_2 - n_1) + i\kappa_2}{(n_2 + n_1) + i\kappa_2}, \qquad \tilde{t} = \frac{2n_1}{(n_2 + n_1) + i\kappa_2} \quad \text{...(12.44)}$$

The complex nature of $\tilde{r}$ and $\tilde{t}$ indicate that the reflected and transmitted waves undergo phase shift relative to the incident wave. To obtain the phase shift we write $\tilde{r}$ and $\tilde{t}$ in polar form. Doing so we have

$$\tilde{r} = r e^{i\varphi_r}, \quad r = \left[\frac{(n_2 - n_1)^2 + \kappa_2^2}{(n_2 + n_1)^2 + \kappa_2^2}\right]^{1/2}, \quad \tan\varphi_r = \frac{2n_1\kappa_2}{(n_2 - n_1)^2 + \kappa_2^2} \quad \text{...(12.45)}$$

$$\tilde{t} = te^{i\varphi_t}, \quad t = \frac{2n_1}{\left[(n_2+n_1)^2+\kappa_2^2\right]^{1/2}}, \quad \tan\varphi_t = -\frac{\kappa_2}{n_2+n_1} \qquad \text{...(12.46)}$$

The reflectance R and transmittance T at the dielectric-conducting interface is given by

$$R = \tilde{r}\tilde{r}^* = |\tilde{r}|^2 = \frac{(n_2-n_1)^2+\kappa_2^2}{(n_2+n_1)^2+\kappa_2^2} \qquad \text{...(12.47)}$$

$$T = 1-R = \frac{4n_1n_2}{(n_2+n_1)^2+\kappa_2^2} \qquad \text{...(12.48)}$$

Since the transmitted wave in the conducting medium is ultimately absorbed, the transmittance is also called absorption A. Thus $A = 1 - R$.

$$A = \frac{4n_1n_2}{(n_2+n_1)^2+\kappa_2^2}, \qquad R = 1-A = 1-\frac{4n_1n_2}{(n_2+n_1)^2+\kappa_2^2} \qquad \text{...(12.49)}$$

For a good conductor $\frac{\sigma}{\omega\varepsilon} >> 1$. The propagation vector $\tilde{k}(=k'+ik'')$ is related to the complex refractive index $\tilde{n}(=n+i\kappa)$ through the relation $\tilde{n} = \frac{c}{\omega}\tilde{k}$ or $n+i\kappa = \frac{c}{\omega}(k'+ik'')$ or $n = \frac{c}{\omega}k'$, $\kappa = \frac{c}{\omega}k''$ where, $k' = k'' = \sqrt{\frac{\omega\mu\sigma}{2}}$. This shows that $n = \kappa = \frac{c}{\omega}\sqrt{\frac{\omega\mu\sigma}{2}} = \sqrt{\frac{\sigma}{2\varepsilon_0\omega}} >> 1$. When these approximations are applied to the interface of air ($n_1 = 1$) and good conductor (metals $n_2 = \kappa_2$), the expressions for A and R become

$$A = T = \frac{2}{\kappa_2} = 2\sqrt{\frac{2\varepsilon_0\omega}{\sigma}}, \quad R = 1-A = 1-2\sqrt{\frac{2\varepsilon_0\omega}{\sigma}} \qquad \text{...(12.50)}$$

This formula is known as *Hagen-Rubens* formula. Let us apply this formula to some air-conductor interfaces.

Air-silver interface: $\sigma(silver) = 6\times10^7\,(\Omega\text{m})^{-1}$

Reflectance at frequency $\omega = 4 \times 10^{15}$ rad/s is

$$R = 1-2\sqrt{\frac{2\varepsilon_0\omega}{\sigma}} = 1-2\sqrt{\frac{2\times8.85\times10^{-12}\times4\times10^5}{6\times10^7}} = 1-0.0687 = 0.9313$$

Thus silver is good reflector at optical frequency $\omega = 4 \times 10^{15}$ rad/s. At lower frequency ($\omega = 6.28 \times 10^{10}$ rad/s) the reflectivity is even more and comes out to be $R = 0.9996$ and $A = 0.00039$. At optical frequency ($\omega = 10^{15}$ rad/s), the reflectivity of aluminium ($\sigma = 38.2\times10^6\ \Omega^{-1}\text{m}^{-1}$) is $R = 0.76$ and $A = 0.24$ and at lower frequency $\omega = 10^9$ rad/s, $R = 0.99976$ and $A = 0.00024$. Thus aluminium is a good reflector at lower frequency but not at optical frequency.

12.4. THEORY OF DISPERSION

Experimental measurements of refractive index of transparent materials in visible region of electromagnetic radiation showed that (*i*) for a given wavelength of radiation, the refractive index n is different for different materials (*ii*) for a given material, refractive index n is different for different wavelengths. *The variation of refractive index of a substance with wavelength is known as dispersion.* It is observed that both n and $dn/d\lambda$ decrease in magnitude as λ increases. *The decrease of refractive index with increasing wavelength is called normal dispersion.* The variation of n with λ is shown in the Fig. 12.13.

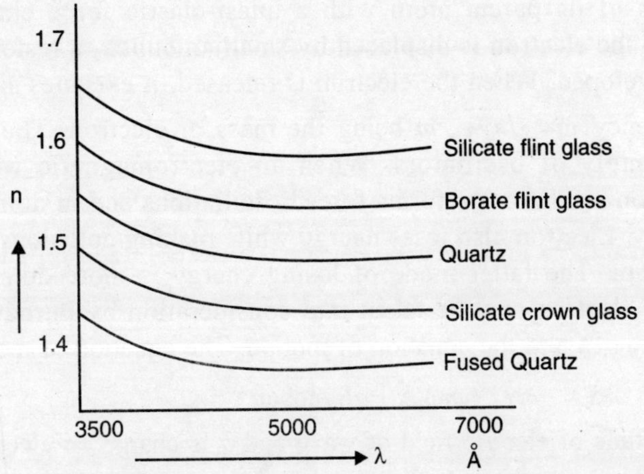

Fig. 12.13. Variation of refractive index with wavelength of light.

In 1836, Cauchy showed that the variation of n with wavelength λ can be represented by formula

$$n = A + \frac{B}{\lambda^2} + \frac{C}{\lambda^4} \qquad \text{...(12.51)}$$

Where A, B and C are constants characteristic of the medium. For most of the substances, only two terms of the above formula are sufficient to describe the dependence of n on λ. Thus

$$n = A + \frac{B}{\lambda^2}, \qquad \frac{dn}{d\lambda} = -\frac{2B}{\lambda^3} \qquad \text{...(12.52)}$$

Hartman suggested that the refractive index of glass is given by

$$n = n_0 + \frac{A}{(\lambda - \lambda_0)^{1.2}}, \quad n_0 \text{ and } \lambda_0 \text{ are constants.} \qquad \text{...(12.53)}$$

When the measurement of refractive index of a transparent substance is extended to infra-red region, it is observed that the medium absorbs strongly a band of wavelengths, called *absorption band.* A peculiar thing that is found in the absorption band is that the refractive index increases as wave length increases. This phenomenon is called *anomalous dispersion.* In this section, we shall give a classical explanation of the phenomenon of dispersion.

Gladstone and Dale showed that the refractive indices of gases obey the rule

$$\frac{n-1}{\rho} = \text{constant} \qquad ...(12.54)$$

Where ρ is density of gas.

12.4.1 Classical Theory of Dispersion

An electromagnetic wave of frequency ω consists of oscillating electric and magnetic fields. In framework of classical physics a substance consists of molecules in which each electron is bound to the nucleus of its parent atom with a quasi-elastic force characterized by a force constant, say s. When the electron is displaced by small amount x, a restoring force proportional to displacement is developed. When the electron is released, it executes simple harmonic motion with resonance frequency $\omega = \sqrt{s/m}$, m being the mass of electron. Thus, a substance may be modelled as an assembly of oscillators. When an electromagnetic wave passes through a substance, each electron oscillator performs forced oscillations and in doing so it radiates energy and hence loses energy. Electron also loses energy while making collisions with the neighbouring particles of the medium. The latter mode of losing energy is more dominant than the former. The loss in energy of electron may be taken into consideration by introducing a damping term, proportional to velocity ($\dot{x}$) into the equation of motion. The equation of motion of electron is

$$m\ddot{x} = -m\gamma\dot{x} - m\omega_0^2 x + qE_0 \cos\omega t \qquad ...(12.55)$$

Where E_0 is amplitude of electric field of wave and q is charge on electron. We can write eqn. (12.55) as

$$\ddot{x} + \gamma\dot{x} + \omega_0^2 x = \frac{qE_0}{m}\cos\omega t \qquad ...(12.56)$$

For mathematical convenience we write this equation in complex form given below.

$$\ddot{\tilde{x}} + \gamma\dot{\tilde{x}} + \omega_0^2 \tilde{x} = \frac{qE_0}{m} e^{-i\omega t} \qquad ...(12.57)$$

In fact eqn. (12.56) is the real part of eqn. (12.57). Let us write the solution of eqn. (12.57) of the form

$$\tilde{x} = \tilde{x}_0 e^{-i\omega t} \qquad ...(12.58)$$

When $\tilde{x}$ from (12.58) is substituted in (12.57) we get

$$\tilde{x}_0 = \frac{q}{m} \cdot \frac{E_0}{\omega_0^2 - \omega^2 - i\gamma\omega} \qquad ...(12.59)$$

The displacement of electron can be written in the form

$$\tilde{x} = \frac{q}{m} \cdot \frac{E_0 e^{-i\omega t}}{\omega_0^2 - \omega^2 - i\gamma\omega} \qquad ...(12.60)$$

A deviation of electron from the equilibrium position results in a dipole moment given by

$$\tilde{p} = q\tilde{x} = \frac{q^2}{m} \cdot \frac{1}{\omega_0^2 - \omega^2 - i\gamma\omega}\tilde{E} \quad \text{where} \quad \tilde{E} = E_0 e^{-i\omega t} \qquad ...(12.61)$$

We assume that the medium in which the electromagnetic wave is propagating is a rarefied medium (gas) in which the electric field acting on the electron may be taken equal to that of the wave. Let there be N electrons per unit volume. The polarization (dipole moment per unit volume) in the medium is

$$\tilde{P} = N\tilde{p} = Nq\tilde{x} = \frac{Nq^2}{m} \cdot \frac{1}{\omega_0^2 - \omega^2 - i\gamma\omega}\tilde{E} \qquad \text{...(12.62)}$$

In a molecule all the electrons do not experience the same force constant and the same damping. Let a fraction f_k of electrons have resonance frequency ω_k and damping constant γ_k. Of course $\sum_k f_k = 1$. Incorporating this fact, the expression for polarization $\tilde{P}$ becomes

$$\tilde{\mathbf{P}} = \sum_k N f_k \tilde{\mathbf{p}}_k = \frac{Nq^2}{m} \sum_k \frac{f_k}{\omega_k^2 - \omega^2 - i\gamma_k\omega}\tilde{\mathbf{E}} \qquad \text{..(12.63)}$$

The symbol f_k is called oscillator strength. The polarization $\tilde{P}$ is related to electric field $\tilde{E}$ through the relation

$$\tilde{\mathbf{P}} = \varepsilon_0(\tilde{\varepsilon}_r - 1)\tilde{\mathbf{E}} \qquad \text{...(12.64)}$$

Where $\tilde{\varepsilon}_r$ is complex dielectric constant. Comparison of eqns. (12.64) and (12.63) gives

$$\tilde{\varepsilon}_r = 1 + \frac{Nq^2}{m\varepsilon_0} \sum_k \frac{f_k}{\omega_k^2 - \omega^2 - i\gamma_k\omega} \qquad \text{...(12.65)}$$

Since the refractive index n is related to dielectric constant $\tilde{\varepsilon}_r$ through the relation

$$\tilde{n}^2 = \tilde{\varepsilon}_r \qquad \text{...(12.66)}$$

We have

$$\tilde{n}^2 = \tilde{\varepsilon}_r = 1 + \frac{Nq^2}{m\varepsilon_0} \sum_k \frac{f_k}{\omega_k^2 - \omega^2 - i\gamma_k\omega}$$

$$= 1 + \frac{Nq^2}{\varepsilon_0 m} \sum_k \frac{f_k(\omega_k^2 - \omega^2)}{(\omega_k^2 - \omega^2)^2 + \gamma_k^2\omega^2} + i\frac{Nq^2}{\varepsilon_0 m} \sum_k \frac{f_k\gamma_k\omega}{(\omega_k^2 - \omega^2)^2 + \gamma_k^2\omega^2} \qquad \text{...(12.67)}$$

Let us write $\tilde{n}$ and $\tilde{\varepsilon}_r$ as

$$\tilde{n} = n + i\kappa \quad \text{and} \quad \tilde{\varepsilon}_r = \varepsilon' + i\varepsilon'' \qquad \text{...(12.68)}$$

Here n is conventional *index of refraction* and k is called *extinction coefficient.*

Equation (12.67) can now becomes

$$n^2 - \kappa^2 = \varepsilon' = 1 + \frac{Nq^2}{\varepsilon_0 m} \sum_k \frac{f_k(\omega_k^2 - \omega^2)}{(\omega_k^2 - \omega^2)^2 + \gamma_k^2\omega^2} \qquad \text{...(12.69)}$$

$$2n\kappa = \frac{Nq^2}{\varepsilon_0 m}\sum_k \frac{f_k\gamma_k\omega}{(\omega_k^2-\omega^2)^2+\gamma_k^2\omega^2} \quad ...(12.70)$$

From eqns. (12.69) and (12.70) we can find n and κ. These are the dispersion relations for dilute gases. In such media damping term is small *i.e.* $\gamma_k \to 0$ and $\kappa \to 0$. Thus, for dilute gases refractive index n is a real quantity. For the rarefied medium ($\gamma_k \to 0$ and $\kappa \to 0$) the refractive index is given by

$$n = 1+\frac{Nq^2}{\varepsilon_0 m}\sum_k \frac{f_k(\omega_k^2-\omega^2)}{(\omega_k^2-\omega^2)^2} \quad \text{(rarefied medium)} \quad ...(12.71)$$

We can easily see that at driving frequencies less than resonance frequency ($\omega < \omega_k$), the second term on the right hand side of eqn. (12.71) is positive, and hence $n > 1$. Similarly, at frequencies greater than resonance frequency ($\omega > \omega_k$), the second term on the right hand side of eqn. (12.71) is negative, and hence $n < 1$.

The equation of plane wave propagating in the medium in z-direction is of the form

$$\tilde{E} = E_0 e^{i(kz-\omega t)} \quad ...(12.72)$$

Where the k is the propagation vector and is now a complex number. Writing

$$\tilde{k} = k' + ik'' \quad ...(12.73)$$

And remembering that $\tilde{k} = \frac{\omega}{c}\tilde{n}$ *i.e.* $(k'+ik'') = \frac{\omega}{c}(n+i\kappa)$ we have

$$k' = \frac{\omega}{c}n \quad \text{and} \quad k'' = \frac{\omega}{c}\kappa \quad ...(12.74)$$

In terms of $k'(n)$ and $k''(\kappa)$ the equation of electromagnetic wave becomes

$$\tilde{E} = E_0 e^{-k''z} e^{-i(k'z-\omega t)} = E_0 e^{-\omega\kappa z/c} e^{i[(\omega n z/c)-\omega t]} \quad ...(12.75)$$

The exponential term $\exp i\left(\frac{\omega n}{c}z - \omega t\right)$ represents a wave travelling with phase velocity $v = \frac{c}{n}$.

Notice that the amplitude of the wave decreases exponentially with z and the imaginary part of complex refractive index viz. κ occurs in the amplitude term. Hence, the imaginary part of refractive index is responsible for the attenuation of the wave. The intensity of the wave is proportional to the square of amplitude and we have

$$I \propto e^{-2\omega\kappa/c}$$

or $$I \propto e^{-\beta z}, \quad \beta = \frac{2\omega\kappa}{c} \quad ...(12.76)$$

The quantity β is called the *absorption coefficient.*

The curves showing the frequency-dependence of conventional refractive index n and of extinction coefficient κ, which is connected with absorption coefficient $\beta(= 2\omega\kappa/c)$ are shown in

Fig. 12.14. The refractive index n rises gradually with increasing frequency ω of the wave and then suddenly drops near the resonance frequency ω_k. Notice that in this region, the imaginary part κ, which describes power absorption, rises and attains maximum value when the driving frequency coincides with the resonance frequency ω_k. The sudden fall of index of refraction n in the vicinity of resonance frequency ω_k is called *anomalous dispersion.* The region where κ is large is called the region of absorption.

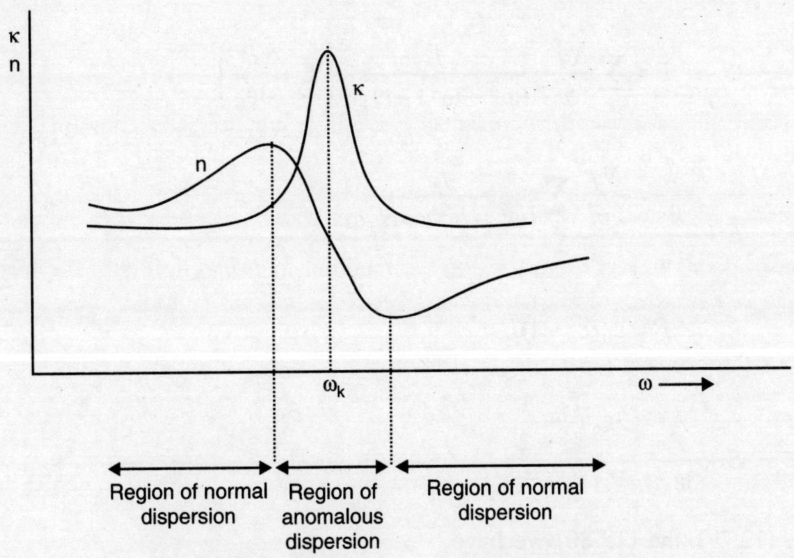

Fig. 12.14. Variation of n and κ with frequency.

For transparent materials, the resonant frequency ω_k lies in ultraviolet region and for visible radiation the driving frequency $\omega << \omega_k$. Then we can make the following approximation.

$$\frac{1}{\omega_k^2 - \omega^2} = \frac{1}{\omega_k^2\left(1 - \frac{\omega^2}{\omega_k^2}\right)} = \frac{1}{\omega_k^2}\left(1 - \frac{\omega^2}{\omega_k^2}\right)^{-1} \cong \frac{1}{\omega_k^2}\left(1 + \frac{\omega^2}{\omega_k^2}\right)$$

Then

$$n' = 1 + \frac{Nq^2}{2\varepsilon_0 m}\sum_k \frac{f_k}{\omega_k^2}\left(1 + \frac{\omega^2}{\omega_k^2}\right)$$

$$= 1 + \left(\frac{Nq^2}{2\varepsilon_0 m}\sum_k \frac{f_k}{\omega_k^2}\right) + \left(\frac{Nq^2}{2\varepsilon_0 m}\sum_k \frac{f_k}{\omega_k^4}\right)\omega^2, \qquad \omega = \frac{2\pi c}{\lambda}$$

$$= A + \frac{B}{\lambda^2} \qquad ...(12.77)$$

Where the constant A is called coefficient of refraction and B is called the coefficient of absorption. Formula (12.75) is known as *Cauchy's formula.*

12.4.2 Dispersion in Dense Media (Solids and Liquids)

For dense materials, the electric field acting on an oscillator is not the same as the external electric field of the wave. The interaction of neighbouring molecules on the oscillator under question can be taken into account by replacing **E** by local electric field which is given by $\left(\mathbf{E}+\dfrac{\mathbf{P}}{3\varepsilon_0}\right)$. The expression for polarization given by eqn. (12.63) now becomes

$$\tilde{P}=\sum_k \frac{Nq^2}{m}\cdot\frac{f_k}{(\omega_k^2-\omega^2)-i\gamma_k\omega}\left(\tilde{E}+\frac{\tilde{P}}{3\varepsilon_0}\right) \quad ...(12.78)$$

or
$$\frac{\tilde{P}}{\tilde{E}+\dfrac{\tilde{P}}{3\varepsilon_0}}=\frac{Nq^2}{m}\sum_k\frac{f_k}{(\omega_k^2-\omega^2)-i\gamma_k\omega} \quad ...(12.79)$$

Since
$$\tilde{P}=\varepsilon_0(\tilde{\varepsilon}_r-1)\tilde{E}$$

Therefore,
$$\frac{\tilde{P}}{\tilde{E}+\dfrac{\tilde{P}}{3\varepsilon_0}}=3\varepsilon_0\frac{\tilde{\varepsilon}_r-1}{\tilde{\varepsilon}_r+2} \quad ...(12.80)$$

From eqns. (12.79) and (12.80) we have

$$\frac{\tilde{\varepsilon}_r-1}{\tilde{\varepsilon}_r+2}=\frac{Nq^2}{3\varepsilon_0 m}\sum_k\frac{f_k}{(\omega_k^2-\omega^2)-i\gamma_k\omega} \quad ...(12.81)$$

or
$$\frac{\tilde{n}^2-1}{\tilde{n}^2+2}=\frac{Nq^2}{3\varepsilon_0 m}\sum_k\frac{f_k}{(\omega_k^2-\omega^2)-i\gamma_k\omega} \quad ...(12.82)$$

The number density of electrons is proportional to the number of atoms per unit volume, which in turn is proportional to volume density ρ of substance, so we can write above equation as

$$\frac{\tilde{n}^2-1}{\tilde{n}^2+2}\cdot\frac{1}{\rho}=\text{constant.}=A\ \text{(say)} \quad ...(12.83)$$

This relation is known as *Lorentz-Lorentz* formula.

QUESTIONS AND PROBLEMS

1. Obtain the boundary conditions that field vectors **E, D, B** and **H** satisfy at the boundary of two media.
2. Plane electromagnetic waves are incident normally on a plane interface of two non-conducting (dielectric) media. Derive *Fresnel's equations* for reflection and transmission of waves at the interface.
3. Discuss the phenomena of reflection and refraction (transmission) when electromagnetic waves are incident obliquely at the plane interface of two non-conducting media. Consider the cases the incident wave is plane polarized with E-vector (*i*) parallel to the plane of incidence (*ii*) perpendicular to the plane of incidence.
4. Derive Brewster's law on the basis of electromagnetic wave theory of light.
5. Discuss the phenomenon of total internal reflection on the basis of electromagnetic theory of light.
6. Plane electromagnetic waves are incident normally on a plane surface of conducting medium (metal). Discuss the phenomenon of reflection and transmission (absorption) at the interface.
7. Explain the meaning of dispersion. Discuss the frequency dependence of index of refraction and the coefficient of absorption. What is anomalous dispersion?
8. Obtain Cauchy's formula for the phenomenon of dispersion.

Appendix—*Vector Calculus*

1. DIFFERENTIATION OF VECTORS

If to each value of some scalar t there corresponds a vector **A** then **A** is said to be vector function of scalar variable t and is denoted by $\mathbf{A}(t)$. Let $\mathbf{A}(t)$ and $\mathbf{A}(t + \delta t)$ represent the vector function corresponding to the scalar variables t and $t + dt$ respectively. Let $\mathbf{A}(t + \delta t) - \mathbf{A}(t) = \delta\mathbf{A}$.

The limit of the quotient

$$\lim_{\delta t \to 0} \frac{\mathbf{A}(t+\delta t) - \mathbf{A}(t)}{\delta t} = \lim_{\delta t \to 0} \frac{\delta \mathbf{A}}{\delta t}$$

provided it exists, is called the derivative of vector **A** with respect to t and is denoted by $d\mathbf{A}/dt$. The derivative of a vector is also a vector.

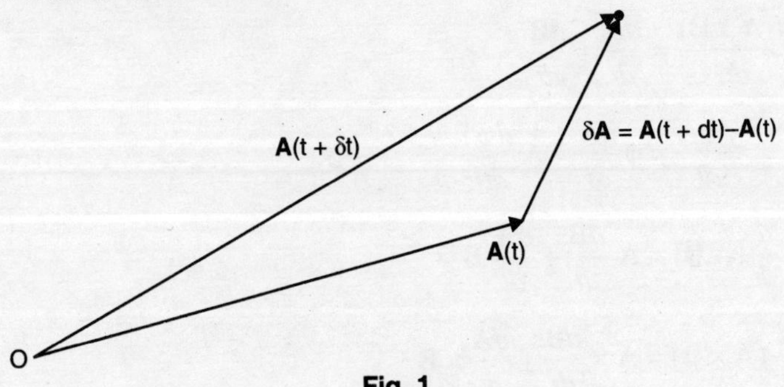

Fig. 1

Thus

$$\frac{d\mathbf{A}}{dt} = \lim_{\delta t \to 0} \frac{\mathbf{A}(t+\delta t) - \mathbf{A}(t)}{\delta t} = \lim_{\delta t \to 0} \frac{\delta \mathbf{A}}{\delta t}$$

If $A_1(t)$, $A_2(t)$ and $A_3(t)$ are the components of vector **A** then

$$\frac{d\mathbf{A}}{dt} = \frac{dA_1}{dt}\mathbf{i} + \frac{dA_2}{dt}\mathbf{j} + \frac{dA_3}{dt}\mathbf{k} \qquad ...(1)$$

$$\mathbf{A}(t) = A_1(t)\mathbf{i} + A_2(t)\mathbf{j} + A_3(t)\mathbf{k}$$

Time derivative of position $\mathbf{r}(t)$ of a moving particle: Let $\mathbf{r}(t)$ and $\mathbf{r}(t + \delta t)$ be the position vectors of the particle at time t and $t + \delta t$. The displacement $\delta\mathbf{r}$ of the particle is given by

$$\delta\mathbf{r} = \mathbf{r}(t + \delta t) - \mathbf{r}(t)$$

The limit of the quotient $\delta\mathbf{r}/\delta t$ as δt tends to zero is called the velocity $\mathbf{v}$ of the particle

$$\mathbf{v} = \lim_{\delta t \to 0} \frac{\delta\mathbf{r}}{\delta t}$$

and is denoted by

$$\mathbf{v} = \frac{d\mathbf{r}}{dt} = \mathbf{i}\frac{dx}{dt} + \mathbf{j}\frac{dy}{dt} + \mathbf{k}\frac{dz}{dt}$$

The acceleration of the particle is

$$\mathbf{a} = \frac{d\mathbf{v}}{dt} = \ddot{\mathbf{r}} \qquad \text{...(2)}$$

2. RULES OF VECTOR DIFFERENTIATION

In the following **A** and **B** are vector functions of scalar variable t, **c** is a constant vector, and φ is a scalar function.

$$\frac{d\mathbf{c}}{dt} = 0 \qquad \text{...(3)}$$

$$\frac{dk\mathbf{A}}{dt} = k\frac{d\mathbf{A}}{dt} \qquad \text{...(4)}$$

$$\frac{d(\mathbf{A} \pm \mathbf{B})}{dt} = \frac{d\mathbf{A}}{dt} \pm \frac{d\mathbf{B}}{dt} \qquad \text{...(5)}$$

$$\frac{d\varphi\mathbf{A}}{dt} = \varphi\frac{d\mathbf{A}}{dt} + \mathbf{A}\frac{d\varphi}{dt} \qquad \text{...(6)}$$

$$\frac{d}{dt}(\mathbf{A}.\mathbf{B}) = \mathbf{A}.\frac{d\mathbf{B}}{dt} + \frac{d\mathbf{A}}{dt}.\mathbf{B} \qquad \text{...(7)}$$

$$\frac{d}{dt}(\mathbf{A} \times \mathbf{B}) = \mathbf{A} \times \frac{d\mathbf{B}}{dt} + \frac{d\mathbf{A}}{dt} \times \mathbf{B} \qquad \text{...(8)}$$

3. PARTIAL DIFFERENTIATION

Let $\varphi(x, y, z)$ be a scalar function of space coordinates x, y and z. The partial derivatives of φ with respect to x, y and z are respectively defined by

$$\frac{\partial\varphi}{\partial x} = \lim_{\delta x \to 0} \frac{\varphi(x + \delta x, y, z) - \varphi(x, y, z)}{\delta x}$$

$$\frac{\partial \varphi}{\partial y} = \lim_{\delta y \to 0} \frac{\varphi(x, y+\delta y, z) - \varphi(x, y, z)}{\delta y}$$

$$\frac{\partial \varphi}{\partial z} = \lim_{\delta z \to 0} \frac{\varphi(x, y, z+\delta z) - \varphi(x, y, z)}{\delta z}$$

If the variables x, y and z change by dx, dy and dz respectively, the change in function is given by

$$d\varphi = \frac{\partial \varphi}{\partial x} dx + \frac{\partial \varphi}{\partial y} dy + \frac{\partial \varphi}{\partial z} dz \qquad ...(9)$$

Similarly, the change in vector function $\mathbf{A}(x, y, z)$ is given by

$$\mathbf{dA} = \frac{\partial \mathbf{A}}{\partial x} dx + \frac{\partial \mathbf{A}}{\partial y} dy + \frac{\partial \mathbf{A}}{\partial z} dz \qquad ...(10)$$

In particular if $\mathbf{r} = x\mathbf{i} + y\mathbf{j} + z\mathbf{k}$ then the differential $\mathbf{dr}$ is given by

$$\mathbf{dr} = \frac{\partial \mathbf{r}}{\partial x} dx + \frac{\partial \mathbf{r}}{\partial y} dy + \frac{\partial \mathbf{r}}{\partial z} dz = dx\,\mathbf{i} + dy\,\mathbf{j} + dz\,\mathbf{k} \qquad ...(11)$$

4. SCALAR AND VECTOR FIELDS

If to each point in a certain region of space there corresponds a physical quantity, the latter is called a *field* or *point function* and is said to be defined in that region. The field is scalar or vector depends whether the corresponding quantity is scalar or vector. If we heat a block of solid matter at one place, each point in the solid has some definite temperature. In the steady state the temperature distribution in the solid is a scalar field *i.e.* $\theta = \theta(x, y, z)$. Similarly, the electrostatic potential around a charged body is another example of scalar field. The surface over which the scalar field has the same value is called the *level surface.* If the scalar field is potential, the corresponding level surface is called the *equipotential surface*. The velocity of a moving fluid varies from point to point in space *i.e.* velocity is function of space coordinates x, y, z. The velocity field is an example of vector field. The electric field around a charged body and the magnetic field around a current carrying conductor are other examples of vector fields.

5. GRADIENT OF A SCALAR FIELD

Let $\varphi(x, y, z)$ be a scalar field. The relation $\varphi(x, y, z) = c$, where c is a constant, represents a surface in three-dimensional space. Similarly, $\varphi'(x, y, z) = c'$ also represents another surface. Let P and Q are two points on the surfaces $\varphi = c$ and $\varphi' = c'$ and $\varphi' - \varphi = \Delta\varphi$. Let us denote the distance PQ by Δr. Then

$$\lim_{\Delta r \to 0} \frac{\Delta \varphi}{\Delta r} \equiv \frac{\partial \varphi}{\partial r}$$

is called the directional derivative of φ (x, y, z) in the direction PQ.

Let $PN = \Delta n$ be the normal to the surface $\varphi\ (x, y, z) = c$ at point P and **n** the unit vector along PN. From the Fig. 2.

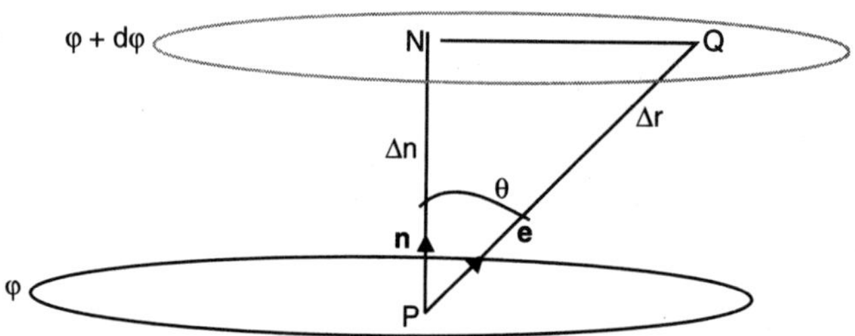

Fig. 2. Gradient of a scalar field.

$$\Delta n = \Delta r \cos\theta \qquad \therefore \frac{\partial n}{\partial r} = \cos\theta$$

and
$$\frac{\partial \varphi}{\partial r} = \frac{\partial \varphi}{\partial n}\frac{\partial n}{\partial r} = \frac{\partial \varphi}{\partial n}\cos\theta$$

The directional derivative is maximum when $\theta = 0$ *i.e.* the maximum rate of change of φ occurs in the direction normal to the surface.

$$\left(\frac{\partial \varphi}{\partial r}\right)_{\max} = \frac{\partial \varphi}{\partial n} \qquad ...(12)$$

Now, we define or a vector whose magnitude is equal to the maximum rate of change of $\varphi(x, y, z)$ and direction is along the normal to the surface $\varphi(x, y, z) = c$. This vector is called the **gradient of** φ and is written as **grad** φ.

$$grad\ \varphi = (\partial\varphi/\partial n)\ \mathbf{n}$$

If **e** is unit vector along PQ then the directional derivative of φ can be written as

$$(\partial\varphi/\partial r) = (\partial\varphi/\partial n)\ (\mathbf{n}.\mathbf{e}) = (grad\ \varphi).\ \mathbf{e}$$

This relation reads that the component of grad φ in a direction is equal to the directional derivative in that direction. Thus, the components of grad φ along the coordinate axes are

$$(grad\,\varphi)\cdot\mathbf{i} = \frac{\partial\varphi}{\partial x},\ (grad\,\varphi)\cdot\mathbf{j} = \frac{\partial\varphi}{\partial y},\ (grad\ \varphi)\cdot\mathbf{k} = \frac{\partial\varphi}{\partial z}$$

This shows that the vector *grad* φ can be expressed as

$$grad\ \varphi = \frac{\partial\varphi}{\partial x}\mathbf{i} + \frac{\partial\varphi}{\partial y}\mathbf{j} + \frac{\partial\varphi}{\partial z}\mathbf{k} \qquad ...(13)$$

6. VECTOR DIFFERENTIAL OPERATOR DEL ∇

The vector differential operator *del* ∇ is defined by

$$\nabla \equiv \mathbf{i}\frac{\partial}{\partial x} + \mathbf{j}\frac{\partial}{\partial y} + \mathbf{k}\frac{\partial}{\partial z} \qquad ...(14)$$

From the very definition we see that the operator del is a vector as well as a differential operator. When it operates on a scalar field, it gives a vector field. If $\varphi(x, y, z)$ is a scalar field then

$$\nabla\varphi = \frac{\partial\varphi}{\partial x}\mathbf{i} + \frac{\partial\varphi}{\partial y}\mathbf{j} + \frac{\partial\varphi}{\partial z}\mathbf{k} \qquad ...(15)$$

is a vector called *gradient of* φ abbreviated as *grad* φ.

If **A** (x, y, z) is a vector field then the dot product of ∇ and **A** is called *divergence of* **A** or *div* **A** and is given by

$$div\ \mathbf{A} = \nabla\cdot\mathbf{A} = \frac{\partial A_1}{\partial x} + \frac{\partial A_2}{\partial y} + \frac{\partial A_3}{\partial z} \qquad ...(16)$$

The vector product of operator ∇ with vector field **A** (x, y, z) is called *curl of* **A** and is given by

$$curl\ \mathbf{A} = \nabla\times\mathbf{A} = \left(\mathbf{i}\frac{\partial}{\partial x} + \mathbf{j}\frac{\partial}{\partial y} + \mathbf{k}\frac{\partial}{\partial z}\right)\times(A_1\mathbf{i} + A_2\mathbf{j} + A_3\mathbf{k}) = \begin{vmatrix} \mathbf{i} & \mathbf{j} & \mathbf{k} \\ \frac{\partial}{\partial x} & \frac{\partial}{\partial y} & \frac{\partial}{\partial z} \\ A_1 & A_2 & A_3 \end{vmatrix} \qquad ...(17)$$

Definitions:

1. A vector field **A** is **solenoidal** if its divergence is zero *i.e.* div $\mathbf{A} \equiv \nabla.\mathbf{A} = 0$
2. A vector field **A** is **irrotational (conservative)** if its curl is zero *i.e.* curl $\mathbf{A} \equiv \nabla\times\mathbf{A} = 0$

7. VECTOR IDENTITIES

In following vector identities, ***A*** and ***B*** are vector fields, φ and ψ are scalar fields.

1. $\nabla(\varphi + \psi) = \nabla\varphi + \nabla\psi$
2. $\nabla\cdot(\mathbf{A} + \mathbf{B}) = \nabla\cdot\mathbf{A} + \nabla\cdot\mathbf{B}$
3. $\nabla\times(\mathbf{A} + \mathbf{B}) = \nabla\times\mathbf{A} + \nabla\times\mathbf{B}$
4. $\nabla(\varphi\,\psi) = \psi\,\nabla\varphi + \varphi\,\nabla\psi$
5. $\nabla\cdot(\varphi\,\mathbf{A}) = \mathbf{A}\cdot\nabla\varphi + \varphi\,\nabla\cdot\mathbf{A}$
6. $\nabla\times(\varphi\,\mathbf{A}) = (\nabla\varphi)\times\mathbf{A} + \varphi\,\nabla\times\mathbf{A}$
7. $\nabla\cdot(\mathbf{A}\times\mathbf{B}) = \mathbf{B}\cdot\nabla\times\mathbf{A} - \mathbf{A}\cdot\nabla\times\mathbf{B}$
8. $\nabla\cdot\nabla\mathbf{A} = \nabla^2\mathbf{A}$
9. $\nabla\times\nabla\varphi = 0$ *curl grad* $\varphi = 0$
10. $\nabla\cdot\nabla\times\mathbf{A} = 0$ *div curl* $\mathbf{A} = 0$
11. $\nabla\times\nabla\times\mathbf{A} = \nabla(\nabla\cdot\mathbf{A}) - \nabla^2\mathbf{A}$

In order to derive above identities we shall change our notations for the sake of convenience. The unit vectors **i, j, k** will be replaced by unit vectors $\mathbf{e}_1$, $\mathbf{e}_2$, $\mathbf{e}_3$ respectively. The space coordinates x, y, z will be denoted by x_1, x_2, x_3 respectively. In terms of new notations the expressions for *grad*, *div* and *curl* become

$$\nabla \equiv \mathbf{e}_1 \frac{\partial}{\partial x} + \mathbf{e}_2 \frac{\partial}{\partial y} + \mathbf{e}_3 \frac{\partial}{\partial z} = \sum \mathbf{e}_1 \frac{\partial}{\partial x_1}$$

$$\nabla \cdot \mathbf{A} = \left(\mathbf{e}_1 \frac{\partial}{\partial x_1} + \mathbf{e}_2 \frac{\partial}{\partial x_2} + \mathbf{e}_3 \frac{\partial}{\partial x_3} \right) \cdot \mathbf{A} \equiv \sum \left(\mathbf{e}_1 \cdot \frac{\partial}{\partial x_1} \right) \mathbf{A}$$

$$\nabla \times \mathbf{A} \equiv \left(\mathbf{e}_1 \frac{\partial}{\partial x_1} + \mathbf{e}_2 \frac{\partial}{\partial x_2} + \mathbf{e}_3 \frac{\partial}{\partial x_3} \right) \times \mathbf{A} \equiv \sum \mathbf{e}_1 \times \frac{\partial}{\partial x_1}$$

1. $\nabla(\varphi + \psi) = \sum \mathbf{e}_1 \frac{\partial}{\partial x_1}(\varphi + \psi) = \sum \mathbf{e}_1 \frac{\partial \varphi}{\partial x_1} + \sum \mathbf{e}_1 \frac{\partial \psi}{\partial x_1} = \nabla\varphi + \nabla\psi$

2. $\nabla \cdot (\mathbf{A} + \mathbf{B}) = \sum \mathbf{e}_1 \cdot \frac{\partial}{\partial x_1}(\mathbf{A} + \mathbf{B}) = \sum \mathbf{e}_1 \cdot \frac{\partial \mathbf{A}}{\partial x_1} + \sum \mathbf{e}_1 \cdot \frac{\partial \mathbf{B}}{\partial x_1} = \nabla \cdot \mathbf{A} + \nabla \cdot \mathbf{B}$

3. $\nabla \times (\mathbf{A} + \mathbf{B}) = \sum \mathbf{e}_1 \times \frac{\partial}{\partial x_1}(\mathbf{A} + \mathbf{B}) = \sum \mathbf{e}_1 \times \frac{\partial \mathbf{A}}{\partial x_1} + \sum \mathbf{e}_1 \times \frac{\partial \mathbf{B}}{\partial x_1} = \nabla \times \mathbf{A} + \nabla \times \mathbf{B}$

4. $\nabla(\varphi\psi) = \sum \mathbf{e}_1 \frac{\partial}{\partial x_1}(\varphi\psi) = (\sum \mathbf{e}_1 \frac{\partial \varphi}{\partial x_1})\psi + \varphi(\sum \mathbf{e}_1 \frac{\partial \psi}{\partial x_1}) = \psi\nabla\varphi + \varphi\nabla\psi$

5. $\nabla \cdot (\varphi \mathbf{A}) = \sum \mathbf{e}_1 \cdot \frac{\partial}{\partial x_1}(\varphi \mathbf{A}) = \sum \mathbf{e}_1 \cdot \left(\frac{\partial \varphi}{\partial x_1} \mathbf{A} + \varphi \frac{\partial \mathbf{A}}{\partial x_1} \right) = \left(\sum \mathbf{e}_1 \frac{\partial \varphi}{\partial x_1} \right) \cdot \mathbf{A} + \varphi \sum \mathbf{e}_1 \cdot \frac{\partial \mathbf{A}}{\partial x_1}$

   $= \mathbf{A}.\nabla\varphi + \varphi\nabla.\mathbf{A}$

6. $\nabla \times (\varphi \mathbf{A}) = \sum \mathbf{e}_1 \times \frac{\partial}{\partial x_1}(\varphi \mathbf{A}) = \sum \mathbf{e}_1 \times \left(\frac{\partial \varphi}{\partial x_1} \mathbf{A} + \varphi \frac{\partial \mathbf{A}}{\partial x_1} \right) = \left(\sum \mathbf{e}_1 \frac{\partial \varphi}{\partial x_1} \right) \times \mathbf{A} + \varphi \sum \mathbf{e}_1 \times \frac{\partial \mathbf{A}}{\partial x_1}$

   $= \nabla\varphi \times \mathbf{A} + \varphi\nabla \times \mathbf{A}$

7. $\nabla \cdot (\mathbf{A} \times \mathbf{B}) = \sum \mathbf{e}_1 \cdot \frac{\partial}{\partial x_1}(\mathbf{A} \times \mathbf{B}) = \sum \mathbf{e}_1 \cdot \left(\frac{\partial \mathbf{A}}{\partial x_1} \times \mathbf{B} + \mathbf{A} \times \frac{\partial \mathbf{B}}{\partial x_1} \right)$

   $= \sum \mathbf{e}_1 \cdot \frac{\partial \mathbf{A}}{\partial x_1} \times \mathbf{B} + \sum \mathbf{e}_1 \cdot \mathbf{A} \times \frac{\partial \mathbf{B}}{\partial x_1}$

   $= \sum \mathbf{e}_1 \times \frac{\partial \mathbf{A}}{\partial x_1} \cdot \mathbf{B} - \sum \mathbf{e}_1 \cdot \frac{\partial \mathbf{B}}{\partial x_1} \times \mathbf{A}$

   $= (\nabla \times \mathbf{A}) \cdot \mathbf{B} - \sum \mathbf{e}_1 \times \frac{\partial \mathbf{B}}{\partial x_1} \cdot \mathbf{A} = \mathbf{B} \cdot \nabla \times \mathbf{A} - \mathbf{A} \cdot \nabla \times \mathbf{B}$

8. $\nabla \cdot \nabla \mathbf{A} = \left(\sum \mathbf{e}_1 \cdot \frac{\partial}{\partial x_1} \right) \left(\sum \mathbf{e}_1 \frac{\partial}{\partial x_1} \right) \mathbf{A} = \sum \frac{\partial}{\partial x_1} \frac{\partial \mathbf{A}}{\partial x_1} = \sum \frac{\partial^2 \mathbf{A}}{\partial x_1^2} = \nabla^2 \mathbf{A}$

9. $\nabla \times (\nabla\varphi) = \left(\sum \mathbf{e}_1 \times \frac{\partial}{\partial x_1} \right) \left(\sum \mathbf{e}_1 \frac{\partial \varphi}{\partial x_1} \right) = \sum \mathbf{e}_1 \times \mathbf{e}_1 \frac{\partial^2 \varphi}{\partial x_1^2} = 0$

10. $$\nabla \cdot \nabla \times \mathbf{A} = \left(\sum \mathbf{e}_1 \cdot \frac{\partial}{\partial x_1} \right) \left(\sum \mathbf{e}_1 \times \frac{\partial \mathbf{A}}{\partial x_1} \right) = \sum \sum \mathbf{e}_1 \cdot \mathbf{e}_1 \times \frac{\partial^2 \mathbf{A}}{\partial x_1 \partial x_1} = 0$$

11. $$\nabla \times (\nabla \times \mathbf{A}) = \left(\sum \mathbf{e}_1 \times \frac{\partial}{\partial x_1} \right) \left(\sum \mathbf{e}_1 \times \frac{\partial \mathbf{A}}{\partial x_1} \right) = \sum \sum \mathbf{e}_1 \times \left(\mathbf{e}_1 \times \frac{\partial}{\partial x_1} \frac{\partial \mathbf{A}}{\partial x_1} \right)$$

$$= \sum \sum \left[\left(\mathbf{e}_1 \cdot \frac{\partial}{\partial x_1} \frac{\partial \mathbf{A}}{\partial x_1} \right) \mathbf{e}_1 - (\mathbf{e}_1 \cdot \mathbf{e}_1) \frac{\partial}{\partial x_1} \frac{\partial \mathbf{A}}{\partial x_1} \right]$$

$$= \sum \sum \left[\mathbf{e}_1 \frac{\partial}{\partial x_1} \left(\mathbf{e}_1 \cdot \frac{\partial \mathbf{A}}{\partial x_1} \right) - \left(\mathbf{e}_1 \cdot \frac{\partial}{\partial x_1} \right) \left(\mathbf{e}_1 \frac{\partial \mathbf{A}}{\partial x_1} \right) \right]$$

$$= \nabla (\nabla \cdot \mathbf{A}) - \nabla^2 \mathbf{A}$$

Solved Examples

***Example* 1:** *The position vector* **r** *of a particle varies with time t according to the relation*

$$\mathbf{r}(t) = (\sin^2 t)\,\mathbf{i} + (\cos^2 t)\,\mathbf{j}$$

Find its velocity and acceleration at time $t = \pi/4$.

Solution:

Velocity $\mathbf{v} = d\mathbf{r}/dt = (2 \sin t \cos t)\,(\mathbf{i} - \mathbf{j})$

At $t = \pi/4$ $\mathbf{v} = \mathbf{i} - \mathbf{j}$

Acceleration $\mathbf{a} = d\mathbf{v}/dt = (2 \cos 2t)\,(\mathbf{i} - \mathbf{j})$

and at $t = \pi/4$, $\mathbf{a} = 0$

***Example* 2:** *A particle is moving in a circle. Show that its velocity is perpendicular to the radius of the circle.*

Solution: Let the position vector of the particle referred to the center of the circle be **r**.

$$\mathbf{r}\cdot\mathbf{r} = r^2 = \text{constant}$$

$$d/dt\,(\mathbf{r}\cdot\mathbf{r}) = 0$$

$$\mathbf{r}\cdot d\mathbf{r}/dt = 0$$

$$\mathbf{r}\cdot\mathbf{v} = 0$$

Hence the radius vector of the particle is perpendicular to velocity.

***Example* 3:** *Find the gradient of scalar field $\varphi = xy + yz + zx$ at point (1,1,1).*

Solution: $$\nabla\varphi = \frac{\partial\varphi}{\partial x}\mathbf{i} + \frac{\partial\varphi}{\partial y}\mathbf{j} + \frac{\partial\varphi}{\partial z}\mathbf{k} = (y + z)\,\mathbf{i} + (x + z)\,\mathbf{j} + (y + x)\,\mathbf{k}$$

$\nabla\varphi$ at point (1,1,1) is

$$(\nabla\varphi)_{1,1,1} = 2\,(\mathbf{i} + \mathbf{j} + \mathbf{k})$$

Its magnitude is $2\sqrt{3}$.

***Example* 4:** *Show that the following vector field is solenoidal.*

$\mathbf{A} = (1 + 2xy)\mathbf{i} - y^2z\,\mathbf{j} + (z^2y - 2zy + 1)\mathbf{k}$

Solution: $div\mathbf{A} = \frac{\partial}{\partial x}(1+2xy) - \frac{\partial}{\partial y}(y^2z) + \frac{\partial}{\partial z}(z^2y - 2zy + 1) = 2y - 2yz + 2yz - 2y = 0$

Hence, **A** is **solenoidal.**

***Example* 5:** *Show that the vector field*

$\mathbf{A} = xy^2z\,\mathbf{i} + x^2yz\,\mathbf{j} + (1/2)x^2y^2\mathbf{k}$

is irrotational.

Solution:

$$curl\ \mathbf{A} = \begin{vmatrix} \mathbf{i} & \mathbf{j} & \mathbf{k} \\ \frac{\partial}{\partial x} & \frac{\partial}{\partial y} & \frac{\partial}{\partial z} \\ xy^2z & x^2yz & \frac{1}{2}x^2y^2 \end{vmatrix}$$

$$= (x^2y - x^2y)\mathbf{i} + (xy^2 - xy^2)\mathbf{j} + (2xyz - 2xyz)\mathbf{k}$$

$$= 0$$

Hence, **A** is **irrotational** field.

***Example* 6:** *Show that* $\nabla r^n = n\,r^{n-2}\,\mathbf{r}$ *where* **r** *is position vector of point (x, y, z).*

Solution:

$$\nabla r^n = \mathbf{i}\frac{\partial r^n}{\partial x} + \mathbf{j}\frac{\partial r^n}{\partial y} + \mathbf{k}\frac{\partial r^n}{\partial z}$$

$$= nr^{n-1}\left(\mathbf{i}\frac{\partial r}{\partial x} + \mathbf{j}\frac{\partial r}{\partial y} + \mathbf{k}\frac{\partial r}{\partial z}\right) \qquad \text{since } r^2 = x^2 + y^2 + z^2$$

$$= nr^{n-1}\left(\frac{x}{r}\mathbf{i} + \frac{y}{r}\mathbf{j} + \frac{z}{r}\mathbf{k}\right) \qquad \text{since } \frac{\partial r}{\partial x} = \frac{x}{r}, \frac{\partial r}{\partial y} = \frac{y}{r}, \frac{\partial r}{\partial z} = \frac{z}{r}$$

$$= nr^{n-2}\,\mathbf{r}$$

***Example* 7:** *Show that* $\nabla.\ \mathbf{r} = 3$ *where* **r** *is radius vector of point (x, y, z).*

Solution:

$$\nabla \cdot \mathbf{r} = \frac{\partial x}{\partial x} + \frac{\partial y}{\partial y} + \frac{\partial z}{\partial z} = 1 + 1 + 1 = 3$$

***Example* 8:** *Show that* $\nabla.(\mathbf{r}/r^3) = 0$

Solution: $\nabla \cdot r^{-3}\,\mathbf{r} = \nabla\, r^{-3}.\mathbf{r} + r^{-3}\,\nabla.\mathbf{r}$

$$= -\,3\,r^{-5}\,\mathbf{r}.\mathbf{r} + 3r^{-3}$$

$$= 0$$

***Example* 9:** *Show that* $\nabla \cdot r^n \mathbf{r} = (n + 3)\, r^n$.

Solution: $\nabla \cdot r^n \mathbf{r} = \nabla r^n \cdot \mathbf{r} + r^n\, \nabla \cdot \mathbf{r} = n\, r^{n-2}\, \mathbf{r} \cdot \mathbf{r} + 3r^n = (n + 3)r^n$

***Example* 10:** *Show that* $\nabla^2 r^n = n\,(n + 1)\, r^{n-2}$

Solution:

$$\begin{aligned}\nabla^2 r^n &= \nabla \cdot \nabla\, r^n = \nabla \cdot n\, r^{n-2}\, \mathbf{r} = n\, \nabla \cdot r^{n-2}\, \mathbf{r} = n\,(\nabla\, r^{n-2} \cdot \mathbf{r} + r^{n-2}\, \nabla \cdot \mathbf{r}) \\ &= n\,[(n-2)\, r^{n-4}\, \mathbf{r} \cdot \mathbf{r} + 3\, r^{n-2}] \\ &= n\,[\,(n-2)\, r^{n-2} + 3\, r^{n-2}\,] \\ &= n\,(n + 1)\, r^{n-2}\end{aligned}$$

***Example* 11:** *If* $\mathbf{A} = \varphi$ *grad* ψ *show that* $\mathbf{A}$ *.curl* $\mathbf{A} = 0$.

Solution: Let *grad* $\psi = \mathbf{B}$ Then $\mathbf{A} = \varphi \mathbf{B}$

Now, *curl* $\mathbf{A}$ = *curl* $(\varphi \mathbf{B})$

$= \varphi$ *curl* $\mathbf{B} + (\nabla \varphi) \times \mathbf{B}$

$= \varphi$ *curl (grad* ψ) $+ \nabla \varphi \times \nabla \psi$

$= 0 + \nabla \varphi \times \nabla \psi$

$\mathbf{A} \cdot$*curl* $\mathbf{A} = \varphi\, (\nabla \psi) \cdot (\nabla \varphi) \times (\nabla \psi) = 0$ (property of scalar triple product)

***Example* 12:** *For a rotating rigid body, show that* curl $\mathbf{v} = 2\boldsymbol{\omega}$ *where* $\boldsymbol{\omega}$ *is the angular velocity of the body and* $\mathbf{v}$ *is the linear velocity of a point with position vector* $\mathbf{r}$ *relative to some origin on the axis of rotation.*

Solution: We know that $\mathbf{v} = \boldsymbol{\omega} \times \mathbf{r} = \begin{vmatrix} \mathbf{i} & \mathbf{j} & \mathbf{k} \\ \omega_1 & \omega_2 & \omega_3 \\ x & y & z \end{vmatrix}$

$$\nabla \times \mathbf{v} = \begin{vmatrix} \mathbf{i} & \mathbf{j} & \mathbf{k} \\ \dfrac{\partial}{\partial x} & \dfrac{\partial}{\partial y} & \dfrac{\partial}{\partial z} \\ (z\omega_2 - y\omega_3) & (x\omega_3 - z\omega_1) & (y\omega_1 - z\omega_2) \end{vmatrix}$$

$$= (\omega_1 + \omega_1)\, \mathbf{i} + (\omega_2 + \omega_2)\, \mathbf{j} + (\omega_3 + \omega_3)\, \mathbf{k}$$

$$= 2\,(\omega_1 \mathbf{i} + \omega_2 \mathbf{j} + \omega_3 \mathbf{k}) = 2\, \boldsymbol{\omega}$$

***Example* 13:** *Show that* $(\mathbf{a} \cdot \nabla)\, \mathbf{r} = \mathbf{a}$.

Solution:

$$\begin{aligned}(\mathbf{a} \cdot \nabla)\mathbf{r} &= (a_1 \mathbf{i} + a_2 \mathbf{j} + a_3 \mathbf{k}) \cdot (\mathbf{i}\, \partial/\partial x + \mathbf{j}\, \partial/\partial y + \mathbf{k}\, \partial/\partial z)\mathbf{r} \\ &= (a_1 \partial/\partial x + a_2 \partial/\partial y + a_3 \partial/\partial z)\,(x\mathbf{i} + y\mathbf{j} + z\mathbf{k}) \\ &= a_1 \mathbf{i} + a_2 \mathbf{j} + a_3 \mathbf{k} \\ &= \mathbf{a}\end{aligned}$$

***Example* 14:** *Show that* $\nabla(\mathbf{a} \cdot \mathbf{r}) = \mathbf{a}$.

Solution:

$$\begin{aligned}\nabla(\mathbf{a} \cdot \mathbf{r}) &= (\mathbf{i}\, \partial/\partial x + \mathbf{j}\, \partial/\partial y + \mathbf{k}\, \partial/\partial z)(a_1 x + a_2 y + a_3 z) \\ &= \mathbf{i} a_1 + \mathbf{j} a_2 + \mathbf{k} a_3 \\ &= \mathbf{a}\end{aligned}$$

***Example* 15:** *Show that* $d\varphi = \nabla\varphi.d\mathbf{r}$ *where* $\mathbf{r} = x\mathbf{i} + y\mathbf{j} + z\mathbf{k}$ *and* φ *is function of x, y and z.*

Solution:

$$\nabla\varphi\cdot d\mathbf{r} = \left(\mathbf{i}\frac{\partial\varphi}{\partial x} + \mathbf{j}\frac{\partial\varphi}{\partial y} + \mathbf{k}\frac{\partial\varphi}{\partial z}\right)\cdot(\mathbf{i}dx + \mathbf{j}dy + \mathbf{k}dz)$$

$$= \frac{\partial\varphi}{\partial x}dx + \frac{\partial\varphi}{\partial y}dy + \frac{\partial\varphi}{\partial z}dz = d\varphi$$

***Example* 16:** *Show that* $r^n\mathbf{r}$ *is an irrotational vector for any value of n but solenoidal only for* $n = -3$ *where* $\mathbf{r}$ *is position vector of point (x, y, z).*

Solution:

$$\nabla\times(r^n\,\mathbf{r}) = \nabla r^n \times \mathbf{r} + r^n\,\nabla\times\mathbf{r}$$

$$= nr^{n-2}\,\mathbf{r}\times\mathbf{r} + 0$$

$$= 0$$

Hence, $r^n\mathbf{r}$ is irrotational vector for any value of n.

$$\nabla.\,(r^n\,\mathbf{r}) = (n+3)r^n$$

Divergence of the given vector is zero only for $n = -3$ and hence, the vector is solenoidal only for this value of n.

8. INTEGRATION OF VECTOR FUNCTIONS

A vector function $\mathbf{A}(t)$ is said to be the *primitive* of the vector function $\mathbf{a}(t)$ if $A(t)$ is differentiable and

$$\frac{d\mathbf{A}(t)}{dt} = \vec{a}(t)$$

The set of all primitive functions of $\mathbf{a}(t)$ is called *indefinite integral* of the vector function of scalar argument $\mathbf{a}(t)$ *i.e.*

$$\int \mathbf{a}(t)\,dt = \mathbf{A}(t) + \mathbf{C} \qquad ...(18)$$

where $\mathbf{A}(t)$ is one of the primitive functions of $\mathbf{a}(t)$ and $\mathbf{C}$ is an arbitrary constant vector.

The following properties hold true for integrals of vector functions:

1. $\int\alpha\,\mathbf{a}(t)dt = \alpha\int\mathbf{a}(t)dt$, α is a numerical constant. ...(19)
2. $\int[\mathbf{a}(t) + \mathbf{b}(t)]dt = \int\mathbf{a}(t)dt + \int\mathbf{b}(t)dt$
3. If $\mathbf{a}(t) = a_1(t)\mathbf{i} + a_2(t)\mathbf{j} + a_3(t)\mathbf{k}$ then
   $\int\mathbf{a}(t)dt = \mathbf{i}\int a_1(t)dt + \mathbf{j}\int a_2(t)dt + \mathbf{k}\int a_3(t)dt$

9. TANGENTIAL LINE INTEGRAL OF A VECTOR FIELD

Consider a curve C in a vector field (x, y, z). Divide the curve into small segments $\Delta\mathbf{r}_1$, $\Delta\mathbf{r}_2$........$\Delta\mathbf{r}_i$.........$\Delta\mathbf{r}_n$. Let $\mathbf{A}_1$, $\mathbf{A}_2$,.......$\mathbf{A}_i$.......$\mathbf{A}_n$ be the vector fields at the initial points of these segments. Now, form the sum of scalar products like

$$\mathbf{A}_1\cdot\Delta\mathbf{r}_1 + \mathbf{A}_2.\Delta\mathbf{r}_2 + \ldots\ldots\ldots\ldots\mathbf{A}_i.\Delta\mathbf{r}_i\ldots\ldots + \mathbf{A}_n\cdot\Delta\mathbf{r}_n$$

or $\quad \Sigma\,\mathbf{A}_i\cdot\Delta\mathbf{r}_i$

and let $\Delta \mathbf{r}_i \to 0$. Then the limit of this sum (if it exists) is called the tangential line integral of vector **A** along the curve C and is written as $\int \mathbf{A}.d\mathbf{r}$. Thus

$$\int_C \mathbf{A}.d\mathbf{r} = \lim_{\Delta r \to 0} \sum \mathbf{A}_i.\Delta r_i$$

In cartesian components form the line integral is written as

$$\int_C \mathbf{A}.d\mathbf{r} = \int_C (A_1 dx + A_2 dy + A_3 dz) \qquad ...(20)$$

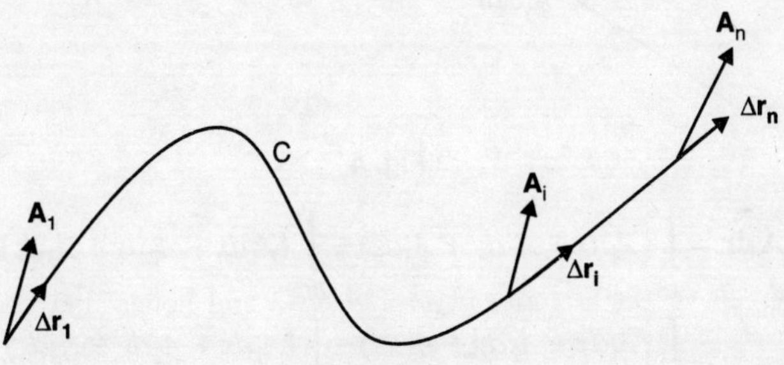

Fig. 3

If the curve C is a closed one then the line integral of **A** is written as

$$\oint_C \mathbf{A} \cdot \mathbf{dr}$$

and is called the *circulation* of vector field **A**.

If the closed line integral of vector field **A** is zero then **A** is said to be **conservative** field.

If a particle moves in a force field $F(x, y, z)$ along the curve C from point P to Q then the line integral of F represents the work done by the force in moving the particle from P to Q.

***Example* 1:** *Compute* $\int \mathbf{A}.d\mathbf{r}$ *where* $\mathbf{A} = (y^2 - z^2)\,\mathbf{i} + 2yz\,\mathbf{j} + x^2\,\mathbf{k}$ *along the curve* $x = t$, $y = t^2$, $z = t^3$, $0 \le t \le 1$.

Solution:

$$\int \mathbf{A}.d\mathbf{r} = \int (A_1 dx + A_2 dy + A_3 dz)$$
$$= \int (y^2 - z^2)dx + \int 2yz dy - \int x^2 dz$$
$$= \int_0^1 (t^4 - t^6)dt + 4\int_0^1 t^6 dt - 3\int_0^1 t^4 dt = \frac{1}{35}$$

***Example* 2.** *Calculate the line integral of the vector field*

$$\mathbf{A} = (2xz + 3y^2)\,\mathbf{j} + 4yz^2\,\mathbf{k}$$

around the boundary of the rectangle formed by lines $y = 0$, $y = 1$, $z = 0$, $z = 1$.

Solution:

$$\oint_{ABCD} \mathbf{A}.\mathbf{dr} = \oint_{ABCD} (A_1 dx + A_2 dy + A_3 dz)$$

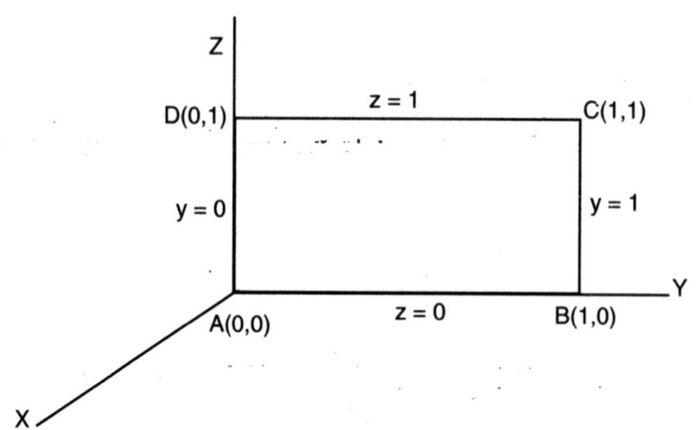

Fig. 4

$$\oint_{ABCDA} \mathbf{A}\cdot\mathbf{dr} = \int_{AB} (A_1dx + A_2dy + A_3dz) + \int_{BC} (A_1dx + A_2dy + A_3dz) +$$

$$\int_{CD} (A_1dx + A_2dy + A_3dz) + \int_{DA} (A_1dx + A_2dy + A_3dz)$$

$$= I_1 + I_2 + I_3 + I_4$$

Now $$I_1 = \int_{AB} (A_1dx + A_2dy + A_3dz)$$

Here $$A_1 = 0 \;\therefore I_1 = \int_{AB} (2xz + 3y^2)dy + \int_{AB} (4yz^2)dz$$

Along AB, $x = 0$, $z = 0$, $dz = 0$, limit of y, $y = 0 \to 1$

$\therefore$ $$I_1 = \int_0^1 3y^2 dy = 1$$

Along BC, $x = 0$, $y = 1$, $dy = 0$ limit of z, $z = 0 \to 1$

$$I_2 = \int_0^1 4yz^2 dz = \int_0^1 4z^2 dz = \frac{4}{3}$$

Along CD, $x = 0$, $z = 1$, $dz = 0$,limit of y, $y = 1 \to 0$

$$I_3 = \int_1^0 3y^2 dy = -1$$

Along DA, $x = 0$, $y = 0$, $dy = 0$, limit of z, $z = 1 \to 0$

$$I_4 = \int_1^0 4yz^2 dz = 0$$

Hence $I = 1 + 4/3 - 1 + 0 = 4/3$

***Example* 3:** *A particle moves from origin to point (1,2) under the influence of a force* $\mathbf{F} = (x\mathbf{i} + y\mathbf{j})$. *Calculate the work done by the force if the particle moves*

1. *from O to A and then to C*
2. *from O to B and then to C*
3. *straight to C.*

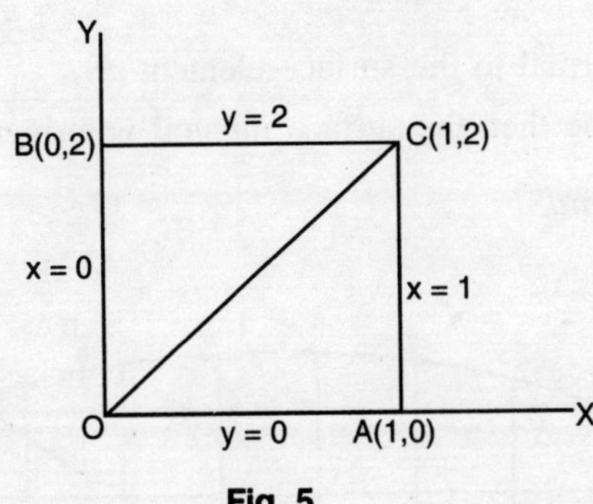

Fig. 5

Solution: $W = \int (F_1 dx + F_2 dy) = \int (xdx + ydy)$

1. Path *OAC*

$$W_{OAC} = W_{OA} + W_{AC}$$

Along *OA*, $y = 0$, $dy = 0$, limit of x, $x = 0 \rightarrow 1$

$$W_{OA} = \int_0^1 xdx = \frac{1}{2}$$

Along $AC x = 1$, $dx = 0$, limit of y, $y = 0 \rightarrow 2$,

$$W_{AC} = \int_0^2 ydy = 2$$

$$W_{OAC} = \frac{5}{2}$$

In the similar way we can calculate $W_{OBC} = 5/2$ and W_{OC} along the straight line *OC* comes out to be 5/2.

Here we see that the work done by the force is independent of the path. Such forces are called conservative forces.

10. NORMAL SURFACE INTEGRAL OR FLUX OF A VECTOR FIELD

Let *S* be a surface in a vector field $\mathbf{A}(x, y, z)$. Divide the surface into a large number of elementary surfaces $\Delta\mathbf{S}_1$, $\Delta\mathbf{S}_2$,................ ....$\Delta\mathbf{S}_i$,......$\Delta\mathbf{S}_n$. Let $\mathbf{A}_1$, $\mathbf{A}_2$, ...$\mathbf{A}_i$,..........$\mathbf{A}_n$ represent the vector field at the middle points of these surface elements. Now form the sum of scalar products such as

$\mathbf{A}_1 \cdot \Delta\mathbf{S}_1 + \mathbf{A}_2 \cdot \Delta\mathbf{S}_2 + \ldots \ldots\ldots\ldots\ldots \mathbf{A}_i \cdot \Delta\mathbf{S}_i \ldots\ldots\ldots\ldots \mathbf{A}_n \cdot \Delta\mathbf{S}_n.$

or $\quad \Sigma\, \mathbf{A}_i \cdot \Delta\mathbf{S}_i$

In the limit $\Delta\mathbf{S}_i \to 0$, the value of the above is called the normal surface integral of vector **A** or flux of vector **A** through the surface S and is denoted by

$$\int_S \mathbf{A}\cdot d\mathbf{S} \quad \text{or} \quad \int_S \mathbf{A}\cdot\mathbf{n}dS = \lim_{\Delta S\to 0} \sum_i \mathbf{A}_i \cdot \Delta S_i$$

where **n** is unit vector normal to the surface element $d\mathbf{S}$.

If the surface is closed one then the surface integral is written as

$$\oint_S \mathbf{A}\cdot\mathbf{n}dS \quad \text{or} \quad \oiint_S \mathbf{A}\cdot\mathbf{n}dS$$

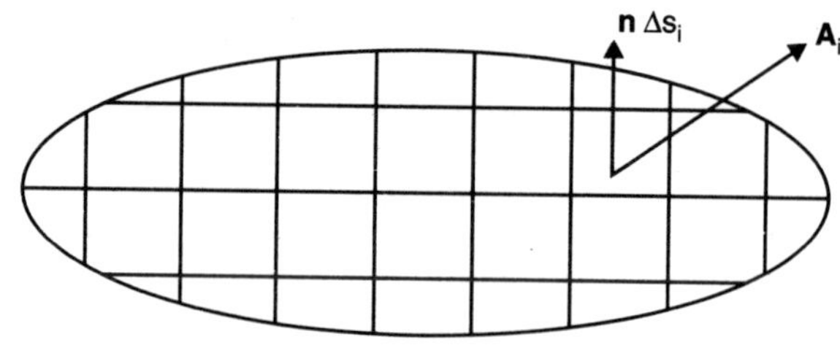

Fig. 6

In cartesian components form, the surface integral is written as

$$\int_S \mathbf{A}\cdot d\mathbf{S} = \int_S (A_1 dS_1 + A_2 dS_2 + A_3 dS_3)$$

$$= \iint (A_1 dydz + A_2 dxdz + A_3 dxdy) \quad \ldots(21)$$

where $dS_1 = dydz$ is the projection of $d\mathbf{S}$ onto the yz-plane etc.

If we imagine an area S in a fluid moving with velocity **v**, then the surface integral $\int \mathbf{v}.d\mathbf{S}$ represents the volume of fluid crossing per sec through the surface S. The surface integral of a vector is also called the **flux** of the vector field.

The flux of a vector reverses sign when the orientation of the surface is changed (that is, when the orientation of the normal **n** to the surface is changed.)

11. METHOD OF CALCULATING FLUX OR NORMAL SURFACE INTEGRAL OF VECTOR FIELD

Suppose that we have to calculate the flux of vector field $\mathbf{A}(x, y, z)$ over a surface S described by equation $\varphi\,(x, y, z) = 0$. First, find the unit vector **n** normal to the surface from the formula

$$\mathbf{n} = \frac{\nabla\varphi}{|\nabla\varphi|}$$

Second, compute **A**·**n**. Project the surface S onto one of the coordinate planes, say xy-plane. If $dxdy$ is the projected area then

$$dxdy = dS \cos \gamma$$

where γ is the angle which the vector **n** makes with z-axis. Thus,

$$dS = \frac{dxdy}{\cos\gamma} = \frac{dxdy}{\mathbf{n}\cdot\mathbf{k}}$$

If R is the region of projection of surface S onto xy-plane, then

$$\int_S \mathbf{A}\cdot\mathbf{n}dS = \iint_R (\mathbf{A}\cdot\mathbf{n})\left(\frac{dxdy}{\cos\gamma}\right) = \iint_R (\mathbf{A}\cdot\mathbf{n})\left(\frac{dxdy}{\mathbf{n}.\mathbf{k}}\right)$$

***Example* 1:** *Calculate the flux of vector field* $\mathbf{A} = (k/r^3)\,\mathbf{r}$ *over the surface of sphere of radius R having centre at the origin.*

Solution: The vector **A** is everywhere normal to the surface of the sphere. Hence, $\mathbf{A}\cdot\mathbf{n} = A = k/r^2$.

$$\oint \mathbf{A}.\mathbf{n}dS = \oint AdS = \oint \frac{k}{R^2}dS = \frac{k}{R^2}\oint dS = \frac{k}{R^2}(4\pi R^2) = 4\pi k$$

***Example* 2:** *Compute the flux of the vector field* $\mathbf{A} = y^2\mathbf{i} + (2xy + z^2)\mathbf{j} + 2yz\,\mathbf{k}$ *through the surface of the cube formed by the planes* $x = 0, y = 0, z = 0, x = 1, y = 1, z = 1$.

Solution: Six planes form a cube. So, we have to calculate the contributions to the total flux from all the six faces. The total flux through the faces of the cube is

$$\oint_{CUBE} \mathbf{A}\cdot\mathbf{n}dS = \iint_{face\ ADHE} \mathbf{A}\cdot\mathbf{n}dydz + \iint_{face\ BCGF} \mathbf{A}\cdot\mathbf{n}dydz + \iint_{face\ ABCD} \mathbf{A}\cdot\mathbf{n}dxdz + \iint_{face\ EFGH} \mathbf{A}\cdot\mathbf{n}dxdz + \iint_{face\ ABFE} \mathbf{A}\cdot\mathbf{n}dxdy + \iint_{face\ DCGH} \mathbf{A}\cdot\mathbf{n}dxdy$$

$$= I_1 + I_2 + I_3 + I_4 + I_5 + I_6$$

At the face ADHE, $x = 0$, $\mathbf{n} = -\mathbf{i}$, $\mathbf{A}\cdot\mathbf{n} = \mathbf{A}\cdot(-\mathbf{i}) = -y^2$, $y = 0 \rightarrow 1$, $z = 0 \rightarrow 1$

$$I_1 = \iint \mathbf{A}\cdot\mathbf{n}dydz = -\int_0^1\int_0^1 y^2dydz = -\int_0^1 y^2dy\int_0^1 dz = -\frac{1}{3}$$

At the face BCGF, $x = 1$, $0 \le y \le 1$, $0 \le z \le 1$, $\mathbf{n} = \mathbf{i}$, $\mathbf{A}\cdot\mathbf{n} = y^2$

$$I_2 = \iint \mathbf{A}\cdot\mathbf{n}dydz = \int_0^1\int_0^1 y^2dydz = \frac{1}{3}$$

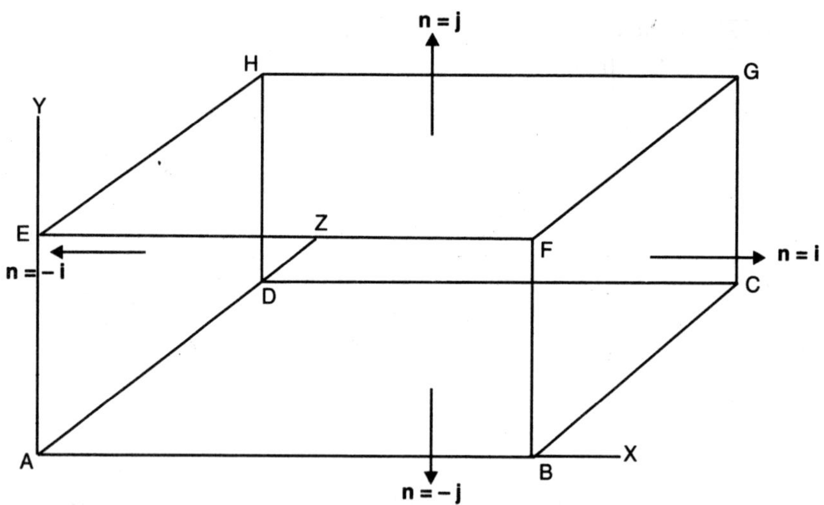

Fig. 7

At the face ABCD, $y = 0$, $0 \le x \le 1$, $0 \le z < 1$, $\mathbf{n} = -\mathbf{j}$, $\mathbf{A\cdot n} = \mathbf{A}\cdot(-\mathbf{j}) = -(2xy + z^2) = -z^2$

$$I_3 = \iint \mathbf{A\cdot n}\,dxdz = -\int_0^1\int_0^1 z^2 dxdz = -\frac{1}{3}$$

At the face EFGH, $y = 1$, $0 \le x \le 1$, $0 \le z < 1$, $\mathbf{n} = \mathbf{j}$, $\mathbf{A\cdot n} = \mathbf{A\cdot j} = 2xy + z^2 = 2x + z^2$

$$I_4 = \iint \mathbf{A\cdot n}\,dxdz = \int_0^1\int_0^1 (2x + z^2)dxdz = \int_0^1 \left[2xz + \frac{z^3}{3}\right]_0^1 dx = \int_0^1 (2x + \frac{1}{3})dx = \frac{4}{3}$$

At the face ABFE, $z = 0$, $0 \le x \le 1$, $0 \le y \le 1$, $\mathbf{n} = -\mathbf{k}$, $\mathbf{A\cdot n} = \mathbf{A}\cdot(-\mathbf{k}) = -2yz = 0$

$$I_5 = \iint \mathbf{A\cdot n}\,dxdy = 0$$

At the face DCGH, $z = 1$, $0 \le x \le 1$, $0 \le y \le 1$, $\mathbf{n} = \mathbf{k}$, $\mathbf{A\cdot n} = \mathbf{A\cdot k} = 2yz = 2y$

$$I_6 = \iint \mathbf{A\cdot n}\,dxdy = 2\int_0^1\int_0^1 y\,dxdy = 2\int_0^1 dx \int_0^1 y\,dy = 1$$

Hence, the total flux through the faces of the cube = 2

***Example* 3:** *Evaluate* $\int \mathbf{A\cdot n}\, dS$ *where*

$$\mathbf{A} = 4xz\,\mathbf{i} - y^2\mathbf{j} + yz\,\mathbf{k}$$

and S is the surface of the cube bounded by the planes $x = 0$, $x = 1$, $y = 0$, $y = 1$, $z = 0$, $z = 1$.

Solution: See the figure of the previous example.

At the face ADHE, $x = 0$, $0 \le y \le 1$, $0 \le z \le 1$, $\mathbf{A\cdot n} = 0$

Flux through this face $I_1 = 0$

At the face BCGF, $x = 1$, $0 \le y \le 1$, $0 \le z \le 1$, $\mathbf{A\cdot n} = 4xz = 4z$. Flux through this face

$$I_2 = \iint \mathbf{A\cdot n}\,dS = \int_0^1\int_0^1 4z\,dydz = 2$$

At the face ABCD, $y = 0$, $0 \le x \le 1$, $0 \le z \le 1$, $\mathbf{A}\cdot\mathbf{n} = 0$

The flux through this face

$$I_3 = 0$$

At the face EFGH, $y = 1$, $0 \le x \le 1$, $0 \le z \le 1$, $\mathbf{A}\cdot\mathbf{n} = -1$

The flux through this face

$$I_4 = \iint \mathbf{A}\cdot\mathbf{n}dS = -\int_0^1\int_0^1 dydz = -1$$

At the face ABEF, $z = 0$, $0 \le x \le 1$, $0 \le y \le 1$, $\mathbf{A}\cdot\mathbf{n} = 0$

$$I_5 = 0$$

At the face DCGH, $z = 1$, $0 \le x \le 1$, $0 \le y \le 1$, $\mathbf{A}\cdot\mathbf{n} = yz = y$

The flux through this face

$$I_6 = \iint \mathbf{A}\cdot\mathbf{n}dS = \int_0^1\int_0^1 ydxdy = \frac{1}{2}$$

Total flux = 3/2

Example 4: *Evaluate* $\int \mathbf{A}\cdot\mathbf{n}\, dS$ *where*

$\mathbf{A} = (x - 2z)\,\mathbf{i} + (x + 3y + z)\,\mathbf{j} + (5x + y)\,\mathbf{k}$ *and S is the surface of the plane* $x + y + z = a$ *between the coordinate planes.*

Solution: Equation of the plane $\varphi(x, y, z) = 0$

$$x + y + z - a = 0$$

Unit vector normal to the plane is

$$\mathbf{n} = \frac{\nabla\varphi}{|\nabla\varphi|} = \frac{\mathbf{i}+\mathbf{j}+\mathbf{k}}{\sqrt{3}}$$

And $\quad \cos\gamma = \mathbf{n}\cdot\mathbf{k} = 1/\sqrt{3}, \qquad \mathbf{A}\cdot\mathbf{n} = (7x + 4y - z)/\sqrt{3}$

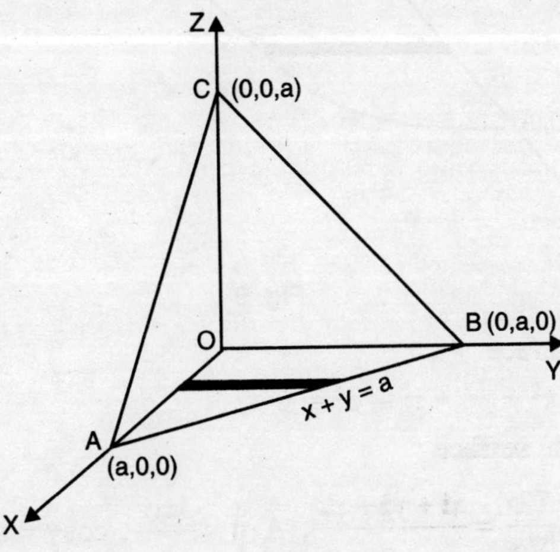

Fig. 8

Projection of the given plane on xy-plane is a triangular region OAB shown in the Fig. 8. Hence,

$$\int_S \mathbf{A}\cdot\mathbf{n}dS = \iint_R \frac{1}{\sqrt{3}}(7x+4y-z)\bigg|_{z=a-x-y} \frac{dxdy}{1/\sqrt{3}}$$

$$= \int_0^a \int_0^{a-x} (8x+5y-a)dxdy$$

$$= \int_0^a dx \int_0^{a-x} (8x+5y-a)dy$$

$$= \frac{5}{3}a^3$$

***Example* 5:** *Compute the flux of the vector field*

$$\mathbf{A} = yz\,\mathbf{i} + xz\,\mathbf{j} + xy\,\mathbf{k}$$

through the part of the sphere $x^2 + y^2 + z^2 = a^2$ *located in the first octant.*

Solution:

$$\text{Flux} = \int_S \mathbf{A}\cdot\mathbf{n}dS = \iint_R \mathbf{A}\cdot\mathbf{n}\frac{dxdy}{\cos\gamma}$$

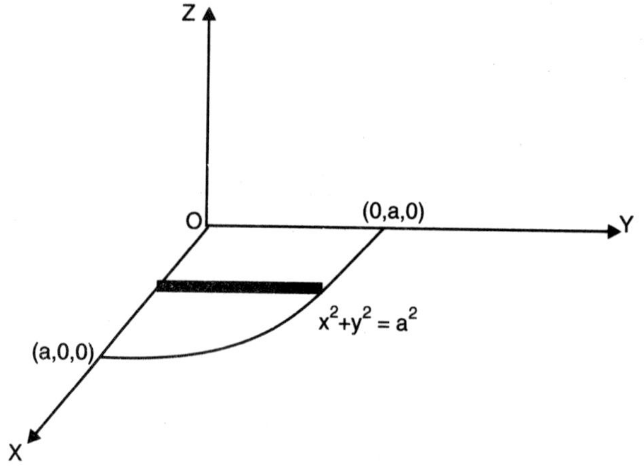

Fig. 9

Equation of the given surface

$$\varphi\,(x, y, z) = x^2 + y^2 + z^2 - a^2 = 0$$

Unit vector normal to the surface

$$\mathbf{n} = \frac{\nabla\varphi}{|\nabla\varphi|} = \frac{x\mathbf{i} + y\mathbf{j} + z\mathbf{k}}{a},\quad \mathbf{A}\cdot\mathbf{n} = \frac{3xyz}{a},\quad \cos\gamma = \mathbf{n}\cdot\mathbf{k} = \frac{z}{a}$$

The projection of the part of the sphere in question onto the xy-plane is a circle $x^2 + y^2 = a^2$

$$\text{Flux} = \iint_R \mathbf{A}\cdot\mathbf{n}\frac{dxdy}{\cos\ \gamma} = \iint_R 3xyz\frac{dxdy}{(z/a)}$$

$$= 3\int_0^a \int_{y=0}^{y=\sqrt{a^2-x^2}} xydxdy = 3\int_0^a xdx\left(\frac{y^2}{2}\right)_0^{\sqrt{a^2-x^2}} = \frac{3}{2}\int_0^a x(a^2-x^2)dx = \frac{3}{8}a^4$$

12. VOLUME INTEGRAL

Let **A** be a vector field and V a volume in the field. Divide the volume into a large number of elementary volumes $\Delta V_1, \Delta V_2, \ldots\ldots\Delta V_i\ldots\ldots\ldots\Delta V_n$, then the limit of the sum

$$\lim_{\Delta V\to 0}\sum_i \mathbf{A}_i\Delta V_i$$

is called the volume integral of vector **A** and is written as

$$\int_V \mathbf{A}dV \text{ or } \iiint \mathbf{A}dV \quad \ldots(22)$$

13. DIVERGENCE OF A VECTOR FIELD

Let S be a closed surface enclosing a volume V in the vector field **A** (x, y, z). The flux of the vector field through the surface S is $\oint_S \mathbf{A}\cdot\mathbf{n}dS$. The flux per unit volume is $\frac{1}{V}\oint_S \mathbf{A}\cdot\mathbf{n}dS$. Now suppose that the surface S shrinks to an interior point P then the limit

$$\lim_{S\to 0}\frac{1}{V}\oint_S \mathbf{A}\cdot\mathbf{n}dS$$

is defined as the divergence of the vector field A at the point P. Thus

$$div\mathbf{A} = \lim_{S\to 0}\ \frac{1}{V}\oint_S \mathbf{A}\cdot\mathbf{n}dS \quad \ldots(23)$$

that is, flux per unit volume through an infinitesimally small closed surface is called divergence of the vector field.

Let us calculate the divergence of a vector field **A** (x, y, z) in Cartesian coordinates. For definiteness we can take the vector field **A** as the velocity field of a moving fluid. Consider a rectangular box with its coterminous edges dx, dy and dz completely immersed in the fluid. We take the coordinate axes parallel to the edges of the box. Let $\mathbf{A}_1$, $\mathbf{A}_2$ and $\mathbf{A}_3$ be the components of the velocity field at the centre of the box.

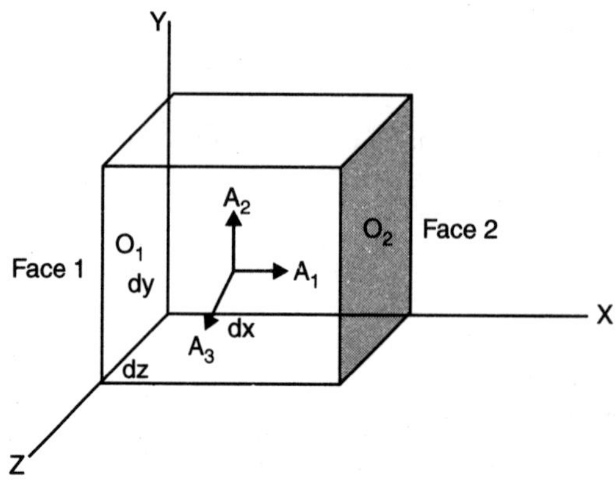

Fig. 10. Divergence of a vector field.

The value of $\mathbf{A}_1$ at the centre O_1 of the face 1 is

$$\mathbf{A}_1 - \frac{1}{2}\frac{\partial \mathbf{A}_1}{\partial x} dx$$

and at the centre O_2 of the face 2 is

$$\mathbf{A}_1 + \frac{1}{2}\frac{\partial \mathbf{A}_1}{\partial x}$$

The flux of vector **A** through the face 1 is

$$\left(\mathbf{A}_1 - \frac{1}{2}\frac{\partial \mathbf{A}_1}{\partial x} dx\right).(-\mathbf{i}dydz)$$

$$= -\left(A_1 - \frac{1}{2}\frac{\partial A_1}{\partial x} dx\right) dydz$$

and the flux through the face 2 is

$$\left(\mathbf{A}_1 + \frac{1}{2}\frac{\partial \mathbf{A}_1}{\partial x} dx\right).(+\mathbf{i}dydz)$$

$$= \left(A_1 + \frac{1}{2}\frac{\partial A_1}{\partial x} dx\right) dydz$$

The total flux of vector field **A** in x-direction is

$$\frac{\partial A_1}{\partial x} dxdydz.$$

Similarly, we can calculate the total flux in y and z directions and these come out to be

$$\frac{\partial A_2}{\partial y} dxdydz \quad \text{and} \quad \frac{\partial A_3}{\partial z} dxdydz.$$

The total flux of vector **A** through all faces of the box is

$$\left(\frac{\partial A_1}{\partial x}+\frac{\partial A_2}{\partial y}+\frac{\partial A_3}{\partial z}\right)dxdydz$$

By definition, total flux per unit volume is called the divergence of the vector field. Hence

$$div\mathbf{A}=\frac{\partial A_1}{\partial x}+\frac{\partial A_2}{\partial y}+\frac{\partial A_3}{\partial z}\equiv\nabla\cdot\mathbf{A} \quad ...(24)$$

A vector whose divergence vanishes is called a **solenoidal vector**.

14. CURL OF A VECTOR FIELD

Let C be a closed curve enclosing a surface S in a vector field $\mathbf{A}(x, y, z)$. The closed line integral of **A** around the boundary C of the surface is

$$\oint_C \mathbf{A}\cdot d\mathbf{r}$$

Now the surface is so oriented that the circulation has maximum value. The maximum line integral per unit area is

$$\frac{1}{S}\oint_C \mathbf{A}\cdot d\mathbf{r}$$

Now suppose that the periphery of the surface S shrinks to an interior point P, then the value of the limit

$$\lim_{S\to 0}\frac{1}{S}\oint_C \mathbf{A}\cdot d\mathbf{r}$$

is defined as the component of curl in the direction normal to the area i.e.

$$(curl\mathbf{A})\cdot\mathbf{n}=\lim_{S\to 0}\frac{1}{S}\oint_S \mathbf{A}\cdot d\mathbf{r} \quad ...(25)$$

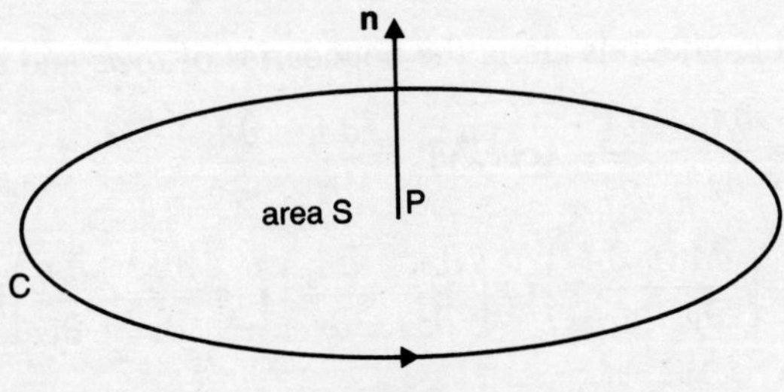

Fig. 11

Now let us find an expression for the curl of a vector in cartesian coordinates. Consider an element of area $d\mathbf{S}$ in an arbitrary orientation. Project $d\mathbf{S}$ onto the coordinate planes. Let the areas dS_1 (= $dydz$), dS_2 (= $dzdx$) and dS_3 (= $dxdy$) be the projections of $d\mathbf{S}$ on the coordinate planes. Obviously

$$d\mathbf{S} = dydz\ \mathbf{i} + dzdx\ \mathbf{j} + dxdy\ \mathbf{k}$$

Let us calculate the line integral of vector **A** along the periphery of the area *dxdy* first. Suppose that the components **A** at the center of this arca are $\mathbf{A}_1$, $\mathbf{A}_2$ and $\mathbf{A}_3$. Since, $\mathbf{A}_3$ is normal to the boundary of the area *dxdy*, it contributes nothing to the line integral .

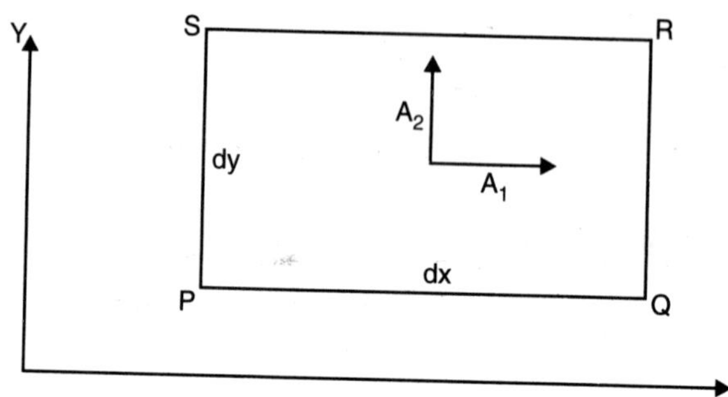

Fig. 12. Curl of a vector field.

The line integral of vector **A** along the boundary of the rectangle is

$$\oint_{PQRS} \mathbf{A}\cdot d\mathbf{r} = \left(A_1 - \frac{1}{2}\frac{\partial A_1}{\partial y}dy\right)dx + \left(A_2 + \frac{\partial A_2}{\partial x}dx\right)dy - \left(A_1 + \frac{1}{2}\frac{\partial A_1}{\partial y}dy\right)dx - \left(A_2 - \frac{\partial A_2}{\partial x}dx\right)dy$$

$$= \left(\frac{\partial A_2}{\partial x} - \frac{\partial A_1}{\partial y}\right)dxdy$$

The line integral per unit area is

$$\left(\frac{\partial A_2}{\partial x} - \frac{\partial A_1}{\partial y}\right)$$

By definition this is the *z*-component of curl **A.** Thus

$$(curl\mathbf{A})_z = \frac{\partial A_2}{\partial x} - \frac{\partial A_1}{\partial y}$$

Similar calculations of line integrals along the boundaries of *dydz* and *dzdx* will give

$$(curl\mathbf{A})_x = \frac{\partial A_3}{\partial y} - \frac{\partial A_2}{\partial z},\ (curl\mathbf{A})_y = \frac{\partial A_1}{\partial z} - \frac{\partial A_3}{\partial x}$$

Hence
$$curl\,\mathbf{A} = \left(\frac{\partial A_3}{\partial y} - \frac{\partial A_2}{\partial z}\right)\mathbf{i} + \left(\frac{\partial A_1}{\partial z} - \frac{\partial A_3}{\partial x}\right)\mathbf{j} + \left(\frac{\partial A_2}{\partial x} - \frac{\partial A_1}{\partial y}\right)\mathbf{k}$$

$$curl\mathbf{A} \equiv \nabla \times \mathbf{A} = \begin{vmatrix} \mathbf{i} & \mathbf{j} & \mathbf{k} \\ \frac{\partial}{\partial x} & \frac{\partial}{\partial y} & \frac{\partial}{\partial z} \\ A_1 & A_2 & A_3 \end{vmatrix} \qquad ...(26)$$

Physical meaning of curl A: Consider a fluid rotating with angular velocity ω about an axis. Let **v** be the velocity of a fluid particle and *r* the radius of its circular path. From the definition, the component of curl **v** normal to the plane of rotation is equal to the closed line integral of **v** per unit area

$$(curl\ \mathbf{v})\cdot\mathbf{n} = \lim_{S\to 0}\frac{1}{S}\oint \mathbf{v}.d\mathbf{r} \qquad \text{where } S = \pi r^2$$

$$= \lim_{S\to 0}\frac{1}{\pi r^2}\oint v dr = \frac{v}{\pi r^2}(2\pi r) = 2(v/r) = 2\omega$$

Thus the curl of velocity vector is twice the angular velocity. In fluid dynamics *curl* **v** is called the ***vorticity.***

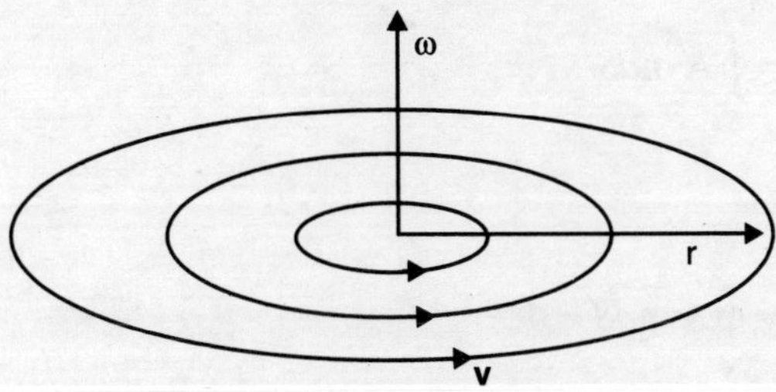

Fig. 13. Rotating fluid.

INTEGRAL THEOREMS

15. GAUSS'S DIVERGENCE THEOREM

The theorem states that the flux of a vector **A** *through a closed surface S is equal to the volume integral of div* **A** *over the region V bounded by the surface S:*

$$\oint_S \mathbf{A}\cdot\mathbf{n}dS = \int_V div\mathbf{A}dV \qquad \text{...(30)}$$

Proof: The flux of vector **A** through the surface *S* is

$$\Phi = \oint_S \mathbf{A}\cdot\mathbf{n}dS$$

Divide the volume *V* into two regions by a common surface S_{12}. The region 1 is bounded by surfaces S_1 and S_{12} and the region 2 by surfaces S_2 and S_{12}. The sum of fluxes of vector *A* through the bounding surfaces of the two sub-regions is

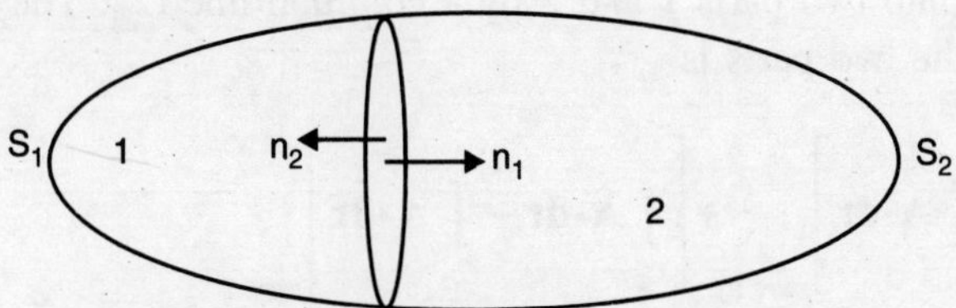

Fig. 14. Gauss's divergence theorem.

$$\int_{S_1} \mathbf{A}\cdot\mathbf{n}dS + \int_{S_{12}} \mathbf{A}\cdot\mathbf{n}dS + \int_{S_2} \mathbf{A}\cdot\mathbf{n}dS + \int_{S_{12}} \mathbf{A}\cdot\mathbf{n}dS$$

Since $\mathbf{n_1} = -\mathbf{n_2}$, the second and the fourth integrals in the above expression cancel out. Therefore, the total flux of **A** from the regions 1 and 2 is

$$\int_{S_1} \mathbf{A}\cdot\mathbf{n}dS + \int_{S_2} \mathbf{A}\cdot\mathbf{n}dS = \oint_S \mathbf{A}\cdot\mathbf{n}dS = \Phi$$

This result is independent of the mode and the number of divisions into which the volume V is subdivided. Let us divide the volume V into a large number of sub-regions and add the fluxes from each region. The result is

$$\sum_i \oint_{S_i} \mathbf{A}_i\cdot\mathbf{n}_i dS_i = \oint_S \mathbf{A}\cdot\mathbf{n}dS$$

or $$\sum_i \frac{\oint_{S_i} \mathbf{A}_i\cdot\mathbf{n}_i dS_i}{\Delta V_i}\Delta V_i = \oint_S \mathbf{A}\cdot\mathbf{n}dS = \Phi$$

where ΔV_i is the volume of the region bounded by i^{th} surface. In the limit $\Delta V_i \to 0$ the left hand side of above equation becomes the volume integral of *div* **A.** Hence,

$$\int_V div\,\mathbf{A}dV = \oint_S \mathbf{A}\cdot\mathbf{n}dS \qquad ...(27)$$

16. STOKE'S THEOREM

The theorem states that the line integral of a vector **A** *around a closed curve C is equal to the normal surface integral of curl of* **A** *over the surface S bounded by the curve C.*

$$\oint_C \mathbf{A}\cdot\mathbf{dr} = \int_S curl\mathbf{A}\cdot\mathbf{n}dS \qquad ...(28)$$

Proof: The circulation of vector A around a closed curve C is given by

$$\text{circulation} \quad \Gamma = \oint_C \mathbf{A}\cdot\mathbf{dr}$$

Divide the surface S into two parts 1 and 2 by a common line C_{21}. The sum of the circulations along the boundaries of the two parts is

$$\left[\int_{C_1} \mathbf{A}\cdot\mathbf{dr} + \int_{C_{12}} \mathbf{A}\cdot\mathbf{dr}\right]_{part\ 1} + \left[\int_{C_2} \mathbf{A}\cdot\mathbf{dr} + \int_{C_{12}} \mathbf{A}\cdot\mathbf{dr}\right]_{part\ 2}$$

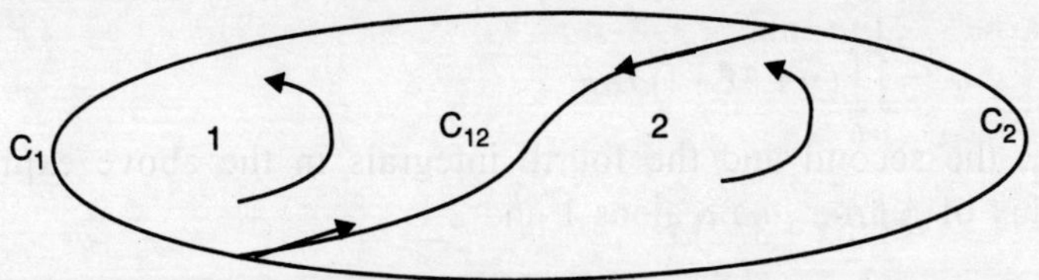

Fig. 15. Stokes' Theorem.

In the above expression, the first two terms represent the circulation around the boundary of region 1 and the last two terms around the boundary of region 2. In calculating the circulation of the vector A around the boundary of region 1, the line C_{12} is traversed anticlockwise whereas in calculating the circulation around the boundary of region 2, it is traversed clockwise. Therefore, the second and the fourth integrals are equal but opposite in sign and sum to zero. Thus, the sum of the circulations along the boundary of regions 1 and 2 reduces to

$$\int_{C_1} \mathbf{A}\cdot d\mathbf{r} + \int_{C_2} \mathbf{A}\cdot d\mathbf{r}$$

This result is independent of the mode and the number of divisions into which the surface S is divided. Dividing the surface S into a large number of parts and adding the circulation around the boundary of each part we get the same result. Thus

$$\sum_i \oint_{i^{th}\ curve} \mathbf{A}\cdot d\mathbf{r} = \oint_C \mathbf{A}\cdot d\mathbf{r}$$

$$\sum_i \left[\frac{1}{\Delta S_i} \oint_{i^{th}\ curve} \mathbf{A}\cdot d\mathbf{r}\right]\Delta S_i = \oint_C \mathbf{A}\cdot d\mathbf{r}$$

where ΔS_I is the area of the *i*th subregion. In the limit $\Delta S_i \to 0$ the term inside the square bracket becomes curl **A.** Hence

$$\int_S curl\mathbf{A}\cdot\mathbf{n}dS = \oint_C \mathbf{A}\cdot d\mathbf{r}$$

***Example* 1:** *Verify divergence theorem for the vector field*

$$\mathbf{A} = xy\ \mathbf{i} + 2yz\ \mathbf{j} + 3zx\ \mathbf{k}$$

taking the region of integration bounded by the faces $x = 0,\ y = 0,\ z = 0,\ x = 1,\ y = 1,\ z = 1.$

Solution: $\quad div\ \mathbf{A} = y + 2z + 3x$

$$\int_V div\mathbf{A}dV = \int_0^1\int_0^1\int_0^1 (y + 2z + 3x)dxdydz$$

$$= \int_0^1\int_0^1 (yz + z^2 + 3xz)_0^1 \quad dxdy$$

$$= \int_0^1 \int_0^1 (y + 3x + 1) dx dy$$

$$= \int_0^1 (3x + 3/2) dx$$

$$= 3$$

In order to evaluate surface integral of vector **A** refer to the Fig. (16).

$$\oint \mathbf{A} \cdot \mathbf{n} dS = \iint_{ADHE} \mathbf{A} \cdot (-\mathbf{i}) dydz + \iint_{BCGF} \mathbf{A} \cdot (\mathbf{i}) dydz + \iint_{ABFE} \mathbf{A} (-\mathbf{j}) dxdz$$

$$+ \iint_{DCGH} \mathbf{A} \cdot (\mathbf{j}) dxdz + \iint_{ABCD} \mathbf{A} \cdot (-\mathbf{k}) dxdy + \iint_{EFGH} \mathbf{A} \cdot \mathbf{k}\, dxdy$$

$$= I_1 + I_2 + I_3 + I_4 + I_5 + I_6$$

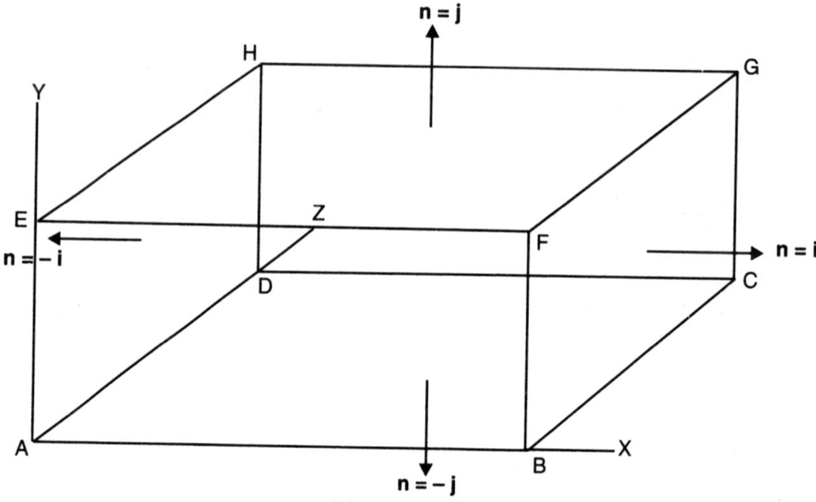

Fig. 16

The values of these integrals come out to be 0, 1/2, 0, 1, 0 and 3/2. Hence

$$\oint_S \mathbf{A} \cdot \mathbf{n} dS = 3$$

This verifies the divergence theorem.

Example 2: *Prove Stokes' theorem for the vector*

$$\mathbf{A} = (x + y, x - z, y + z)$$

taken over the triangle cut from the plane $3x + 2y + z = 6$ by the coordinate planes.

Solution: Refer to the Fig. 17. The circulation of **A** around the closed curve ABCA is given by

$$\oint_{ABCA} \mathbf{A} \cdot d\mathbf{r} = \int_{AB} \mathbf{A} \cdot d\mathbf{r} + \int_{BC} \mathbf{A} \cdot d\mathbf{r} + \int_{CA} \mathbf{A} \cdot d\mathbf{r} = I_1 + I_2 + I_3$$

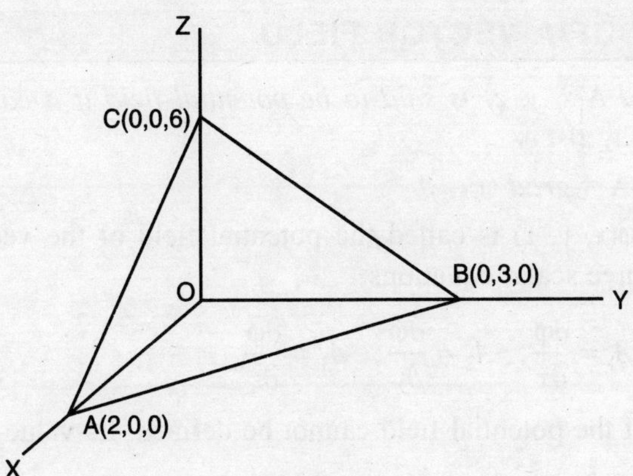

Fig. 17

Along AB, $z = 0$, $3x + 2y = 6$, $2 \geq x \geq 0$, $0 \leq y \leq 3$.

$$A_1 = x + y = 3 - x/2,\ A_2 = x - z = (6 - 2y)/3$$

$$I_1 = \int_{AB} \mathbf{A}\cdot d\mathbf{r} = \int A_1 dx + \int A_3 dy + \int A_3 dz$$

$$I_1 = \int_2^0 A_1 dx + \int_0^3 A_2 dy = \int_2^0 \left(3 - \frac{x}{2}\right) dx + \int_0^3 \frac{6-2y}{3} dy = -2$$

Along BC, $x = 0$, $2y + z = 6$, $3 \geq y \geq 0$, $0 \leq z \leq 6$.

$$A_1 = x + y = 0 + y,\ A_2 = x - z = -z = 2y - 6,\ A_3 = y + z = (6 + z)/2$$

$$I_2 = \int_{BC} \mathbf{A}\cdot d\mathbf{r} = \int A_1 dx + \int A_2 dy + \int A_3 dz = 0 + \int_3^0 (2y-6) dy + \int_0^6 \frac{6+z}{2} dz = 36$$

Along CA, $y = 0$, $3x + z = 6$, $0 \leq x \leq 2$, $6 \geq z \geq 0$

$$A_1 = x + y = x,\ A_2 = x - z,\ A_3 = y + z = z$$

$$I_3 = \int_{CA} \mathbf{A}\cdot d\mathbf{r} = \int A_1 dx + \int A_2 dy + \int A_3 dz = \int_0^2 x dx + 0 + \int_6^0 z dz = -16$$

$$\therefore \quad \oint \mathbf{A}\cdot d\mathbf{r} = -2 + 36 - 16 = 18$$

Now $curl\, \mathbf{A} = 2\,\mathbf{i}$

Unit vector normal to the plane $\varphi = 3x + 2y + z - 6 = 0$ is

$$\mathbf{n} = \frac{\nabla\varphi}{|\nabla\varphi|} = \frac{3\mathbf{i} + 2\mathbf{j} + \mathbf{k}}{\sqrt{14}}, \quad \cos\gamma = \mathbf{n}\cdot\mathbf{k} = \frac{1}{\sqrt{14}}, \quad curl\,\mathbf{A}\cdot\mathbf{n} = 2\mathbf{i}\cdot\mathbf{n} = \frac{6}{\sqrt{14}}$$

The projection of the surface onto xy-plane is the triangular region OAB.

$$\int_S curl\,\mathbf{A}\cdot\mathbf{n}dS = \iint_{\Delta OAB} \frac{6dxdy}{\sqrt{14}\cos\gamma} = \iint_{\Delta OAB} 6dxdy = 6(3) = 18$$

17. POTENTIALITY OF A VECTOR FIELD

Definition: *A vector field* $\mathbf{A}(x, y, z)$ *is said to be potential field if it can be expressed as gradient of some scalar field* $\varphi(x, y, z)$ *i.e.*

$$\mathbf{A} = grad\ \varphi \qquad ...(29)$$

The scalar function $\varphi(x, y, z)$ is called the potential field of the vector field. Equation (29) is equivalent to following three scalar equations

$$A_1 = \frac{\partial \varphi}{\partial x}, \quad A_2 = \frac{\partial \varphi}{\partial y}, \quad A_3 = \frac{\partial \varphi}{\partial z} \qquad ...(30)$$

The absolute value of the potential field cannot be defined. Its value can be determined only up to an additive constant.

Since *curl grad* $\varphi = 0$, the criterion for vector field $\mathbf{A}$ (x, y, z) to be a potential field is

$$curl\ \mathbf{A} = 0$$

Therefore, the line integral of a potential field is independent of path and depends on the initial and the final points of the path.

$$\int_P^Q \mathbf{A}\cdot d\mathbf{r} = \int_P^Q grad\,\varphi \cdot d\mathbf{r} = \int_P^Q d\varphi = \varphi(Q) - \varphi(P)$$

The potential function $\varphi(x, y, z)$ corresponding to the vector field $\mathbf{A}(x, y, z)$ is defined by

$$\varphi(x, y, z) = \int_{P_0}^{P} \mathbf{A}\cdot d\mathbf{r} \qquad ...(31)$$

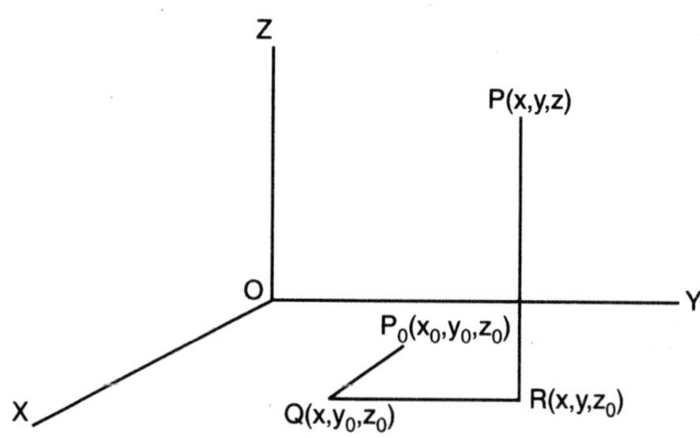

Fig. 18

where $P_0(x_0, y_0, z_0)$ is some fixed point and $P(x, y, z)$ is the point where potential φ is defined. In terms of components of vector $\mathbf{A}$ we can write the above equation as

$$\varphi(x, y, z) = \int (A_1 dx + A_2 dy + A_3 dz)$$

In eqn. (35) the first integral is evaluated along the path P_0Q parallel to x-axis, the second integral along the path QR parallel to y-axis and the third integral along the path RP parallel to z-axis. Thus

$$\varphi(x, y, z) = \int_{x_0}^{x} A_1 dx + \int_{y_0}^{y} A_2 dy + \int_{z_0}^{z} A_3 dz \qquad ...(32)$$

***Example* 1:** *Show that the field*

$$\mathbf{A} = 2xyz\,\mathbf{i} + x^2z\,\mathbf{j} + x^2y\,\mathbf{k}$$

is a potential field. Obtain its potential function.

Solution: It can be shown that *curl* **A** = 0, hence the given field is a potential field. Now the potential function is given by

$$\varphi(x, y, z) = \int_0^x (2xyz)_{y=0,z=0}\,dx + \int_0^y (x^2 z)_{x=0}\,dy + \int_0^z x^2 y\,dz$$

$$= 0 + 0 + x^2yz + c$$

Hence, the potential function is $\varphi = x^2yz + c$, where c is a constant.

***Example* 2:** *The electric field at any point (x, y, z) is given by*

$$\mathbf{E} = 2x\,\mathbf{i} + 2y\,\mathbf{j} + 2z\,\mathbf{k}$$

Derive the equation for the equipotential surface.

Solution: The equation of equipotential surface is

$$\varphi(x, y, z) = \int_0^x 2x dx + \int_0^y 2y dy + \int_0^z 2z dz = x^2 + y^2 + z^2$$

$$x^2 + y^2 + z^2 = c$$

where c is a constant.

18. GREEN'S THEOREM IN A PLANE

Let S be a region bounded by a simple closed curve C and $P(x, y)$ and $Q(x, y)$ be continuous functions having continuous partial derivatives. Then

$$\oint_C (P dy - Q dx) = \iint_S \left(\frac{\partial P}{\partial x} + \frac{\partial Q}{\partial y} \right) dx dy \qquad ...(33)$$

Proof: Let C be a closed curve in xy-plane. Now

$$\iint_S \frac{\partial Q}{\partial y}\, dx dy = \int \left[Q(x, y) \right]_{y_1}^{y_2} dx$$

$$= \int_a^b \left[Q(x, y_2) - Q(x, y_1) \right] dx$$

$$= \int_a^b Q(x, y_2)\, dx - \int_a^b Q(x, y_1)\, dx$$

$$= -\left[\int_a^b Q(x, y_1)\, dx + \int_b^a Q(x, y_2)\, dx\right]$$

$$= -\oint_C Q(x, y)\, dx$$

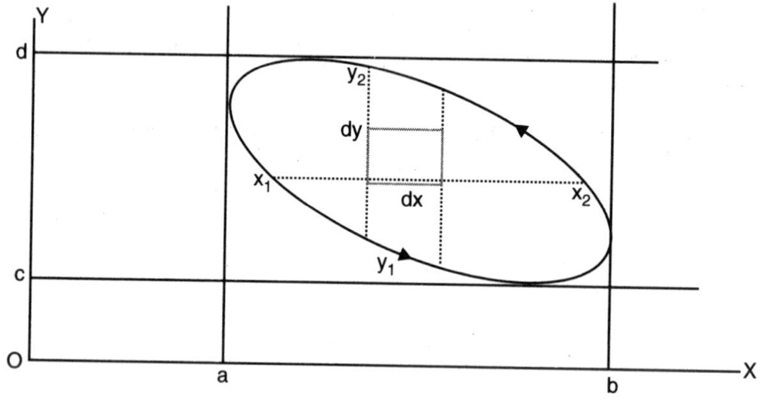

Fig. 19. Green's theorem in a plane.

Similarly,

$$\iint_S \frac{\partial P}{\partial x} dxdy = \int_c^d \left[P(x, y)\right]_{x_1}^{x_2} dy$$

$$= \int_c^d P(x_2, y)dy - \int_c^d P(x_1, y)dy$$

$$= \int_c^d P(x_2, y)dy + \int_d^c P(x_1, y)dy$$

$$= \oint_C P(x, y)dy$$

Hence, $$\iint_S \left(\frac{\partial P}{\partial x} + \frac{\partial Q}{\partial y}\right) dxdy = \oint_C (Pdy - Qdx)$$

19. GREEN'S THEOREM IN 3D-SPACE

Gauss's divergence theorem states that

$$\int_V \nabla \cdot \mathbf{A} dV = \oint_S \mathbf{A} \cdot \mathbf{n} dS$$

Putting $\mathbf{A} = \varphi\nabla\psi$ where φ and ψ are scalars, we have

$$\int \nabla\cdot(\varphi\nabla\psi)\,dV = \oint \varphi\nabla\psi\cdot\mathbf{n}dS$$

$$\int\left(\varphi\nabla^2\psi + \nabla\varphi\cdot\nabla\psi\right)dV = \oint \varphi\nabla\psi\cdot\mathbf{n}dS \qquad \text{...(34)}$$

$$= \oint \varphi\frac{\partial\psi}{\partial n}dS \qquad \text{...(35)}$$

This is the Green's theorem of first kind. Interchanging φ and ψ in above equations we have

$$\int\left(\psi\nabla^2\varphi + \nabla\psi\cdot\nabla\varphi\right)dV = \oint \psi\nabla\varphi\cdot\mathbf{n}dS \qquad \text{...(36)}$$

$$= \oint \psi\frac{\partial\varphi}{\partial n}dS \qquad \text{...(37)}$$

Subtracting (34) from (36) we have

$$\int\left(\varphi\nabla^2\psi - \psi\nabla^2\varphi\right)dV = \oint(\varphi\nabla\psi - \psi\nabla\varphi)\cdot\mathbf{n}dS \qquad \text{...(38)}$$

$$= \oint\left(\varphi\frac{\partial\psi}{\partial n} - \psi\frac{\partial\varphi}{\partial n}\right)dS \qquad \text{...(39)}$$

Equations (38) and (39) are known as Green's theorem of second kind.

Special cases:

1. When the scalar φ is constant, eqn. (38) becomes

$$\int \nabla^2\psi dV = \oint \nabla\psi\cdot\mathbf{n}dS \qquad \text{...(40)}$$

2. When the scalar ψ is constant then

$$\int \nabla^2\varphi dV = \oint \nabla\varphi\cdot\mathbf{n}dS \qquad \text{...(41)}$$

3. If φ and ψ satisfy Laplace's equations $\nabla^2\varphi = 0$ and $\nabla^2\psi = 0$. In view of these equations we can write eqn. (38) as

$$\oint \varphi\nabla\psi\cdot\mathbf{n}dS = \oint \psi\nabla\varphi\cdot\mathbf{n}dS \qquad \text{...(42)}$$

$$\oint \varphi\frac{\partial\psi}{\partial n}dS = \oint \psi\frac{\partial\varphi}{\partial n}dS \qquad \text{...(43)}$$

***Example* 1:** *Show that the integral*

$$\frac{1}{2}\oint_C (xdy - ydx)$$

represents the area of the region bounded by the closed curve C. Use this result to obtain the area of ellipse.

Solution: Green's theorem in a plane is

$$\oint_C (Pdy - Qdx) = \iint_S \left(\frac{\partial P}{\partial x} + \frac{\partial Q}{\partial y} \right) dxdy \qquad ...(44)$$

Comparing the given integral with eqn. (44) we have

$$P = x/2 \, , \; Q = y/2, \; \frac{\partial P}{\partial x} = \frac{1}{2}, \; \frac{\partial Q}{\partial y} = \frac{1}{2} \qquad ...(45)$$

In view of (45) we can write (1) as

$$\frac{1}{2}\oint_C (xdy - ydx) = \iint_S \left(\frac{1}{2} + \frac{1}{2} \right) dxdy = \iint_S dxdy$$

= area of region bounded by C

For an ellipse $x = a \cos t, \; y = b \sin t \, , \; 0 < t < 2p$

$$A = \frac{1}{2}\oint (xdy - ydx)$$

$$= \frac{1}{2}\int_0^{2\pi} \{(a\cos t)(b\cos t) - (b\sin t)(-a\sin t)\}\, dt$$

$$= \frac{ab}{2}\int_0^{2\pi} dt = \pi ab$$

***Example* 2:** *Verify Green's theorem for the functions*

$$P(x,y) = x^2 y, \; Q(x,y) = y^2 x$$

over the region bounded by the circle $x^2 + y^2 = a^2$ *or* $x = a \cos t, \; y = a \sin t,$ *where* $0 \le t \le 2p$

Solution: Green's theorem

$$\oint_C (Pdy - Qdx) = \iint_S \left(\frac{\partial P}{\partial x} + \frac{\partial Q}{\partial y} \right) dxdy$$

$$P = x^2 y, \; Q = y^2 x, \; \frac{\partial P}{\partial x} = 2xy, \; \frac{\partial Q}{\partial y} = 2yx$$

Now

$$\oint (Pdy - Qdx) = \oint (x^2 ydy - y^2 xdx)$$

$$= a^4 \int_0^{2\pi} \sin t \, \cos t \; dt = 0$$

And $$\iint_S \left(\frac{\partial P}{\partial x} + \frac{\partial Q}{\partial y} \right) dxdy = \iint_S 2xydxdy$$

Changing to polar coordinates through the transformation equations $x = r\cos\theta, \; y = r\sin\theta$ and $dxdy = rd\theta dr$ we have

$$\iint_S \left(\frac{\partial P}{\partial x} + \frac{\partial Q}{\partial y} \right) dxdy = 2\int_0^a \int_0^{2\pi} (r\cos\theta)(r\sin\theta) r d\theta dr$$

$$= 2\int_0^a r^3 dr \int_0^{2\pi} \sin\theta \ \cos\theta \, d\theta = 0$$

***Example* 3:** *Prove the following relations*

$$\oint_S \varphi \mathbf{n} \, dS = \int_V \nabla\varphi \, dV$$

$$\oint_S \mathbf{n} \times \mathbf{F} dS = \int_V \nabla \times \mathbf{F} dV$$

$$\oint_C \varphi \, dr = \oint_S \mathbf{n} \times \nabla\varphi \, dS$$

Proof:

1. Let $\mathbf{A} = \mathbf{c}\varphi$ where c is an arbitrary constant vector.

$$\nabla \cdot \mathbf{A} = \nabla \cdot (\mathbf{c}\varphi) = (\nabla \cdot \mathbf{c})\varphi + \mathbf{c} \cdot (\nabla\varphi) = \mathbf{c} \cdot \nabla\varphi$$

According to Gauss's divergence theorem

$$\oint_S \mathbf{A} \cdot \mathbf{n} dS = \int_V \nabla \cdot \mathbf{A} dV$$

$$\oint_S \mathbf{c}\varphi \cdot \mathbf{n} dS = \int_V \mathbf{c} \cdot \nabla\varphi dV$$

$$\mathbf{c} \cdot \oint_S \varphi \mathbf{n} dS = \mathbf{c} \cdot \int_V \nabla\varphi dV$$

Since c is arbitrary we have

$$\oint_S \varphi \mathbf{n} dS = \int_V \nabla\varphi dV$$

2. Let $\mathbf{A} = \mathbf{c} \times \mathbf{F}$ where $\mathbf{c}$ is an arbitrary constant vector. According to Gauss's divergence theorem

$$\oint_S \mathbf{A} \cdot \mathbf{n} dS = \int_V \nabla \cdot \mathbf{A} dV$$

$$\oint_S (\mathbf{c} \times \mathbf{F}) \cdot \mathbf{n} dS = \int_V \nabla \cdot (\mathbf{c} \times \mathbf{F}) dV$$

$$\oint_S \mathbf{c} \cdot (\mathbf{F} \times \mathbf{n}) dS = -\int_V \mathbf{c} \cdot (\nabla \times \mathbf{F}) dV$$

$$\mathbf{c} \cdot \oint_S \mathbf{n} \times \mathbf{F} dS = \mathbf{c} \cdot \int_V \nabla \times \mathbf{F} dV$$

Since c is arbitrary we have

$$\oint_S \mathbf{n} \times \mathbf{F} dS = \int_V \nabla \times \mathbf{F} dV$$

3. Let $\mathbf{A} = \varphi\mathbf{c}$ where $\mathbf{c}$ is an arbitrary constant vector.

$$\nabla \times \mathbf{A} = \nabla \times (\varphi\, \mathbf{c}) = \nabla\varphi \times \mathbf{c} + \varphi\nabla \times \mathbf{c} = \nabla\varphi \times \mathbf{c}$$

Now according to Stokes' theorem

$$\oint_C \mathbf{A}\cdot d\mathbf{r} = \int_S \nabla \times \mathbf{A} \times \mathbf{n}\, dS$$

$$\oint_C \varphi\mathbf{c}\cdot d\mathbf{r} = \int_S \nabla\varphi \times \mathbf{c}\cdot\mathbf{n}\, dS$$

$$\mathbf{c}\cdot\oint_C \varphi d\mathbf{r} = -\int_S \mathbf{c} \times \nabla\varphi\cdot\mathbf{n}\, dS$$

$$\mathbf{c}\cdot\oint_C \varphi d\mathbf{r} = -\int_S \mathbf{c}\cdot\nabla\varphi \times \mathbf{n}\, dS = \mathbf{c}\cdot\int_S \mathbf{n} \times \nabla\varphi dS$$

Since $\mathbf{c}$ is arbitrary we have

$$\oint_C \varphi d\mathbf{r} = \int_S \mathbf{n} \times \nabla\varphi dS$$

***Example* 4:** *Show that* $\oint_S \mathbf{r}\cdot dS = 3V$.

where V is the volume enclosed by the surface S.

Solution: According to divergence theorem

$$\oint_S \mathbf{r}\cdot\mathbf{n}dS = \int_V \nabla\cdot\mathbf{r}dV = \int_V 3dV = 3V$$

***Example* 5:** *Show that* $\oint_S \frac{\mathbf{r}}{r^2}\cdot d\mathbf{S} = \int_V \frac{1}{r^2} dV.$

Solution: According to Gauss's divergence theorem

$$\oint_S \frac{\mathbf{r}}{r^2}\cdot d\mathbf{S} = \int_V div\left(\frac{\mathbf{r}}{r^2}\right) dV = \int_V \frac{1}{r^2} dV$$

***Exmaple* 6:** *Show that* $\oint_S \mathbf{n}\cdot curl\,\mathbf{F} dS = 0$.

Solution: According to Gauss's theorem

$$\oint_S curl\,\mathbf{F}\cdot\mathbf{n}dS = \int_V div(curl\,\mathbf{F})dV = 0$$

***Example* 7:** *Show that*

$\oint_S \mathbf{n}\cdot d\mathbf{S} = 0,$ *where* $\mathbf{n}$ *is unit vector normal to* $d\mathbf{S}$.

Solution: According to Gauss's divergence theorem

$$\oint_S \mathbf{a}\cdot\mathbf{n}dS = \int_V div\,\mathbf{a}\,dV \text{ where } \mathbf{a} \text{ is a constant vector}$$

Since **a** is arbitrary we have

$$\oint_S \mathbf{n}\cdot d\mathbf{S} = 0$$

***Example* 8:** *Show that*

$$\oint_C \mathbf{r}\cdot d\mathbf{r} = 0.$$

Solution: $\oint_C \mathbf{r}\cdot d\mathbf{r} = \int_S curl\ \ \mathbf{r}\cdot d\mathbf{S} = 0$

***Example* 9:** *Apply Gauss's divergence theorem to show that*

$$\oint_S \left\{\left(x^3 - yz\right)\mathbf{i} - 2x^2 y\mathbf{j} + 2\mathbf{k}\right\}\cdot\mathbf{n}dS = \frac{1}{3}a^5$$

where S denotes the surface of the cube bounded by planes $x = 0, x = a, y = 0, y = a, z = 0, z = a.$

Solution: $\nabla\cdot\mathbf{A} = \frac{\partial}{\partial x}\left(x^3 yz\right) + \frac{\partial}{\partial y}\left(-2x^2 y\right) + \frac{\partial}{\partial z}(2) = x^2$

According to divergence theorem

$$\oint_S \mathbf{A}\cdot\mathbf{n}dS = \int_V \nabla\cdot\mathbf{A}dV = \int_V x^2 dV = \int_{x=0}^{a}\int_{y=0}^{a}\int_{z=0}^{a} x^2\,dxdydz = \frac{1}{3}a^5$$

20. SOLID ANGLE

Consider an element of surface **dS** at point **r** referred to origin O. Construct a cone with **dS** as base and O as apex and draw a sphere of unit radius around the point. The numerical value of the surface on the unit sphere lying within the cone is called the solid angle subtended by the surface **dS** at point O. Solid angle is expressed in steradians. Let the normal at **dS** make an angle ψ with the radius vector **r.** The projection of **dS** on a spherical surface of radius r is $dS_{sphere} = dS\cos\psi$.

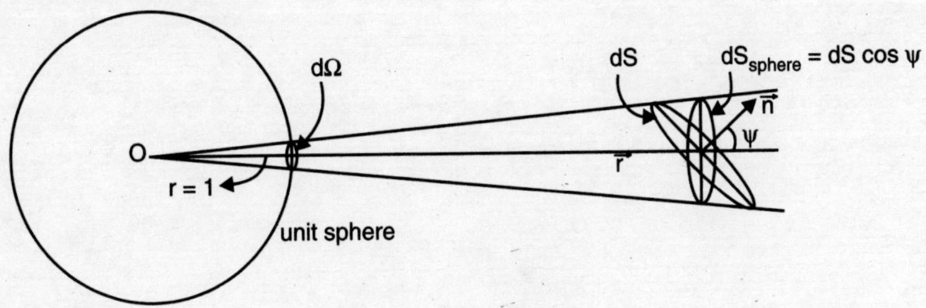

Fig. 20. Solid angle.

Let $d\Omega$ denote the solid angle subtended at O by the surface dS. It is evident from the Fig. (20) that

$$\frac{d\Omega}{1^2} = \frac{dS_{\text{sphere}}}{r^2} = \frac{dS\cos\psi}{r^2} = \frac{\mathbf{r}\cdot\mathbf{n}dS}{r^3}$$

Where $\mathbf{n}$ is unit vector normal to surface $\mathbf{dS}$.

From above equation, $$d\Omega = \frac{dS_{\text{sphere}}}{r^2} = \frac{dS\cos\psi}{r^2} = \frac{\mathbf{r}\cdot\mathbf{n}dS}{r^3} \qquad ...(46)$$

The solid angle subtended by a finite surface S is given by

$$\Omega = \int_S d\Omega = \int_S \frac{dS_{\text{sphere}}}{r^2} = \int_S \frac{dS\cos\psi}{r^2} = \int_S \frac{\mathbf{r}\cdot\mathbf{n}dS}{r^3} \qquad ...(47)$$

A closed surface includes the entire surface area of the unit sphere drawn about an interior point. Hence, the solid angle subtended by a closed surface at an interior point is equal to 4π. Thus,

$$\Omega = \oint_S d\Omega = \oint_S \frac{dS_{\text{sphere}}}{r^2} = \oint_S \frac{dS\cos\psi}{r^2} = \oint_S \frac{\mathbf{r}\cdot\mathbf{n}dS}{r^3} = 4\pi \qquad ...(48)$$

In terms of spherical polar coordinates, an element of surface on a sphere of radius r is

$$dS_{\text{sphere}} = r^2 \sin\theta \; d\theta \; d\varphi$$

Therefore, the solid angle subtended by this surface at the centre of sphere is

$$d\Omega = \frac{dS_{\text{sphere}}}{r^2} = \sin\theta \; d\theta \; d\varphi \qquad ...(49)$$

Total solid angle subtended by the whole surface of sphere at its centre is

$$\Omega = \oint_S d\Omega = \int_{\theta=0}^{\pi} \int_{\varphi=0}^{2\pi} \sin\theta \; d\theta \; d\varphi = 4\pi \qquad ...(50)$$

OOO